Real Questions

Reading and Writing Genres

Real Questions

Reading and Writing Genres

Kathryn Evans

Bridgewater State University

Bedford/St. Martin's

Boston ◆ New York

For Bedford/St. Martin's

Senior Executive Editor: Leasa Burton
Senior Developmental Editor: Adam Whitehurst
Production Editor: Jessica Gould
Assistant Production Manager: Joe Ford
Executive Marketing Manager: Molly Parke
Editorial Assistant: Nicholas McCarthy
Copy Editor: Jamie Thaman
Indexer: Melanie Belkin
Photo Researcher: Connie Gardner
Permissions Manager: Kalina K. Ingham
Art Director: Lucy Krikorian
Text Design: Claire Seng-Niemoeller
Cover Design: Donna Dennison
Cover Art: Question (Ask the Magic Box), 2010. Polaroid composite.
 © Patrick Winfield.
Composition: Graphic World Inc.
Printing and Binding: RR Donnelley and Sons

President, Bedford/St. Martin's: Denise B. Wydra
Presidents, Macmillan Higher Education: Joan E. Feinberg and Tom Scotty
Editor in Chief: Karen S. Henry
Director of Development: Erica T. Appel
Director of Marketing: Karen R. Soeltz
Production Director: Susan W. Brown
Associate Production Director: Elise S. Kaiser
Managing Editor: Shuli Traub

Manufactured in the United States of America.

8 7 6 5 4 3
f e d c b a

For information, write: Bedford/St. Martin's, 75 Arlington Street, Boston, MA 02116
 (617-399-4000)

ISBN 978-0-312-60121-8

Acknowledgments

To my parents, Beverly and Travis Evans,
who have always encouraged me to learn.

Preface for Instructors

If you ask your students to describe their favorite music, their list of likes might readily include whole genres—"I really love alt country" or "I mostly listen to dubstep." Many students are keenly aware of how to distinguish musical genres and subgenres. In music, an understanding of genre helps students refine their tastes, develop fluency, and participate more fully in discussions with their friends and with the outside world.

In the writing classroom, however, students are more likely to need guidance in becoming genre-sensitive readers and writers. Many students believe that there is a set of decontextualized rules for writing, and they try to follow these rules when they write. Understanding, instead, that writers choose among genres and conventions as tools to make the greatest impact empowers students to share their own points of view in ways that matter most to them. The goal of *Real Questions* is to help students engage more fully with their own reading and writing by understanding a broader range of rhetorical strategies and contexts.

Real Questions promotes genre as a subject of inquiry in the writing classroom by placing it in the context of engaging topics that students connect to personally, topics that let them see how genre changes with different audiences and purposes. *Real Questions* encourages students to approach genre as another choice that every writer faces by presenting them with a wider range of genres than is found in most textbooks—creative nonfiction, newspaper and magazine articles, blogs, Twitter posts, brochures, infographics, excerpts from self-help books, and public service announcements, as well as more challenging academic and civic writing.

An Accessible Introduction to Genre

Featuring a substantial three-part introduction to reading and writing processes, *Real Questions* encourages students to think rhetorically by treating genre as an adaptation to their particular purposes, media, messages, and audiences. The first part, **What Is Genre and How Can It Help You?,** opens the text by helping students reach a working definition of genre and framing genre as part of the rhetorical situation. Following that, **Strategies for Critical Thinking, Reading, and Writing** provides instruction on reading and writing strategies as well as guidance in writing summaries, reflections, and rhetorical analyses—three types of writing that can bolster students' confidence in interacting with texts and understanding writing as a series of choices that are informed by genre.

The third section, **Writing Genres,** walks students through seven commonly assigned types of writing: arguments, op-eds and letters to the editor, creative nonfiction, blogs, brochures, and presentations (available online in e-Pages). Featuring checklists and excerpted texts, this section illustrates conventions typical of particular genres, but above that it encourages students to see the conventions of genre as a platform for experimentation by highlighting how genres have evolved and continue to evolve to fit rhetorical needs. This section features diverse examples of moves common to each genre as well as annotated student writing that models these moves and presents them in the context of writing that students will do in class and in their daily lives.

Themes and Readings That Inspire

The **five thematic chapters** in *Real Questions* tap into students' personal experiences — with loving others, with navigating relationships on- and offline, with pursuing happiness, and with negotiating social responsibility. These topics are familiar and interesting to students, but they also represent universal questions that connect writers to the world at large.

By helping students bridge personal experiences with academic topics and writing situations, these themes demonstrate our connections to one another. The **62 reading selections** in *Real Questions* represent an expansive range of genres that demonstrate for students the ways that writers adapt genres to almost any writing situation imaginable. For example:

- In "Act the Way You Want to Feel," blogger Gretchen Rubin takes advantage of the Internet's reach to explore strategies for achieving happiness.

- In an excerpt from *Eating Animals,* Jonathan Safran Foer employs strategies from narrative journalism and creative nonfiction to ponder the personal question of whether we should eat meat.

- In the e-Pages, the White House's "1 Is 2 Many" public service announcement leverages the ethos of professional athletes to raise young men's awareness of domestic violence.

And because genres exist in a web of other genres, five sets of **linked readings** illustrate for students how genres respond in conversation to other genres: how academic articles inspire critiques, how press releases are turned into news articles, and how letters to the editor can respond to op-eds.

Genre-sensitive Discussion and Writing Prompts

Real Questions promotes reading and writing strategies that are genre sensitive. Each reading selection is accompanied not only by a biographical headnote that provides background and context for students, but also a label that prompts student to think about the type of writing they are about to read. Rather than promote an idea that genres are simple categories, these **genre labels** consider not only writing conventions, but also the medium of original publication and, in some cases, whether the selection represents a hybrid of multiple genres. In addition, each reading begins with a **Focus on Genre** section that points out particular rhetorical strategies modeled in the reading to come.

The end-of-reading questions ask students to think critically about both the message of each selection and the specific choices each writer makes, while additional prompts in each chapter and an Appendix titled Publishing Your Writing encourage students to use genre to guide their own writing.

- **Making Connections** questions highlight rhetorical moves across different genres and ask students to consider, among other things, why certain moves are more effective in some genres than in others. These questions reinforce students' genre awareness by asking them to fine-tune their understanding of how specific genres work (both when they reflect convention and when they don't).
- **Writing: Your Turn** questions put students to work evaluating, reflecting, and summarizing the reading as well as challenging them to create their own genre pieces related to the reading.
- **Pulling It All Together** questions end each chapter with longer writing prompts that further students' work in writing genres, many of which are cross-referenced to walk-throughs from the Writing Genres section.
- Students are encouraged to use an **Appendix** that provides some advice for where to seek publication for their writing, reinforcing the message in *Real Questions* that composing for real purposes and real audiences will help students invest more personally in their writing.

Attention to Visual and Multimedia Genres

A composition textbook focused on genre would not be complete without consideration of visual and multimedia genres. Each thematic chapter opens with a **Case Study** that orients students to the chapter's theme by featuring a visual example that distills the nature of the topic and provides a springboard for discussion of the chapter theme. In addition,

Visualizing Genre portfolios feature artifacts from real life that highlight issues of genre, from bumper stickers and food packaging to greeting cards and public service announcements. The Case Studies and Visualizing Genre features are also available online in the e-Pages so that students can examine the art in color and in larger sizes.

e-Pages for *Real Questions*

Some aspects of genre are best experienced beyond the printed page — for instance, listening to an audio essay from NPR's *This I Believe* illustrates different strategies for appealing to audiences, and analyzing a video presentation on climate change encourages new considerations for organizing evidence. To help extend what students read and learn in *Real Questions* to the kinds of media they are most familiar with and excited by, we have added compelling multimodal selections to *Real Questions*. For a complete list of e-Pages, see the book's table of contents. Instructors can also use the free tools accompanying the e-Pages to upload a syllabus, readings, and assignments to share with the class.

You and your students can access the e-Pages from a tab on the *Student Site for Real Questions* at **bedfordstmartins.com/realquestions /epages**. Students receive access automatically with the purchase of a new book. If the activation code printed on the inside back cover of the student edition is expired, students can purchase access at the student site. Instructors receive access information in a separate e-mail with access to all of the resources on the student site. You can also log in or request access information at the student site.

Acknowledgments

I am indebted to many people for their support of this project. My students — the people for whom I wrote this book — have given me feedback that has improved the book significantly. I'm likewise grateful to the students who revised their work to be published in this book and its online companion: Dave Cook, Rikimaru Kataoka, Devin McGuire, Jean Kesner Mervius, Amy Peterson, Kirsten Ridlen, and Sara Snider. For the many ways they have provided help and support, I'm also grateful to Shannon Rosenblat, Kyle Giacomozzi, WM Scott, Sean Janson, Danielle Oliveira Gelehrter, Anne Bray, Maureen Jecrois, and all the current and former consultants at Bridgewater State University's Writing Studio.

Bridgewater State University's Center for the Advancement of Research and Scholarship (CARS) generously provided funding that enabled me to write much of this book. My research assistant, Greta Marszalkowski, provided significant help and support during one of the most labor-intensive stages of work. My colleagues at Bridgewater and elsewhere have likewise been generous in their support, and I'm especially grateful to Bruce Machart and Philip Eubanks for their helpful feedback on parts of this book.

I'm thankful for the many scholars who have devoted their careers to thinking and writing about genre. In writing and revising this book, I was especially influenced by Mary Jo Reiff and Anis Bawarshi's suggestion that, rather than drawing on whole genres, students might be well served by drawing on constellations of strategies used in a range of genres.[1]

Special thanks are due to my teachers, who have directly and indirectly contributed to this book in numerous ways. Many thanks to Paul Prior, not only for providing feedback on What Is Genre and How Can It Help You?, but also for teaching me that genre is vitally important—knowledge that has guided my thinking and teaching for many years. Thanks to Gail Hawisher for teaching me how to teach—especially for teaching me that it's important to help students see the reasons underlying what they're being asked to do. Deep gratitude is due to the late Greg Colomb for teaching me the power of using contrasting examples to enable students to make inductions—inductions that, through discussion, can become explicit knowledge that students draw on when they decide whether or not to make particular rhetorical moves in particular rhetorical situations.

I'm thankful for the many people at Bedford/St. Martin's who have made this book possible. Leasa Burton helped me conceptualize the book and patiently encouraged me to actually write it; without her persistence, insight, and feedback, the book wouldn't exist. I'm also grateful to Adam Whitehurst, who devoted an untold number of hours to making this book a reality, and whose unfailing support helped me survive the process of writing it. Thanks are likewise due to the many other people at Bedford/ St. Martin's who have dedicated both time and thought to this project: Jessica Gould, project editor; Jamie Thaman, copyeditor; Claire Seng-Niemoeller, designer; Molly Parke, executive marketing manager; Margaret Gorenstein, text researcher; and Connie Gardner, art researcher. Finally, I would like to thank Joan Feinberg, Karen Henry, Steve Scipione, and Denise Wydra for their contributions to this project.

I'm very grateful to Dawn Formo, Catherine Cucinella, and Lynne Stallings for writing a superb Instructor's Manual, and thanks are due to Carla Maroudas for her many contributions. I feel blessed to have an Instructor's Manual that not only guides instructors through practical matters but also makes insightful connections among different parts of the book and, ultimately, has much to teach instructors about teaching.

---

[1] See, for example, "Tracing Discursive Resources: How Students Use Prior Genre Knowledge to Negotiate New Writing Contexts in First-Year Composition" in the July 2011 issue of *Written Communication*, pp. 312–337.

For their helpful and detailed feedback, I'm grateful to a number of reviewers: Trela Anderson, Fayetteville State University; Susan Bailor, Front Range Community College; Lisa Bickmore, Salt Lake Community College; Elizabeth Canfield, Virginia Commonwealth University; Julie Nelson Christoph, University of Puget Sound; Andrew Davis, Georgia State University; Susan Davis, Arizona State University; Garry Engkent, Seneca College of Applied Arts and Technology; Jennifer Giaconia, University of Akron; Rachel Golland, St. Thomas Aquinas College; Carol Hawkins, Colby College; Randall Jedele, Des Moines Area Community College; Kathryn Kerr, Illinois State University; Elizabeth Kubek, Benedictine University; Carla Kungl, Shippensburg University; Rachel Lewis, El Camino College; Linda C. Macri, University of Maryland; Elizabeth Gassel Perkins, Darton College; Lynn Reid, Fairleigh Dickinson University; Jennifer Scheidt, Palo Alto College; Mary Sheridan-Rabideau, University of Wyoming; David Stock, University of Wisconsin–Madison; Catherine Stoynoff, University of Akron; Matthew Thiele, University of Alabama; Shaina Trapedo, University of California, Irvine; Stephanie Turner, University of Wisconsin–Eau Claire; Anna Varley, University of Arizona; Stephanie Wade, Stony Brook University; Tamora Whitney, Creighton University; and Michele Wollenzier, Kent State University.

Special thanks to my mother, Beverly Evans, for all the love, support, and encouragement she provided throughout this project. I'm also very grateful to my father, Travis Evans, for the insightful feedback he provided alongside his love and support. I never could have finished this project without the patience and many sacrifices made by my husband, Paul Rohr, who worked tirelessly to make sure I had time to write, and who gave me perceptive and meticulous feedback on every section of this book, over and over. Finally, I'm grateful to my daughters, Maya and Bryn Evohr. Thank you, Maya, for your unwavering faith, encouragement, and enthusiasm for this project. Thank you, Bryn, for your love and patience — and for pulling me back down to earth and reminding me of what's most important in life.

Kathryn Evans

You Get More Choices for *Real Questions*

Bedford/St. Martin's offers resources and format choices that help you and your students get even more out of the book and your course. To learn more about or order any of the products below, contact your Bedford/St. Martin's sales representative, e-mail sales support (sales_support@bfwpub .com), or visit the Web site at **bedfordstmartins.com**.

Let Students Choose Their Format

Students can purchase *Real Questions* in e-book formats for computers, tablets, and e-readers. For more details, visit **bedfordstmartins.com/ebooks**.

Value Packages

Add more value to your text by packaging one of the following resources with *Real Questions*. To learn more about package options, contact your sales representative or visit **bedfordstmartins.com/realquestions/catalog**.

Package a handbook with *Real Questions* and make sure your students have all the help they need with sentence-level issues, documentation guidelines, and more.

- To order *The Everyday Writer*, by Andrea A. Lunsford, packaged with this book, use ISBN 978-1-4576-5639-2.
- To order *A Writer's Reference for Multimodal Projects*, by Diana Hacker and Nancy Sommers, packaged with this book, use ISBN 978-1-4576-5640-8.

Bedford's *i-series* visual tutorials introduce students to principles of composition through visual examples, interactive annotations, and activities they can complete online.

- *ix: visualizing composition 2.0* (available online) helps students put into practice key rhetorical and multimodal concepts. To order *ix: visualizing composition* packaged with the print book, use ISBN 978-1-4576-4313-2.
- *i-claim: visualizing argument 2.0* (available online) shows students how to analyze and compose arguments in words, images, and sounds with six tutorials, an illustrated glossary, and more than seventy multimedia arguments. To order *i-claim: visualizing argument* packaged with the print book, use ISBN 978-1-4576-4324-8.
- *i-cite: visualizing sources* (available online as part of *Re:Writing Plus*) brings research to life through an animated introduction, four tutorials, and hands-on source practice. To order *i-cite: visualizing sources* packaged with the print book, use ISBN 978-1-4576-4323-1.

VideoCentral (available online) is a growing collection of videos for the writing class that captures real-world, academic, and student writers talking about how and why they write. VideoCentral can be packaged for free with *Real Questions*. To order VideoCentral packaged with the print book, use ISBN 978-1-4576-4315-6.

Re:Writing Plus (available online) gathers all of Bedford/St. Martin's premium digital content for composition into one online collection. It includes hundreds of model documents, the first ever peer-review game, and VideoCentral. *Re:Writing Plus* can be purchased separately or packaged with the print book at a significant discount. To order *Re:Writing Plus* packaged with *Real Questions*, use ISBN 978-1-4576-4314-9.

Student Site for Real Questions

bedfordstmartins.com/realquestions
Free and open resources for *Real Questions* provide students with easy-to-access reference materials, visual tutorials, and support for working with sources.

- Three free tutorials from *ix visual exercises* by Cheryl Ball and Kristin Arola
- *TopLinks* with reliable online sources
- *The Bedford Bibliographer:* a tool for collecting source information and making bibliographies in MLA, APA, and *Chicago* styles

Instructor Resources

You have a lot to do in your course. Bedford/St. Martin's wants to make it easy for you to find the support you need—and get it quickly.

The *Instructor's Manual for Real Questions* is available not only in the Instructor's Edition but also as a PDF that can be downloaded from **bedfordstmartins.com/realquestions**. In addition to chapter overviews and teaching tips, the Instructor's Manual includes background readings in teaching genre and useful suggestions for classroom activities.

TeachingCentral (**bedfordstmartins.com/teachingcentral**) offers the entire list of Bedford/St. Martin's print and online professional resources in one place. You'll find landmark reference works, sourcebooks on pedagogical issues, award-winning collections, and practical advice for the classroom—all free for instructors.

Bedford Bits (**bedfordbits.com**) collects creative ideas for teaching a range of composition topics in an easily searchable blog. A community of teachers—leading scholars, authors, and editors—discuss revision, research, grammar and style, technology, peer review, and much more. Take, use, adapt, and pass the ideas around. Then, come back to the site to comment or share your own suggestion.

Contents

e For readings that go beyond the printed page, see bedfordstmartins.com/realquestions/epages.

1 How Can Our Relationships Change and Grow? 122

e bedfordstmartins.com/realquestions/epages

🄴 bedfordstmartins.com/realquestions/epages

4   When Is Eating a Social Issue?   420

[e] bedfordstmartins.com/realquestions/epages

Real Questions

Reading and Writing Genres

What Is Genre and How Can It Help You?

We are surrounded by genres. From Facebook status updates to college application essays, from the texts you send friends to the lab reports you'll write for professors, genres are everywhere. If so many different types of writing count as genres, you might be wondering what exactly a genre is. On the most basic level, a genre is a type of writing (or speech) that you can distinguish from other types based on different patterns of language use — patterns that have evolved in part from the common purposes shared by many of the people who have used the genre over time. In the "Writing Genres" section, you'll see genre in a more nuanced light, but this gives us a good start.

It's useful to understand how genres work because writing effectively involves adapting the way you write when you move from one genre to another. (Even when writing a single genre, it's good to adapt what you write to the unique situation at hand.) Ultimately, then, the phrase "good writing" doesn't mean following a fixed set of rules every time you write (although it often gets used this way); rather, "good writing" means being flexible enough to constantly adapt your writing to your genre, purpose, and audience. The more flexible you are, the more likely you are to accomplish your purposes as a writer.

The genres that will be the most important to you will probably be the ones used in a community you want to join. The better you understand how those genres work, the easier it will be for you to think and act like a member of that community and, ultimately, to have an influence.

What Band Names Can Teach Us about Genre

As suggested, genres can be thought of as patterns of language use, or typical moves people make to accomplish often-shared purposes; however, genres aren't recipes to be followed. Although writers who use a genre tend to make similar sets of moves, they often choose a *subset* of moves to adapt their work to specific situations. They may also borrow moves commonly made in other genres; this can be a useful strategy since many genres share overlapping purposes.

To gain insight into how you might choose moves when you use a genre, consider band names as a case study in genre. When you look at the following list of band names,[1] try taking a few notes (in your mind or on paper) to help you see patterns. Which names are similar, and how? Which names are different, and how? Why do you think these names were chosen?

We Were Promised Jet Packs	Outrageous Things Said Casually
Electric Courage Machine	Dead by Sunrise
Fleshgod Apocalypse	Raygun
Dinosaur Pile-Up	Cymbals Eat Guitars
Micachu and the Shapes	The Smith Westerns
The Dead Weather	Whyzdom
Joy Orbison	The Christopher Walk-Ins
Javelin	The Van Gobots
Florence and the Machine	Peter Wolf Crier
Broken Records	We Fell to Earth
The Terror Pigeon Dance Revolt!	Ginsu Wives
The Big Pink	Rain Machine
And So I Watch You from Afar	Allo Darlin'
I Fight Dragons	Freelance Whales
Wild Moccasins	The Peelies
Golden Silvers	Elizabeth and the Catapult
Romance on a Rocketship	Get Back Guinozzi!
Beans on Toast	The Temper Trap
The Second Hand Marching Band	Fever Ray
Floating Action	The xx
Them Crooked Vultures	Boyz IV Men
Tinted Windows	Atoms for Peace
Edward Sharpe & the Magnetic Zeros	Nick Jonas and the Administration

What patterns did you notice? Now take a minute to jot down the names of your favorite bands. Do you see any of the same patterns?

One pattern you may or may not have noticed is that many band names make allusions, in this case references to actors, painters, other musicians, and even types of robots, guns, and knives. If you caught any of these allusions, they might have amused you—and amusing potential listeners is a good strategy for making them interested in a band. Another move made to engage our interest is the use of sentences that are clearly untrue (e.g., "I Fight Dragons," "We Were Promised Jet Packs," "Cymbals Eat Guitars," and "We Fell to Earth"). A similar move is to use adjective-noun combinations

---

[1] Band names are excerpted from "Best American New Band Names" (p. 37) in *The Best American Nonrequired Reading* (2010), edited by Dave Eggers and published by Houghton Mifflin Harcourt.

that don't make sense. How, for example, could weather be dead? How could whales be freelance, silver be golden, or vultures crooked? The incongruity may pique the interest of potential listeners. People who name bands also make other moves, but you get the idea: there's an overarching purpose shared by people who use a genre, and they choose from among a variety of moves to help them accomplish that purpose.

Thinking of moves as the building blocks of genre will make it easier for you to recognize the typical moves made in the genres you use. Your heightened awareness, in turn, will enable you to see more options when you write — and to make deliberate choices about which moves to use in which situations. The following questions about moves highlight the choices you can make when crafting texts in any genre:

- Are you drawing on *enough moves* of the genre to enable readers to recognize the genre and thus to make sense of your text? (For example, if people see your band's name but can't tell that it's a band name, you've got problems.)

- Have you drawn on an *appropriate subset of moves* given the audience you're trying to reach and the specific purposes you're trying to accomplish? (For example, if you want your band name to serve two purposes — sparking interest in the band *and* suggesting what type of music the band plays — then some names will work better than others.)

- Have you considered *experimenting with moves typically made in other genres*? Because many genres share overlapping purposes, a move typically made in one genre might be useful in another. (For example, one move made across genres is to use concrete objects as symbols, as in the band name "Beans on Toast.")

Unfortunately the success of the moves you make isn't guaranteed; allusions, for example, assume prior knowledge that readers may or may not have. Nonetheless, if you see writing as choosing from among a constellation of moves made across genres — rather than as a rote activity in which you mimic all the conventions of a single genre wholesale — then you'll be better able to use genres to accomplish your purposes.

How Genres Make Reading and Writing Easier

In addition to helping us accomplish specific purposes, genres ease the cognitive burden on readers and writers; our familiarity with them helps us read and write more efficiently. If we're reading or writing a genre that we've encountered before, we draw on our previous encounters with that genre to help us in our current encounter.

For example, if you've read many news articles, you've probably come to know (even if you're not aware that you know it) that the most important information is generally placed at the beginning of the article. Even if this knowledge is tacit, it helps you navigate news articles; you probably don't, for instance, feel obligated to finish every article you start. Consider another example: if you're looking at dozens of sociology research reports to see which ones are most relevant to an academic argument you're writing, you'll notice that the authors' key points appear in their abstracts. Knowing this about the genre, you might decide to take a first pass through all the reports just to look at the abstracts. After you select a relevant subset of reports based on the abstracts, only then would you go back and read those reports. Knowing a convention of the genre (that abstracts summarize key findings) saves you time and allows you to focus your search for sources.

Just as genres can make a reader's experience easier, so too can they make your experience as a writer easier. For example, if you know where readers expect certain information to appear, you don't have to spend time wondering where to put it. Knowing what readers tend to expect also helps you make a variety of other choices. This knowledge can help you decide how much — and what type of — evidence to use, whether to make an argument implicitly or explicitly, and whether to quote sources or paraphrase them, among many other choices.

Not only can genre help you make decisions when you write, but it can also help you generate ideas. Reading and thinking about the list of band names, for example, might help you generate a band name of your own. Genres also foster habits of mind — that is, ways of thinking that are valued by a community. After reading and writing many pieces in a genre — especially a genre used by members of a community that you want to join — you'll be better able to generate ideas that they'll find interesting and important.

Strategies for Reading and Writing Any Genre

As you study new disciplines in college, and later as you begin to do the reading and writing you'll be called on to do in most jobs, you'll almost inevitably encounter new genres. Although some of these genres may seem difficult at first, don't worry; the more time you spend reading and writing them, the more comfortable you'll feel.

For an example of how you can learn to become comfortable with a genre, consider David Sedaris's experience with poetry, which he discusses in his introduction to *The Best American Nonrequired Reading* (2010). Sedaris begins by informing us that he likes only limericks, which, he says, "are basically dirty jokes that rhyme" (xvii). He goes on to tell us what he thinks of other poetry:

> The other kinds of poetry, the kind written entirely in lowercase letters, or the kind where a single sentence is broken into eight different lines, I find confounding. I think I was out sick the day we learned to read them, and it never occurred to me that I could catch up, or, heaven forbid, teach myself.
>
> . . . It's easy to believe when looking at such things that parts of them are missing, that words and commas got erased or were blown away, like one of those church signs after a strong wind. The bits that are left function as clues, the poem itself not a story, but a problem, something to be sweated over and solved. Why not make things easier and just say what you mean? Why be all, well, *poetical* about it?

Sedaris's attitude, however, begins to shift after he downloads a podcast called *Poetry Off the Shelf*, which enables him to encounter more poetry:

> I originally downloaded it thinking, not of myself, but of [my boyfriend Hugh's] mother, who likes serious things. I was going to force her to sit in a chair with my iPod on, but then I ran out of books to listen to. Company was coming, I had a day's worth of house work ahead of me, so I thought, *What the hell.*
>
> The first podcast that I listened to featured the late James Schuyler. . . . After listening to him twice, I listened to a short analysis offered by the podcast's host, and the week's special guest. A few small references went over my head, but otherwise, I seem to have gotten everything. Equally surprising is that it never felt like work. . . .

Notice that Sedaris listened to the poet twice. If you reread a piece of writing (or listen to it more than once), you'll be much better equipped to make sense of it. Also note that Sedaris learned a bit more from listening to the podcast's host and the guest; hearing what others have to say about a piece of writing can provide you with insight you can use when you encounter other pieces that draw on that genre. Indeed, Sedaris goes on to encounter more poetry that he understands and enjoys:

> In the next podcast, I discovered Robert Hayden. . . . From Robert Hayden I moved to Philip Larkin, then to Fanny Howe and Robert Lowell. The more I'm exposed to, the more enraptured I become, the world feeling both bigger and smaller at the same time. *Poetry*, I think. *Where has it been all my life!* I said to Hugh, "I feel like I've discovered a whole new variety of meat.
>
> And
>
> it's
>
> free!"

Sedaris is more eloquent than most when he describes the process of becoming comfortable with a genre, but the process he describes is typical. If you, like Sedaris, encounter a genre that's "something to be sweated over and solved," you too will prevail if you keep engaging with the genre and with others who use it.

One of the most helpful ways to engage with a genre is to read sample after sample of it and look for patterns. In other words, do the same thing you probably did when you read the list of band names. In addition to looking for patterns, ask yourself which samples of the genre better accomplish their purposes for their intended audiences—and why. Being able to see why some samples are more effective than others will help you when you produce the genre.

Once you have samples of a genre—whether it's one you need for your new major, your new job, or any other purpose—you can use the following questions to gain insight into the genre. The questions are arranged in categories that highlight key patterns; if you can discuss some of the categories with people who write the genre, you'll have even more insight to draw on when you write the genre yourself.

Routine Practices and the Roles of Others

- What are the *routine practices* people engage in as they produce the genre?[2] Are other genres read or written in the process of producing this one? How many people are directly or indirectly involved? What role does formal or informal discussion play? What about other activities (e.g., work on white boards or other modalities)? Does one person write, get feedback, and revise, or do several people write? Are the roles that others play in the production of the genre publicly recognized?

Audience and Purpose

- What are the *recurrent purposes* that authors who use the genre are trying to accomplish? What do they want readers to do or think? Might they have multiple purposes?

- Who is the *audience?* What do readers expect, and why are they reading the genre? Is the audience composed of different readers who might have different purposes? Is the audience often rushed when encountering the genre? Are people likely to read a piece in this genre in its entirety, or might they skip reading it or read just part of it? Are they likely to read sections in order, or might they

---

[2] Genres can be thought of not just as words alone but as words embedded within the repeated practices that people engage in as they produce, receive, and use those words.

read sections out of order (perhaps looking at a list of references first or reading a conclusion before the body)? Is the genre used differently when it's targeted to audiences in different cultures (e.g., different countries or companies)?

Subject Matter, Development, and Organization

- What *subject matter* does the genre typically address? What subject matter does the genre tend *not* to address?

- How do pieces in the genre tend to be *structured?* Is the genre flexible enough to allow for variation, or do particular types of information tend to be put in a certain order? Do writers have any typical ways of signaling how a piece is organized?

- How are *ideas developed?* What types of information tend to be included? Are there narratives? If evidence is used, is there a typical type of it, or are multiple types used?

- If *points* are made, are they typically made explicitly (stated directly) or implicitly (so that the audience has to "read between the lines"), or is the genre flexible enough that some samples make points explicitly while others do so implicitly?

Assumptions

- What *assumptions* do writers typically make about the subject matter? What's taken for granted as being true? What's assumed to be good or bad?

- Is there a *relationship between readers and writers* that's typically assumed? What roles are readers assumed to play? What roles are writers assumed to play (e.g., an expert instructing a novice, a subordinate deferring to a superior)?

Language and Design

- What type of *language* is commonly used? Do certain words, phrases, or sentence structures tend to recur? Is the tone typically formal, semi-formal or informal, or does it vary? Is active or passive voice usually used, or does it vary?

- What are common elements of *visual design?* Do writers typically use subheadings, photos, charts, icons, or other graphics? How are graphic elements typically related to text? What purposes do they serve?

You'll think of even more questions to ask and answer as you delve deeper into a new genre. When you begin writing the genre yourself, you'll find it especially helpful to get feedback on what you write.

If you use particular genres often enough, and interact often with others who use them, you'll become increasingly confident when you read and write those genres. If you engage with multiple genres over time, you'll probably also notice some subtle aspects of how genres work: they can change over time, they reflect and perpetuate assumptions and beliefs, and they each have unique limitations — things they can't help you accomplish. Knowing this will help you to respond to any changes, assumptions, or limitations you notice and, ultimately, to become even better equipped to craft language.

Using This Book

This book will help you deepen your understanding of genre in several ways. Each numbered chapter features readings from a variety of genres, followed by questions that highlight how the writers' choices were shaped by genre, audience, and purpose. As you consider these writers' choices, you'll start to see choices when you write, and you'll gain insight into which ones will be more likely to help you accomplish your purposes. You'll put your insights into practice at the end of each reading and chapter, where you can select which genres you want to use to explore the central questions of that chapter.

The chapters with readings are prefaced by two chapters of in-depth writing advice that you can refer back to as you write. The initial chapter discusses general strategies you can use for critical thinking, reading, and writing, and it describes three types of writing that will help you critically engage with any genre you read. The subsequent chapter discusses specific genres; by illustrating how writing looks similar — and different — as you move from one genre to another, this chapter will help you become a more flexible writer, one who knows how to adapt words to the unique situation that's at hand every time you write.

Strategies for Critical Thinking, Reading, and Writing

Your success in college — and in life — will be shaped not only by *what* you think, read, and write but also by *how* you think, read, and write. Tweaking how you engage in these activities can help you generate more ideas, critique what you read, and write more effectively. To this end, the following sections will provide you with specific strategies for critical thinking, active reading, and engaged writing — strategies that you can use with any genre. Following these sections you'll find discussions of three types of writing — summary, reflection, and rhetorical analysis — that can prompt you to read more actively and develop ideas worth writing about.

Critical Thinking

You've probably heard the term "critical thinking." At its core, critical thinking means bringing a questioning mind-set to everything you read, write, and think. Why is this important?

Consider Tom Bartlett's words in the *Chronicle of Higher Education's* blog *Percolator*. Although Bartlett focuses on what you might read in the discipline of psychology, what he says applies to other disciplines as well:

> For decades, literally, there has been talk about whether what makes it into the pages of psychology journals — or the journals of other disciplines, for that matter — is actually, you know, true. Researchers anxious for novel, significant, career-making findings have an incentive to publish their successes while neglecting to mention their failures. It's what the psychologist Robert Rosenthal named "the file drawer effect." So if an experiment is run ten times but pans out only once, you trumpet the exception rather than the rule. Or perhaps a researcher is unconsciously biasing a study somehow. Or maybe he or she is flat-out faking results, which is not unheard of. . . .
>
> [I]t's not just social psychology that has to deal with this issue. Recently, a scientist named C. Glenn Begley attempted to replicate 53 cancer studies he deemed landmark publications. He could only replicate six. Six! Last December

I interviewed Christopher Chabris about his paper titled "Most Reported Genetic Associations with General Intelligence Are Probably False Positives." Most![1]

Regardless of whether you're reading a research report or a restaurant review, a news article or a Facebook status update, what you're reading was written by a particular person in a particular place at a particular time. If you change any part of this equation — if you swap out the person, the place, or the time — what you read would be different; there is no single "truth."

To shed light on how this is possible, consider that words — either spoken or written — are in many ways like photographs. For example, if you took photos in your dining hall and had to pick one to share with your class, your photo might feature students happily chatting over lunch, or it might feature a slump-shouldered student eating alone in a corner. Alternatively, you might share a close-up of some food with your class — perhaps a photo of a crisp colorful salad or a photo of some over-cooked broccoli. You would choose which photos to take, and which one to share, from among many possibilities. Your ultimate choice of photos would be colored by your opinion of the dining hall (among other things), and your opinion of the dining hall would be shaped by layers of other influences, including what kind of food you ate before you came to college, whether the food served in the dining hall aligns with your values, and whether you had much choice in meal plans.

When people write, they are similarly influenced by layers of context — context that shapes how (or if) they conduct research on a topic, the sources (if any) they choose to cite, and the words they choose when they write, among many other things. It's thus important to think critically about the words that come your way — whether those words come from the mouth of a professor, the pages of a magazine or a peer-reviewed journal, or the screen of your phone or computer. The following strategies will help you think critically about the words you encounter:

- *Ask if there's evidence to support any claims being made — and, if so, how that evidence was selected from among the many other pieces of evidence that could have been used instead.* If an example is used, is it a typical example? If quotations are used, do they come from only one or two sources? If there are statistics, how might they have been selected from among other statistics to advance a particular perspective?

---

[1] From "Is Psychology about to Come Undone?" posted on April 17, 2012.

- *If evidence is being used, how much context for that evidence is given?* Could a quotation have been taken out of context? Could an action described by an author have been taken out of context? If a description of context is included, is the context described in enough depth to provide a sense of how that context is unique (and thus how the evidence embedded in that context might differ from other pieces of evidence)?

- *Similarly, if research is being reported, ask how the methods of conducting that research might have affected the results.* If research was conducted with human subjects in a lab, would the results hold true outside the lab? If so, would they hold true for everyone in every situation? If you're reading about a survey, did it have many respondents? How many demographics did the respondents represent? What additional information might have been yielded by interviewing people? If people were interviewed, how might their words have been influenced by their view of the person interviewing them (among other things)? If you're reading about something researchers observed, how might what they noticed have been shaped by their values, beliefs, and culture?

- *Critically evaluate the credibility of the authors you read as well as the authors they cite.* Is an author an expert? If so, do his or her views represent those held by most other experts? Regardless of whether an author is an expert, does he or she have a stake in advancing a particular perspective?

- *Consider other possible explanations that might (at least partially) account for a phenomenon being discussed.* Could something else have led to this phenomenon? Could there have been not just one but several things that might have contributed? If causality is being claimed, could it have worked in the opposite direction as well—that is, X contributes to Y but Y also contributes to X?

In sum, ask yourself how a topic might be more complex than acknowledged by the words on the page. Is there a claim that something is always true when it might be true only sometimes? Is it true only for some people or only in some situations?

In addition to questioning the words you encounter with your eyes and ears, question the words in your head. Keep an open mind, and expect your opinions and ideas to evolve as you read and write. If your ideas don't evolve, you're not learning. You might have seen one or both of the following bumper stickers, both of which make important points:

If you haven't changed your mind lately, how can you be sure you still have one?

Don't believe everything you think.

Active Reading

Bringing a questioning mind-set to what you think, read, and write will be easier if you see reading as more than just receiving knowledge. Indeed, readers don't simply extract meaning from words; readers *construct* meaning through the ways they interact with words. You can deepen how you interact with words by asking yourself questions such as these:

- What is the author responding to? What prompted him or her to write?
- What do you think is the author's purpose in writing? What does he or she want readers to do or think?

Through the process of thinking about what an author is responding to and what motivates him or her to write, you'll think of more questions to ask yourself (and the author) — and asking questions is key to gaining insight.

Also, try looking for connections between what you're reading and your own prior knowledge and experience. Finding connections to your experience can deepen your insight into what you read. In addition, look for connections to other things you've read — in the same class, in other classes, or on your own. Do other things you've read, along with your own experience, seem to validate what you're reading? Call it into question? Validate part of it but call other parts into question?

The more connections you see between your life and what you read, the more thoughtfully you'll be able to read and write (and to think about the world more generally). The strategies discussed in this section will help you see more connections, question what you read, and develop your own insightful ideas in response to what you read. When you decide which strategies to use, bear in mind your purposes for reading; for instance, you might be reading because you need to write an essay about a text, or you might be reading just to see if a text is worth using as one of many sources. Considering your purposes for reading — along with the genre and difficulty of a text — will help you decide which of the following strategies are worth trying.

Before You Read

Experienced readers often use these strategies before reading.

Preview the reading.   Quickly glance through the pages to see how many parts to the reading there are. Depending on the genre you're reading, you might find it helpful to take a peek at the abstract or introduction, the conclusion, any headings and subheadings, any graphics or illustrations, and the bibliography if there is one. Even if you take just a minute to do this, you'll get a sense of what the parts are and how they fit together, which makes reading easier.

Make predictions about what you're going to read.   You can make predictions based on either your preview or something you might know about the author's purpose or the context in which the author wrote. Making predictions can bring focus and a sense of purpose to your reading. (The accuracy of your predictions doesn't matter.)

While You Read

Although you may not be used to writing in books (or annotating what you read on a screen), this practice is essential for understanding, remembering, and responding to a text as insightfully as possible. Think about which of the following strategies will work for you.

Consider developing your own set of symbols.   In the margins, you might use an exclamation point for something that surprises you, a check mark for something you agree with, a question mark for something that confuses you, a question mark with an exclamation point for something you disagree with, and so on. You might also experiment with stars or other symbols. Have fun figuring out a system that works for you.

Highlight or underline important words.   Or draw a vertical line down the margin beside passages you think are important.

Write words in the margins.   Note any one or more of the following:

- What the author is doing (e.g., summarizing in one paragraph, making a claim and providing evidence in another paragraph)
- Why you agree or disagree with something
- What specific questions or concerns you might have (e.g., "Why does the author use this type of evidence?" or "There's probably lots of evidence supporting the opposite view!")
- Possible implications of what the author is saying (e.g., "If this policy were implemented, wouldn't that make ____ more likely?")
- How what the author says is connected to what other authors have said (e.g., "Uses a different kind of evidence than Gonzalez" or "Makes a point similar to Boyd's")
- How credible an author's sources are (e.g., "Bibliography cites a news article — not the most credible source")
- How you might use something from the reading in your own writing (e.g., "Quote this," "Paraphrase this," or "Critique this").

Flag key pages to look at again later.   Most bookstores and office supply stores sell small paper or plastic flags that stick on pages. Flagging pages can save you time when you write; you might spend less time hunting for an important passage that you remember, or you might be reminded of an important passage you wouldn't have remembered. Besides writing on flags (e.g., "Cite this"), you could develop your own color-coded system — perhaps green for something important that you agree with, yellow for something you think is only partially true, and red for something you want to critique.

Draw horizontal lines to divide a reading into sections, and consider labeling each section.   You could do so according to topic or what you think the author is trying to accomplish. Dividing a work into sections can help you distinguish different parts of the whole and better see how a work is organized. (Some genres, of course, are already divided into sections by headings and subheadings.)

Take some notes on what you're reading or make a more structured outline.   You might simply jot down a couple of ideas that interest you, or you might list all the author's points, perhaps with one or two levels of indentation to show what's subordinate to what (if relevant). Being able to see, on a single piece of paper, what the most important points are — and how those points are related to one another — may help you better understand, critique, and remember a reading.

Any one of these strategies will enable you to bring more of your own ideas into dialogue with what you read — and that's the ultimate goal of reading.

It will also be useful for you to think about strategies you can use if, say, you have to read something by the next day but you also have three midterms, or if you're going through a crisis and can't focus long enough to read something carefully. If a text would normally take an hour to read carefully but you can only muster up ten minutes, don't just read for ten minutes and only get a sixth of the way through; instead, consider reading the first sentence or two of all the key paragraphs in the text. Depending on the genre, you'll probably get more out of the reading by using this approach.

After You Read

Compared to the time you spend reading a text, the time you spend with a text *after* your initial reading can sometimes provide the most bang for the buck. You can use your post-reading time in any of the following ways (depending on your purpose as a reader).

Try skimming something right after you finish reading it.   Even if you take just a few minutes to glance at a couple things you marked, you'll probably be better able to remember what you read, and you might realize that some points were more or less important than you had initially thought. You might also be able to see connections between points that were too subtle to notice on the first reading.

Carefully reread something that you plan to write about before you write.   This is crucial if you want to write something insightful rather than just regurgitate information or make a simplistic argument. A careful rereading of a text often reveals nuances that even the most experienced readers wouldn't notice the first time around. In fact, experienced readers often reread a text multiple times if they plan to write about it.

Use writing as a tool to develop insight into what you've read.   You might, for example, write a brief reflection (p. 27), a summary (p. 23), or a rhetorical analysis (p. 31) of a text before you go on to write, say, a letter to the editor or another genre of argument that draws on that text. The insight you gain through writing the first piece will enable your second piece of writing to be more thoughtful.

In sum, the more deeply and often you interact with the words you read, the more insight you'll gain in response to those words.

Engaged Writing

Just as you'll gain more insight into a reading if you take more than one pass through it, so too will your writing be more insightful if you take more than one pass through it.

If you don't have as much time as you'd like to write a piece, make a deliberate decision about how to allot that time. If you have five hours to produce an essay, try not to spend all five hours writing a draft. Instead, consider your genre, audience, and purpose and make a deliberate decision about how much time to spend preparing, how much time to spend drafting, and how much time to spend making changes to what you write. Note that many if not most published writers spend more time preparing to write and making changes than they do actually writing an initial draft.

Although writing is often described as a process with stages that happen both before and after the initial draft is written, you might find that the stages are somewhat artificial and that they overlap. That's fine; in fact, it's good to question what anyone tells you about writing because every writer, and every situation, is different. The important truth to remember is this: if you care about a piece of writing, it's helpful to have a process that consists of more than one activity.

The activities described in this section are presented in a certain order, but you can try them in any order — and at different points during your writing process. For example, you might find an idea under "Before You Draft" to be more helpful when implemented while you're writing or revising — or to be helpful during all three of these activities. Indeed, writers often find themselves looping back to some of the same activities again and again; this is generally necessary to produce writing that successfully communicates what you want to convey.

Before You Draft

The time you spend thinking before you draft can significantly affect the quality of what you write — and it can save you both time and frustration during the process. Spending a bit of time generating ideas and planning before you draft could potentially save you hours in writing time. Consider trying a couple of the following strategies (in any order) to help you generate ideas to write about.

Reread any sources you're thinking of using.   Recall that rereading is crucial if you want to go beyond regurgitating what your sources have said. If you'll be using sources, rereading is perhaps the single most important thing you can do before you write.

Articulate what you think your specific purpose(s) in writing will be.   Your primary purpose might be to get readers to consider your ideas, to enable them to better understand others, to entertain them, to inform them about something you think is important, or any number of other purposes.

Select a genre appropriate to your purpose, and try reading samples of other writing in that genre.   You'll notice patterns — moves writers make that repeat across the samples you read. You'll also notice differences — adaptations that each writer makes to tailor his or her writing to the specific situation. Reading writing samples will give you ideas about which moves you want to emulate, adapt, or avoid.

Talk about your topic with someone.   Talking and writing are interconnected in many ways. People often think of new ideas or further develop their ideas when they talk to others.

Brainstorm a list of possible ideas to write about.   Don't censor yourself; write down all your ideas, regardless of how obvious or silly they may seem. You might write phrases, sentences, or questions that you are genuinely curious about. Questions that you don't know the answers to are especially useful in prompting you to think beyond the obvious. Also consider other prewriting strategies your instructor may have taught you, including writing a discovery draft or freewriting (continuously writing about whatever ideas come to mind). You can go back later and discard some of these ideas.

If you're using a thesis-driven genre, consider crafting a working thesis. A working thesis (an overview of your main point) will help to guide your thinking and planning. It can be written at any point and can be repeatedly refined as your thinking continues to evolve.

After you're satisfied with the number and depth of ideas you've generated, consider which ones work best together as a focused whole. Some ideas, though good, might be better ignored or put in another piece of writing so that the piece at hand can have a sharper focus. Also think about which ideas fit the scope of your project; for example, perhaps half of your ideas would work together as a focused whole, but only a quarter of them will work with your planned length.

You may have trouble assessing how many ideas "translate" into how many pages. That depends on whether you'll discuss those ideas in depth (sacrificing breadth) or whether you'll favor breadth (sacrificing depth). In many cases, discussing fewer ideas in greater depth leaves readers with a fuller understanding than they would get from a quick, superficial discussion of more ideas. (With some genres, such as blog posts, you may even decide to sacrifice both depth and breadth, opting for a one- or two-sentence post.) Regardless of what you decide about depth and breadth, you'll want it to be a deliberate decision.

Once you've decided on the scope of what you'll write, consider doing a few of these activities to plan your writing.

Imagine two or three different ways to organize your ideas, and pick the organization you think is best based on your purpose, audience, and genre.   Making an outline or a list of how you want to order your ideas will help you find a logical order, and that will make writing easier.

Make a list of possible objections or points of confusion that readers might have.   Should you concede a point in an argument, specify when and where something happened in a creative nonfiction piece, or provide a definition in a brochure or blog post? (Although some writers like to anticipate readers' responses only when they revise, others like to do so at several points throughout the process of writing a piece.)

Decide how to design your work based on genre, purpose, and audience.   You might use headings and subheadings, bulleted lists, photos, charts, tables, or graphs, or you might simply leave extra white space between sections. Design can significantly affect how readers respond to what you write, so it's something you'll want to consider.

While You Draft

No matter how carefully a writer plans, first drafts are messy and imperfect. No writers—not even published writers—produce first drafts that reflect what they're capable of.

In addition to being a messy activity, writing is a generative activity; no matter how many ideas you think of ahead of time, you'll continue to generate ideas as you write (especially if you're "unplugged" from your phone and computer). Given the generative and messy nature of writing, you might find some of these ideas helpful.

Try not to get stuck worrying about things like grammar, spelling, and punctuation.   These can be adjusted later, when you edit your work; worrying about them now might stifle your ideas. If you're writing on a screen, consider turning off the spelling and grammar checkers at this point. Letting go of the little things can free you up to keep generating ideas.

Realize that you don't have to write your draft in order.   It might be useful to write your introduction after you've written the body paragraphs or to save a tricky middle paragraph until last.

If you get stuck, take a break.   You might talk about what you're writing with someone, do a bit of exercise, get some water, or eat a snack. Any of these activities can spark your brain. At the very least, try writing a different section of your draft. You'll probably find that any problems you encounter will be easier to solve after you've had some time away from them.

Consider unplugging from your phone and the Internet.   If your ideas aren't coming as quickly as you'd like, or they seem a bit obvious and superficial, try unplugging. This is one of the most common pieces of advice that experienced writers give novice writers (and it might also be worth considering at other points in your reading and writing process as well). Being able to concentrate on your writing without interruption can enable you to see more connections and develop more nuanced ideas.

If you can see more than one way to manipulate a passage, consider copying and pasting that passage and then changing one of the copies.
Writers often find it easier to make choices if they actually see the alternatives side by side.

After You Draft

Although some students' post-drafting process consists of hitting Print and looking for a stapler, the more you do after you finish drafting, the more likely you are to be truly happy with what you've written.

Before you alter your draft, however, think about doing two things that may make it easier for you to make changes. First, consider copying your draft and pasting it into a new document that you can then alter. Knowing that your original draft is still intact can make it easier to experiment with radical changes; if you make a change and end up not liking what you did, you can always go back to your original draft.

Second, consider printing your draft. Because printed pages have a higher resolution than some screens, many people find that they notice more problems when they read printouts. In addition, printing a draft allows you to lay all the pages in front of you so that you can see every page at once — a strategy that enables you to notice issues with focus and organization that you might not otherwise notice. (If you don't have access to a printer, a second choice would be to zoom out on your screen, which will allow you to see your draft two or more pages at a time.)

Once you have a printout of your draft, three activities are generally recommended: revising, editing, and proofreading. Although these activities can overlap, thinking of them as distinct — and at least trying to do each one of them in a separate pass — can help writers be more thorough, usually resulting in an end product that is considerably better than the first draft.

Revise.   When writers revise, they're generally looking for big-picture issues that can be seen only by looking at the text as a whole (rather than by looking at individual sentences or paragraphs in isolation). When you revise, you might sharpen your focus, reorganize your work, or more fully develop your ideas. Revision results in substantial changes rather than superficial tinkering.

Revision is a good time to ask yourself how well you succeeded in accomplishing your purposes as a writer. If your primary audience is a professor, it's also a good time to reread an assignment description (or at least to glance at the parts you underlined or highlighted).

As you revise, try to see your draft through readers' eyes. If possible, have others read what you wrote, and ask them specific questions about how well they think the draft fulfills your purpose. Also try pointing them toward specific passages you have questions about. Here are a few questions to think about as you revise:

- *What could you move?* Is there something in the middle of your piece that might receive more emphasis if you moved it to the beginning?

If you're writing a point-first argument, is there a better-articulated version of your thesis in the conclusion that might be moved to the introduction? Are there any paragraphs or sentences you could move somewhere else to sharpen your focus or to provide a more logical order for readers? Some writers find that making a "reverse outline" of a draft (outlining it *after* they finish writing) can be a useful tool for seeing which parts might be better moved elsewhere.

- *Are there any passages that you want to expand?* Just as main characters in movies get more screen time than minor characters, you'll generally want your most important ideas to be more prominent than your minor ideas. Where might readers appreciate more support or explanation? What passages might you expand to help readers see the importance of your topic?

- *Could you cut or condense any passages?* Try to muster up the strength to cut paragraphs or passages that don't fit your overall focus, that are repetitious, or that may not be effective given your audience and purpose. If you haven't kept a copy of your first draft, you might find it easier to cut or condense passages if you paste copies of them into a "scrap heap" at the bottom of your document (or into another document). That way, what you've worked hard to write won't be lost if you decide to add it back or use it in something else you write.

Edit.   While revision tends to involve looking at your piece as a whole, editing tends to involve looking at smaller parts of your work, often focusing on clarity or emphasis in light of your audience, purpose, and genre. If a piece is important enough to edit, consider some of these questions:

- *Could you break a long sentence into two? Could you combine two shorter sentences into one?* Breaking a sentence into two (or three) might help you clarify points or better emphasize ideas. Conversely, you might combine two shorter sentences so that a relationship between ideas is more apparent. You might also decide to combine or divide sentences so that you have more variety in sentence structure and length.

- *Are there any words that might be replaced with other words?* Would another word be more accurate or less likely to offend readers? If you're using a thesis-driven genre, are there any key words in your thesis that you could repeat in your body paragraphs to sharpen your focus? If you're not using a thesis-driven genre, could you replace any words that don't reflect your focus with words that do?

- *Would you want to add any words*, perhaps to qualify an idea, create emphasis, sharpen your focus, or clarify a point?

- *Could you create more emphasis or sharpen your focus by deleting any words?* Is there an unimportant phrase occupying the position of emphasis at the end of a sentence? Are there any words that don't fit your focus? If so, press the Delete key.

- *How might you fiddle with punctuation to clarify relationships between ideas, add emphasis, or take away emphasis?* Are there occasional commas that might be replaced with dashes? Are there any phrases between dashes that might be better demoted to parenthetical remarks? Could adding a semicolon between two sentences emphasize their relationship or encourage readers to continue reading (so that they're less likely to be confused)? Could adding a comma create emphasis or help readers see which words go together, thus making for a smoother reading experience?

Proofread.   While editing involves fiddling with words and sentences to make them better achieve your purpose, proofreading is focused on correcting typos, punctuation glitches, and grammatical errors. Some readers see errors as a sign of disrespect or carelessness, so you'll want to proofread carefully. You might find one or more of these strategies helpful:

- *Read what you wrote aloud, or ask someone to read it to you.* Using your ears as well as your eyes can help you notice errors that you might not otherwise catch.

- Turn your spelling and grammar checkers back on, but *don't assume they will find all the glitches.* The grammar checker might be wrong and the spell checker won't catch errors such as "there" instead of "their."

- *Have on hand a dictionary and a grammar handbook (or the online equivalents)* to check any word-choice issues or possible punctuation and grammatical glitches. Web searches can also help, especially if you consult more than one source.

- If a piece of writing is short and important, *try reading it backwards.* You might read the last word, then the second-to-last word, and so on, or you might read the last sentence, then the second-to-last sentence, and so on. Many students find that the latter approach is especially useful in finding sentence fragments. Reading backwards can often prevent a common problem: seeing what you think you wrote rather than what you really did write.

- After you do a round or two of proofreading on your own, *consider asking a friend, roommate, or writing center consultant to look at what you've written.* This strategy is especially helpful if, through no fault of your own, you tend to have errors that you don't catch; for example, it's a useful work-around for multilingual writers and people with learning disabilities. (If you have a learning disability or are a multilingual writer and you can't find anyone to look at your work, consider telling your readers about your situation so that they don't feel disrespected.)

The more passes you take through your writing, the more it will reflect the depth of thought you're capable of. To this end, the following text box will provide you with a useful reference to consult after you finish a draft.

Break It Down

If you write something and read it over only once before submitting it, your work won't reflect your true intelligence. Almost all writers—including professional writers—overlook problems and miss opportunities to strengthen their work any time they reread a draft. This is simply the limitation of the human brain; we're very smart, but we can only do so much at once.

To produce writing that better reflects your true intelligence, read your work more than once before you submit it. Consider a "break-it-down" approach in which you *read your work one time for each area you're developing as a writer.* One writer, for instance, might read her work once to see if it's focused, another time to see if she could provide more evidence, and still another time to look for comma splices. Another writer might read his work once for organization, once for transitions, and once for typos.

In collaboration with a classmate, professor, or writing center consultant, use the space that follows to list issues to consider each time you reread a piece of your work. Use pencil, since the list will change as you develop as a writer (and as you move from one genre to another).

Personalized list of issues to focus on:

_____

_____

_____

_____

Reading your work one time for each of these issues can lead to significant improvements in your writing.

Writing to Prompt Active Reading

There are many types of writing that foster active reading, including summaries, reflections, and rhetorical analyses. The following sections discuss useful strategies for these three types of writing. In addition, they include sample student work with annotations that you'll find useful when it's your turn to write about what you've read.

Instead of reading the sections that follow in one sitting, you'll probably find it more helpful to read about each type of writing just before you do it.

Writing Summaries

When you summarize a piece you've read, you'll often gain insights into the piece that you wouldn't have otherwise gained. Summaries are written for several purposes; for instance, writers often embed them into a variety of genres, perhaps summarizing a work to orient readers before they go on to critique that work or summarizing others' work to provide context for their own work — to show readers how their own work fits into a larger conversation. Stand-alone summaries, in contrast, are generally written to save readers time — to allow them to get an accurate sense of what an author has written without having to read it themselves. Stand-alone summaries can also help readers decide whether they want to read the work being summarized or help them decide whether they truly understand what they've read. The following ideas will help you write effective summaries.

Before You Write

What you do before you write can significantly affect the quality of your summary.

Consider outlining the piece you're summarizing. To help you create your outline of the piece you've read, try drawing horizontal lines between sections and labeling each section (e.g., "introduction and main point," "examples to support main point," or "subpoint").

To get a sense of which points are especially important, it's often useful to focus on the title, the opening and closing of the piece, the opening and closing sentences of paragraphs, and any headings or graphics that are included.

In addition to noting main points and subordinate points in your outline, note how the author develops the piece. If explicit points are made, how does the author support them? If points are made implicitly, what does the author do to provide clues about what the main and subordinate ideas are?

Reread the piece you're summarizing to see if your outline missed anything. Even if your outline is thorough, rereading the piece will help you pick up additional nuances not apparent in the first reading.

Plan your summary before you write. You might take the outline of the piece you're summarizing and rework it into an outline of your summary, bearing the following points in mind:

- *You'll want to cut less important information.* For example, rather than recounting every piece of evidence the author uses, you'll want to focus on the main points. You can then briefly describe how those main points are supported (e.g., anecdotes, statistics, or case studies).
- *Consider how you want to organize your summary.* Your summary doesn't have to follow the organization of the piece you're summarizing. For instance, if the author you're summarizing waits several paragraphs to define a key term, you may decide not to wait, instead providing the definition at the beginning of your summary. Similarly, if the author waits until the end to state the main point, you may decide to state it at the beginning of your summary. (Organization is shaped by genre and purpose; since your summary will be a different genre than the piece you're summarizing, and since you may intend it to serve a different purpose, you might decide to organize it differently.)

While You Write

Adapt the following points to your audience, purpose, and genre as needed. If you're embedding your summary into a larger piece (as opposed to writing a stand-alone summary), you might skip some of these ideas.

At the beginning of your summary, state the author and title, and then paraphrase the author's main idea. If the piece is part of something larger, such as a magazine or journal, also include where it was published. You may also want to mention the genre of the piece and its intended audience. This information is often provided in the first few sentences of a stand-alone summary, although another option would be to preface this information by briefly discussing why the piece you're summarizing is important or interesting.[2]

---

[2] Note that Trent Batson does this at the beginning of his "Response to Nicholas Carr's 'Is Google Making Us Stupid?'" on p. 584.

Consider discussing the author's subordinate ideas, making sure to distinguish them from the main idea (if it's relevant to the genre of the piece you're summarizing). For an example of how you might do this, see the annotated summary that follows this section.

Mention how the author came up with his or her ideas and how those ideas are developed. This might be through anecdotes, illustrative statistics, real or hypothetical examples, and/or discussion of research conducted by the author or by others. You'll usually want to avoid summarizing examples, in most situations opting instead to simply describe the types of examples used. For an illustration, see the annotated summary that follows this section.

Try to avoid extensive quotation of the piece you're summarizing. The point of a summary is to condense a piece, not to reproduce parts of it. In some situations, it's fine to quote sparingly; in others (especially if you're writing for an audience of scientists or social scientists), readers may expect you to avoid quotation altogether

Try to reiterate the author's name throughout your summary. You might say, for example, "Ching argues," "Ching describes," "Ching suggests," or "Ching claims." If you don't reiterate the author's name (or use pronouns referring to the author), readers might be misled into thinking that some of the author's ideas are your own.

Carefully consider whether to discuss your own views. Many readers expect summaries to reflect the views of the author being summarized, not the views of the person writing the summary. (There are some exceptions; for example, if you're embedding a summary into a critique, you'll obviously need to discuss your response to the work you're summarizing.)

After You Write

Revise your summary. Take one last look at the piece you're summarizing to make sure your summary represents it as accurately as possible. Do a final check to see if you want to add, cut, or move any information. You might add, cut, or move sentences or even whole paragraphs.

Edit and proofread your summary. See if you need to fiddle with any words or adjust any punctuation to add emphasis or clarify your meaning. Then check for typos and formatting glitches so that your readers don't get distracted from the content of your summary.

Sample Summary

Devin McGuire

Summary of *The Relationship Cure* Excerpt

When we think of bids we think of auctions, or a dollar amount on *The Price Is Right*. In the self-help excerpt of *The Relationship Cure*, however, John Gottman and Joan DeClaire define a bid as "the fundamental unit of emotional communication" (p. 147), or a request for an emotional connection. They tell us that relationships grow bid by bid, "one encounter at a time" (p. 149). They also tell us that if we can't recognize and respond to bids, our relationships may be in jeopardy.

A bid can be nonverbal—a look, a touch, a gesture—or it can be verbal; it's any expression that says "I want to feel connected to you" (p. 147). Some examples of bids are the following:

"Knock-knock."

"That's a pretty dress."

"Do you mind if I sit here?"

"What are you doing for lunch today?" (p. 149)

Gottman and DeClaire base some of their information on Gottman's clinical practice and some on years of research observing couples through a two-way mirror in the University of Washington's "Love Lab," a "comfortable weekend hideaway . . . [where couples can] simply relax and do whatever they would normally do during a typical weekend at home together" (p. 154). Based on these observations and a ten-year follow-up of the couples, Gottman and DeClaire provide a few statistics, including one about bidding and divorce: "husbands headed for divorce disregard their wives' bids for connection 82 percent of the time, while husbands in stable relationships disregard their wives' bids just 19 percent of the time" (p. 147).

Gottman and DeClaire also discuss more specific consequences of the bidding patterns found in the research (and in Gottman's clinical practice). They look at many types of relationships, including not only couples but also siblings, parents and children, coworkers, and friends. They don't stick to exposition but they also go to dialogue format, quoting a conversation that brings the reader into the parent-teen situation and shows how communication breaks

Opening paragraph. This paragraph clearly states the authors' names, the title of the text being summarized, and the main idea. Providing this information early helps orient readers.

Source of authors' ideas. Here McGuire mentions how the authors came up with their ideas. This information helps readers decide how much to trust those ideas.

Development of authors' ideas. McGuire tells readers how the authors have chosen to convey their ideas.

down when people don't respond to each other's bids. The authors then provide a makeover dialogue that gives an example of how people might respond to each other's bids and thus improve their relationships.

Finally, Gottman and DeClaire tell us there are three main responses to a bid:

1. *Turning toward: a positive response to another's bids for emotional connection.* A positive response to a bid might be a laugh, a nod, a question, or participation in a conversation. Gottman and DeClaire say that if a bid is an invitation, a positive response could be either to accept the invitation or to refuse the invitation but still accept the bid for emotional connection.

2. *Turning against: a negative or argumentative response to another's bid*, or just a mean reply. Turning against a bid pushes the bidder away, causing him or her to bid less for that emotional connection with the responder.

3. *Turning away: acting preoccupied or ignoring another's bid.* A person who turns away from a bid might not bother to look at the bidder, might not say anything in response to the bid, or might say something unrelated.

Gottman and DeClaire say that consistently turning against and away from bids can lead to disaster: the ending of friendships; divorce; and distance between coworkers, siblings, and parents and children. But the authors give hope; turning against or turning away isn't a concrete trait within anyone's personality, and Gottman and DeClaire leave us with an understanding that it's never too late to start responding in a positive manner and to reconnect with lost loved ones; it's the only bid worth winning.

> **Summary of subordinate ideas.** In this section, McGuire paraphrases the authors' subordinate ideas without relying on extensive quotation or getting bogged down in specific examples.

> **Repetition of authors' names.** Mentioning the authors' names frequently helps readers understand whose ideas are whose. We're not misled into thinking that McGuire is telling us about his own ideas.

Writing Reflections

A reflection is a response to or interpretation of something you've read, experienced, or observed. Writing a reflection can be a gratifying way to express your thoughts and feelings, and it can also help you clarify those thoughts and feelings, generate new ideas, and deepen your understanding of an issue.

While many genres are written to bring about a change in readers, often the audience of a reflection is not just the readers but also the writer him- or herself. Because reflections can help you both refine and document your thoughts, you might find it useful to reread them later — especially since, after writing one, you might be asked to produce a piece in a more formal genre, drawing on the insights discussed in your reflection.

Because this book asks you to write reflections on what you've read, the ideas that follow are geared toward helping you write reflections on reading selections. If you're ever asked to reflect on something you've observed or experienced, simply adapt these ideas to your situation.

Before You Write

Read the text that you'll reflect on actively rather than passively.   You might flag pages, highlight passages, make a list of questions about the text, or take notes in the margins or on a separate piece of paper.

Reread the piece you'll reflect on.   When you reread, focus on finding ideas that you might be interested in responding to, or focus on developing a more nuanced understanding of the reading.

Generate ideas to write about.   If you don't have a writing assignment that asks specific questions to prompt your thinking, consider doing one of the following:

- If the reading taught you something, changed your perspective, broadened your understanding, or made you feel a certain way, discuss why you had the response you did.
- Explain how the reading relates to something you've experienced. Discuss how your experience sheds light on the reading or how the reading sheds light on your experience.
- Quote a passage you think is especially meaningful, and explain why you think it's important.
- Discuss your interpretation of what the reading means (especially if it's a genre that tends not to make explicit points, such as creative nonfiction).
- Reflect on the author's purpose and how well you think he or she succeeded in achieving that purpose.
- Agree with, disagree with, qualify, or extend a point made by the author, and explain your reasoning.
- Discuss any questions you're left with after finishing the reading.
- Speculate about one or two implications of what the author is saying.

Plan your reflection.   Although your planning may not be as elaborate as it is when you write other genres, take a minute to think about which ideas are most worth discussing and how you want to organize those ideas.

While You Write

Make sure you're truly engaging with the text.   This is perhaps the most important thing to do while writing. Help readers understand how your thoughts are connected to the reading. For example, avoid saying that the reading reminds you of an experience you had and then spending the rest of your time discussing that experience. Instead, you might explain *why* the reading reminds you of that experience and *how* the reading helps you better understand what you experienced. Regardless of what you choose to discuss in your reflection, keep coming back to the text you've read.

Develop your ideas.   Put yourself in your readers' shoes; try to provide enough elaboration on your thoughts so that readers can fully understand and appreciate your ideas.

Feel free to use the pronoun "I."   Although some students are taught in high school that they shouldn't use "I" when they write, this pronoun is useful in many genres — including reflections.

After You Write

Revise.   Which ideas would benefit from even more explanation? Could you engage with the reading even more, perhaps more fully explaining the connections between your thoughts and the text? Are there any passages that could be moved or omitted to sharpen your focus?

Edit and proofread.   If you've used quotations (as many students do), most readers will expect you to

- *introduce your quotations* (e.g., use attribution tags, such as "Lopez writes"),
- *include page numbers* (so readers can find the passage being quoted if they want to see the context of the quotation),
- *double- or triple-check the accuracy of all quotations* (important for anything you write).

In addition, you might want to play with some of the wording or punctuation to better emphasize or clarify ideas. Finally, correct typos or grammatical glitches so that readers don't get distracted by them.

Sample Reflection

Sara Snider

Lappé Reflection

As an avid nutrition advocate and a tuition-paying college student, I respond to Anna Lappé's 2009 article about the Real Food Challenge with hope and pride that young people are fighting for their right to real food and a sustainable environment. This work piques my interest for a variety of reasons and it also reminds me of an experience I had last semester. I attended the annual Sustainable Dinner at Loyola University Chicago, which consisted of vegetables and grains grown at the student-run farm on Loyola's Recreation and Ecology Campus in Woodstock, Illinois. This dinner, sponsored by the Gannon Center for Women and Leadership, also included keynote speeches in which students and professors shared their experiences with sustainable farming and the importance of local food sources for both personal and environmental health. I think this event is an example of what Lappé means when she writes about a new social movement striving to achieve greater food consciousness.

It inspires me to learn that college students are, in a sense, leading the way on this important issue. Aramark, one of the three major food providers Lappé mentions, is the food service employed by Loyola. I agree with Lappé's assertion that in a free market, college students are customers who deserve to get what they pay for. College tuition and fees at both private and public institutions are rising, and students at every institution take part in a system characterized by a give-and-take mentality. Students give the university tuition and other funds, and in return students are entitled to certain services. Meals are an important service that students at every university in the United States consume. Local food choices, especially produce, are usually fresher than their counterparts, and therefore most likely higher in nutritional quality. Further, nutrition is central to health, and health is essential for the highest levels of learning. It is safe to say that individuals usually enroll in college to learn or enhance their knowledge, and so every

The pronoun "I." Reflections are frequently meant to be your personal take on a text you have read. Snider uses first person throughout her reflection to highlight how the article she read was personally significant.

Connection back to the reading. Rather than end the paragraph with the description of the dinner she attended, Snider tells us how the dinner relates to the reading.

student deserves to have a variety of healthy and sustainable food choices regardless of the institution they attend.

A particular quote about companies like Aramark from Anim Steel strikes me and reflects my own experience: "no matter how committed many [food service] companies say they are, they can only go as far as students push them" (qtd. in Lappé 455). Aramark made notable changes in terms of sustainability, food transportation, and food origin at Loyola last year, but only after the Unified Student Government Association stepped in and proposed new policies on behalf of Loyola students. A few of those changes include a trayless dining system, sustainable seafood purchases in partnership with the Monterey Bay Aquarium's Seafood Watch program, and a fryer oil recycling program.

Support for claims. Snider uses her own knowledge to support a claim made in the reading. This is another useful strategy for making connections between the reading and personal knowledge/experience.

Many of these sustainability initiatives align directly with those of the Real Food Challenge. The central positive result of these changes is that college students are receiving more nutritious food options while also conserving resources and reducing greenhouse gas emissions that have rapidly advanced climate change. Another positive aspect of sustainable aspirations at college campuses is the rising notion that young people truly have a voice in our society. Student action is a primary cause of such sustainability measures not only at Loyola, but around the nation due to the nature and impact of the Real Food Challenge.

Loyola University Chicago Sustainability Statement:
www.campusdish.com/NR/rdonlyres/4C399444-325F-4E29-8D50
-A8C772ACD1CC/0/SustainabilityCOMMITMENT.pdf

Writing Rhetorical Analyses

When you write a rhetorical analysis of something you've read, you're examining the effects of how the author uses language in light of his or her purpose, audience, and genre. There are at least two reasons it's useful to examine how language is used. First, language shapes thought, and being aware of how language can be manipulated will help you prevent your thoughts from being manipulated. Second, examining how language is used can help you grow as a writer; when you look at how others use language, you gain insight into more ways that *you* can use it.

You might write a rhetorical analysis as a stand-alone essay, or you might embed one into an op-ed, a letter to the editor, a blog post, or any other genre.[3] The purpose of a rhetorical analysis is generally to help readers see the text being analyzed in a new light. Your analysis might enable readers to better appreciate a text, or it might alert them to problems in the text that they missed. Of course, you might also write a mixed rhetorical analysis—one that does both. When you write a rhetorical analysis, it often helps to start with one of these two groups of questions:

- What patterns do you see in how the author uses language? What are the effects of those patterns? How might those patterns be related to the author's audience, purpose, and genre?

- How effectively do you think the author uses language given his or her purpose, audience, and genre? Why should readers care about how effectively or ineffectively the author uses language?

A rhetorical analysis is generally considered to be a type of argument; you'll essentially be making an argument about how language is being used and, if your rhetorical analysis is a stand-alone essay, developing that argument through a set of subpoints (subarguments).

Before You Write[4]

Read the text you're analyzing actively rather than passively.   You might flag pages, highlight passages, make a list of questions about the text, or take notes in the margins or on a separate sheet of paper.

Generate ideas to write about.   If you don't have a writing assignment that asks you to address specific aspects of the text, consider some of the questions in the text box that follows this section.

Reread the text you're analyzing in light of what you're planning to write about.   Or, if you still haven't decided what to write about, reread

---

[3] For example, in Bonnie Liebman's newsletter interview "In Your Face: How the Food Industry Drives Us to Eat" (p. 481), Kelly Brownell examines how the language of advertising encourages us to eat too much, but this is only one piece of his broader argument that obesity should be addressed at the policy level instead of being left as a problem for individuals to solve by themselves. Rhetorical analyses, then, can be useful not only in making arguments about the effects of language use but in making other arguments as well.

[4] The ideas described in this list are activities to experiment with, not a prescription of steps you must take. You might skip some of these activities, do them in a different order, intersperse a few of them with other activities not listed here, or do some of them recursively (coming back to do them again after engaging in other activities).

for the purpose of discovering a point worth making. If you've read a text only once, you're more likely to make an obvious argument that won't help readers see the text in a new light.

Plan your rhetorical analysis.   This will make writing it quicker and easier. To plan (and generate more ideas), you might write a discovery draft, pick out the ideas you like, and think about the order of those ideas before going on to write your "real" draft. After or instead of writing a discovery draft, you might experiment with the following activities:

- *Try developing a working thesis (an overview of your argument), a list of subpoints, and a list of passages that support those subpoints.* You could do this in any order; you might start with several passages from the text and from there develop subpoints and a thesis, or you might already have a thesis in mind that can guide you in developing subpoints and finding passages to use as supporting evidence. For examples of a thesis statement, subpoints, and evidence, see the sample rhetorical analysis that follows this section.

- *Decide how you want to order your subpoints.* Try putting your subpoints in a logical order based on how they relate to one another, how important they are to your overarching argument, and/or how receptive you think your audience will be to each point.

While You Write

Consider how familiar your audience will be with the text you're analyzing. If readers may not have read the text, try to give them enough background information on it—and on the passages you're quoting—to help them feel oriented. (Also note that even when the reader is a professor who knows the text, he or she may want you to contextualize the text, along with the specific passages that you quote.) See the sample rhetorical analysis for examples of how to do this.

Try to keep a sharp focus.   If readers see how all your paragraphs work together to support your thesis, they won't get distracted by wondering how things connect. This also holds true if the sentences in each paragraph work together to support the main point of the paragraph. A useful strategy for helping readers see the connections between sentences and paragraphs is to repeat key words or synonyms in your transitions and throughout your body paragraphs. (This strategy can work for both implicit and explicit arguments.) See the sample rhetorical analysis for examples.

Try to provide enough evidence.   For your analysis to be more persuasive, try to provide multiple pieces of evidence to support most of your subpoints. Much of your evidence will probably consist of quotations and analysis of those quotations.[5]

Consider how deep to go when you analyze quotations.   Readers may need you to go into depth to explain *how* a quotation supports a claim. (If it's obvious how all your quotations support your claims, your claims may be too simple.) When you quote a passage, you'll often need to call readers' attention to a few individual words within the passage and explain how those words work to convey a particular effect. See the sample rhetorical analysis for examples.

After You Write

Revise your rhetorical analysis.   Consider the following:

- *Confirm that you've provided enough context for the text you're analyzing, as well as the individual passages you're quoting,* so that readers will feel oriented.

- *See if you can refine your thesis and the main points of your paragraphs* so that they can be even more specific and nuanced. Recall that readers often lose interest in simple, obvious points.

- *See if you can sharpen your focus even more* so that readers can quickly see
  - o how your body paragraphs relate to your thesis,
  - o how each body paragraph relates to the previous paragraph,
  - o how sentences within a paragraph relate to each other.

  You might sharpen the focus by adding key words, cutting irrelevant words, and/or moving words or passages from one place to another.

- *Consider which parts of your rhetorical analysis need to be expanded.* See which claims could use even more evidence, and which quotations could benefit from a more in-depth analysis.

- *Make sure your claims aren't too strong.* Since a rhetorical analysis is your interpretation, try to avoid verbs like "prove," which imply that there is a single definitive interpretation. Instead, try verbs such as "suggests," "illustrates," "implies," or even "seems." You might also consider qualifying some claims (e.g., "for some readers, this word might bring to mind ____"). In addition, you might acknowledge alternative interpretations by using phrases such as "although some

---

[5] In a few cases, you might also be able to analyze an author's use of language without direct quotation (e.g., if you're describing how a text is organized and discussing the effects of that organization, or if you're pointing to something the author has chosen *not* to do).

readers might take ___ to mean ____, it could also be interpreted to suggest ____." If your claims are too strong for the evidence you're using, your credibility might be undermined.

Edit and proofread your rhetorical analysis. Most readers will expect you to do the following:

* *Introduce your quotations* (see the sample rhetorical analysis for examples).
* *Indent long quotations* ("long" is over four lines for MLA, which is the citation style you may be expected to use).
* *Include page numbers* for all quotations, so that readers can refer to the text you're analyzing if they want to see the words in their original context.
* *Double- or triple-check the accuracy* of all quotations; it's easy to mistype or omit a word.

In addition, you might want to play with your sentence structure, wording, or punctuation to emphasize or clarify important ideas. Finally, look for any typos or grammatical glitches that could distract readers and undermine your credibility.

Questions to Consider before Writing Your Rhetorical Analysis

Some of these questions will help you generate ideas for your rhetorical analysis. See which ones prompt you to look at the text in a new light.

YOUR RESPONSE TO THE TEXT

* What is your response to the text, either intellectually or emotionally? Trace your response back to what the author is doing. (Of course, your response will also be shaped by other influences, such as your beliefs, values, and experiences.)

GENRE, AUDIENCE, AND PURPOSE

* What do you take to be the author's purpose(s)? How can you tell?
* What type of audience does the author seem to be addressing? How can you tell?
* Given the audience and purpose of the text, did the author select an appropriate genre to use? Why or why not? Is the author drawing on more than one genre, and if so, why?

CONTINUED >

Questions to Consider before Writing Your Rhetorical Analysis, continued

- What are the conventions of the genre used by the author, and which of those conventions does the author choose to use, adapt, or not use? What purpose(s) do those conventions seem to serve?

FOCUS, ORGANIZATION, AND DEVELOPMENT

- Does the text have a sharp focus? If so, how is the focus maintained? If not, what diffuses the focus? What is the effect of the sharp (or diffused) focus?
- How is the text organized, and how does the author signal the organization? Does he or she provide an overview? Use transitions or subheadings? Why do you think the author chose to organize the text the way he or she did?
- If the text you're analyzing is a persuasive genre, does the author provide evidence? If so, what kind of evidence? Could the evidence be interpreted in a different way? What kinds of evidence does the author choose not to include? Is there any counterevidence?
- If the text you're analyzing isn't an explicitly persuasive genre, how is the text developed? What types of information or ideas are included, and how might they affect readers?
- Does the author recognize complexity in cases where readers might expect complexity to be recognized? Does he or she see things as being simple or nuanced? Does he or she anticipate and address potential objections or sweep things under the rug?

PERSONA OF THE AUTHOR

- Consider how the author comes across (e.g., knowledgeable, friendly, trustworthy, tentative, vulnerable). What does the author do to project that persona? How might the author's persona affect readers?
- How would you describe the author's tone (attitude toward the topic and toward readers)? How can you tell? What do you think is the effect of the author's tone?

ASSUMPTIONS MADE BY THE AUTHOR

- What does the author assume to be good or bad? True or false? How can you tell? What information does the author choose to include or omit? Does the author write from a particular person's point of view, conveying only that person's perspective? What are the connotations of the words chosen (e.g., does a reporter say that a source "noted" something or that the source "claimed" something)?

Questions to Consider before Writing Your Rhetorical Analysis, continued

VIVID LANGUAGE

- Some genres prize vivid language more than others. If you're reading creative nonfiction, blog posts, or journalistic genres (among others), consider the author's use of specific detail. Are nouns and verbs specific?[6] What are the effects of the specific details?
- Does the author use any analogies, including similes or metaphors? Does the author appeal to any of the five senses? Is there any dialogue? Do sentences tend to be long and wordy, or are short sentences and paragraphs occasionally used?

EMPHASIS

- Does the author succeed in emphasizing the words and ideas that are most relevant to his or her purpose?
- Does the author use color or graphic elements (e.g., photographs, charts, tables, bulleted lists, subheadings) to draw attention to important information?
- Does he or she use antitheses (juxtapositions of opposite ideas, as in "not X but Y")? What about other sentence structures that can add emphasis?
- How does the author use punctuation, which can be a powerful tool for emphasis?

Sample Rhetorical Analysis

Kirsten Ridlen

Is Brent Staples a Threat, or a Victim?

A Rhetorical Analysis of "Black Men and Public Space"

At twenty-two years old, Brent Staples was confronted with the implications of his race when a young white woman ran from him as he walked idly and innocently behind her along a silent city street. Upon some reflection of the incident, Staples suggests that although "there seemed to be a discreet, uninflammatory distance between

---

[6] For example, consider Brent Staples's nouns and verbs when he refers to "New Yorkers hunching toward nighttime destinations" (p. 226) rather than "people walking toward nighttime destinations."

us . . . [t]o her, the youngish black man—a broad six feet two inches with a beard and billowing hair, both hands shoved into the pockets of a bulky military jacket—seemed menacingly close" (p. 224). It seems his race alone proves enough to identify him as a threat. He relates this and similar incidents in his essay "Black Men and Public Space." This essay, first published in *Ms.* Magazine in 1986, addresses an audience largely populated by the same kind of women on the other side of these experiences. As Staples reveals through his elegant and at times ironic diction—and through his careful presentation of his character and antithetical contrasts between perceptions and reality—he is not a threat; rather he is the victim of a stigma that ultimately threatens his safety.

> **Thesis.** Note that Ridlen's thesis makes an argument about Staples's use of language. She argues that Staples presents himself as a victim rather than a threat—and she tells us *how* he does this (through his diction, characterization, and use of contrasting statements).

With his elegant diction, Staples casts himself not as a threat but as a well-educated and clever man. His easy use of words like "affluent," "errant," and "quarry" (p. 224) is evidence of a high-class education and contradicts the assumption that he is a lowlife offender. His diction illustrates his cleverness when he ironically describes the woman who ran away from him: "My first victim was a woman—white, well dressed, probably in her early twenties" (p. 224). The ironic use of the word "victim" insinuates the hostility with which he is met on the street, for the woman is not an actual victim of an actual threat but only a perceived victim of a perceived threat. Staples's sophisticated diction continues: "It was in the echo of the terrified woman's footfalls that I first began to know the unwieldy inheritance I'd come into—the ability to alter public space in ugly ways" (p. 224). What he satirically calls his "unwieldy inheritance" is merely the pedigree of a race marked by a history of prejudicial aversion. With his clever diction, Staples implicitly argues against the sort of stigma he addresses in this essay by disproving the stereotype.

> **Introduction to quotation.** Rather than begin the sentence with a quotation, Ridlen orients readers by suggesting *why* she's quoting Staples here (to show us another example of his sophisticated diction). When we go on to read the quotation, we know what we're supposed to get out of it.

More explicitly, Staples uses antithetical statements to identify misperceptions of him and immediately negate them with redeeming facts. Regarding his first encounter with the terrified woman, he says: "It was clear she thought herself the quarry of a mugger, a rapist, or worse. Suffering a bout of insomnia, however, I was stalking sleep, not defenseless wayfarers" (p. 224). The woman suspects he is after a violent opportunity when in truth, he only seeks a placid sleep. This contrast between opposites stresses the difference between the woman's perception and his reality. In the same vein, Staples

> **Contextualization.** Here Ridlen mentions the context in which a quotation appears in Staples's essay. This contextual information helps readers feel oriented when they read the quotation that follows.

describes himself as "a softy who is scarcely able to take a knife to a raw chicken — let alone hold one to a person's throat" (p. 224), and so emphasizes the opposing extremes of his perceived identity and his actual identity. In truth, he is harmless.

Staples further emphasizes his harmlessness by establishing his character as good-natured and patient, though disheartened. He says, "I grew accustomed to but never comfortable with people crossing to the other side of the street rather than pass me" (p. 224). He provides another glimpse into his character when he tells us about the time he entered a jewelry store and the proprietor appeared, "eyes bulging nearly out of her head," with an "enormous red Doberman pinscher straining at the end of a leash" (p. 225). Rather than retaliating, Staples writes that he "nodded, and bade her good night," and he says that he now takes "precautions to make [himself] less threatening" (p. 226). His better-man manners prevail, even though these people preemptively push him to the metaphorical margins of society for crimes he'll never commit.

Staples eloquently communicates the effects of how he's treated. People alienate him and make him unwelcome among them, until it feels criminal enough for a black man to share their public space. Staples writes that there is "no solace against the kind of alienation that comes of being ever the suspect, a fearsome entity with whom pedestrians avoid making eye contact" (p. 225). He also tells us, "I learned to smother the rage I felt at so often being taken for a criminal." Words like "alienation" and "rage" emphasize the depth of the wounds he has received. Thus, in the ultimate reversal, this terrified public proves the "assailant," Brent Staples, and black men like him, the victims.

Indeed, Staples suggests that rather than being a threat to potential victims, he's actually a victim of the belief that he's a threat; he observes that "being perceived as dangerous is a hazard in itself" (p. 224). He explains:

> I only needed to turn a corner into a dicey situation, or crowd some frightened, armed person in a foyer somewhere, or make an errant move after being pulled over by a policeman. Where fear and weapons meet — and they often do in urban America — there is always the possibility of death. (p. 224)

Focus. Ridlen keeps her argument focused by breaking her overarching argument into subpoints such as this one. By opening paragraphs with subpoints that use some of the key words (or synonyms) from her thesis, she helps readers feel oriented.

Analysis of quotations. Rather than move on to a new point after the quotation in the previous sentence, Ridlen analyzes the quotation; she tells us how it supports the point she's arguing in this paragraph.

One might consider the fight-or-flight principles of fear. Though the scene that opened this essay gave an example of a woman *fleeing* the perceived threat, Staples goes on to address the much more alarming possibility of a fight—a potentially lethal one. There have been several cases in recent U.S. history of innocent black men who have been murdered by men claiming to have acted in self-defense. In 2010, DJ Henry, an unarmed black college student from Massachusetts, was killed by a white police officer, Aaron Hess. In 2012, seventeen-year-old Trayvon Martin, an unarmed black Florida teen, was killed while walking to his father's house from a convenience store by George Zimmerman, a white community watch coordinator, for so-called "suspicious behavior." In both of these instances, and many more, these gunmen shot to kill without any legitimate threat to their lives. Although these deaths hadn't yet happened when "Black Men and Public Space" was written, Staples's awareness of the possibility of death shapes his life.

For this reason, Staples whistles. Like a hiker forewarning a bear, he whistles, so as not to provoke the deadly wrath of the startled majorities.

Writing Genres

This chapter discusses not only genres of argument, including op-eds and letters to the editor, but also creative nonfiction, blogs, and brochures. You'll find that these different genres will enable you to accomplish different purposes. Genres of argument allow you to take a stance on an issue — to make a case for something you believe in. Letters to the editor and op-eds allow you, in addition, to make arguments in a public forum, where more people will encounter your ideas. Creative nonfiction is a powerful vehicle for fostering empathy — for showing readers what it's like to be someone else. Blogs can enable you to accomplish a variety of purposes, including entertaining readers and persuading them to consider your ideas. Finally, brochures are useful if you want to provide information or promote a product, service, or organization.

The sections on these genres will show you how to use language to have an influence — to actually affect the people who read what you write. Each section calls attention to audience and purpose; focus, organization, and development; language; and design. Each section highlights moves you can make to help you accomplish your purposes and provides examples of those moves. At the end of each section, you'll find a list of reading selections that illustrate the genre, as well as an annotated sample of the genre with key moves highlighted and explained. Each section is prefaced by a "Quick Checklist" providing an overview of key points — points that take the form of questions highlighting the choices available to you when you write.

As you write each genre, try to see it in light of other genres. Recall that a move commonly made in one genre might also be useful in another. For example, op-eds, creative nonfiction, and blogs often open with a catchy phrase or an original idea that entices people to keep reading. As you learn more about the genres described in this chapter, you'll notice still more moves that you might use across genres. Noticing these moves — and thinking about them in terms of the purposes they can help you accomplish — will ultimately enable you to use a variety of genres more effectively, including not only the ones described in this book but also the many others you'll encounter as you navigate college and life.

Writing arguments

If you want others to consider your ideas, it's good to know how to make an argument. Unless you think the world is perfect — and will remain so — you'll want to make your arguments as compelling as possible. "Argument" in this sense doesn't refer to a fight or conflict; it refers to taking a stance — to making a point rather than simply reporting information. Many arguments aim to persuade, while others aim to share insight into a topic.

There are many genres of argument, including not only those that professors will ask you to read and write but also reviews, op-eds, letters to the editor, political speeches, self-help books, advertisements, fund-raising letters, cover letters, proposals, and legal briefs, to name just a few. You'll encounter arguments everywhere: on Facebook, Twitter, Google+, and e-mail; in books and essays; on billboards and bumper stickers; in your mailbox; in print and online newspapers and magazines; and in blogs, brochures, and flyers.

You'll notice many of the same moves appearing in different genres of argument, but you'll also notice significant variation across genres and within a genre. These differences will be discussed in the sections that follow, along with ideas for how you might adapt an argument to a variety of situations — how you might, in other words, make a compelling case and ultimately have an influence.

Quick Checklist

PURPOSE AND AUDIENCE

How similar are the members of your audience? Do they tend to share many of the same assumptions, and will they generally share the same purpose in reading your argument? Might many members of your audience be relatively open to your argument, or might they be reluctant? Are they likely to read your entire argument or skip part or all of it? (p. 44)

ORGANIZATION, FOCUS, AND DEVELOPMENT

Title. Does your title reflect the focus of your argument? (p. 44)

Thesis. Have you tailored your thesis to the genre and audience? Is it implicit or explicit? If explicit, where does it appear? Is your thesis stating something that's already obvious to your readers? How specific is your thesis? How much complexity does it recognize? Have you reread and reconsidered any sources you're drawing on before crafting the final version of your thesis? (p. 45)

Quick Checklist, continued

Focus: thesis and body paragraphs. Will readers be able to see the connections between your thesis and your body paragraphs? Have you considered using a consistent string of repeated key words and synonyms to connect your body paragraphs to your thesis? Have you made a deliberate decision about whether to use body paragraphs to list examples that support your thesis or to develop reasoned subarguments that you then support? (p. 49)

Paragraph focus. Will readers be able to see how the sentences within a paragraph are related to the main point of that paragraph? (p. 51)

Evidence. Have you provided evidence appropriate for your audience, purpose, and genre of argument? How *much* evidence have you provided? What *type* of evidence have you provided (e.g., quotations, quotations accompanied by analysis, examples, hypothetical scenarios, case studies, statistics, primary research you conducted yourself, and/or citations of others' research? Given your audience's expectations, have you gone into enough detail explaining/analyzing your evidence? (p. 52)

Source use. Did you establish the credibility of your sources (appropriate in many genres)? Have you made an informed choice about whether to include or avoid direct quotations? If you included direct quotations, did you introduce them and provide page numbers (appropriate in many genres)? If you used long quotations, did you use block format, starting them on a new line and indenting them? Have you used a citation style (e.g., MLA, APA, or Chicago) appropriate to your genre, purpose, and audience? (p. 54)

Recognition of complexity. If appropriate for your genre, audience, and purpose, have you recognized complexity (e.g., acknowledged more than one side of an issue, anticipated readers' objections, and qualified your claims)? (p. 55)

EFFECTIVE LANGUAGE

Transitions. If appropriate, have you used transitions to show readers how the different parts of your argument are connected? (p. 57)

Level of formality. Have you used an appropriate level of formality (e.g., used Standard English when it's expected)? When appropriate, have you avoided judgmental words, such as "ridiculous" and "outrageous"? (p. 58)

"Person." Have you decided to use or avoid pronouns such as "I," "you," and "we," based on genre, audience, and purpose? (p. 58)

DESIGN

If appropriate, have you used subheadings, bulleted lists, photos, charts, tables, or other graphics to emphasize or support your argument? (p. 58)

Purpose and Audience

As noted above, your purpose in making an argument may be to persuade your audience of a particular point, or it may be to share an insight — to encourage your audience to think more deeply about an issue. Your purpose might be to argue, among other things, that something is beneficial or problematic; that an important term should be redefined; that taking a specific action could help address a problem; that one thing contributes to causing something else; that some things are similar or different; that something has important implications; that people should change their behavior; that something is more complicated than previously thought; or that someone is wrong, partially wrong, partially right, or right. (If your argument agrees with someone else's, however, it's good to have your own "value add" — something that extends the original argument.)

Regardless of your purpose, you'll want to adapt your argument to your audience. How reluctant an audience is, for instance, might influence whether you make an argument implicitly or explicitly, or whether you state your thesis at the beginning or the end. Similarly, you'll want to consider whether your audience is likely to read your entire argument or whether readers might skip part or all of it. If you don't feel confident that your audience will read your entire piece, you may want to make some additional moves to communicate your points — for example, providing photos, easy-to-read charts, or subheadings. (Note, however, that even readers who are obligated to read your entire piece often appreciate such graphic elements.) You'll also want to bear in mind that you may have a diverse audience; in many cases, for example, not all readers will share the same assumptions or have the same purpose in reading your argument. Strategies for addressing a variety of audiences will be discussed in more detail in the following sections.

Organization, Focus, and Development

Craft a title that establishes the focus of your argument.   Although titling conventions vary across genres of argument, titles typically establish the topic and often specify the writer's argument. Consider, for example, the following titles:

- "Is Google Making Us Stupid?"
- *"Pediatrics* Gets It Wrong about 'Facebook Depression'"
- "Social Media Addiction: Engage Brain before Believing"
- *Alone Together: Why We Expect More from Technology and Less from Each Other*

Note that titles of academic arguments often use a colon followed by a subtitle summarizing the argument. Regardless of whether you're using an academic genre, however, you'll want your title to establish a clear focus for your piece.

Tailor your thesis to your situation.   Your thesis is the backbone of your argument, the central claim that you're making. Where it appears and whether it will be explicit or implicit depends on your purpose, audience, and genre. If you're writing an academic argument for a class, some professors may expect an implicit thesis, but many will expect to see your thesis at the end (not the beginning) of your introduction. Other professors may expect to see your thesis in your conclusion. Although you can often predict professors' expectations based on discipline, there can be some variation even within a discipline. If you're not sure where to put your thesis, ask; this is important because if the thesis isn't where readers expect it, they may have difficulty finding it and thus may be confused about the point of your argument.

In some nonacademic arguments, you might find still more variation in thesis placement. Some genres (especially short ones) may state the thesis in the opening sentence rather than at the end of the introduction. You may even find a thesis placed elsewhere, perhaps early in the body of an essay. If you're writing an unfamiliar genre of argument, read several samples of that genre to see where thesis statements tend to appear (or if they tend to be implicit rather than explicit).

If you're writing a nonacademic genre or writing for a professor who doesn't have a preference, you might consider stating the thesis at the end of your introduction if you think most people will be open to your argument but in the conclusion if you think they might not be receptive. Delaying the thesis until the end (after you've provided evidence) is a strategy that often allows an audience to be more open-minded when encountering the body of an argument. Imagine, for instance, that you're an education major who's done research on how students respond to professors' comments on their writing — and imagine that many students you interviewed felt demoralized by their professors' comments. Now imagine that you had the opportunity to present your research to an audience of professors and that you wanted them to thoughtfully consider your thesis (something to the effect of "If you aim for a relatively equal balance of positive and negative comments, students may be more receptive to those comments"). Consider which of the following three approaches you might take: (1) opening with an explicit version of your thesis, (2) spending most of your time describing students' responses and ending with your thesis, or (3) opting not to state your thesis explicitly and instead simply providing evidence (describing students' responses). Although there's not necessarily a right answer, in this and many other situations you'll be well served by making an informed choice among alternatives.

After you consider the *location* of your thesis, you'll want to think about the *type* of thesis appropriate for your audience. Consider, for example, the following questions:

- *How obvious* will your audience think your thesis is? (You'll usually want to avoid telling people things that seem obvious to them. If you're worried that your thesis is too obvious, try recasting it, e.g., "Although many people believe ____ is obvious, their behavior doesn't always reflect that belief.")

- *How specific* should your thesis be, given the situation? (If your thesis is specific rather than general, it's often easier to keep a sharp focus and marshal compelling evidence. However, there are also times when a more general thesis may be appropriate. For instance, if you're addressing the audience of professors previously described and you decide to state your thesis explicitly, a general thesis like "Professors may benefit from knowing how students respond to their comments" may be more effective than a more specific thesis such as "Professors should provide students with a relatively equal balance of positive and negative comments.")

- *How much complexity* should your thesis acknowledge? Some audiences are more likely to see complexity than others. If your audience sees complexity that your thesis doesn't acknowledge, your credibility may be undermined. (See p. 59 for an example of a thesis statement that recognizes complexity.)

If you're writing for an academic audience, it will be useful to know that many professors expect thesis statements to do the following:

- Make an arguable claim rather than stating a fact
- Make a claim that is narrow rather than broad
- Make a claim that recognizes complexity — that doesn't make a simple "pro" or "con" argument or assume that all people have the same experience of a phenomenon

Consider the following thesis statements from a first-year composition class, each of which the professor thought was better than the previous one.

Not an arguable claim:

People spend more time using social media today than they did a decade ago.	This is a well-documented fact, not a claim that a reasonable person might disagree with.

Makes a claim but is too broad, obvious, and simplistic:

Technology is beneficial to our society.	There are so many different kinds of technology that it would take at least a few hundred pages to provide adequate support for this claim. Even if the thesis were adequately supported, few people would disagree with it, and many would think it's obvious and simplistic.

Somewhat narrower but still too broad and simplistic:

Technology is beneficial to our society because it provides entertainment, helps us maintain relationships, and helps us be safer in emergencies.	The reasons provided narrow the thesis somewhat, but these reasons — entertainment, relationships, and safety — cover a lot of ground and aren't closely connected to each other. In addition, many readers would think that this thesis is obvious and that it doesn't acknowledge complexity.

Narrower but makes a blanket claim:

Social media alters our views of others and hinders our interpersonal communication skills.	"Social media" is narrower than "technology," and the claims about altering views of others and hindering communication skills are logically related; the writer isn't covering too much ground. Moreover, this thesis doesn't state an obvious point; regardless of whether or not readers agree, it will probably provoke thought. The problem is that it doesn't recognize complexity. Some readers may bristle at the blanket claim implying that everyone has the same experience of social media.

More nuanced and thus more likely to persuade more readers:

Even though social media can connect people, it can also alter our views of others and hinder our interpersonal communication skills.	This thesis recognizes complexity in two ways. First, it acknowledges that social media isn't all bad—an important move given that many readers will have positive experiences with social media and might feel alienated if their experience isn't acknowledged. Second, this thesis claims that social media "can" alter our views of others and hinder our interpersonal communication skills—not that it always does. This minor revision may make the writer seem more credible in the eyes of many readers. This same effect could have also been achieved in other ways, such as "it sometimes alters" or "it alters some people's views."

Equally nuanced while also distinguishing the writer's idea from others' ideas:

Although many have realized that social media can connect people, they often don't realize that social media can also alter our views of others and hinder our interpersonal communication skills.	Many genres of argument emphasize that the writer's thesis goes beyond what others believe or have previously argued. The writer's thesis is motivated; the underlying idea is this: "There's a good reason for me to make this argument at this time, and that reason is to tell others something important that they may not know." Writers who want to make this move may find it useful to begin thesis statements with words like "Although" or to include words like "but" in the middle of the thesis.

Crafting a good, thought-provoking thesis can be difficult. Many students find that they're better able to develop a thought-provoking thesis if they carefully reread their sources or look at their data again. Indeed, it can be very useful to revisit your sources or data with a specific focus. You might focus your rereading around

- a question,
- a hypothesis,
- a point of confusion (a specific "mystery"—something that genuinely stumps you about the topic).

If you're using secondary sources (such as the reading selections in this book), it will be helpful to look for connections between readings. Does one reading, for instance, shed light on another reading in some way? Does it contradict another reading? Does it suggest that another reading may not fully acknowledge complexity?

If you're working from primary sources (research that you have conducted yourself, such as surveys or interviews), it will be helpful to look at your data again; when doing so, focus on looking for patterns and contradictions. Which pieces of the data are consistent with other pieces? Do some pieces contradict others? Do some pieces contradict what other researchers have found? If so, how would you explain the contradiction? Explaining contradictions, or seeming contradictions, can often lead to good, nuanced thesis statements.

Regardless of whether you're reexamining primary or secondary sources to develop a thesis, keep an open mind. Your argument might, and perhaps should, change as you revisit your sources; at the very least, it should recognize more complexity. Recognizing additional layers of complexity — layers that aren't immediately apparent — often results in a more thought-provoking thesis that genuinely teaches the audience something.

Try to keep the main ideas of paragraphs (sometimes called topic sentences) focused around your thesis. Regardless of genre, you'll find that effective arguments rarely lack focus; the main points of paragraphs rarely wander away from the thesis. This tends to be true regardless of whether the thesis is explicit or implicit; even with an implicit thesis, readers draw inferences about how paragraphs are connected, and if they don't see the connections, they may feel disoriented.[1]

It is often the case that writers think their argument is focused — that their body paragraphs relate to their thesis — but readers disagree. This is generally because writers have spent so much time thinking about their specific argument that they see connections more easily. For this reason, it can be helpful to think of yourself as being smarter than the reader. Readers often need more hand-holding than you might expect.

A useful hand-holding strategy is to notice key words in your thesis and to use those same words (or synonyms) throughout your body paragraphs. When you're finished writing, it can help to underline, circle, or highlight the key words in your thesis and body paragraphs and then confirm that they go together, or form a consistent "lexical string." Consider the lexical string formed by the previously discussed thesis and the following paragraph openings.

---

[1] Note, however, that expectations about focus — like other expectations — can vary across cultures.

Thesis (with key words highlighted):

> Although many have realized that social media can connect people, they often don't realize that social media can also alter our views of others and hinder our interpersonal communication skills.

Paragraph openings (with key words highlighted):

> One way social media can alter our view of others is that many people carefully select the photos they share; shared photos don't always represent a person's actual life.

> Social media can also alter our view of others because when we chat and post status updates, we don't usually discuss complex feelings, and yet those feelings are an important part of who we are.

> Because we're not used to discussing complex feelings in social media and because we may think of people as they are represented in their photos, we may feel uncomfortable when complex feelings come up in our interpersonal interactions. We may not know what to do or say. [Goes on to give an example.]

> Another example of a heavy social media user feeling uncomfortable with interpersonal interaction is discussed by [author's name].

Having a consistent lexical string (such as the highlighted words) in your thesis and paragraph openings is perhaps one of the most important things you can do to help readers see the connections between your thesis and body paragraphs.

Notice that with the exception of the last paragraph, the writer's paragraphs are organized around subarguments rather than a list of examples. In other words, instead of opening paragraphs with sentences such as "One example is . . ." and "Another example is . . . ," the paragraphs open with sentences that provide different reasons explaining why the thesis is valid. When you provide reasons that divide your argument into subarguments, you'll be able to make claims that are more specific than the claim made in your thesis, thus preventing repetition yet maintaining focus.[2]

Although paragraphs often open by stating the main idea, main ideas can also be implicit, or they might be stated at the end of the paragraph

---

[2] Also note that providing reasons in specific subarguments can help you make a more nuanced argument. (Simply saying "One example of [thesis] is . . ." and "Another example of [thesis] is . . . " generally doesn't reflect a nuanced argument.) To transform a list of undifferentiated examples into reasoned subarguments, ask yourself how each example is similar to and different from the other examples. (Of course, in some situations, a straightforward thesis supported by a list of examples can be effective; just make a deliberate decision based on an analysis of your situation.)

(or occasionally in the middle). Regardless of whether or where the main idea is stated, using a consistent string of key words in your thesis and body paragraphs will help readers see connections.

Try to keep your body paragraphs focused. Just as readers typically expect the main ideas of paragraphs to relate to your thesis, so too do they generally expect the sentences within a paragraph to relate to the point of that paragraph. If they don't see how the sentences within a paragraph are connected, they may feel disoriented or confused.

Consider the following two versions of a body paragraph from a first-year composition paper arguing about the benefits of technology. In both versions, the point of the paragraph is stated in the first sentences and the first half of the paragraph maintains focus. One of the versions, however, shifts focus in the middle. See which version you prefer.

Version 1	Version 2
Some people believe that technology is making them lazy and stupid, but one thing they don't realize is that they are the ones responsible for their own behavior. For example, if you have a class assignment to finish and you have your Facebook window open, someone is going to chat with you. So before that happens, you can go offline on Facebook, so you can finish the assignment. I love technology; I use it all the time, but I know when it's too much. Those who are against technology are missing out. My uncle Joe and his wife live their life technology free. They have only a car and a TV, and they think everything else is junk. They don't own anything electronic whatsoever. When their daughter got injured at cheerleading practice, they were the last ones to know about the accident because they don't own a cell phone. They made their choice to be anti-technology and to have the disadvantages that come with it.	Some people believe that technology is making them lazy and stupid, but one thing they don't realize is that they are the ones responsible for their own behavior. For example, if you have a class assignment to finish and you have your Facebook window open, someone is going to chat with you. So before that happens, you can go offline on Facebook, so you can finish the assignment. If you do not and get caught up in the distraction, it is not the technology's fault. And your true friends will always be there for you whenever you need them. Everyone has a choice whether to use the technology or not; we also have the choice to prevent technology addiction from happening to us. Know your limit. In reality, we don't want to end up like the humans in the Disney movie *WALL-E*, who just sit in front of a computer and have everything done for them. I love technology; I use it all the time, but I know when it's too much.

Which version do you prefer? Do you think the paragraph that shifts focus (the first one) is less effective in conveying the main point of the paragraph? In your own writing, if you can keep the sentences in each paragraph focused around the main idea of that paragraph, it will prevent readers from losing track of your point. When paragraphs maintain a sharp focus on a point, that point receives more emphasis.

Provide evidence appropriate for the genre of argument you're using.   Providing evidence to support claims is one of the key moves made in arguments across genres. What varies from genre to genre is the type and amount of evidence used. Some genres of argument may dispatch with evidence quickly, in a short paragraph. Other genres will provide extended support for a claim, marshaling evidence in longer paragraphs — or perhaps discussing an important piece of evidence over the course of two or more paragraphs.

Just as the *amount* of evidence varies across genres, so too does the *type* of evidence. Some genres of argument tend to use quotations, often accompanied by analysis, while others tend to avoid quotation and instead use statistics, case studies, analogies, hypothetical scenarios, or citations or summaries of research. Still other genres tend to use a combination of different types of evidence, and many are flexible enough to allow writers significant latitude in choosing and combining types of evidence. If you're writing for a professor and you're not sure what type(s) of evidence he or she is expecting, be sure to ask. It also helps to read several examples of the genre you plan to use.

Following are two versions of a passage from professor Sherry Turkle's *Alone Together: Why We Expect More from Technology and Less from Each Other* (p. 593), a reading selection in this book that uses data from the author's research to make an argument aimed at a lay audience. One version of the passage provides evidence and one doesn't; see if you find one version more persuasive:

Version 1	Version 2
We are overwhelmed across the generations. Teenagers complain that parents don't look up from their phones at dinner and that they bring their phones to school sporting events. Parents say they are ashamed of such behavior but quickly get around to explaining, if not justifying, it. They say they are more stressed than ever as they try to keep up with e-mail and messages. They always feel behind.	We are overwhelmed across the generations. Teenagers complain that parents don't look up from their phones at dinner and that they bring their phones to school sporting events. Hannah, sixteen, is a solemn, quiet high school junior. She tells me that for years she has tried to get her mother's attention when her mother comes to fetch her after school or after dance lessons. Hannah says, "The car will start; she'll be driving still looking down, looking at her messages, but still no hello." We will hear others tell similar stories.

	Version 2 *(continued)*
	Parents say they are ashamed of such behavior but quickly get around to explaining, if not justifying, it. They say they are more stressed than ever as they try to keep up with e-mail and messages. They always feel behind. They cannot take a vacation without bringing the office with them; their office is on their cell phone.[4]
	[4] Diana B. Gant and Sara Kiesler, "Blurring the Boundaries: Cell Phones, Mobility and the Line Between Work and Personal Life," in *Wireless World: Social and Interactional Aspects of the Mobile Age*, ed. N. G. R. H. Brown (New York: Springer, 2001).

Did you find the passage with evidence to be more persuasive? This passage (the second one) is the one that Turkle really wrote (pp. 594–95). Note that Turkle provides not one but two types of evidence: a quotation from a participant in her own research as well as a citation of someone else's research. Readers of many genres often find that more than one *piece* of evidence — and more than one *type* of evidence — can be more persuasive.

Note that providing evidence isn't a simple matter of doing it or not doing it. Many inexperienced writers ask themselves the yes-no question "Have I provided evidence?" but it's better to avoid this question and instead ask yourself questions like these:

- Given my audience and purpose, how could my evidence be even more persuasive?
- What if I included more *pieces* of evidence?
- What if I included more *types* of evidence?
- What if I kept the same evidence but went into more detail explaining it?
- What if I used graphic elements to add or better emphasize evidence (e.g., included photographs or tables, provided subheadings, converted an unbulleted list to a bulleted list)?

Using evidence effectively — in a way consistent with the genre you're writing — is key to persuading readers. Taking a good, hard look at your evidence will be one of the most important things you do when you revise.

Incorporate sources appropriately. Sources are cited in many genres of argument not only to provide direct evidence but also to establish the context for an argument or to discuss a point the writer is critiquing. If you're citing sources to provide evidence, it's especially important to select credible sources. Your credibility as a writer rests largely on the credibility of your sources. To show readers that your sources are credible, try making a move like the one Nicholas Carr makes in "Is Google Making Us Stupid?" (p. 574):

> "We are not only *what* we read," says Maryanne Wolf, a developmental psychologist at Tufts University and the author of *Proust and the Squid: The Story and Science of the Reading Brain.* "We are *how* we read." (para. 8)

When you let your readers know that a source is credible, as Carr does, they are more likely to be persuaded by your argument.

You'll also want to cite sources in a way that's consistent with your audience's expectations. Direct quotation is often used in journalistic arguments and academic arguments in the humanities. However, quotation is generally avoided in many science and social science genres; instead writers typically paraphrase sources or use footnotes or endnotes to point readers to sources.

When you're using a genre that tends to quote, the following ideas will help you establish your credibility and make it easier for you to integrate another author's words into your own words:

- *Introduce quotations* (in most but not all genres). Instead of using a "floating" quotation (one that takes up a whole sentence), consider integrating quotations into sentences that contain some of your own words, such as "Martinez notes that [quotation]". In many genres of argument, it's also appropriate to establish the credibility of the source when you introduce a quotation (e.g., "Maria Martinez, a neuroscience professor at MIT, notes that . . .").

- *Provide a page number* if you're using an academic genre; not doing so can undermine your credibility and may constitute plagiarism in academic contexts. (Note, however, that page numbers aren't always used in nonacademic genres.) Page numbers make it easier for readers to find the quotation if they want to read it in its original context.

- *Use ellipsis points* [. . .] to indicate that you've omitted some of the author's words from the quotation.

- *Use square brackets* [ ] to indicate that you've added some of your own words to a quotation. You might want to add information for clarification, or you might want to replace a pronoun with a name.

- *Be sure to double- or triple-check your version of the quotation against the original.* It's very common for writers to mistype quotations.

Also note that when you include long quotations,[3] you'll be expected to set those quotations apart from the rest of your text by indenting them in block format, as John Grohol does in the following passage when he paraphrases what other authors say before going on to critique them:

> Here's what the [authors] had to say about "Facebook depression":
>
> > Researchers have proposed a new phenomenon called "Facebook depression," defined as depression that develops when preteens and teens spend a great deal of time on social media sites, such as Facebook, and then begin to exhibit classic symptoms of depression. . . .
>
> Time and time again [however] researchers are finding much more nuanced relationships between social networking sites and depression. In the Selfhout et al. (2009) study they cite, for instance, the researchers only found the correlation between the two factors in people with *low quality* friendships. (p. 645)

Like block quotations in many genres, Grohol's quotation is sandwiched: rather than being plopped in the middle of the paragraph and then abandoned, it's prefaced by an introduction and followed by a discussion commenting on the quotation. This is an approach you'll find helpful when writing arguments across a variety of genres.

Whether or not you use direct quotation, you'll almost certainly be expected to use the citation style appropriate to your genre of argument. Common citation styles include MLA, APA, and Chicago; if you're not sure which style to use, ask.

Regardless of the citation style you use, citing sources is an important strategy for providing evidence, establishing a context for your argument, or referring to what others say before critiquing them. The more skilled you are at integrating sources, the better able you'll be to command readers' respect.

Recognize an appropriate degree of complexity.   Recall that recognizing complexity in appropriate situations can bolster your credibility. Genres of argument written for academic audiences tend to recognize complexity, while genres written for laypeople sometimes do and sometimes don't. If you're using an academic genre of argument — or even one of many nonacademic genres — recognizing complexity is useful not just in your thesis but throughout your argument. Consider, for example, the following two versions of a passage from Nicholas Carr's "Is Google

---

[3] What counts as a long quotation varies from one citation style to another. In MLA, a long quotation is one that's over four lines; in APA, it's over forty words, and in Chicago, it's eight or more lines.

Making Us Stupid?"; see whether you prefer the version that recognizes complexity or the version that doesn't:

Version 1	Version 2
The advantages of having [the web provide] immediate access to such an incredibly rich store of information are many, and they've been widely described and duly applauded. . . . But [those advantages come] at a price. (para. 4)	The web has a high cost to our society.

Recognizing that there's more than one side to an issue can prevent readers from thinking that you haven't carefully considered the issue from all angles.

When you recognize both sides of an issue (while still sticking to your argument), you're in effect acknowledging potential objections that readers may have — and acknowledging these objections may defuse them. (It can sometimes silence the "yeah, but . . ." voice in readers' minds.) Another strategy for acknowledging potential objections, and thus recognizing complexity, is to use language similar to the following:

- Readers might interpret this quotation to mean ____, but interpreted in the context of ____, it implies ____.
- Although this data could be interpreted to suggest ____, a thorough analysis of it suggests ____.
- Although only a small number of case studies were conducted, these cases nonetheless paint a vivid picture of how ____ can sometimes ____.
- Although this research doesn't definitively demonstrate ____, it nonetheless suggests ____.

You can recognize complexity not only by anticipating potential objections but also by qualifying your claims and using speculative language, as in the following examples:

- ____ may contribute to ____.
- ____ may result in part from ____.
- It's possible that ____.
- ____ tends to ____.
- It can be argued that ____.

- This passage implies / suggests ____.
- The researchers speculate that ____.
- These results may suggest ____.

When you're using a genre that tends to recognize complexity, consider your verbs. The preceding examples, for instance, avoid verbs like "prove" and instead favor verbs such as "suggest," "imply," "can," "may," "might," "hypothesize," and "speculate." Although many of the verb phrases in the examples are longer (e.g., "may result" instead of "result"), recognition of complexity often trumps streamlined prose. Although there will be times when you find it appropriate to state a claim authoritatively — without qualification — it's nonetheless useful to consider the language writers use to acknowledge complexity. Indeed, few things are black and white; there are many shades of gray, and you'll have more credibility if you can anticipate when your audience will see those shades of gray.

Effective Language

Consider using transitions to guide readers through your argument. Many genres of argument use transitions to show how a sentence is related to previous sentences — and how a paragraph is related to previous paragraphs and to the thesis. Transitional words and phrases that suggest an additive relationship include "also," "in addition," "not only . . . but also," "more," "moreover," "another [reason / problem, etc.]," "yet another," "still another," "for example," "for instance," and "further" (e.g., "this problem is further illustrated . . . ").

Not only can words like these help you transition from one similar point to another, but they can also help you develop the same point over the course of several paragraphs. For example, if one paragraph states a claim and provides one type of evidence, the next paragraph could open with a phrase such as "Still more evidence . . ." Making a move like this can enable you to provide more evidence and thus make a more compelling argument.

To establish a contrasting relationship between ideas, consider transitional words such as "however," "although," "while," "whereas," "nonetheless," "nevertheless," "yet," "in contrast," and "a counterexample." Of course, not all relationships are simply additive or contrasting. For example, if you quote somebody who provides a relatively simple explanation of a phenomenon and you follow that quotation with another one that better recognizes complexity, you might say "[second author's name] points out that the phenomenon is more complex . . ." Specifying how ideas are related can make it easier for readers to navigate your argument.

Adapt your level of formality to the genre of argument you are using.   How formal or informal your argument seems to readers depends largely on the extent to which you use the conventions of Standard English and on the degree of judgment implied by your words. When using many genres of argument, you'll be expected to use Standard English; be sure to edit and proofread carefully to make sure you don't miss anything. Your credibility may suffer if the English you use is more informal than what your audience expects.

Your audience may also assess your level of formality based on whether or not you use judgmental words. When using formal genres of argument, it's especially important to avoid words such as "ridiculous," "bad," "lazy," "disgusting," "outrageous," "greedy," "money-grubbing," "cheap," and "apathetic"; these words and others like them can prompt readers to dismiss you as being biased or judgmental. It's good to avoid words like these unless you're using an informal genre or writing to an audience of friends you know well.

Use the "person" appropriate for your genre.   Pronouns such as "I," "you," and "we" tend to be used in some genres of argument but avoided in others. Still other genres provide writers the latitude to choose the pronouns they feel work best in their specific situation. As usual, if you're not sure what's appropriate, you'll find that reading samples of a genre before using it may shed light on the situation.

Design

Just as your words will be shaped by the genre of argument you use, so too will the design elements of your work; you'll find tremendous variation in design as you move from one genre of argument to another. As you look at samples of the genre you plan to use, consider the use of subheadings, bulleted lists, white space, photos, charts, and other graphics.

Don't feel, however, that you have to slavishly imitate other samples of your genre. Graphic elements such as photos and tables can provide compelling evidence to support claims in a variety of genres, and you may want to consider importing such elements into your own argument even if they're not common in the genre you're using. Similarly, you may want to consider using subheadings in your argument even if they're not common in that genre; not only can subheadings help you structure your argument as you write, but they can also be useful tools to emphasize your points and guide readers through the pieces of your argument.

Sample arguments*	
"The Good, the Bad, and the Technological"	p. 59
The Relationship Cure	p. 146

* Note that some of the readings on this list draw on original research to make arguments, while others draw on secondary sources. Also note that reading selections not listed here could be interpreted as arguments.

Sample Argument

David Cook

The Good, the Bad, and the Technological: Technology and Its Impacts

Facebook. Twitter. Tumblr. Reddit. Wikipedia. These are just some of the ways that we are connected to the world at large through the Internet. With this and more, there are many ways to access large amounts of information and entertainment in a very short time. At the same time, constantly being "wired in" and being exposed to so much at once results in a number of negative impacts on health and mental and physical well-being and yet, despite how serious some of the impacts can be, there is still great good to be found in these advances.

Thesis. Rather than state a fact, Cook's thesis makes an argument—it states a claim that others might disagree with. Note that instead of making a simplistic argument that technology is good or bad, Cook recognizes complexity, a move that is likely to make him seem more credible in the eyes of many readers.

One unexpected result of being "wired in" is the loss of an essential bodily function. Linda Stone wrote about a phenomenon called "Email Apnea," which she defines as "a temporary absence or suspension of breathing, or shallow breathing, while doing email" (624). This calls back to the common disorder of sleep apnea, the temporary cessation of breathing while in deep sleep, which in rare cases can be fatal. Although limiting one's breathing (consciously or otherwise) while awake is usually nonfatal, it can still have long-lasting health consequences. Stone spoke to Dr. Margaret Chesney of the National Institutes of Health, who said that, in short, holding our breath "contributes significantly to stress-related diseases" and that, through the process of our bodies reabsorbing some of the chemicals present, "our biochemistry is thrown off" (624). This doesn't necessarily apply just to e-mail, either. There have been plenty of times when a text message conversation can also trigger a change in breathing or an elevated heart rate: be it a conflict with a significant other, or waiting for the response of a parent after sending a report of some less-than-stellar grades. With the inner workings of our bodies disrupted in even the slightest ways, our bodies enter "fight or flight" mode when there is nothing to actually fight or fly from. This constant state of readiness increases our stress levels, and given how stressful our day-to-day lives can already be, the added stress can only serve to aggravate an already frustrating situation.

> **Focus.** Cook helps readers see how his body paragraphs are connected to his thesis by starting body paragraphs with subarguments that advance his overarching argument. His paragraph openings are generally more specific than his thesis, which helps him avoid repetition while still maintaining focus.

Of course, there is more than texting and e-mail that can cause negative effects on a person. A report published by the American Academy of Pediatrics discusses a disorder they termed "Facebook depression," which is defined as "depression that develops when preteens and teens spend a great deal of time on social media sites" (638). Although this report has been critiqued by John Grohol, who raises a valid point that the authors "can't differentiate between correlation and causation" (645), this should not lead to an outright dismissal of the argument. Although the simple act of using a social media site isn't enough to cause someone to display symptoms of depression, the interactions that take place on them can and have. Cyberbullying, according to the *Pediatrics* article, is "deliberately using digital media to communicate false, embarrassing, or hostile information about another person," and the authors call it the "most common online risk" for users of social media sites (637).

> **Transitions.** Cook transitions from one paragraph to another by first referring back to the previous paragraph and then going on to state the topic of the paragraph at hand. Because both this paragraph and the previous one advance his thesis, he maintains focus on both the paragraph and the whole-text level.

> **Evidence.** Cook quotes a credible source as evidence to support the claim he's making in this paragraph. However, he is careful to balance quotations so that they don't overwhelm his own analysis.

With the emphasis placed on using electronic resources in school, it is easier for children to be targets of bullying, which now extends beyond the closing bell of school. Because of this, there have been a number of news stories recently about young people who have committed suicide because of severe, pervasive cyberbullying. The bullying that takes place on Facebook can just as easily take place on Google+, or could have taken place on Myspace when that was a big player in the social media game. If this bullying is combined with "sexting," or the sending of sexually explicit photos, a simple case of children being children can quickly turn very, very illegal. Though "Facebook depression" may be nothing more than a made-up term to stir up media pundits and parental groups, depression that may be caused or aggravated by interactions on Facebook is a very real phenomenon.

An increased amount of bullying and possible exploitation of young people, along with a failure to breathe properly, are certainly very severe consequences of our society's increased reliance on technology. However, every major human innovation has led to some kind of negative consequence: the discovery of fire by the ancients eventually led to the "Zippo raids" of the Vietnam War, and the harnessing of nuclear power led to the creation of the weapons that devastated Japan at the end of World War II. And yet, fire still serves to keep us warm on the coldest of summer nights in the woods, and nuclear energy powers many cities and communities in a relatively clean and efficient way. With the increased presence of technology, it is easier for friends to stay connected across long distances, and finding information in archives that might otherwise be inaccessible (again due to distance) can be invaluable for both students and professional researchers.

The benefits can and often do outweigh the negatives. There can be no good without the bad—it's a fact of life. What we must do is learn how to deal with the negative impacts of our increased reliance on technology and settle them with the many, many positive impacts these innovations can and do have on our daily lives.

Strong conclusion. Cook uses the first two sentences of his conclusion to refer back to his thesis, thus maintaining the focus of his essay. He then goes a layer deeper by answering the "so what" question—imagine him asking himself, "So what? What should we do about this good-bad mix that we face?" He then answers the question, thus preventing his conclusion from being a simple reiteration of his thesis.

Writing op-eds and letters to the editor

Letters to the editor and op-eds (sometimes called opinion pieces) are widely read genres that enable you to have a public voice — to shape opinion and possibly prompt action. Most print and online newspapers publish op-eds and letters to the editor. In addition, letters to the editor are also published in online and print magazines and newsletters. Your voice, then, may reach many people and thus make a difference.

When you write an op-ed or a letter to the editor, you'll make several of the same moves that you'll make when writing arguments for professors: you'll make a specific claim (rather than simply relating facts), you'll probably support that claim with evidence, and you may recognize complexity. However, you'll probably use shorter sentences and paragraphs and tie your argument to something recent, thus letting readers know why you're writing now instead of another time.

Note that not all publications accept op-eds from people who aren't on their staff; many do, however — including many college newspapers. If the venue you're targeting doesn't accept outside op-eds, you can always write a letter to the editor. Before you write either genre, however, be sure to go to the venue's Web site to check specific guidelines; different venues have different requirements, including length limits. You'll often find that letters to the editor should be fewer than 200 or 250 words and that op-eds should be between 500 and 800 words — but these limits vary from venue to venue, and some accept longer pieces for their Web sites.

Just as length varies from venue to venue, so too does subject matter, type of evidence, tone, and the choice of whether or not to use the first person ("I"). Be sure to read several examples from the venue you're targeting *before* you begin writing. The more your letter or op-ed reflects the length, tone, and style of that venue, the better are your chances of getting published and having an influence. Note that some town and college newspapers publish almost every letter they receive, if not in print then online.

Quick Checklist

PURPOSE AND AUDIENCE

Who is the audience of the newspaper, magazine, or online venue you're targeting? Regardless of audience beliefs and demographics, have you considered which strategies you'll use to entice busy readers to keep reading? (p. 64)

Quick Checklist, continued

ORGANIZATION, FOCUS, AND DEVELOPMENT

Headline. Does your headline establish the focus of your argument? Will it draw readers into your piece? (p. 65)

Opening and closing sentences. Have your opening sentences captured readers' attention? Do they clearly state your point and establish and its timeliness? Have your closing sentences driven home your point as compellingly as possible? (p. 66)

Main ideas of paragraphs. Are most or all paragraphs focused around one idea? If not, can you cut less relevant information, move information, or divide paragraphs so that each idea receives more emphasis? (p. 67)

Reasons and evidence. Have you provided appropriate reasons and evidence to support your points? If you're citing a source for your evidence, is it credible? Have you considered telling readers what your source is so that they're more likely to trust it? (p. 68)

Recognition of complexity. If you think readers will see complexity, have you recognized that complexity? Have you anticipated and addressed potential objections? (p. 69)

Providing information about yourself. If relevant, have you established your expertise or provided information about yourself to increase your credibility in the eyes of readers? (p. 70)

Appealing to readers' emotions. Would appealing to readers' emotions be appropriate in your situation? Could doing so make your point more compelling? (p. 70)

EFFECTIVE LANGUAGE

Vivid writing. Have you used some short sentences and paragraphs to better emphasize your points and ease the burden on readers? Have you provided specific detail instead of speaking in generalities? Have you (especially in op-eds) considered other strategies for making your language vivid? (p. 71)

Respectful tone. Have you avoided judgmental words (such as "ridiculous" and "outrageous") so that readers won't dismiss you as being biased or angry? (p. 72)

CONTINUED >

Quick Checklist, continued

Standard English.   Have you edited and proofread carefully so that typos and grammatical glitches don't undermine your credibility? Have you asked at least one other person to read your piece to catch what you missed? (p. 72)

DESIGN

Have you considered design elements—such as italics and bulleted lists—that can help you better emphasize what's important? What about photos, maps, or other visual aids (sometimes used in op-eds)? (p. 72)

Purpose and Audience

Op-eds and letters to the editor have a wide variety of purposes. The purpose of a letter to the editor might be to raise awareness of an issue, to influence people's opinions or actions, to let readers know about an organization or event they think is important, or to respond to something previously published in that venue. Op-eds, on the other hand, aren't typically used to respond to something previously published or to inform readers of events or organizations. Like letters to the editor, however, op-eds *are* commonly used to raise awareness of an issue and to influence people's opinions or actions.

Audiences who read these genres vary tremendously; if you're writing a letter to *Rolling Stone*, for example, it's a safe assumption that your audience will be very different than if you were writing to the *Wall Street Journal*. When you read other letters and op-eds in the publication you're targeting, you'll be able to make inferences about who your readers will be, including their average age, socioeconomic status, education level, and political beliefs. If you're not sure who the publication's target audience is after reading it, look at the ads in a print edition; these will help you infer much about the audience.

Although audience demographics vary from venue to venue, readers of op-eds and letters to the editor generally have one important thing in common: they don't always read every letter and op-ed published because they're often in a hurry, quickly skimming headlines and possibly the first sentence or two to decide whether to continue reading. Strategies you can use to address this situation will be discussed in the following sections.

Organization, Focus, and Development

Craft a headline that establishes the focus of your argument and engages readers' attention. Although headlines are sometimes changed by editors, it's still good practice to craft one you like. Consider the following op-ed headlines:

- "Let's cut the fat on obesity commentary in the U.S."
- "Justice for dead miners trumped by corporate influence"
- "UW's planned photoshoot sorry attempt at 'diversity'"
- "End Sex Week extremism"
- "Nigeria's latest frustration"
- "The vegetarian delusion"

Although some publications don't include headlines for letters to the editor, many do. If you're writing a letter, your headline will often begin with "Letter to the Editor," followed by a colon and a more specific title. The following list provides examples of specific letter titles.

- "Student dialogue needed to improve hourly wage"
- "Humans v. Zombies is not going anywhere"
- "Hunting helps go green"
- "Parking priorities"
- "Contraception controversy"
- "Hands off D.C.'s war memorial"
- "Citizens against 'Citizens United'"

Note that conventions for headlines vary from venue to venue; a few venues, for instance, capitalize all important words in opinion and letter headlines, while many others capitalize only the first word, along with proper names if there are any. Similarly, some venues favor full sentences while others favor phrases. You'll want to observe the conventions used in the venue you're targeting.

You'll also want to make a deliberate decision about whether to state your argument in the headline (as opposed to stating your topic). When making this decision, think about whether stating your argument will increase or decrease the odds that most of your audience will continue to read. Regardless of what you decide, try to make your headline as engaging as possible so that your audience is compelled to keep reading.

Carefully craft your opening and closing sentences. Consider these strategies:

- *Try to open with a short, attention-grabbing sentence.* Although opening with a punchy sentence isn't always a move made in letters (or even in all op-eds), this move can be a powerful way to compel people to continue reading.

- *Clearly state the point (or at least the focus) of your piece early.* If people don't see where your piece is going, they're unlikely to continue reading.

- *Make sure your point is timely*—that readers see the reason you're making this point at this time. Try to tie your point to something recent: perhaps an event that just happened, a study that has just been released, a holiday or an anniversary of an important milestone, or something that has been published in the newspaper, newsletter, or magazine that you're writing to.[4]

- *Use your closing sentences to drive home your point as compellingly as possible.* If you're having trouble driving home your point in a way that doesn't just repeat your opening, try stating a more specific version of your point. In some cases, you may also want to refer readers to an additional resource or issue a call to action.

The following two examples, which include both opening and closing paragraphs, illustrate the different ways that writers can make these moves.

Letter to the editor, "Take pride in our community":

The beauty of fall now surrounds us—so does litter and garbage.

As the leaves fall and plants begin to die, what becomes most apparent to me are the beer cans, pop bottles and fast food containers. What is obvious in this town is not its beauty, but the deplorable acceptance and tolerance of litter and improperly disposed of garbage. Is this an acceptable standard of living just because we are a college town?

---

[4] If you have an argument you want to make but can't think of anything recent to "hook" it to, it's usually easy to find news or a recently published study relevant to your topic. You might try www.google.com/alerts; simply type the name of the topic you want to write about into the top box. You might also look at recent press releases at www.eurekalert.org; just click on whatever topic you are interested in. Another resource for press releases is www.sciencedaily.com; scroll all the way down to the bottom of the page to find a search box where you can type in a subject that interests you.

. . .

It saddens me that my children and guests of this community have to see garbage around them when we live in such a beautiful place — almost heaven, West Virginia.

Who will help us clean up this town? Our family cannot do it alone. It takes a village, and this village is failing.[5]

Op-ed, "Justice for dead miners trumped by corporate influence":

It appears that the Massey Energy Company may have gotten away with nearly 30 negligent homicides.

. . .

It seems that, yet again, corporate influence supersedes human life in modern-day America; but that won't deter the determined supporters of the 29 men, who plan to fight the injustices for years to come.

One of those supporters, United Mine Workers of America's President Cecil E. Roberts, was appropriately adamant that suitable consequences have yet to be handed down when he was recently interviewed by the *New York Times*.

"Until someone goes to jail, there will be no justice done here."[6]

Although many op-eds and letters state their main points in the opening sentence, others take a few sentences (occasionally longer) to establish a context for the argument. Either way, you'll usually want to make sure that a timely point is clear early in your piece and that it's driven home at the end. Lack of a clear, timely point is perhaps the most common pitfall (especially in op-eds), so pay special attention to this when you revise. For another example of how to make a point timely, see the annotated op-ed on p. 73.

Keep your paragraphs focused around one main idea. If you avoid discussing multiple ideas in a paragraph and instead focus on just one, your ideas will receive more emphasis. On the following page, consider the two versions of a letter to the editor entitled "MSU should take next green step"; the first version (the one that was published) provides evidence for two different ideas in a single paragraph, while the second version takes two paragraphs to develop the material. See which version you prefer.

---

[5] Written by Natasha Diamond and published in the *Daily Athenaeum* on October 8, 2011.

[6] Written by Doug Walp and published in the *Daily Athenaeum* on January 9, 2012.

Version 1	Version 2
I personally have a friend who has asthma, and being a student on this campus has made her condition much worse. There are 37 people who die coal-related deaths in Ingham County every year, according to the Clean Air Task Force. MSU Beyond Coal has been growing every year, with more than 8,000 signatures collected overall and about 3,000 just in the current semester. MSU Beyond Coal has held numerous rallies and events in order to gain the attention of the administration, and we seem to finally be doing it.[7]	I personally have a friend who has asthma, and being a student on this campus has made her condition much worse. My friend isn't the only one affected by coal pollution; there are 37 people who die coal-related deaths in Ingham County every year, according to the Clean Air Task Force. MSU Beyond Coal has been growing every year, with more than 8,000 signatures collected overall and about 3,000 just in the current semester. MSU Beyond Coal has held numerous rallies and events in order to gain the attention of the administration, and we seem to finally be doing it.

If you find yourself discussing more than one idea in a paragraph, there are several solutions: you could divide the paragraph into two, cut the information that doesn't fit, or move some of the information to another paragraph. Sometimes a combination approach works best; you might, for instance, divide the paragraph in two *and* omit a sentence. If you think about paragraph focus as you plan, write, and revise, you'll be able to craft sharply focused paragraphs, thus better emphasizing each of your ideas.

Provide reasons and evidence to support your points.   Providing reasons and evidence is perhaps your best tool for persuading readers. Consider the following examples.

> **Letter to the editor, "Educational gap shows Teach for America is still important":**
>
> [Teach for America is an organization worth considering after you graduate.] I first heard of TFA during my senior year. As I walked up Bascom Hill, I saw a sign that said, "Nine-year-olds in low-income communities are already three grade levels behind their peers in high-income communities." Then came "Only one in 10 students growing up in poverty will have the opportunity to attend this school. Teach for all 10."[8]

---

[7] Written by Tobias Roth and published in the *State News* on December 4, 2011.

[8] Written by Maurice Thomas and published in the *Badger Herald* on October 3, 2011.

Op-ed, "Fix the military from within":

[Inequality persists within the military. . . . Army spouses] are afforded benefits such as housing, health care, identification cards, access to morale and welfare programs, and survivor benefits because the military knows that sacrifices of service members also entail the sacrifices of their loved ones.

That is, if you're straight. If you're a lesbian like Luz Bautista, U.S. Navy Petty Officer 1st Class, the military can't recognize your marriage or your family because of the Defense of Marriage Act (DOMA).[9] Bautista was stationed in San Diego with her spouse, also in the service, and they raised their six-year-old son together there.

When Bautista received orders to relocate to Illinois, she knew that meant separating from her family; the military only accommodates heterosexual spouses and families together. Her partner was required to remain in San Diego with their son. Lack of federal marriage recognition meant the military had the right to separate Bautista's family and deny them all other benefits, even after DADT's repeal. I forgot to mention, Bautista was pregnant with her family's second child. As they say in the Army, "that's all jacked-up."[10]

As you probably noticed, the longer length limit of op-eds can enable writers to provide more detailed evidence, but letters to the editor typically provide evidence as well. In general, the more specific your evidence, the more likely it is to persuade readers.

Note that in some situations, readers may take your evidence more seriously if you tell them where you got it, as the author of the op-ed "Justice for dead miners . . ." does when he tells us that his evidence comes from an "independent report filed by the Department of Labor's Mine Safety and Health Administration on Dec. 6." If in doubt, tell readers your sources. If they don't know where your evidence comes from, many of them will have less trust in you — often significantly less trust. In addition to telling readers where you got your evidence, it's also useful to take information only from credible sources; as with other genres, your credibility rests largely on the credibility of your sources.

Recognize complexity when appropriate. Not all letters and op-eds recognize complexity, but many do. Consider this passage from an op-ed entitled "Let's cut the fat on obesity commentary in the U.S.":

[The obesity epidemic is *not* the fault of food manufacturers, advertisers, or TV-chef celebrities.] For those who subscribe to logical thinking, it seems starkly apparent — each individual is responsible for the personal choices they make,

---

[9] In 2011, the Obama administration announced it would no longer defend DOMA, in part because of public opinion such as that expressed in this letter.

[10] Written by Katie Miller and published in the *Yale Daily News* on November 11, 2011.

> including eating and exercise habits. . . . The . . . exception to this is there are still some social boundaries in place that overwhelm some individuals' free will.[11] [Provides an example.]

Acknowledging that your argument doesn't hold true for everybody is, in effect, a way to anticipate readers' objections and thus defuse them. Just remember to return to your argument, perhaps with a phrase such as "Despite this . . .".

Consider providing information about yourself to further establish your credibility.   You might provide information about yourself in a brief bio at the end (e.g., "[Your name] . . . is a biology major at . . .") or in the text itself, as the author does in the letter entitled "Educational gap shows Teach for America is still important":

> Raised by a single mother in a low-income African American community in Milwaukee, I knew the importance of caring, committed teachers firsthand. I wouldn't have become a proud Badger without Ms. Meyer telling me I could achieve my dream . . . or Ms. Ebel telling me I should reach higher and apply for the district's gifted middle school program. That's why I decided to join Teach for America (TFA) after graduating. . . .

While some writers use their experience to establish their credibility, others divulge information about themselves that's counter to what readers might expect; if, for example, people in your situation don't typically believe something that you believe, the fact that even *you* believe it can make your argument more compelling. Consider, for instance, the following passage from a letter to the editor entitled "Race and background important for admissions":

> I am white, I am Jewish, and I am from the East Coast. I have no business being a fan of affirmative action because in many instances I fall into the over-represented minority category. Yet I'm still a fan of using race, among other things, as a tiebreaker in admission decisions. This is the way to bring more variety of race to a school that desperately needs it.[12]

Divulging information about yourself can prompt readers to take your argument more seriously.

Consider appealing to emotion as another means of persuading readers. Letters and op-eds sometimes appeal to readers' emotions more often than other genres of argument. Many readers care about how events and

---

[11] Written by Doug Walp and published in the *Daily Athenaeum* on January 23, 2012.

[12] Written by Zack Goldberg and published in the *Badger Herald* on December 8, 2009.

circumstances affect others—and if they know how others are affected, they can often, at least to some extent, share others' pain or happiness. This emotional investment can make them more receptive to a writer's point.

Consider the following excerpt of a letter from a Muslim student, entitled "FLAME ad promotes negative stereotype of Muslims":

> I was saddened and hurt to read the advertisement, which included quotes such as "Anti-Semitism is integral to Muslim culture" and "[encouraging children to emulate Nazis] is . . . standard practice in the Muslim world. To kill Jews, to become a martyr, is the highest goal. . . ."
>
> Seeing one of our campus's most read publications, in the very popular Wednesday edition, publish an ad that accuses me and my family of being bigots, hate mongers and uncivilized took all the air out of the room I was in.[13]

If it wouldn't be relevant to discuss your own emotions, remember the strategy used in "Educational gap shows Teach for America is still important": the author tells us about a sign reading "Only one in 10 students growing up in poverty will have the opportunity to attend this school. Teach for all 10." Although the author himself was on the positive side of the statistic, many readers will feel empathy for the students who weren't. Regardless of how you appeal to readers' emotions, there are many situations in which doing so can make your argument more compelling.

Effective Language

Write as vividly as you can.   Although you're more likely to encounter vivid language in an op-ed than in a letter, such language can be effective in both genres. Consider the following passage from the op-ed "UW's planned photoshoot sorry attempt at 'diversity,'" which uses short sentences and paragraphs, asks questions, provides detail, and makes an analogy:

> You guaranteed a fun time at the photo session, and there will be dancing. Can I ask you to consider that bribing hundreds of students of color with bagels to pose for the diversity camera isn't really all that different than just picking up a black person and throwing him in the picture? I mean, aren't you just photoshopping our reality?
>
> I will not be eating your bagels.[14]

The detail in the last sentence is especially effective; saying "I will not be eating your bagels" instead of "I will not be attending your photo session" makes the point more vividly.

---

[13] Written by Sami Ghani and published in the *Badger Herald* on October 20, 2011.

[14] Written by Dakota Alcantara-Camacho and published in the *Badger Herald* on November 9, 2010.

Use a respectful tone.   A respectful tone can prompt readers to take you more seriously, while a disrespectful or hostile tone can prompt them to dismiss you as being either biased or too angry to think straight. In most cases, you'll want to avoid words such as "ridiculous," "outrageous," "lazy," "disgusting," "greedy," "money-grubbing," "cheap," and "apathetic." Although there are times when an angry tone might be appropriate, a respectful tone will generally help readers be more open to your ideas.

Use Standard English in your letter or op-ed.   Like using a respectful tone, using Standard English will generally help you come across as being more professional and credible. Be sure to edit and proofread carefully to make sure you don't miss anything, and have at least one other person read your piece before you submit it.

Design

Photos, maps, or other visual aids can command readers' attention; although rarely included alongside letters, visual aids like these are sometimes included alongside op-eds. For instance, "Justice for dead miners trumped by corporate influence" was accompanied by a photo of someone looking at a memorial wreath decorated with white hearts, which probably bore the names of the dead miners. Photos like this are likely not only to catch a reader's eye but also to engage a reader's emotion.

In addition to using visual aids, consider using italics and bulleted lists if appropriate. Italics can emphasize important words, while bulleting a list rather than enumerating it in paragraph form can help you better emphasize each item in the list. For instance, a letter to the editor entitled "A letter of thanks" expresses gratitude toward many organizations that helped the author's university during and after two fires, but rather than listing each organization in paragraph form, separated by commas, the author uses a column that lists each organization on a new line. When you format lists this way, each item is surrounded by white space both to the left *and* to the right (and on top and on the bottom if you skip lines between each item). When something is set apart by white space, it receives much more emphasis.

In sum, consider these design tools (and others like them):

- Photos, maps, or other visual aids
- Italics
- Bulleted lists

If you use design elements such as these, your letter or op-ed may be more likely to be read — and, when read, may have a greater impact.

Sample op-eds

"Meeting great expectations"	p. 73
"The Vegetarian Delusion"	p. 545
"How to Survive the Age of Distraction"	p. 566

Sample letters to the editor

"Understanding Flaws Eases Discussion"	p. 75
"Eating Vegetarian and Making a Difference"	p. 548

Sample Op-Ed

Meeting great expectations

Published 12 Oct 2011 by Katherine Taylor

From *The Daily Texan*

I would be excited for the Texas Book Festival, which is the weekend of Oct. 22, if I could remember the last time I read a book for pleasure. I miss reading, and because my majors — [Plan II[15] and rhetoric and writing] — are as liberal artsy as can be, this should come as a surprise.

Timeliness. Taylor opens her op-ed by relating her topic to a current event. Making this typical move increases the likelihood of getting published.

In the past week alone, I read 75 pages about our declining education system, 30 pages of my U.S. history textbook, 90 pages from a rhetorical theory handbook, and a 25-page narrative, and this wasn't even all the reading I was supposed to do for my classes. I skipped two whole classes worth of reading because I knew I simply didn't have time to do it.

Evidence. Taylor provides evidence by giving readers an actual page count that she sees as being too high. After providing this evidence, she makes a move that you might consider when your own evidence is drawn from the experience of just one person: she suggests that person's experience is representative — that the problem involves many people, not just one.

I have a feeling I'm not the only one this happens to. For some reason, professors seem to think that assigning upward of 100 pages per week to read is a feasible task for students. Multiply that times five classes, and that's 500 pages per week. If it takes me three minutes to read each page — a conservative number, as

---

[15] Plan II is an interdisciplinary honors program at the University of Texas at Austin.

textbooks are often complicated and take much more time to read, annotate and highlight—that's 25 hours of reading per week. On top of that, teachers expect us to engage with the material, too. Add assignments, papers, and tests to this equation and the time it takes to study and prepare for each of those, and there is no time left at all.

Do teachers not realize that even if all I did was school, I still wouldn't be able to get all my reading done? We're all balancing jobs, internships, volunteer work, student organizations, and occasionally friends, too. Sometimes we even frequent that small strip of street dedicated to hedonism and a lack of inhibitions that is fondly referred to as "Dirty Sixth." Whatever it is, on top of the reading load you undoubtedly carry, you have a real life as well.

So this load of reading each week becomes even more impossible. I feel like my professors are setting me up to fail. Since I know I don't have time to do everything, I learn the art of reading only the beginning and end of chapters. I learn which classes have reading that is unnecessary. Wikipedia becomes my best friend. Reading is no longer about soaking up knowledge but about cannibalizing information as quickly as possible.

Now, even if I do have time when I could read for fun again, I can't. I simply feel too guilty. No matter how hard I try to finish it, I always have reading I could be doing for school, so that's the reading I limit myself to. When I go home for breaks, my brain is so tired from all my textbooks and rhetorical analyses that I cry out for mindless engagements and end up reading literary trash such as the "Twilight" series just so I don't have to think.

As a kid, I read all the time. The *New Yorker* just celebrated the 50th anniversary of one of my favorite childhood books: *The Phantom Tollbooth*. My sixth-grade English class read parts of it and ended up using the plot to hold a debate over an age-old query: Which is better, numbers or letters? I still remember that debate. I still wonder which one is better and if we could ever truly live without one of them.

When was the last time that happened with reading for school? I probably couldn't summarize half of what I read for the past week,

Paragraph focus. Taylor keeps this paragraph focused by discussing only one reason that she thinks the reading load is too heavy.

Credibility. As she does in her opening paragraph, Taylor provides information about herself—information that might make her seem more credible in the eyes of some readers. These readers might think, "If even someone who loves to read thinks there's too much reading, then there really might be too much reading."

much less the past three years. My heroes used to be Heidi, Anne of Green Gables, and Laura Ingalls Wilder. Now, with the heavy weight of unmet expectations on our shoulders, it is no wonder that the heroes of today's college student are the things that help us forget our failures: Shiner, Smirnoff, and Sixth Street.

Taylor is a Plan II and rhetoric and writing senior.

Driving home the point. Like many other op-ed authors, Taylor leaves us with a vivid closing that encapsulates her argument. The vividness of this closing comes largely from her use of specific details (the two lists).

Sample Letter to the Editor

Josh Moss

Understanding Flaws Eases Discussion

I was chewing with my mouth closed. It was the second day of my freshman year, and I was eating at Gordon Commons with someone I had just met from my dorm. "That's weird," he said.

"What's weird?" I responded.

"I thought all Jews chewed with their mouths open."

This was my introduction to the University of Wisconsin. I, a Jewish student from New York City (yes, the city; not Long Island, Westchester, or New Jersey), had just encountered the most odd — but still offensive — stereotype about my heritage. I could have become angry. I could have accused him of anti-Semitism. I could have said he had no idea how to deal with people who were not raised the way he was or thought the way he did. But I didn't. I calmly stated that I thought it was probably a stereotype that wasn't true and went on talking. Why did I do this? Because I realized I would be living with this person for the next year, so it would be better to get to know the person before I judged him from one comment alone.

An unconventional opening. This opening helps Moss connect with his intended audience of fellow college students. Although many letters open by stating the writer's point, the anecdote shows Moss's personal connection to the issue he discusses.

Far too often the debates on campus issues surrounding the sundry of different student racial and religious backgrounds rely not on legitimate dialogue and interaction but on cheap accusations, flawed forums, and all without addressing the single most obvious reason there is not a healthy debate on this topic on campus: the self-segregation of each group on this campus.

Let's be honest with each other on this issue. As a Jewish student who lived in Sellery my freshman year, I was separated from almost every other Jewish student on this campus, as the vast

Focus. Although Moss doesn't state his argument in the first paragraph, he nevertheless states it relatively early in the letter. This prevents readers from being confused about what his point is. Note that the rest of Moss's letter maintains the focus on this point.

majority of them live in private dorms. There can be no good dialogue between Jewish students and non-Jewish students if they don't live together or see each other.

Likewise, it is not a surprise that many students of Asian descent mingle mainly with other students of Asian descent, or that African American students often interact with other students who are also African American or that Hispanic students associate with other Hispanic students, and the list could go on. There can never be a true campus debate on any issue that is race-based until we realize we're not even having a debate in the same room. We don't live with each other, and for the most part, we separate ourselves from each other. And often the only time we come together is to accuse each other of offending another party.

If we only come together to speak about these issues when there is controversy, then this conversation will always fail to find a consensus. What we need is to talk about this when tempers are not high and when we are just living our lives. And this cannot happen with the segregation of students on this campus. I don't have an actual solution to stop this from happening now and in the future. I just want this to be part of the debate and for people to recognize why all previous debates have failed.

As for the student who was shocked that a Jewish student chewed food with his mouth closed, four years later, he is now one of my dearest and closest friends. I realized he wasn't anti-Semitic or naive at all. He just had not met many Jews before and held an extremely odd stereotype. But neither of us overreacted. We talked. We realized we both were flawed human beings. And we happened to see each other on a daily basis for almost a year. And that made all the difference.

Evidence. Here Moss provides evidence to support his argument that interaction rather than separation is key. Providing evidence to support this claim increases his odds of persuading readers.

Writing creative nonfiction

Creative nonfiction can refer to many types of writing, from personal narrative to memoirs to opinionated essays. These forms may even overlap with other genres. Although some people may disagree on whether a particular piece should be classified as creative nonfiction, a general guideline is provided by the word "creative," which in this case refers to the use of literary writing techniques—such as figurative language, flashbacks, and dialogue—to tell a story that is true.

Some critics of creative nonfiction have questioned whether the use of literary techniques obscures the facts too much for the genre to be considered true nonfiction. Although people may disagree on the extent to which writers should use their imaginations in creative nonfiction, many agree that it's acceptable to reconstruct dialogue and use artistic license as long as a piece sticks to the "essential truth." For example, if you're using your imagination rather than a perfectly accurate memory to reconstruct dialogue, that dialogue would generally be seen as the essential truth if it accurately reflects people's values and ways of speaking. However, if you put formal words in the mouth of someone who generally speaks informally—or if you have a person express a viewpoint he or she doesn't hold—then you wouldn't be sticking to the essential truth.

To write successful creative nonfiction, it might help to think of your piece as having two separate aspects: the experience itself and the way you choose to tell it. There are many different ways to tell the same story: you might relate events in chronological order or use flashbacks; you might add detail or omit detail; you might use more dialogue or less dialogue; you might use just one scene or give readers a series of related scenes. It's useful to imagine several different versions of your piece—and, if you have time, to consider writing several different versions. The power of your essay should come not just from the story but also from the way you tell it—and imagining different versions will help you gain insight into more powerful ways of crafting your story.

Quick Checklist

PURPOSE AND AUDIENCE

Your essay will be more likely to affect your audience if you're consciously aware of your purpose as a writer. Do you want to entertain readers? Expose an injustice? Honor someone's memory? Raise awareness of an important issue or phenomenon? Communicate ideas that might make someone's life easier? Provide insight into the complexity of life or relationships? (p. 79)

CONTINUED >

Quick Checklist, continued

ORGANIZATION, FOCUS, AND DEVELOPMENT

Scenes and summary.   Are scenes the backbone of your essay? Do you use summary only minimally? (p. 79)

Organization.   Do you organize your scenes around a chronological time line, or do you use flashbacks and/or start the essay *in medias res*? Why? (p. 81)

Focus.   Have you maintained a sharp focus? Does each scene advance the purpose of your essay? (p. 81)

Title.   Is the focus of your essay reflected in your title? Note that some writers like to craft their title after they're sure of their focus. (p. 82)

Pacing.   Have you condensed less important moments and drawn out more important moments? (p. 82)

EFFECTIVE LANGUAGE

Showing rather than telling.   Have you used details to *show* your readers what's important instead of coming right out and telling them? If you do any telling, is it done sparingly? (p. 83)

Avoiding overwriting.   Have you avoided telling readers that "the yellow, round orb of the sun stealthily and smoothly creeps into the azure blue early morning sky"? (p. 85)

Vivid, specific verbs.   Are there any places where more specific verbs might help you advance your purpose as a writer? (p. 85)

Avoiding clichés.   Have you cut the clichés that seem to insert themselves into writers' early drafts? (p. 86)

Polished language.   Have you revised, edited, and proofread as a courtesy to readers? (p. 87)

DESIGN

Scene breaks.   Will readers be able to tell where one scene ends and another one begins? How? (p. 87)

Paragraphing when speakers change.   Have you started new paragraphs when the speaker changes so that readers can more easily follow dialogue? (p. 87)

Purpose and Audience

While some genres target very specific audiences, creative nonfiction tends to be written for a fairly broad audience. The same creative nonfiction piece, for example, might move a struggling high-school student, a middle-aged office manager, and an elderly retired doctor. Indeed, one purpose of creative nonfiction is to show people what it's like to be someone else. Whatever gender you are, whatever race you are, and whatever age you are, there is something unique about you — some aspect of your life that isn't shared by others or that, if shared, isn't necessarily seen by others in the same way. When you share a carefully chosen aspect of your experience with a broad audience, there will be people in that audience who will grow from reading what you've written; you might change, in big or small ways, the way your readers look at the world or at other people. Indeed, creative nonfiction can be a powerful vehicle for fostering empathy, especially if your narrative centers around characters as much as or more than plot.

If you want to make your creative nonfiction piece as powerful as it has the potential to be, it will help if you are consciously aware of your purpose as a writer. Do you want to entertain readers? Expose an injustice? Honor someone's memory? Raise awareness of an important issue or phenomenon? Communicate ideas that might make someone's life easier? Provide insight into the complexity of life or relationships? If you are consciously aware of your purpose, you'll be better able to fulfill that purpose.

Organization, Focus, and Development

Being aware of your purpose will help you decide how to organize, focus, and develop your piece. To this end, some of the following strategies may be helpful.

Organize your piece around scenes; use summary only minimally. If you use scenes as the backbone of your piece, your writing will be more powerful. Think of a scene in a play: the curtain opens, some very specific action happens, and the curtain closes. Scenes in creative nonfiction are similar; they provide detailed descriptions of action (often including dialogue), and *they happen in a single place at a single time*.

Unlike scenes, summaries describe general conditions or beliefs, background information, repeated actions, or less important action. Because summaries depict generalities rather than specifics, *they do not take place in a single time and location*. Specificity is lost, thus making it harder for readers to be there with the characters.

Because your piece will lose power if there's more summary than scene, it's important to be able to distinguish the two. To help you make the distinction, consider an example of summary taken from Amy Peterson's "Fine Lines" (p. 88), an essay she wrote during her first year in college; note that this summary works because it's so vivid and because it's only a small piece of Peterson's essay:

> Some people think this kind of thing just happens. That there's just a psychotic break and someone just loses it. When you're in it, though, time slows down. The actual act that is perceived as "crazy" isn't the worst part; it's the agonizingly drawn-out loss of total control. It's the feeling of climbing an immense and wobbly ladder when you're terrified of heights, and the whole contraption teeters on the edge of oblivion. Anticipation always feels worse than the actual fall.

Here Peterson is *not* giving us a scene describing a specific panic attack that happens at a particular time and place; instead, she's summarizing what it's like to have a panic attack. Although the summary contributes much to Peterson's piece,[16] it can't carry the entire essay by itself. The essay is carried by the scenes, one of which opens as follows:

> I don't take the stairs. I can't trust my shaky legs to make it the whole way down in one piece. So I sit in the elevator and compose myself. At the bottom I calmly cross the road to some gas station, your typical Cumberland Farms type setup. The frigid wind at my back almost wills me through the door.

We can tell this is going to be a scene because Peterson is describing a very specific series of actions that take place at a single time and location. Without this level of specificity, readers can get lost in a sea of abstraction.

A scene might be a paragraph, several paragraphs, or even several pages. When you write your own creative nonfiction piece, you'll want to think about it not just as a series of paragraphs but instead as a series of scenes that ultimately work together to help you achieve your purpose. (You might, alternatively, decide that your purpose can be well served by writing just one scene.)

---

[16] One reason this summary works while others fall flat is this: the specificity often missing in summary is provided by Peterson's metaphor: "It's the feeling of climbing an immense and wobbly ladder when you're terrified of heights, and the whole contraption teeters on the edge of oblivion."

To make sure you have more scene than summary, read your draft carefully, looking for summaries that could be replaced by scenes. If your readers encounter scenes—if they see action unfolding as if they were witnessing it on a stage—your words will be more likely to stay with them even after they have finished reading your essay.

Be aware of alternatives to chronological organization.   Some creative nonfiction pieces are organized chronologically: this happened first, then this, then this. Organizing by chronology isn't bad—especially if you omit irrelevant events—but in some cases the following alternatives are useful:

- Starting *in medias res* (a Latin phrase meaning "into the middle of things")
- Using flashbacks

The opening of Mary Karr's memoir *The Liars' Club* provides an example of an *in medias res* opening, for we are placed in the middle of the action, with no idea how we got there:

> My sharpest memory is of a single instant surrounded by dark. I was seven, and our family doctor knelt before me where I sat on a mattress on the bare floor . . .

Karr doesn't open with background information; she doesn't tell us why the doctor is kneeling before her. Instead, she puts us right in the middle of the scene, sparking our desire to continue reading to find out what's happening. This is a technique you can use too; if you find that your opening doesn't grab your attention as much as it could, keep reading until you find a better passage to use as your opening.

See "Fine Lines" (p. 88) for another example of an *in medias res* opening, and see "The Waltz" (p. 298) for an example of flashbacks. In addition to advancing your purpose, such techniques can make your piece more interesting. (Flashbacks, however, can confuse readers if they are not signaled well. If you do decide to use them, carefully study the techniques other writers have used to signal the beginnings and endings of the flashbacks.)

Maintain focus.   While in argumentative writing authors often organize their work around an explicit thesis, in many subgenres of creative nonfiction there is no thesis; instead, writers often want their audiences to read between the lines. Thus, maintaining focus in this genre can be more difficult.

To help maintain your focus, try writing down an explicit statement of purpose on a separate piece of paper (not part of your essay); then read your essay and ask yourself the following question as you go through it scene by scene: "To what extent does this scene advance my purpose? What about this next scene?" Then read the essay another time, this time focusing on paragraphs within a scene: "To what extent does this paragraph advance my purpose? What about this next paragraph?" You might even read it yet again, this time focusing on each sentence — and one more time, focusing on individual words. Experienced writers delete words, sentences, paragraphs, and scenes that are beautifully written but do not advance their purpose. Lack of focus is one of the most common pitfalls for writers new to this genre, so be vigilant in looking for irrelevant details and scenes.

Craft a title that reinforces your focus.   As with most genres, you'll want the title of your piece to reflect the focus of your writing. The title "Patching Holes" is a good example, for both the title and the essay (p. 127) bring our attention to the literal and figurative focus of the piece: the holes that the narrator's father punches in the walls and the figurative holes that he creates in family relationships. You can craft your title at any point before, during, or after you draft your piece. Some writers like to develop the title after they have finished (or at least begun) a piece so that they have a clearer idea of what their focus is.

Manipulate your pacing.   Pacing, an especially important aspect of creative nonfiction, refers to how quickly or slowly a scene progresses. You can — and should — manipulate the length of each passage to reflect its importance. You can manipulate the pacing of each passage by deciding whether to

- condense a moment,
- describe a moment in "real time," or
- draw a moment out, making your description of it last longer than it did in real time.

This is a difficult decision — one that can stump even the best of writers, especially in early drafts. Ultimately, the decision depends on whether your purpose is advanced or undermined by altering the pacing of a particular passage. Is the passage simply establishing some background so that readers can appreciate a more important moment, or is it describing a key moment in the piece? You might choose to draw out key moments for a variety of reasons: to create a mood, to convey the complexity of a character, to depict the nuances of a relationship, or to create suspense. In the tenth paragraph of "Patching Holes," for example, we learn that Long's father had an accident at work. It is not until paragraph 18, however, that we learn he'll live. Forcing us to wait to find out his fate advances Long's purpose as a writer; it forces us to wear her shoes.

Compare Long's pacing to that of another student's when she learns that her father, who has Alzheimer's, is at the police station: "As I approached my back door, I found a note tacked to it that read: 'Call the Police Station.' I silently panicked. Nervous, I made the call and found out that, luckily, my father was fine." This writer would have done well to draw out this scene. For instance, she could have told us what she was thinking as she made the call, described how she dropped the receiver as she was dialing, or told us how many times the phone rang before it was answered. If it advances your purpose to draw out certain moments, try rereading Long's description of what happens between the time she hears about her father's accident and the time she learns he'll live (paras. 10–18). These paragraphs illustrate strategies you can use to draw out your own pacing.

The key to good pacing in your own work is to *make deliberate choices among a variety of alternatives*. Don't just go with the pacing you happened to end up with in your first draft. Instead, imagine different versions of each scene — one that's condensed a bit, one that's condensed a lot, one that's drawn out a bit, and one that's drawn out a lot. Then decide, based on the purpose and importance of each scene, which version you like best. You'll often find that drawing out important scenes helps readers become more immersed in what you've written.

Effective Language

Show, don't tell.   "Show, don't tell" is perhaps the most commonly given advice for this genre. Compare the following two ways a writer might describe the town of Dalton, Maine: one version simply *tells* us what the town is like, while the other *shows* us through details — details that allow us to infer for ourselves what the town is like:

Version 1	Version 2
Dalton is an extremely harsh and cold town.	It's a fishing town where the fish fight back. Faces are chapped, lips are cracked, and smiles bleed.

While the first example uses an adverb ("extremely") and adjectives ("harsh" and "cold") to *tell* us what Dalton is like, the second example is so effective in *showing* us what Dalton is like that it doesn't need to tell us.[17] In this genre, if you do a good job showing readers, you generally won't need to tell them; in fact, telling can undermine the power of a piece. *To avoid telling, make your nouns and verbs do the work; avoid excessive use of adjectives and adverbs.* Note, for instance, that many of the key words in the second passage are nouns and verbs: "fish fight back" and "smiles bleed."

To further avoid telling, try not to come right out and say "This experience taught me that _____" or "I felt _____"; lessons and feelings are often more powerful if you let readers figure things out for themselves through specific details that you provide. Compare the different versions of the following two passages. In the first versions, the authors simply tell us how they feel, while in the second versions they provide details that let us figure it out for ourselves:

Version 1	Version 2
I felt extremely nervous and panicky.	I can recall pressure. A tight knot forming in my chest. It starts in my throat and spreads, cancerous, until I can't breathe. I'm Alice down the rabbit hole and I can't quite find the right cake to eat and suddenly everything is tiny.[18]
I feel sad because my father doesn't show his love for me.	Sometimes I count his words: 45 for the dog; none for me. I'd be leaning my back on the kitchen sink, one foot crossed over the other, arms folded across my chest, dressed in my black ensemble with hair freshly dyed with cherry Kool-Aid watching my father greet my dog. I wish I could teach her not to like him as much as she does, like the way I taught her to sit. I wish I could say to him, "Hey, asshole, I'm your little girl, remember?" I wait patiently. "Did you eat your supper, puppy? Are you hungry? Oh, you're a good little girl." He glances up at me, then back at the dog. "Didja feed her?" he'd ask. "No," I'd say, and walk away, wondering if I should count "didja" as one word or two.[19]

---

[17] Thankfully, the second example is the real one; it is taken from Mandy Simoneau's "Paper Fish," published in Bridgewater State's *The Bridge, vol. I.*

[18] From "Fine Lines" (p. 88).

[19] From "Patching Holes" (p. 128).

Note that in the second (real) versions, the authors don't actually tell us how they feel. In the first example, the author instead describes what is happening in her body and then compares herself to Alice in the rabbit hole. In the second example, the author provides dialogue and describes actions (counting words, watching her father greet the dog). If you find yourself telling readers how you feel, consider replacing that telling by using one or more of these strategies yourself:

- Describing what is happening in the body
- Describing actions (that people take or want to take)
- Providing dialogue

Although there are times when a bit of telling works, too much telling is one of the most common pitfalls experienced by writers new to this genre. If you are vigilant in replacing unnecessary telling with showing, your work will be more compelling.

Avoid overwriting.   Not only can using too many adjectives and adverbs result in too much telling, but it can also lead to overwriting. Writer Sandra Glahn discusses overwriting in a blog post entitled "Murder Your Modifiers":[20]

> Mark Twain said, "If you catch an adjective, kill it." Stephen King said, "I believe the road to hell is paved with adverbs."
>
> So why do these guys detest modifiers?
>
> Because they flag places where wordiness reigns. New writers usually have to cut their stories by ten to fifty percent before editors take them seriously. A surefire symptom of overwriting is using an abundance of modifiers.

Glahn then says she pulled down a dust-covered issue of her favorite writing magazine, *The Writer*, and read Max Keele's parody of overwriting: "When the yellow, round orb of the sun stealthily and smoothly creeps into the azure blue early morning sky, one may wonder why the sun didn't simply rise; it would have saved a good deal of trouble for all concerned."

Glahn wisely tells us that if we feel the need to modify every verb with an adverb and every noun with an adjective, we're "not picking the right words to begin with."

Use vivid, specific verbs.   If you want to "pick the right words to begin with," look at your verbs. Vivid, specific verbs appear in many genres, but

---

[20] From her blog *Aspire 2*. Retrieved July 18, 2012, from http://aspire2.blogspot.com/2008/06/murder-your-modifiers.html.

many writers consider them one of the hallmarks of creative nonfiction. Compare the following versions (key verbs are italicized):

Version 1	Version 2
Over and over in my head, I *heard* my coach's voice: "Shut down number three."	My coach's voice *echoed* in my head: "Shut down number three."[21]
Elsewhere—in SoHo, for example, where sidewalks are narrow and where there *are* tightly spaced buildings—things can get very taut indeed.	Elsewhere—in SoHo, for example, where sidewalks are narrow and tightly spaced buildings *shut out* the sky—things can get very taut indeed.[22]

The more specific the verbs, the easier it is for readers to imagine what you're describing. This is true for nouns as well.

Avoid clichés. Avoiding clichés is especially important in creative nonfiction, for readers of this genre expect originality. Here are some examples of how a writer might revise a cliché:

Version 1	Version 2
A tear rolled down my cheek.	A tear arose from hidden ducts, and, clutching my helmet, I heard it hit the frozen earth.[23]
Although I take Luvox and go through life with my heart in my throat, most people don't know that I have OCD until I tell them.	For all this, however, for all the Luvox and the neurons and the occasional field trips to the fetal position, most people don't know that I have OCD until I tell them.[24]
My father is all bark but no bite; he lets my mother punish us.	My father is the bark but my mother does the biting. She lunges at me. The belt in her hand is high in the air.[25]

If readers have heard an expression many times, it loses much of its effectiveness.

---

[21] From a student essay by Merisa Leatherman.
[22] From "Black Men and Public Space" (p. 224).
[23] From a student essay by Matthew Moreau.
[24] From "The Waltz" (p. 304).
[25] From a student essay by Pernell Grazette.

Try to make your language sound polished.   Although many creative nonfiction pieces use slang, dialect, or informal language (especially but not exclusively in dialogue), you'll still want to be clear. Typos and jumbled sentence structure can distract readers. You don't necessarily have to use Standard English—sentence fragments are common in this genre, for example—but do revise, edit, and proofread as a courtesy to readers.

Design

As with any genre, it's not only the words that are important; it's also how the words are laid out on the page. Where you put the words is an important way of preventing confusion, of telling readers what goes with what. In this genre, it's especially important to use white space to indicate which paragraphs go together to make a scene and to clarify which lines of dialogue go with which speaker.

Signal scene breaks.   If two scenes are close in time, you can signal the beginning of the new scene with the simple use of a transitional phrase. However, if there's a significant shift in time or place, many writers use a blank line to signal the shift to readers. (See "Fine Lines" for an example.) In addition to extra white space, some writers use asterisks or other symbols to show where one scene ends and the next one begins. In some cases, writers may also use numbers, titles, or even dates.

Begin a new paragraph when the speaker changes.   As you can see at the end of "Fine Lines," starting a new paragraph when the speaker changes allows the writer to avoid repeating "I said" and "they said," thus allowing readers to focus more on the dialogue itself. Even if you do choose to include attribution tags (e.g., "I said," "she said"), starting a new paragraph when the speaker changes helps readers to more quickly and easily follow the dialogue.

Sample creative nonfiction pieces (or pieces with strong elements of creative nonfiction):

Sample Creative Nonfiction

Amy Peterson

Fine Lines

An evocative title. "Fine Lines" has a double meaning that emphasizes the complexity of the writer's point.

How it all began I'm not too sure. It always becomes a haze once the madness sets in. Everything tends to come back in bits and pieces, just a series of chronological facts that don't mean a thing separately. I can recall pressure. A tight knot forming in my chest. It starts in my throat and spreads, cancerous, until I can't breathe. I'm Alice down the rabbit hole and I can't quite find the right cake to eat and suddenly everything is tiny. I'm too big for the space I'm in, and the doorway to the outside definitely can't accommodate me. There is not enough space or oxygen in the entire atmosphere to make me feel calm. I hear this is called a panic attack. What it's called is irrelevant though; when it takes over the last thing you're concerned with is what it's called.

An opening that draws readers in. Works of creative nonfiction often begin *in medias res*, a Latin phrase meaning "into the middle of things." In this opening sentence, for instance, we're not sure what "it" refers to; our curiosity may compel us to keep reading, and we're spared potentially boring background information.

Some people think this kind of thing just happens. That there's a psychotic break and someone just loses it. When you're in it though, time slows down. The actual act that is perceived as "crazy" isn't the worst part; it's the agonizingly drawn-out loss of total control. It's the feeling of climbing an immense and wobbly ladder when you're terrified of heights, and the whole contraption teeters on the edge of oblivion. Anticipation always feels worse than the actual fall.

I don't take the stairs. I can't trust my shaky legs to make it the whole way down in one piece. So I sit in the elevator and compose myself. At the bottom I calmly cross the road to some gas station, your typical Cumberland Farms type set up. The frigid wind at my back almost wills me through the door. It is a simple transaction: find package of razors, give the cashier money, walk away. He smiles at me as he slides me my change. I grin back. How ironic. After all, facades are always better when they're nice pretty ones.

Finding an empty stall was easy. Everyone was away at dinner except for my roommates. Somehow I get an individual blade out of the unassuming white case. I place it against my forearm. Moments later a wet, scarlet line appears. It's funny how people assume this hurts because I never feel a thing. Nothing resembling pain anyway.

Shifts in scene. Although academic genres often call for smooth transitions that refer back to the thesis and previous paragraph, creative nonfiction allows writers to use extra space (or other means) to indicate a change in scene.

The pressure lifts and a peaceful deep breath refills my lungs. The ladder finally tips and I can float with no thought of hitting bottom. As sick as this may seem, that red line is one I walk all the time. It is the thin line between who I am and who I should be. It feels like zero gravity, the sweet madness that washes over you when you let go.

> **Craft.** Note the repetition of "line" and the shift in meaning. Though inexperienced writers often think creative nonfiction is a simple genre that just involves telling a story, it is actually a highly complex genre requiring much craft on the part of the writer.

All better.

This time I take the stairs up to the room. Gingerly I make it step by awkward step up the four flights. When I come through the door everyone is there.

"Hey!" they greet me.

"Hi." *Shit, I better sound happier.*

"What's wrong?"

Deny. Deny. DENY.

"Nothing."

"There has to be something. Come on, you look really upset."

"I'm fine. I mean, I feel much better now. I'm tired though. Just go to dinner without me."

They really don't need to know. It's not that important.

> **"Show, don't tell."** In this genre writers tend to make points implicitly rather than explicitly; they use details to allow readers to figure things out for themselves. This writer, for example, could have omitted the dialogue and just said, "I had friends who cared about me. Unfortunately, I minimized my problem and did not take advantage of the support they could have given me." Luckily for us as readers, the writer allows us to infer this point rather than coming right out and telling us.

Writing blogs

Good blogs are fun to read, and they can also be fun to write. Although there's no recipe for writing a good blog — just as there's no recipe for any genre — this section provides you with strategies for making your blog engaging to readers.[26]

Engaging blogs are often written in a casual, conversational tone — a tone that enables readers to see the personality of the writer. Engaging blogs also tend to avoid the "echo chamber," meaning that posts tend to be original, not just echoes of what others have said. Posts generally focus on a single idea, which makes it easier for readers to quickly grasp what bloggers want to communicate. Bloggers try to boil ideas down to their essence by getting rid of anything extraneous. (Blog posts, then, are often shorter than many other genres; some posts may even consist of a few well-chosen words.)

To further engage readers' interest, bloggers like to use lively, vivid language and make their posts "scannable" — that is, they try to ease the burden for busy readers who scan the page rather than reading every word. Finally, many bloggers take advantage of the serial nature of blogging; rather than seeing a post in isolation, they see individual posts as part of something bigger. They might, for instance, make a deliberate decision about whether to develop a point in one post or over a series of posts.

Blogging offers you a unique opportunity to develop as a writer. It's true that the more you use a genre, the better you'll tend to get at using it — but you probably won't use many genres, say, fifty times a year. You might, however, write fifty blog posts in a year, and your fiftieth will probably be better than your first.

Because your blog will have many posts, you don't need to worry about making each one perfect. Even longtime bloggers who feel adept using the genre realize that some posts are better than others — and that that's OK. It's not going to ruin your blog if you publish a few posts that aren't your best.

Another advantage of blogs is that they tend to be less ephemeral than some other genres, including many Internet genres. Although some readers do encounter (and forget) blog posts right after they're written, others find them in web searches, often long after they were written. Moreover, because blogging software allows blogs to feature easily accessible archives, readers who find a post they like will often look at other posts to that blog. Your blog posts, then, may reach more people and have a longer shelf life than you expect.

---

[26] Although blogging is a medium that enables writers to publish a variety of genres (including essays and news articles), blogs are also considered a genre; an experienced blogger might characterize some but not other blogs as being prototypically "bloggy."

Quick Checklist

PURPOSE AND AUDIENCE

Have you written each post while keeping in mind its purpose (e.g., to inform, to teach, to entertain, to inspire, to provoke thought and debate, to persuade, to prompt action)? (p. 92)

ORGANIZATION, FOCUS, AND DEVELOPMENT

Title.   Have you crafted post titles that reflect the focus of each post and that engage readers' attention? (p. 93)

Focus.   Is each post focused around one idea (so that readers aren't left wondering, "What am I supposed to get out of this post")? (p. 94)

Avoiding the "echo chamber."   Is each post focused around something that's original and new to readers? (p. 94)

Organization as part of a series.   Have you considered the organization of your blog as a *series* of posts? Did you think about writing a series of posts to accomplish a particular purpose? Did you consider using a day of the week (e.g., Fun Fridays) to help you organize and generate content? (p. 97)

Organization of posts.   Have you decided how to organize individual posts based on your purpose and audience? Would it be better to move what you have at the end of a post to the beginning, or vice versa? What about the middle? (p. 97)

Length.   Have you decided how long a post should be based on your purpose and audience? Do you need to add a quotation to inspire readers to click a link? Do you need to provide an example? Could you say the same thing in fewer words? Could you break a long post into two? (p. 98)

Disclosures.   If relevant, have you disclosed anything that might influence you to depict people or things in a different light than you otherwise might? (p. 99)

EFFECTIVE LANGUAGE

Conversational tone.   Have you let your personality show through in a conversational tone? (p. 99)

Vivid language.   Have you used vivid language whenever possible? Is there any way you could replace a general phrase with a concrete detail? (p. 99)

Polished English.   Have you made the level of English you're using sound polished? Although you'll probably use a conversational tone (and possibly slang or dialect), you don't want readers to be distracted by typos or jumbled sentence structure. (p. 101)

CONTINUED >

Quick Checklist, continued

DESIGN

Have you made your post "scannable"? Have you used short paragraphs and other techniques for providing plenty of white space? If relevant, have you considered photos, bulleted/numbered lists, or bold typeface (used sparingly)? (p. 102)

Purpose and Audience

Unlike social media genres that are usually read by a diverse set of acquaintances, blogs tend to be read by people who share the blogger's interests. You might target a broad audience of anyone in the world who shares your interests, or you might choose to address an audience comprising yourself and/or a handful of relatives and close friends. (Some blogging software even allows you to restrict readership.) Even though it's fair to assume most readers will share your interests, you'll still want to craft posts that hold their attention — especially because people who read online tend to zip from site to site, often scanning rather than reading word by word.

When you address your readers, you might have a variety of purposes. One might be self-expression — to express a perspective on something you care about. You might also be writing to connect with others. Indeed, people often connect in the blogosphere, where you'll find one or more communities for almost any area of interest you can imagine — from communities of vegetable gardeners to communities of Call of Duty players. You can connect with people who share your interests in any of the following ways:

- Linking to others' blogs[27]
- Quoting their blogs
- Commenting on their blogs
- Responding to their comments on your blog

Besides writing for the purposes of connecting with others and self-expression, you might blog for a variety of other purposes: to inform, to

---

[27] Note that when you link to other blogs, some bloggers (usually experienced ones) will know that you did so because of software that calls their attention to links. When they see that you've linked to them, they may occasionally be prompted to look at your blog. Even if they don't, many of them will feel validated by the attention being given to their words.

teach, to entertain, to inspire, to provoke thought and debate, to persuade, to prompt action, or to promote services or products (like the hand-knitted scarves you're selling in your Etsy shop or the robots you built in your garage last summer). Some writers also use blogging to help them remember things they might otherwise forget. You might write one post to help you remember an insight, another to make readers laugh, and still another to share an informative link — and, of course, a post might have multiple purposes.

Regardless of what your purpose is, try to hold it in mind while you're writing. The more you're aware of the purpose of a post, the more likely you are to keep a sharp focus — to craft each sentence with your purpose in mind. When you do that, each post is more likely to fulfill its purpose.

Organization, Focus, and Development

Craft titles that reflect your focus and engage readers' attention.   Titles aren't as important if you're writing for an audience of parents or friends (who will probably be interested in whatever you say regardless of the title), but you'll want to craft titles carefully if you're hoping to attract a lot of readers. This is especially true for the titles of individual posts, which show up in search results. Seeing an interesting title can prompt readers to click the link.

The following list includes both blog titles (in bold) and titles of individual posts (in quotation marks); seeing the variety of topics — and the different types of titles — may help you come up with some titles of your own:

> *Zen Habits . . . Breathe*
>
> "Would You Rather Be Right or Happy?"
>
> "A Survival Guide for Beating Information Addiction"
>
> *Whatever: Still Running against the Wind*
>
> "I've Apparently Invented the Word 'Assnard'"
>
> "Gaaah This Song Is in My Head and the Only Way to Get It Out of Mine Is to Put It in Yours"
>
> *17 and Baking*
>
> "Gelato Withdrawals"
>
> "Announcing Sugar High Fridays — Browned Butter"
>
> *A VC [Venture Capitalist]: Musings of a VC in NYC*
>
> "Fun Friday: Startup Creation Stories"
>
> "The Board of Directors — Selecting, Electing, and Evolving"

Citizen Jane Politics: Vote Like a Girl

"Understanding the National Debt, in 10 Seconds Flat"

"Facebook and Politics: Speak Your Mind without Losing Your Friends"

Sh*t My Kids Ruined (or otherwise made filthy, distasteful, gross or painful)

"Parenting Tip #462"

"Epic Ruination"

When writing your own titles, you might find the following points helpful:

- *Try to craft post titles that are specific* (e.g., "The Board of Directors — Selecting, Electing, and Evolving" rather than "The Board of Directors").
- *Occasionally consider using numbers as one way to make post titles more vivid and specific* (e.g., "Parenting Tip #462"). Also useful — if not overused — are titles such as "5 Ways to . . . ," "3 Reasons . . . ," and so on.
- *Consider asking a question to draw readers in* (e.g., "Would You Rather Be Right or Happy?").
- *If relevant, consider suggesting how readers might benefit from reading a post* (e.g., "A Survival Guide . . ." and "Understanding . . . in 10 Seconds Flat").

Even if you have great content in your posts, you might not attract a lot of readers unless you have titles that are engaging and that give readers an accurate sense of what each post is about.

Try to keep each post focused.   While your blog as a whole might address a fairly broad range of topics, as *Whatever* does, bloggers typically focus individual posts around a single idea. You don't want befuddled readers to think, "What am I supposed to get out of this post? Why am I being told these unrelated things?" If you find yourself discussing different ideas or pieces of information, consider omitting everything that readers might see as being unrelated. You can always take what you cut and use it as the basis for another post.

Try to write content that's original and new to readers; avoid adding to what bloggers call the echo chamber.   There are several ways to avoid the echo chamber:

- *Link to something that's new to most of your readers.* When you link, it's often a good idea to explain why your link is important, perhaps by highlighting how readers might learn something new after clicking.

- *Juxtapose quotations, stories, or links to shed light on the relationship between them—especially when you think there's a relationship readers may not be aware of* (e.g., "The Democratic/Republican party claims that X is important [link to a page on the party's Web site], but here's how they vote [link to voting record]"). Juxtaposing information is a common move made in blogs—a move that often prompts readers to see something in a new light.

- *Post a photo readers haven't seen before.* You might use a photo to engage readers' emotions, to make or support a point, or simply to share something you think is interesting or beautiful.

- *Tell a story readers haven't heard.* Consider this story from *Sweet Up 'n Down,* the blog of college student and salesclerk Kristen Wolfe:

> Yesterday I had a pair of brothers in my store. . . . They were talking about finding a game for the younger one, and he was absolutely insisting it be one with a female character. I don't know how many of y'all play games, but that isn't exactly easy. Eventually, I helped the brothers pick a game called Mirror's Edge. The youngest was pretty excited about the game, and then he specifically asked me, "Do you have any girl color controllers?" . . . He grabbed the purple one, and informed me purple was his FAVORITE.
>
> The boys had been taking awhile, so their father eventually comes in. He sees the game, and the controller, and starts in on the youngest about how he needs to pick something different. Something more manly. Something with guns and fighting, and certainly not a purple controller. . . . Eventually it turns into a full blown argument complete with Dad threatening to whoop his son if he doesn't choose different items.
>
> That's when big brother stepped in. He said to his Dad, "It's my money, it's my gift to him. If it's what he wants, I'm getting it for him, and if you're going to hit anyone for it, it's going to be me." Dad just gives his oldest son a strong stern stare down, and then leaves the store. Little brother is crying quietly, I walk over and ruffle his hair (yes, this happened all in front of me). I say, "I'm a girl, and I like the color blue, and I like shooting games. There's nothing wrong with what you like. Even if it's different than what people think you should." I smile, he smiles back (my heart melts!). Big brother then leans down, kisses little brother on the head, and says, "Don't worry dude." They check out and leave, and all I can think is how *awesome* big brother is, how sweet little brother is, and how Dad ought to be ashamed for trying to make his son any other way.

What if instead of telling the story, Wolfe had simply stated an opinion we've probably all heard before: "people should tolerate difference"? By telling us something we *haven't* heard before, Wolfe increases the odds that people will be interested in reading her post. (Indeed, the post, entitled "Dear Customer Who Stuck Up for His Little Brother," went viral and was reposted in numerous other venues, including the *Huffington Post*.)

- *Consider using a post to showcase an original example of another genre.* Blogging is an especially flexible genre, and one way bloggers take advantage of this flexibility is to integrate other genres into their posts. You might find blog posts that include poems, song lyrics, and advice lists, among other genres. Many readers appreciate the variety provided by this interweaving of genres, especially if the writing in the other genres is original and engaging. Consider this advice list, excerpted from Maggie Mason's *Mighty Girl: Famous among Dozens.* Note that because some list items have been omitted, the excerpt doesn't start with number 1, nor are the numbers sequential; nevertheless, the list—taken from the post "20 Things I Wish I'd Known at 20"—illustrates several strategies you can use when integrating lists (or other genres) into your blog:

> 14. **Let your passion shape your profession.** You know that thing your dad says? "If work wasn't hard, they wouldn't pay you to do it." Please. There are professional rock stars, astronauts, puppy trainers, and bloggers.
>
> 18. **Don't be intimidated.** World travelers are just people who bought plane tickets. Pulitzer Prize winners are people who sit alone and write. You can break the most profound accomplishment down to a series of mundane tasks.
>
> 19. **Choose good company.** Ask yourself if a person makes you better or drains your life force. If the answer is B, you're busy next time they call. And the time after that.

Mason makes this list sound new and interesting in several ways. Rather than just regurgitating common knowledge, she disagrees with the commonly held belief that "If work wasn't hard, they wouldn't pay you to do it." She also makes the list within the list sound new and interesting by juxtaposing words we've never seen together: "astronauts, puppy trainers, and bloggers."

When Mason does give us advice we might have heard before ("Don't be intimidated"), she makes it sound fresh by giving us an original example ("World travelers are just people who bought plane tickets"). She uses a similar strategy when she tells us to "Choose good company"—to avoid people who drain our life force. Instead of following this advice with a general statement we've heard before ("Don't spend time with those people"), she gives us a specific example: "you're busy next time they call. And the time after that."

If you're ever stuck for something to post, consider Mason's strategy of integrating another genre—whether it be an advice list, a letter, or any other genre. As long as the writing in the other genre doesn't add to the echo chamber, you'll be likely to spark some interest.

Consider the organization of your blog as a *series* of posts.   Rather than trying to tackle too much in one post, many bloggers take advantage of the serial nature of blogs. Here are some ways you can do this:

- *Consider breaking what you had originally conceptualized as one post into two or more.* Here's an example: If you want to give people reasons to vote for a certain gubernatorial candidate, make a deliberate decision about whether to discuss your reasons in a single post or in a series of posts. If you write about your reasons in a series of posts, you'll be able to go into a bit more detail to explain each reason — *and* each post will still be shorter than your original "monster" post. Many bloggers find that using a shorter length can force them to distill their thoughts and thus express them more clearly.

    Of course, if your reasons for supporting your candidate can be quickly summarized, you may opt to mention all of them in a single post after all. You might, for example, decide to provide a short bulleted list of reasons with one statistic to illustrate each reason. The important thing is to make a deliberate decision between alternatives.

- *You can also take advantage of the serial nature of blogs by organizing some of your posts around a day of the week* (e.g., "Wordless Wednesdays" might feature pictures, or "Fun Fridays" might feature weekly jokes). In some blogs with a wide readership, one day of the week is devoted to quoting and discussing readers' comments. There are many ways you could use a day of the week to help you organize (and generate) some of your content.

Make deliberate decisions about how to organize individual posts.   Just as you should consider how to organize your blog as a series of posts, so too should you consider how to organize individual posts. Bear in mind that readers flitting from site to site are unlikely to continue reading a post if they're not sure where it's going.

If your purpose is to inform, you'll probably decide to state the most important information at the beginning rather than at the end, just as journalistic genres tend to do. If your purpose is to persuade, consider making your point in the first sentence or two of your post rather than making readers wade through an introductory paragraph. (Unlike readers of academic genres, blog readers don't necessarily expect an argument to be contextualized before it's stated. Your previously published posts may already provide some context. Moreover, the fact that readers have found their way to your post suggests that they're already interested in the topic and thus probably don't need much context to be persuaded of its importance.)

Although you might usually decide to state your point early, there are certain situations in which you might decide to delay it. In *Mighty Girl*, for instance, Mason has a post entitled "Library Portraits Project: Golden Gate Valley Branch," and she doesn't tell us her point until the end. She opens the post with a beautiful photo taken in a San Francisco library, and she follows it with four more lovely photos, also taken in San Francisco libraries. It's only in a brief paragraph at the end that she finally states her point: she asks readers who love libraries to write letters in support of restoring their funding, and she provides a link to resources to help them do so. How do you think the post might have affected readers differently if Mason had made her request at the beginning of the post? Why do you think she delayed her point?

You might also want to consider delaying your point if you think a lot of readers will disagree with you. You might decide to tell a story first and then mention the point of the story afterwards, only after the story has (you hope) opened readers' minds. You may also decide to let a story speak for itself, not explicitly mentioning the point of the story at all.

Although most posts convey a point or a main idea at the beginning, here's what you really need to know: when you consider alternatives rather than using the first organizational pattern that comes to mind, you're more likely to make a choice that will better help you accomplish your purpose.

Decide how long you want each post to be.   Depending on the purpose and audience of a post, you might want it to be very short, or you might want it to be a bit longer so that you can go into some detail to support a point, tell a story, or provide a bit more information. Before writing a very long post, however, bear in mind that you risk getting the "tl;dr" response from some readers ("too long; didn't read"). Also bear in mind what blogger Raam Dev says in a post entitled "Say Less":

> When you say less, you *emphasize* more.
>
> You may not be able to *say* more, but what you do say will be heard.
>
> Half attention becomes full attention.
>
> Scanned writing becomes writing that is read.
>
> Discarded opinions become opinions that are taken into consideration.

Like journalists trying to get the attention of readers pulled in a dozen different directions, bloggers also benefit from being succinct. If you can make the same point in fewer words, consider doing so. If you can't, recall that dividing one post into two or three is often a good strategy.

If relevant, disclose things that—if discovered by readers—might undermine your credibility. This is also important for ethical reasons; blogging, like other genres, should be an ethical endeavor. A good example of disclosure can be found in Katherine Mangu-Ward's guest post to Megan McArdle's *Atlantic* blog. The post, entitled "IRS to Mom and Pop: Drop Dead," depicts "be-suited superlawyers* at the Institute for Justice (IJ)" as heroes, but the blogger acknowledges that her depiction of these lawyers might be influenced by her friendship with several of them. The asterisk after the word "superlawyers" guides readers to this sentence at the end of the post: "Disclosure: I am friends with this particular IJ suit hanger, plus a few other dudes over there. You should be too." Like Mangu-Ward, you should disclose anything that might influence you to depict people or things in a more positive (or negative) light than you otherwise might.

Effective Language

Try to use a conversational tone and let your personality show. Some blogs do have a formal, professional tone, but if you look at some of the most successful blogs, you'll find that many of the sentences are informal; they sound as if the blogger is having a casual conversation with a friend. Consider the following example from "IRS to Mom and Pop: Drop Dead":

> Look at this dude! He does his taxes at a table covered in a lace doily for crying out loud. In a sweater. Sure, he uses a typewriter. . . . But—and this is the important thing—forcing this guy to spend a thousand bucks on continuing education . . . isn't likely to mean more accurate returns overall.

A breezy, conversational tone can help you engage a reader's interest. A conversational tone also helps readers who don't know you see you as a real person—as someone they might like to get to know.

Try to use lively, vivid language whenever possible. Because Internet readers often zip from site to site, successful bloggers realize they need to earn readers' attention on a sentence-by-sentence basis: if the first sentence is vivid, readers are more likely to continue on to the second; and if the second sentence is vivid, they're more likely to continue on to the third—and so on. To make your language vivid, you'll find it helpful to experiment with some of the following strategies:

- *Try using specific detail.* Recall how specific *Mighty Girl's* list was. Also consider the original and altered passages from Justin Huang's "How to Fit into an American Apparel Deep V-Neck T-Shirt Size XS," a post to his blog *I Am Yellow Peril*. Do you prefer the original passages with the specific detail or the altered passages without the detail?

Original Passage	Altered Passage
Under my bed was a landfill of candy wrappers and greasy fast food bags. I'd say the majority of my eating was done sitting on my toilet, quickly cramming food into my mouth while running the faucet, in case anyone might hear.	I had an eating disorder. I ate lots of unhealthy food in secret.
[E]very time I overate, I found the nearest toilet. The back of my right hand is still scarred with teeth marks.	I still have scars as a result of purging after I overate.

Many readers find that the details in Huang's original passages help them better visualize what he's describing.

- *Try occasionally using questions to draw in readers.* In addition to using questions as titles of posts, many bloggers use them in the body of their posts. Consider the opening of "Alexandra Wallace Is Worse than Japanese Tsunamis," posted to Huang's *I Am Yellow Peril*:

  > How do you piss off 4,000,000,000 people in 3 minutes? Like this: [link to video that Huang found offensive]

  Note that this question is vivid largely because it's so specific. Think about why Huang uses numbers rather than simply asking "How do you make a lot of people mad quickly?" More general questions can often engage readers too, as long as they're not overused. Asking questions can encourage people to read further for answers and can also invite comments to your blog.

- *Consider using analogies (comparisons).* If you can avoid clichéd comparisons such as "I'm happy as a clam," using analogies is another strategy that can help you craft more vivid posts. In "How to Fit into an American Apparel Deep V-Neck T-Shirt Size XS," Huang tells us "I really wish I could burst into song like Jennifer Hudson in those Weight Watchers commercials and sing about healthy weight loss plans. This was not the case." Using analogies can be so effective that there's even a blog, "Washington Could

Learn a Lot from __(insert noun)__," that builds each post around an analogy. Consider the following post, entitled "Washington Could Learn a Lot from Marathon Runners":

> Marathons are named after this one time where a guy ran until he died. Naturally, humans sought to recreate this event minus the dying. Supposedly, this is an enjoyable thing. Either way Washington could learn a lot from it.
>
> When you run a death trot, beg our pardon, marathon, you have to be in it for the long haul. You don't run full speed ahead the whole time; you have to pace yourself if you want to finish. Otherwise, and I think we've pretty clearly established this, you die. Currently Washington has no plans for the long haul. Our debt is 15 trillion dollars and growing. . . .

Crafting an original, vivid analogy increases your odds of attracting readers — and makes it more likely that they'll remember your point.

- *Think about using humor as another tool to make your posts vivid.* You probably noticed humor in some of the previously quoted passages, but consider one more; this passage is from *Wesleying*, a group blog written by students at Wesleyan University:

> [T]he *Times'* coverage gives quite the shout-out to Wesleyan's own Biology department, specifically Professor Michael Singer, known for his studies on caterpillars and, less prominently, deep appreciation for soul and funk music.

Much of the humor here comes from an unexpected juxtaposition; when we read "known for his studies on caterpillars and . . . ," we're expecting the next phrase to mention something else Singer studies — and we may smile when we realize that our expectations have been played with. Using an unexpected juxtaposition, or any other type of humor, can be an effective way to make your writing vivid. (If you're having trouble using humor, don't worry — just use another strategy to engage readers.)

- *Consider quoting someone else's vivid language.* You can use bloggers' tendency to quote to your advantage: if you're stuck, let someone else be vivid for you.

Try to make whatever register of English you use sound polished. Even though you'll probably be using a conversational tone, you'll still want to be clear. Typos and jumbled sentence structure generally distract readers and can undermine your credibility. You don't necessarily have to use Standard English — sentence fragments are common in blogs, and some blogs are written in dialect or slang—but do revise, edit, and proofread as a courtesy to readers.

Design

Bloggers often talk about the importance of making posts scannable. Indeed, making posts scannable is perhaps the most important design aspect to consider when you blog. Recall that Internet readers generally don't read word by word; instead, their eyes tend to scan quickly down the page, using white space (empty space) to help them quickly pick out a few words or images to glance at. If it's hard for readers to scan down the page, they may go somewhere else. You can make a post scannable in any one of the following ways:

- *Make your paragraphs short* (or at least relatively short), and indicate the beginning of new paragraphs by skipping a line rather than indenting. One- or two-sentence paragraphs are common in blogs. Adding a couple more sentences is fine too, but exercise caution when using the long paragraphs typical in academic genres. Using shorter paragraphs enables you to provide more white space, which makes the page more inviting and allows more words to jump into a reader's line of sight.

- *Use block (indented) quotations* with white space above and below. Though writers using print genres tend to indent quotations only if they're long, bloggers often use block format even for short quotations. The white space around block quotations can attract a reader's eye and emphasize the words you're quoting.

- *Consider using bulleted or numbered lists* with white space above and below each item. Like using short paragraphs and block quotations, using bulleted or numbered lists can create more white space to attract a reader's eye and create emphasis. Think twice before getting rid of the white space between items in a list.

- *Consider bolding important words* (such as the first phrase or sentence of items in a list). Readers' eyes tend to be drawn toward bolded text; just be sure not to overuse it.

- *Use pictures.* A well-chosen photograph can engage a reader's interest and draw his or her eye down the page.

While all these strategies can be helpful, it's the ones that allow you to provide white space that are the most crucial. White space is important because it prevents readers from getting overwhelmed by long streams of unbroken text or by images crammed next to each other with no room to breathe.

If you use white space to make your posts scannable — and if readers are interested in what you have to say — then your blog may find a larger audience than you had anticipated!

Sample blog posts

Sample Blog Post

New York Times on Drunk Fruit Flies, Wooly Bear Caterpillars, and Prof. Michael Singer

> **Attention-grabbing yet focused title.** This title tells us exactly what the post will be about but also cleverly strings together seemingly unrelated things to create reader interest.

Zach Schonfeld, *Wesleying*[28]

If you're hungover as hell, you may have more in common with the average fruit fly than you think. According to a recent *New York Times* piece, the fruit flies species *Drosophila melanogaster* consumes yeast-produced alcohol and, well, get drunk as a defense against parasites. "*Drosophila melanogaster* thrives on rotting fruit [because] it has evolved special enzymes that quickly detoxify alcohol," demonstrated a recent Emory University study.

> **Avoiding the echo chamber.** Schonfeld continues to draw readers in to the post with an unexpected, original idea. Originality is a hallmark of the genre.

What the hell does this have to do with Wes?

> **Scannability.** Short paragraphs make it easier for readers to quickly scan the post. Also, note that the conversational tone is typical — and that the sentence addresses the target audience (Wesleyan University students).

Err, for one thing, Emory's esteemed 18th president, one William M. Chace (not to be confused with this epic-stached gentleman), also served as Wesleyan's own fourteenth president, where he reduced faculty size, taught a whole lot of James Joyce, and presided over the Mummy Incident of 1990.

> **Inclusion of links.** Many blogs link to outside sources to allow readers to explore topics and references in greater detail. This link allows the author to reference something potentially unfamiliar to readers without having to explain it.

---

[28] *Wesleying* (www.wesleying.org) is a group blog written by students at Wesleyan University.

For another, the *Times'* coverage gives quite the shout-out to Wesleyan's own Biology department, specifically <u>Professor Michael Singer,</u> known for his studies on caterpillars and, less prominently, deep appreciation for soul and funk music. Apparently Emory's study on fruit flies bears significant comparison to Wesleyan studies [of] self-medicating wooly bear caterpillars, which make significant use of toxic plant leaves:

> "This article is exciting in several ways," said Michael Singer, a biologist at Wesleyan University who was not involved in the study. Over the years, scientists have gathered a few examples of animals medicating themselves. Chimpanzees eat plants with antiparasitic compounds when they get intestinal worms, for example. Dr. Singer and his colleagues have shown that woolly bear caterpillars go out of their way to feed on toxic plant leaves when parasitic flies lay eggs in them.

That said, no other study — including Singer's — suggests evidence of animals using alcohol to medicate themselves.

For more on fruit flies you can scope the *New York Times* article <u>here</u>, but for more on Wesleyan studies of wooly bear caterpillars, see <u>this paper</u> via PLoS ONE, on "Increased Ingestion of Plant Toxins by Parasitized Caterpillars." Spoiler alert: the "experiments show that the ingestion of plant toxins called pyrrolizidine alkaloids improves the survival of parasitized caterpillars by conferring resistance against tachinid flies."

Quotation. Quotations are common in blog posts. Note that bloggers typically indent quotations, even when they're short. Indenting quotations helps readers scan posts more quickly — and it also serves to emphasize the words being quoted.

Writing brochures

You've probably noticed brochures in many different locations: in your doctor's office, at information booths, in your bank, at trade shows, at career fairs, and in university department offices and counseling centers, to name just a few. Brochures are often used to promote products, services, and organizations; they are useful tools in marketing and public relations. They're also commonly used to provide readers with information that can help them—information ranging from how to deal with depression to how to care for a sprained ankle. If you have information that you think might help people, or if you want to promote something, consider writing a brochure.

Quick Checklist

PURPOSE AND AUDIENCE

Have you articulated the purpose of the brochure to yourself as specifically as possible? How can you best achieve this purpose given your readers' situation?

ORGANIZATION, FOCUS, AND DEVELOPMENT

Cover. Will your cover draw the attention of your target audience? Does it feature a photo or an interesting graphic? Does your title reflect the focus of your brochure? Does it suggest reader benefits if appropriate? (p. 107)

Focus. Does your brochure focus on a relatively narrow topic? (p. 107)

Sections. Have you divided your brochure into several sections, each of which has a narrow focus? Have you crafted a heading for each section that will prompt readers to look at that section? (p. 108)

Subsections. If appropriate, have you further divided sections into subsections? Have you crafted an interesting or informative subheading for each subsection? (p. 108)

Logical organization. Have you put your sections and subsections in an order that would make sense to most readers? (p. 108)

Reasons and evidence. If you make any suggestions to readers, have you mentioned the reasons underlying those suggestions? If you make any claims, have you provided evidence? Have you considered telling readers the source of your information? Is the source credible? (p. 109)

CONTINUED >

Quick Checklist, continued

Specific examples.   If appropriate, have you provided examples? (p. 110)

Recognition of complexity.   If appropriate, have you anticipated and addressed potential objections? If you're making a suggestion that isn't a cure-all, have you acknowledged that? Have you acknowledged that some of what you're discussing may not apply to everyone? (p. 110)

EFFECTIVE LANGUAGE

Short sentences and paragraphs.   Have you considered dividing long sentences and paragraphs into shorter ones? Have you eliminated any unnecessary words so that readers can navigate the brochure more quickly? (p. 111)

Parallel structure.   Have you used parallel structure in lists? (p. 111)

Word choice.   Have you avoided words that might make readers feel judged or stigmatized? (p. 112)

Standard English.   Have you edited and proofread carefully so that typos and grammatical glitches don't undermine your credibility? Have you asked others to read your brochure to catch what you missed? (p. 112)

DESIGN

White space.   Have you used enough white space to emphasize important ideas and to make your brochure look inviting? (p. 113)

Photos and other graphics.   If possible, have you used photos or other graphics to communicate information or add visual interest? (p. 113)

Alignment.   Have you made an informed decision about whether to center your text or align it along the left or right margin (or along both margins)? Left alignment often works best in brochures. (p. 114)

Contrast.   Is there enough contrast to provide appropriate emphasis, create visual interest, and communicate your organization? (p. 114)

Purpose and Audience

When you write a brochure, your purpose might be to inform or to persuade — or to persuade through providing information. It's often helpful to articulate your purpose to yourself as specifically as you can. If, for example, you're writing a brochure about an organization that you belong to, your primary goal might not actually be to inform people about your organization; it might be to persuade them to join, or to persuade them to donate money. The more specifically you can articulate your purpose, the easier it will be to accomplish that purpose.

Your purpose will also be easier to accomplish if you consider the situation in which potential readers will encounter your brochure. For example, someone who sees a sorority's brochure on a rack surrounded by other brochures is in a very different situation than someone who is rushing that sorority and is given the brochure by a sorority member whom she hopes will become her "sister." Though you can sometimes feel reasonably confident that a reader will open your brochure, there are many situations in which you'll need to entice a potential reader to take that first step. The following sections will provide you with specific strategies for prompting readers to take this first step, as well as strategies for communicating effectively with them after they've opened the brochure.

Organization, Focus, and Development

Make your cover inviting since it will be the first thing readers see. Consider both graphics and words for your cover. Photos are perhaps the most commonly used graphic. For instance, the cover of a brochure entitled *Personal Best: Positive Performance for Athletes* features soft-focus sepia photos of a male hurdler and a female tennis player. If passersby don't read the title of the brochure, their attention might be caught by these photos—and if they're athletes, the photos might inspire them to look at the title of the brochure and perhaps pick it up.

In addition to considering a photo (or other image), try to craft a title that communicates the brochure's contents and, if appropriate, that also suggests reader benefits (how readers will benefit from opening the brochure). For example, a brochure entitled *Allergies: Help Is on the Way* might attract more readers than a brochure simply entitled *Allergies*. Similarly, *Getting What You Want from Sleep* may be more inviting than just *Sleep*.

If your brochure will be displayed on a rack rather than handed to people, check to see how much of the cover will show. You may find that only the top third of your brochure will be visible. If this is the case, you'll want the top third to be compelling on its own, without having to rely too heavily on the bottom two-thirds.

Keep a sharp focus. Brochures are generally not collections of unrelated facts; the information presented is typically focused around achieving a specific, narrow purpose. If you try to cover too much ground, you may not be able to go into enough depth to adequately inform or persuade readers. For example, instead of a brochure entitled *Problems College Students May Encounter,* it might be better to have one brochure on stress, one on homesickness, and one on navigating financial aid.

Divide your brochure into logical sections labeled with headings. If a brochure is an undifferentiated sea of paragraphs and long lists, people will be less likely to read it—and if they do read it, they might be less likely to remember what they read. Instead of one or two long sections, try dividing your brochure into several sections. People who pick it up will probably at least glance at your headings, and if they find any of them interesting, they'll probably start reading the body text underneath that heading. If there aren't many headings, readers may not be prompted to read as much of the body text as they otherwise would. Note that in addition to drawing your readers into your body text, headings make it easier for them to locate and reread information they find useful.

Consider further dividing each section of your brochure into subsections. After you've divided your brochure into sections, see if it might be appropriate to further divide those sections into subsections. It's often easier for readers to process several subsections, each of which has a narrow focus, than it is for them to process one longer section with a broader focus. For instance, the first section of *Maybe I Have a Friend with an Eating Disorder*, entitled "Difficulties Often Associated with an Eating Problem," lists thirty-three signs that could indicate a problem. Rather than discussing all thirty-three signs in one undivided section, however, the brochure divides the section into subsections, grouping similar signs together. Subsections are labeled with the subheadings "Behavior[al]," "Emotional," "Psychological," "Social," and "Physical" to guide readers through five shorter lists. If you find yourself with a long list or with a long string of paragraphs, see if you can make a similar move.

Organize your sections and subsections logically. It may sound obvious to say that readers appreciate information in a logical order, but less-than-perfect organization is common. Consider a brochure entitled *Depression & Anxiety*, which includes a section called "Understanding Depression." In what order would you put these three subsections?

> Types of Depression
>
> Responding to Depression
>
> Recognizing the Symptoms of Depression

Many readers would want to know what the symptoms of depression are before they learn what to do about those symptoms—and they might also want to learn the symptoms before reading about the different types of depression. Unfortunately, the order listed here is the actual order in the brochure. If you're not sure how to order sections and subsections, one of the following suggested organizations might be helpful. (Note that not all suggestions will apply to all brochures.)

- Consider discussing *signs or symptoms* before discussing what can be done about them.
- Consider organizing your brochure around *the order of questions a reader might have.* Some brochures even have a section entitled "Frequently Asked Questions," but you could organize your brochure around the order of an imagined reader's questions regardless of whether or not you include an actual FAQ.
- If your brochure discusses a problem readers might have, consider making the following moves very early:
  - *Establish how common the problem is* (if it is common), possibly providing statistics and mentioning the source where you obtained the statistics.
  - *Show that you understand a reader's situation* before you suggest solutions. For example, one of the first sections of the brochure *Personal Best: Positive Performance for Athletes* is entitled "Life as a Student Athlete Is Intense," and the section opens with this sentence: "Students who are not involved in athletics probably don't understand how demanding a daily schedule can be for us." If readers feel understood, they may be more receptive to the suggestions that come later.
- If appropriate, consider ending the brochure with one of the following:
  - A list of resources, such as books or Web sites, where readers can learn more
  - A reiteration of the most important point
  - A call to action (e.g., "The key is to tell someone.")

A well-organized brochure will help readers navigate information more easily and may prevent them from feeling confused.

Provide reasons and credible evidence if your purpose is to persuade. For example, the brochure *Cycle of Violence* (p. 174), aimed at readers who are living with a batterer, provides advice as well as the reason underlying the advice: "Get away . . . [and don't] say you are leaving. This may put you in more danger." If readers know the reason underlying a suggestion, they're more likely to take that suggestion to heart.

Providing evidence to support your claims can also make your brochure more persuasive. For example, the brochure *Depression & Anxiety* claims that "Almost everybody has [experienced] a time when life was a little overwhelming, when stress or anxiety seemed to be at a high level, or when they felt a little down or depressed." The brochure then supports this claim with evidence: "The . . . American College Health Association Survey found 93% of students report[ed] feeling 'overwhelmed' sometime in the past year, including 48% who said they were at times so depressed it was difficult to function." Many readers will find this brochure more persuasive not only because the claim is supported but also because the brochure mentions the source of the supporting evidence. Note that this is a credible source; it's not a statistic from a random dot-com Web site. Providing evidence from a credible source, along with the reasons underlying any suggestions, will make your brochure more compelling.

Provide specific examples when appropriate.   Specific examples can illustrate the ideas or information you're providing. Compare the following two versions of some advice given in *Maybe I Have a Friend with an Eating Disorder*; see if you prefer version 1 (which *doesn't* provide a specific example) or version 2 (which *does* provide an example). Note that the difference is italicized.

Version 1	Version 2
Use "I" statements [when talking to a friend with an eating disorder]. These involve comments which convey your thoughts, feelings, and reactions. Using "you" statements tends to convey judgments about the other person, causing your friend to become defensive.	Use "I" statements. These involve comments which convey your thoughts, feelings, and reactions (i.e., *"I heard you throwing up last night and I am concerned"* [as opposed to "You were throwing up last night"] . . .). Using "you" statements tends to convey judgments about the other person, causing your friend to become defensive.

Many readers would prefer version 2 (the version that was published). When you provide specific examples in cases like this, readers are more likely to understand and remember your points.

Recognize complexity when appropriate.   Like many other genres, brochures sometimes recognize complexity. They sometimes anticipate potential objections, for example, and they sometimes acknowledge that a solution isn't perfect or that advice that helps one person may not help another. Making moves like these can prompt readers to put more trust in you. (It's often difficult for people to trust simplistic blanket statements and unqualified claims about perfect solutions.)

Consider how *Cycle of Violence* (p. 174) anticipates a potential objection in the first sentence: "You can't control what your partner does. But you can take steps to be safer." Just as acknowledging potential objections can bolster your credibility, so too can acknowledging complexity in other ways; consider, for instance, a passage from a brochure entitled *Alternative Health*:

Do These Methods Work?

It depends! No single method works for everyone, even people who have the same condition. Your backache may be relieved by massage or chiropractic. Someone else's may not.

Millions of people in all parts of the world use these methods. Acupuncture has been used in China for more than 2,000 years to treat a range of conditions with great success. It can even block enough pain to serve as the only form of anesthesia during medical procedures.

Note that although the passages from both *Alternative Health* and *Cycle of Violence* recognize complexity, they don't *end* with the recognition of complexity; instead, they end by returning to the focus of the brochure.

Effective Language

Favor short sentences and paragraphs. Because many readers find brochures with long paragraphs to be uninviting, consider breaking long paragraphs into two or three, or perhaps converting some of the material to a bulleted list. Similarly, think about breaking up long sentences. You might need to divide one sentence into two or three, or you might be able to eliminate unnecessary words to shorten a sentence. To see how eliminating words can affect a sentence, compare the two versions of the following sentence from *Depression & Anxiety*. See which version you prefer:

Version 1	Version 2
[T]here are . . . things that we can do to reduce the likelihood of a depressive episode or to keep the disorder from surfacing.	There are things we can do to prevent depression.

Version 1 (the one that was actually published) would be appropriate in an academic genre because it conveys a more nuanced point; however, brochure readers often appreciate shorter sentences. In addition to helping people more easily read your brochure, shorter sentences can help you better emphasize your points.

Use parallel structure in any lists you provide. Although it's good to use parallel structure in any genre, it's especially important in brochures; lists are common in this genre, and using parallel structure in lists can sometimes be tricky. Regardless of whether a list is bulleted or in sentence form, avoid nonparallel lists like the one in this sentence: "Stress can often be relieved by physical activities such as walking, skiing, and to swim." Although the problem here is obvious, lack of parallel structure can sometimes be harder to spot. Consider this list from the brochure *Maybe I Have a Friend with an Eating Disorder*:

Psychological [Difficulties often Associated with an Eating Problem]

- Perfectionism
- Preoccupation with food
- Rigid eating schedule
- Alternate between being in control of eating and "letting go"

As with any list that lacks parallel structure, this one could be revised in more than one way: the last item in the list could be changed to a noun phrase (like those in the first three items), *or* the first three items could be changed to verb phrases (like the one in the last item). It's helpful to consider all the possibilities when revising your lists for parallel structure.

Consider how your word choice may affect your audience.   The words you choose can imply positive or negative assumptions about readers. If possible, try to avoid words that might make readers feel judged. Compare the following two versions of a passage from *Personal Best: Positive Performances for Athletes*. If you were a student athlete, which one would you prefer?

Original Passage	Altered Passage
If we make poor choices . . . we suffer the consequences. . . . What we forget sometimes is that a wrong decision about alcohol or drugs can carry more negative consequences than a lost game. You can't recover from a drunk driving conviction like you can from a batting slump, for example.	What we forget sometimes is that a decision to use drugs or alcohol can carry more negative consequences than a lost game. You can't recover from a drunk driving conviction like you can from a batting slump, for example.

Although not all athletes would be bothered by the words "poor choices," some might be — and their response to words like these could make them less receptive to the message.

Use Standard English in your brochure.   Using Standard English will help you come across as being more professional and credible. Be sure to edit and proofread carefully to make sure you don't miss anything, and ask others to read your brochure before you make it available to your intended audience.

Design

Design is even more important in brochures than it is in some other genres. Good design can prompt people to read more of your brochure, provide emphasis, help readers better remember what they've read, and make it easier for readers to find information if they decide to reread your brochure.

Use plenty of white space. "White space" is a term used to describe empty space (even if it has a colored background); it's the space where no words or images appear. Lack of enough white space is perhaps the biggest pitfall in brochure writing, for if words and images are crammed next to each other with no room to breathe, a brochure may look uninviting to some readers, potentially prompting them to put it down.

In addition to making your brochure look inviting, white space allows you to better emphasize what's important; words with white space on one or more sides receive more emphasis than words surrounded by other words. One reason people tend to look at headings, subheadings, and bulleted lists even when they don't read body text is that these elements are surrounded by white space. White space is also a tool that can enable opening and closing sentences of paragraphs to receive more emphasis; if you skip lines between paragraphs instead of indenting, opening sentences will have white space above them, and closing sentences will have white space below them.

When you use white space, try to use more of it above some words than there is below. This helps readers quickly see which parts of your brochure go with other parts. Consider the following example:

First Heading

Imagine that this is the first body paragraph. Notice that this body paragraph is closer to the first heading than it is to the second heading.

Second Heading

This is the second body paragraph. If there were a third heading below, this body paragraph would be closer to the second heading than to the third.

After you finish writing and designing your brochure, look at it again to see if any parts of it need more white space. You can make room for more white space if you cut words, put some words in a smaller font, or adjust your margins (although you'll want to make sure that there's enough room between each panel of your brochure). White space can make or break your brochure, so it's worth taking the time to tinker with it.

Use photos or other graphics if possible. Because photos can add visual interest, convey emotion, and communicate points, they're worth considering for the inside of your brochure as well as for the cover.

Many readers are especially interested in photos of someone or something moving, such as the photo of a woman doing an airborne jumping jack on the cover of a brochure entitled *Move More: Feel Great!* Pictures that show emotion on people's faces can also be compelling.

Note that high-resolution photographs generally look clearer and sharper. You could use a photo taken by you or someone you know, or you could use a high-resolution photo you find on the Internet; if you do a search for "free stock images," you may be able to find some pictures that will work for your brochure. If you find a photo or other graphic that you like, consider making it bigger than you'd originally planned; the bigger size may be even more compelling.

You might also consider adding bolded captions underneath your photos. Many readers look at bolded captions before body text, and you can take advantage of this tendency by using captions to make a point. For example, the inside of *Move More: Feel Great!* features a picture of a young man walking and a caption that quotes him as saying. "A brisk walk can calm me down when I'm feeling stressed." Although some readers might find this quotation a bit corny, the caption conveys a point — and it's more likely to be read than the body copy.

Make informed decisions about alignment.   Alignment refers to where your words and graphics line up on the page: left, right, both left and right, or center. This is important because some alignments are easier to read than others.

If you experiment with different alignments, you'll probably find that left alignment works best in a brochure's relatively narrow columns. Centered text can be difficult to read because each line starts in a slightly different place. Text that lines up along both margins can be difficult to read, especially in narrow columns, because the amount of spacing between the words varies (to enable the right side to be as straight as the left side). Many designers recommend left alignment not only for body text but also for headings and subheadings. You may also decide to align the left side of any graphics you include with the invisible line on the left that is formed by your words.

Make sure your brochure has enough contrast to provide emphasis, create visual interest, and communicate your organization.   Imagine a brochure with no contrast — that is, a brochure in which everything looks the same, perhaps because there are no graphics and all words are in 10-point font, with nothing bolded. A brochure like this wouldn't have much visual interest, nor would it help readers to quickly see the hierarchy of what's important and what's subordinate. You can create contrast in a variety of ways:

- *Make some words and graphics bigger than others.* For example, try making your headings bigger than your body text. (Note that body text in brochures often looks more professional if it's *smaller* than 12 points.) You might also try making one photo or graphic element much bigger than another; the contrast can add visual interest.

- *Use bold (and italics if applicable) for still more emphasis.* Bold is generally used to distinguish headings and subheadings from body text. It's also commonly used to emphasize photo captions and key terms.

  Either bold or italics can be used to emphasize important ideas in your body text. Using italics rather than bold in body text often results in a cleaner, less busy look. Using bold rather than italics is likely to prompt people to read your text out of order, since eyes are generally drawn to bolded text first. Depending on your purpose, this may be desirable or undesirable. The important thing is to be consistent and to avoid overusing bold and italics; doing so can diffuse your emphasis.

- *Consider using contrasting fonts.* Although having too many fonts can be distracting, it's common to see body text in a serif font and headings and subheadings in a sans serif font. A serif is a very short line finishing off the main stroke of a letter. For example, in a serif font, the top of the letter "i" has a little line extending to one side, and the bottom of the letter has a slightly longer line extending to both sides.

  Serif fonts commonly used in body copy include Times New Roman, Bookman, Garamond, and New Century Schoolbook. Sans serif fonts that you might see in headings and subheadings include Arial, Syntax, Formata, and Myriad. Of course, you might find other fonts that you like.

- *Consider using contrasting colors or shades for emphasis and visual interest.* For instance, you might use a gray or lightly colored background for parts of your brochure. You might also decide to make your headings and subheadings a different color than your body copy or to include colored horizontal or vertical rules (lines) that contrast with the color of your body copy. As with any means of providing contrast, you'll generally want to avoid slight differences; using light gray as the background for one section and slightly lighter gray in another section may seem like a mistake rather than a deliberate choice. If the contrast is sharp enough, however, it can add visual interest, create emphasis, and help readers differentiate parts of your brochure.

Sample brochures

Sample Brochure

Social Phobia (Social Anxiety Disorder):

Always Embarrassed

Are you afraid of being judged by others or of being embarrassed all the time? Do you feel extremely fearful and unsure around other people most of the time? Do these worries make it hard for you to do everyday tasks like run errands, or talk to people at work or school?

If so, you may have a type of anxiety disorder called social phobia, also called social anxiety disorder.

National Institute of Mental Health
U.S. DEPARTMENT OF HEALTH AND HUMAN SERVICES
National Institutes of Health

Cover. The cover of the brochure tries to catch the attention of the target audience (people with social phobia) in two ways. First, it uses a short, easy-to-understand subtitle ("Always Embarrassed"), which is emphasized by a contrasting shade (white). Second, it asks key questions that, if readers say "yes" to, may prompt them to open the brochure.

Social Phobia (Social Anxiety Disorder)

What is social phobia?

Social phobia is a strong fear of being judged by others and of being embarrassed. This fear can be so strong that it gets in the way of going to work or school or doing other everyday things.

Everyone has felt anxious or embarrassed at one time or another. For example, meeting new people or giving a public speech can make anyone nervous. But people with social phobia worry about these and other things for weeks before they happen.

People with social phobia are afraid of doing common things in front of other people. For example, they might be afraid to sign a check in front of a cashier at the grocery store, or they might be afraid to eat or drink in front of other people, or use a public restroom. Most people who have social phobia know that they shouldn't be as afraid as they are, but they can't control their fear. Sometimes, they end up staying away from places or events where they think they might have to do something that will embarrass them. For some people, social phobia is a problem only in certain situations, while others have symptoms in almost any social situation.

Social phobia usually starts during youth. A doctor can tell that a person has social phobia if the person has had symptoms for at least 6 months. Without treatment, social phobia can last for many years or a lifetime.

Subheadings. The bolded subheadings throughout the brochure break the content down into easy-to-process chunks rather than present readers with a giant sea of text. Subheadings also enable readers to quickly scan the brochure and skip to another section if the one they're reading doesn't feel relevant to them.

What are the signs and symptoms of social phobia?

People with social phobia tend to:

- Be very anxious about being with other people and have a hard time talking to them, even though they wish they could
- Be very self-conscious in front of other people and feel embarrassed
- Be very afraid that other people will judge them
- Worry for days or weeks before an event where other people will be
- Stay away from places where there are other people
- Have a hard time making friends and keeping friends
- Blush, sweat, or tremble around other people
- Feel nauseous or sick to their stomach when with other people.

Bulleted list. A common feature of brochures, bulleted lists work to emphasize important information. They also help readers to scan that information quickly.

What causes social phobia?

Social phobia sometimes runs in families, but no one knows for sure why some people have it, while others don't. Researchers have found that several parts of the brain are involved in fear and anxiety. By learning more about fear and anxiety in the brain, scientists may be able to create better treatments. Researchers are also looking for ways in which stress and environmental factors may play a role.

White space. A key design element, white space works to make brochures more scannable. (Words surrounded by other words don't jump into a reader's line of sight the way that words surrounded by white space do.)

How is social phobia treated?

First, talk to your doctor about your symptoms. Your doctor should do an exam to make sure that another physical problem isn't causing the symptoms. The doctor may refer you to a mental health specialist.

Social phobia is generally treated with psychotherapy, medication, or both.

Section overview. Many readers find section overviews helpful, especially if a section is longer than others.

Psychotherapy. A type of psychotherapy called cognitive behavior therapy is especially useful for treating social phobia. It teaches a person different ways of thinking, behaving, and reacting to situations that help him or her feel less anxious and fearful. It can also help people learn and practice social skills.

Medication. Doctors also may prescribe medication to help treat social phobia. The most commonly prescribed medications for social phobia are anti-anxiety medications and antidepressants. Anti-anxiety medications are powerful and there are different types. Many types begin working right away, but they generally should not be taken for long periods.

Antidepressants are used to treat depression, but they are also helpful for social phobia. They are probably more commonly prescribed for social phobia than anti-anxiety medications. Antidepressants may take several weeks to start working. Some may cause side effects such as headache, nausea, or difficulty sleeping. These side effects are usually not a problem for most people, especially if the dose starts off low and is increased slowly over time. **Talk to your doctor about any side effects you may have.**

A type of antidepressant called monoamine oxidase inhibitors (MAOIs) are especially effective in treating social phobia. However, they are rarely used as a first line of treatment because when MAOIs are combined with certain foods or other medicines, dangerous side effects can occur.

It's important to know that although antidepressants can be safe and effective for many people, they may be risky for some, especially children, teens, and young adults. A "black box"—the most serious type of warning that a prescription drug can have—has been added to the labels of antidepressant medications. These labels warn people that antidepressants may cause some people to have suicidal thoughts or make suicide attempts.

Different levels of subheadings. Like section overviews, second-level headings are useful in longer sections. They highlight how those sections are organized and help readers find more detailed information quickly.

Focus. As in many genres, paragraphs in brochures tend to be focused on one idea (in this case, antidepressants as one possible treatment for social phobia). Sections are typically focused on slightly broader topics (e.g., all the treatments for social phobia), while brochures as a whole tend to be focused on topics that are broader still (e.g., social phobia).

Anyone taking antidepressants should be monitored closely, especially when they first start treatment with medications.

Another type of medication called beta-blockers can help control some of the physical symptoms of social phobia such as excessive sweating, shaking, or a racing heart. They are most commonly prescribed when the symptoms of social phobia occur in specific situations, such as "stage fright."

Some people do better with cognitive behavior therapy, while others do better with medication. Still others do best with a combination of the two. Talk with your doctor about the best treatment for you.

Left alignment. Note that the body text of many brochures is aligned on the left margin but not on the right. This makes the brochure's narrow columns easier to read.

What is it like having social phobia?

"In school I was always afraid of being called on, even when I knew the answers. When I got a job, I hated to meet with my boss. I couldn't eat lunch with my co-workers. I worried about being stared at or judged, and worried that I would make a fool of myself. My heart would pound and I would start to sweat when I thought about meetings. The feelings got worse as the time of the event got closer. Sometimes I couldn't sleep or eat for days before a staff meeting.

I'm taking medicine and working with a counselor to cope better with my fears. I had to work hard, but I feel better. I'm glad I made that first call to my doctor."

Contrasting shades. Like other types of contrast, the use of different shades can create visual interest. It can also signal to readers that the information in the shaded area is different in some way.

National Institute
of Mental Health

Contact us to find out more about Social Phobia
(Social Anxiety Disorder).

National Institute of Mental Health
Science Writing, Press & Dissemination Branch
6001 Executive Boulevard
Room 8184, MSC 9663
Bethesda, MD 20892-9663
Phone: 301-443-4513 or
  1-866-615-NIMH (6464) toll-free
TTY: 301-443-8431 or
  1-866-415-8051 toll-free
E-mail: **nimhinfo@nih.gov**
Website: **www.nimh.nih.gov**

Resources. Many brochures provide readers with one or more resources they can consult for more information (e.g., phone numbers, web addresses, book titles). This information is typically found on the back cover or the second-to-last panel.

U.S. DEPARTMENT OF HEALTH AND HUMAN SERVICES
National Institutes of Health
NIH Publication No. TR 10-4678
Revised 2010

Author. The name of the person and / or organization that produced the brochure is typically provided on the bottom of the back cover. Readers are more likely to trust information if they know where it comes from.

1

How can our relationships change and grow?

Can we bridge the parent-child
communication gap?
Creative nonfiction, page **127**   Self-help book, page **163**

How can we train our mates?
Humor column, page **138**

What types of talking matter most?
Self-help book, page **146**

How can we protect ourselves
from violent relationships?
Brochure, page **174**   Scholarly research report, page **183**

Human relationships are incredibly complex — even more so than they might appear at first glance. Think about how many areas of study and genres discuss how we live with and love one another; from love songs to magazine quizzes, from sociology to psychoanalysis, we spend a lot of time taking stock, evaluating, and recording the health and development of our relationships with one another.

Consider the last time you had a fight with a friend or partner: How did the fight affect you? Did you consult a magazine article for help sorting out the conflict? Did you listen to a favorite sad song to help you cope? Perhaps you flipped or scrolled through old photo albums to remind you of better times. In each of these cases, you were seeking out a specific genre for a specific purpose — whether that purpose was advice or reminiscence or insight — and each of these genres, in its own way, provides a portrait of how relationships can grow and change. Like these genres you may have encountered, the genres in this chapter provide portraits of how relationships can evolve — portraits that shed light on the complexity of both relationships and the genres that discuss them.

Case Study in Genre and Relationships:
"The Relationship Status Update"

It's only natural that the dominance of technology today would provide us with new genres for monitoring, recording, and evaluating our relationships. Online dating sites abound, offering singles greater opportunities to select specific criteria they want in a partner. Facebook's

Timeline lets us track relationships as they happen: friends are added, photos document the time spent with those we care about, and relationship statuses inform others about changes in our romantic availability.

As it becomes more common to record our lives online, so too does it become more common for technology-enabled genres to influence how our relationships develop. Couples can discover infidelity by reading their partners' texts, fights can all too easily become public, and we can even be horrified about what our mothers might find out about us by adding us as friends. The infographic shown here, posted to the blog of the market research firm Lab 42, uses data obtained through social media to provide statistics about how technology (among other things) influences the ways that our relationships begin, develop, and end.

As a genre, infographics are a hybrid: they provide statistics resembling those you might see in a more serious report, but they also use icons in a graphic format that displays those statistics with more visual force. "The Relationship Status Update" combines statistics with icons to give readers an idea, before they've even read the statistics themselves, of what those statistics represent.

To see this infographic in color, visit the e-Pages for *Real Questions* at **bedfordstmartins .com/epages**.

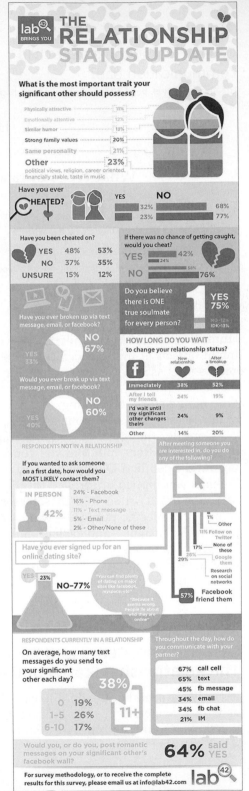

Questions for Critical Reading

1. What was your response to this infographic? What do you take to be its purpose, and to what extent do you think it accomplished this purpose?
2. Genres draw on, influence, and refer to other genres. How effectively do you think the reference to another genre works in the title "The Relationship Status Update"? Did this title succeed in drawing you in to the rest of the infographic? Why or why not?
3. Genres influence—and are influenced by—assumptions, and the specific ways that individuals use those genres may reveal (and perpetuate) even more assumptions. What assumptions do you see in "The Relationship Status Update"? Do you think it's fair to make these assumptions? Why or why not?
4. As you look at "The Relationship Status Update," do the graphic elements guide your eye toward the statistical information? Do the graphic elements help you find and understand the information more easily? Why or why not?
5. How does the infographic as a whole work to tie together a loose assortment of statistical information? How well does it allow you to see how each set of statistics might be related? Why?
6. Imagine that, instead of an infographic, this information were presented as a news article. How might a news article show connections between the sets of statistics that the infographic can't? Which presentation would you be more interested in reading, the infographic or a news article (or both)? Why?

Consider the information represented in the infographic as you read this chapter, which includes other genres that attempt to explain or influence how we relate to the people we care about.

About the Readings

Human relationships are at once both universal and personal, and each of the readings in this chapter in some way addresses this duality while also offering its own perspective. In the first reading selection, "Patching Holes," Andi Long uses creative nonfiction to illustrate her own complicated father-daughter relationship while also exploring more broadly what daughters need from fathers and what daughters' duties to fathers are. In the newspaper column "What Shamu Taught Me about a Happy Marriage," Amy Sutherland likewise draws extensively on personal experience, although she's less interested in documenting her relationship with her husband than she is in discussing what animal trainers have taught her about how to improve romantic relationships. Sutherland uses humor to suggest that when it comes to building relationships, we have a lot more in common with animals than we might like to admit.

Unlike Sutherland and Long, the next two reading selections don't go into depth discussing the authors' own personal experience; rather, they were written to help readers apply research-based advice to their own lives. To accomplish this purpose, they use examples drawn from research (and other examples) to help readers make more universal advice personal. John Gottman and Joan DeClaire's self-help book *The Relationship Cure* argues that relationships grow "bid by bid," through our responses to each other in a series of mundane interactions—and it gives examples of how we might improve our relationships by acting differently in these mundane interactions. Deborah Tannen's self-help book *You're Wearing That? Understanding Mothers and Daughters in Conversation* likewise uses a variety of examples to explore how relationships go wrong and how they can be improved. Although Tannen focuses on mother-daughter relationships, what she says can be applied to other relationships as well.

Unlike these two book excerpts, Diane Davis's brochure *Cycle of Violence* examines relationships that go through negative, not positive, changes. Also unlike the two book excerpts, the brochure genre used by Davis doesn't allow for a wide variety of extended examples. Rather, the author distills what she thinks people in violent relationships need to know, informing readers about how violent relationships can go through cycles of change—and how they can succeed in escaping from these relationships. The selection that closes the chapter, "When We Hurt the Ones We Love: Predicting Violence against Women from Men's Mate Retention," also discusses how relationships can deteriorate. As an academic research report, however, this selection provides much more detail, including not only citations of previously conducted research but also details about the authors' own research. The authors ultimately use what they learned through their own research to argue that there are early warning signs that a relationship might become violent—signs that women can use to predict and thus avoid violence.

As a set, the readings in this chapter use different genre conventions to demonstrate the complexity of relationships while also highlighting universal aspects of relationships. As you read, think about how each writer uses the conventions of his or her genre to talk both broadly and specifically about relationships in flux.

🄴 For additional readings in online and multimedia genres related to the chapter theme, see the e-Pages online at **bedfordstmartins.com /realquestions/epages.**

Patching Holes

Andi Long

"[T]here's something there with my dad that I want," Long tells us. "Something that I want so badly to understand and fix." Long's creative nonfiction piece about her relationship with her father was published in 2004 in the first volume of the *Bridge*, an award-winning journal of student work published by Bridgewater State University. Long wrote the piece for a creative nonfiction class when she was a student at Bridgewater State.

Focus on Genre   Many nonfiction genres, including much academic and workplace writing, tend to make points explicitly; writers in these genres typically state their points as clearly as they can, often at or toward the beginning of what they are writing. Creative nonfiction writers, however, often make points implicitly, requiring us to read between the lines. As you read "Patching Holes," consider what points Long is making and how she goes about making them. Also consider how her piece might have been different had she made her points explicitly. Given your assessment of her purpose and audience, do you think her essay would have been more — or less — effective if she had made her points explicitly? Why?

◄○►

makes you think that everything's not all right, but immediately I thought he was dead. Or I thought a chain saw cut him up. Or I thought — maybe the worst thought? — that he got sucked into his chipper.

My sister was always emotional. She cried over everything. I tried to calm her down, to get her to tell me what happened, while from the other end of the phone I sat, rolling my eyes at her. "I don't know how bad it is," she said through her dramatic sobs, "but he's at the South Shore Hospital." I told her I'd be there soon, leaving my writing for later. And I was annoyed. This phone call, as urgent as it was, had ruined my routine. It made me stop in the middle of the paragraph that I was revising, that I was getting so proud of, and I had to save, mid-sentence, the unfinished draft, and drive.

On the way to the hospital I tried my mom's cell phone. Voicemail. I tried my brother. Voicemail. I kept driving, not in a panic, just driving, wondering what had happened. Wondering how my life might change when I got to the hospital.

I pulled into the lot, unsure of where to park, walked into the front revolv- ing doors and went up to the Clinique-green desk that said "Information" in four different languages. There was an older woman with a blue volunteer button and a mauve smock sitting behind the desk. I gave her my dad's name, and she typed it into her computer, typing with just her index fingers, and I watched how her wrinkles made her fingers fatter than they probably were in youth, how her wedding band pinched and made the fat of her finger puff out a bit, wondering how she'd ever get the ring off, and noticing that her hands shook a lot like my dad's. "I'm sorry, dear," she said. "He's been transferred." She couldn't tell me what happened or what condition he was in. Just that he was now at the Beth Israel in Boston. I knew it couldn't be good.

I got to the hospital after a long, traffic-filled drive up the expressway and a dozen cell phone calls with no answers. I was amazed at how calm I was. How I didn't even care that there was traffic. How I didn't cry. How I sung along to my Ani DiFranco albums while thinking of how I would react. What I would say if my dad was dead. What I would wear to his funeral. Wondering if Bryan, my boyfriend, would get to stand with me in the family line, if he'd have his hand on my back the whole time, rubbing it, and smiling little, reassuring smiles at me. I didn't know if boyfriends could do that, or if it was reserved just for hus- bands. For legal, lifetime companions.

I got to the hospital and met up with my mom, brother, sister, and aunt. They told me that he fell out of his tree, fell 40 feet right to the ground, because his rope broke in half. I tried to picture 40 feet in my mind, but I couldn't, couldn't gauge it. I couldn't visualize 480 inches stacked up one on top of another, reaching up high, pointing at the sky like tree branches. I couldn't picture my dad collapsing all of those 480 inches. I couldn't picture them breaking in half from the weight of his body, his chain saw, his boots and

15

his belt. When I tried to picture it, it was in slow motion and silent. It was a graceful fall. A slow, foot-first fall. Maybe even a jump.

He was in surgery now, and the doctors thought he'd be okay. It was a miracle, they all said, and Bryan told me how just the week before, at my brother's wedding, that my dad was talking about his trees and how if you fall 15 feet you're done. Dead. Gone. But he, somehow, 25 feet higher, was alive.

I didn't cry that night. I'm not sure what that says about me or my dad or how I feel about him. I was in this weird state where I didn't know how I felt. I was sad. I was scared. I didn't care. I wished it was worse than it was. I was just confused, disoriented. My dad could have died, I kept telling myself. And I didn't know how I would have felt. I didn't know if it would be relief or pain, grief or anger, passivity or deep sadness.

I went to the hospital again. He was on morphine—a lot of morphine—and was crying because he was in so much pain. He was talking about the pharaohs and how they were trying to steal his arm. He called me down close to his face, and whispered in my ear: "Don't let them take it, Andrea. I need it." Later when the nurses were in the room he was yelling and swearing, screaming at the nurses: "Fucking pharaohs! Get them away! I'm not selling my arm!" And I couldn't help—maybe because I was immature, maybe because I was nervous, maybe because it really was funny, maybe because I was embarrassed—I couldn't help but laugh.

He came home after a while. I forget how long it was. But all summer it was my job (mine because part-time work is not as important as full-time work, and, being the youngest and in school, I only had a part-time job) to take care of him. But I also took the job on without much hesitation. I went to their house at six every morning to find my dad sleeping. I got close, made sure he was breathing, and then played with my dog. He'd call me from his bedroom when he woke up, slurring my name so it just sounded like a bunch of vowels strung together, and ask me to do various things: fluff his pillow, get more blankets, take blankets off, take away his pillow, change his socks, help him up, crank the metal screws that were going straight through his left arm, change his bandages, clean the pus from the holes in his body, get him drinks, bring him the plastic jug to piss in, empty it into the toilet, roll him over. It was exhausting, but I did it.

A lot of people were surprised by my nursing duties. Scores of people who know about my dad and me told me that I should let him lay there alone and suffer. Dozens of people told me that a man like him didn't deserve a daughter like me. But I felt this obligation, this subtle obligation, that I almost enjoyed, to stay there with him.

I've heard a lot of girls' stories about their fathers. And there's something there between dads and daughters, something that's just not there with

20

mothers. If my mother was sick, I thought, I wouldn't have gone. But there's something there with my dad that I want. Something that I so badly want to understand and to fix. And fixing him, or nursing him, or whatever it was that I was doing to him, was my way of beginning.

After a good, long month he got out of his bed and started standing. He wanted to go outside, he told me, so I (who stand just five feet tall and can hardly carry anything more than two gallons of milk in the house at one time) carried the wooden gliding rocker from the living room outside to the front yard. I picked the chair up and it glided forward, then back, in my hands, and my body was awkward over it, trying to grip it and keep it still. I carried it down the stairs, almost falling, trying to squeeze through the front door with this chair, without letting the cat out, without letting the bees in, without tripping, and I put it on the front steps. I helped him down next. We got down the stairs and into the chair, and he sat back, mumbled, slurred, sighed, and spit. "Aeeah," he said, and I understood now that that was my name, "geh'me a hat." I went back up the stairs, found an old baseball cap, came down the stairs, outside, and put it on his head. "No," he said, after I went in and came out again, "geh'me ma' tree hat." I rolled my eyes, went back in, into the bedroom, and found his hat, a green one with yellow embroidery: "Simple Tree Man." I got it for him for Christmas one year but had never seen him wear it. It was covered with dust, so I cleaned it, brought it out, and set it on his head. A few minutes later he wanted an O'Doul's. A few minutes later, another. Then new socks. Then a blanket. Then a wet towel. I put the towel on his lap and he pulled me in toward him. "You're a sweetheart," he said, speaking even more clearly than he had before the fall, staring at me. "A real sweetheart."

I never heard him use either word: "Sweet" or "Heart." I had never been that   25
close to his face. I stared at him like that for a long time, his eyes glazed over from the oxycontin and morphine, and noticed the gray hues in his eyes that I never noticed before. I wish there was someone walking by who could have taken a picture in that moment: my dad, hurt, casted, broken, with my chin in his large, shaking hand, holding me, the daughter who I was convinced he had no use for, close to his face. I just looked at him, loving the moment, then shook out of it, said, "Cut the shit, Tom," and walked up the stairs, smiling the whole way, and sat in the kitchen over a cup of coffee, smiling, because my dad thought I was a sweetheart.

I continued for the rest of that summer to care for him until he was able to walk, then drive, then, finally, work. And I thought we were fixed. I thought maybe now he would take care of me. But when he got better and didn't need me anymore, when his hands worked again and when his speech was comprehensible, he started swearing again, started punching things again, and, the moment that made me know that it was over, when he threatened to kick me out of the house (which I hadn't lived in, mind you, for three years) because

I got in a fight with my mother, I knew he was better again. And that I wasn't a sweetheart. And that things would go back, back three months, back with holes to patch, like nothing had ever happened.

Questions for Critical Reading

1. What was your response to "Patching Holes"? What do you think was Long's purpose in writing it, and to what extent do you think it accomplishes this purpose?

2. Long implies dissatisfaction with her relationship with her father. As a creative nonfiction writer, however, she does not explicitly tell us that his actions hurt her; instead her hurt is implied. Read the following two passages and consider whether you prefer the first one (the original passage that just implies Long's hurt) or the second one (an altered version that makes the point explicitly).

Original Passage	Altered Passage
Maya, my dog, is perched on the top step, tail wagging, looking down the stairs and waiting for [my father] to come up. He bends down, slowly, to greet her, meeting his face with hers. "Oh, hello my little girl! Did you miss me today? Did you? How was your day? Aw, you're a good little girl! Hello!" This goes on for about ten minutes. Sometimes I count his words: 45 for the dog; none for me. I'd be leaning my back on the kitchen sink, one foot crossed over the other, arms folded across my chest, dressed in my black ensemble with hair freshly dyed with cherry Kool-Aid watching my father greet my dog. I wish I could teach her not to like him as much as she does, like the way I taught her to sit. I wish I could say to him, "Hey, asshole, I'm your little girl, remember?" I wait patiently. "Did you eat your supper, puppy? Are you hungry? Oh, you're a good little girl." He glances up at me, then back at the dog. "Didja feed her?" he'd ask. "No," I'd say, and walk away, wondering if I should count "didja" as one word or two. (paras. 3–5)	My father pays more attention to my dog than to me, and that hurts me deeply.

Considering Long's purpose and audience, would you say that the implicit or the explicit version is more effective? Why? In what situations might you as a writer want to make points explicitly? implicitly?

3. As you saw, the altered passage in the preceding question simply *tells* us how Long felt, while the original one subtly *shows* us how she felt through the use of detail. Long uses this technique of showing rather than telling in several other passages; indeed, "show, don't tell" is common advice given to both fiction and creative nonfiction writers (although it is generally inappropriate in academic writing). Find two or three other passages—ones you especially like—in which Long shows rather than tells. How might the points made in these passages have been conveyed more explicitly? Develop your own altered versions. (It can be instructive—as well as great fun—to revise passages to make them worse.)

4. Consider Long's use of fragments (incomplete sentences). Although fragments in academic and professional genres can undermine a writer's credibility, they are generally accepted in genres such as advertising, blogs, and creative nonfiction. Long, for example, writes the following:

> For my dad, the shaking is a nuisance. It makes eating difficult. Writing nearly impossible. (para. 2)

(You can identify a fragment by tacking "It is true that" onto the beginning of a sentence. If the original phrase makes sense with this temporary addition, it is in fact a sentence; if it doesn't make sense, it is actually a fragment. Consider this tacking-on strategy when you read these altered sentences: "It is true that, for my dad, the shaking is a nuisance"; "It is true that it makes eating difficult"; and "It is true that writing nearly impossible." Since the last phrase doesn't make sense, we know it's a fragment.)

Long uses fragments in several passages. Consider each of the following passages alongside versions that eliminate the fragments; see which ones you prefer:

Original Passage	Altered Passage
An accident for my dad, the arborist, could have meant a lot of things. In the past it meant torn rotator cuffs, twice, in both shoulders. It also meant a broken rib once. Once a cut leg. A sliced arm. A lost finger. (para. 11)	An accident for my dad, the arborist, could have meant a lot of things. In the past it meant torn rotator cuffs, twice, in both shoulders. It also meant a broken rib once. Once it meant a cut leg. Another time it meant a sliced arm. Still another time it meant a lost finger.

Original Passage	Altered Passage
On the way to the hospital I tried my mom's cell phone. Voicemail. I tried my brother. Voicemail. (para. 14)	On the way to the hospital I tried my mom's cell phone, but I got her voice-mail. I tried my brother, but again I got voicemail.

Which passages do you find more effective, and why? Take a few minutes to find more fragments, and revise them so that they are complete sentences. Trade revisions with some classmates, and come up with a theory about why fragments tend to appear more frequently in some genres than in others. When in your own writing might you want to use fragments, and when might you want to avoid them? Your instructor may ask you to share your insights with the class.

Making Connections

5. Readers of academic and professional genres tend to be more interested in content than in craft; many of them are reading primarily to learn and to assess ideas rather than to appreciate the originality and beauty of the language. In contrast, when people read creative nonfiction such as "Patching Holes" and journalistic writing such as Amy Sutherland's "What Shamu Taught Me about a Happy Marriage" (p. 138), they often appreciate the way a writer carefully manipulates and crafts language. One way to craft language is through using very specific detail. Think about why both Long and Sutherland use detail in the original passages below; compare these passages to altered versions that are more general.

Original Passage	Altered Passage
I tried to picture 40 feet in my mind, but I couldn't, couldn't gauge it. I couldn't visualize 480 inches stacked up one on top of another, reaching up high, pointing at the sky like tree branches. I couldn't picture my dad collapsing all of those 480 inches. I couldn't picture them breaking in half from the weight of his body, his chain saw, his boots and his belt. (Long, para. 17)	I tried to picture 40 feet in my mind, but I couldn't, couldn't gauge it. I couldn't visualize how high that was. I couldn't picture my dad collapsing from that height.

connections

Original Passage	Altered Passage
[My husband] hovers around me in the kitchen asking if I read this or that piece in *The New Yorker* when I'm try-ing to concentrate on the simmering pans. He leaves wadded tissues in his wake. He suffers from serious bouts of spousal deafness but never fails to hear me when I mutter to myself on the other side of the house. "What did you say?" he'll shout. (Sutherland, para. 5)	[My husband] hovers around me in the kitchen when I'm trying to con-centrate on cooking. He's a slob. He suffers from serious bouts of spousal deafness but never fails to hear me when I mutter to myself on the other side of the house.

For you as a reader, what was the effect of the detail in the original passages? Which passages did you prefer, and why?

6. Like writers across a variety of genres, Long uses dashes [—] throughout "Patching Holes." So too does Amy Sutherland in "What Shamu Taught Me about a Happy Marriage" (p. 138), as do John Gottman and Joan DeClaire in their self-help book *The Relationship Cure.* Consider the following passages from each work to see if you can articulate a principle describing when and how dashes are used.

"Patching Holes"

Other nights—nights when there is no storm in sight—are loud. (para. 6)

"What Shamu Taught Me about a Happy Marriage"

I wanted—needed—to nudge him a little closer to perfect, to make him into a mate who might annoy me a little less, who wouldn't keep me waiting at restaurants, a mate who would be easier to love. (para. 6)

The Relationship Cure

[E]ven our best efforts to connect can be jeopardized as a result of one basic problem: failure to master what I call the "bid"—the fundamental unit of emotional communication. . . . A bid can be a question, a gesture, look, a touch—any single expression that says, "I want to feel connected to you." (paras. 2–3)

How would you explain the use of dashes in these examples? When might you want to use dashes in your own writing?

Writing: Your Turn

1. Write a rhetorical analysis of "Patching Holes." In your analysis, try answering the following question: How effective do you find "Patching Holes" as a piece of creative nonfiction, and why? You might consider, as evidence to support your claim, any combination of the following: Long's use of dialogue, varied sentence lengths, fragments, repetition, symbolism, present tense, and detail (especially detail that shows rather than tells). Since one purpose of rhetorical analysis is to help readers see the text you're analyzing in a new light, give your analysis to some classmates to see if you have accomplished this purpose. If you haven't, ask for revision suggestions. If you have, ask what you might do to better accomplish this purpose. For ideas on writing a rhetorical analysis, see p. 31.

2. Write your own piece of creative nonfiction about a family relationship (either one that involves you or one that you've observed). Give your draft to some classmates and ask them where you might use even more detail to show rather than tell when you revise. For other strategies you can use when writing creative nonfiction, see p. 77.

What Shamu Taught Me about a Happy Marriage

Amy Sutherland

"[Y]ou don't get a sea lion to balance a ball on the end of its nose by nagging," Sutherland informs us. "The same goes for the American husband." Sutherland, a journalist with a master's degree from Northwestern University, wrote the following column for the *New York Times* in 2006. Inspired by the positive response, she used it as the basis for her latest book, *What Shamu Taught Me about Life, Love, and Marriage* (2009).

Focus on Genre One textual feature that tends to vary across genres is paragraph length, which can shape a reader's experience significantly. Paragraphs in academic genres—the genres most of your professors will expect you to use—tend to be longer, often to fulfill readers' expectations that claims will be supported with ample evidence. However, in journalistic writing such as Sutherland's column, you'll often find medium and short paragraphs, sometimes even one-sentence paragraphs.

Paragraphs in journalistic genres may be shorter for several reasons—one of which is that readers of these genres tend to expect less evidence. In addition, short paragraphs allow writers to achieve greater emphasis. Short paragraphs are also useful in journalistic writing for yet another reason: imagine yourself as a reader with a big newspaper but little time. Assuming that there are two articles of equal interest, would you be more likely to read the one with long paragraphs or the one with short paragraphs?

As you read, see if you find Sutherland's variation in paragraph length to be effective. Also consider when you would want to experiment with short paragraphs in your own writing—and when you wouldn't.

◄○►

A s I wash dishes at the kitchen sink, my husband paces behind me, irritated. "Have you seen my keys?" he snarls, then huffs out a loud sigh and stomps from the room with our dog, Dixie, at his heels, anxious over her favorite human's upset.

In the past I would have been right behind Dixie. I would have turned off the faucet and joined the hunt while trying to soothe my husband with bromides like, "Don't worry, they'll turn up." But that only made him angrier, and a simple case of missing keys soon would become a full-blown angst-ridden drama starring the two of us and our poor nervous dog.

Now, I focus on the wet dish in my hands. I don't turn around. I don't say a word. I'm using a technique I learned from a dolphin trainer.

I love my husband. He's well read, adventurous and does a hysterical rendition of a northern Vermont accent that still cracks me up after 12 years of marriage.

But he also tends to be forgetful, and is often tardy and mercurial. He hovers around me in the kitchen asking if I read this or that piece in *The New Yorker* when I'm trying to concentrate on the simmering pans. He leaves wadded tissues in his wake. He suffers from serious bouts of spousal deafness but never fails to hear me when I mutter to myself on the other side of the house. "What did you say?" he'll shout.

These minor annoyances are not the stuff of separation and divorce, but in sum they began to dull my love for Scott. I wanted—needed—to nudge him a little closer to perfect, to make him into a mate who might annoy me a little less, who wouldn't keep me waiting at restaurants, a mate who would be easier to love.

So, like many wives before me, I ignored a library of advice books and set about improving him. By nagging, of course, which only made his behavior worse: he'd drive faster instead of slower; shave less frequently, not more; and leave his reeking bike garb on the bedroom floor longer than ever.

We went to a counselor to smooth the edges off our marriage. She didn't understand what we were doing there and complimented us repeatedly on how well we communicated. I gave up. I guessed she was right—our union was better than most—and resigned myself to stretches of slow-boil resentment and occasional sarcasm.

Then something magical happened. For a book I was writing about a school for exotic animal trainers, I started commuting from Maine to California, where I spent my days watching students do the seemingly impossible: teaching hyenas to pirouette on command, cougars to offer their paws for a nail clipping, and baboons to skateboard.

I listened, rapt, as professional trainers explained how they taught dolphins to flip and elephants to paint. Eventually it hit me that the same techniques might work on that stubborn but lovable species, the American husband.

The central lesson I learned from exotic animal trainers is that I should reward behavior I like and ignore behavior I don't. After all, you don't get a sea lion to balance a ball on the end of its nose by nagging. The same goes for the American husband.

Back in Maine, I began thanking Scott if he threw one dirty shirt into the hamper. If he threw in two, I'd kiss him. Meanwhile, I would step over any soiled clothes on the floor without one sharp word, though I did sometimes kick them under the bed. But as he basked in my appreciation, the piles became smaller.

I was using what trainers call "approximations," rewarding the small steps toward learning a whole new behavior. You can't expect a baboon to learn to flip on command in one session, just as you can't expect an American husband to begin regularly picking up his dirty socks by praising him once for picking up a single sock. With the baboon you first reward a hop, then a bigger hop, then an even bigger hop. With Scott the husband, I began to praise every small act every time: if he drove just a mile an hour slower, tossed one pair of shorts into the hamper, or was on time for anything.

I also began to analyze my husband the way a trainer considers an exotic animal. Enlightened trainers learn all they can about a species, from anatomy to social structure, to understand how it thinks, what it likes and dislikes, what comes easily to it and what doesn't. For example, an elephant is a herd animal, so it responds to hierarchy. It cannot jump, but can stand on its head. It is a vegetarian.

The exotic animal known as Scott is a loner, but an alpha male. So hier-   15
archy matters, but being in a group doesn't so much. He has the balance of a gymnast, but moves slowly, especially when getting dressed. Skiing comes naturally, but being on time does not. He's an omnivore, and what a trainer would call food-driven.

Once I started thinking this way, I couldn't stop. At the school in California, I'd be scribbling notes on how to walk an emu or have a wolf accept you as a pack member, but I'd be thinking, "I can't wait to try this on Scott."

On a field trip with the students, I listened to a professional trainer describe how he had taught African crested cranes to stop landing on his head and shoulders. He did this by training the leggy birds to land on mats on the ground. This, he explained, is what is called an "incompatible behavior," a simple but brilliant concept.

Rather than teach the cranes to stop landing on him, the trainer taught the birds something else, a behavior that would make the undesirable behavior impossible. The birds couldn't alight on the mats and his head simultaneously.

At home, I came up with incompatible behaviors for Scott to keep him from crowding me while I cooked. To lure him away from the stove, I piled up parsley for him to chop or cheese for him to grate at the other end of the kitchen island. Or I'd set out a bowl of chips and salsa across the room. Soon I'd done it: no more Scott hovering around me while I cooked.

I followed the students to SeaWorld San Diego, where a dolphin trainer introduced me to least reinforcing syndrome (L.R.S.). When a dolphin does something wrong, the trainer doesn't respond in any way. He stands still for a few beats, careful not to look at the dolphin, and then returns to work. The idea is that any response, positive or negative, fuels a behavior. If a behavior provokes no response, it typically dies away.

In the margins of my notes I wrote, "Try on Scott!"

It was only a matter of time before he was again tearing around the house searching for his keys, at which point I said nothing and kept at what I was doing. It took a lot of discipline to maintain my calm, but results were immediate and stunning. His temper fell far shy of its usual pitch and then waned like a fast-moving storm. I felt as if I should throw him a mackerel.

Now he's at it again; I hear him banging a closet door shut, rustling through papers on a chest in the front hall and thumping upstairs. At the sink, I hold steady. Then, sure enough, all goes quiet. A moment later, he walks into the kitchen, keys in hand, and says calmly, "Found them."

Without turning, I call out, "Great, see you later."

Off he goes with our much-calmed pup.

After two years of exotic animal training, my marriage is far smoother, my husband much easier to love. I used to take his faults personally; his dirty clothes on the floor were an affront, a symbol of how he didn't care enough about me. But thinking of my husband as an exotic species gave me the distance I needed to consider our differences more objectively.

I adopted the trainers' motto: "It's never the animal's fault." When my training attempts failed, I didn't blame Scott. Rather, I brainstormed new strategies, thought up more incompatible behaviors and used smaller approximations. I dissected my own behavior, considered how my actions might inadvertently fuel his. I also accepted that some behaviors were too entrenched, too instinctive to train away. You can't stop a badger from digging, and you can't stop my husband from losing his wallet and keys.

* * *

Professionals talk of animals that understand training so well they eventually use it back on the trainer. My animal did the same. When the training techniques worked so beautifully, I couldn't resist telling my husband what I was up to. He wasn't offended, just amused. As I explained the techniques and terminology, he soaked it up. Far more than I realized.

Last fall, firmly in middle age, I learned that I needed braces. They were not only humiliating, but also excruciating. For weeks my gums, teeth, jaw and

Questions

sinuses throbbed. I complained frequently and loudly. Scott assured me that I would become used to all the metal in my mouth. I did not.

One morning, as I launched into yet another tirade about how uncomfort-   30
able I was, Scott just looked at me blankly. He didn't say a word or acknowledge my rant in any way, not even with a nod.

I quickly ran out of steam and started to walk away. Then I realized what was happening, and I turned and asked, "Are you giving me an L.R.S.?" Silence. "You are, aren't you?"

He finally smiled, but his L.R.S. has already done the trick. He'd begun to train me, the American wife.

Questions for Critical Reading

1. Did you find any techniques to try in your own relationships when you read Sutherland's description of how she trained her husband (e.g., coming up with incompatible behaviors and rewarding desirable behaviors while ignoring undesirable ones)? If Sutherland persuaded you that these techniques are worth trying, what strategies did she use to do so? Point to a couple of passages that you find especially compelling, and explain why. If you weren't persuaded to try any of Sutherland's techniques, explain why not.

2. Do you think some of Sutherland's readers would be more likely to enjoy her column than others? Do you think some might take offense? Why or why not?

3. Consider the way Sutherland varies her paragraph length in the following passage, and speculate about why she might have done this:

> Professionals talk of animals that understand training so well they eventually use it back on the trainer. My animal did the same. When the training techniques worked so beautifully, I couldn't resist telling my husband what I was up to. He wasn't offended, just amused. As I explained the techniques and terminology, he soaked it up. Far more than I realized. . . .
>
> One morning, as I launched into yet another tirade about how uncomfortable I was, Scott just looked at me blankly. He didn't say a word or acknowledge my rant in any way, not even with a nod.
>
> I quickly ran out of steam and started to walk away. Then I realized what was happening, and I turned and asked, "Are you giving me an L.R.S.?" Silence. "You are, aren't you?"
>
> He finally smiled, but his L.R.S. has already done the trick. He'd begun to train me, the American wife. (paras. 28–32)

Why do you think Sutherland uses paragraphs of different lengths? Can you articulate a principle that might help you as a writer decide when to try a short paragraph? a medium one? a long one?

4. Many genres—including journalistic writing, creative nonfiction, and advertising—sometimes use humor as a strategy to draw in readers. To what extent does "What Shamu Taught Me about a Happy Marriage" succeed in entertaining you through its use of humor? What other purposes might Sutherland's use of humor accomplish?

Making Connections

5. Reflect on the ways in which Sutherland and Andi Long (p. 127) use dialogue, and imagine each piece without dialogue. What do you think is the effect of the dialogue in each piece? In which genres and for what purposes might you want to use dialogue in your own writing?

6. Consider the following two passages, one from Long's creative nonfiction piece "Patching Holes" and one from Sutherland's column; see if you can come up with a theory about why Long develops her piece largely through providing details (without telling us what those details mean), while Sutherland not only gives us details but also tells us what they mean:

"Patching Holes"

[My sister] was never one to begin a conversation with, "Everything's all right, but . . ." so I didn't know if everything was all right. I guess that phrase just makes you think that everything's not all right, but immediately I thought he was dead. Or I thought a chain saw cut him up. Or I thought—maybe the worst thought? —that he got sucked into his chipper. (para. 12)

"What Shamu Taught Me about a Happy Marriage"

The central lesson I learned from exotic animal trainers is that I should reward behavior I like and ignore behavior I don't. After all, you don't get a sea lion to balance a ball on the end of its nose by nagging. The same goes for the American husband.

Back in Maine, I began thanking Scott if he threw one dirty shirt into the hamper. If he threw in two, I'd kiss him. Meanwhile, I would step over any soiled clothes on the floor without one sharp word, though I did sometimes kick them under the bed. But as he basked in my appreciation, the piles became smaller. (paras. 11–12)

Why do you think Sutherland tells us what her point is ("The central lesson I learned . . ."), while Long doesn't?

7. Think about Sutherland's and Long's organization; both authors make us wait to find out key information. First consider Sutherland's opening; she begins by telling us about an interaction she is having with her husband, but we don't know *why* she's telling us this until the third paragraph:

As I wash dishes at the kitchen sink, my husband paces behind me, irritated. "Have you seen my keys?" he snarls, then huffs out a loud sigh and stomps from the room with our dog, Dixie, at his heels, anxious over her favorite human's upset.

In the past I would have been right behind Dixie. I would have turned off the faucet and joined the hunt while trying to soothe my husband with bromides like, "Don't worry, they'll turn up." But that only made him angrier, and a simple case of missing keys soon would become a full-blown angst-ridden drama starring the two of us and our poor nervous dog.

Now, I focus on the wet dish in my hands. I don't turn around. I don't say a word. I'm using a technique I learned from a dolphin trainer. (paras. 1–3)

What if Sutherland had begun her piece with the sentence "I'm training my husband as one would train a dolphin"? Why might she have waited to tell us this information?

Long also waits to tell us important information, but her delay has a very different effect, as you'll see when looking at paragraphs 10–18. Long begins this passage by describing a phone call she received: "A big sniff, a hollow hello, and loud sobs followed by a nasally, 'Dad had an accident at work today.'" It's not until eight paragraphs later that we learn Long's father will live. How might her piece have affected you differently had she cut to the chase instead of making you wait so many paragraphs for this information? Imagine yourself writing creative nonfiction or a column like Sutherland's; in what situations might you consider making readers wait to find out key information?

Writing: Your Turn

1. Try your hand at writing a humorous piece such as "What Shamu Taught Me about a Happy Marriage." Sutherland achieves humor largely through the use of incongruity (e.g., hyenas who pirouette or killer whales who help people improve their marriages), but you should feel free to use any other strategies you think might work.

    Give your piece to a few classmates to see if it makes them laugh or smile, and get their feedback on how you might make it even funnier when you revise. Also ask them about other ideas they might have for strengthening your piece. Humorous pieces can be difficult to pull off, so don't let your classmates off the hook if their primary feedback is "I liked it." You might try pointing them to passages you're unsure of and asking them specific questions about those passages. After you revise, consider submitting your piece to your campus newspaper.

2. Write a rhetorical analysis of "What Shamu Taught Me about a Happy Marriage." You might discuss issues of audience, considering whether the piece might appeal to some readers more than others. You could also consider the effects of Sutherland's style: she uses a variety of sentence structures; she writes both short and long sentences; she writes both short and long paragraphs; and she varies how she transitions from paragraph to paragraph. Of

course, you might also notice other aspects of Sutherland's writing to discuss instead.

When you're done writing, give your draft to a classmate and have him or her read it out loud; this can prompt you to give yourself good feedback, just as one of your classmates might. After the piece is read aloud, ask a few classmates to read your draft silently so that they can gain more insight into how your piece could be even stronger. You might ask them if they can see *how* you came up with the interpretation you did. If they're not sure how you came up with your interpretations, you might decide to analyze your quotations in more depth. For suggestions on writing a rhetorical analysis, see p. 31.

From *The Relationship Cure*

John Gottman and Joan DeClaire

In *The Relationship Cure* (2001), John Gottman and Joan DeClaire suggest that relationships grow "bid by bid," through our responses to each other in a series of mundane interactions. Gottman, the primary author, is an emeritus psychology professor from the University of Washington who has spent decades researching human relationships and publishing academic articles on his findings. Note that when the pronoun "I" appears, it refers to Gottman.

Focus on Genre   *The Relationship Cure* is a self-help book intended not for an academic audience of professors and researchers but for an audience of laypeople (nonexperts). The following excerpt, juxtaposed with the academic selection at the end of this chapter, illustrates some of the characteristics that tend to distinguish academic from nonacademic writing. This is an important distinction because, throughout your college and post-college career, you'll be called on to do both types of writing.

One difference between most academic and nonacademic genres is authors' tendency to cite sources. You'll notice that Gottman and DeClaire don't cite their sources, instead using general phrases such as "studies show." In contrast, people writing for academic audiences generally specify who did the research, how and when they did it, and where it was published. As you read Gottman and DeClaire, notice how you respond to passages that use phrases such as "studies show" rather than citing specific sources. Are there any instances in which you might like to look at the studies referred to?

Also think about what Gottman and DeClaire's thesis (main point) is; identify one or more key sentences in the text where you think they state their thesis.

Finally, consider how Gottman and DeClaire use evidence to support their claims. What kinds of evidence do they use, and how persuasive do you find it?

◄O►

Whether people are struggling to save a marriage, to cooperate in a family crisis, or to build rapport with a difficult boss, they usually have one thing in common: They need to share emotional information that can help them feel connected. . . .

Sharing such information through words and behavior is essential for improving any significant relationship. This includes bonds with our kids, our siblings, our friends, our coworkers. But even our best efforts to connect can be jeopardized as a result of one basic problem: failure to master what I call the "bid" — the fundamental unit of emotional communication. . . .

A bid can be a question, a gesture, a look, a touch — any single expression that says, "I want to feel connected to you." A response to a bid is just that — a positive or negative answer to somebody's request for emotional connection.

At the University of Washington, my research colleagues and I recently discovered how profoundly this bidding process affects relationships. We learned, for example, that husbands headed for divorce disregard their wives' bids for connection 82 percent of the time, while husbands in stable relationships disregard their wives' bids just 19 percent of the time. Wives headed for divorce act preoccupied with other activities when their husbands bid for their attention 50 percent of the time, while happily married wives act preoccupied in response to their husbands' bids just 14 percent of the time.

When we compared how often couples in the two groups extended bids and responded to them, we found another significant difference. During a typical dinner-hour conversation, the happily married people engaged one another as many as one hundred times in ten minutes. Those headed for divorce engaged only sixty-five times in that same period. On the surface the contrast may seem inconsequential, but taken together over a year, the additional moments of connection among the happy couples would be enough to fill a Russian novel.

We also found that this high rate of positive engagement paid off in tremendous ways. For example, we now know that people who react positively to one another's bids have greater access to expressions of humor, affection, and interest during arguments. It's almost as if all the good feelings they've accumulated by responding respectfully and lovingly to one another's bids form a pot of emotional "money in the bank." Then, when a conflict arises, they can draw on this reservoir of good feeling. It's as if something inside unconsciously says, "I may be mad as hell at him right now, but he's the guy who listens so attentively when I complain about my job. He deserves a break." Or, I'm as angry as I've ever been with her, but she's the one who always laughs at my jokes. I think I'll cut her some slack."

Having access to humor and affection during a conflict is invaluable because it helps to de-escalate bad feelings and leads to better understanding. Rather than shutting down communication in the midst of an argument, people who can stay present with one another have a much better opportunity to resolve issues through their conflicts, repair hurt feelings, and build positive regard. But this good work must begin long before the conflict starts: it's got to be grounded in those dozens of ordinary, day-to-day exchanges of emotional information and interest that we call bids.

And what happens when we habitually fail to respond positively to one another's bids for emotional connection? Such failure is rarely malicious or mean-spirited. More often we're simply unaware of or insensitive to others' bids for our attention. Still, when such mindlessness becomes habitual, the results can be devastating.

I've seen such results in my clinical practice at the Gottman Institute, where I've counseled many people who describe their lives as consumed by loneliness. They feel lonely despite their proximity to many significant people in their lives—lovers, spouses, friends, children, parents, siblings, and coworkers. Often they seem surprised and greatly disappointed at the deterioration of their relationships.

"I love my wife," one client says of his faltering marriage, "but our relationship feels empty somehow." He senses that the passion is waning, that the romance is drifting away. What he can't see are all the opportunities for closeness that surround him. Like so many other distressed, lonely people, he doesn't mean to ignore or dismiss his spouse's bids for emotional connection. It's just that the bids happen in such simple, mundane ways that he doesn't recognize these moments as very important.

Clients like these typically have trouble at work, as well. Although they're often skilled at forming collegial bonds when they first start a job, they tend to focus totally on the tasks at hand, often to the detriment of their relationships with coworkers. Later, when they're passed over for a promotion, or when they discover they have no influence on an important project, they're baffled. And they often feel betrayed and disappointed by their colleagues and bosses as a result.

Such feelings of disappointment and loss also crop up in these clients' relationships with friends and relatives. Many describe peers, siblings, and children as disloyal, unworthy of trust. But when we dig deeper, we find a familiar pattern. These clients seem unaware of the bids for connection that their friends and relatives have been sending them. So it's no wonder that their loved ones feel no obligation to continue their support.

People who have trouble with the bidding process also have more conflict—conflict that might be prevented if they could simply acknowledge one another's emotional needs. Many arguments spring from

10

misunderstandings and feelings of separation that might have been avoided if people would have the conversations they need to have. But because they don't, they argue instead. Such conflicts can lead to marital discord, divorce, parenting problems, and family feuds. Friendships fade and deteriorate. Adult sibling relationships wither and die. Kids raised in homes filled with chronic conflict have more difficulty learning, getting along with friends, and staying healthy. People who can't connect are also more likely to suffer isolation, as well as dissatisfaction and instability in their work lives. Any of these problems can create a tremendous amount of stress in people's lives, leading to all sorts of physical and mental health problems.

But our findings about the bidding process give me a tremendous amount of hope. They tell me that people who consistently bid and respond to bids in positive ways have an astounding chance for success in their relationships. . . .

BID BY BID: HOW TO BUILD BETTER RELATIONSHIPS ONE STEP AT A TIME

Writer Anne Lamott tells the story of her ten-year-old brother agonizing over a   15
school report he had to write about birds. Frozen by the size and complexity of the task, he turned to his dad for help. She writes, "My father put his arm around my brother's shoulder and said. 'Bird by bird, buddy. Just take it bird by bird.'"

So it is with our ties to friends, family, and coworkers. Complex, fulfilling relationships don't suddenly appear in our lives fully formed. Rather, they develop one encounter at a time.

If you could carefully observe and analyze those encounters—as my research colleagues and I have done—you would see how each one is made up of many smaller exchanges. There's a bid and a response to that bid. Like cells of the body or bricks of a house, such exchanges are the primary components of emotional communication. Each exchange contains emotional information that can strengthen or weaken connections between people. Here are some examples. . . .

"Knock-knock."
"Who's there?"

"Are you busy tonight?"   20
"Maybe . . . Maybe not . . ."

Bids and responses to bids can be big, overblown, cathartic events such as those we see in the movies:
"Will you marry me, Violet?"
"I will, Jack, I will!"

Or they can be the small, mundane exchanges of everyday life: 25
"Get me a beer while you're up, okay?"
"Sure, do you want anything else? Any chips?"
Bids can be subtle: *"That's a pretty dress."*
Or they can be straight ahead: *"I want to make love to you."* . . .
Bids allow strangers to get acquainted: *"Do you mind if I sit here?"*   30
And they're essential for longtime friends or partners who want to stay
close: *"I've missed you so much. Let's go somewhere and talk!"*
    Positive responses to a bid typically lead to continued interaction, often
with both parties extending more bids to one another. Listening to this kind of
exchange is kind of like watching a Ping-Pong game in which both players are
doing very well.
"What are you doing for lunch today?"
"I brought a sandwich. Want to join me outside?"
"Sure. But I need to get something from the deli first. Need anything?"   35
*"Yeah, get me a Dr. Pepper. Maybe I'll bring those pictures from my family
reunion?"*
"Sure. I'd love to see them. And we can plan the party for Peg."
"Yeah, we better get started on that."
    But a negative response to a bid typically shuts down emotional communica-
tion. All bids cease. The game is over. People want to pick up their Ping-Pong
paddles and go home.
"What are you doing for lunch today?"   40
"Lunch? Who's got time for that?"
"Maybe some other time then."
"Yeah, some other time."
    But our research shows that "some other time" rarely happens. In fact, the
probability that a person will attempt to re-bid once an initial bid has been
rejected is close to zero. That's not to say people need to accept every lunch
date that comes along. But they can refuse specific invitations while still accept-
ing the bid for emotional connection.
"What are you doing for lunch today?"   45
"I wish I had time for lunch. I've got to finish this report. What are you up to?"
*"I brought a sandwich. I thought I'd go sit outside. But I have to go by the deli
for a Coke. Want me to bring something back for you?"*
*"That would be nice. Can you get me a ham on rye and a Dr. Pepper?
Oh—and catch some rays for me while you're out there, okay?"*
"Sure thing."
    Bids typically grow in intensity and frequency as a relationship grows and   50
deepens. Think about the steps you might take in making a friend on the
job. Your initial bid might be a software question on your first day. That leads

to a joke—politically correct, of course—over cubicle walls. Your potential friend laughs and invites you to lunch. Conversation centers on fairly routine, work-related issues. But then one day, after you've had a few breaks together, you take the risk of asking him how he *really* feels about the boss. He tells you, and you end up asking him for some career advice. A few months later, when you find out that your favorite project has been canned, you're enraged! Where do you go to blow off steam? To his office, of course. You trust him. You can say whatever's on your mind. It won't come back to haunt you. As the years go by, you start getting together on weekends to watch the game. You have him and his wife over for dinner. He learns all about your family, your childhood, your passions, your fears. It's hard to remember what life was like before you met him. You always open his e-mail first. And now you tell him *all* your jokes.

How did it become possible? One small interaction at a time. And how do you keep it afloat? By continuing to make bids to one another for connection, and by continuing to respond to one another's bids, moment by moment, in positive ways.

While the process sounds simple, most people can think of many relationships in their lives that have gone awry because of failed bidding or failed responses to bids.

Below you'll see an example in which the bidding process goes badly, resulting in interactions that hinder the development of the relationship. Then you'll read a bidding "makeover"—the same scenario, but with a few adjustments in key exchanges that take the conversation into new territory, leading the relationship into a more positive realm. . . .

Let's take a look at one of the most challenging pairings of all: the parent-teen relationship.

Roger is a salesman who spends a lot more time than he'd like on the road. 55 Each time he comes home from a trip and greets his daughter, Hannah, now thirteen, she seems to have grown another inch taller.

Hannah believes her dad when he says "I missed you," because she used to feel that way about him, too. But ever since she started middle school, that feeling is fading. There are just so many things to think about—friends, school projects, the track team, high school next year. Sure, she loves her dad, but he's not the top item on her agenda anymore.

One night, as Roger's flying home, he reads an ad for Cirque de Lune—"an animal-free circus that blends the pageantry of the Big Top with the antics of street theater," the ad says. The ticket prices are sky-high, but Hannah would love it, Roger muses—especially the "animal-free" part. She's been talking a lot about animal rights lately. He tears out the ad and sticks it in his pocket.

At breakfast the next morning he says. "Hey, sweetie, have you ever heard about this show called Cirque de Lune?"

"Nope."

"Well, it's kind of like a circus."   60

"Daddy, you know how I feel about circuses."

"No, this one's different. No animals. More like theater. Lots of acrobats and costumes. It's supposed to be really something. I think you'd like it."

"Hmm . . . maybe."

"Go get the ad that's in my jacket pocket over there," he says, pointing. Hannah, intrigued now, does just that.

"Oooh. It looks cool," she says, as she peruses the description.   65

"So I'm thinking I should get tickets," Roger says. "Just you and me. Next Saturday night."

"Next Saturday?"

"Yeah. You got a hot date or something?" Roger says, teasing.

"Well, that's the night of Rachel Iannelli's slumber party."

"Oh, she probably has slumber parties all the time," Roger says, good-   70
naturedly. "Besides, that's the only night I'm going to be in town while it's here."

"But I really wanted to go to Rachel's party . . ."

"Honey, you girls have these parties nearly every weekend."

"No we don't."

"Well, okay. Maybe not every weekend. But I thought this was something special you and I could do together."

"But I don't want to go that night."   75

"Because your friends are more important."

"No. It's just that this is Rachel Iannelli's party and she's never invited me to one before and—"

"Okay, if that's a higher priority for you, fine. Go."

"So now I'm in trouble."

"No, you're not in trouble. I'm just disappointed, that's all. We don't have   80
all that much time to spend together."

"And that's supposed to be my fault?"

"No, it's not your fault. It's nobody's fault. Forget it. Forget I mentioned it. Go to your damned slumber party."

With that, Roger crumples up the ad, and Hannah leaves the breakfast table in tears—not exactly the scenario Roger had in mind.

Could it have gone differently? Let's take a look, picking up the scene where Hannah tells Roger about Rachel's slumber party.

"Oh, she probably has slumber parties all the time." Roger says, good-   85
naturedly. "Besides, that's the only night I'm going to be in town while it's here."

"But I really wanted to go to Rachel's party . . ."

"Now, whose party is it?"

"Rachel Iannelli. She's this new girl who Dana's always hanging with. Dana thinks she's really cool."

"You mean Dana—your best friend Dana?"

"Yep. And Dana's always spending the night over there. Kelly and Laura, too."   90

"Oh. Is this the first time Rachel has invited you to one of these parties?"

"Yeah."

"So it feels kind of important to you to go because you really like hanging out with Dana and Kelly and Laura."

"Yeah. I was feeling like they didn't like me anymore or something. But I think Rachel just doesn't know me that well. I really want to go."

"And it's the same night as this show. I feel kind of disappointed about that."   95

"Me, too. Because the show looks really neat, Daddy. And it's so nice that you want to take me."

"I really do want to take you. But maybe we could think of something else to do together. Like during the day on Saturday, instead."

"Really?"

"Yeah. Then you could go to Rachel's party."

"And you could take Mom to this circus instead. I bet she'd really like it, too."   100

"I think you're right. That's a great idea. So you be thinking about what you want to do together next Saturday afternoon. Just the two of us, okay?"

"Okay, Daddy. Thanks."

So Roger didn't get to take Hannah to Cirque de Lune, but he did get what he was bidding for—an opportunity to spend time with his daughter. Not only that, but he got the chance to do something parents too rarely do: He got to show Hannah that he's interested in her world, and that he really does understand how she's feeling. That's called emotional connection.

TURNING POINTS: THE CHOICES WE MAKE IN RESPONDING TO BIDS

My insights into the process of bidding for emotional connection are a result of many years of observing human interaction in a variety of real-life settings. My research colleagues and I have studied the dynamics of friendships, parent-child relationships, adult siblings, and couples in all stages of marriage and child rearing.

The group with whom I've always been most fascinated is the one I call   105
"marital masters"—folks who are so good at handling conflict that they make marital squabbles look like fun. It's not that these couples don't get mad and disagree. It's that when they disagree, they're able to stay connected and engaged with each other. Rather than becoming defensive and hurtful, they

pepper their disputes with flashes of affection, intense interest, and mutual respect. Amazingly, they seem to have access to their sense of humor even when they're arguing. In this way, their conflict actually becomes fruitful—a resource for discovery and problem solving, another place to demonstrate the overriding passion and respect in their relationships.

How do they do it, I've wondered. It seemed that they must have some kind of secret weapon against elements like contempt, criticism, defensiveness, and stonewalling—the factors that we discovered could destroy all kinds of relationships. What is it that allows couples to continue to react with good humor and affection despite the typical stresses of family life? If I could find the answer to this question, I might have a key to helping people build and sustain better emotional connections, not only in marriage, but in all sorts of significant relationships. The answer came, in part, when I started to look at the link between conflict and bidding behavior among sixty married couples who volunteered to spend the weekend alone together at our family research facility on the University of Washington campus. Affectionately dubbed "The Love Lab," the place includes a small studio apartment in a parklike setting on the University of Washington campus. From the apartment's large picture window, couples can watch pleasure boats float through the Montlake Cut, a canal that connects Seattle's Portage Bay to Lake Washington.

The apartment is furnished like a comfortable weekend hideaway. There's a kitchen, a dining area, a hide-a-bed, a television, and a VCR. Study couples bring along groceries to cook, games to play, movies to watch. They're asked to simply relax and do whatever they would normally do during a typical weekend at home together. The only difference is that we have stationed scientific observers behind a two-way mirror in the kitchen to observe every interaction that takes place. Four video cameras mounted on the walls and microphones attached to the couples' clothes capture all their movements, all their conversations. The couples also wear sensors on their bodies to monitor signs of stress such as a rise in heart rate or increased sweating. (To preserve the couple's privacy, we don't monitor them between 9:00 P.M. and 9:00 A.M., nor do cameras follow them to the bathroom. They also get a half hour of privacy to walk in the park that surrounds the lab.)

We learned that people typically respond to another's bids for connection in one of three ways: They turn toward, turn against, or turn away. By correlating these three types of behavior with the status of their relationships ten years later, we were able to show how each of these types of behavior affect people's connections over the long term. In a nutshell, here's what we learned:

1. Turning toward.   To "turn toward" one another means to react in a positive way to another's bids for emotional connection. One person makes a funny comment, for example, and the other person laughs. A man points to an impressive car as it passes by, and his friend nods as if to say. "I agree. That's quite a car!" A father asks his son to pass the ketchup, and his son does so in a kind, accommodating way. A woman muses about a vacation she'd like to take, and her coworker joins in. He asks her questions, adds his opinions, lends colorful details to a trip they imagine together.

What happens in relationships where people consistently turn toward one   110
another's bids for connection? Our analysis shows that, over time, they develop stable, long-lasting relationships rich in good feelings for one another. Like the "marital masters," they also seem to have easier access to humor, affection, and interest in one another during conflict, a factor that allows them to stay connected emotionally, solve problems, and avoid the downward spiral of negative feelings that destroy relationships.

2. Turning against.   People who turn against one another's bids for connection might be described as belligerent or argumentative. For example, if a man fantasized about owning a passing sports car, his friend might reply, "On your salary? Dream on!"

Turning against often involves sarcasm or ridicule. In one instance in our marriage lab, a wife gently asked her husband to put down his newspaper and talk to her.

"And what are we going to talk about?" he sneered.

"Well, we were thinking of buying a new television," she offered. "We could talk about that."

But his next response was just as mean: "What do *you* know about televi-   115
sions?" he asked. After that, she said nothing at all.

This woman's withdrawal is typical in situations when one person habitually turns against another, we discovered. After all, who wants to be ridiculed or snapped at? We also found that this pattern of hostility followed by suppression of feelings is destructive to relationships. Among married couples, the pattern leads to divorce later on. Among adult siblings, such behavior is linked to being emotionally distant from one another and having a less supportive relationship. In addition, studies show that such hostility is also harmful to relationships among friends, coworkers, and other relatives.

Interestingly, the married couples in our study who habitually displayed this behavior did not divorce as quickly as couples whose main habit of interaction was for one partner to turn away. But eventually the majority of them did split up.

3. Turning away.   This pattern of relating generally involves ignoring another's bid, or acting preoccupied. A person in these instances might comment and point to that impressive sports car, but his friend wouldn't bother to look up. Or he might look up and say something unrelated, such as, "What time do you have?" Or, "Do you have change for a five-dollar bill?" . . .

In one poignant example from our marriage lab, the wife apologized to her husband for a mistake she made in preparing dinner that night. She raised the issue three times during the course of the evening, obviously wanting him to let her off the hook. But all three times the husband met his wife's comments with silence and looked away.

Another husband said, "Dinner's almost ready," while his wife divided   120
her attention between reading and watching TV. She didn't respond. So he went over to the couch where she sat and said, "How's your book, hon?" She ignored him again. He then kissed her twice, and she was unresponsive to his kisses. "Is that book good?" he asked. Finally she said, "Yes, it has some nice pictures in it." That was their entire exchange.

Consistently turning away from one another's bids is clearly bad for relationships, our research has revealed. In our studies of children's friendships, for example, the young children who couldn't engage one another in shared fantasy failed to develop lasting bonds.

In our marriage studies, we found that turning away on a regular basis is actually destructive. Partners who displayed this pattern of interaction in the apartment lab often became hostile and defensive with each other—particularly when they discussed an area of continuing disagreement. This behavior typically results in early divorce among married couples.

Studies done on the dynamics of parent-child, adult friendship, adult sibling, and coworker relationships lead us to believe that it's destructive to other relationships as well.

THE GOOD NEWS ABOUT CONNECTING

Failure to connect can hinder your career. It can interfere with friendships. It can weaken your relationships with relatives, including your kids. It can even ruin your marriage.

But here's the good news: Connecting is *not* magic. Like any other skill, it   125
can be learned, practiced, and mastered. And there's never been a better time to master these skills. Recent scientific discoveries about the emotional brain, along with the latest observational studies of human interaction, have helped us to form a body of scientifically proven advice for connecting with one another and improving the quality of our lives.

That's not to say that connecting more effectively will solve all our problems. I'm reminded of a woman who came to me for marriage counseling shortly after a major career change. The problems she faced were significant:

She had new financial pressures, anxiety about the future, and she dearly missed the friends she used to work with. But when I asked her about her marriage—which was to be the focal point of our session—she said, "That's what puzzles me. My husband and I are doing fine. So why do I feel so anxious and depressed?"

At that point I had to tell her. "Feeling connected to your husband isn't going to fix all your problems. It won't fill your bank account. It won't land you the perfect job, and it won't make you stop missing your friends. But it will make the two of you feel closer as you go through this transition together. And that's as good as it gets."

That's the beauty of feeling emotionally connected to others. Whatever you're facing—serious illness, divorce, job loss, grief over the death of a loved one—you don't have to face it alone. Sharing your experience with other people who express understanding and empathy may be helpful in ways we're only beginning to understand. Consider, for example, studies of survival rates among cancer patients who participate in peer support groups. With all other factors equal, those who take part in the group support typically outlive those who don't.

As healing as connecting can be, it doesn't happen automatically. Even when people are highly motivated, it takes a certain amount of conscious effort and diligence. A good example is the communication that typically takes place between mother and infant. In one study, researchers found that mothers misread their fussy babies' bids 70 percent of the time. The mother might think the baby is hungry when he's not, for instance. Or she might start to bounce the baby, only to find that the stimulation upsets him more. Consequently the mother must switch strategies, trying something different to meet her baby's needs. As she does so, both she and the baby learn more about each other's cues. Her willingness to keep trying, even when things aren't going well, ensures that the relationship will get better over time.

So it is in relationships between spouses, friends, relatives, and coworkers. 130 If both parties are willing to hang in there, pay attention, and change direction when they make mistakes, chances are they can improve the relationship. Having to apologize, make adjustments, or "patch things up" is not necessarily the sign of a bad fit. It's a sign that people value one another and are willing to work through the rough spots to stick together. It's by weathering conflicts that marriages, families, friendships, and work teams grow strong. . . .

Building better emotional connections is like any other valuable life goal, in that it requires attention and sustained effort. But I'm certain that few other endeavors can promise a reward as rich as connecting does. Through it, we learn to know, express, and understand the shared meaning we find in one another's experience.

Questions

Questions for Critical Reading

1. What was your initial response to this excerpt from *The Relationship Cure*? Did Gottman and DeClaire succeed in persuading you that you can improve your relationships by paying attention to how you bid and respond to bids? See if you can trace your response back to one or two specific passages, and explain why they affected you the way they did.

2. Which sentence or sentences did you identify as Gottman and DeClaire's thesis (main point), and why? Why do you think they explicitly state their thesis rather than letting readers infer it? In what genres and situations do you think you'll want to explicitly tell readers your point?

3. Although the evidence used in some self-help books consists primarily of anecdotes (stories about real or hypothetical people), *The Relationship Cure* provides different types of evidence, including not only anecdotes but also hypothetical dialogues, general references to previously conducted research, and data from Gottman's own research, including statistics. Providing multiple types of evidence is a strategy used in many academic genres too; it's likely that, over the course of your college career, you'll encounter many situations in which you'll use this strategy yourself.

   Take a few minutes to identify some examples of different types of evidence. Do you find the authors' use of multiple types of evidence to be persuasive? Do you think you would have responded differently to the selection if it had provided only one type of evidence? Why or why not?

4. Although self-help books such as *The Relationship Cure* differ from academic genres in many respects, you'll nonetheless notice several of the same moves being made across genres.

   In addition to marshaling evidence, *The Relationship Cure* makes another move commonly found in the academic genres you'll be writing: it establishes exigence. Exigence is established when readers are persuaded that there's a need for what the author is writing; imagine someone reading your work and asking, "So what?" or "Why should I care?" If your writing successfully addresses these questions, you have established exigence.

   Note that there are different ways of establishing exigence. You might establish positive exigence, as Gottman and DeClaire do early in the selection by telling us why we should care about sharing emotional information:

   > Sharing [emotional] information through words and behavior is essential for improving any significant relationship. (para. 2)

   They make a similar move in their final paragraph:

   > Through [building better emotional connections], we learn to know, express, and understand the shared meaning we find in one another's experience. (para. 131)

You might also establish negative exigence, as the authors do both at the beginning and the end of the selection. Consider, for example, the opening of their final section:

> Failure to connect can hinder your career. It can interfere with friendships. It can weaken your relationships with relatives. . . . It can even ruin your marriage. (para. 124)

Does the authors' use of both positive and negative exigence work to persuade you that their topic is indeed important? In what situations might *you* want to establish positive exigence, negative exigence, or both? Now consider how you might organize your writing; if you establish exigence, where would you do it?

5. Consider Gottman's methodology, or the methods he used to conduct his research. Descriptions of methodology can help you critically evaluate research results, ultimately enabling you to decide how seriously to take them.

    The level of detail in a methodology section generally depends on the genre; in nonacademic genres such as *The Relationship Cure*, these sections (if they exist at all) are usually brief. In academic genres, however, readers expect methodology sections to be more detailed, in part because they believe methodology affects results and they may want to assess the results carefully. Although Gottman and DeClaire aren't writing for an academic audience, it's still a good exercise in critical thinking to consider how Gottman's methodology might have influenced his research results. Here's how Gottman describes his methodology:

    > I started to look at the link between conflict and bidding behavior among sixty married couples who volunteered to spend the weekend alone together at our family research facility. . . . Affectionately dubbed "The Love Lab," the place includes a small studio apartment. . . .
    >
    > [Study couples are] asked to simply relax and do whatever they would normally do during a typical weekend at home together. The only difference is that we have stationed scientific observers behind a two-way mirror in the kitchen to observe every interaction that takes place. Four video cameras mounted on the walls and microphones attached to the couples' clothes capture all their movements, all their conversations. The couples also wear sensors on their bodies to monitor signs of stress such as a rise in heart rate or increased sweating. (paras. 106–7)

    If you had been a participant in Gottman's research, do you think you would have acted differently in the Love Lab than you would normally act? If so, how? If you think the research participants would have acted differently in the Love Lab, to what extent do you think Gottman's results are valid?

6. Recall that unlike most academic genres, genres written for popular audiences often use phrases such as "studies show" rather than referring to

specific studies. Gottman and DeClaire, for instance, mention studies of cancer patients' survival rates but don't tell us who conducted these studies:

> Consider . . . studies of survival rates among cancer patients who participate in peer support groups. With all other factors equal, those who take part in the group support typically outlive those who don't. (para. 128)

If Gottman and DeClaire had been using an academic genre, they would have told us who conducted these studies; indeed, Gottman is a widely published researcher who consistently cites sources in his academic writing. Why do you think Gottman cites sources in his academic writing but not here?

Making Connections

7. In addition to citation practices and the amount of detail in methodology descriptions, there are other differences that tend to distinguish academic from nonacademic writing—differences that, unfortunately for college students who are expected to use academic genres, may be hard to notice. Word choice is one example. Gottman and DeClaire use words such as "cure," "discovered," and "proven," but most people writing for academic audiences tend to avoid such words, believing that they imply absolute, certain knowledge. To reflect what they see as the tentative nature of knowledge, they might say that their research "suggests" something rather than that they have "discovered" or "proven" something. Likewise, instead of using the word "cure," they might discuss how to "address" a problem. (Of course there are exceptions to this general pattern, and practices vary across disciplines and genres.)

Like attention to word choice, qualifying your claim can often help you address an academic audience. When you qualify a claim, you're acknowledging that it may not always be true. Consider the academic research report at the end of this chapter, "When We Hurt the Ones We Love: Predicting Violence against Women from Men's Mate Retention" (p. 183). Note how the authors qualify what they say through their verb choices (italicized):

> Although many mate retention behaviors *appear to be* innocuous romantic gestures (e.g., displaying resources, giving flowers), some *may be* harbingers of violence. . . . The general discussion outlines future directions for research that *are likely to* result in a more comprehensive understanding of partner violence against women. (para. 1, italics added)

Bearing in mind that such seemingly insignificant word choices reflect important core beliefs, look at this sentence from *The Relationship Cure* and consider how you would translate it for an academic audience:

> Recent scientific discoveries about the emotional brain, along with the latest observational studies of human interaction, have helped us to form a body of

scientifically proven advice for connecting with one another and improving the quality of our lives. (para. 125)

If you were adapting this for an academic audience, what would you say? Take a few minutes to write a different version, and then trade with some classmates to compare notes. Your instructor may ask that a few examples be shared with the whole class.

8. In light of the previous question, also consider the title of *The Relationship Cure*. How does this title differ from that of the scholarly research report "When We Hurt the Ones We Love: Predicting Violence against Women from Men's Mate Retention"?

Take a minute to adapt the title *The Relationship Cure* for an academic audience. This may be a bit difficult because titling conventions can vary from one academic discipline to another and even from one journal to another, but give it your best shot. Since Gottman is an emeritus psychology professor, assume you're addressing an audience of academics in that discipline, and write your title after you consider what might appeal to that audience.

After you've written the title, trade with the person next to you so that you can compare notes. Do you think your classmate's title might appeal to an audience of psychology professors? Why or why not? Your instructor may ask for some volunteers to share and explain their titles.

Writing: Your Turn

1. Being sure to credit Gottman and DeClaire, use the excerpt from *The Relationship Cure* to write a brochure that gives relationship advice. You may decide to write a brochure for a broad audience, or you may decide to write one targeted to a particular group, such as parents experiencing problems with their children, employees experiencing problems with coworkers, or college students experiencing problems in romantic relationships.

After you do the first round of writing and designing your brochure, give it to some of your classmates for feedback on how to make it even stronger. You might ask them questions such as the following:

- Does the brochure highlight the most important information from the reading selection?
- Is there any information that could be further explained?
- How could the brochure be revised to better meet the needs of the intended audience?
- How could the design of the brochure be fine-tuned to make it easier for readers to notice the most important information?

After you revise your brochure, distribute it to at least a few people who aren't in your class so that they can benefit from what you've written. For strategies to use when writing brochures, see p. 105.

2. Write a reflection in which you discuss Gottman and DeClaire's advice. Do you agree that paying attention to bidding might help people improve their relationships? Do you think Gottman and DeClaire have "the" solution, as their title suggests? Do you think they have part of a solution? If so, what other pieces to the solution might there be? Do Gottman and DeClaire give any counterproductive advice, or any advice that might be useful for only some people in some situations? After you write your reflection, trade with a few classmates to see which of their ideas are different from yours and to get their feedback on how your reflection might be revised. For strategies you might find useful in writing a reflection, see p. 27.

From *You're Wearing That?*
Understanding Mothers and
Daughters in Conversation

Deborah Tannen

Like Gottman and DeClaire, Georgetown linguistics professor Deborah Tannen tells us that we can improve our relationships by thinking about how we communicate with each other. Like Gottman, Tannen is a well-known scholar who publishes both academic work and books for lay-people. *You're Wearing* That? discusses insights she gleaned from a variety of sources, including her own research. Although the book focuses on how mothers and daughters can improve their communication, Tannen tells us in her preface that much of what she says "is also true of talk between mothers and sons, fathers and daughters, and fathers and sons."

Focus on Genre   Like the previous reading selection, this one is excerpted from a self-help book written by an expert for an audience of nonexperts. Also like the previous selection, this selection illustrates strategies you will use in many of the academic genres that you'll be called on to write in college. As you read, note where Tannen states her thesis and where she states the point of each section. Looking at the paragraphs immediately above and below the subtitles will help you identify these key sentences, just as this strategy will help you identify thesis statements and section overviews when you read many other genres.

As you read, also consider how Tannen uses evidence to support her claims. Some of her examples are comparatively brief, but one of them makes up almost an entire section. Think about why she uses examples of different lengths — and when you might want to do the same.

Finally, consider how Tannen transitions from paragraph to paragraph; the strategies she uses to do so are used by writers across a variety of genres and may also be useful to you. Does Tannen help you understand how paragraphs are related? If so, how does she do this?

◄○►

163

BLENDING INTIMACY AND INDEPENDENCE: NEW WAYS OF TALKING

As my mother got progressively weaker from lung disease, I visited her and my father more and more often. The weaker she got, the more time I spent helping her, caring for her. One afternoon, during a visit, I lay down on the couch to take a brief nap. Before succumbing to the plunge into sleep, I felt a movement at my legs. Briefly opening my eyes, I saw my mother, one hand on her cane, the other carrying a small blanket she had brought from the foot of her bed. Still gripping her cane, she used the other hand to spread the blanket over my legs. I can't tell this story without tearing up. It is one of my most precious memories from the last years of my mother's life.

But it's easy to imagine a teenage girl (even me when I was one) reacting very differently in the same situation. She might even snap, "For crying out loud, Mom, I'm not a baby anymore. I can figure out for myself if my legs are cold!" Any gesture or remark that is comforting in one context can be cloying or annoying in another. And this is especially true for remarks or gestures that a mother makes in order to help or protect her child. That is what was so precious to me about my mother bringing a blanket to cover my legs as I napped: In that gesture, she was still watching over me, protecting me. But protection is a two-edged sword, and this accounts for many mismatches between daughters' and mothers' perspectives. Where a mother sees protection and connection, a daughter may see a limit to her freedom and invasion of her privacy. It is hard for daughters to understand the depth of their mothers' desire to protect them, and it is hard for mothers to understand that their expressions of concern can undermine their daughters' confidence and seem like criticism rather than caring.

I have tried in this book to explain why conversations between mothers and grown daughters can be among the most comforting but also the most hurtful we'll ever have. I have tried, too, to show how understanding why this is so, and seeing conversations from the other's point of view, can minimize the hurt and maximize the healing. Although what works for one mother-daughter pair may not work for another, there are principles that can provide guidance for all. In this last chapter I'll show how women have found that new ways of talking can improve their relationships with their daughters and mothers.

And Now For Something Different

When a conversation takes a turn we don't like, we usually think of ourselves as reacting to an offense that the other person initiated. We rarely stop and think about whether the other person was reacting to us, or what further response our reaction will provoke. Regardless of who first diverted a conversation from a pleasant to a tense one, either can head off a familiar argument by changing the way she responds. Vivian Gornick's memoir provides an example.

Gornick and her mother are walking together when her mother says, "So I'm reading the biography you gave me." The book was about Josephine Herbst, "a thirties writer, a stubborn willful raging woman grabbing at politics and love and writing, in there punching until the last minute." Gornick is delighted to hear her mother has been reading the book. But when her mother begins to speak, Gornick realizes that they are headed toward an argument:

> "Oh!" I smile in wide delight. "Are you enjoying it?"
> "Listen," she begins. The smile drops off my face and my stomach contracts. That "listen" means she is about to trash the book I gave her to read. She is going to say, "What. What's here? What's here that I don't already know? I *lived* through it. I know it all. What can this writer tell me that I don't already know? Nothing. To *you* it's interesting, but to me? How can this be interesting to me?"

Gornick and her mother have had so many conversations over their years together that her prediction of how her mother will speak is exactly right. And she can also predict how she herself will react:

> "Listen," my mother says now in the patronizing tone she thinks is conciliatory. "Maybe this is interesting to you, but not to me. I lived through all this. I know it all. What can I learn from this? Nothing. To you it's interesting. Not to me."
> Invariably, when she speaks so, my head fills with blood and before the sentences have stopped pouring from her mouth I am lashing out at her. "You're an ignoramus, you know nothing, only a know-nothing talks the way you do. The point of having lived through it, as you say, is only that the background is familiar, so the book is made richer, not that you could have written the book. People a thousand times more educated than you have read and learned from this book, but *you* can't learn from it?"

It's easy to understand why Gornick would be inclined to react this way: She'd be reflecting back the same dismissive, scornful tone in which her mother spoke to her. And the angry reaction would be only natural, since her mother's scorn for the book rejects her daughter's gesture of connection in recommending a book she liked—as well as casting aspersions on her daughter's judgment.

This time, however, the argument does not ensue, because Gornick reacts differently, both verbally and physically. Instead of leaping into the fray with her mother, she steps back and changes the tone of their exchange. She also makes a physical connection by touching her reassuringly:

> I turn to my mother, throw my left arm around her still solid back, place my right hand on her upper arm, and say, "Ma, if this book is not interesting to you, that's fine. You can say that." She looks coyly at me, eyes large, head half-turned; *now* she's interested. "But don't say it has nothing to teach you. That

there's nothing here. That's unworthy of you, and of the book, and of me. You demean us all when you say that."

By reacting differently than she usually did, Gornick gets her mother's attention and changes the course of the conversation. After a long silence, her mother makes a very different sort of remark: "That Josephine Herbst," Mrs. Gornick says. "She certainly carried on, didn't she?" At that, her daughter is "relieved and happy." She hugs her mother, who goes on, "I'm jealous. I'm jealous she lived her life, I didn't live mine."

Vivian Gornick changed the way her mother spoke to her by changing the way she spoke to her mother. A key difference in her new response was that it focused attention on the hurtful implications of her mother's remarks rather than simply reacting to them—and reacting in kind. In this, she did what the anthropologist Gregory Bateson called "metacommunication," that is, talking about talk. Metacommunication can be an especially powerful way to reframe a conversation, because it requires you to step out of the interaction and look at it from the outside. This in itself provides a measure of calm, and a new perspective.

Much of the power of Vivian Gornick's metacommunication resided in calling attention to the effect her mother's words had on her. It is common—indeed automatic—to assume that the effects of others' words always reflect their intentions. But that assumption is not always accurate. Checking it out is [a] useful form of metacommunicating—and of stepping out of the frame.

In telling me how she improved her relationship with her mother, one woman mentioned a simple step, but one that simply doesn't occur to many of us: When something her mother says hurts her feelings, she asks her mother what she means:

> She makes a statement and I don't know whether she's signifying, you know, what her come-from is, and rather than just speculate and just let it hang there, it's like, "What do you mean by that?" or "Do you intend that to be hurtful, do you intend for that to be—What's your come-from on that?"

In other words, the daughter went on, "I took it in a certain way, and she may or may not have meant it that way." By asking her mother to clarify her intentions rather than silently absorbing what to her was a hurtful metamessage, this woman opened a dialogue that improved their relationship. It also let her mother know the effect of her words—whether or not she intended to have that effect.

When we find ourselves having one of our least favorite conversations and feel trapped in it, seeing no way out, it is helpful to remember that if we speak

10

differently than we usually do, the other person will have to react differently too. I can't guarantee that the outcome will always be as satisfying as it was in these examples, but at the very least it will remind us that we have it in our power to change the paths that conversations take.

Change the Script

[J]ust being aware of the dynamics that drive conversations is often all that is needed for individuals to find more enjoyment and less irritation in talking to their mothers or daughters. A woman who wrote to me after reading my analysis of the double meaning of caring and criticizing explained how this worked for her. In the past, she said, she had dreaded holidays because she knew that her mother would be critical, and that she would explode in response. Her mother seemed to treat her like a thirteen-year-old rather than a middle-aged woman with a master's degree and a successful career. After she read the chapter, nothing changed—except the way she interpreted her mother's remarks. And that changed everything. Just reframing her mother's comments as expressions of caring rather than criticizing was all that was needed to change the way she experienced her visits home.

For example, the woman showed her mother a new purchase that she was pleased with: two pairs of socks, one black and one dark navy, made of supersoft fabric that was warm to boot. The next day she wore one of the pairs of socks, and she pointed out to her mother how well they matched her outfit. Her mother responded, "Are you sure you're not wearing one of each color?" The woman explained to me how her reaction had changed:

> My immediate thought was "What do you think? That I can't make sure I'm wearing socks of the same color? What kind of incompetent do you think I am?" It's just the sort of thing that would have set me off in the past. But I stopped to think for a moment and realized that she loves me and wants to make sure I look good, or didn't embarrass myself with mismatched socks. I became almost tender toward her for caring in such a small but touching way.

It was a perfect setup for her daughter to take offense—until she reframed her understanding of her mother's intentions.

One of my students, Jessie, also found that reframing how she thought about her mother led her to talk to her in new ways, with happy results for them both. Here's how she described in a class assignment the dynamics in her family and the way she began to reframe them:

> This past summer I stayed home with my parents. . . . I found myself having dinner with my parents every night. My father has always dominated every relationship in the family, and it became especially clear to me in the past few

months just how often my mother is excluded and cast aside in family debates
as we all tend to side with my father. One night we spent nearly an hour
arguing against my mother on some topic, barely letting her say a word and
condemning anything she said. I really did agree with my father, but I noticed
that my brother and sister also side with him and my mother has always been
the odd man out.

Jessie reevaluated how she reacted to her mother after class material inspired
her to view the dynamics from her mother's perspective. We had discussed in
class how mothers are often left out when daughters align with their fathers. As
a result of this discussion, Jessie made a change:

After this summer I realized how out of the loop my mother feels; my father
has always been the "favorite" parent to talk to and spend time with, while my
mother is constantly trying to be involved in our lives, and my siblings and I
see her as intrusive and nagging. I made a conscious effort to spend more time
with my mother and to align myself with her whenever possible. She really
appreciated my interest in her life and we are closer now as a result. Simply
being conscious of certain actions can completely change the emotions and
dynamics within a family unit.

Jessie's experience shows how looking at a relationship in a new way can lead
to new ways of talking and acting—and improving the relationship.

I am always impressed by individuals' abilities to devise ways to improve
communication with those they love once they understand the processes that
are causing distress. Though all relationships between mothers and daughters
share many characteristics, as I discovered in my research and have shown in
this book, each relationship is unique, so no easy solutions will work for all, as
daughters and mothers try to find the amount of connection that feels right,
without invoking the specters of criticism and intrusion. It might at first seem
maddening that there is no correct answer to the question "How much connection is right?" But really, it's good that there isn't, so each family can find
the amount that is right for them.

The challenge is greatest when the amount that is comfortable for one is   15
uncomfortable for the other. Yet again, understanding the dynamics can help.
I'll explain with an analogy to a nonverbal process described by Edward Hall,
an anthropologist who analyzed cross-cultural differences in the use of space.
When two people have different senses of how close to stand while having a
conversation, the one who expects to stand closer will move in to adjust the
space between them, but the one who expects to stand farther away will back
off to create the distance that seems appropriate to her. As one inches forward
in order to get comfortable, the other inches back for the same reason. Together
they move across the room until one is pinned against a wall—or nearly pushed

down a flight of stairs. The same can happen in relationships between mothers and daughters. If one—let's say the mother, because it is usually, but not always, the mother—seeks a bit more closeness than the daughter is comfortable with, the daughter will perceive her mother as encroaching and will back off, thereby prodding her mother to intensify her efforts to get closer, and so on, until they end up at the edge of a cliff, if not tumbling over it.

Like moving closer or farther away to adjust the physical space between us as we talk, we tend to try harder and do more of the same when we are uncomfortable with a conversation—or a relationship. But consider the results of doing that: Each step you take to get comfortable drives the other to take a step in the direction you don't want her to go. And consider the very different results that would ensue if you did something that seems at first counterintuitive: If you stop moving closer, the other person will stop moving farther away. Conversely, if you stop backing up, the other person will stop moving toward you. There may be a moment of discomfort as you stand firm or even take a step in the other direction, but it's surely better than moving inexorably and pointlessly across a room—or into an abyss. That is how doing something different can break a hurtful cycle, or unwind spiraling conversations.

Questions for Critical Reading

1. Were you ultimately persuaded that mother-daughter relationships (and possibly other relationships) can be improved through using the strategies Tannen describes? If so, what did Tannen do to persuade you? If not, what might she have done differently?

2. Like many of the academic genres you'll be expected to write, the chapter excerpted here features an introduction that ends with a thesis (in this case, an overview of the argument made in the chapter). Consider Tannen's thesis:

> In this . . . chapter I'll show how women have found that new ways of talking can improve their relationships with their daughters and mothers. (para. 3)

Why do you think Tannen provides readers with this overview instead of just discussing her examples?

Also consider why Tannen puts her thesis at the *end* of her introduction, where it's prefaced by the story about her mother putting a blanket over her legs—and by her caveat that "[a]lthough what works for one mother-daughter pair may not work for another, there are principles that can provide guidance for all" (para. 3). Why do you think Tannen prefaces her thesis like this instead of simply stating it at the very beginning of the chapter? When in your own writing might you choose to place a thesis at the end of an introduction?

3. Just as Tannen provides an overview of her chapter, she also provides an overview of each section. Take a few minutes to see if you can find where she provides the overviews for "And Now for Something Different" (p. 164) and "Change the Script" (p. 167). Where did you find the overviews, and how did you identify them? Why do you think Tannen provides these overviews?

4. Since you'll be expected to use evidence throughout your college career (and very possibly throughout your post-college career), think about how Tannen uses evidence. She provides comparatively brief examples to support claims, but she also provides an extended example: the supporting evidence taken from Vivian Gornick's memoir (pp. 165–166). Take a few minutes to consider the Gornick example and to find a shorter example to compare it to. Why do you think Tannen uses examples of such different lengths? Did both examples work for you as a reader? Why or why not?

5. Like writers across many genres, Tannen doesn't simply throw us example after example; instead, she transitions from one piece of evidence to another, showing us how her examples—and the points they illustrate—are connected. A key strategy she uses to craft transitions is to *start a paragraph by referring back to the previous paragraph.* Let's look at an example:

> It was a perfect setup for her daughter to take offense—until she *reframed* her understanding of her mother's intentions.
> One of my students, Jessie, *also* found that *reframing* how she thought about her mother led her to talk to her in new ways. (paras. 12–13, italics added)

Note that there are actually two strategies Tannen uses to link the paragraphs: she uses the word "also," and she repeats versions of the word "reframe." Thus, readers immediately know that the paragraph about Jessie is going to provide additional evidence to support the claim about reframing made in the previous paragraph.

Take a few minutes to find another example of a transition that guides you from the main point of one paragraph to the main point of another. Bear in mind that a point might be developed over the course of two (or more) paragraphs, in which case a transition typically clarifies that the second paragraph is a continuation of the point discussed in the previous paragraph. After you find an example of a transition you like, share it with some classmates and explain how it shows the relationship between paragraphs.

Did the transition you found work for your classmates too? Why or why not? (Some readers see connections that others don't.) Your instructor might ask someone from your group to share an example with the class.

Making Connections

6. Using quotations—and introducing them effectively—can be key to advancing your purposes as a writer. The way you introduce your quotations will vary depending on your genre, audience, and purpose. To shed light on different strategies you can use, consider these excerpts from Tannen's chapter, Gottman and DeClaire's self-help book *The Relationship Cure* (p. 146), and Long's creative nonfiction piece "Patching Holes" (p. 127). Notice the similarities and differences in how these writers integrate quotations:

Tannen:

In telling me how she improved her relationship with her mother, one woman mentioned a simple step, but one that simply doesn't occur to many of us: When something her mother says hurts her feelings, she asks her mother what she means:

> [When my mother] makes a statement [that hurts me] . . . , rather than just speculate and just let it hang there, [I'll ask], "What do you mean by that?" or "Do you intend that to be hurtful, do you intend for that to be—What's your come-from on that?"

In other words, the daughter went on, "I took it in a certain way, and she may or may not have meant it that way." By asking her mother to clarify her intentions rather than silently absorbing [her hurt], this woman opened a dialogue that improved their relationship. (para. 9)

Gottman and DeClaire:

[A] negative response to a bid typically shuts down emotional communication. All bids cease. . . . People want to pick up their Ping-Pong paddles and go home.

> *"What are you doing for lunch today?"*
>
> *"Lunch? Who's got time for that?"*
>
> *"Maybe some other time, then."*
>
> *"Yeah, some other time."*

But our research shows that "some other time" rarely happens. (paras. 39–45, italics original)

Long:

> "You're a sweetheart," he said, speaking even more clearly than he had before the fall, staring at me. "A real sweetheart." (para. 24)

Which writers told us the point of the quotation before we even read the quotation? What other similarities and differences did you notice?

In what situations might you want to use Tannen's style of integrating quotations? Gottman and DeClaire's style? Long's? Why?

7. Regardless of the genre(s) being read, professors appreciate it when students see connections between readings; seeing connections can help you formulate more sophisticated thesis statements (and engage in critical thinking more generally). Reading Tannen in light of Gottman and DeClaire (p. 146), for example, can be instructive.

Writing

Although Tannen doesn't mention Gottman's concept of the bid (an attempt to make an emotional connection with someone), we can see many examples of bids in the examples she discusses. In the last sentence of paragraph 5, for instance, she notes that a daughter makes a "gesture of connection" in recommending a book to her mother. The mother, however, comments that she doesn't like the book — a comment that Gottman would see as a rejection of the daughter's bid. The problem, he would say, stems largely from the fact that the mother didn't recognize the daughter's bid as a bid; if she had, she would have probably responded differently.

What other bids and responses do you see in Tannen's examples? What can we learn by considering how Gottman's concept of bidding seems to affect the communication in Tannen's examples?

Writing: Your Turn

1. Consider Tannen's ideas for improving relationships alongside Gottman and DeClaire's ideas (p. 146). Drawing on both sources, make an argument about how people might improve their relationships. You could synthesize information from both sources to develop a thesis that goes beyond regurgitating what the sources say, or you could respond to both sources with your own take on how to improve communication — perhaps extending, qualifying, or critiquing the sources' ideas. Decide who you want your audience to be, and tailor your argument to that audience.

   After you finish writing and doing a round of revision on your own, give your argument to some classmates. Tell them who your intended audience is, and ask them questions such as these:

   • How could I better tailor what I wrote to my intended audience?

   • Where could I add more evidence?

   • How could I make the evidence I already have even more persuasive?

   • How could I sharpen the focus? (Your classmates might suggest that you revise your thesis — and/or the main points of your paragraphs — to be more specific. They might also suggest that you more explicitly show readers how the different pieces of your argument are connected.)

   After you revise, give what you wrote to some of your intended readers to see how they respond. For ideas on writing an argument, see p. 42.

2. Write a dialogue illustrating one of Tannen's strategies for improving communication; then write a reflection that discusses which strategy you're illustrating and why you think that strategy is important.

   Share your dialogue and reflection with some classmates. You might ask them the following questions, along with any other questions you have:

   • How could my dialogue better illustrate the strategy I'm trying to illustrate?

- Does my reflection succeed in explaining how the strategy might help people?
- Which passages in my reflection could be explained in more depth?

Revise based on your classmates' feedback. For ideas on writing a reflection, see p. 27.

3. Write a reflection speculating on how the selection you just read might compare to one of Tannen's other books, many of which you can peek at on Amazon.com. A few of her other books for laypeople include the following:

- *That's Not What I Meant! How Conversational Style Makes or Breaks Relationships*
- *You Just Don't Understand: Women and Men in Conversation*
- *I Only Say This Because I Love You: Talking to Your Parents, Partner, Sibs, and Kids When You're All Adults*

Pick one of these titles and view the table of contents or any other section that interests you. Based on this material, speculate on how the book you peeked at might be similar to or different from *You're Wearing* That?

After you finish your reflection, exchange drafts with a few classmates so that you can learn from their ideas—and so that you can get feedback on which parts of your reflection they would like to hear more about. For ideas on writing a reflection, see p. 27.

Cycle of Violence

Diane Davis

While other selections in this chapter discuss relationships in terms of how they can change for the better, the brochure that follows addresses relationships in terms of the negative cycles they can go through. Author Diane Davis, MA, specifically addresses readers who have experienced domestic violence (battering), which she says can include physical violence and/or emotional abuse. Unlike the other reading selections, which assume that relationships are worth maintaining, *Cycle of Violence* might prompt some readers to consider ending relationships before they degenerate even further.

The brochure, written in 2000, continues to be distributed by ETR Associates. ETR is a nonprofit organization that, according to its Web site (www.etr.org), is dedicated to "improv[ing] the physical, social and emotional health of individuals, families and communities."

Focus on Genre   Brochures can be a difficult genre to produce; potential readers may or may not pick up any given brochure, and if they do, they may not read all of it. The stakes of writing an effective brochure can be high. Many brochures discuss — and help people cope with — crucial problems in society, yet to be effective and quickly appeal to readers, most brochures are short and thus cannot provide as much information as the problem addressed in the brochure may warrant.

As you read *Cycle of Violence,* consider both its design and its content, especially in terms of how readers in the targeted audience might respond to it. Imagine what it would look like folded up, what might prompt someone to pick it up, and whether it might change — or even save — someone's life.

◄O►

Cycle of
Violence

What Is the "Cycle of Violence"?

In a violent relationship, the same things may happen over and over again.

Not all relationships follow this "cycle of violence." But many go through these 3 stages:

THE TENSION-BUILDING STAGE

No matter what you do, you can't please your partner. Your partner may shout, blame, criticize, threaten, call you names or refuse to speak to you.

THE EXPLOSION

The explosion can be verbal, physical and/or sexual (rape). The batterer may scream, yell, shove, slap, hit, punch, kick, break things, or even use weapons to frighten you.

THE "I'M SORRY" STAGE

After the explosion, batterers may be sorry and promise it will never happen again. Some may cry or bring you flowers and gifts. Some may threaten to kill themselves or you, if you leave.

Things may be calm for a while. Then the cycle begins again.

> Not all batterers say "I'm sorry."
> And an apology doesn't mean you
> are safe from the violence.

1

What You Can Do

**You can't control what your partner does.
But you can take steps to be safer.**

When tension starts building:

- Pay attention to your feelings. Are you tense, fearful or on edge?

- Don't minimize or deny the danger.

- Don't try to argue or reason. You **can't** change a batterer's mind or behavior.

- Get away if you can. Don't say you are leaving. This may put you in more danger.

During the explosion:

- The most important thing is to protect yourself.

- Get away, if you can.

- Try to avoid unsafe areas in your home. Stay away from the kitchen (where knives are kept), the basement or garage (where tools are stored) and any rooms with guns. Avoid rooms with hard surfaces and only one exit, such as the bathroom.

- If you are being hit, protect your face with your hands and arms. If you are knocked down, curl up in a ball on the floor and continue to protect your face and head.

If you hear "I'm sorry":

- Know that no matter what the batterer says, without professional help the violence will happen again.

- Get help for yourself. Find out how to be safer when the violence happens again.

2

What to Know

Battering is *not* your fault. The batterer is the one who has the problem and who needs to get help.

You might feel confused. Many women who are battered feel ashamed, afraid, guilty or humiliated. They think they should be able to make it stop. They can't.

Violence is dangerous and unpredictable. It may not follow a cycle. If it does, the time between explosions tends to get shorter. In the future there may be no "I'm sorry" stage.

Violence will get worse. Without professional help, the violence will keep happening. Over time it will get worse. In time, the batterer may kill you or himself, or both of you.

Violence Is Against the Law

- If your partner hits you, report it to the police as soon as you can.
- The police can come to you or you can go to them. They will talk to you in person and file a report.
- If you have been injured, they may take pictures of your injuries.
  - They may arrest your partner.

Don't listen to anyone who tells you the abuse is your fault. No one ever deserves to be battered.

Ways to Get Help

- **Call the women's crisis line** in your community. They can tell you what resources are available. Or call the National Domestic Violence Hotline at 1-800-799-7233.

- **Make a list of family and friends** who could help in an emergency. Ask what they would be willing to do (transportation, shelter, money, etc.).

- **Join a support group.** You will learn more about domestic violence. Groups for battered women can give you information, comfort and support.

- **Find out your legal rights.** There are ways to keep a batterer away from you, your home and your children. Call a women's shelter or the County Bar Association to learn what to do.

- **Get counseling.** Find a counselor who understands domestic violence and is sensitive to those who've been through it. Ask a woman's shelter to refer you to someone.

- **Go to a shelter** (a place where you and your children can stay for a while). Shelters offer safety, counseling and support while you decide what to do next.

What Children Need to Know

**Children know that fighting is going on, even if you think they don't.
Denying it or not talking about it upsets them even more.**

- Talk to them and let them tell you how they feel.

- Tell them the fighting is *not their fault*.

- Tell them to *stay out* of the fighting.

- Talk about where they can hide *inside* the home (in a closet, under the bed, in a room that has a lock on the door).

- Talk about where they can hide *outside* the home (garage, neighbors' or friends' homes).

- Talk about whom they can go to for help (grandparents, other relatives, neighbors, friends, police).

- Teach older children how to call 9-1-1. Practice what to say when they call. ("Daddy is hitting Mommy. We live at… Hurry!")

How Batterers Can Get Help

THERAPY GROUPS

Batterers *must* get professional help to stop the cycle of violence.

- They have to want to stop.

- They must agree to weekly sessions in a therapy group for batterers for at least 1 year. Therapists trained in domestic violence lead these groups. They try to help batterers change their violent behavior.

ALCOHOL / DRUG TREATMENT PROGRAMS

Using alcohol and other drugs can add to violent behavior. But even with treatment for drug or alcohol abuse, a batterer still needs help to stop battering.

Even with counseling,
violent patterns are hard to break.
So you need to get help for yourself
and have plans to stay safe.

5

6

What Is Domestic Violence?

Abusing a partner physically, emotionally or sexually is called domestic violence. It is also called "battering."

- Battering is physical force used to control or hurt someone. Batterers hit, slap, kick, push or sexually assault (rape) the other person.

- Emotional abuse is also a form of violence. Threats, shouting, name calling and other verbal abuses are used to frighten the other person.

Violence isn't normal In fact, battering is against the law.

Written by Diane Davis, MA.

 1-800-321-4407

www.etr.org   Title No. R848

Questions

Questions for Critical Reading

1. Do you think Davis's brochure might succeed in helping some readers in abusive relationships feel more confident that they can address the problem? Why or why not?

2. Although both men and women can be in abusive relationships, Davis is writing for an audience of women. Take a minute to identify and think about the passages that assume a female audience. Which passages did you find?

   How would Davis's brochure have been different if she'd chosen to address an audience of both men and women? If you were Davis and you decided that both sexes could benefit from a brochure on abusive relationships, what would you do — and how would you do it?

3. Like spoken words, written words imply attitudes toward others. Depending on the extent to which readers feel respected by writers, the writing in genres such as brochures may be more — or less — likely to help a reader. Take a minute to identify a couple of passages that seem to reflect Davis's attitude toward her intended audience. What does her attitude seem to be? Does she come across as understanding and supportive? condescending and judgmental? somewhere in between, or some of both? Why do you interpret her attitude the way you do?

4. Recall that to have credibility with readers, writers across genres often qualify their claims; rather than making a blanket statement, they may acknowledge that a claim is their own opinion, or they may acknowledge that a phenomenon they are discussing doesn't always happen. On the first panel of Davis's brochure, for instance, she uses the word "may" to qualify a claim. As you look at her original sentence next to an altered version, think about why she might have qualified this claim:

Original Passage	Altered Passage
[T]he same things may happen over and over again. (panel 1)	[T]he same things happen over and over again.

Not only does the word "may" help establish Davis's credibility (she's not making a simplistic blanket claim), but it might also work to persuade a broader audience. In the altered passage, a reader who *isn't* having the same things happen over and over might disregard the brochure, thinking that it doesn't apply to his or her situation.

   Given the importance — and the multiple functions — of qualifying a claim, you'll probably want to make this move in some of your own writing. For additional examples of this move, take a minute to glance at *Cycle of Violence.* What other qualified claims do you see? Why do you think Davis qualified these claims?

5. Although many writers qualify claims, these same writers may sometimes choose not to do so in light of their purpose, audience, and genre. Consider three of Davis's unqualified statements:

> [A]n apology doesn't mean you are safe from the violence. (panel 1)

> You **can't** change a batterer's mind or behavior. (panel 2; boldface original)

> Battering is *not* your fault. (panel 3; italics original).

Find other examples of unqualified claims in *Cycle of Violence*. Given the situation of many readers, do you think any of these blanket claims are appropriate, or do you think Davis should have qualified them? Why?

Making Connections

6. Unlike many other genres, Davis's brochure *Cycle of Violence* doesn't provide evidence for the claims it makes. For instance, Davis doesn't provide evidence for her claim that "an apology doesn't mean you are safe from the violence" (panel 1), nor does she provide evidence for her claim that the "[v]iolence will get worse" (panel 3)—even though there *is* research she could have cited to support these claims. Consider *Cycle of Violence* in light of the excerpts from *The Relationship Cure* (p. 146) and *You're Wearing That?* (p. 163). Why do you think Davis decided to forgo providing evidence while the book authors didn't? If you were Davis, would you have provided evidence? Why or why not?

7. Look at the design of *Cycle of Violence,* and compare it to that of the scholarly research report "When We Hurt the Ones We Love" (p. 183). Consider the use of headings, italics, boldface, bullets, borders, and white space (the blank space between lines). How do you think such design elements influence what gets emphasized?

Although the two documents represent very different genres, each document could have been designed differently. If you were the author/designer of either document, would you alter any aspects of the design to change what gets emphasized? Why or why not?

Writing: Your Turn

1. *Cycle of Violence* uses the brochure genre to offer advice that is quick at hand for people in troubled relationships. Think of a topic that a friend or loved one might need advice on, and write a reflection on how you would offer that advice in brochure form. How would you adapt your brochure to your audience? What images might you include? How would you use white space, headings, and (if applicable) bulleted lists?

After you write your reflection, share it with a few classmates. Point them to some passages you're unsure of, and get their ideas on how you might revise. Also ask them for suggestions on how you might refine the design to better emphasize important ideas. For ideas on brochures, see the "Quick Checklist" on p. 105; for ideas on writing reflections, see p. 27.

2. Write a rhetorical analysis of *Cycle of Violence*; try to help an audience of your classmates see the brochure in a new light. You might consider either or both of the following (along with any additional ideas you have):

- Davis's degree of success in adapting her language to her target audience
- Davis's use of design elements such as headings, white space, bulleted lists, textboxes, boldface, and italics.

Give your rhetorical analysis to some classmates to see if it succeeded in helping them see the brochure in a new light and to get their feedback on how you might provide even more evidence to support your claims (or how you could explain the evidence you already have in more depth). Consider your classmates' feedback when you revise. For ideas on writing a rhetorical analysis, see p. 31.

3. Integrating some or all of the information in *Cycle of Violence* with your own independent research, write an argument about domestic violence. Decide who you want your audience to be, and tailor your argument to that audience. You might argue that domestic violence is commonly misunderstood by the public or that people who are battered are being unjustly blamed. Combining your own research with what you learned from the brochure, you might also argue that the advice in *Cycle of Violence* is incomplete, or that some of the information it presents simplifies a complex phenomenon. Alternatively, you could argue a point not suggested here.

After you finish writing and doing a round of revision on your own, give your argument to some classmates. Tell them who your intended audience is, and ask them questions such as these:

- How could I better tailor what I wrote to my intended audience?
- Where could I add more evidence?
- How could I make the evidence I already have even more persuasive?
- How could I sharpen the focus? (Your classmates might suggest that you revise your thesis — and/or the main points of your paragraphs — to be more specific. They might also suggest that you more explicitly show readers how the different pieces of your argument are connected.)

After you revise, give what you wrote to some of your intended readers to see how they respond. For ideas on writing an argument, see p. 42.

When We Hurt the Ones We Love: Predicting Violence against Women from Men's Mate Retention

Todd K. Shackelford, Aaron T. Goetz,
David M. Buss, Harald A. Euler, and Sabine Hoier

Like the last selection, this one examines relationships that change not for the better but for the worse — significantly worse. The authors consider which actions taken by men may be predictors of violence against women, and they claim that some acts — even those that wouldn't seem to predict violence — may in fact predict violence. The authors hope the danger signs they identify will ultimately reduce violence and help women avoid it. The selection is excerpted from a scholarly research report published in the peer-reviewed social psychology journal *Personal Relationships* in 2005.[1]

Focus on Genre Although many undergraduates find it difficult to understand scholarly genres, especially the extensive citation of research, the more you encounter these genres, the more successfully you'll be able to navigate college.

Before you read a scholarly genre (or any other difficult genre), it's useful to spend a few minutes previewing what you're about to read. Skim the abstract (overview), and look at the headings, subheadings, and bibliography. Spending just one or two minutes previewing will save you time when you read.

As you read this research report, notice when and how the authors cite sources, and think about when you may want to cite sources in your own writing. Also consider, more generally, what the authors' purpose is and to what extent their ability to accomplish that purpose depends on the type of audience that reads the report.

◄o►

---

[1] A peer-reviewed journal is one that sends authors' submissions to several of their peers — other professors and researchers — so that they can weigh in on whether a submission should be published and, if so, what revisions the authors should make.

ABSTRACT

Mate retention behaviors are designed to solve several adaptive problems such as deterring a partner's infidelity and preventing defection from the mating relationship. Although many mate retention behaviors appear to be innocuous romantic gestures (e.g., displaying resources, giving flowers), some may be harbingers of violence. We investigated the associations between male mate retention and violence against women in romantic relationships. In Study 1, 461 men reported their use of mate retention behaviors and separately completed instruments designed to assess violence in their relationships. Study 2 assessed 560 women's reports of their partners' mate retention behaviors and the degree to which their partners used violence against them. As predicted, and across both studies, men's use of particular mate retention behaviors was related positively to female-directed violence. Study 3 secured 2 separate data sources—husbands' reports of their mate retention and wives' reports of their husbands' violence in a sample of 214 individuals forming 107 couples. The results corroborated those of Studies 1 and 2, with particular male mate retention behaviors predicting violence against romantic partners. The general discussion outlines future directions for research that are likely to result in a more comprehensive understanding of partner violence against women.

M ale sexual jealousy is a frequently cited cause of nonlethal and lethal violence in romantic relationships (e.g., Buss, 2000; Daly & Wilson, 1988; Daly, Wilson, & Weghorst, 1982; Dobash & Dobash, 1979; Dutton, 1998; Dutton & Golant, 1995; Walker, 1979, 2000). . . .

Expressions of male sexual jealousy historically may have been functional in deterring rivals from mate poaching (Schmitt & Buss, 2001) and in deterring a mate from a sexual infidelity or outright departure from the relationship (Buss, Larsen, Westen, & Semmelroth, 1992; Daly et al., 1982; Symons, 1979). Buss (1988) categorized the behavioral output of jealousy into different "mate retention" categories and tactics, ranging from vigilance over a partner's whereabouts to violence against rivals (see also Buss & Shackelford, 1997). Performance of mate retention behaviors is assessed by the Mate Retention Inventory (MRI; Buss, 1988). Buss's (1988) taxonomy partitions the behaviors into two general domains: *Intersexual Manipulations*, which includes behaviors

We thank Dan Perlman, Sue Sprecher, and seven anonymous reviewers for comments and suggestions that greatly improved this article. In addition, we thank Steve Hecht and three additional anonymous reviewers for valuable statistical advice. The first and second authors contributed equally.

Correspondence should be addressed to Todd K. Shackelford or Aaron T. Goetz, Florida Atlantic University, Department of Psychology, Davie, FL 33314, e-mail tshackel@fau.edu (TKS); agoetz2@fau.edu (ATG).

directed toward one's partner, and *Intrasexual Manipulations*, which includes behaviors directed toward same-sex rivals. Each domain is partitioned into several categories: Intersexual Manipulations includes the categories *Direct Guarding, Negative Inducements,* and *Positive Inducements.* Intrasexual manipulations includes the category *Public Signals of Possession.* Each mate retention category comprises several mate retention tactics, which, in turn, comprise specific mate retention acts (see Buss, 1988; Buss & Shackelford; and see the Methods subsection under the Studies 1 and 2 section). The current research tests predictions targeting the category level of mate retention behaviors. In a series of exploratory analyses in each study, however, we also address the tactic and act levels of mate retention behaviors.

Because male sexual jealousy has been linked to violence in relationships, and because mate retention behaviors are manifestations of jealousy, men's use of these behaviors is predicted to be associated with violence toward their partners. Indeed, Buss and Shackelford (1997) hypothesized that the use of some mate retention tactics may be early indicators of violence in romantic relationships. Unfortunately, little is known about which specific acts and tactics of men's mate retention efforts are linked with violence. One exception is the study by Wilson, Johnson, and Daly (1995), which identified several predictors of partner violence—notably, verbal derogation of the mate and attempts at sequestration, such as limiting access to family, friends, and income (for related research that is not conducted within an evolutionary framework and that tends to focus on broader, more general predictors of partner violence, see, e.g., Johnson, 1995; Leone, Johnson, Cohan, & Lloyd, 2004; Smith, White, & Holland, 2003; White, Merrill, & Koss, 2001). A goal of the current research is to identify specific behaviors that portend violence in romantic relationships and thereby to contribute to a better understanding of violence against women. Identifying the predictors of partner violence would be theoretically valuable and may provide information relevant to developing interventions designed to reduce partner violence or to help women avoid such violence.

Predictors of violence in romantic relationships

Direct Guarding.   Tactics within the Direct Guarding category of the MRI   5
include Vigilance, Concealment of Mate, and Monopolization of Time. An exemplary act for each tactic is, respectively, "He dropped by unexpectedly to see what she was doing." "He refused to introduce her to his same-sex friends," and "He monopolized her time at the social gathering." Each of these tactics implicates what Wilson and Daly (1992) term "male sexual proprietariness," which refers to the sense of entitlement men sometimes feel that they have over their partners and, more specifically, their partners' sexual behavior. . . .

Wilson et al. (1995) demonstrated that violence against women is linked closely to their partners' autonomy-limiting behaviors. Women who affirmed items such as "He is jealous and doesn't want you to talk to other men" were more than twice as likely to have experienced serious violence by their partners. Of those women who were questioned further about their experiences with serious violence, 56% reported being fearful for their lives and 72% required medical attention following an assault. Because Direct Guarding is associated specifically with men's autonomy-limiting behaviors, we expect the use of Direct Guarding to be related positively to violence in romantic relationships.

Intersexual Negative Inducements.   In addition to Direct Guarding, men sometimes attempt to retain their partners by using Intersexual Negative Inducements. Punish Mate's Infidelity Threat, for example, includes acts such as "He yelled at her after she showed interest in another man." . . . The tactics and acts within this category have a violent theme and, therefore, we expect the use of Intersexual Negative Inducements to be related positively to violence in relationships.

Positive Inducements.   Not all mate retention behaviors are expected to predict positively violence toward partners. Some mate retention behaviors are not in conflict with a romantic partner's interests and, indeed, may be encouraged and welcomed by a partner (Buss, 1988, 2000). One might not expect, for example, that men who attempt to retain their partners by using Positive Inducements will behave more violently toward their partners than men who do not deploy such tactics. For example, men who affirm Love and Care acts (e.g., "I was helpful when she really needed it") and Resource Display acts (e.g., "I bought her an expensive gift") may not be expected to use violence against their partners. Men who have resources might be able to retain their partners using methods that are not available to men lacking resources. Indeed, Daly and Wilson (1988) predicted that men who cannot retain mates through positive inducements may be more likely to resort to violence. Following Daly and Wilson, we expect the use of Positive Inducements to be related negatively to female-directed violence.

Public Signals of Possession.   Tactics within the Public Signals of Possession category include Verbal Possession Signals (e.g., "He mentioned to other males that she was taken"). Physical Possession Signals (e.g., "He held her hand when other guys were around"), and Possessive Ornamentation (e.g., "He hung up a picture of her so others would know she was taken"). Public Signals of Possession reflect male sexual proprietariness and, therefore, we expect the use of Public Signals of Possession to be related positively to female-directed violence. . . .

Summary of current research

. . . With few exceptions, we find the same pattern of results using three   10
independent samples. Moreover, these samples were not just independent but
provided different perspectives (the male perpetrator's, the female victim's,
and a combination of the two) on the same behaviors—men's mate retention
and men's violence against their partners. We identified overlap between the
predictors of violence across the studies. For example, men's use of Emotional
Manipulation, Monopolization of Time, and Punish Mate's Infidelity Threat
predict female-directed violence, according to independent reports provided
by men and women and according to reports provided by husbands and their
wives. The three perspectives also converged on which tactics do not predict
relationship violence. For example, Love and Care and Resource Display consistently fail to predict female-directed violence. . . .

   Some mate retention behaviors involve the provisioning of benefits rather
than the infliction of costs (Buss, 1988; Buss & Shackelford, 1997). Prediction
3 was designed to test Daly and Wilson's (1988) hypothesis that men who are
unable to employ positive inducements such as gift giving and the provisioning
of material resources to retain a mate will be more likely to use violence as a
means of mate retention. Violence against their partners, therefore, was predicted to be related negatively to men's use of Positive Inducements. The current research provides no support for this prediction and, in fact, provides some
evidence for the reverse relationship. Across the three studies, the significant
correlations identified between tactics in the Positive Inducements category and
female-directed violence are exclusively positive. A speculation for these results
is that men faced most severely with the adaptive problem of a partner's defection may ratchet up their use of all mate retention behaviors, both positive
(benefit provision) and negative (cost infliction). . . .

Mate retention tactics as predictors of relationship violence

The tactic Emotional Manipulation was the highest ranking predictor of relationship violence in Study 1, based on men's self-reports, and the second
highest ranking predictor in Studies 2 and 3, based on women's partner reports
and spousal reports, respectively. In addition, Emotional Manipulation was the
only tactic that uniquely predicted violence in Study 1 and one of just three
tactics that uniquely predicted violence in Study 2. The items that comprise
the Emotional Manipulation tactic include "He told her he would 'die' if she
ever left" and "He pleaded that he could not live without her." Such acts seem
far removed from those that might presage violence. The robust relationship
between female-directed violence and men's use of Emotional Manipulation
can be interpreted in at least two ways. Emotional Manipulation may be a

postviolence "apologetic" tactic. Perhaps men who behave violently toward their partners are apologizing and expressing regret for their violent behavior. Indeed, Walker (2000) has observed that, following a violent episode, men often are apologetic, expressing remorse and pleading for forgiveness.

Another possibility is that Emotional Manipulation may occur before relationship violence, making it a true harbinger of violence. Perhaps a man who tells his partner that he would die if she ever left him is so heavily invested in the relationship and perceives that he has so much to lose if the relationship ended, that he reacts violently when the relationship is threatened. Men who are of much lower mate value than their partners, for example, may have so much to lose that they become violent when their partner defects temporarily (i.e., commits a sexual infidelity) or permanently (i.e., ends the relationship). Future research would benefit from determining whether the use of Emotional Manipulation occurs before or after relationship violence. A longitudinal study, for example, could assess men's use of mate retention in the beginning of a relationship and then subsequently assess men's violence against their partners. . . .

Monopolization of Time also was a highly ranked predictor of violence across the three studies. Example acts included in this tactic are "He spent all his free time with her so that she could not meet anyone else" and "He would not let her go out without him." The positive relationship identified in the current studies between Monopolization of Time and violence is consistent with Wilson et al.'s (1995) demonstration that violence against women is linked closely to their partners' autonomy-limiting behaviors. Wilson et al. found that women who affirmed items such as "He tries to limit your contact with family or friends" are twice as likely to have experienced serious violence by their partners. . . .

Mate retention acts as predictors of relationship violence

The highest ranking correlations between single acts and relationship violence   15
are not particularly consistent across the three studies. The data of Studies 1 and 2 are secured from a single data source (men and women, respectively). The data of Study 3 arguably have greater credibility, because reports of mate retention and violence are provided by different data sources. For this reason, and for reportorial efficiency, we limit our discussion of the results of act-level analyses to Study 3. More specifically, we discuss three of the highest ranking correlations between single acts of mate retention and violence, based on husbands' reports of their mate retention and their wives' reports of violence.

The acts "Dropped by unexpectedly to see what my partner was doing" and "Called to make sure my partner was where she said she would be" are the third and fifth highest ranking predictors of violence, respectively. These acts are included in the tactic Vigilance, which is the highest ranking tactic-level predictor of violence in Study 3 and the only tactic that uniquely predicted violence against women. . . .The acts within the Vigilance tactic are examples of autonomy-limiting behaviors—behaviors motivated by male sexual propri- etariness and designed to restrict women's sexual autonomy (Wilson & Daly, 1992). Wilson et al. (1995) demonstrated that men's use of autonomy-limiting behaviors is associated with female-directed violence. Wilson et al. found that 40% of women who affirmed the statement "He insists on knowing who you are with and where you are at all times" reported experiencing serious violence at the hands of their husbands. . . .

Concluding Remarks

. . . Violence directed toward a mate appears to be one manifestation of male sexual proprietariness (Wilson & Daly, 1992). The current studies contribute to knowledge about this pervasive problem on two levels, conceptually and practi- cally. Conceptually, we have identified several expected predictors of men's use of violence, which contributes in some measure to a broader theory of men's use of violence. At a practical level, results of these studies can potentially be used to inform women and men, friends and relatives, of danger signs—the specific acts and tactics of mate retention—that portend the possibility of future violence in relationships in order to prevent it before it has been enacted.

References

Buss, D. M. (1988). From vigilance to violence: Tactics of mate retention in American undergraduates. *Ethology and Sociobiology, 9,* 291–317.

Buss, D. M. (2000). *The dangerous passion.* New York: The Free Press.

Buss, D. M., Larsen, R. J., Westen, D., & Semmelroth, J. (1992). Sex differences in jeal- ousy: Evolution, physiology and psychology. *Psychological Science, 3,* 251–255.

Buss, D. M., & Shackelford, T. K. (1997). From vigilance to violence: Mate retention tac- tics in married couples. *Journal of Personality and Social Psychology, 72,* 346–361.

Daly, M., & Wilson, M. (1988). *Homicide.* Hawthorne, NY: Aldine de Gruyter.

Daly, M., Wilson, M., & Weghorst, J. (1982). Male sexual jealousy. *Ethology and Sociobiol- ogy, 3,* 11–27.

Dobash, R. E., & Dobash, R. P. (1979). *Violence against wives.* New York: The Free Press.

Dutton, D. G. (1998). *The abusive personality.* New York: Guilford Press.

Dutton, D. G., & Golant, S. K. (1995). *The batterer.* New York: Basic Books.

Johnson, M. P. (1995). Patriarchal terrorism and common couple violence: Two forms of violence against women. *Journal of Marriage and the Family, 57,* 283–294.

Leone, J. M., Johnson, M. P., Cohan, C. L., & Lloyd, S. E. (2004). Consequences of male partner violence for low-income women. *Journal of Marriage and Family, 66,* 472–490.

Schmitt, D. P., & Buss, D. M. (2001). Human mate poaching: Tactics and temptations for infiltrating existing mateships. *Journal of Personality and Social Psychology, 80,* 894–917.

Smith, P. H. White, J. W., & Holland, L. J. (2003). A longitudinal perspective on dating violence among adolescent and college-age women. *American Journal of Public Health, 93,* 1104–1109.

Symons, D. (1979). *The evolution of human sexuality.* New York: Oxford University Press.

Walker, L. E. (1979). *The battered woman.* New York: Harper & Row.

Walker, L. E. (2000). *The battered woman syndrome* (2nd ed.). New York: Springer.

White, J. W., Merrill, L. L., & Koss, M. P. (2001). Predictors of premilitary courtship violence in a Navy recruit sample. *Journal of Interpersonal Violence, 16,* 910–927.

Wilson, M., & Daly, M. (1992). The man who mistook his wife for a chattel. In J. Barkow, L. Cosmides, & J. Tooby (Eds.), *The adapted mind* (pp. 289–322). New York: Oxford University Press.

Wilson, M., Johnson, H., & Daly, M. (1995). Lethal and nonlethal violence against wives. *Canadian Journal of Criminology, 37,* 331–361.

Questions for Critical Reading

1. If you previewed the abstract and the headings before you read the research report, do you think your preview helped? Why or why not? In what other situations might you want to preview a reading?

2. What do you take the authors' purpose to be — and to what extent do you think their ability to accomplish it depends on what type of audience reads the report?

3. When you read academic genres such as "When We Hurt the Ones We Love," you may find the writing dense and hard to understand. Rather than giving up, however, consider identifying a few key passages and "translating" them into language that's easier to understand.[2] Read the adaptation of the original passage that follows to get an idea of how you might do this:

Original Passage	Altered Passage
Buss and Shackelford (1997) hypothesized that the use of some mate retention tactics may be early indicators of violence in romantic relationships. Unfortunately, little is known about *which specific acts and tactics* of men's mate retention efforts are linked with violence. . . . A goal of the current research is to identify specific behaviors that portend violence in romantic relationships and thereby to contribute to a better understanding of violence against women. (para. 4; italics original)	Buss and Shackelford speculated that the ways some men try to hang on to their partners might provide an early warning sign that those men could become violent. Unfortunately, we don't know much about *which specific acts and tactics* of men's mate retention efforts are linked with violence. . . . A goal of our research is to identify specific behaviors that could provide a warning of future violence and thus help us better understand violence against women.

---

[2] Although it can be very frustrating to read some academic genres, the more often you read a genre, the easier it is to understand what you read. If you read a genre often enough, it might eventually become so easy to understand that you won't need to translate key passages (especially if you're majoring in the field that uses the genre and if you're in close contact with the professors who live and breathe that genre).

Did you find the altered passage easier to understand? Why or why not? In groups, find another passage and translate it. Your instructor may ask some groups to share their translations (along with the original passages).

4. Many academic authors cite sources as a strategy for supporting their claims. Take a minute to find a few examples in "When We Hurt the Ones We Love." Did the authors make any claims that you found to be more persuasive because they cited sources? How might your response to the authors' claims have been different had they not cited sources?

5. Many academic authors cite sources not only to support their claims but also to argue that there's a gap in our knowledge (an issue or problem that other authors haven't addressed). Typically these authors claim, in their introductions, that their own work will address that gap. Look at the original passage in question 3 again, this time noticing how the authors claim such a gap.

Why do you think the author makes this move? When in your own writing might you want to say that you're addressing a gap in readers' knowledge?

Making Connections

6. Like authors in many academic disciplines, the authors of "When We Hurt the Ones We Love" tend to use the third person (e.g., "he," "she," "they," or people's names). In contrast, the brochure *Cycle of Violence* (p. 174) tends to use the second person ("you"). Take a few minutes to find some specific examples in both reading selections. For you as a reader, what's the effect of the third person in "When We Hurt the Ones We Love"? What's the effect of the second person in *Cycle of Violence*? Why might the authors of each piece have chosen to use the pronouns they did?

Writing: Your Turn

1. Although "When We Hurt the Ones We Love" is intended for a scholarly audience, some of the authors' ideas might be helpful for an audience of laypeople. Using any ideas from the research report that you think might be useful, design a brochure to help readers predict and thus avoid violent relationships. (This brochure would be a good complement to *Cycle of Violence*, which aims to help people *after* violence has occurred.)

After you write and design your brochure, give it to some classmates for feedback. Ask them specific questions about whether they think your brochure would accomplish its intended purpose for an audience who hasn't read "When We Hurt the Ones We Love." It's good to target brochures to an audience who may not be familiar with your sources, since an audience who *is* familiar with your sources may have less need for the brochure. (Unfortunately, since your classmates will have read "When We Hurt the Ones We Love," they might not notice passages in your brochure that could use clarification or elaboration; they might understand much of what you say because they read the research report rather than because the information is clearly explained in your brochure. Nonetheless, if they put themselves in the shoes of someone who hasn't read the research report, they should be able to give you some good feedback.)

After you revise based on your classmates' feedback, give your brochure to someone who isn't in your class to share your knowledge and to gauge his or her response. For ideas on writing and designing brochures, refer to p. 105.

2. Write a summary of "When We Hurt the Ones We Love." Don't worry if you don't understand all the words; just do the best you can. Many people find that summarizing a work helps them to better understand it. When you finish your summary, give it to some classmates and ask them to carefully consider whether your summary reflects the most important points made by the authors. Consider your classmates' ideas — along with new ideas of your own — when you revise. For strategies to use when writing a summary, see p. 23.

3. Write a reflection on "When We Hurt the Ones We Love." Do you think any of the information presented in this research report might actually help people? Why or why not? Give your reflection to some classmates so that they can learn from your ideas and give you feedback for revision. For ideas on writing a reflection, refer to p. 27.

e To see these bumper stickers in color, visit the e-Pages for *Real Questions* at
bedfordstmartins.com/realquestions/epages.

Questions for Critical Reading

1. Bumper stickers are a popular way both to personalize our modes of transportation and to communicate some of our beliefs to others. Think about how the bumper stickers in this portfolio provide insight into the ways people think about relationships. What do these bumper stickers tell you about strangers who might be driving in front of you, and what do you think these strangers intend to communicate?

2. Consider the bumper stickers in this portfolio in light of this point, which actually appeared on a bumper sticker:

> # BUMPER STICKERS
> ## are an ineffectual means
> of communicating my nuanced views
> on a variety of issues that cannot
> be reduced to a simple pithy slogan

To what extent do you think the bumper stickers in this portfolio are ineffectual due to the limitations of the genre?

3. Consider the use of contrast in the design of the bumper stickers. Designers can provide contrast in a number of ways, including the use of contrasting colors, font sizes, and shapes. How do you think the use of contrast influences what gets emphasized in each bumper sticker?

4. Think about a relationship in your life that is valuable to you (whether it is loving, contentious, or complex). How would you design a bumper sticker to describe it? What text would you use? What sorts of visual touches might you add?

Pulling It All Together

ARGUMENT

Drawing on two or more of the selections in this chapter, and perhaps also on your personal experience or independent research, make an argument about relationships. You might formulate your own question to respond to, or you might respond to either one of the following questions:

- To what extent might it be possible to improve a relationship? How might one go about doing so?

- How might someone decide whether to try to change a relationship or to end it?

You could make an argument that has the potential to apply to a variety of relationships, or you could focus your argument on a particular type of relationship, such as friendships, romantic partnerships, parent-child relationships, sibling relationships, or any other type of relationship (including those between people who aren't related by blood but who nonetheless consider themselves a family).

Think of a specific audience you want to address, and target your argument to that audience. Bear in mind that many readers will find your argument more persuasive if you recognize complexity rather than making black-and-white, cut-and-dried claims. (Recognizing complexity will add to your credibility because many readers will see you as having examined the issue from all sides rather than simply ignoring potential objections to your claims.) Also carefully consider how you use evidence, along with how you focus and organize your work.

After you draft your argument, give it to some classmates for feedback. Use the "Quick Checklist" on p. 42 to formulate a list of questions to ask them. However, for guidance in actually writing and revising your argument, see the entire section that starts on p. 42.

BLOG POSTS

Drawing on some of the selections in this chapter, and perhaps also on your personal experience or independent research, write a series of blog posts reflecting on relationships. This is a good option if you have several different ideas to convey—ideas that might be hard to weave together in a single essay. Writing effective blog posts presents different challenges, such as using vivid language and being original enough to inspire busy readers to read your posts.

After you draft your posts, give them to some classmates for feedback. Use the "Quick Checklist" on p. 91 to formulate a list of questions to ask them. However, for guidance in actually writing and revising your posts, see the entire section that starts on p. 90.

DO
I
LOOK
illegal??

exclusively for you
PAPAYA

2

When should we assume the best (or worst) about others?

How do our assumptions affect others?
Creative nonfiction, page **223**

Why do we assume the worst about others?
Online encyclopedia article, page **202**   Research report, page **229**

Why should we assume the best?
Radio essay, page **255**

How do we learn to overcome negative assumptions?
Popular nonfiction, page **207**   Oral history, page **235**
Advice essay, page **249**   Professional resource, page **260**

What might be done to prevent negative assumptions within a society?
Research report, page **229**

Can assumptions save our lives?
Self-help book, page **268**

Think about your first day of your first college class. It is likely that you were sitting in an unfamiliar room with unfamiliar people, being given directions by an unfamiliar professor. Even though your concrete knowledge of your surroundings might have been limited, chances are your brain was filling this gap in knowledge by making assumptions about this new situation: the professor's loud voice was indicative of an authoritarian teaching style; the upright posture of the student next to you signaled that she would be overeager to answer questions; the hair gel and fashion-model appearance of the student across the room suggested that he would be more interested in himself than in his studies.

No matter who we are, we've probably assumed the worst about someone else. Most of us, in turn, have had the experience of people assuming the worst about us. This chapter explores the complexity underlying people's assumptions about each other. You'll ultimately be asked to evaluate whether making assumptions (or trying to defer assumptions) can be done intelligently, and to consider when our assumptions should and should not guide our actions.

Ways of thinking about this issue will be provided by the readings in this chapter—readings from a wide variety of genres. Because different genres tend to have different approaches to addressing this issue, reading a variety of genres will help you gain deeper insight into this complex topic.

Case Study in Genre and Assumptions: Attribution Theory

A case study in how genre shapes the presentation of this topic is provided by "Attribution Theory," an online encyclopedia article by David Straker from ChangingMinds.org. As an encyclopedia article, "Attribution Theory" illustrates both the value and the limitations of encyclopedias. Many encyclopedias focus on breadth rather than depth of coverage; that is, they often provide a little bit of information about many different topics rather than in-depth information about a narrow topic. Although genres like this provide a useful way for readers to get an introductory overview of a topic that's new to them, many encyclopedia articles tend to represent complex material in a simple way. This simplified representation may be even more common in online encyclopedias, whose readers may be jumping from one Web site to another.

Because encyclopedias often favor breadth over depth and may simplify complex material, many professors recommend that students not cite encyclopedias in their writing. Some students, however, may find it useful to read online encyclopedias (with a critical eye) to get an introductory overview of a topic before going on to read more complex material that they cite in their writing.

As you read the following encyclopedia article, think about which ideas you'd like to know more about, and critically assess the extent to which the article represents complex phenomena in a simple way.

To read and answer questions about this case study online, visit the e-Pages for *Real Questions* at **bedfordstmartins.com/realquestions /epages.**

Attribution Theory

DESCRIPTION

We all have a need to explain the world, both to ourselves and to other people, attributing *cause* to the events around us. This gives us a greater sense of control. When explaining behavior, it can affect the standing of people within a group (especially ourselves).

When another person has erred, we will often use *internal attribution*, saying it is due to internal personality factors. When we have erred, we will more likely use *external attribution*, attributing causes to situational factors rather than blaming ourselves. And vice versa. We will attribute our successes internally and the successes of our rivals to external "luck."

Our attributions are also significantly driven by our emotional and motivational drives. Blaming other people and avoiding personal recrimination are very real *self-serving attributions*. We will also make attributions to defend what we perceive as attacks. We will point to injustice in an unfair world. People with a high need to avoid failure will have a greater tendency to make attributions that put themselves in a good light.

We will even tend to blame victims (of us and of others) for their fate as we seek to distance ourselves from thoughts of suffering the same plight.

We will also tend to ascribe less variability to other people than ourselves, seeing ourselves as more multifaceted and less predictable than others. This may well be because we can see more of what is inside ourselves (and spend more time doing this).

In practice, we often tend to go through a two-step process, starting with an automatic internal attribution, followed by a slower consideration of whether an external attribution is more appropriate. As with <u>Automatic Believing</u>, if we are hurrying or are distracted, we may not get to this second step. This makes internal attribution more likely than external attribution.

RESEARCH

Roesch and Amirkham (1997) found that more experienced athletes made less self-serving external attributions, leading them to find and address real causes and hence [enabling them] to improve their performance.

SO WHAT?

Using It

Beware of losing trust by blaming others (i.e., making internal attributions about them). Also beware of making excuses (external attributions) that lead you to repeat mistakes and lead to Cognitive Dissonance in others when they are making internal attributions about you.

Defending

Watch out for people making untrue attributions.

SEE ALSO

<u>Correspondent Inference Theory</u>, <u>Covariation Model</u>, <u>Fundamental Attribution Error</u>, <u>Actor-Observer Difference</u>, <u>Ultimate Attribution Error</u>, <u>Idealization</u>, <u>Post Hoc</u>, <u>Self-Determination Theory</u>
http://www.as.wvu.edu/~sbb/comm221/chapters/attrib.htm

CONTINUED >

Attribution Theory, continued

References

Heider, F. (1958). *The psychology of interpersonal relations.* New York: Wiley.

Jones, E. E. and Davis, K. E. (1965). From acts to dispositions: The attribution process in social psychology. In L. Berkowitz (ed.), *Advances in Experimental Social Psychology* (Volume 2, pp. 219–266). New York: Academic Press.

Kammer, D. (1982). Differences in trait ascriptions to self and friend: Unconfounding intensity from variability. *Psychological Reports, 51,* 99–102.

Kelley, H. H. (1967). Attribution theory in social psychology. In D. Levine (ed.), *Nebraska Symposium on Motivation* (Volume 15, pp. 192–238). Lincoln University of Nebraska Press.

Roesch, S. C., and Amirkham, J. H. (1997). Boundary conditions for self-serving attributions: Another look at the sports pages. *Journal of Applied Social Psychology, 27,* 245–261.

Questions for Critical Reading

1. Did "Attribution Theory" prompt you to question any of the assumptions you've made about others? Do you think it explains any of the assumptions others have made about you? Why or why not? Point to a specific passage and explain why it succeeded — or didn't succeed — in prompting you to consider why people make the attributions they do.

2. When you read or write, it's useful to be aware of whether the genre you're working with tends to favor breadth (brief coverage of many ideas) or depth (a thorough exploration of fewer ideas). Although many genres tend to favor depth over breadth, encyclopedia articles such as "Attribution Theory" illustrate one advantage of the breadth-over-depth approach: readers are exposed to many ideas and thus have many possible avenues to pursue for further research. Of the many ideas mentioned briefly in "Attribution Theory," which ones would you be most interested in learning more about? Why?

3. Like many encyclopedia articles, "Attribution Theory" tends not to recognize complexity as much as an article in an academic genre would. Consider, for instance, this blanket statement: "We will attribute our successes internally and the successes of our rivals to external 'luck'" (para. 2). This sentence assumes that we're all the same — that we all believe our successes are solely the result of a good quality about us and that we all believe our rivals' success to be the result of luck. Readers of some genres are used to such blanket statements, but readers of academic genres tend to see writers who make blanket statements as being less credible. If you were writing for an academic audience, how would you recast this sentence to avoid the blanket statement?

4. Encyclopedia articles generally don't give the kind of advice that "Attribution Theory" does at the end: "Beware of losing trust by blaming others (i.e., making internal attributions about them). Also beware of making excuses

(external attributions) that lead you to repeat mistakes" (para. 8). If you were the author of the article, would you omit this advice if someone told you it wasn't typical for the genre or would you decide to bend the genre and keep the advice? Why?

Making Connections

5. Recall that citation practices vary significantly across genre. Unlike "Attribution Theory," the sociology research report "Mere Exposure and Racial Prejudice" (p. 229) cites sources for any information that isn't commonly known, as the authors do in the final paragraph when they discuss "longer prison sentences and more frequent death sentences for convicted criminals who have a more prototypical Black appearance (Blair et al., 2004; Eberhardt et al., 2006)." One reason academic readers appreciate such citations is that they may want to find and read some of the sources cited. Citing sources can also bolster the writer's credibility because it not only lets readers know that the writer has researched the topic but also lets readers gauge the trustworthiness of the sources. If you were to rework "Attribution Theory" for an academic audience, which information would you cite?

6. Both "Attribution Theory" and Julie Schwartz Gottman's "An Abbreviated History and Overview of Gottman Method Couples Therapy" (p. 260) discuss how people's attributions shape the extent to which they assume the best or worst about others. The encyclopedia article discusses only one axis of attribution theory: internal attributions (the belief that a cause originates within a person) and external attributions (the belief that a cause originates in the situation or environment).

    Gottman, using a genre of professional discourse that tends to recognize more complexity, mentions an additional axis of attribution theory: the belief that the cause of something is stable (likely to be permanent) and the competing belief that the cause is unstable (temporary). Gottman describes a hypothetical example in which a woman believes a negative comment made by her husband has a temporary cause; the woman believes he made the comment not because he's a jerk (permanent) but because he happened to be in a bad mood that day (temporary). Believing the cause to be a temporary bad mood, the woman does not assume the worst about her husband. Instead, she merely says, "Whoa, what side of the bed did you get up on this morning?" (para. 19).

    If you were the author of "Attribution Theory," would you discuss this additional layer of complexity (the temporary vs. permanent axis of the theory)? Why or why not?

If you think "Attribution Theory" might explain some of the assumptions that you make about others or that others make about you, consider delving more deeply into this topic on your own. A bit of additional research will help you make more sense not only of your interactions with others but also of some of the readings in this chapter.

About the Readings

Now that you've thought a bit about why we make the assumptions we do, you're ready to consider how this topic is addressed by authors working in other genres. Some genres—including Studs Terkel's oral history "C. P. Ellis," Brent Staples's creative nonfiction piece "Black Men and Public Space," and popular nonfiction books such as Malcolm Gladwell's *Blink* and Gavin de Becker's *Gift of Fear*—enable authors to provide us with in-depth accounts of real people's experiences—experiences both making assumptions about others and having others make assumptions about them.

Other genres, such as Zebrowitz et al.'s research report "Mere Exposure and Racial Prejudice" and Julie Schwartz Gottman's introduction to a book for clinical therapists "An Abbreviated History and Overview of Gottman Method Couples Therapy," draw on multiparticipant research to discuss common patterns of behavior, with few if any examples of specific people's experiences.

Still other genres, such as Amel S. Abdullah's advice essay "Assuming the Best of Others" and Sarah Adams's radio essay "Be Cool to the Pizza Dude," draw on religious ideology and personal experience, respectively, to support well-considered philosophies regarding the assumptions we make about others.

Taken together, these selections illustrate that our assumptions about others aren't always under our conscious control but that we *can* become more aware of them and thus change them. Even radical change, the readings suggest, is possible. The readings also suggest that deciding whether to assume the best or worst about someone—or whether to defer making assumptions—is a complex issue that doesn't necessarily have easy answers.

As you explore the genres in this chapter, think about how the authors' choices were shaped by their audiences and purposes. Some authors, for example, write with the primary purpose of helping readers better understand something, while others want to change people's behavior. Several want to accomplish both purposes. Consider what the authors' primary and secondary purposes might be, and think about how the choices they made were shaped by these purposes.

Also reflect on how the authors reinforce, complicate, and contradict one another's points, and notice how your answers to the central questions addressed by this chapter may shift as you read, becoming more nuanced as you encounter more genres and more points of view.

[e] For additional readings in online and multimedia genres related to the chapter theme, see the e-Pages online at **bedfordstmartins.com /realquestions/epages**.

From *Blink*

Malcolm Gladwell

In *Blink*, respected journalist Malcolm Gladwell teaches an audience of well-educated laypeople about rapid cognition, or what he calls "thin slicing" — the ability to rapidly form first impressions based only on thin slices of experience. Gladwell notes that thin slicing, which takes only two seconds, can be useful or dangerous. In the following excerpt, he examines how thin slicing gone wrong can prompt us to make unwarranted assumptions about others, positive and negative. He ultimately argues that we can and should address this problem. Gladwell is a staff writer for the *New Yorker* and is the best-selling author of four books, including *The Tipping Point* (2005) and *Outliers* (2008).

Focus on Genre   Gladwell draws on strategies used in multiple genres, interweaving narrative (stories) with exposition (explanation) to ultimately make a researched argument. Notice how he organizes his writing in terms of his points; while some books for laypeople and academic texts make points first and then provide examples, Gladwell reverses this order; he often tells a story about a person and relays the point of the story only after he's done telling it. When you read point-last writing such as this, it's helpful to try to figure out the points as you read rather than waiting for the author to tell you at the end. This reading strategy will serve you well regardless of the genre you're reading.

◄○►

THE WARREN HARDING ERROR: WHY WE FALL FOR TALL, DARK, AND HANDSOME MEN

Early one morning in 1899, in the back garden of the Globe Hotel in Richwood, Ohio, two men met while having their shoes shined. One was a lawyer and lobbyist from the state capital of Columbus. His name was Harry Daugherty. He was a thick-set, red-faced man with straight black hair, and he was brilliant. He was the Machiavelli of Ohio politics, the classic behind-the-scenes fixer, a shrewd and insightful judge of character or, at least, political opportunity. The second man was a newspaper editor from the small town of Marion, Ohio, who was at that moment a week away from winning election to the Ohio state senate. His name was Warren Harding. Daugherty looked over at Harding and was instantly overwhelmed by what he saw. As the journalist Mark Sullivan wrote, of that moment in the garden:

> Harding was worth looking at. He was at the time about 35 years old. His head, features, shoulders and torso had a size that attracted attention; their proportions to each other made an effect which in any male at any place would justify more than the term handsome—in later years, when he came to be known beyond his local world, the word "Roman" was occasionally used in descriptions of him. As he stepped down from the stand, his legs bore out the striking and agreeable proportions of his body; and his lightness on his feet, his erectness, his easy bearing, added to the impression of physical grace and virility. His suppleness, combined with his bigness of frame, and his large, wide-set rather glowing eyes, heavy black hair, and markedly bronze complexion gave him some of the handsomeness of an Indian. His courtesy as he surrendered his seat to the other customer suggested genuine friendliness toward all mankind. His voice was noticeably resonant, masculine, warm. His pleasure in the attentions of the bootblack's whisk reflected a consciousness about clothes unusual in a small-town man. His manner as he bestowed a tip suggested generous good-nature, a wish to give pleasure, based on physical well-being and sincere kindliness of heart.

In that instant, as Daugherty sized up Harding, an idea came to him that would alter American history: Wouldn't that man make a great President?

Warren Harding was not a particularly intelligent man. He liked to play poker and golf and to drink and, most of all, to chase women; in fact, his sexual appetites were the stuff of legend. As he rose from one political office to another, he never once distinguished himself. He was vague and ambivalent on matters of policy. His speeches were once described as "an army of pompous phrases moving over the landscape in search of an idea." After being elected to the U.S. Senate in 1914, he was absent for the debates on women's suffrage and Prohibition—two of the biggest political issues of his time. He advanced steadily from local Ohio politics only because he was pushed by his wife, Florence, and stage-managed by the scheming Harry Daugherty and because, as he grew older, he grew more and more irresistibly distinguished-looking. Once, at a banquet, a supporter cried out, "Why, the son of a bitch *looks* like a senator," and so he did. By early middle age, Harding's biographer Francis Russell writes, his "lusty black eyebrows contrasted with his steel-gray hair to give the effect of force, his massive shoulders and bronzed complexion gave the effect of health." Harding, according to Russell, could have put on a toga and stepped onstage in a production of *Julius Caesar*. Daugherty arranged for Harding to address the 1916 Republican presidential convention because he knew that people only had to see Harding and hear that magnificent rumbling voice to be convinced of his worthiness for higher office. In 1920, Daugherty convinced Harding, against Harding's better judgment, to run for the White House. Daugherty wasn't being facetious. He was serious.

"Daugherty, ever since the two had met, had carried in the back of his mind the idea that Harding would make a 'great President,'" Sullivan writes. "Sometimes, unconsciously, Daugherty expressed it, with more fidelity to exactness, 'a great-*looking* President.'" Harding entered the Republican convention that summer sixth among a field of six. Daugherty was unconcerned. The convention was deadlocked between the two leading candidates, so, Daugherty predicted, the delegates would be forced to look for an alternative. To whom else would they turn, in that desperate moment, if not to the man who radiated common sense and dignity and all that was presidential? In the early morning hours, as they gathered in the smoke-filled back rooms of the Blackstone Hotel in Chicago, the Republican party bosses threw up their hands and asked, wasn't there a candidate they could all agree on? And one name came immediately to mind: Harding! Didn't he *look* just like a presidential candidate? So Senator Harding became candidate Harding, and later that fall, after a campaign conducted from his front porch in Marion, Ohio, candidate Harding became President Harding. Harding served two years before dying unexpectedly of a stroke. He was, most historians agree, one of the worst presidents in American history.

1. The Dark Side of Thin-Slicing

Many people who looked at Warren Harding saw how extraordinarily handsome and distinguished-looking he was and jumped to the immediate—and entirely unwarranted—conclusion that he was a man of courage and intelligence and integrity. They didn't dig below the surface. The way he looked carried so many powerful connotations that it stopped the normal process of thinking dead in its tracks.

The Warren Harding error is the dark side of rapid cognition. It is at the root of   5
a good deal of prejudice and discrimination. It's why picking the right candidate
for a job is so difficult and why, on more occasions than we may care to admit,
utter mediocrities sometimes end up in positions of enormous responsibility. Part
of what it means to take thin-slicing and first impressions seriously is accepting the
fact that sometimes we can know more about someone or something in the blink
of an eye than we can after months of study. But we also have to acknowledge
and understand those circumstances when rapid cognition leads us astray.

2. Blink in Black and White

If you have a strongly pro-white pattern of associations, for example, there is
evidence that that will affect the way you behave in the presence of a black
person. It's not going to affect what you'll choose to say or feel or do. In all
likelihood, you won't be aware that you're behaving any differently than you
would around a white person. But chances are you'll lean forward a little less,
turn away slightly from him or her, close your body a bit, be a bit less expres-
sive, maintain less eye contact, stand a little farther away, smile a lot less,
hesitate and stumble over your words a bit more, laugh at jokes a bit less. Does
that matter? Of course it does. Suppose the conversation is a job interview. And
suppose the applicant is a black man. He's going to pick up on that uncertainty
and distance, and that may well make him a little less certain of himself, a little
less confident, and a little less friendly. And what will you think then? You may
well get a gut feeling that the applicant doesn't really have what it takes, or
maybe that he is a bit standoffish, or maybe that he doesn't really want the
job. What this unconscious first impression will do, in other words, is throw the
interview hopelessly off course.

Or what if the person you are interviewing is tall? I'm sure that on a conscious level we don't think that we treat tall people any differently from how we
treat short people. But there's plenty of evidence to suggest that height—
particularly in men—does trigger a certain set of very positive unconscious
associations. I polled about half of the companies on the Fortune 500 list—the
list of the largest corporations in the United States—asking each company
questions about its CEO. Overwhelmingly, the heads of big companies are,
as I'm sure comes as no surprise to anyone, white men, which undoubtedly
reflects some kind of implicit bias. But they are also almost all tall: in my sample,
I found that on average, male CEOs were just a shade under six feet tall. Given
that the average American male is five foot nine, that means that CEOs as a
group have about three inches on the rest of their sex. But this statistic actually
understates the matter. In the U.S. population, about 14.5 percent of all men
are six feet or taller. Among CEOs of Fortune 500 companies, that number is
58 percent. Even more striking, in the general American population, 3.9

percent of adult men are six foot two or taller. Among my CEO sample, almost a third were six foot two or taller.

. . . Of the tens of millions of American men below five foot six, a grand total of ten in my sample have reached the level of CEO, which says that being short is probably as much of a handicap to corporate success as being a woman or an African American. (The grand exception to all of these trends is American Express CEO Kenneth Chenault, who is both on the short side—five foot nine—and black. He must be a remarkable man to have overcome *two* Warren Harding errors.)

Is this a deliberate prejudice? Of course not. No one ever says dismissively of a potential CEO candidate that he's too short. This is quite clearly the kind of unconscious bias that the IAT [Implicit Association Test] picks up on.* Most of us, in ways that we are not entirely aware of, automatically associate leadership ability with imposing physical stature. We have a sense of what a leader is supposed to look like, and that stereotype is so powerful that when someone fits it, we simply become blind to other considerations. . . . Have you ever wondered why so many mediocre people find their way into positions of authority in companies and organizations? It's because when it comes to even the most important positions, our selection decisions are a good deal less rational than we think. We see a tall person and we swoon.

3. Taking Care of the Customer

The sales director of the Flemington Nissan dealership in the central New Jersey   10
town of Flemington is a man named Bob Golomb. Golomb is in his fifties, with short, thinning black hair and wire-rimmed glasses. He wears dark, conservative suits, so that he looks like a bank manager or a stockbroker. Since starting in the car business more than a decade ago, Golomb has sold, on average, about twenty cars a month, which is more than double what the average car salesman sells. On his desk Golomb has a row of five gold stars, given to him by his dealership in honor of his performance. In the world of car salesmen, Golomb is a virtuoso.

Being a successful salesman like Golomb is a task that places extraordinary demands on the ability to thin-slice. Someone you've never met walks into your dealership, perhaps about to make what may be one of the most expensive purchases of his or her life. Some people are insecure. Some are nervous. Some know exactly what they want. Some have no idea. Some know a great deal about cars and will be offended by a salesman who adopts a patronizing tone. Some are desperate for someone to take them by the hand and make sense of what seems to them like an overwhelming process. A salesman, if he or she

---

*The IAT is a computerized test designed to help people assess whether they have any biases they aren't aware of; go to https://implicit.harvard.edu/implicit/demo to see the variety of tests available.

is to be successful, has to gather all of that information—figuring out, say, the dynamic that exists between a husband and a wife, or a father and a daughter—process it, and adjust his or her own behavior accordingly, and do all of that within the first few moments of the encounter.

Bob Golomb is clearly the kind of person who seems to do that kind of thin-slicing effortlessly. He has a quiet, watchful intelligence and a courtly charm. He is thoughtful and attentive. He's a wonderful listener. He has, he says, three simple rules that guide his every action: "Take care of the customer. Take care of the customer. Take care of the customer." . . .

There is another even more important reason for Golomb's success, however. He follows, he says, another very simple rule. He may make a million snap judgments about a customer's needs and state of mind, but he tries never to judge anyone on the basis of his or her appearance. He assumes that everyone who walks in the door has the exact same chance of buying a car.

"You cannot prejudge people in this business," he said over and over when we met, and each time he used that phrase, his face took on a look of utter conviction. "Prejudging is the kiss of death. You have to give everyone your best shot. A green salesperson looks at a customer and says, 'This person looks like he can't afford a car,' which is the worst thing you can do, because sometimes the most unlikely person is flush," Golomb says. "I have a farmer I deal with, who I've sold all kinds of cars over the years. We seal our deal with a handshake, and he hands me a hundred-dollar bill and says, 'Bring it out to my farm.' We don't even have to write the order up. Now, if you saw this man, with his coveralls and his cow dung, you'd figure he was not a worthy customer. But in fact, as we say in the trade, he's all cashed up. Or sometimes people see a teenager and they blow him off. Well, then later that night, the teenager comes back with Mom and Dad, and they pick up a car, and it's the other salesperson that writes them up."

What Golomb is saying is that most salespeople are prone to a classic Warren   15
Harding error. They see someone, and somehow they let the first impression they have about that person's appearance drown out every other piece of information they manage to gather in that first instant. Golomb, by contrast, tries to be more selective. He has his antennae out to pick up on whether someone is confident or insecure, knowledgeable or naïve, trusting or suspicious—but from that thin-slicing flurry he tries to edit out those impressions based solely on physical appearance. The secret of Golomb's success is that he has decided to fight the Warren Harding error.

4. Spotting the Sucker

Why does Bob Golomb's strategy work so well? Because Warren Harding errors, it turns out, play an enormous, largely unacknowledged role in the car-selling business. Consider, for example, a remarkable social experiment conducted in the 1990s by a law professor in Chicago named Ian Ayres. Ayres put together a team of thirty-eight people—eighteen white men, seven white women, eight black women, and five black men. Ayres took great pains to make them appear as similar as possible. All were in their mid-twenties. All were of average attractiveness. All were instructed to dress in conservative casual wear: the women in blouses, straight skirts, and flat shoes; the men in polo shirts or button-downs, slacks, and loafers. All were given the same cover story. They were instructed to go to a total of 242 car dealerships in the Chicago area and present themselves as college-educated young professionals (sample job: systems analyst at a bank) living in the tony Chicago neighborhood of Streeterville. Their instructions for what to do were even more specific. They should walk in. They should wait to be approached by a salesperson. "I'm interested in buying this car," they were supposed to say, pointing to the lowest-priced car in the showroom. Then, after they heard the salesman's initial offer, they were instructed to bargain back and forth until the salesman either accepted an offer or refused to bargain any further—a process that in almost all cases took about forty minutes. What Ayres was trying to do was zero in on a very specific question: All other things being absolutely equal, how does skin color or gender affect the price that a salesman in a car dealership offers?

    The results were stunning. The white men received initial offers from the salesmen that were $725 above the dealer's invoice (that is, what the dealer paid for the car from the manufacturer). White women got initial offers of $935 above invoice. Black women were quoted a price, on average, of $1,195 above invoice. And black men? Their initial offer was $1,687 above invoice. Even after forty minutes of bargaining, the black men could get the price, on average, down to only $1,551 above invoice. After lengthy negotiations, Ayres's black men still ended up with a price that was nearly $800 higher than Ayres's white men were offered without having to say a word. . . .

    [The car salespeople] were silently picking up on the most immediate and obvious fact about Ayres's car buyers—their sex and their color—and sticking with that judgment even in the face of all manner of new and contradictory evidence. They were behaving just like the voters did in the 1920 presidential election when they took one look at Warren Harding, jumped to a conclusion, and stopped thinking. In the case of the voters, their error gave them one of the worst U.S. Presidents ever. In the case of the car salesmen, their decision to quote an outrageously high price to women and blacks alienated people who might otherwise have bought a car.

5. Think about Dr. King

What should we do about Warren Harding errors? The kinds of biases we're talking about here aren't so obvious that it's easy to identify a solution. If there's a law on the books that says that black people can't drink at the same water fountains as white people, the obvious solution is to change the law. But unconscious discrimination is a little bit trickier. The voters in 1920 didn't think they were being suckered by Warren Harding's good looks any more than Ayres's Chicago car dealers realized how egregiously they were cheating women and minorities or boards of directors realize how absurdly biased they are in favor of the tall. If something is happening outside of awareness, how on earth do you fix it?

The answer is that we are not helpless in the face of our first impressions. [20] They may bubble up from the unconscious—from behind a locked door inside of our brain—but just because something is outside of awareness doesn't mean it's outside of control. It is true, for instance, that you can take the Race IAT or the Career IAT as many times as you want and try as hard as you can to respond faster to the more problematic categories, and it won't make a whit of difference. But, believe it or not, if, before you take the IAT, I were to ask you to look over a series of pictures or articles about people like Martin Luther King or Nelson Mandela or Colin Powell, your reaction time would change. Suddenly it won't seem so hard to associate positive things with black people. "I had a student who used to take the IAT every day," [Mahzarin] Banaji says. "It was the first thing he did, and his idea was just to let the data gather as he went. Then this one day, he got a positive association with blacks. And he said, 'That's odd. I've never gotten that before,' because we've all tried to change our IAT score and we couldn't. But he's a track-and-field guy, and what he realized is that he'd spent the morning watching the Olympics."

Our first impressions are generated by our experiences and our environment, which means that we can change our first impressions—we can alter the way we thin-slice—by changing the experiences that comprise those impressions. If you are a white person who would like to treat black people as equals in every way—who would like to have a set of associations with blacks that are as positive as those that you have with whites—it requires more than a simple commitment to equality. It requires that you change your life so that you are exposed to minorities on a regular basis and become comfortable with them and familiar with the best of their culture, so that when you want to meet, hire, date, or talk with a member of a minority, you aren't betrayed by your hesitation and discomfort. Taking rapid cognition seriously—acknowledging the incredible power, for good and ill that first impressions play in our lives—requires that we take active steps to manage and control those impressions.

CONCLUSION: LISTENING WITH YOUR EYES: THE LESSONS OF *BLINK*

At the beginning of her career as a professional musician, Abbie Conant was in Italy, playing trombone for the Royal Opera of Turin. This was in 1980. That summer, she applied for eleven openings for various orchestra jobs throughout Europe. She got one response: The Munich Philharmonic Orchestra. "Dear Herr Abbie Conant," the letter began. In retrospect, that mistake should have tripped every alarm bell in Conant's mind.

The audition was held in the Deutsches Museum in Munich, since the orchestra's cultural center was still under construction. There were thirty-three candidates, and each played behind a screen, making them invisible to the selection committee. Screened auditions were rare in Europe at that time. But one of the applicants was the son of someone in one of the Munich orchestras, so, for the sake of fairness, the Philharmonic decided to make the first round of auditions blind. Conant was number sixteen. She played Ferdinand David's Konzertino for Trombone, which is the warhorse audition piece in Germany, and missed one note (she cracked a G). She said to herself, "That's it," and went backstage and started packing up her belongings to go home. But the committee thought otherwise. They were floored. Auditions are classic thin-slicing moments. Trained classical musicians say that they can tell whether a player is good or not almost instantly—sometimes in just the first few bars, sometimes even with just the first note—and with Conant they knew. After she left the audition room, the Philharmonic's music director, Sergiu Celibidache, cried out, "That's who we want!" The remaining seventeen players, waiting their turn to audition, were sent home. Somebody went backstage to find Conant. She came back into the audition room, and when she stepped out from behind the screen, she heard the Bavarian equivalent of whoa. *"Was ist'n des? Sacra di! Meine Goetter! Um Gottes willen!"* They were expecting Herr Conant. This was Frau Conant.

It was an awkward situation, to say the least. Celibidache was a conductor from the old school, an imperious and strong-willed man with very definite ideas about how music ought to be played—and about who ought to play music. What's more, this was Germany, the land where classical music was born. Once, just after the Second World War, the Vienna Philharmonic experimented with an audition screen and ended up with what the orchestra's former chairman, Otto Strasser, described in his memoir as a "grotesque situation": "An applicant qualified himself as the best, and as the screen was raised, there stood a Japanese before the stunned jury." To Strasser, someone who was Japanese simply could not play with any soul or fidelity music that was composed by a European. To Celibidache, likewise, a woman could not play the trombone. . . .

There were two more rounds of auditions. Conant passed both with flying colors. But once Celibidache and the rest of the committee saw her in the flesh, all those long-held prejudices began to compete with the winning first impression they had of her performance. She joined the orchestra, and Celibidache stewed. A year passed. In May of 1981, Conant was called to a meeting. She

25

was to be demoted to second trombone, she was told. No reason was given. Conant went on probation for a year, to prove herself again. It made no difference. "You know the problem," Celibidache told her. "We need a man for the solo trombone."

Conant had no choice but to take the case to court. In its brief, the orchestra argued, "The plaintiff does not possess the necessary physical strength to be a leader of the trombone section." Conant was sent to the Gautinger Lung Clinic for extensive testing. She blew through special machines, had a blood sample taken to measure her capacity for absorbing oxygen, and underwent a chest exam. She scored well above average. The nurse even asked if she was an athlete. The case dragged on. The orchestra claimed that Conant's "shortness of breath was overhearable" in her performance of the famous trombone solo in Mozart's *Requiem*, even though the guest conductor of those performances had singled out Conant for praise. A special audition in front of a trombone expert was set up. Conant played seven of the most difficult passages in the trombone repertoire. The expert was effusive. The orchestra claimed that she was unreliable and unprofessional. It was a lie. After eight years, she was reinstated as first trombone.

But then another round of battles began—that would last another five years—because the orchestra refused to pay her on par with her male colleagues. She won, again. She prevailed on every charge, and she prevailed because she could mount an argument that the Munich Philharmonic could not rebut. Sergiu Celibidache, the man complaining about her ability, had listened to her play Ferdinand David's Konzertino for Trombone under conditions of perfect objectivity, and in that unbiased moment, he had said, *"That's who we want!"* and sent the remaining trombonists packing. Abbie Conant was saved by the screen.

1. A Revolution in Classical Music

[O]ver the past few decades, the classical music world has undergone a revolution. In the United States, orchestra musicians began to organize themselves politically. They formed a union and fought for proper contracts, health benefits, and protections against arbitrary firing, and along with that came a push for fairness in hiring. Many musicians thought that conductors were abusing their power and playing favorites. They wanted the audition process to be formalized. That meant an official audition committee was established instead of a conductor making the decision all by himself. In some places, rules were put in place forbidding the judges from speaking among themselves during auditions, so that one person's opinion would not cloud the view of another. Musicians were identified not by name but by number. Screens were erected between the committee and the auditioner, and if the person auditioning cleared his or her throat or made any kind of identifiable sound—if they were wearing heels, for example, and stepped on a part of the floor that wasn't carpeted—they were ushered out and given a new number. And as these new rules were put in place around the country, an extraordinary thing happened: orchestras began to hire women.

In the past thirty years, since screens became commonplace, the number of women in the top U.S. orchestras has increased fivefold. "The very first time the new rules for auditions were used, we were looking for four new violinists," remembers Herb Weksleblatt, a tuba player for the Metropolitan Opera in New York, who led the fight for blind auditions at the Met in the mid-1960s. "And all of the winners were women. That would simply never have happened before. Up until that point, we had maybe three women in the whole orchestra. I remember that after it was announced that the four women had won, one guy was absolutely furious at me. He said, 'You're going to be remembered as the SOB who brought women into this orchestra.'"

What the classical music world realized was that what they had thought   30
was a pure and powerful first impression—listening to someone play—was in fact hopelessly corrupted. "Some people look like they sound better than they actually sound, because they look confident and have good posture," one musician, a veteran of many auditions, says. "Other people look awful when they play but sound great. Other people have that belabored look when they play, but you can't hear it in the sound. There is always this dissonance between what you see and hear. The audition begins the first second the person is in view. You think, Who is this nerd? Or, Who does this guy think he is?—just by the way they walk out with their instrument."

Julie Landsman, who plays principal French horn for the Metropolitan Opera in New York, says that she's found herself distracted by the position of someone's mouth. "If they put their mouthpiece in an unusual position, you might immediately think, Oh my God, it can't possibly work. There are so many possibilities. Some horn players use a brass instrument, and some use nickel-silver, and the kind of horn the person is playing tells you something about what city they come from, their teacher, and their school, and that pedigree is something that influences your opinion. I've been in auditions without screens, and I can assure you that I was prejudiced. I began to listen with my eyes, and there is no way that your eyes don't affect your judgment. The only true way to listen is with your ears and your heart."

In Washington, D.C., the National Symphony Orchestra hired Sylvia Alimena to play the French horn. Would she have been hired before the advent of screens? Of course not. The French horn—like the trombone—is a "male" instrument. More to the point, Alimena is tiny. She's five feet tall. In truth, that's an irrelevant fact. As another prominent horn player says, "Sylvia can blow a house down." But if you were to look at her before you really listened to her, you would not be able to hear that power, because what you saw would so contradict what you heard. There is only one way to make a proper snap judgment of Sylvia Alimena, and that's from behind a screen.

2. A Small Miracle

There is a powerful lesson in classical music's revolution. Why, for so many years, were conductors so oblivious to the corruption of their snap judgments? Because we are often careless with our powers of rapid cognition. We don't know where our first impressions come from or precisely what they mean, so we don't always appreciate their fragility. Taking our powers of rapid cognition seriously means we have to acknowledge the subtle influences that can alter or undermine or bias the products of our unconscious. Judging music sounds like the simplest of tasks. It is not, any more than sipping cola or rating chairs or tasting jam is easy. Without a screen, Abbie Conant would have been dismissed before she played a note. With a screen, she was suddenly good enough for the Munich Philharmonic.

And what did orchestras do when confronted with their prejudice? They solved the problem, and that's the second lesson of *Blink*. Too often we are resigned to what happens in the blink of an eye. It doesn't seem like we have much control over whatever bubbles to the surface from our unconscious. But we do, and if we can control the environment in which rapid cognition takes place, then we can control rapid cognition. We can prevent the people fighting wars or staffing emergency rooms or policing the streets from making mistakes.

The fact that there are now women playing for symphony orchestras is not 35 a trivial change. It matters because it has opened up a world of possibility for a group that had been locked out of opportunity. It also matters because by fixing the first impression at the heart of the audition—by judging purely on the basis of ability—orchestras now hire better musicians, and better musicians mean better music. And how did we get better music? Not by rethinking the entire classical music enterprise or building new concert halls or pumping in millions of new dollars, but by paying attention to the tiniest detail, the first two seconds of the audition.

When Julie Landsman auditioned for the role of principal French horn at the Met, the screens had just gone up in the practice hall. At the time, there were no women in the brass section of the orchestra, because everyone "knew" that women could not play the horn as well as men. But Landsman came and sat down and played—and she played well. "I knew in my last round that

I had won before they told me," she says. "It was because of the way I performed the last piece. I held on to the last high C for a very long time, just to leave no doubt in their minds. And they started to laugh, because it was above and beyond the call of duty." But when they declared her the winner and she stepped out from behind the screen, there was a gasp. It wasn't just that she was a woman, and female horn players were rare, as had been the case with Conant. And it wasn't just that bold, extended high C, which was the kind of macho sound that they expected from a man only. It was because they *knew* her. Landsman had played for the Met before as a substitute. Until they listened to her with just their ears, however, they had no idea she was so good. When the screen created a pure *Blink* moment, a small miracle happened, the kind of small miracle that is always possible when we take charge of the first two seconds: they saw her for who she truly was.

Questions for Critical Reading

1. Did Gladwell succeed in persuading you that we can — and should — take control of the first two seconds and thus avoid making wrong assumptions? If so, how did he persuade you? If not, where did he go wrong?

2. As you may have noticed, the points of the stories about Warren Harding, Bob Golomb, and Abbie Conant are stated only after the stories are told; these points aren't disclosed until paragraphs 4–5, 15, and 33–34, respectively. How would you summarize the point of each story? If you, like Gladwell, were writing to an audience of laypeople to communicate an argument about rapid cognition, would you have chosen point-last organization for all three stories? Why or why not?

3. Like authors of many genres, Gladwell draws on both primary and secondary research to make his argument. ("Primary" refers to research conducted by the author; "secondary" refers to research conducted by others but cited by the author.) Gladwell could have relied only on secondary research; for example, he could have chosen to make his argument without polling about half the Fortune 500 companies (see para. 7) or without interviewing Bob Golomb (see para. 14). How persuasive did you find the additional evidence that Gladwell was able to provide based on his own research? Why? When might you as a writer want to do a bit of your own research in addition to citing others' work?

4. Authors across genres are faced with the choice of whether to present information in paragraph form or in a more visual form, such as a graph, pie chart, bulleted list, or table. For example, when Gladwell discusses Ayres's research on how gender and skin color affect what people pay for a car, he could have presented the dollar amounts quoted by the salespeople in a table, perhaps

Connections

with one column each for white men, white women, black women, and black men. Instead, however, he presents the information in paragraph form. Consider the following passage:

> The white men received initial offers from the salesmen that were $725 above the dealer's invoice (that is, what the dealer paid for the car from the manufacturer). White women got initial offers of $935 above invoice. Black women were quoted a price, on average, of $1,195 above invoice. And black men? Their initial offer was $1,687 above invoice. (para. 17)

If you had written *Blink*, how would you have chosen to present this information, given your audience and purpose? Why?

5. You've probably noticed that authors in various genres will occasionally use a quotation within a quotation, a strategy that can sometimes help them better achieve their purpose. (If you choose to do this yourself, note that writers following U.S. conventions generally signal the quotation within a quotation by using single quotation marks. If the quotation within a quotation ends the sentence, there would be three quotation marks—one single followed by a double.) Consider why Gladwell might have chosen to use a quotation within a quotation at the end of this passage:

> "The very first time the new rules for auditions were used, we were looking for four new violinists," remembers Herb Weksleblatt, a tuba player for the Metropolitan Opera in New York, who led the fight for blind auditions at the Met in the mid-1960s. "And all of the winners were women. That would simply never have happened before. Up until that point, we had maybe three women in the whole orchestra. I remember that after it was announced that the four women had won, one guy was absolutely furious at me. He said, 'You're going to be remembered as the SOB who brought women into this orchestra.'" (para. 29)

If you were Gladwell, would you have chosen to use the quotation within the quotation, or would you have simply ended the quotation one sentence earlier? Why?

Making Connections

6. Readers of some (not all) genres tend to have relatively flexible expectations about pronoun usage. Although the choice of which pronouns to use—or whether to use pronouns at all—may seem trivial, such subtleties can shape readers' responses. Consider why three writers in this chapter choose to refer to people by using words such as "we" and "our" rather than "they" or "their" (or the noun "people"). You can see examples in the following passages—one from *Blink*, one from David Straker's online encyclopedia article (p. 202), and one from Amel S. Abdullah's advice essay (p. 249). Compare the original passages to the altered passages to see if the changes in pronouns affect your response. (Differences are italicized.)

Original Passage	Altered Passage
Our first impressions are generated by *our* experiences and *our* environment, which means that *we* can change *our* first impressions — *we* can alter the way *we* thin-slice — by changing the experiences that comprise those impressions. (Gladwell, para. 21)	*People's* first impressions are generated by *their* experiences and *their* environment, which means that *they* can change *their* first impressions — *they* can alter the way *they* thin-slice — by changing the experiences that comprise those impressions.
We will even tend to blame victims (of *us* and of others) for their fate as *we* seek to distance *ourselves* from thoughts of suffering the same plight. (Straker, para. 4)	*People* will even tend to blame victims (of *themselves* and of others) for their fate as *they* seek to distance *themselves* from thoughts of suffering the same plight.
Feeling hurt or annoyed, *we* dream up scenarios that blame the people who have hurt *us*. (Abdullah, para. 5)	Feeling hurt or annoyed, *people* dream up scenarios that blame the people who have hurt *them*.

Although Gladwell, Straker, and Abdullah are using different genres, some aspects of their rhetorical situations may be similar. Why might they have chosen to use pronouns such as "we" and "our" rather than "they" or "their" (or the noun "people")? Which versions of the passages do you prefer? Why?

7. Regardless of the genre you choose to use, punctuation can be a powerful tool for emphasis. When you read the following excerpts from *Blink* and Sarah Adams's radio essay "Be Cool to the Pizza Dude" (p. 255), see if you notice a pattern in how they use colons [:], and consider when you might want to use them yourself.

Blink

In that instant, as Daugherty sized up Harding, an idea came to him that would alter American history: Wouldn't that man make a great President? (para. 1)

And as these new rules were put in place around the country, an extraordinary thing happened: orchestras began to hire women. (para. 28)

"Be Cool to the Pizza Dude"

If I have one operating philosophy about life it is this: "Be cool to the pizza delivery dude" (para. 1)

Let's face it: We've all taken jobs just to have a job because some money is better than none. (para. 3)

How would you describe the common elements in these examples? In what situations might you use colons in your own writing?

Writing: Your Turn

1. Write a summary of the excerpt from *Blink,* making sure to distinguish between Gladwell's overarching argument and his subpoints. When you finish your summary, give it to some classmates and ask them for feedback on whether it accurately distills Gladwell's most important points. Consider your classmates' ideas — along with ideas of your own — when you revise. For strategies to use when writing a summary, see p. 23.

2. You might recall that Gladwell mentions the Implicit Association Test (paras. 9 and 20), a computerized test designed to help individuals assess whether they might have a preference for a particular demographic (e.g., male, female, black, white, young, old). Go to https://implicit.harvard.edu/implicit/demo to take an IAT yourself, and write a reflection on your experience of taking the test. In your reflection, you might discuss one or more of the following: what it was like to take the test, what you think of your results, and what you think of the IAT's overall validity. Share your reflection with your classmates so that they can learn from your experience and so that you can get ideas for revision. For ideas on writing a reflection, see p. 27.

Black Men and Public Space

Brent Staples

This classic piece, originally published over two decades ago in *Ms.* magazine, discusses the author's experience as a black man who has "learned to smother the rage" he feels when people assume he's a criminal. Staples tells us that "being perceived as dangerous is a hazard in itself" — something we know is still true today due to the number of innocent, unarmed black men who continue to be killed by people who assume the worst of them.

Currently a member of the *New York Times* editorial board, Staples has published numerous editorials and reviews. He is also the author of an acclaimed memoir, *Parallel Time: Growing Up in Black and White* (1994).

Focus on Genre In "Black Men and Public Space," Staples draws on strategies used in several genres, especially creative nonfiction. You'll notice a common creative nonfiction move in his final paragraph, which ends with a symbolic image — a reference to the cowbells that hikers wear in bear country. To appreciate this reference, it will help to know that hikers wear cowbells to warn bears of their presence, so that the bears aren't surprised and are thus less likely to pose a threat to the hikers. As you read, consider Staples's purpose in referring to the cowbell, as well as his overall purpose in writing the essay.

◄O►

My first victim was a woman—white, well dressed, probably in her early twenties. I came upon her late one evening on a deserted street in Hyde Park, a relatively affluent neighborhood in an otherwise mean, impoverished section of Chicago. As I swung onto the avenue behind her, there seemed to be a discreet, uninflammatory distance between us. Not so. She cast back a worried glance. To her, the youngish black man—a broad six feet two inches with a beard and billowing hair, both hands shoved into the pockets of a bulky military jacket—seemed menacingly close. After a few more quick glimpses, she picked up her pace and was soon running in earnest. Within seconds she disappeared into a cross street.

That was more than a decade ago. I was twenty-two years old, a graduate student newly arrived at the University of Chicago. It was in the echo of that terrified woman's footfalls that I first began to know the unwieldy inheritance I'd come into—the ability to alter public space in ugly ways. It was clear that she thought herself the quarry of a mugger, a rapist, or worse. Suffering a bout of insomnia, however, I was stalking sleep, not defenseless wayfarers. As a softy who is scarcely able to take a knife to a raw chicken—let alone hold one to a person's throat—I was surprised, embarrassed, and dismayed all at once. Her flight made me feel like an accomplice in tyranny. It also made it clear that I was indistinguishable from the muggers who occasionally seeped into the area from the surrounding ghetto. That first encounter, and those that followed, signified that a vast, unnerving gulf lay between nighttime pedestrians—particularly women—and me. And I soon gathered that being perceived as dangerous is a hazard in itself. I only needed to turn a corner into a dicey situation, or crowd some frightened, armed person in a foyer somewhere, or make an errant move after being pulled over by a policeman. Where fear and weapons meet—and they often do in urban America—there is always the possibility of death.

In that first year, my first away from my hometown, I was to become thoroughly familiar with the language of fear. At dark, shadowy intersections, I could cross in front of a car stopped at a traffic light and elicit the *thunk, thunk, thunk, thunk* of the driver—black, white, male, or female—hammering down the door locks. On less traveled streets after dark, I grew accustomed to but never comfortable with people crossing to the other side of the street rather than pass me. Then there were the standard unpleasantries with policemen, doormen, bouncers, cabdrivers, and others whose business it is to screen out troublesome individuals *before* there is any nastiness.

I moved to New York nearly two years ago and I have remained an avid night walker. In central Manhattan, the near-constant crowd cover minimizes tense one-on-one street encounters. Elsewhere—in SoHo, for example, where sidewalks are narrow and tightly spaced buildings shut out the sky—things can get very taut indeed.

After dark, on the warren-like streets of Brooklyn where I live, I often see   5
women who fear the worst from me. They seem to have set their faces on neutral, and with their purse straps strung across their chests bandolier-style they forge ahead as though bracing themselves against being tackled. I understand, of course, that the danger they perceive is not a hallucination. Women are particularly vulnerable to street violence, and young black males are drastically overrepresented among the perpetrators of that violence. Yet these truths are no solace against the kind of alienation that comes of being ever the suspect, a fearsome entity with whom pedestrians avoid making eye contact.

It is not altogether clear to me how I reached the ripe old age of twenty-two without being conscious of the lethality nighttime pedestrians attributed to me. Perhaps it was because in Chester, Pennsylvania, the small, angry industrial town where I came of age in the 1960s, I was scarcely noticeable against a backdrop of gang warfare, street knifings, and murders. I grew up one of the good boys, had perhaps a half-dozen fistfights. In retrospect, my shyness of combat has clear sources.

As a boy, I saw countless tough guys locked away; I have since buried several, too. They were babies, really—a teenage cousin, a brother of twenty-two, a childhood friend in his mid-twenties—all gone down in episodes of bravado played out in the streets. I came to doubt the virtues of intimidation early on. I chose, perhaps unconsciously, to remain a shadow—timid, but a survivor.

The fearsomeness mistakenly attributed to me in public places often has a perilous flavor. The most frightening of these confusions occurred in the late 1970s and early 1980s, when I worked as a journalist in Chicago. One day, rushing into the office of a magazine I was writing for with a deadline story in hand, I was mistaken for a burglar. The office manager called security and, with an ad hoc posse, pursued me through the labyrinthine halls, nearly to my editor's door. I had no way of proving who I was. I could only move briskly toward the company of someone who knew me.

Another time I was on assignment for a local paper and killing time before an interview. I entered a jewelry store on the city's affluent Near North Side. The proprietor excused herself and returned with an enormous red Doberman pinscher straining at the end of a leash. She stood, the dog extended toward me, silent to my questions, her eyes bulging nearly out of her head. I took a cursory look around, nodded, and bade her good night.

Relatively speaking, however, I never fared as badly as another black male   10
journalist. He went to nearby Waukegan, Illinois, a couple of summers ago to work on a story about a murderer who was born there. Mistaking the reporter

for the killer, police officers hauled him from his car at gunpoint and but for his press credentials would probably have tried to book him. Such episodes are not uncommon. Black men trade tales like this all the time.

Over the years, I learned to smother the rage I felt at so often being taken for a criminal. Not to do so would surely have led to madness. I now take precautions to make myself less threatening. I move about with care, particularly late in the evening. I give a wide berth to nervous people on subway platforms during the wee hours, particularly when I have exchanged business clothes for jeans. If I happen to be entering a building behind some people who appear skittish, I may walk by, letting them clear the lobby before I return, so as not to seem to be following them. I have been calm and extremely congenial on those rare occasions when I've been pulled over by the police.

And on late-evening constitutionals I employ what has proved to be an excellent tension reducing measure: I whistle melodies from Beethoven and Vivaldi and the more popular classical composers. Even steely New Yorkers hunching toward nighttime destinations seem to relax, and occasionally they even join in the tune. Virtually everybody seems to sense that a mugger wouldn't be warbling bright, sunny selections from Vivaldi's *Four Seasons*. It is my equivalent of the cowbell that hikers wear when they know they are in bear country.

Questions for Critical Reading

1. What do you think might have been Staples's purpose in writing this piece and submitting it to *Ms.* (a magazine targeting a readership of well-educated left-leaning women)? For you as a reader, did the piece fulfill what you take to be its purpose? Why or why not?

2. Throughout his career as a journalist, Staples has often chosen *not* to draw on personal experience. Indeed, he could have written this piece without doing so. He could have, for instance, focused only on others' experiences, as he does in paragraph 10 when he recounts the story of the black male reporter hauled away at gunpoint. Had Staples chosen not to discuss his personal experience, how might his piece have affected you differently? How might you as a writer decide when to draw on personal experience and when not to?

3. As you've probably noticed, writers across genres sometimes use dashes to help them achieve their purposes. Consider, for example, the effect of the dashes in the following two passages:

> Where fear and weapons meet—and they often do in urban America—there is always the possibility of death. (para. 2)

At dark, shadowy intersections, I could cross in front of a car stopped at a traffic light and elicit the *thunk, thunk, thunk, thunk* of the driver—black, white, male, or female—hammering down the door locks. (para. 3)

In the first example, Staples could have replaced his dashes with commas or parentheses; in the second example, he could have replaced his dashes with parentheses—yet he chose not to. How might these two passages have affected you differently if Staples hadn't used dashes? Why do you think he used them in these sentences?

Making Connections

4. The way Staples ends his essay provides an interesting contrast to the way Malcolm Gladwell ends his popular nonfiction book (p. 207)—and examining this contrast may help you develop some ideas for deciding how to end your own pieces. Unlike Staples, Gladwell explicitly refers to his main point when he ends *Blink*; he writes, "When the screen [hiding the identity of Julie Landsman] created a pure *Blink* moment, a small miracle happened, the kind of small miracle that is always possible when we take charge of the first two seconds: they saw her for who she truly was" (para. 36). Here Gladwell explicitly connects his final example to his overarching point that we can take charge of the first two seconds—that we can control our first impressions (and thus avoid wrong assumptions).

In contrast, Staples ends with a move made by many creative nonfiction writers: he leaves us with a symbolic image that implicitly reinforces the focus of his essay. Describing what he does to prevent people from assuming the worst about him, he tells us that he whistles melodies from classical composers, noting that this whistling is his "equivalent of the cowbell that hikers wear when they know they are in bear country" (para. 12).

What do you take to be the point of this ending, and how does it reinforce Staples's purpose as a writer? Why might Staples have chosen to end with a symbolic image rather than stating his point more explicitly, as Gladwell does? How might you as a writer decide when to end an essay by referring to your point explicitly and when to end by referencing it more implicitly?

5. Although Staples draws on many strategies used by creative nonfiction writers, he also draws on strategies used by writers who try to persuade readers of an explicit point. Just as Amel S. Abdullah does in her advice essay "Assuming the Best of Others" (p. 249), Staples addresses potential objections that a reader might have before going on to maintain his point. Consider why both writers might have made this move:

"Black Men and Public Space"

I understand, of course, that the danger [women] perceive is not a hallucination. Women are particularly vulnerable to street violence, and young black

males are drastically overrepresented among the perpetrators of that violence. Yet these truths are no solace against the kind of alienation that comes
of being ever the suspect. (para. 5)

"Assuming the Best of Others"

Making "seventy excuses" [for other people's bad behavior] does not mean
that we should ignore or dismiss bad or hurtful behavior, but that we should
try to understand the circumstances behind it when it occurs. (para. 4)

Neither author had to address potential objections, but both chose to make
this move anyway. For you as a reader, did this move add to the persuasive-
ness of the each author's point? Why or why not? When might you as a
writer want to address potential objections?

Writing: Your Turn

1. Write a rhetorical analysis of "Black Men and Public Space," discussing how
effective you find the writing to be, given Staples's audience and purpose.
Many students find that writing a rhetorical analysis helps them to better
understand writers' choices and thus to see more alternatives in their own
writing. Share your analysis with some of your classmates so that they can gain
insight into ways of using language and so that they can give you suggestions
for revision. For ideas on how to write a rhetorical analysis, see p. 31.

2. Drawing on your personal experience, write a creative nonfiction piece about
a time (or times) when someone assumed the worst about you or a time
when you assumed the worst about someone else. Try to represent your
experience in a way that speaks to others — that makes it relevant to someone
other than yourself. (Your goal might, for example, be to change how your
readers behave or to get them to understand what it's like to be in your
shoes.) Share your piece with your classmates, and if they say it speaks to
them, consider submitting it to your campus newspaper or literary journal.
For ideas on writing creative nonfiction, see p. 77.

Mere Exposure and Racial Prejudice: Exposure to Other-Race Faces Increases Liking for Strangers of That Race

Leslie A. Zebrowitz, Benjamin White, and Kristin Wieneke

"Mere Exposure and Racial Prejudice" suggests that there's a way to pre vent people from assuming the worst about others of a different race. It reports on research conducted at Brandeis University and was originally published in *Social Cognition*, a scholarly journal published by the International Social Cognition Network.

Focus on Genre   The following excerpt of a sociology research report includes the abstract (an overview printed before the text of the article) and the final paragraph of the conclusion (excerpted from a section entitled "General Discussion"). Note that reading only certain sections of a scholarly article is a common strategy among academic readers. If these sections reveal that an article is relevant to the readers' interests, they'll often read the rest of it. This selective reading strategy may help you when you do your own research.

One challenge of reading academic work like "Mere Exposure" is the often-unfamiliar vocabulary. In the excerpt that follows, key terms include "subliminal" (seen too quickly to be noticed on a conscious level) and "supraliminal" (seen long enough to be noticed). If you encounter other terms assuming specialized knowledge you don't have, experiment with this strategy: instead of stopping to puzzle over unfamiliar words and phrases, just keep reading, focusing on the phrases that do make sense. You can always take a second pass through the selection after reading it once to get the gist of it.

◄○►

ABSTRACT

White participants were exposed to other-race or own-race faces to test the generalized mere exposure hypothesis in the domain of face perception, namely that exposure to a set of faces yields increased liking for similar faces that have never been seen. In Experiment 1, rapid supraliminal exposures to Asian faces increased White participants' subsequent liking for a different set of Asian faces. In Experiment 2, subliminal exposures to Black faces increased White participants' subsequent liking for a different set of Black faces. The findings are consistent with prominent explanations for mere exposure effects as well as with the familiar face overgeneralization hypothesis that prejudice derives in part from negative reactions to faces that deviate from the familiar own-race prototype.

GENERAL DISCUSSION

The present findings would seem to have significant applied value. First, the documentation of an effect using supraliminal faces demonstrates the generalizability of the results to real world exposures. Second, other research has shown that basic mere exposure effects are non-trivial, extending beyond marks on a rating scale. For example, mere exposure has been shown to increase incipient smiles toward previously exposed faces (Harmon-Jones & Allen, 2001), increase willingness to help an individual to whom one was exposed (Burger, Soroka, Gonzago, Murphy, & Somervell, 2001), and increase agreement with the judgments of an individual whose face had been subliminally exposed (Bornstein, Leone, & Galley, 1987). Generalized mere exposure effects are likely to have similar consequences. If so, then simple interventions, such as showing more racial minority faces on television and public billboards, could enhance White people's initial evaluative reactions toward unknown members of racial outgroups as well as positive behavioral responses toward newly encountered individuals of that race. It could also temper the negative reactions that accrue to individuals who, regardless of race, have a more prototypical other-race appearance. Such effects are not trivial, including both longer prison sentences and more frequent

This research was supported by Grants MH066836 and K02MH72603 from the National Institute of Mental Health to the first author. The content is solely the responsibility of the authors and does not necessarily represent the official views of the National Institute of Mental Health or the National Institutes of Health. The authors thank Yuko Yotsumoto and Masako Kikuchi for their help programming the software to run Experiment 2.

Correspondence concerning this article should be addressed to Leslie A. Zebrowitz, Department of Psychology, MS 062, Brandeis University, Waltham, MA 02454. E-mail: Zebrowitz@brandeis.edu.

death sentences for convicted criminals who have a more prototypical Black appearance (Blair et al., 2004; Eberhardt et al., 2006). Interventions designed to increase exposure to other-race faces would seem particularly important given the finding that repeated exposure to own-race faces can foster decreased liking for faces of another race (Smith et al., 2007). Ameliorative effects of other-race exposure would be consistent with recent evidence that inter-group contact can reduce prejudice even when the ideal conditions specified by Allport (1954) are not met (Pettigrew & Tropp, 2006).

REFERENCES

Allport, G. W. (1954). *The nature of prejudice.* Oxford, England: Addison-Wesley.

Blair, I. V., Judd, C. M., & Chapleau, K. M. (2004). The influence of Afrocentric facial features in criminal sentencing. *Psychological Science, 15,* 674-679.

Bornstein, R. F., Leone, D. R., & Galley, D. J. (1987). The generalizibility of subliminal mere exposure effects: Influence of stimuli perceived without awareness on social behavior. *Journal of Personality and Social Psychology, 53,* 1070-1079.

Burger, J. M., Soroka, S., Gonzago, K., Murphy, E., & Somervell, E. (2001). The effect of fleeting attraction on compliance to requests. *Personality and Social Psychology Bulletin, 27,* 1378-1586.

Eberhardt, J. L., Davies, P. G., & Purdie-Vaughns, V. J. (2006). Looking death-worthy: Perceived stereotypicality of black defendants predicts capital-sentencing outcomes. *Psychological Science, 17,* 383-386.

Harmon-Jones, E., & Allen, J. J. B. (2001). The role of affect in the mere exposure effect: Evidence from psychophysiological and individual differences approaches. *Personality and Social Psychology Bulletin, 27,* 889-898.

Pettigrew, T. F., & Tropp, L. R. (2006). A meta-analytic test of intergroup contact theory. *Journal of Personality and Social Psychology, 90,* 751-783.

Smith, P. K., Dijksterhuis, A., & Chaiken, S. (2007). Subliminal exposure to faces and racial attitudes: Exposure to whites makes whites like blacks less. *Journal of Experimental Social Psychology,* doi:10.1016/j.jesp.2007.01.006.

Questions for Critical Reading

1. Although this reading selection may have been difficult for you since you're not part of the target audience, there are strategies you can use to make more sense of it. Take a few minutes to reread the conclusion and underline the words and phrases most familiar to you. Talk about what you underlined with a classmate and then discuss whether the ideas resonate with your own experience. Do you think the authors might be right? Why or why not?

After you talk to your classmates, your instructor may ask you to participate in a whole-class discussion about whether the authors do indeed have insights that could reduce racial prejudice.

2. Since the key findings of research reports are discussed in their abstracts, readers use abstracts to decide whether or not they want to read other sections of the article and, if so, what questions they will bring to the reading. If you were a sociologist, would you want to read more of this article? Why or why not? What questions would you bring to your reading?

3. Writers across genres often use repetition to drive home a point or to emphasize similarities, but repetition can also be used to emphasize difference. Consider how the authors repeat exact words as well as sentence structure in their abstract, and compare what they've written to an altered version that doesn't repeat the sentence structure. Although only one phrase in the second sentence has been moved, see if you have an opinion about which version would work better in the abstract.

Original Passage	Altered Passage
In Experiment 1, rapid supraliminal exposures to Asian faces increased White participants' subsequent liking for a different set of Asian faces. In Experiment 2, subliminal exposures to Black faces increased White participants' subsequent liking for a different set of Black faces.	In Experiment 1, rapid supraliminal exposures to Asian faces increased White participants' subsequent liking for a different set of Asian faces. Subliminal exposures to Black faces increased White participants' subsequent liking for a different set of Black faces in Experiment 2.

If you were one of the authors, would you lobby for one version over the other? Why or why not?

4. Although extensive citation of others' research can be distracting for readers new to academic genres, recall that citation is a hallmark of academic genres—one that generally allows authors to better fulfill their purposes. (Note, however, that citation styles vary from discipline to discipline.) Consider the effect of the authors' citations in the following passage from their conclusion:

> [O]ther research has shown that basic mere exposure effects are non-trivial, extending beyond marks on a rating scale. For example, mere exposure has been shown to increase incipient smiles toward previously exposed faces (Harmon-Jones & Allen, 2001), increase willingness to help an individual to whom one was exposed (Burger, Soroka, Gonzago, Murphy, & Somervell, 2001), and increase agreement with the judgments of an individual whose face had been subliminally exposed (Bornstein, Leone, & Galley, 1987).

For you as a reader, what was the effect of the citations? How would your response to "Mere Exposure" have been different if the authors hadn't referred to others' research?

Making Connections

5. Recall that writers across genres often add to their persuasive power by explaining *why* an idea or piece of information is important. Consider how this move is made in both "Mere Exposure" and Malcolm Gladwell's *Blink* (p. 207):

> **"Mere Exposure"**
>
> The present findings would seem to have significant applied value. First, the documentation of an effect using supraliminal faces demonstrates the generalizability of the results to real world exposures. (para. 2)
>
> **Blink**
>
> The fact that there are now women playing for symphony orchestras is not a trivial change. It matters because it has opened up a world of possibility for a group that had been locked out of opportunity. It also matters because by fixing the first impression at the heart of the audition—by judging purely on the basis of ability—orchestras now hire better musicians, and better musicians mean better music. (para. 35)

How would you have responded differently to "Mere Exposure" and *Blink* had the authors not included these passages explaining the importance of their topics? Think about the last piece of writing that you submitted; how did you establish the importance of your topic (or, if you didn't, how could you have)?

6. Average sentence length, like average paragraph length, often varies from genre to genre. The longest sentences in academic genres, for instance, tend to be longer than those in many other genres. Compare the first sentence of "Mere Exposure" to the first sentences of the public service anouncement (PSA) "United by Mission" (p. 287):

> **"Mere Exposure"**
>
> White participants were exposed to other-race or own-race faces to test the generalized mere exposure hypothesis in the domain of face perception, namely that exposure to a set of faces yields increased liking for similar faces that have never been seen.
>
> **"United by Mission"**
>
> We come from different places. We come to different conclusions. But underneath it all, we share a passion for improving the human condition.

Considering the different purposes and audiences of each passage—as well as the different situations in which readers encounter these sentences—why might the authors of the two passages have chosen to use such different sentence lengths? When might you as a writer want to keep your sentences on the shorter side, and when might you choose to use longer sentences?

Writing

Writing: Your Turn

1. Academic genres are often hard for students because they're written for experts who are familiar with jargon and can more easily process complex ideas and information. Recall that one strategy for navigating academic genres is to "translate" important passages into language that can be more easily understood. To this end, translate the two-paragraph excerpt of "Mere Exposure" so that it might be more easily understood by first-year college students. After you finish, share what you've written with some classmates to see how well your translation worked. Ask them what they think is gained and lost in the translation, and consider their ideas when you revise.

2. If you were persuaded by Zebrowitz, White, and Wieneke's claim that seeing more minority faces in the public sphere would help combat bias, identify a newspaper or magazine that you feel underrepresents a particular population and write a letter to the editor arguing that this underrepresentation is a problem that should be rectified. Before you submit your letter for publication, ask your classmates how it might be even more persuasive, and consider their feedback when you revise. For ideas on writing a letter to the editor, see p. 62.

C. P. Ellis

Studs Terkel

A classic text written in 1980, "C. P. Ellis" discusses Ellis's experience as a former Ku Klux Klan (KKK) leader who comes to realize that his assumptions about blacks (and Jews and Catholics) are dead wrong. Ultimately, "C. P. Ellis" provides us with insight into how a person can end up being deeply prejudiced — and what it takes for that person to begin overcoming prejudice.

Ellis's story was originally included in Studs Terkel's *American Dreams: Lost and Found*. Terkel was a well-known oral historian, radio broadcaster, and author. His books include *Working: People Talk about What They Do All Day and How They Feel about What They Do* (1974) and *"The Good War": An Oral History of World War II* (1984), for which he won the Pulitzer Prize for General Nonfiction.

Focus on Genre   "C. P. Ellis" is an oral history; Terkel interviewed C. P. Ellis and then wrote down and edited a version of what Ellis told him. Thus, the following narrative is written in the first person ("I") from Ellis's point of view, even though it was actually written down by Terkel. Oral history, then, is an especially complex genre — one shaped by the genres that interviewees draw on when they talk to historians as well as by the genres that historians draw on when they write. As you read "C. P. Ellis," consider the ways that Terkel might have manipulated Ellis's narrative and thus shaped your experience as a reader.

◄○►

We're in his office in Durham, North Carolina. He is the business manager of the International Union of Operating Engineers. On the wall is a plaque: "Certificate of Service, in recognition to C. P. Ellis, for your faithful service to the city in having served as a member of the Durham Human Relations Council. February 1977."

At one time, he had been president (exalted cyclops) of the Durham chapter of the Ku Klux Klan.

He is fifty-three years old.

My father worked in a textile mill in Durham. He died at forty-eight years old. It was probably from cotton dust. Back then, we never heard of brown lung. I was about seventeen years old and had a mother and sister depending on somebody to make a livin'. It was just barely enough insurance to cover his burial. I had to quit school and go to work. I was about eighth grade when I quit.

My father worked hard but never had enough money to buy decent clothes. When I went to school, I never seemed to have adequate clothes to wear. I always left school late afternoon with a sense of inferiority. The other kids had nice clothes, and I just had what Daddy could buy. I still got some of those inferiority feelin's now that I have to overcome once in a while.

I loved my father. He would go with me to ball games. We'd go fishin' together. I was really ashamed of the way he'd dress. He would take this money and give it to me instead of putting it on himself. I always had the feeling about somebody looking at him and makin' fun of him and makin' fun of me. I think it had to do somethin' with my life.

My father and I were very close, but we didn't talk about too many intimate things. He did have a drinking problem. During the week, he would work every day, but weekends he was ready to get plastered. I can understand when a guy looks at his paycheck and looks at his bills, and he's worked hard all the week, and his bills are larger than his paycheck. He'd done the best he could the entire week, and there seemed to be no hope. It's an illness thing. Finally you just say: "The heck with it. I'll just get drunk and forget it."

My father was out of work during the depression, and I remember going with him to the finance company uptown, and he was turned down. That's something that's always stuck.

My father never seemed to be happy. It was a constant struggle with him just like it was for me. It's very seldom I'd see him laugh. He was just tryin' to figure out what he could do from one day to the next.

After several years pumping gas at a service station, I got married. We had to have children. Four. One child was born blind and retarded, which was a real additional expense to us. He's never spoken a word. He doesn't know me when

5

I go to see him. But I see him, I hug his neck. I talk to him, tell him I love him. I don't know whether he knows me or not, but I know he's well taken care of. All my life, I had work, never a day without work, worked all the overtime I could get and still could not survive financially. I began to say there's somethin' wrong with this country. I worked my butt off and just never seemed to break even.

I had some real great ideas about this great nation. (Laughs.) They say to abide by the law, go to church, do right and live for the Lord, and everything'll work out. But it didn't work out. It just kept gettin' worse and worse.

I was workin' a bread route. The highest I made one week was seventy-five dollars. The rent on our house was about twelve dollars a week. I will never forget: outside of this house was a 265-gallon oil drum, and I never did get enough money to fill up that oil drum. What I would do every night, I would run up to the store and buy five gallons of oil and climb up the ladder and pour it in that 265-gallon drum. I could hear that five gallons when it hits the bottom of that oil drum, splatters, and it sounds like it's nothin' in there. But it would keep the house warm for the night. Next day you'd have to do the same thing.

I left the bread route with fifty dollars in my pocket. I went to the bank and   10
I borrowed four thousand dollars to buy the service station. I worked seven day a week, open and close, and finally had a heart attack. Just about two months before the last payments of that loan. My wife had done the best she could to keep it runnin'. Tryin' to come out of that hole, I just couldn't do it.

I really began to get bitter. I didn't know who to blame. I tried to find somebody. I began to blame it on black people. I had to hate somebody. Hatin' America is hard to do because you can't see it to hate it. You gotta have somethin' to look at to hate. (Laughs.) The natural person for me to hate would be black people, because my father before me was a member of the Klan. As far as he was concerned, it was the savior of the white people. It was the only organization in the world that would take care of the white people. So I began to admire the Klan.

I got active in the Klan while I was at the service station. Every Monday night, a group of men would come by and buy a Coca-Cola, go back to the car, take a few drinks, and come back and stand around talkin'. I couldn't help but wonder: Why are these dudes comin' out every Monday? They said they were with the Klan and have meetings close-by. Would I be interested? Boy, that was an opportunity I really looked forward to! To be part of somethin'. I joined the Klan, went from member to chaplain, from chaplain to vice-president from vice-president to president. The title is exalted cyclops.

The first night I went with the fellas, they knocked on the door and gave the signal. They sent some robed Klansmen to talk to me and give me some instructions. I was led into a large meeting room, and this was the time of my life! It was thrilling. Here's a guy who's worked all his life and struggled all his life to be something, and here's the moment to be something. I will never forget it. Four robed Klansmen led me into the hall. The lights were dim, and the only thing you could see was an illuminated cross. I knelt before the cross. I had to make certain vows and promises. We promised to uphold the purity of the white race, fight communism, and protect white womanhood.

After I had taken my oath, there was loud applause goin' throughout the buildin', musta been at least four hundred people. For this one little ol' person. It was a thrilling moment for C. P. Ellis.

It disturbs me when people who do not really know what it's all about are   15 so very critical of individual Klansmen. The majority of 'em are low-income whites, people who really don't have a part in something. They have been shut out as well as the blacks. Some are not very well educated either. Just like myself. We had a lot of support from doctors and lawyers and police officers.

Maybe they've had bitter experiences in this life and they had to hate somebody. So the natural person to hate would be the black person. He's beginnin' to come up, he's beginnin' to learn to read and start votin' and run for political office. Here are white people who are supposed to be superior to them, and we're shut out.

I can understand why people join extreme right-wing or left-wing groups. They're in the same boat I was. Shut out. Deep down inside, we want to be part of this great society. Nobody listens, so we join these groups.

At one time, I was state organizer of the National Rights party. I organized a youth group for the Klan. I felt we were getting old and our generation's gonna die. so I contacted certain kids in schools. They were havin' racial problems. On the first night, we had a hundred high school students. When they came in the door, we had "Dixie" playin'. These kids were just thrilled to death. I begin to hold weekly meetin's with 'em, teachin' the principles of the Klan. At that time, I believed Martin Luther King had Communist connections. I began to teach that Andy Young was affiliated with the Communist party.

I had a call one night from one of our kids. He was about twelve. He said: "I just been robbed downtown by two niggers." I'd had a couple of drinks and that really teed me off. I go downtown and couldn't find the kid. I got worried. I saw two young black people. I had the .32 revolver with me. I said: "Nigger, you seen a little young white boy up here? I just got a call from him and was told that some niggers robbed him of fifteen cents." I pulled my pistol out and put it right at his head. I said: "I've always wanted to kill a nigger and I think I'll make you the first one." I nearly scared the kid to death, and he struck off.

This was the time when the civil rights movement was really beginnin' to   20
peak. The blacks were beginnin' to demonstrate and picket downtown stores.
I will never forget some black lady I hated with a purple passion. Ann Atwater.
Every time I'd go downtown, she'd be leadin' a boycott. How I hated—pardon
the expression, I don't use it much now—how I just hated that black nigger.
(Laughs.) Big, fat, heavy woman. She'd pull about eight demonstrations, and
first thing you know they had two, three blacks at the checkout counter. Her
and I have had some pretty close confrontations.

I felt very big, yeah. (Laughs.) We're more or less a secret organization.
We didn't want anybody to know who we were, and I began to do some
thinkin'. What am I hidin' for? I've never been convicted of anything in my
life. I don't have any court record. What am I, C. P. Ellis, as a citizen and
a member of the United Klansmen of America? Why can't I go to the city
council meeting and say: "This is the way we feel about the matter? We don't
want you to purchase mobile units to set in our schoolyards. We don't want
niggers in our schools."

We began to come out in the open. We would go to the meetings, and
the blacks would be there and we'd be there. It was a confrontation every time.
I didn't hold back anything. We began to make some inroads with the city
councilmen and county commissioners. They began to call us friend. Call us at
night on the telephone: "C. P., glad you came to that meeting last night." They
didn't want integration either, but they did it secretively, in order to get elected.
They couldn't stand up openly and say it, but they were glad somebody was
sayin' it. We visited some of the city leaders in their home and talk to 'em
privately. It wasn't long before councilmen would call me up: "The blacks are
comin' up tonight and makin' outrageous demands. How about some of you
people showin' up and have a little balance?" I'd get on the telephone: "The
niggers is comin' to the council meeting tonight. Persons in the city's called me
and asked us to be there."

We'd load up our cars and we'd fill up half the council chambers, and the
blacks the other half. During these times, I carried weapons to the meetings,
outside my belt. We'd go there armed. We would wind up just hollerin' and
fussin' at each other. What happened? As a result of our fightin' one another,
the city council still had their way. They didn't want to give up control to the
blacks nor the Klan. They were usin' us.

I began to realize this later down the road. One day I was walkin' downtown and a certain city council member saw me comin'. I expected him to
shake my hand because he was talkin' to me at night on the telephone. I had
been in his home and visited with him. He crossed the street. Oh shit, I began
to think, somethin's wrong here. Most of 'em are merchants or maybe an

attorney, an insurance agent, people like that. As long as they kept low-income whites and low-income blacks fightin', they're gonna maintain control.

I began to get that feeling after I was ignored in public. I thought: Bullshit,   25 you're not gonna use me any more. That's when I began to do some real serious thinkin'.

The same thing is happening in this country today. People are being used by those in control, those who have all the wealth. I'm not espousing communism. We got the greatest system of government in the world. But those who have it simply don't want those who don't have it to have any part of it. Black and white. When it comes to money, the green, the other colors make no difference. (Laughs.)

I spent a lot of sleepless nights. I still didn't like blacks. I didn't want to associate with 'em. Blacks, Jews, or Catholics. My father said: "Don't have anything to do with 'em." I didn't until I met a black person and talked with him, eyeball to eyeball, and met a Jewish person and talked to him, eyeball to eyeball. I found out they're people just like me. They cried, they cussed, they prayed, they had desires. Just like myself. Thank God, I got to the point where I can look past labels. But at that time, my mind was closed.

I remember one Monday night Klan meeting. I said something was wrong. Our city fathers were using us. And I didn't like to be used. The reactions of the others was not too pleasant: "Let's just keep fightin' them niggers."

I'd go home at night and I'd have to wrestle with myself. I'd look at a black person walkin' down the street, and the guy'd have ragged shoes or his clothes would be worn. That began to do somethin' to me inside. I went through this for about six months. I felt I just had to get out of the Klan. But I wouldn't get out.

Then something happened. The state AFL-CIO received a grant from the   30 Department of HEW, a $78,000 grant: how to solve racial problems in the school system. I got a telephone call from the president of the state AFL-CIO. "We'd like to get some people together from all walks of life." I said: "All walks of life? Who you talkin' about?" He said: "Blacks, whites, liberals, conservatives, Klansmen, NAACP people."

I said: "No way am I comin' with all those niggers. I'm not gonna be associated with those type of people." A White Citizens Council guy said: "Let's go up there and see what's goin' on. It's tax money bein' spent." I walk in the door, and there was a large number of black and white liberals. I knew most of 'em by face 'cause I seen 'em demonstratin' around town. Ann Atwater was there. (Laughs.) I just forced myself to go in and sit down.

The meeting was moderated by a great big black guy who was bushy-headed. (Laughs.) That turned me off. He acted very nice. He said: "I want you all to feel free to say anything you want to say." Some of the blacks stood up and say it's white racism. I took all I could take. I asked for the floor and I cut loose. I said, "No, sir, it's black racism. If we didn't have niggers in the schools, we wouldn't have the problems we got today."

I will never forget. Howard Clements, a black guy, stood up. He said: "I'm certainly glad C. P. Ellis come because he's the most honest man here tonight." I said: "What's that nigger tryin' to do?" (Laughs.) At the end of that meeting, some blacks tried to come up shake my hand, but I wouldn't do it. I walked off.

Second night, same group was there. I felt a little more easy because I got some things off my chest. The third night, after they elected all the committees, they want to elect a chairman. Howard Clements stood up and said: "I suggest we elect two co-chairpersons." Joe Beckton, executive director of the Human Relations Commission, just as black as he can be, he nominated me. There was a reaction from some blacks. Nooo. And, of all things, they nominated Ann Atwater, that big old fat black gal that I just hated with a purple passion, as co-chairman. I thought to myself: Hey, ain't no way I can work with that gal. Finally, I agreed to accept it, 'cause at this point, I was tired of fightin', either for survival or against black people or against Jews or against Catholics.

A Klansman and a militant black woman, co-chairmen of the school committee. It was impossible. How could I work with her? But after about two or three days, it was in our hands. We had to make it a success. This give me another sense of belongin', a sense of pride. This helped this inferiority feelin' I had. A man who has stood up publicly and said he despised black people, all of a sudden he was willin' to work with 'em. Here's a chance for a low-income white man to be somethin'. In spite of all my hatred for blacks and Jews and liberals, I accepted the job. Her and I began to reluctantly work together. (Laughs.) She had as many problems workin' with me as I had workin' with her. 35

One night, I called her: "Ann, you and I should have a lot of differences and we got 'em now. But there's somethin' laid out here before us, and if it's gonna be a success, you and I are gonna have to make it one. Can we lay aside some of those feelin's?" She said: "I'm willing if you are." I said: "Let's do it."

My old friends would call me at night: "C. P., what the hell is wrong with you? You're sellin' out the white race." This begin to make me have guilt feelin's. Am I doin' right? Am I doin' wrong? Here I am all of a sudden makin' an about-face and tryin' to deal with my feelin's, my heart. My mind was beginnin' to open up. I was beginnin' to see what was right and what was wrong. I don't want the kids to fight forever.

We were gonna go ten nights. By this time, I had went to work at Duke University, in maintenance. Makin' very little money. Terry Sanford give me this ten days off with pay. He was president of Duke at the time. He knew I was a Klansman and realized the importance of blacks and whites getting along.

I said: "If we're gonna make this thing a success, I've got to get to my kind of people." The low-income whites. We walked the streets of Durham, and we knocked on doors and invited people. Ann was goin' into the black community. They just wasn't respondin' to us when we made these house calls. Some of 'em were cussin' us out. "You're sellin' us out, Ellis, get out of my door. I don't want to talk to you." Ann was gettin' the same response from blacks: "What are you doin' messin' with that Klansman?"

One day, Ann and I went back to the school and we sat down. We began   40 to talk and just reflect. Ann said: "My daughter came home cryin' every day. She said her teacher was makin' fun of me in front of the other kids." I said: "Boy, the same thing happened to my kid. White liberal teacher was makin' fun of Tim Ellis's father, the Klansman. In front of other peoples. He came home cryin'." At this point—(he pauses, swallows hard, stifles a sob)—I begin to see, here we are, two people from far ends of the fence, havin' identical problems, except hers bein' black and me bein' white. From that moment on, I tell ya, that gal and I worked together good. I begin to love the girl, really. (He weeps.)

The amazing thing about it, her and I, up to that point, had cussed each other, bawled each other, we hated each other. Up to that point, we didn't know each other. We didn't know we had things in common.

We worked at it, with the people who came to these meetings. They talked about racism, sex education, about teachers not bein' qualified. After seven, eight nights of real intense discussion, these people, who'd never talked to each other before, all of a sudden came up with resolutions. It was really somethin', you had to be there to get the tone and feelin' of it.

At that point, I didn't like integration, but the law says you do this and I've got to do what the law says, okay? We said: "Let's take these resolutions to the school board." The most disheartening thing I've ever faced was the school system refused to implement any one of these resolutions. These were recommendations from the people who pay taxes and pay their salaries. (Laughs.)

I thought they were good answers. Some of 'em I didn't agree with, but I been in this thing from the beginning, and whatever comes of it, I'm gonna support it. Okay, since the school board refused, I decided I'd just run for the school board.

I spent eighty-five dollars on the campaign. The guy runnin' against me   45 spent several thousand. I really had nobody on my side. The Klan turned against me. The low-income whites turned against me. The liberals didn't particularly like me. The blacks were suspicious of me. The blacks wanted to support me, but they couldn't muster up enough to support a Klansman on the school board. (Laughs.) But I made up my mind that what I was doin' was right, and I was gonna do it regardless what anybody said.

It bothered me when people would call and worry my wife. She's always supported me in anything I wanted to do. She was changing, and my boys were too. I got some of my youth corps kids involved. They still followed me.

I was invited to the Democratic women's social hour as a candidate. Didn't have but one suit to my name. Had it six, seven, eight years. I had it cleaned, put on the best shirt I had and a tie. Here were all this high-class wealthy candidates shakin' hands. I walked up to the mayor and stuck out my hand. He give me that handshake with that rag type of hand. He said: "C. P., I'm glad to see you." But I could tell by his handshake he was lyin' to me. This was botherin' me. I know I'm a low-income person. I know I'm not wealthy. I know they were sayin': "What's this little ol' dude runnin' for school board?" Yet they had to smile and make like they're glad to see me. I begin to spot some black people in that room. I automatically went to 'em and that was a firm handshake. They said: "I'm glad to see you, C. P." I knew they meant it—you can tell about a handshake.

Every place I appeared, I said I will listen to the voice of the people. I will not make a major decision until I first contacted all the organizations in the city. I got 4,640 votes. The guy beat me by two thousand. Not bad for eighty-five bucks and no constituency.

The whole world was openin' up, and I was learnin' new truths that I had never learned before. I was beginnin' to look at a black person, shake hands with him, and see him as a human bein'. I hadn't got rid of all this stuff. I've still got a little bit of it. But somethin' was happenin' to me.

It was almost like bein' born again. It was a new life. I didn't have these sleepless nights I used to have when I was active in the Klan and slippin' around at night. I could sleep at night and feel good about it. I'd rather live now than at any other time in history. It's a challenge. 50

Back at Duke, doin' maintenance, I'd pick up my tools, fix the commode, unstop the drains. But this got in my blood. Things weren't right in this country, and what we done in Durham needs to be told. I was so miserable at Duke, I could hardly stand it. I'd go to work every mornin' just hatin' to go.

My whole life had changed. I got an eighth-grade education, and I wanted to complete high school. Went to high school in the afternoons on a program called PEP—Past Employment Progress. I was about the only white in the class, and the oldest. I begin to read about biology. I'd take my books home at night, 'cause I was determined to get through. Sure enough, I graduated. I got the diploma at home.

I come to work one mornin' and some guy says: "We need a union." At this time I wasn't pro-union. My daddy was anti-labor too. We're not gettin' paid much, we're havin' to work seven days in a row. We're all starvin' to death. The next day, I meet the international representative of the Operating Engineers. He give me authorization cards. "Get these cards out and we'll have an election." There was eighty-eight for the union and seventeen no's. I was elected chief steward for the union.

Shortly after, a union man come down from Charlotte and says we need a full-time rep. We've only got two hundred people at the two plants here. It's just barely enough money comin' in to pay your salary. You'll have to get out and organize more people. I didn't know nothin' about organizin' unions, but I knew how to organize people, stir people up. (Laughs.) That's how I got to be business agent for the union.

When I began to organize, I began to see far deeper. I began to see people   55
again bein' used. Blacks against whites. I say this without any hesitancy: management is vicious. There's two things they want to keep: all the money and all the say-so. They don't want these poor workin' folks to have none of that. I begin to see management fightin' me with everything they had. Hire antiunion law firms, badmouth unions. The people were makin' a dollar ninety-five an hour, barely able to get through weekends. I worked as a business rep and was seein' all this.

Last year, I ran for business manager of the union. He's elected by the workers. The guy that ran against me was black, and our membership is seventy-five percent black. I thought: Claiborne, there's no way you can beat that black guy. People know your background. Even though you've made tremendous strides, those black people are not gonna vote for you. You know how much I beat him? Four to one. (Laughs.)

The company used my past against me. They put out letters with a picture of a robe and a cap: Would you vote for a Klansman? They wouldn't deal with the issues. I immediately called for a mass meeting. I met with the ladies at an electric component plant. I said: "Okay, this is Claiborne Ellis. This is where I come from. I want you to know right now, you black ladies here, I was at one time a member of the Klan. I want you to know, because they'll tell you about it."

I invited some of my old black friends. I said: "Brother Joe, Brother Howard, be honest now and tell these people how you feel about me." They done it. (Laughs.) He said: "I know what C. P. Ellis come from. I knew him when he was. I knew him as he grew, and growed with him. I'm tellin' you now: follow, follow this Klansman." (He pauses, swallows hard.) "Any questions?" "No," the black ladies said. "Let's get on with the meeting, we need Ellis." (He laughs and weeps.) Boy, black people sayin' that about me. I won one thirty-four to forty-one. Four to one.

It makes you feel good to go into a plant and butt heads with professional union busters. You see black people and white people join hands to defeat the racist issues they use against people. They're tryin' the same things with the Klan. It's still happenin' today. Can you imagine a guy who's got an adult high school diploma runnin' into professional college graduates who are union busters? I gotta compete with 'em. I work seven days a week, nights and on Saturday and Sunday. The salary's not that great, and if I didn't care, I'd quit. But I care and I can't quit. I got a taste of it. (Laughs.)

I tell people there's a tremendous possibility in this country to stop wars, the battles, the struggles, the fights between people. People say: "That's an impossible dream. You sound like Martin Luther King." An ex-Klansman who sounds like Martin Luther King. (Laughs.) I don't think it's an impossible dream. It's happened in my life. It's happened in other people's lives in America.

I don't know what's ahead of me. I have no desire to be a big union official. I want to be right out here in the field with the workers. I want to walk through their factory and shake hands with that man whose hands are dirty. I'm gonna do all that one little ol' man can do. I'm fifty-two years old, and I ain't got many years left, but I want to make the best of 'em.

When the news came over the radio that Martin Luther King was assassinated, I got on the telephone and begin to call other Klansmen. We just had a real party at the service station. Really rejoicin' 'cause that son of a bitch was dead. Our troubles are over with. They say the older you get, the harder it is for you to change. That's not necessarily true. Since I changed, I've set down and listened to tapes of Martin Luther King. I listen to it and tears come to my eyes 'cause I know what he's sayin' now. I know what's happenin'.

POSTSCRIPT: *The phone rings. A conversation.*

"This was a black guy who's director of Operation Breakthrough in Durham. I had called his office. I'm interested in employin' some young black person who's interested in learnin' the labor movement. I want somebody who's never had an opportunity, just like myself. Just so he can read and write, that's all."

Questions for Critical Reading

1. In general, oral history is one of the genres that tends not to make points explicitly. However, oral history, like all historical narratives, must necessarily include some information and exclude other information — and historians' choices of what to include and exclude are influenced by their beliefs and the beliefs that they (consciously or unconsciously) want readers to hold. Terkel is especially masterful in his ability to select a coherent set of details to include — details that ultimately result in a sharply focused narrative. Many of the details he includes in the first few pages of "C. P. Ellis," for instance, suggest a point about the reason Ellis joined the KKK. What do you take to be this point? Were you persuaded that Ellis (and possibly others like him) did indeed join the KKK for the reasons Terkel implies? Why or why not?

2. Terkel provides us not only with a coherent set of details suggesting why Ellis joined the KKK but also with a coherent set of details suggesting how Ellis was ultimately able to change his mind about the KKK and stop assuming the worst of people he perceived as different. How would you explain some of the reasons that Ellis (at least according to Terkel's narration) changed his attitude and behavior? Do you think that such a dramatic turnaround might be possible for others who consistently assume the worst about people they perceive as being different? If so, what (if anything) might be done to make such turnarounds more likely?

3. Regardless of genre, many readers find that paragraph endings are places of special emphasis. Considering the following passage, look at the place Terkel chose to end the first paragraph, and compare that paragraph ending to the ending of the first paragraph in the altered version. Note that the words — and the order of those words — are exactly the same; the only difference is the paragraph break.

Original Passage	Altered Passage
The other kids had nice clothes, and I just had what Daddy could buy. *I still got some of those inferiority feelin's now that I have to overcome once in a while.*	The other kids had nice clothes, and I just had what Daddy could buy. I still got some of those inferiority feelin's now that I have to overcome once in a while. *I loved my father. He would go with me to ball games.*
I loved my father. He would go with me to ball games. We'd go fishin' together. I was really ashamed of the way he'd dress. . . . I always had the feeling about somebody looking at him and makin' fun of him and makin' fun of me. I think it had to do somethin' with my life. (paras. 2–3; emphasis added)	We'd go fishin' together. I was really ashamed of the way he'd dress. . . . I always had the feeling about somebody looking at him and makin' fun of him and makin' fun of me. I think it had to do somethin' with my life.

How might your response as a reader have been different if Terkel had chosen the paragraph break in the altered passage? Which paragraph break do you think better helps Terkel accomplish this purpose?

Making Connections

4. Writers across genres experiment with how much evidence they use to support their claims. In several passages, both Terkel and Brent Staples (p. 223)

provide multiple pieces of evidence to support implied claims. Consider Staples's use of not one or two but *three* examples to support his claim that people are afraid of him:

> At dark, shadowy intersections, I could cross in front of a car stopped at a traffic light and elicit the *thunk, thunk, thunk, thunk* of the driver—black, white, male, or female—hammering down the door locks. On less traveled streets after dark, I grew accustomed to but never comfortable with people crossing to the other side of the street rather than pass me. Then there were the standard unpleasantries with policemen, doormen, bouncers, cabdrivers, and others whose business it is to screen out troublesome individuals *before* there is any nastiness. (para. 3)

Similarly, Terkel includes not one but many examples to paint a picture of Ellis's poverty:

> I was about seventeen years old and had a mother and sister depending on somebody to make a livin'. [There] was just barely enough insurance to cover [my father's] burial. I had to quit school and go to work. (para. 1)

> I got married. We had to have children. Four. One child was born blind and retarded, which was a real additional expense to us. . . . All my life, I had work, never a day without work, worked all the overtime I could get and still could not survive financially. (para. 7)

> I will never forget: outside of this house was a 265-gallon oil drum, and I never did get enough money to full up that oil drum. What I would do every night, I would run up to the store and buy five gallons of oil and climb up the ladder and pour it in that 265-gallon drum. I could hear that five gallons when it hits the bottom of that oil drum, splatters, and it sounds like it's nothin' in there. (para. 9)

Imagine Staples's and Terkel's passages with only one piece of evidence. Would you have been less persuaded? How might you as a writer gauge when you need not one but multiple pieces of evidence?

5. The genre of oral history allows Terkel to go into great detail about one person's experience; in contrast, academic genres such as "Mere Exposure" (p. 229) tend to mention numerous studies and then go on to report the results of a particular study, all without discussing the lived experience of any people. By reading works in both genres, then, you had the benefit of both approaches. If you had just read one of the two, do you think your insight into prejudice and how to combat it would be as deep? Why or why not? How will you gauge when it will be instructive to read multiple genres rather than just one?

Writing: Your Turn

1. Just as Terkel did, conduct a recorded interview of someone that sheds light on the experience of being prejudiced or the experience of being the target of

Writing

prejudice. (Note that depending on your college's or university's policy, your professor may tell you that you need permission from its Institutional Review Board to conduct the interview.) After the interview, write your own oral history using some of Terkel's strategies — especially using paragraph breaks for emphasis and carefully selecting which parts of the interview to transcribe and which parts to omit.

Share your oral history with some or all of your classmates so that they can get a sense of what it's like to be in someone else's shoes. After your classmates read your oral history, ask them what they took away from it, and gauge the extent to which you succeeded in conveying the points you wanted to make. See http://dohistory.org/on_your_own/toolkit/oralHistory.html for tips on doing an oral history.

2. Find another example of an oral history of someone who assumed the worst about others or who had the experience of others assuming the worst about him or her.[1] Find one written more recently than Terkel's (1980); you'll probably notice that the genre has evolved, as genres tend to do. Oral history has evolved in part because of technology; some recent histories, for instance, include video or at least a photograph. Another difference is that the interviewer's questions are now often included.

After reading several pages of your chosen oral history, reflect on how the more recent conventions shape your experience as a reader; for instance, how did the picture (or video) and inclusion of interview questions affect your response to the oral history? (If the history you found didn't include the questions or a picture or video, reflect instead on how your response might have been different if such elements had been included.) For ideas on how to write a reflection, see p. 27.

---

[1] It will probably be easier to find oral histories of people who have been the target of uncharitable assumptions. You might start by looking at repositories of oral histories hosted by universities and organized by topic; do a web search for "oral history repository," or go to http://bancroft.berkeley.edu/ROHO/collections/subjectarea/index.html and click on such topics as "Suffragists," "Human Rights/Relations Commission" (under "Politics and Government"), "Disability Rights and Independent Living Movement," or "Self-Advocacy Movement" (under "Social Movements").

Assuming the Best of Others

Amel S. Abdullah

Written by translator and freelance writer Amel S. Abdullah, "Assuming the Best of Others" appears on the Web site of the Shaw University mosque. In it, Abdullah argues that rather than assuming the worst of others, we should be "keeping all possibilities in mind when judging another person's actions."

Focus on Genre   "Assuming the Best of Others" is a religious advice essay; it aims to persuade readers to change the way they think and behave. Although Abdullah briefly quotes an early Muslim as the source of her advice, readers of different faiths, or no faith, may find her essay persuasive. As you'll notice in the following excerpt, Abdullah's essay has much in common with other genres of persuasive writing. As you read, consider her choice of pronouns, her use of real and hypothetical examples, her anticipation of potential objections, and her acknowledgment of the difficulty of what she's asking for. If you find her essay persuasive, try to articulate why.

◄O►

Today, I read the true story of a young woman who was feeling upset with her old childhood friends, who hadn't bothered to call or write to her in the years since they had graduated from high school. Although she believed they didn't really deserve it, she decided to get in touch with them instead. Imagine her shock when she discovered that they were both long dead—one killed in a car accident, and the other a victim of cancer.

Utterly humbled by the news, the woman wished for nothing more than to be able to turn back time, hug her friends and relive their most special moments together. Naturally, she regretted her anger, which had been misplaced, and realized the importance of keeping all possibilities in mind when judging another person's actions.

One of the early Muslims advised, "If a friend among your friends errs, make seventy excuses for them. If your hearts are unable to do this, then know that the shortcoming is in your own selves."

Making "seventy excuses" does not mean that we should ignore or dismiss bad or hurtful behavior, but that we should try to understand the circumstances behind it when it occurs. In the woman's case, she was lacking the information she needed to make a correct judgment about her friends, who were not trying to hurt her at all.

Sometimes it happens that we have no way of knowing another person's 5 circumstances, either because we are separated from that person by distance (like the woman and her friends), or because we cannot truly understand what motivates people unless we are actually living their lives and thinking their thoughts, which is impossible. Feeling hurt or annoyed, we dream up scenarios that blame the people who have hurt us.

Sometimes it's hard not to be angry, especially when someone is acting strangely or seems to be ignoring you, which can happen just as you have done something nice, such as loaning that person money or helping him through a difficult situation. Feeling betrayed, you might start to believe that the person is selfish and regret ever getting involved. But this is where your sense of compassion comes in. Walk in your friend's shoes a bit, and you might find that he feels ashamed for having needed and accepted help. A private person, he wishes that you didn't know so many details about his life. And if he owes you money, perhaps he is worried about paying you back on time.

Think about the reason why your friend sought help in the first place. Whether he has lost his job, is getting divorced, has a sick child, or is facing some other trouble, it's very likely that this thing is causing him great anxiety. Part of being a good friend means that we have to give people space to express their emotions and learn not to take things personally if they stop confiding in us for a while. Instead of feeling offended, we can support troubled friends by

Questions

checking on them frequently, inviting them to our homes for companionship, and doing what we can to change their outlook into a positive one.

The next time you are faced with odd behavior and you find yourself assuming something bad about someone you love, respect or admire, remember that false assumptions lead to false conclusions, and that it is not a bad idea at all to try making "seventy excuses" for the person in question. My recommendation? Get a notebook and actually go through the process of writing down the excuses—all seventy of them. By the time you finish this exercise, you will have explored many sides of the issue at hand and probably learned something new about yourself, too.

A final word here. There will be times when the truth is not pretty, and you may find that someone has intentionally done something wrong, deceitful or hurtful. When possible, do your best to repair the situation, and keep making excuses. You never know—maybe your own good character will be the influence needed to inspire permanent change in that person's life.

Questions for Critical Reading

1. Did Abdullah succeed in persuading you that it's a good idea to make seventy excuses for people who err? Why or why not? How would you describe the strategies she used to try to persuade you?

2. Recall that regardless of the genre you're writing, the choice of which pronouns you use can shape readers' responses. Just as changing "we" to "they" can affect readers' responses, so too can changing "we" to "you." Compare the following passage from Abdullah's essay to an altered passage that uses the pronoun "you" instead of the pronoun "we" (relevant pronouns are italicized):

Original Passage	Altered Passage
Part of being a good friend means that *we* have to give people space to express their emotions and learn not to take things personally if they stop confiding in *us* for a while. Instead of feeling offended, *we* can support troubled friends by checking on them frequently, inviting them to *our* homes for companionship, and doing what *we* can to change their outlook into a positive one. (para. 7)	Part of being a good friend means that *you* have to give people space to express their emotions and learn not to take things personally if they stop confiding in *you* for a while. Instead of feeling offended, *you* can support troubled friends by checking on them frequently, inviting them to *your* homes for companionship, and doing what *you* can to change their outlook into a positive one.

Given Abdullah's purpose and audience, do you think her choice to use "we" rather than "you" was a good one? Why or why not?

3. Recall that in a variety of persuasive genres, one of the most important strategies writers use to persuade readers is to provide examples. Readers of some persuasive genres are accustomed to hypothetical (rather than real) examples, while readers of other genres tend to be less persuaded by hypothetical examples. You may have noticed that in "Assuming the Best of Others," Abdullah uses both real and hypothetical examples. Compare the following two passages, considering whether you find her real example and her hypothetical example to be equally persuasive:

Real example

Today, I read the true story of a young woman who was feeling upset with her old childhood friends, who hadn't bothered to call or write to her in the years since they had graduated from high school. Although she believed they didn't really deserve it, she decided to get in touch with them instead. Imagine her shock when she discovered that they were both long dead—one killed in a car accident, and the other a victim of cancer. (para. 1)

Hypothetical example

Sometimes it's hard not to be angry, especially when someone is acting strangely or seems to be ignoring you, which can happen just as you have done something nice, such as loaning that person money or helping him through a difficult situation. Feeling betrayed, you might start to believe that the person is selfish and regret ever getting involved. But this is where your sense of compassion comes in. Walk in your friend's shoes a bit, and you might find that he feels ashamed for having needed and accepted help. A private person, he wishes that you didn't know so many details about his life. And if he owes you money, perhaps he is worried about paying you back on time. (para. 6)

Would you have been more persuaded if the hypothetical example had been a real one, or does the combination of one real and one hypothetical example work for you? In what situations might you want to use real examples, hypothetical examples, or a combination of both?

Making Connections

4. Although it may seem counterintuitive, when writers try to persuade readers to change their attitudes or behavior, they often acknowledge the difficulty of the change. Abdullah makes this move when she notes that "[s]ometimes it's hard not to be angry" (para. 6).

Unlike Abdullah, who is directly addressing the people she wants to change, Julie Schwartz Gottman *doesn't* acknowledge the difficulty of the change she describes in "An Abbreviated History and Overview of Gottman Method Couples Therapy" (p. 260). In this book chapter, written for therapists who want to help couples change how they think about each other,

Gottman doesn't mention whether the change she is proposing would be hard, easy, or somewhere in between:

> In [Gottman Method Couples Therapy], couples are taught to change their habit of mind. Rather than looking for their partners' flaws, sins, and omissions, couples are taught to watch for the positives in their partners—the behaviors, words, and glances that should be appreciated but are more often overlooked. (para. 15)

Given their different audiences, why might Abdullah have acknowledged that "[s]ometimes it's hard" while Gottman did not? When might you as a writer want to acknowledge the difficulty of something you propose?

5. Recall that Abdullah opens "Assuming the Best of Others" with the narrative about the young woman who assumed the worst about her friends, just as Gladwell opens the excerpt from *Blink* with the narrative about Warren Harding (p. 207). Given their audiences and purposes, why might both authors have chosen to open with narratives such as these? When might you as a writer want to open with a narrative?

Writing: Your Turn

1. Write an argument in which you agree with, disagree with, extend, or qualify Abdullah's point. Although it might seem easiest to agree with her, arguing that an author makes a valid point can sometimes be more difficult than extending, qualifying, or disagreeing with a point. (When students choose the latter options, they're often inclined to use more evidence to support their argument, but when they agree, they're sometimes tempted to simply summarize the author's evidence.) If you agree with Abdullah, try to find additional evidence; you might, for example, draw on Gladwell, Staples, and/or Terkel. Address your argument to an audience of your classmates, and get their feedback on how you might revise it to make it even more persuasive. For ideas on writing an argument, see p. 42.

2. Using "Assuming the Best of Others" as a model, write your own advice essay on the topic of making assumptions. To illustrate your advice, draw on one or more of the readings in this chapter or, as Abdullah does, draw on a religious figure. To decide, consider the audience you're targeting; drawing on a religious figure (or text) makes sense if your target audience practices that religion. You might also draw on experience—either your own or that of family members, friends, or acquaintances.

Your essay will be more persuasive if your advice is sharply focused rather than vague. Note that rather than advising us to assume the best about others in general, Abdullah advises us, more specifically, to assume the best about someone when that person does something that results in hurt or angry feelings. Abdullah makes her point still more specific by giving us a strategy for assuming the best: making seventy excuses. Your readers may be more likely to follow your advice if you can make it as specific as Abdullah's.

Give your essay to some classmates to get their feedback on how your advice could be even more specific — and on how your evidence could be even more persuasive. After you revise, submit your essay to a venue that your target audience will likely encounter — for example, your campus newspaper, an online forum, or a newsletter published by a group you're affiliated with. Because an advice essay is a type of argument, see p. 42 for strategies you can use when you write.

Be Cool to the Pizza Dude

Sarah Adams

In the radio address that follows, Sarah Adams explains why she assumes the best about the "pizza delivery dude." Adams's essay was broadcast in 2005 on National Public Radio (NPR) as part of the series *This I Believe,* in which contributors discuss the core beliefs that guide their lives. After its broadcast, the essay was also included in the book *This I Believe: The Personal Philosophies of Remarkable Men and Women* (2007). Adams is currently a professor of English at Olympic College in Washington.

Focus on Genre   The *This I Believe* series of radio addresses considers submissions from anyone. Adams, who had never written a radio address before, told the radio producer that her essay "had been rattling around" in her head — that she "just needed the assignment." Her experience is a good example of how genre can be generative — of how writing within the constraints imposed by a specific situation can help people generate ideas worth sharing. The constraints that Adams faced were many; because her listeners might be driving, getting ready to leave in the morning, or doing any number of other daily activities, she would have wanted her essay to be brief and to be easily understood by people who were doing something else. As you read the essay, consider how these constraints might have shaped her choices as a writer.

Also, bear in mind that writers in many genres sometimes use a specific person (or place or thing) to represent a larger category. As you read, try to decide if the pizza dude represents a broader category of people or whether he is really just a pizza dude.

◄o►

I f I have one operating philosophy about life it is this: "Be cool to the pizza delivery dude; it's good luck." Four principles guide the pizza dude philosophy.

Principle 1: Coolness to the pizza delivery dude is a practice in humility and forgiveness. I let him cut me off in traffic, let him safely hit the exit ramp from the left lane, let him forget to use his blinker without extending any of my digits out the window or towards my horn because there should be one moment in my harried life when a car may encroach or cut off or pass and I let it go. Sometimes when I have become so certain of my ownership of my lane, daring anyone to challenge me, the pizza dude speeds by me in his rusted Chevette. His pizza light atop his car glowing like a beacon reminds me to check myself as I flow through the world. After all, the dude is delivering pizza to young and old, families and singletons, gays and straights, blacks, whites and browns, rich and poor, vegetarians and meat lovers alike. As he journeys, I give safe passage, practice restraint, show courtesy, and contain my anger.

Principle 2: Coolness to the pizza delivery dude is a practice in empathy. Let's face it: We've all taken jobs just to have a job because some money is better than none. I've held an assortment of these jobs and was grateful for the paycheck that meant I didn't have to share my Cheerios with my cats. In the big pizza wheel of life, sometimes you're the hot bubbly cheese and sometimes you're the burnt crust. It's good to remember the fickle spinning of that wheel.

Principle 3: Coolness to the pizza delivery dude is a practice in honor and it reminds me to honor honest work. Let me tell you something about these dudes: They never took over a company and, as CEO, artificially inflated the value of the stock and cashed out their own shares, bringing the company to the brink of bankruptcy, resulting in 20,000 people losing their jobs while the CEO builds a home the size of a luxury hotel. Rather, the dudes sleep the sleep of the just.

Principle 4: Coolness to the pizza delivery dude is a practice in equality.   5 My measurement as a human being, my worth, is the pride I take in perform-ing my job—any job—and the respect with which I treat others. I am the equal of the world not because of the car I drive, the size of the TV I own, the weight I can bench press, or the calculus equations I can solve. I am the equal to all I meet because of the kindness in my heart. And it all starts here—with the pizza delivery dude.

Tip him well, friends and brethren, for that which you bestow freely and willingly will bring you all the happy luck that a grateful universe knows how to return.

Questions for Critical Reading

1. "Be Cool to the Pizza Dude" employs many strategies used by creative nonfiction writers. One such strategy is to have a small detail represent something larger; when Adams says "Tip [the pizza dude] well" (para. 6), she is perhaps advising us, more generally, to *treat* the pizza dude well. You might also believe, by the same token, that the "pizza dude" symbolizes something larger. Do you believe this or not? Identify specific passages that support your interpretation, and explain how they do so.

2. Given that Adams wrote her essay as a radio address, what choices do you think she might have made so that she could better achieve her purpose as a writer? How might she have written the essay differently if she'd been writing for an audience of readers rather than listeners?

3. Unlike books for laypeople that often begin chapters with a narrative, and unlike academic articles that often state the point at the end of the introduction, Adams makes her point in the very first sentence. She immediately tells us, "If I have one operating philosophy about life it is this: 'Be cool to the pizza delivery dude; it's good luck.'" How might you have responded differently to her essay had she instead opened by discussing the context leading up to her point? How might you have responded had she instead opened with a narrative, perhaps a story about an interaction she had with a pizza delivery dude?

Making Connections

4. Recall that writers across genres strategically use detail. Take, for example, the following passages from "Be Cool to the Pizza Dude" and Brent Staples's "Black Men and Public Space" (p. 223). Consider how the authors' use of detail (italicized) affects you as a reader:

   "Black Men and Public Space"

   [Women who fear the worst from me] seem to have set their faces on neutral, and *with their purse straps strung across their chests bandolier-style*, they forge ahead as though bracing themselves against being tackled. (para. 5)

   "Be Cool to the Pizza Dude"

   Sometimes when I have become so certain of my ownership of my lane, daring anyone to challenge me, the pizza dude speeds by me in his *rusted Chevette*. (para. 2)

   Staples chose to tell us that the women who fear him have "purse straps strung across their chests bandolier-style," even though some of them were probably carrying briefcases, backpacks, tote bags, or short-strapped purses.

Writing

Similarly, Adams chose to tell us that the pizza dude speeds by in a "rusted Chevette," even though in reality she may have seen several pizza dudes in different models of cars; she could have said "speeds by me in his car." Why do you think Staples and Adams chose to use the details they did? What other examples of specific details can you find in Adams's writing, and what purpose do you think they serve?

5. Recall that writers across genres often use an antithesis (the juxtaposition of contrasting ideas, often signaled by words such as *instead*, *rather*, or *not*, as in "not X but Y"). Adams uses antitheses in "Be Cool to the Pizza Dude," as does Julie Schwartz Gottman in "An Abbreviated History and Overview of Gottman Method Couples Therapy" (p. 260), a book chapter that describes, for an audience of therapists, an approach that could be used to help couples assume the best about each other. Consider why Adams and Gottman might have chosen to use antitheses in the following passages. Compare the original passages to altered ones that don't use antitheses:

Original Passage	Altered Passage
I am the equal of the world not because of the car I drive, the size of the TV I own, the weight I can bench press, or the calculus equations I can solve. I am the equal to all I meet because of the kindness in my heart. (Adams, para. 5)	I am the equal to all I meet because of the kindness in my heart.
The relationship begins to feel like a port in a storm, not the storm itself. (Gottman, para. 15)	The relationship begins to feel like a port in a storm.

Why do you think Adams and Gottman use antitheses? Do you prefer the passages with or without antitheses? When might you as a writer choose to use an antithesis?

Writing: Your Turn

1. Write a *This I Believe* essay that discusses the topic of making assumptions about others. Just as Adams did, state a specific belief related to this topic, and go on to illustrate your belief by discussing an event (or events) from your life. As per the *This I Believe* guidelines, your essay should be fewer than five hundred words. For ideas on how to write it, see "essay guidelines" (under the "participate" link at Thisibelieve.org). For more ideas, consider reading or listening to other *This I Believe* essays, which you can access via the "listen" link at Thisibelieve.org. After you write the first draft of your essay, ask your classmates for feedback on whether you used enough specific

detail (and on anything else they notice). After you revise, submit your essay by going to the *This I Believe* Web site and clicking on "participate" and then "submit your essay." Note that, after a review process that could take up to eight weeks, all essays meeting the submission guidelines will be publicly available on the Web site. Unless you grant permission for use of your last name, only your first name, city, and state will be provided to people who search the essay collection.

2. Write a reflection that discusses any connections you see between "Be Cool to the Pizza Dude" and one of the other reading selections in this chapter. (Looking for connections between readings often helps people develop insights they might not otherwise have.) Share your reflection with your classmates so that they can benefit from what you've learned and so that you can get ideas for revision. For tips on writing a reflection, see p. 27.

An Abbreviated History and Overview of Gottman Method Couples Therapy

Julie Schwartz Gottman

In this introduction to *The Marriage Clinic Casebook*, Julie Schwartz Gottman describes an approach to couples counseling that, she claims, can help couples who assume the worst about each other start assuming the best. Although this approach is intended for couples, it could potentially be used by anyone who wants to start assuming the best about others.

Gottman is the cofounder (with John Gottman) of the Gottman Relationship Institute, which provides counseling to couples and training to mental health professionals. She is also the coauthor of *And Baby Makes Three* (2008) and *Ten Lessons to Transform Your Marriage* (2007).

Focus on Genre   This book introduction is written for an audience of clinicians — professional therapists who counsel couples wanting to improve their relationships. This audience has much in common with an audience of academics; both audiences are experts with graduate degrees who can navigate complex material. Gottman's audience of professional practitioners, however, also has something in common with an audience of laypeople: both groups include many people who care more about how they might *use* knowledge than where that knowledge comes from — unlike an audience of academics, who generally care very much about where knowledge comes from. This difference in values is reflected in different citation practices. As you read, notice how Gottman cites sources only occasionally, and consider whether you'd be interested in knowing where she got more of her information.

◄○►

One summer 10 years ago, John and I sat in our canoe off the shore of Orcas Island. The sea rippled as we paused from paddling to sit and gaze into the deep forest descending to the shore.

"I wonder what would happen if we created a workshop that helped couples," John said. "We've got this beautiful data. It shows we can create change. . . ."

"Wouldn't that be *incredible*?" I replied in my usual hyperbolic style. "To actually use this to *really* help people instead of just a few in the lab?"

"We'd have to build a workshop. We'd explain the theory and do exercises to lead couples through the interventions from the lab. We'd start with building friendship, forming a base for their working with conflict the next day. Only this time they'd learn different skills, the ones that work."

We both knew from Jacobson's (1984) analysis of his behavioral couple therapy outcome that one year after therapy only 33% of couples in therapy were in the nondistressed range of marital satisfaction, and that 35–50% of those couples relapsed after 2 years, leaving a dismal 17% success rate. What if we could improve on that?

We were very excited and with atypical speed paddled quickly back to shore, trudged back up the hill to our cabin, climbed up to the loft, and set to work.

A month later the manual was completed. . . . We also created a workshop to train clinicians how to do couple therapy based on John's research and my years with clients. . . . In 1998, advanced trainings were offered, and from the clinicians who participated, 16 were asked to form the Marriage Clinic.

Referrals were made, clients were seen, and in our bimonthly consultation meetings, we wrestled with the dilemmas our couples faced—affairs, childhood trauma, depression, outbreaks of violence, attention deficit disorders, chronic illnesses, troubled children, distressed stepchildren—in short, the problems that you as a clinician face daily when you walk into your office.

Three years ago, John suggested to the group that we write a book for clinicians. It would describe case studies, the most difficult ones, and guide clinicians through the complexities of applying what we came to call "Gottman Method Couples Therapy" (GMCT) to their work. We were aghast. Most of us felt we didn't know enough. In characteristic fashion, at 3 A.M. one night, John wrote up a tentative book proposal, handed it to me the next morning, and said, "Look, it's easy, you can do it." I blanched.

The Marriage Clinic group also hesitated, wanting to wait and learn more first.

Another 2 years passed. Finally, after collectively ushering nearly 4,000 couples through workshops and/or therapy, we agreed to write up some cases. Those cases are presented here.

BASE PRINCIPLES

Following is a brief summary of some basic principles. (For an in-depth description, see Gottman, 1999.) GMCT is based on the Sound Relationship House theory (SRH; formerly known as the Sound Marital House theory). Following a 14-year longitudinal study of over 700 couples, John Gottman learned that the couples who successfully kept their relationships together worked on three primary objectives: They sustained their romance through the fundamentals of friendship, they managed their conflicts well, and they created a shared sense of meaning that knitted their lives together. There were also a number of corrosive forces that they tried to squelch, namely, the "Four horsemen of the apocalypse": criticism, contempt, defensiveness, and stonewalling. They worked hard to honor each other's dreams and laugh when perpetual issues raised their hoary heads. They also balanced the negative and positive interactions they had, so that there were five times as many positive as negative interactions during conflict and nearly 20 positive interactions to every negative one during peaceful times. From the study of these couples internally through physiological readings and externally through second-by-second videotaped coding, we learned the details of the SRH theory.

Imagine a house subdivided into seven levels, bottom to top. We begin with the foundation, which consists of the first three levels. These levels sustain friendship and depth of connection, which in turn fuel romance, passion, and good sex.

The First Level: Love Maps

Love maps represent our knowledge of our partner's internal world. Who are our partner's best friends, colleagues, enemies, allies? What are our partner's favorite books, movies, restaurants, travel destinations? What are our partner's dreams, hopes, nightmares, aspirations? What are our partner's most embarrassing moments from childhood? Their funniest moments? Couples who have distanced from one another don't know the answers, or what they know may be years old and outdated. In GMCT, clinicians give couples a list of questions to ask one another that help them update their love maps. In the workshop these questions are printed on cards, and couples play with the cards, guessing at the answers to the questions and gently correcting each other when wrong answers are given. By asking the questions, couples encounter each other as constantly changing and growing new worlds to be explored.

The Second Level: Fondness and Admiration

This level involves voicing our feelings of care and respect for our partners. As human beings, we need to feel loved, just as we need food and water. Yet many

15

couples neglect to express their love. Consequently, partners feel lonely, uncared for, and invisible. Criticism and contempt compound the problem. Some couples think their partners will appreciate "constructive advice" or criticism—that it will foster improvements in their partners and in their relationships. The reality is that it does quite the opposite—it tears at the fabric of the partners' beliefs that they are loved and respected. It mirrors back to the partners negative reflections of themselves. Contempt, or criticism poisoned with superiority and sarcasm, name calling, or mockery, is worse still. Contempt is the antithesis of respect; thus it destroys feeling loved and shreds self-respect. Contempt even predicts infectious illness in its recipient. Couples in distressed relationships often feel battered by contempt. Expressions of fondness and admiration can help to heal these relationships. In GMCT, couples are taught to change their habit of mind. Rather than looking for their partners' flaws, sins, and omissions, couples are taught to watch for the positives in their partners—the behaviors, words, and glances that should be appreciated but are more often overlooked. Then they are coached to voice their appreciations in either words or touch. The more fondness and admiration are expressed, the more partners see one another as a refuge from the harsh realities of the world outside. The relationship begins to feel like a port in a storm, not the storm itself.

The Third Level: Turning Toward

This level contributes the small nuts and bolts that hold the SRH together. These are those moments when one partner makes a bid for connection to which the other partner positively responds. For example, look at the following turning toward moment between a couple named Joe and Adele.

> Joe: Wow, look at those whitecaps on the sea.
> Adele: Yeah, they sure are huge.

That was a bid for attention that the partner turned toward. Bids for attention can be negatively responded to as well, by either turning away or turning against. Turning away might sound like this:

> Joe: Wow, look at those whitecaps on the sea.
> Adele: (*reads her book without looking up*)

Turning against could be like this:

> Joe: Wow, look at those whitecaps on the sea.
> Adele: Would you stop interrupting me? I'm trying to read!

The bids may be for attention, affection, conversation, humor, emotional support, and so on. The number of these moments and the way they are responded to predict with good accuracy whether or not a couple will stay together or separate. Successful couples usually turn toward one another when bids for connection are made. Couples who separate don't. When seeking to heal their relationships, couples must learn to recognize when these bids for connection are made and how to respond to them positively. Often when couples finally reach therapists (usually, 6 years after first noticing the distress in their relationships), so many bids for connection have failed that couples no longer trust each other enough to even attempt another bid. The therapist can begin by gently interceding, structuring conversations in which couples write down the specifics of how each partner would prefer to receive attention. Couples can also try to do one positive thing for their partner each week, while the recipient guesses what that one thing was. Slowly, couples can rebuild the third level of their SRH by increasing the frequency of turning toward one another.

Together, love maps, fondness and admiration, and turning toward form a solid foundation of trust that underlies friendship and intimacy. Love maps help partners to feel individually known and interesting; fondness and admiration nourish partners' feeling loved and respected; and turning toward moves couples closer together as responders to each other's needs. When these three levels are strong, there is room for passion and sexual intimacy to grow and deepen.

The Fourth Level: Positive Sentiment Override

Also known as the positive perspective, this level is the bonus achieved when the first three levels have been solidly built. It is a concept originally suggested by Weider and Weiss (1980). It describes an overall color or mood of the relationship. It also refers to the way in which one partner interprets neutral statements made by the other partner. For example, if Joe says, "You left the fan on in the bathroom again," Adele might reply, "Oh, right. I'll go switch it off" (positive sentiment override), or "Stop trying to control me, as if you never leave anything on" (negative sentiment override). In the first case, the response is acceptance; in the second, it's counterattack and defensiveness. In *negative sentiment override* a person has "a chip on the shoulder" and is hypervigilant for negativity from the partner. When positive sentiment override is in place, even negative statements can be responded to with neutrality; in other words, one partner gives the other partner the benefit of the doubt. If Joe says, "I hate how you burned this toast," Adele might reply, "Whoa, what side of the bed did you get up on this morning?" The attribution is entirely different; a temporary emotional state of the partner is presumed to underlie negativity, not a lasting negative partner trait. Sentiment override, positive or negative, is determined by the quality of friendship and intimacy. If partners have been trampled by the four horsemen, haven't asked each other a personal question in many months, and typically ignore each other's bids for connection, negative sentiment override will sour the relationship. On the other hand, if partners have continually updated their love maps of one another, frequently expressed fondness and admiration, and regularly turned toward one another in the small moments, positive sentiment override will sweeten it. Negative sentiment override can be reversed by strengthening the first three levels of the SRH and minimizing the presence of the four horsemen.

References

Gottman, J. M. (1999). *The marriage clinic: A scientifically based marital therapy.* New York: Norton.

Jacobson, N. S. (1984). Variability in outcome and clinical significance of behavioral marital therapy: A reanalysis of outcome data. *Journal of Consulting and Clinical Psychology, 52*(4), 497–504.

Weider, G. B., & Weiss, R. L. (1980). Generalizability theory and the coding of marital interactions. *Journal of Consulting and Clinical Psychology, 48*(4), 469–477.

Questions for Critical Reading

1. Imagine yourself as a couples therapist, part of Gottman's target audience. Would you believe her claim that, through the approach she describes, couples who assume the worst about each other can indeed be helped to assume the best about each other? Why or why not?

2. Regardless of the genre you're reading, it's useful to consider whether an author's ideas might be applied more broadly than the author assumes. Do you think any of the relationship strategies Gottman discusses could be applied more broadly — for example, that you or other people (even if they're single) might use these strategies to more frequently assume the best about friends and family members? Why or why not?

3. Like other book introductions, Gottman's provides readers with an overview of what they need to know to better understand the book. Before providing this overview, Gottman makes a move that's not uncommon in book introductions: she tells us the story of how the book came to exist (paras. 1–11). How would you have responded if she had skipped the story and instead started with the overview: "Following is a brief summary of some basic principles" (para. 12)? If you were Gottman, how would you have started the book? Why?

4. As mentioned previously, Gottman only occasionally tells us where she got her information; she doesn't cite sources as often as she would if she were writing for an academic audience. (Academics devote much of their day to reading scholarly sources and assessing how much they should trust any given piece of knowledge — an assessment that informs the research they do, since their goal is generally to create new knowledge. A professional audience like Gottman's,

in contrast, may be less interested in creating new knowledge than in putting what's already known into practice; such an audience generally devotes most of the day to practicing their profession—to working as a clinical therapist, doctor, social worker, lawyer, teacher, and so on. Since some members of professional audiences may care more about what the knowledge is than where it came from, they don't necessarily expect extensive citation.)

Given the audience she's writing for, it's not surprising that Gottman doesn't tell us where she learned about the connection between contempt and infectious illness; she simply informs us that "[c]ontempt even predicts infectious illness in its recipient" (para. 15). If she were writing for an academic audience, she would have probably cited a source here. Find an example of another idea or piece of information that Gottman would have cited if she were writing for an academic audience, and explain how a citation would have benefited that audience. Were there any places where *you* as a reader would have appreciated knowing where Gottman got her information? Why or why not?

5. You'll encounter semicolons [;] in a variety of genres. As a writer, you might find that they can prompt readers to move on to the next independent clause more quickly than a period would. (An independent clause is simply a clause with a subject and a verb that could stand alone as a sentence.) Consider the semicolon in the following passage:

> When positive sentiment override is in place, even negative statements can be responded to with neutrality; in other words, one partner gives the other partner the benefit of the doubt. (para. 19)

Why do you think Gottman used a semicolon when a period would have also been correct? Drawing on your insight, consider the following passage, and see if you can find two sentences that you might want to connect with a semicolon:

> Three years ago, John suggested to the group that we write a book for clinicians. It would describe case studies, the most difficult ones, and guide clinicians through the complexities of applying what we came to call "Gottman Method Couples Therapy" (GMCT) to their work. We were aghast. Most of us felt we didn't know enough. (para. 9)

Check in with a few of your classmates to see how their choices compare with yours. Why did they choose to put their semicolons where they did? Why did you choose to put yours where you did?

Making Connections

6. Although they are writing different genres for different audiences, both Gottman and Sarah Adams (author of the radio essay "Be Cool to the Pizza Dude" on p. 255) use numbers to divide their writing into sections. Gottman, for instance, includes subheadings such as the following:

- The First Level: Love Maps
- The Second Level: Fondness and Admiration
- The Third Level: Turning Toward
- The Fourth Level: Positive Sentiment Override

Similarly, Adams numbers her principles:

- Principle 1: Coolness to the pizza delivery dude is a practice in humility and forgiveness.
- Principle 2: Coolness to the pizza delivery dude is a practice in empathy.
- Principle 3: Coolness to the pizza delivery dude is a practice in honor and it reminds me to honor honest work.
- Principle 4: Coolness to the pizza delivery dude is a practice in equality.

Imagine each writer's work without the numbers. Would you prefer their writing with or without the numbered phrases preceding the colons? Why? When might you as a writer want to consider using numbers to divide your work into sections?

Writing: Your Turn

1. Using the ideas from Gottman's work that you find most compelling, write a brochure for couples who want to assume the best about each other more often. Be sure to cite Gottman so that she gets credit for her ideas and so that interested readers can look at her work for themselves. Ask your classmates how your brochure might be even more persuasive, and take their feedback into account when you revise. Distribute the revised brochure to at least ten people. For ideas on how to write a brochure, see p. 105.

2. Write a reflection in which you speculate about whether negative sentiment override (para. 19) affects not just romantic relationships but also other relationships. Have you ever felt that you were the victim of a friend or family member's negative sentiment override? Do you think the way you treat others has ever been affected by negative sentiment override? Share your reflection with your classmates so that they can learn from your ideas and so that you can get ideas for revision. For tips on writing a reflection, see p. 27.

3. Write a reflection discussing whether you believe, as Gottman claims in paragraph 19, that negative sentiment override can be reversed by strengthening the first three levels of the Sound Relationship House she describes. Try learning more about someone else's internal world (para. 14), expressing admiration for that person (para. 15), and/or turning toward that person's bids more often (paras. 16–18)—and write about what you learn from your experiment. If you feel comfortable, share your reflection with your classmates so that they can learn from your experience and give you ideas for revision. For ideas on writing a reflection, see p. 27.

From *The Gift of Fear*

Gavin de Becker

A well-known expert on violent behavior, Gavin de Becker argues that we can predict, and thus often prevent, violent behavior. In the following excerpts from *The Gift of Fear*, he argues that instead of ignoring our instincts as we often do, we should listen to them — even if we can't explain them. Following de Becker's advice would mean sometimes assuming the worst about people — sometimes acting as if people will hurt us — but he claims that safety trumps all. De Becker is currently a senior fellow at the UCLA School of Public Affairs, and he has also served on the President's Advisory Board at the United States Department of Justice.

Focus on Genre   *The Gift of Fear* is a self-help book for a general audience. In it, de Becker gives us advice that, he hopes, will prompt us to stop denying our instincts that some people aren't trustworthy. Many of the strategies he uses as a writer, then, are designed to persuade us — to convince us that we should behave in certain ways and not others. As you read, think about whether or not you are persuaded, and try to trace your reaction to what de Becker does and doesn't do as a writer. Think about, for instance, the way he uses examples, anticipates readers' objections, and establishes point of view (tells stories through the perspective of a particular person).

◄○►

China Leonard's story is not about violence. It is, however, about life and death, and about the denial of intuition. She and her young son, Richard, had just settled into the preop room at St. Joseph's Hospital, where Richard was soon to have minor ear surgery. He usually had a barrage of questions for doctors, but when the anesthesiologist, Dr. Joseph Verbrugge Jr., came into the room, the boy fell silent. He didn't even answer when Dr. Verbrugge asked if he was nervous. "Look at me!" the doctor demanded, but Richard didn't respond.

The boy obviously disliked the abrupt and unpleasant doctor, and China felt the same way, but she also felt something more than that. A strong intuitive impulse crossed her mind: "*Cancel the operation,*" it boldly said, "*Cancel the operation.*" She quickly suppressed that impulse and began a mental search for why it was unsound. Setting aside her intuition about Dr. Verbrugge in favor of logic and reason, she assured herself that you can't judge someone by his personality. But again, that impulse: "*Cancel the operation.*" Since China Leonard was not a worrier, it took some effort to silence her inner voice. "Don't be silly," she thought, "St. Joseph's is one of the best hospitals in the state, It's a teaching hospital; it's owned by the Sisters of Charity, for Christ's sake. You just have to assume this doctor is good."

With her intuition successfully beaten down, the operation went forward as scheduled, and Richard died during the minor procedure. It is a sad story that teaches us that the words "I know it" are more valuable than the words "I knew it."

Later, it was revealed that some of Dr. Verbrugge's colleagues had also been concerned about him. They said he was inattentive to his work, and, most seriously, there were at least six occasions when colleagues reported that he appeared to be sleeping during surgeries. For the hospital staff, these were clear signals, but I can't be certain what China and her son detected. Their concern—whatever it was—was justified by the boy's death, and I accept that as good enough.

There were people right at the operating table who heard and then vetoed their intuition. The surgeon told Verbrugge that Richard's breathing was distressed, but Verbrugge did nothing effective. A nurse said she was getting concerned with the boy's distress but "chose to believe" that Verbrugge was competent.

One of the doctors who reviewed how people had performed in that operating room could have been speaking about denial in general when he astutely said: "It's like waking up in your house with a room full of smoke, opening the window to let the smoke out, and then going back to bed."

IN THE PRESENCE OF DANGER

"This above all, to refuse to be a victim."   —*Margaret Atwood*

He had probably been watching her for a while. We aren't sure—but what we do know is that she was not his first victim. That afternoon, in an effort to get all her shopping done in one trip, Kelly had overestimated what she could comfortably carry home. Justifying her decision as she struggled with the heavy bags, she reminded herself that making two trips would have meant walking around after dark, and she was too careful about her safety for that. As she climbed the few steps to the apartment building door, she saw that it had been left unlatched (again). Her neighbors just don't get it, she thought, and though their lax security annoyed her, this time she was glad to be saved the trouble of getting out the key.

She closed the door behind her, pushing it until she heard it latch. She is certain she locked it, which means he must have already been inside the corridor.

Next came the four flights of stairs, which she wanted to do in one trip. Near the top of the third landing, one of the bags gave way, tearing open and dispensing cans of cat food. They rolled down the stairs almost playfully, as if they were trying to get away from her. The can in the lead paused at the second floor landing, and Kelly watched as it literally turned the corner, gained some speed, and began its seemingly mindful hop down the next flight of steps and out of sight.

"Got it! I'll bring it up," someone called out. Kelly didn't like that voice.   10
Right from the start something just sounded wrong to her, but then this friendly-looking young guy came bounding up the steps, collecting cans along the way.

He said, "Let me give you a hand."

"No, no thanks, I've got it."

"You don't look like you've got it. What floor are you going to?"

She paused before answering him. "The fourth, but I'm okay, really."

He wouldn't hear a word of it, and by this point he had a collection of cans   15
balanced between his chest and one arm. "I'm going to the fourth floor too," he said, "and I'm late—not my fault, broken watch—so let's not just stand here. And give me that." He reached out and tugged on one of the heavier bags she was holding. She repeated, "No, really, thanks, but no, I've got it."

Still holding on to the grocery bag, he said, "There's such a thing as being *too* proud, you know."

For a moment, Kelly didn't let go of that bag, but then she did, and this seemingly insignificant exchange between the cordial stranger and the recipient of his courtesy was the signal—to him and to her—that she was willing to trust him. As the bag passed from her control to his, so did she.

"We better hurry," he said as he walked up the stairs ahead of Kelly. "We've got a hungry cat up there."

Even though he seemed to want nothing more at that moment than to be helpful, she was apprehensive about him, and for no good reason, she thought. He was friendly and gentlemanly, and she felt guilty about her suspicion. She didn't want to be the kind of person who distrusts everybody, so they were next approaching the door to her apartment.

"Did you know a cat can live for three weeks without eating?" he asked. "I'll   20 tell you how I learned that tidbit: I once forgot that I'd promised to feed a cat while a friend of mine was out of town."

Kelly was now standing at the door to her apartment, which she'd just opened.

"I'll take it from here," she said, hoping he'd hand her the groceries, accept her thanks, and be on his way. Instead, he said, "Oh no. I didn't come this far to let you have another cat food spill." When she still hesitated to let him in her door, he laughed understandingly. "Hey, we can leave the door open like ladies do in old movies. I'll just put this stuff down and go. I promise."

She did let him in, but he did not keep his promise.

*   *   *

At this point, as she is telling me the story of the rape and the whole three-hour ordeal she suffered, Kelly pauses to weep quietly. She now knows that he killed one of his other victims, stabbed her to death.

All the while, since soon after we sat down knee to knee in the small gar-   25 den outside my office, Kelly has been holding both my hands. She is twenty-seven years old. Before the rape, she was a counselor for disturbed children, but she hasn't been back to work in a long while. That friendly looking young man had caused three hours of suffering in her apartment and at least three months of suffering in her memory. The confidence he scared off was still hiding, the dignity he pierced still healing.

Kelly is about to learn that listening to one small survival signal saved her life, just as failing to follow so many others had put her at risk in the first place. She looks at me through moist but clear eyes and says she wants to understand every strategy he used. She wants me to tell her what her intuition saw that saved her life. But she will tell me.

"It was after he'd already held the gun to my head, after he raped me. It was after that. He got up from the bed, got dressed, then closed the window. He glanced at his watch, and then started acting like he was in a hurry."

"I gotta be somewhere. Hey, don't look so scared. I promise I'm not going to hurt you." Kelly absolutely knew he was lying. She knew he planned to kill her, and though it may be hard to imagine, it was the first time since the incident began that she felt profound fear.

He motioned to her with the gun and said, "Don't you move or do anything. I'm going to the kitchen to get something to drink, and then I'll leave. I promise. But you stay right where you are." He had little reason to be concerned that Kelly might disobey his instructions because she had been, from the moment she let go of that bag until this moment, completely under his control. "You know I won't move," she assured him.

But the instant he stepped from the room, Kelly stood up and walked after   30
him, pulling the sheet off the bed with her. "I was literally right behind him, like a ghost, and he didn't know I was there. We walked down the hall together. At one point he stopped, and so did I. He was looking at my stereo, which was playing some music, and he reached out and made it louder. When he moved on toward the kitchen, I turned and walked through the living room."

Kelly could hear drawers being opened as she walked out her front door, leaving it ajar. She walked directly into the apartment across the hall (which she somehow knew would be unlocked). Holding a finger up to signal her surprised neighbors to be quiet, she locked their door behind her.

"I knew if I had stayed in my room, he was going to come back from the kitchen and kill me, but I don't know how I was so certain."

"Yes, you do," I tell her.

She sighs and then goes over it again. "He got up and got dressed, closed the window, looked at his watch. He promised he wouldn't hurt me, and that promise came out of nowhere. Then he went into the kitchen to get a drink, supposedly, but I heard him opening drawers in there. He was looking for a knife, of course, but I knew way before that." She pauses. "I guess he wanted a knife because using the gun would be too noisy."

"What makes you think he was concerned about noise?" I ask.   35

"I don't know." She takes a long pause, gazing off past me, looking back at him in the bedroom. "Oh . . . I do know. I get it, I get it. Noise was the thing—that's why he closed the window. That's how I knew."

Since he was dressed and supposedly leaving, he had no other reason to close her window. It was that subtle signal that warned her, but it was fear that gave her the courage to get up without hesitation and follow close behind the man who intended to kill her. She later described a fear so complete that it replaced every feeling in her body. Like an animal hiding inside her, it opened to its full size and stood up, using the muscles in her legs. "I had nothing to do with it," she explained. "I was a passenger moving down that hallway."

What she experienced was real fear, not like when we are startled, not like the fear we feel at a movie, or the fear of public speaking. This fear is the powerful ally that says, "Do what I tell you to do." Sometimes, it tells a person to play dead, or to stop breathing, or to run or scream or fight, but to Kelly it said, "Just be quiet and don't doubt me and I'll get you out of here."

Kelly told me she felt new confidence in herself, knowing she had acted on that signal, knowing she had saved her own life. She said she was tired of being blamed and blaming herself for letting him into her apartment. She said she had learned enough in our meetings to never again be victimized that way.

"Maybe that's the good to come from it," she reflected. "The weird thing is,   40
with all this information I'm actually less afraid walking around now than I was before it happened—but there must be an easier way people could learn."

The thought had occurred to me. I know that what saved Kelly's life can save yours. In her courage, in her commitment to listen to intuition, in her determination to make some sense out of it, in her passion to be free of unwarranted fear, I saw that the information should be shared not just with victims but with those who need never become victims at all. I want this book to help you be one of those people.

Because of my sustained look at violence, because I have predicted the behavior of murderers, stalkers, would-be assassins, rejected boyfriends, estranged husbands, angry former employees, mass killers, and others, I am called an expert. I may have learned many lessons, but my basic premise in these pages is that you too are an expert at predicting violent behavior. Like every creature, you can know when you are in the presence of danger. You have the gift of a brilliant internal guardian that stands ready to warn you of hazards and guide you through risky situations.

I've learned some lessons about safety through years of asking people who've suffered violence, "Could you have seen this coming?" Most often they say, "No, it just came out of nowhere," but if I am quiet, if I wait a moment, here comes the information: "I felt uneasy when I first met that guy . . ." or "Now that I think of it, I was suspicious when he approached me," or "I realize now I had seen that car earlier in the day."

Of course, if they realize it now, they knew it then. We all see the signals because there is a universal code of violence. You'll find some of what you need to break that code in the following chapters, but most of it is in you.

SURVIVAL SIGNALS

"People should learn to see and so avoid all danger. Just as a wise man
keeps away from mad dogs, so one should not make friends with evil men."
— *Buddha*

Kelly had been apprehensive from the moment she heard the stranger's voice,   45
and now she wants me to tell her why. More than anything else, it was just the
fact that someone was there, because having heard no doors open before the
man appeared, Kelly knew (at least intuitively) that he must have been waiting
out of sight near the entry hall. Only as we spoke did she realize that when he
said he was going to the fourth floor, he didn't offer why. It was Kelly who had
filled in the blanks, concluding that he was visiting the Klines, who lived across
the hall from her. Now, as we are talking, she realizes that if the Klines had
admitted a guest over the intercom, she'd have heard the loud buzz of the electric lock being released, and Mrs. Kline would have been at the top of the stairs,
already well into a high-volume conversation with her visitor. It was because of
all this that Kelly's intuition sent her the signal to be wary.

Kelly tells me that she didn't listen to herself because there wasn't anything
she saw in the man's behavior to explain the alarm she felt. Just as some things
must be seen to be believed, some must be believed to be seen. The stranger's
behavior didn't match Kelly's image of a rapist's behavior, and she could not
consciously recognize what she didn't recognize. Neither can you, so one way
to reduce risk is to learn what risk looks like.

The capable face-to-face criminal is an expert at keeping his victim from
seeing survival signals, but the very methods he uses to conceal them can
reveal them.

Forced Teaming

Kelly asks me what signals her attacker displayed, and I start with the one I call
"forced teaming." It was shown through his use of the word "we" ("We've got a
hungry cat up there"). Forced teaming is an effective way to establish premature trust because a *we're-in-the-same-boat* attitude is hard to rebuff without
feeling rude. Sharing a predicament, like being stuck in a stalled elevator or
arriving simultaneously at a just-closed store, will understandably move people
around social boundaries. But forced teaming is not about coincidence; it is
intentional and directed, and it is one of the most sophisticated manipulations.
The detectable signal of forced teaming is the projection of a shared purpose or
experience where none exists: "Both of us"; "We're some team"; "How are we
going to handle this?"; "Now we've done it," etc.

David Mamet's film *House of Games* is a wonderful exploration of cons and
con artists that shows forced teaming at work. A young soldier enters a Western Union office late one evening; he is anxious about whether the money he
needs for a bus ticket will arrive there before Western Union closes. Another
man is there, apparently in the same predicament. The two commiserate while
waiting, and then the man tells the soldier, "Hey, if my money comes in first, I'll

give you whatever amount you need. You can send it to me when you get back to the base." The soldier is moved by this kindness, but the stranger brushes it off, saying, "You'd do the same for me."

In fact, the stranger is *not* in the same boat, is not expecting any money to   50
be wired. He is a con artist. Predictably, the soldier's money is the only to arrive, and when the Western Union office closes, he insists that the stranger accept some of his cash. The best cons make the victim want to participate.

Kelly did not consciously recognize what her intuition clearly knew, so she couldn't apply the simple defense for forced teaming, which is to make a clear refusal to accept the concept of partnership: "I did not ask for your help and I do not want it." Like many of the best defenses, this one has the cost of appearing rude. Kelly now knows it is a small cost, comparatively speaking.

Safety is the preeminent concern of all creatures and it clearly justifies a seemingly abrupt and rejecting response from time to time. Anyway, rudeness is relative. If while waiting in some line, a person steps on our foot a second time, and we bark, "Hey!" we don't call our response rude. We might even feel we showed restraint. That's because the appropriateness of our response is relative to the behavior that provoked it. If people would view forced teaming as the inappropriate behavior It is, we might feel less concern about appearing rude in response. . . .

Charm and Niceness

Charm is another overrated ability. Note that I called it an ability, not an inherent feature of one's personality. Charm is almost always a directed instrument, which, like rapport building, has motive. To charm is to compel, to control by allure or attraction. Think of charm as a verb, not a trait. If you consciously tell yourself, "This person is trying to charm me," as opposed to "This person is charming," you'll be able to see around it. Most often, when you see what's behind charm, it won't be sinister, but other times you'll be glad you looked.

So many signals, I tell Kelly, are in the face. She intuitively read the face of her attacker, as she is now reading mine, as I am now reading hers. University of California at San Francisco psychologist Paul Eckman says, "The face tells us subtleties in feelings that only a poet can put into words." One way to charm is with the smile, which Eckman calls the most important signal of intent. He adds that it is also "the typical disguise used to mask the emotions."

University of California at Los Angeles psychiatrist Leslie Brothers says, "If I   55
am trying to deceive someone, that person has to be just a bit smarter than I am in order to see through my deceit. That means you have sort of an arms race."

The predatory criminal does all he can to make that arms race look like détente. "He was so nice" is a comment I often hear from people describing the man who, moments or months after his niceness, attacked them. We must learn and then teach our children that niceness does not equal goodness. Niceness is a decision, a strategy of social interaction; it is not a character trait. People seeking to control others almost always present the image of a nice person in the beginning. Like rapport building, charm, and the deceptive smile, unsolicited niceness often has a discoverable motive.

Kelly nods and reminds me that her attacker was "very nice." I tell her about a rhyme by Edward Gorey, the master of dark humor:

> *The proctor buys a pupil ices*
> *And hopes the boy will not resist,*
> *When he attempts to practice vices*
> *Few people even know exist.*

Yes, the proctor is nice enough to buy some sweets for the boy, and he is nice in lots of other ways, but that is not a credential of his good intent. . . .

Too Many Details

People who want to deceive you, I explain to Kelly, will often use a simple technique that has a simple name: too many details. The man's use of the story about the cat he left unfed in a friend's apartment: too many details. His reference to leaving the door open, "like ladies do in old movies": too many details. His volunteering that he is always late ("broken watch, not my fault"): too many details.

When people are telling the truth, they don't feel doubted, so they don't feel the need for additional support in the form of details. When people lie, however, even if what they say sounds credible to you, *it doesn't sound credible to them*, so they keep talking.

60

Each detail may be only a small tack he throws on the road, but together they can stop a truck. The defense is to remain consciously aware of the context in which details are offered.

Context is always apparent at the start of an interaction and usually apparent at the end of one, but too many details can make us lose sight of it. Imagine gazing out the window of a train as it pulls away from the station. Details move by you, or you by them, slowly at first. As the train gets going a little faster, you see more details, but each one more briefly: an empty playground, a phrase painted in graffiti, some kids playing in the street, a construction site, the steeple of a church, until the train reaches a speed that requires you to let the individual components become . . . a neighborhood. This same transition can occur as a conversation becomes . . . a robbery. Every type of con relies upon distracting us from the obvious.

Kelly had so many details thrown at her that she lost sight of this simple context: The man was an absolute stranger. Whenever the train got going fast enough that she was uncomfortable, whenever she might have seen what was happening, like his taking the shopping bag from her hand even though she said no, he slowed the train down with some new irrelevance. He used catchy details to come to be perceived as someone familiar to her, someone she could trust. But she knew him artificially; she knew the con, not the con man.

The person who recognizes the strategy of Too Many Details sees the forest while simultaneously being able to see the few trees that really matter. When approached by a stranger while walking on some city street at night, no matter how engaging he might be, you must never lose sight of the context: He is a stranger who approached you. A good exercise is to occasionally remind yourself of where you are and what your relationship is to the people around you. With a date who stays beyond his welcome, for example, no matter how jokey or charming he may be, a woman can keep herself focused on context simply by thinking, "I have asked him to leave twice." The defense for too many details is simple: Bring the context into conscious thought.

Typecasting

Another strategy used by Kelly's rapist is called typecasting. A man labels a woman in some slightly critical way, hoping she'll feel compelled to prove that his opinion is not accurate. "You're probably too snobbish to talk to the likes of me," a man might say, and the woman will cast off the mantle of "snob" by talking to him. A man tells a woman, "You don't look like someone who reads the newspaper," and she sets out to prove that she is intelligent and well-informed. When Kelly refused her attacker's assistance, he said, "*There's such thing as being too proud, you know,*" and she resisted the label by accepting his help.

Typecasting always involves a slight insult, and usually one that is easy to refute. But since it is the response itself that the typecaster seeks, the defense is silence, acting as if the words weren't even spoken. If you engage, you can win the point, but you might lose something greater. Not that it matters what some stranger thinks anyway, but the typecaster doesn't even believe what he says is true. He just believes that it will work.

Loan Sharking

The next signal I explain to Kelly is one I call loan sharking: "He wanted to be allowed to help you because that would place you in his debt, and the fact that you owe a person something makes it hard to ask him to leave you alone." The more traditional loan shark gladly lends one amount but cruelly collects much more. Likewise, the predatory criminal generously offers assistance but is always calculating the debt. The defense is to bring two rarely remembered facts into consciousness: He approached me, and I didn't ask for any help. Then, though a person may turn out to be just a kindly stranger, watch for other signals.

We are all familiar with the stranger who offers to help a woman with her groceries; most often he is a fairly unsophisticated loan shark looking to pick someone up. The debt he records in his ledger can usually be paid off quite easily, just a little talk will do it. But he has something in common with the predatory criminal who imposes his counterfeit charity into someone's life: motive. There is no spiritually minded movement dedicated to lightening the burden of American women by carrying their groceries. At its best, loan sharking is a strategy on a par with asking a woman, "Do you come here often?" At its worst, it exploits a victim's sense of obligation and fairness.

I haven't focused here on the criminal who simply walks up, displays a weapon, and demands money. That's because he is distinctly more obvious than those who use the strategies I've described.

It's important to clarify that forced teaming, too many details, charm, nice- 70 ness, typecasting, and loan sharking are all in daily use by people who have no sinister intent. You might have already recognized several of these strategies as those commonly used by men who want little more than an opportunity to engage a woman in conversation. I don't mean to cramp the style of some crude Casanova, but times have changed, and we men can surely develop some approaches that are not steeped in deceit and manipulation.

The Unsolicited Promise

For the next signal, I ask Kelly to go back to that moment when she was reluctant to let her attacker into her apartment. He had said, "I'll just put this stuff down and go. I *promise*."

The unsolicited promise is one of the most reliable signals because it is nearly always of questionable motive. Promises are used to convince us of an intention, but they are not guarantees. A guarantee is a promise that offers some compensation if the speaker fails to deliver; he commits to make it all right again if things don't go as he says they would. But promises offer no such collateral. They are the very hollowest instruments of speech, showing nothing more than the speaker's desire to convince you of something. So, aside from meeting all unsolicited promises with skepticism (whether or not they are about safety), it's useful to ask yourself: Why does this person need to convince me? The answer, it turns out, is not about him—it is about you. The reason a person promises something, the reason he needs to convince you, is that he can see that you are not convinced. You have doubt (which is a messenger of intuition), likely because there is reason to doubt. The great gift of the unsolicited promise is that the speaker tells you so himself!

In effect, the promise holds up a mirror in which you get a second chance to see your own intuitive signal; the promise is the image and the reflection of your doubt. Always, in every context, be suspicious of the unsolicited promise. When Kelly's rapist told her he would leave after he got something to drink from the kitchen, he detected her doubt, so he added, "I promise."

Here's the defense: When someone says "I promise," you say (at least in your head) "You're right, I am hesitant about trusting you, and maybe with good reason. Thank you for pointing it out."

Discounting the Word "No"

It is late, and I suggest to Kelly that we'll discuss the rest tomorrow, but she 75 wants another signal before we stop. Like every victim of a truly awful crime, she is anxious to make some sense of it, to understand it, to control it. So I speak to her about one more signal, perhaps the most universally significant one of all: a man's ignoring or discounting the concept of *no*. Kelly's rapist ignored it several times, in various forms. First she said no, she didn't want his help. Then she showed him no when she didn't immediately let go of the bag.

Actions are far more eloquent and credible than words, particularly a short and undervalued word like "no," and particularly when it's offered tentatively or without conviction. So when Kelly said no but then agreed, it wasn't really no anymore. "No" is a word that must never be negotiated, because the person who chooses not to hear it is trying to control you.

In situations in which unsolicited offers of assistance are appropriate, such as approaches by a salesman or flight attendant, it is simply annoying if you have to decline three times. With a stranger, however, refusal to hear "no" can be an important survival signal, as with a suitor, a friend, a boyfriend, even a husband.

Declining to hear "no" is a signal that someone is either seeking control or refusing to relinquish it. With strangers, even those with the best intentions, never, ever relent on the issue of "no," because it sets the stage for more efforts to control. If you let someone talk you out of the word "no," you might as well wear a sign that reads, "You are in charge."

The worst response when someone fails to accept "no" is to give ever-weakening refusals and then give in. Another common response that serves the criminal is to negotiate ("I really appreciate your offer, but let me try to do it on my own first"). Negotiations are about possibilities, and providing access to someone who makes you apprehensive is not a possibility you want to keep on the agenda. I encourage people to remember that "no" is a complete sentence.

The criminal's process of victim selection, which I call "the interview," is 80 similar to a shark's circling potential prey. The predatory criminal of every variety is looking for someone, a vulnerable someone, who will allow him to be in control, and just as he constantly gives signals, so does he read them.

The man in the underground parking lot who approaches a woman as she puts groceries in the trunk of her car and offers assistance may be a gentleman or he may be conducting an interview. The woman whose shoulders tense slightly, who looks intimidated and shyly says, "No, thanks, I think I've got it," may be his victim. Conversely, the woman who turns toward him, raises her hands to the Stop position, and says directly, "I don't want your help," is less likely to be his victim.

A decent man would understand her reaction or, more likely, wouldn't have approached a woman alone in the first place, unless she really had some obvious need. If a man doesn't understand the reaction and stomps off dejected, that's fine too. In fact, any reaction—even anger—from a decent man who had no sinister intent is preferable to continued attention from a violent man who might have used your concern about rudeness to his advantage.

A woman alone who needs assistance is actually far better off choosing someone and asking for help, as opposed to waiting for an unsolicited approach. The person you choose is nowhere near as likely to bring you hazard as is the person who chooses you. That's because the possibility that you'll inadvertently select a predatory criminal for whom you are the right victim type is very remote. I encourage women to ask other women for help when they need it, and it's likewise safer to accept an offer from a woman than from a man. (Unfortunately, women rarely make such offers to other women, and I wish more would.)

I want to clarify that many men offer help without any sinister or self-serving intent, with no more in mind than kindness and chivalry, but I have been addressing those times that men refuse to hear the word "no," and that is not chivalrous—it is dangerous.

When someone ignores that word, ask yourself: Why is this person seeking to control me? What does he want? It is best to get away from the person altogether, but if that's not practical, the response that serves safety is to dramatically raise your insistence, skipping several levels of politeness. "I said *NO!*"

When I encounter people hung up on the seeming rudeness of this response (and there are many), I imagine this conversation after a stranger is told "no" by a woman he has approached:

Man: What a bitch. What's your problem, lady? I was just trying to offer a little help to a pretty woman. What are you so paranoid about?

Woman: You're right. I shouldn't be wary. I'm overreacting about nothing. I mean, just because a man makes an unsolicited and persistent approach in an underground parking lot in a society where crimes against women have risen four times faster than the general crime rate, and three out of four women will suffer a violent crime; and just because I've personally heard horror stories from every female friend I've ever had; and just because I have to consider where I park, where I walk, whom I talk to, and whom I date in the context of whether someone will kill me or rape me or scare me half to death; and just because several times a week someone makes an inappropriate remark, stares at me, harasses me, follows me, or drives alongside my car pacing me; and just because I have to deal with the apartment manager who gives me the creeps for reasons I haven't figured out, yet I can tell by the way he looks at me that given an opportunity he'd do something that would get us both on the evening news; and just because these are life-and-death issues most men know nothing about so that I'm made to feel foolish for being cautious even though I live at the center of a swirl of possible hazards *doesn't mean a woman should be wary of a stranger who ignores the word "no."*

Whether or not men can relate to it or believe it or accept it, that is the way it is. Women, particularly in big cities, live with a constant wariness. Their lives are literally on the line in ways men just don't experience. Ask some man you know, "When is the last time you were concerned or afraid that another person would harm you?" Many men cannot recall an incident within years. Ask a woman the same question and most will give you a recent example or say, "Last night," "Today," or even "Every day."

Still, women's concerns about safety are frequently the subject of critical comments from the men in their lives. One woman told me of constant ridicule and sarcasm from her boyfriend whenever she discussed fear or safety. He called her precautions silly and asked, "How can you live like that?" To which she replied, "How could I not?"

I have a message for women who feel forced to defend their safety concerns: tell Mister I-Know-Everything-About-Danger that he has nothing to contribute to the topic of your personal security. Tell him that your survival instinct is a gift from nature that knows a lot more about your safety than he does.

Questions for Critical Reading

1. What did you take to be de Becker's purpose? For you as a reader, was that purpose achieved? Why or why not?

2. Recall that writers in a variety of persuasive genres anticipate readers' objections and, rather than ignoring them, explicitly address them. De Becker does this when he writes, "I want to clarify that many men offer help without any sinister or self-serving intent, with no more in mind than kindness and chivalry, but I have been addressing those times that men refuse to hear the word 'no'" (para. 84). It's as if de Becker imagines a reader saying "But not all men hurt women" and then responds to that reader. What effect does this move have on you as a reader? Does de Becker anticipate and address objections often enough for you, or were there passages that didn't address your objections? Take a couple of minutes to find a passage that succeeds — or doesn't succeed — in addressing your objections, and consider why you responded to it in the way you did.

3. Like many writers across genres, de Becker uses an antithesis (the juxtaposition of opposite ideas) to emphasize his points. Compare the two passages with antitheses to the altered passages that don't have antitheses, and consider whether de Becker uses them effectively:

Original Passage	Altered Passage
Think of charm as a verb, not a trait. If you consciously tell yourself, "This person is trying to charm me," as opposed to "This person is charming," you'll be able to see around it. (para. 53)	Think of charm as a verb. If you consciously tell yourself, "This person is trying to charm me," you'll be able to see around it.
Niceness is a decision, a strategy of social interaction; it is not a character trait. (para. 56)	Niceness is a decision, a strategy of social interaction.

How would you have responded differently if de Becker hadn't used these antitheses? Given his purpose as a writer, why do you think he used them?

4. Recall that readers of many genres tend not to trust writers when they make blanket statements — when they claim or imply, for example, that all people are the same in some way or that something is always true. Consider this blanket statement made by de Becker: "Always, in every context, be suspicious of the unsolicited promise" (para. 73). Did this claim undermine de Becker's credibility in your eyes, or do you think a blanket claim is warranted in this case? Why?

5. When writing across genres, it's useful to be able to manipulate the order of words within a passage — to take a passage you've written and, keeping the same words, simply reorder them. To that end, compare these original passages from *The Gift of Fear* to their altered counterparts, considering the effect of the different word order:

Original Passage	Altered Passage
She wants me to tell her what her intuition saw that saved her life. But she will tell me. (para. 26)	She will tell me what her intuition saw that saved her life. But she wants me to tell her.
Most often, when you see what's behind [someone's] charm, it won't be sinister, but other times you'll be glad you looked. (para. 53)	Sometimes you'll be glad you looked behind [someone's] charm, but most often, when you see what's behind it, it won't be sinister.

Why do you think de Becker might have chosen the word order he did in the original passages? Which passages do you prefer, and why?

Making Connections

6. Rather than providing a series of similar examples, writers across genres often juxtapose *different* types of examples. This strategy can help writers drive home a point or show the complexity of an issue. De Becker, for instance, uses the following (very different) people as examples:

- China Leonard (whose son dies when she doesn't listen to her instincts)
- Kelly (who saves her own life when she does listen to her instincts)

In his book *Blink* (p. 207), Malcolm Gladwell also uses very different people as examples:

- Warren Harding (about whom people assume the best — mistakenly)
- Abbie Conant (about whom people assume the worst — mistakenly)
- Bob Golomb (who assumes the best about people — productively)

What do you think each writer accomplishes by giving us different, rather than similar, types of examples? How might you have responded if de Becker had provided examples only of people who had listened to their instincts — or examples only of people who didn't? How might you have responded if Gladwell had provided only one type of example? When might you as a writer want to provide different types of examples?

7. Writers using different genres often use different means of establishing point of view (POV) — of telling a story or discussing an issue through the filter of a particular person's perspective. For instance, in the oral history "C. P. Ellis" (p. 235), Studs Terkel uses the first person ("I") to relate C. P. Ellis's story, as in the following passage: "Since I changed, I've set down and listened to tapes of Martin Luther King. I listen to it and tears come to my eyes 'cause I know what he's sayin' now. I know what's happenin'" (para. 62).

While Terkel uses the first person to help readers see things through Ellis's eyes, de Becker uses multiple strategies to help us see things through Kelly's eyes. First, he quotes Kelly extensively, which allows him to use both the third person ("she") and, like Terkel, the first person ("I"). In addition, he tells us not only Kelly's actions but also her thoughts and feelings, as in the following passage:

> As she climbed the few steps to the apartment building door, she saw that it had been left unlatched (again). Her neighbors just don't get it, she thought, and though their lax security annoyed her, this time she was glad to be saved the trouble of getting out the key. (para. 7)

Would de Becker's and Terkel's narratives have affected you differently if they hadn't been told from Kelly's and Ellis's points of view? Why or why not?

Writing: Your Turn

1. Write a reflection discussing whether or not you find the excerpts from *The Gift of Fear* to be persuasive, and why. If you find some parts to be more persuasive than others, please explain. Trade reflections with a classmate to share your ideas and get ideas for revision. For ideas on writing a reflection, see p. 27.

2. If you appreciated the information that de Becker provides in the section with subheadings ("Forced Teaming," "Charm and Niceness," "Too Many Details," "Typecasting," "Loan Sharking," "The Unsolicited Promise," and "Discounting the Word 'No'"), use that information to write a brochure. Give your brochure to some classmates to get their feedback on both the content and the design, and consider their feedback when you revise. Share your revised brochure with at least ten people who might appreciate the information (people who have not read *The Gift of Fear* or excerpts from it). For ideas on writing a brochure, see p. 105.

gay (gā) **1.** there once was a time when all "gay" meant was "happy." then it meant "homosexual." now, people are saying "that's so gay" to mean dumb and stupid. which is pretty insulting to gay people (and we don't mean the "happy" people). **2.** so please, knock it off. **3.** go to ThinkB4YouSpeak.com

Ad Council

GLSEN®

 To see these public service announcements in color, visit the e-Pages for *Real Questions* at bedfordstmartins.com/realquestions/epages.

Questions for Critical Reading

1. The purpose of PSAs (public service announcements) is typically to change people's attitudes and/or behavior. Attitudes and behavior stem in part from our responses to difference; people often make uncharitable assumptions about those they perceive to be different. Select two of the PSAs to consider in terms of difference and assumptions. What do they seem to suggest about how we should respond to difference? Why?

2. Note that the "Gay" and "United by Mission" PSAs appeared in print publications and that "Stop the Sag!" and "Violence...It's Not Okay" appeared on billboards. What do the two billboards have in common, and what do the two print ads have in common? To what do you attribute these common elements?

3. Consider a particularly important design element: repetition. What design elements (including shapes and similar images in photos) do you see repeated in each PSA? What is the effect of the repetition in each PSA?

4. Like other genres, PSAs exist in a web of multiple genres, media, and actions. Consider why New York State Senator Eric Adams, one of the "Stop the Sag!" sponsors, might have supplemented his PSA with a column in the *New York Post* entitled "Give 'em a kick in the saggy pants."[2] Here's a passage from Adams's column:

> The communities I represent are ground zero for sagging. Some people may think, What's the big deal? But it's more than someone not wearing a belt on their pants....
>
> Mayor Bloomberg made a comment one day—I think he said we shouldn't be the dress-code police. I think he missed the boat. He's so far up in the building that he doesn't realize what those broken windows are doing on the first floor.
>
> In the society he hangs out in, they don't sag. They laugh at people that sag. And they just say, "Those are the people we'll never hire, who will never date our children." In the universe that he lives in, sagging is not an issue. Would he hire someone that comes in the building sagging? Would he employ them to run his corporation? Would he bring them into City Hall?

Why do you think Adams supplemented the PSA with this column? What can he accomplish with a column that he can't with a PSA?

---

[2] Column published on March 11, 2012; accessed on October 3, 2012 from http://www .nypost.com/p/news/local/give_em_kick_in_the_saggy_pants_B0WFceEhEQnOp91CM5MvpK

Pulling It All Together

ARGUMENT

Drawing on the readings in this chapter, write an argument about making assumptions about people. You might formulate a thesis to address a question you had while reading, or you might address one of these questions:

- To what extent are negative assumptions about others a problem in a specific medium or social setting that you're familiar with? So that you can advance a focused, in-depth argument, discuss just one medium or social setting (e.g., TV or Facebook — or your hometown, college, or high school). Similarly, consider focusing on one group of people (e.g., male, female, young, elderly, rich, poor). Is the problem — either the frequency or the consequences — more or less serious than people generally realize?

- When people habitually make negative assumptions about others, to what extent might it be possible for them to change? If it's possible, how might they go about doing so? To write a focused argument, decide whether you want to address a social issue, such as racism, sexism, or classism, or whether you want to address interpersonal issues, such as those addressed by Gottman and Abdullah.

Address your argument to an audience of classmates, and when you're done writing, ask them if reading your work changed their attitudes or might change their behavior. If they found your work persuasive, ask them how it could be more so; if they didn't, ask them what their objections are so that you can address them in your revision. See p. 42 for ideas on writing an argument.

OP-ED

Write an op-ed discussing people's assumptions about others. You might consider any of the following to help you craft a timely hook:

- a newly released movie, book, or music video that illustrates assumptions people make about others
- a recent study or news story relating to people's assumptions of others
- an event that recently happened to you or someone you know

When you write your op-ed, have a specific purpose in mind; for example, you might want to make readers aware of a pattern of assumptions you see, or you might want them to reexamine their own assumptions (and possibly their behavior). Some op-eds quote or paraphrase sources, so you might consider drawing on some of the readings in this chapter as evidence.

After you finish writing your op-ed, identify specific passages that you want feedback on and ask your classmates for their thoughts on those passages, along with any other revision ideas they have. For ideas on writing an op-ed, see p. 62.

3

What is happiness, and how can we find it?

How do we become happy or unhappy?

How does the self-help industry make
big money off marketing happiness?

How might we practice
making ourselves happy?

Is happiness a political issue?

How can we quantify world happiness?

How Can We Be Happy?

In 2007, social psychologist Adrian White received a lot of press after publishing a study entitled "A Global Projection of Subjective Well-Being: A Challenge to Positive Psychology?" In his study, White ranked the countries of the world by how happy their citizens reported being, and he reported that the happiest country was Denmark, with the United States coming in at number twenty-three. This might surprise people in the United States, since we live in a country where shelves of books are sold promising us the secret to happiness (an Amazon.com search for "happiness" yields over 30,000 results) and where ads on TV, billboards, and the Internet show us what we can buy to increase any joy missing in our lives. Happiness is even built in to our national politics; after all, our Declaration of Independence makes the bold claim that the "pursuit of happiness" is one of the most central human rights.

This chapter explores a variety of ideas about what makes happiness difficult to achieve and, conversely, what makes it possible. Readings from several different genres provide insight into this complex topic, ultimately raising questions such as the following: What can people do to make themselves happier? What obstacles prevent happiness? Why are some people happier than others? What role do poverty and other extreme adversities play in influencing people's levels of happiness? Should governments enact policies to support people in their pursuit of happiness — or at least to prevent conditions that make happiness arguably next to impossible? Who is ultimately responsible for creating conditions in which people can be happy? After reading this chapter, you'll have a more nuanced understanding of this complex topic and of the many ways that people write — and think — about it.

Case Study in Happiness: Maslow's Hierarchy of Needs

If you had to describe what happiness is and offer someone steps to achieve it, how would you do it? You might find it difficult at first because happiness is such an abstract concept. To begin your foray into this topic, think about whether there are any prerequisites to happiness — any conditions that need to be met before people can be happy. To this end, consider the following excerpt from the online encyclopedia article "Maslow's Hierarchy of Needs" by educational psychology professor William Huitt, PhD. Published in Huitt's *Educational Psychology Interactive*, "Maslow's Hierarchy of Needs" summarizes an influential theory that may help readers gain insight into the needs that, according to the theory, must be met before people can find self-fulfillment.

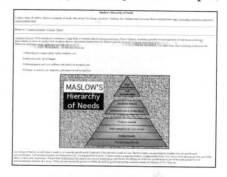

Recall that encyclopedia articles are generally written for the purpose of introducing readers to a topic and that they typically favor breadth over depth of coverage, often simplifying ideas in the process. One way "Maslow's Hierarchy of Needs" simplifies an abstract concept is by presenting it visually. Indeed, diagrams and other visuals are used across genres to illustrate concepts that can be hard to explain in text, as well as to present information with greater impact. As you read, consider how the diagram of the triangle works in tandem with the words to provide a relatively simple, concrete representation of an abstract concept. Also consider whether you agree with Maslow's theory about which needs must be met before people can find self-fulfillment.

To read and answer questions about this case study online, visit the e-Pages for *Real Questions* at **bedfordstmartins.com/realquestions /epages.**

Maslow's Hierarchy of Needs

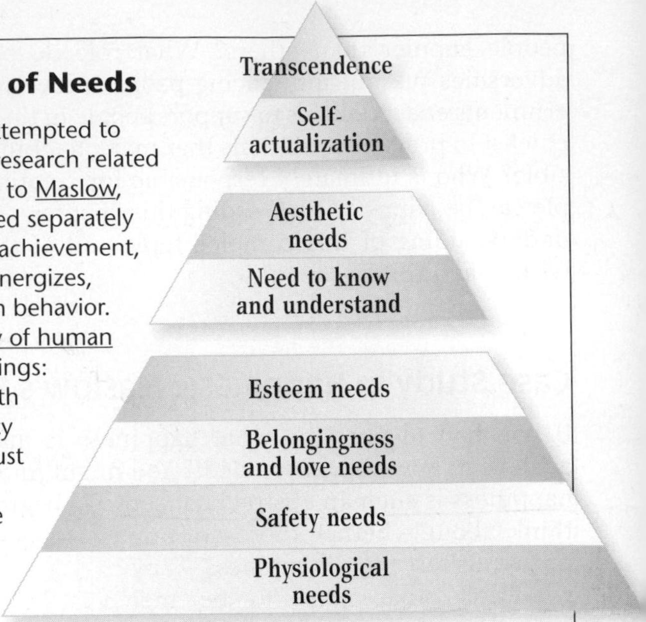

Abraham Maslow (1954) attempted to synthesize a large body of research related to human motivation. Prior to Maslow, researchers generally focused separately on such factors as biology, achievement, or power to explain what energizes, directs, and sustains human behavior. Maslow posited a hierarchy of human needs based on two groupings: deficiency needs and growth needs. Within the deficiency needs, each lower need must be met before moving to the next higher level. Once each of these needs has been satisfied, if at some future time a deficiency is detected, the individual will act to remove the deficiency. The first four levels are:

Transcendence

Self-actualization

Aesthetic needs

Need to know and understand

Esteem needs

Belongingness and love needs

Safety needs

Physiological needs

(margin note: First steps)

1. Physiological: hunger, thirst, bodily comforts, etc.;
2. Safety/security: out of danger;
3. Belongingness and Love: affiliate with others, be accepted; and
4. Esteem: to achieve, be competent, gain approval and recognition.

According to Maslow, an individual is ready to act upon the growth needs if and only if the deficiency needs are met. Maslow's initial conceptualization included only one growth need—self-actualization. Self-actualized people are characterized by (1) being problem-focused [focused on problems outside of the self rather than being ego-centered]; (2) incorporating an ongoing freshness of appreciation of life; (3) a concern about personal growth; and (4) the ability to have peak experiences. Maslow later *differentiated the growth need of self-actualization,* specifically identifying two of the first growth needs as part of the more general level of self-actualization (Maslow & Lowery, 1998) and one beyond the general level that focused on growth beyond that oriented towards self (Maslow, 1971). They are:

(margin note: second steps)

5. Cognitive: to know, to understand, and explore;
6. Aesthetic: symmetry, order, and beauty;
7. *Self-actualization:* to find self-fulfillment and realize one's potential; and
8. *Self-transcendence:* to connect to something beyond the ego or to help others find self-fulfillment and realize their potential.

Maslow's basic position is that as one becomes more *self-actualized and self-transcendent,* one becomes more wise (develops wisdom) and automatically knows what to do in a wide variety of situations. Daniels (2001) suggested that Maslow's ultimate conclusion that the highest levels of self-actualization are transcendent in their nature may be one of his most important contributions to the study of human behavior and motivation. . . .

Maslow published his first conceptualization of his theory over fifty years ago (Maslow, 1943) and it has since become one of the most popular and often cited theories of human motivation.

References

Daniels, M. (2001). *Maslow's concept of self-actualization*. Retrieved February 2004, from http://www.mdani.demon.co.uk/archive/MDMaslow.htm.

Maslow, A. (1943). A theory of human motivation. *Psychological Review, 50*, 370-396. Retrieved June 2001, from http://psychclassics.yorku.ca/Maslow/motivation.htm.

Maslow, A. (1954). *Motivation and personality*. New York: Harper.

Maslow, A. (1971). *The farther reaches of human nature*. New York: The Viking Press.

Maslow, A., & Lowery, R. (Ed.). (1998). *Toward a psychology of being* (3rd ed.). New York: Wiley & Sons.

Questions for Critical Reading

1. To what extent do you agree that basic needs such as food and shelter must be met before people can find self-fulfillment? Do you think that Maslow's theory, as represented in the excerpted encyclopedia article, is too much of an oversimplification to be useful, or do you see value in this representation of his ideas? Why?

2. For you as a reader, does the visual aid of the triangle succeed in providing a concrete representation of an abstract concept? Why or why not?

3. As when analyzing words, when analyzing visuals it can be useful to imagine altered versions. Some versions of Maslow's triangle, for example, include not one but two levels of text within the triangle: the descriptive label (e.g., "Physiological Needs") and, underneath that, examples in smaller type (e.g., "food, water"). Do you think examples in smaller type would have made the diagram more effective for you as a reader, or do you think the more streamlined original version works as is? Why?

4. Regardless of genre, many writers put a lot of thought into making their visuals and their text mutually reinforcing. A tall rectangle, rather than a triangle, could have been selected to house the key words of Maslow's theory. Given the description of the theory in "Maslow's Hierarchy of Needs," do you think this might have been a choice worth considering? Why or why not?

Consider how well Maslow's ideas resonate with your own. For example, if you think it might be true that people who are starving may not be able to find self-fulfillment, then Maslow's theory might serve as a useful caveat (a caution) when you read the other selections in this chapter, some of which imply that we're capable of pursuing and finding happiness at any given time in our lives.

About the Readings

Taken together, the selections in this chapter will provide you with a richer understanding of the many facets of happiness. They'll also help you appreciate the potential dangers of assuming we know everything there is to know about what enables happiness for everyone.

The first selection, "The Waltz," is a creative nonfiction essay that gives us a rich sense of what it's like to live with a relatively common obstacle to happiness, obsessive-compulsive disorder (OCD). OCD is just one of many conditions in which people's brain chemistry makes happiness difficult to achieve, and remembering brain differences when reading the other selections will, like "Maslow's Hierarchy of Needs," provide a useful caveat — a caution against the perhaps incomplete solutions that are proposed to address the problem of unhappiness.

Another useful caveat is provided by the excerpt from Barbara Ehrenreich's *Bright-Sided*, a critique of how the positive psychology movement may lead us to, among other things, ignore the role that circumstances play in people's happiness, thus potentially allowing us to feel comfortable abandoning advocacy for issues such as quality education and health care. When reading about happiness, you'll find that critique is an especially important genre, since assumptions about what enables happiness (circumstances vs. chosen behavior) often drive public policy, as you'll see when you read Arthur Brooks's political argument "Inequality and (Un)Happiness in America." Brooks suggests that U.S. public policy shouldn't include measures such as welfare and higher taxes for the rich because, he argues, poverty doesn't cause unhappiness.

In counterpoint to Brooks's political argument, the press release "University of Leicester Produces the First Ever World Map of Happiness" and the news article based on it, Marina Kamenev's "Rating Countries for the Happiness Factor," suggest that poverty (along with poor health care and education) *does* contribute to unhappiness.

Although these genres provide us with some understanding of national and global levels of happiness, insight into what we can do to improve our individual happiness is provided by several other genres. The excerpt from Martin Seligman's self-help book chapter, "Positive Feeling and Positive Character," suggests that we can be happier by identifying and more frequently using our "signature strengths." The excerpt from Mihaly Csikszentmihalyi's *Flow*, a summary of his seminal social science research, likewise focuses on individual happiness; Csikszentmihalyi describes the common elements in his participants' "optimal experience"—elements, he suggests, that we can integrate into our own personal experiences. Dr. John Ratey's synthesis of medical research, "Depression: Move Your Mood," makes the case that exercise can prompt individual happiness, while a more personal insight is provided by Gretchen Rubin's blog post "Act the Way You Want to Feel." Rubin notes that changing her facial muscles changes her mood—an interesting personal experience that she augments by citing research and quoting an expert. Still more insight into what influences an individual's level of happiness can be gained from reading Mary Pipher's case study "June," an account of how the remembrance of a deceased mother's love helps a young woman overcome adversity and ultimately achieve happiness.

Reading these selections from a variety of genres will help you see how one author's ideas might call another author's ideas into question, and it will ultimately help you gain insight that you may be able to use in your own quest to become happier, to understand others, and to appreciate the role that assumptions about happiness play in national and global arenas.

For additional readings in online and multimedia genres related to the chapter theme, see the e-Pages online at **bedfordstmartins.com /realquestions/epages.**

The Waltz

Mary Beth Ellis

In "The Waltz," Mary Beth Ellis describes what it's like to live with obsessive-compulsive disorder: "The nice ribbons and sharp paper edges are gone, frayed out of existence by fear and flinching and sorrow." By better understanding what it's like to live with fear and sorrow, we gain insight into how complex — and how difficult to achieve — happiness can be for many people. "The Waltz" was published in Random House's *Twentysomething Essays by Twentysomething Writers* (2006).

Focus on Genre   As a work of creative nonfiction, "The Waltz" uses original, artfully crafted language to convey an implicit (unstated) message. As a bonus, Ellis injects humor throughout the piece. As you read, think about Ellis's purpose and how her use of humor may have helped her achieve that purpose. Also note how Ellis communicates characters' emotions; rather than explicitly labeling feelings, she often describes characters' actions. Consider, above all, what she gains by letting us figure things out by ourselves rather than stating an explicit thesis.

◄O►

By order of the resident assistant, I made the appointment with the therapist following a fairly major war with my next-door neighbor in the dorm, an altercation involving her assertion that *Growing Pains* reigned supreme over all the eighties sitcoms of the land. I kicked her wall and put my foot through her prized possession, a Whopper banner swiped from the flagpole of a Burger King, because *everybody* knows that *Family Ties* just absolutely *rocked*, at least until the extraordinarily slappable extra child, Andy, showed up.

"I think I need help with stress management," I said to the therapist. I was perched on the edge of a lavender chair crammed hard with foam and embroidery. It was aggressively comforting, this chair.

A manila file folder marked with my name was open on the psychologist's lap. "I see you've been in therapy before," she said.

That would be my freshman year of high school, when I first became strongly convinced that if I did not touch a doorknob with both hands upon entering or exiting a room, the world would implode in dramatic and fully horrible fashion.

"Yes," I said. I had not told anyone that such matters were my chief concern most days, as I was fully aware they were well within the realm of the totally ridiculous.

5

"Also," said the woman before me with my mental health history spread on her knees, "you seem to have had certain excessive . . . anxieties . . . concerning use of the Internet?"

That, I hadn't quite been able to hide. When you are fourteen and you make furtive attempts to double back to the pew your family was sitting in so you can scrub away the fingerprints, thus leaving no record of your active Catholicism because you are privately terrified that the Ku Klux Klan is after you, people tend to form the conclusion that There Is a Problem.

Activities such as these sprang from the day I posted a gentle rant to an electronic religious discussion group, in which I'd announced to the whole entire Internet that I was Catholic and that, in my very humble opinion, liturgical dance was the worst thing *ever* and that it made me want to injure people with blunt and heavy objects.

Making this pronouncement, I decided with a terrifying and completely unwarranted urgency less than a week after I'd typed it, was not the brightest thing I had ever done. It was bottomlessly stupid; it was *stupid*, and it was going to get me killed. The Klan! They hate Catholics, they *kill* Catholics, and where better to find Catholics than a public forum? Oh God, maybe they *set up the discussion* for the *sole purpose* of finding some! And there were other people . . . just who, I didn't know, but they were out there and they hated Catholics and they were going to kick my ass.

And the liturgical dancers . . . oh God . . . I'd insulted the liturgical dancers   10
of the earth. They were going to find me, me and my family. Right now they
were taking a break from choreographing "Crown Him with Many Crowns" to
call out a hit on me, their vaunted and public enemy. Why didn't I just keep my
mouth shut? Why hadn't I just endured their "Nearer My God to Thee" kick-
lines in silence? I had angered them, belittled their cherished way of life, and
any second now a gauze-wrapped grenade was going to come sailing through
the window. Oh God oh God oh God oh God.

I stayed away from the Internet after that, and not long after came the day
when my mother walked into my room with some laundry to find me breaking
open a floppy disk, slicing apart its filmy guts with a pair of desk scissors. She
stared at me, a stack of bras in one hand, a pile of Umbro shorts in the other.

"Isn't that," she said, "where the computer saves all the stories and essays
you've been writing?"

I glanced down at the torn-away disk label marked with my name—I was
going to tear *that* up next, in very tiny bits, and scatter them in a variety of
trash bags throughout the house, over a course of many trash collection days,
so that no one could piece them together and trace me to it—and looked back
up at her, scissors poised.

She twisted her hands in one of my bra straps. "Why are you doing that?"

"I don't know," I said finally, unable to break her heart and let on that I   15
had gone altogether round the bend and was terrified of the frantic electrons
that were the Internet, where there was no way to tear up anything you
wrote, where God and all His revenge-bent liturgical dancers could find you.
Two days later, I was in another version of where I am now—in a therapist's
office, in the grips of a chair decorated in Modern American Hotel Lobby,
where, for the duration of my high school career, I participated in circular
conversations concerning whether or not I was breast-fed, the monotony of
which was occasionally sprinkled with moments when the therapist wanted
to know, by the way and just out of simple curiosity, if I ever heard voices
belonging to famous people or the Devil or God instructing me to, say, shoot
the president.

"Well," I said now by way of explanation, "you know."

The therapist closed my file. I settled in and prepared to be casually asked
whether I held regular conversations with the Lord of Darkness.

Instead she was eyeing my hands. "You have dry skin," she said.

"I wasn't breast-fed," I said, nodding.

"Dry skin on your hands and nowhere else," she pointed out. "They're   20
chapped almost raw."

"You know what?" I said, rising. "I have a class."

"It's almost as if," she continued, examining her ballpoint pen, "you've been washing them with some fairly strong soap. Pretty often, actually."

Oh dear.

"It's okay if you do," she said.

Ohhhhhhhhhhhh . . .   25

"Do you have a lot of unwanted thoughts and worries, Mary Beth?"

"I'm having some *right now*." I bent down to retrieve my backpack.

"Are those fears over events you intellectually know aren't likely to happen, but you can't stop worrying anyway? And do you feel you need to check and arrange things a lot to relieve the worry—not just leaving the curling iron on, but more out-of-the-ordinary things, like rereading pages in a book over and over, avoiding certain numbers. . . ."

I sat down again. "Three!" I said. "And six!"

"It sounds like you might have obsessive-compulsive disorder."   30

"And I'm afraid that if I sit in a chair that a guy's been sitting in, I will become pregnant!"

"Let's make another appointment so I can administer a screening test."

"I'm afraid I'll catch AIDS from library books!"

"Okay, well, maybe we can skip the screening test."

When one has obsessive-compulsive disorder, insufficient amounts of the   35
neurotransmitter serotonin prevent proper communication between one's orbital cortex and basal ganglia, resulting in unwanted obsessive thoughts, even though the patient is fully cognizant of the inappropriate and nonsensical nature. To sum: The brain is on a constant short circuit and therefore shits a brick. You don't die from OCD. You just wish you would.

Patients can tackle the symptoms of it—the liturgical-dancer panic, the frantic mental urgings to run for the bathroom sink—with behavioral therapy, which involves extensive and intense work on retraining one's brain by forcing oneself to face, even encounter, those aspects of life that one most fears. When the therapist suggested this—she encouraged me to, for instance, wear my boyfriend's boxer shorts for a day without washing them first—I communicated that I'd really rather not by way of throwing up in her floral trash can.

The other course of action is to ingest staggering amounts of government-regulated mind-altering substances. I was all for this.

The Luvox, the "serotonin reuptake inhibitor"—they could have called it Warmed-Over String-Bean Vomit, for all I cared, as long as it curbed the overwhelming urge to carry my own toilet paper into public restrooms because God only knew what kind of AIDS-riddled microbes lurked within the tire-size rolls—tamed the OCD to a manageable if irritating mosquito whine. Life as a

Luvox-sedated obsessive-compulsive is like arising each morning with a slightly pulled calf muscle: You can run, walk, stretch, and kick perfectly well, but not without an eternally twinging reminder, a tiny pinprick of fear. There is always sewage in the serotonin canal.

The OCD flows through my family like a Purell-purchasing version of the Force: My great-grandmother had it. My grandmother had it. I have it. But I also have the gift of receiving a diagnosis in an era when personal problems are quite the thing, as evidenced when my girlhood hero, Mary Lou Retton, told the world that she has an overactive bladder, easily the most important celebrity endorsement of a bodily dysfunction since Jerry Mathers bravely denounced psoriasis. So far, those of us with OCD have netted only former *Double Dare* host Marc Summers, but as awareness increases, we might be able to score us someone on the level of a Loni Anderson or—dare we dream—a Bob Barker.

Everyday life is a soapy film coating seas of panic and second-guessing. We seek   40 constant reassurance from those without OCD that our fears are groundless, thus unwittingly sweeping friends and family members into the sticky, clawing net.

And I'm one of the lucky ones. Some OCD patients, unresponsive to treatment or just plain unaware that there exists a name and a lot of slanty Latin words for what they're feeling and thinking and doing, spend hours before the mirror, parting their hair just . . . exactly . . . right. Others feel forced to hoard mail, sit on every single piece of it, hundreds and hundreds of little Ed McMahons smiling out from beneath the kitchen table, in between piles of 1987 *Peoples*, peering up from behind the television set. There are those compelled to count objects—windowpanes, words, songs on the radio—to a certain number for a certain number of times. Many can't stop tearing out their own hair. Sometimes an OCD patient cannot leave a room without holding a certain word or phrase in his mind. Mothers double over in the fear that they will somehow harm their children; children erase holes in their math homework, frantic that they haven't printed out their numbers in precisely the proper fashion.

Me, I just spend an inordinate amount of time worrying that, virgin status notwithstanding, I will come down either pregnant or HIV-positive. So: a *Hannity & Colmes* session between me and my serotonin . . . holding myself a delicate distance from a gentleman's crotch . . . these are simple things, really.

Try telling that, however, to the gentleman. The experts have informed me that such fears are quite prevalent among OCD patients who have grown up steeped in Catholicism, a religion that kind of frowns upon premarital sex; but if that's really the case, we would have popped up with a Saint Simon of the Antibacterial Soap a long, long time ago.

As I began dating more and more, and the Luvox-pumped serotonin levels went up and up, I wasn't sure if I felt uncomfortable with the nonsex I was having because of the obsessing and compulsing in my head or because of the Blessed Virgin statue on my windowsill. On dates I would toss my hair and lean forward with wide eyes and feign enchantment over butchered acoustical versions of "Gloria"; then I'd return to the dorm, stare up at the stained ceiling, and anxiously await my period. My other friends, when they had pregnancy scares, at least had the preliminary fun of the thing.

Every time I fumbled through a darkened dorm room in search of my underwire bra, I had to sort it out like dirty laundry: Did I feel cascades of unease after I sat up on the couch because I was afraid that HIV had somehow magically leaped into my bloodstream, or because if an anvil came crashing down upon me through the ceiling, it meant big-time hell for me?   45

By the end of my college career, I had it pretty well figured out—when I felt like a slut as I was dropped off, it was the Catholicism; when I merely felt like shooting up a horse tranquilizer, it was the OCD. On a good night I felt only one or the other.

I've been through four boyfriends and two therapists since I was diagnosed, and the only one not currently eyeing me from a distance of at least seven states are the therapists.

The first boyfriend, to his everlasting credit, broke up with me because he was an idiot and a child and was feeling, and I quote, "trapped" after I insisted that he remove the pictures of his ex-girlfriend from his walls. Obsessive-compulsive disorder, whatever—just don't come between him and the woman who'd asked for a restraining order.

The second boyfriend, a little worse. When I explained the condition to him, he had no problem with it as long as his wang was satisfyingly chunged, and when I told him I felt uncomfortable or frightened, he tended to become very, very concerned with how incredibly frustrating all this was for him personally. "I just . . . I just need some time to come to terms with this," he said once after I asked him to stop, tears spilling down my face. He then turned his face toward the wall.

I sent that one packing after he shipped me an anniversary present—we   50
celebrated it in late February—with a card reading "Happy Anniversary to a Great Couple!" and a bag of Valentine's Day candy with the 50-percent-off tag still dangling.

The most earnest one lasted all of seven months. He did his best, God bless him—came to a therapy session with me, looked up the Obsessive-Compulsive Foundation on the Internet—but the problem with him wasn't so much the number of women he'd been with before he began dating me (nine) or the fact that, as a non-Catholic he'd never experienced the faith-based restrictions I faced (nine!); it was more that he'd never been in a relationship with a heavily medicated lady before, even though, to be honest, the only OCD skin off his nose (*nine*), other than the fact that one of us had to have her underwear on at all times and was afraid to sit on certain spots of the bed, was to periodically endure the offhand question "So you did test negative, right? . . . *right*?" (*Nine!*) And so all of a sudden here was this poor fellow in a relationship with a woman who drew her knees to her chest in paroxysms of panic every now and again (NINE!) after definitely not having sex, so I should not have been too horribly shocked when the word came via e-mail one morning: "I've come to the conclusion," he wrote, "that OCD is not something I could spend the rest of my life with."

After I read this, I sat on the floor and cried a whole lot, and then I took myself for a wee-small-hours drive, at the end of which, the odometer, I could not help but notice, stood at 33,033 miles.

For all this, however, for all the Luvox and the neurons and the occasional field trips to the fetal position, most people don't know that I have OCD until I tell them about it; one of the main symptoms of OCD is that its patients rarely exhibit any. We *know* that crabs cannot be transmitted via Blockbuster rentals; we are fully aware that no misfortune shall befall us should we become the sixth person in line rather than the fourth or seventh or twenty-eighth; and for the most part, the dishes get washed and the TPS report gets faxed without anyone knowing that our neurons fear otherwise. Much as the fears loom and snarl on the inside, nearly as bad is the fear that somebody else will know they are there.

I could be sitting right smack next to you in a movie theater, in the pincers of an OCD attack, terrified more than anyone has ever been, and the only sound you will hear, the only sight you will see, is Tom Hanks before you delivering a soliloquy to a volleyball, a thing bad enough all on its own.

For we are actors, consummate and professional actors, we members of the OCD Guild. There should be a separate Oscar ceremony each and every year specifically for obsessive-compulsives. "And the award for Best Excuse upon Getting Caught Backing In and Out of a Doorway Seventeen Times goes to . . ." "The nominees for Outstanding Adeptness at Covering Up the Fact That One Is Counting the Number of Syllables in the Sentence One Is Currently Speaking are . . ."

"Think of the most scared you've every felt," I'll say to people who ask me about it. "It feels like that, only all the time, every single second of every single day." People will cock their heads and conjure up the top of the roller coaster or the day Dad found out about the dent on the Wrangler.

If you're missing a leg, people get that, it's *right there*, they're not going to ask you to help move the couch. Where OCD is concerned, where the absurd

55

meets cover-ups of Watergate dimensions, it's not so self-explanatory. Go ahead, give it a shot: "I'd love to play tennis, Alan, but I can't serve game point because I have a strong aversion to the number three."

It's simpler with women, with friends, with men who repulse me sexually, because once the bottle of wine is half gone and the other party has slipped me a secret of his own, it's not a far leap to slur, "Did I ever tell you that I can't let myself inhale if someone's talking about AIDS, that I'll, like, hold my breath for, like, *ever* because I toooooootally freak out that if I breathe in while someone's even *talking* about it, then I'm afraid that means I'll get it? Iddn't that fucked *up*?" I have no problem broaching the subject under these circumstances, for if the other party freaks and bolts, I can watch him walk away without wondering whether I have just truthed myself right out of a potential groom.

At what point does one inform a budding love interest that one has qualms turning a page in a magazine if the last word of the last paragraph is "death" or "baby" or "positive" or "wrong"? First date? Second? After he's seen you without makeup? Before or after the check? "I'll have the surf and turf, and by the way, in the rare event this evening that your pubic area should brush mine and I run shrieking for the shower, don't take it personally." I feel an obligation to run some sort of public service disclaimer, a PG-13 warning that She's Got Issues; and I feel I need to lay it all out for each potential suitor before he starts building up feelings of the for-life variety. It would not be sporting of me to allow the Serotonin Express to mow him sideways after he has been so foolish.

Sometimes with OCD there are only fear and the fetal position, no washing or checking or counting, just plain old ordinary terror that comes and goes as it pleases. Here, I'll use an example we can all recognize: 60

"Hello, I'm anthrax, and I'll be your OCD trigger today. Worried yet? . . . worried yet? . . . worried yet? . . . No?" What about that box you opened the other day, with the address labels you ordered from New Jersey—you really aren't sure which post office that came through, are you? How about now? . . . No white powder, but then again there doesn't necessarily have to be any, you know . . . Oh, there you go! That's a lovely panic attack, right in the middle of the *Cheers* rerun, very nice. Good girl! Good girl: Get up, look at the labels, think about tossing them out, wash your hands, can't be too careful! Lookit, I'll allow you to watch the first twenty minutes of *Skating with Celebrities* in relative peace, then I'll come back and check on you, okay? I'll see ya. . . . In the meantime—oh dear, is that a headache coming on? Sore throat? Oh, doesn't matter, you know that by the time the symptoms come on, it's too late anyway, you're dead. Wash your *hands*!"

This happens every now and again, when real-life worries and normal-people stresses ooze out of the basal ganglia in the form of some truly fer-weird mental experience. It sucks when this comes to pass, because the OCD, it does this on purpose, digs deep into your psyche, submarines down through sugar-cookie recipes and the brand of socks that don't crunch up when I run and how Colorado smells in the morning; and then it roots out the diamonds, the good stuff, the things that mean the most, and it clamps on and it contaminates.

Months ago, as my thesis deadline closed in, I began to shift uneasily and look over my shoulder every time I prayed the Rosary, suddenly and for no reason at all fearing an apparition from the Virgin Mary, somehow convinced that such an appearance would signal the end of the world. (The OCD is overfond of fretting about the apocalypse, apparently unaware that its arrival would neatly counteract all of the other calamities it usually shrieks about.)

Here was a powerful religious figure whom I normally enjoyed hanging out with, prayer-wise, and the fear spread to going to Communion and then Mass itself. I swept every Mary statue in the house into a box and hid it behind the Christmas decorations, the gold-painted halos and the tiny white hands clinking together as I fled from room to room, beside myself at my feebleness in the face of such illogic: Like the boyfriend who sent me on my way once he realized that his discomfort with the OCD was greater than his love for me, I was shoving away someone I loved and leaned on because I was afraid.

At such times I wish very hard that I had done less learning and more drinking in college, that I had developed the ability to drain large amounts of liquor without having to toss it right back up at the bar. Nights, wandering the blazing house in fear of the Virgin Mary (I felt quieter with the lights on somehow, protected by the blazing glow of the GE bulbs), I would pause before my father's liquor cabinet, arrested by the rows of see-through Scotch and dark, engulfing Jack, square and sturdy in the bottle. The thick phantom sensations of the two times I have been full-blown drunk would slide into my bloodstream and extremities. Anesthetized, dead: It would be so nice, I'd think, running a palm over the decanter lids, to be numb, and hurling. But the Luvox doesn't work as well with alcohol in the system, makes you sleepy, and so I'd keep pacing, next room, next worry-go-round. 65

These phases never last long; they level out, once medications are adjusted and exercise is attended to, and I sink back into the blissful state of normality— to bitch, without impunity, about the mere existence of Jessica Simpson! The sublime joy of going to my dead-end job every morning! Normal is lovely; the grind is a salve. Those of us with OCD live for the days when the counting is unconscious and the flashes of discomfort exist as a mere itch on the anklebone; when the battery-acid fear is far off on the horizon somewhere, and the house may be exited without tossing all the matchbooks in the bathtub first.

That is why, in the aftermath of September 11, I watched with equal parts pity and dark amusement as the nation had a bout of the serotonin grippers. What's this, don't you feel safe in everyday life anymore? Do you fear that the calm Delta fabric print of the seat back in front of you is the last sight you'll ever see? Are you slathering yourself with Germ-X every time you page through the Lands' End catalog? Longing to go about your day worried only that your TiVo commands were set correctly? Pull up a chair and have a Luvox: You've just taken your first step into a freakier world, young Skywalker.

Normal people, people in Nebraska and Delaware and Utah with no prescriptions to fill, were forced to redefine bravery as they beheld cranes lifting entire fire engines from the smoking hole in the concrete that was once the World Trade Center. To me, a person whose most frightening, thick-scariest task was to log on to the Internet so I could close my online account during my liturgical-dancer phase, anyone who ran *at* danger, on *purpose*, was a *god*. Army guys and fire chiefs and police officers — my God, imagine the mean people who must hate *them*. How do they get *up* in the morning? Terrorists . . . death threats . . . smallpox . . . poison in the water supply . . . that was small potatoes, that was amateur hour. I panicked over microorganisms in my juice box way before Tom Brokaw ever did, man, eons and ages before *Newsweek* deemed it fashionable to fling oneself hysterical over baby powder on the bathroom floor.

So, the whole Mary thing.

The Our Lady of Lourdes statue and the Rosaries, they continue to reside   70
with the Tinker Bell Christmas stocking and the *Grandma Got Run Over by a Reindeer* CD. I go to Mass, but I'm typing this quickly, nervous clicks on the keyboard, because the topic gives me the d.t.'s. We continue in a nodding, proper Protestant relationship, the Virgin and I, and probably will until the next fun topic screams down the brain pike.

And . . . that's it?

That's never it. That's OCD: The nice ribbons and sharp paper edges are gone, frayed out of existence by fear and flinching and sorrow.

But what if . . .

And how about . . .

That is how OCD goes, and that is what the life is like: the endless march,   75
the daytime drama with no final episode, on and on with predictable camera angles and ridiculous plots and new actors taking over the same character as the rest of the townsfolk pretend not to notice. Fear, adjust, fear again: The needle skips, the gramophone gets a kick, and the dance, it goes on . . . never as a waltz, though . . . in that dance, you count by threes.

Questions for Critical Reading

1. What do you think Ellis's purpose was in writing this piece? For you as a reader, did she accomplish this purpose? Why or why not?

2. Why do you think that instead of telling us directly what her purpose was, Ellis left us to figure it out by ourselves?

3. Although readers don't expect to encounter humor in every genre, it's not uncommon in creative nonfiction. Do you think Ellis's use of humor helps her achieve her purpose, or do you think she should have avoided humor in an essay about such a serious impediment to happiness? Why?

4. Most writers—regardless of genre—try to maintain a sharp focus. That is, they try to cut words, sentences, or paragraphs that don't relate to their topic. Given that Ellis's topic revolves around her OCD, some readers might find that her opening doesn't establish her focus sharply; other readers, however, might find that it works. Consider her first paragraph, assessing how sharp the focus is for you as a reader:

> By order of the resident assistant, I made the appointment with the therapist following a fairly major war with my next-door neighbor in the dorm, an altercation involving her assertion that *Growing Pains* reigned supreme over all the eighties sitcoms of the land. I kicked her wall and put my foot through her prized possession, a Whopper banner swiped from the flagpole of a Burger King, because *everybody* knows that *Family Ties* just absolutely *rocked*, at least until the extraordinarily slappable extra child, Andy, showed up. (para. 1; emphasis original)

If you were Ellis, would you keep the opening as it is, replace it, or revise it to better illustrate how it relates to OCD? Why?

5. Although flashbacks are common in creative nonfiction, writers sometimes find it difficult to signal when flashbacks begin and end, thus confusing readers. Consider how Ellis signals the beginning of her flashback:

> "Also," said the woman before me with my mental health history spread on her knees, "you seem to have had certain excessive . . . anxieties . . . concerning use of the Internet?"
>
> That, I hadn't quite been able to hide. When you are fourteen and you make furtive attempts . . . (paras. 6–7)

Ellis lets us know that we are entering a flashback in two ways: she refers to her younger age (fourteen), and she changes verb tense (from past—"said the woman"—to past perfect—"I *hadn't* quite been able to hide"). She lets us know we're leaving the flashback in another way: after describing a scene with her mother that's part of the flashback, she twice uses the word "now" (italicized) to help us transition back into the original scene at the therapist's office. Consider whether this strategy works for you as a reader:

"I don't know," I said finally, unable to break [my mother's] heart and let on that I had gone altogether round the bend and was terrified of the frantic electrons that were the Internet. . . . Two days later, I was in another version of where I am *now*—in a therapist's office, in the grips of a chair decorated in Modern American Hotel Lobby, where, for the duration of my high school career, I participated in circular conversations concerning whether or not I was breast-fed, the monotony of which was occasionally sprinkled with moments when the therapist wanted to know . . . if I ever heard voices belonging to famous people or the Devil or God instructing me to, say, shoot the president.

"Well," I said *now* by way of explanation, "you know."

The therapist closed my file. (paras. 15–17)

For you as a reader, are the transitions into and out of the flashback adequately signaled? Why or why not? Why do you think Ellis uses flashbacks?

Making Connections

6. Creative nonfiction writers often imply characters' emotions rather than directly telling readers how characters feel. One way writers imply emotions is by describing actions—either actions characters take or those they feel like taking. Writers in other genres may or may not use this strategy. Consider the following passages from three different genres, and see if you can come up with an explanation for why each writer did or didn't explicitly name the emotions being felt. Each writer's strategy for suggesting emotion is italicized.

Creative nonfiction ("The Waltz")

When the therapist suggested [that I face my fears]—she encouraged me to, for instance, wear my boyfriend's boxer shorts for a day without washing them first—I communicated that I'd really rather not by way of *throwing up in her floral trash can*. (para. 36)

By the end of my college career, I had it pretty well figured out—when I felt like a slut as I was dropped off, it was the Catholicism; when I merely felt like *shooting up a horse tranquilizer*, it was the OCD. (para. 46)

Case study ("June")

June paused and looked at me [and said] "Mom died at the start of my freshman year in high school. It was an awful time to lose her. I had just started my periods. I was clumsy and had bad acne. I had been slightly chubby and then I got fat. I was totally alone."

June blew her nose before continuing. "The year Mom died, I watched the Miss America pageant all by myself. I stared at those thin, poised girls and knew I would never be like that. I had no looks and no talents. Only my mom had loved me as I was. I thought about giving up."

She rubbed her forehead . . . (paras. 10–12)

Blog post ("Act the Way You Want to Feel")

Lately, I've been feeling low. I had various justifications for my blue mood, but just last night it occurred to me—maybe it's due to my persistent case of viral conjunctivitis. . . .

As a consequence of the conjunctivitis, my eyes well up constantly, and I wipe tears off my face many times through the day. Maybe *that's* contributing to my feelings of sadness.

It sounds far-fetched—that *I feel sad* because my eyes are watering as a result of eye inflammation. . . .

[But actions,] even involuntary actions, influence feelings. Studies show that an artificially induced smile can prompt happier emotions. . . (paras. 4–7; emphasis on "that's" in original)

Why might the blog author have chosen to explicitly tell us what emotion she was feeling while the other authors didn't? Take a few minutes to rewrite the passages from "The Waltz" and "June" so that emotions are labeled directly rather than being implied through actions. Then do the reverse for the blog; write a version that replaces the name of the emotion ("low," "sad") with a description of an action. When you're done rewriting, compare notes with a classmate. Do you think the original authors made good choices about how to convey emotion, or do you prefer your revisions? Why?

Writing: Your Turn

1. Write your own creative nonfiction essay about an obstacle to achieving happiness. Just as Ellis does, try to depict emotion through actions rather than by simply naming feelings. Share your work with some of your classmates, and see if they can accurately identify the emotions implied by the actions. For more ideas on writing creative nonfiction, see p. 77.

2. Write a condensed version of two or three sections of "The Waltz." (Sections are signaled by additional white space, such as that between paragraphs 34 and 35.) Condense the sections you selected by explicitly telling readers things that are just implied in the original. For example, you could write "My old therapist was terrible" to replace the passage that reads "I participated in circular conversations concerning whether or not I was breast-fed, the monotony of which was occasionally sprinkled with moments when the therapist wanted to know . . . if I ever heard voices belonging to famous people or the Devil or God instructing me to, say, shoot the president" (para. 15). In addition to being fun, making the writing ineffective in this way might help you gain insight into some of the strategies writers use to enable readers to make inferences. Share your condensed version and the original with a classmate so that he or she can see the stark difference between the two and so that you can get feedback on the changes you made. If your classmate also condensed "The Waltz," discuss who did a better job making the writing worse, and why.

June

From *Reviving Ophelia*

Mary Pipher

"June" is an excerpt from *Reviving Ophelia* (2005), a book written by psychologist Mary Pipher to help an audience of laypeople gain insight into some of the obstacles faced by adolescent girls (and young women). "June" ultimately addresses the question of whether it's possible to be happy in the face of overwhelming adversity. Mary Pipher is a former therapist and the author of eight books, most recently *Seeking Peace. Chronicles of the Worst Buddhist in the World* (2010).

Focus on Genre A case study, "June" is an in-depth account of one person's experience. Although there are many types of case studies, this one is written primarily in narrative form; Pipher relays June's experiences as a story and delays telling us the point of the story until the end. As you read, think about why Pipher might have chosen to organize her writing this way—why she didn't simply state her point at the beginning and then support it by telling us June's story.

Other noteworthy aspects of "June" include the extensive use of quotation and appeals to readers' emotions. As you read, think about why Pipher quoted June so extensively, and why she decided to break June's words into paragraphs in the way that she did.

◄○►

The morning we met, June had worked a double shift at the Kawasaki plant, gone out for breakfast and driven across town to my office. June was big-boned with a round, pockmarked face. She wore her hair short and was dressed in a gray sweat suit. She lumbered into my office and sank onto the couch. She was so physically imposing that I was surprised by her delicate sensibilities.

Her language was personal, precise and earthy. She talked about herself softly and carefully as if psychotherapy, like dentistry, might hurt. She did not, thank goodness, talk like someone who had read too many self-help books.

June said, "I'm here because I am dating someone for the first time in my life. I'm twenty-seven and I've never been kissed. I thought I might need some coaching."

She'd been at Kawasaki for ten years. Her closest friend worked next to her on the assembly line. Dixie was a single parent and June helped her with her kids. She pulled out their school pictures to show me and said they called her Aunt June. "They're real good kids," she said, "once you get to know them."

June had met her boyfriend, Marty, at work too. He was the union rep-   5 resentative for her group of workers. The last three Saturday nights he had dropped by with a pizza and a video. Last Saturday night he put his arm around June. That's when she decided to call me.

I asked her about her family and June sighed. "I was afraid you would bring them up."

"We can wait," I say gently.

"I might as well get it out," she said. "After you hear about my teenage years, you'll understand why I haven't dated much."

June's father was a farm laborer who "never had much to do with me." Her mother was a cook at a rest home. "She was hard-working and fun. She'd bring me treats from the rest home—cookies and crafts that the residents made for me. She showed them my pictures and kept them posted on my activities. Everyone at the home loved her."

June paused and looked at me. "Mom died at the start of my freshman   10 year in high school. It was an awful time to lose her. I had just started my periods. I was clumsy and had bad acne. I had been slightly chubby and then I got fat. I was totally alone."

June blew her nose before continuing. "The year Mom died, I watched the Miss America pageant all by myself. I stared at those thin, poised girls and knew I would never be like that. I had no looks and no talents. Only my mom had loved me as I was. I thought about giving up."

She rubbed her forehead as if to erase some memories too painful to consider. "I don't know how I made it through that year. Dad was never home. I had hardly any clothes. I did what housework and cooking got done and that was precious little. Dad almost never gave me money for groceries. I was fat and hungry at the same time."

I asked her about the kids at school. "They were terrible. Not so much mean, as totally indifferent. I didn't exist for them. I was too ugly and too sad to even be part of the class. I ate by myself and walked to and from school alone. No one would be my lab partner."

She rubbed her big face and continued. "One time a boy approached me in the cafeteria, in front of all the other kids, and asked me to go to a football game. I was such a goof that I thought he meant it. I thought maybe he could see past my appearance and like the real me. So I said sure, if I could get Dad's permission. Then he started laughing. His buddies all whooped it up too. They'd dared him to do it for a joke. He collected ten bucks for just asking me out."

June sighed. "After that I steered clear of boys." 15

Her father married Mercene a year after June's mother died. They took a honeymoon trip to Sun City and brought June salt and pepper shakers for her hope chest. "By then I had no hope," she said flatly.

"My stepmother was tight with money. She only let me wash my hair once a week. I needed to wash it daily it was so greasy, but she didn't want to pay for the water. My teeth were crooked and the school recommended braces. Mercene said, 'I've heard that can cost a thousand dollars. No way we'll spend that kind of money for straight teeth.' Once I cut my foot pretty badly when I was walking beans. She wouldn't pay for the doctor. I limped a little because of that."

I worked hard to remain neutral as June talked about this neglect. June herself had no anger. She continued matter-of-factly. "I was the black sheep. Once my stepbrother asked me why I lived with his family."

I asked how she survived those years when she was rejected at home and at school. "I thought about my mother and how she would have wanted me to behave. I decided that other people's bad behavior was no excuse for mine. I would do the best I could. I talked to Mom in bed at night. I told her about my days. I always tried to have something I was proud of to report to her. I knew she had really loved me, and that got me through a lot. I knew I was lovable and that the people around me were too blind to see it."

She rubbed her broad face with a handkerchief. "At the time I desperately 20 wanted friends. Now I think I learned a lot those years. I learned to take care of myself. I got so that other people's rejection didn't faze me. I had my ideas about right and wrong.

"After high school my life really improved. I started working at Kawasaki. Immediately I felt more accepted. I worked hard and people noticed. Women invited me to eat with them. The men joked around with me. My supervisor took an interest in me. He encouraged me to get my teeth worked on and have my foot evaluated. I wear a brace now that corrected the limp."

June smiled when she spoke of work. "I have a Halloween party every year for all the workers in my area. Fridays I bowl on the union team. I have earned merit raises every year I've worked there. I make good money.

"I've forgiven Dad and Mercene. I'm happy, so what is there to be angry about now? I am happier than they are. I try to do something for them every weekend. I take over a pie or mow their yard."

I asked how she gets along with her father. "Dad can't forgive me for being fat. He really wanted a beautiful daughter."

I thought of June's life. She has a spirit as delicate and strong as a spider-web. She is gifted at forgiving and loving. Because she is unattractive by our cultural standards, she has been devalued by many, including her own father. But somehow she had managed to survive and even thrive through all this adversity. She reminds me of those succulent desert flowers that remain dormant for so many seasons and then bloom lavishly when there is a smattering of rain.

I said to her, "Your father has missed an opportunity to love someone who is marvelous."

We talked about Marty. He's a bulky man who is prematurely balding. June said, "His looks don't matter. I know how hard he works and that he doesn't put anyone down. He's not a complainer."

I suggested that daily she imagine herself successfully kissing him. "It's hard to do what you can't even imagine doing. Once you have the images down, the reality will be easier." I encouraged her to keep her expectations for that first kiss low. "Bells may not ring and the sky may not light up." I quoted Georgia O'Keeffe, totally out of context: "Nobody's good at the beginning."

I pointed out that the relationship was going well. Physical affection was only a small part of a relationship. She was already gifted at loving and forgiving, which were much more important qualities. I predicted that kissing would be easy once she was ready.

When I saw June again, she reported that kissing was great. She asked me if I thought she needed more therapy. "No," I said. "I think you could teach me some lessons about strength through adversity and the importance of forgiveness."

June is a good example of someone who, with almost no luck at all, fashioned a good life for herself. Almost all our psychological theories would predict that June would turn out badly. But as happens more frequently than we psychologists generally acknowledge, adversity built her character. What saved her was her deep awareness of her mother's love. Even though her mother was dead, June felt her mother's spirit was with her. That enabled her to feel valued at a time when she was rejected by everyone. June's belief in her mother's love gave her a sense of purpose. She was determined to live in a way that would make her mother proud.

June had the gift for appreciating what was good in her life. Once she told me, "I always get what I want." Then she winked and said, "But I know what to want." Her life, which might strike some people as difficult or dull, is rich and rewarding. She has friends, money, a boyfriend and the respect of her peers. She has no bitterness or anger because she is basically happy. She's a desert flower opening to the rain.

Questions for Critical Reading

1. What did you take to be Pipher's purpose in writing this case study? For you as a reader, did she succeed in accomplishing this purpose? Why or why not?

2. Recall that writers often decide how to organize their work based on the purposes they're trying to achieve. Why do you think Pipher organized "June" by telling us June's story first and the point of the story last? In considering this question, it may help to think of Pipher as having layers of purposes — a primary purpose of communicating a point about happiness and adversity, and a secondary purpose of trying to get us to feel a certain way about June. How would you explain, more specifically, what Pipher's purposes might have been? Do you think her organization helped her to achieve these purposes? Why or why not?

3. Recall that where you choose to break your paragraphs can shape a reader's experience, sometimes significantly. When writers use point-first organization, they generally decide to start a new paragraph when they're ready to make a new point. However, when they *don't* use point-first organization, they need to look for alternative strategies for deciding when to break a paragraph. Read the two versions of the following passage (one original, one altered by eliminating some paragraph breaks), and see if you can explain why Pipher might have decided to break the paragraphs as she did:

Original Passage	Altered Passage
I asked her about the kids at school. "They were terrible. Not so much mean, as totally indifferent. I didn't exist for them. I was too ugly and too sad to even be part of the class. I ate by myself and walked to and from school alone. No one would be my lab partner." She rubbed her big face and continued. "One time a boy approached me in the cafeteria, in front of all the other kids, and asked me to go to a football game. I was such a goof that I thought he meant it. I thought maybe he could see past my appearance and like the real me. So I said sure, if I could get Dad's permission. Then he started laughing. His buddies all whooped it up too. They'd dared him to do it for a joke. He collected ten bucks for just asking me out." June sighed. "After that I steered clear of boys." (paras. 13–15)	I asked her about the kids at school. "They were terrible. Not so much mean, as totally indifferent. I didn't exist for them. I was too ugly and too sad to even be part of the class. I ate by myself and walked to and from school alone. No one would be my lab partner." She rubbed her big face and continued. "One time a boy approached me in the cafeteria, in front of all the other kids, and asked me to go to a football game. I was such a goof that I thought he meant it. I thought maybe he could see past my appearance and like the real me. So I said sure, if I could get Dad's permission. Then he started laughing. His buddies all whooped it up too. They'd dared him to do it for a joke. He collected ten bucks for just asking me out." June sighed. "After that I steered clear of boys."

Why do you think Pipher decided to break the paragraphs where she did? Do you prefer the original passage (with more paragraph breaks) or the altered passage (with fewer paragraph breaks)? Why?

4. In a variety of genres, you'll need to decide when to quote and when to paraphrase (to summarize what someone said in your own words). Making informed choices about when to quote and when to paraphrase can help you better achieve your purposes as a writer. Compare the following two passages, and consider which version you prefer. Note that the altered version is the opposite of the original; it quotes when the original paraphrases and paraphrases when the original quotes:

Original Passage	Altered Passage
When I saw June again, she reported that kissing was great. She asked me if I thought she needed more therapy. "No," I said. "I think you could teach me some lessons about strength through adversity and the importance of forgiveness." (para. 30)	When I saw June again, she said, "Kissing was great." She asked me, "Do you think I need more therapy?" I said that she didn't and that she could teach me some lessons about being strong during hard times and forgiving those who have done us wrong.

Which passage do you prefer? Why do you think Pipher might have chosen to quote what she did? How might you as a writer decide when to quote and when to paraphrase?

Making Connections

5. Quotation is used across genres for a variety of purposes, including to appeal to readers' emotions and to provide evidence for claims. Compare the purposes of the quotations in the following two passages, one from "June" and one from *Flow* (p. 319), Mihaly Csikszentmihalyi's account of his research on "optimal experience":

"June"

[June said,] "My stepmother was tight with money. She only let me wash my hair once a week. I needed to wash it daily it was so greasy, but she didn't want to pay for the water. My teeth were crooked and the school recommended braces. Mercene said, 'I've heard that can cost a thousand dollars. No way we'll spend that kind of money for straight teeth.' Once I cut my foot pretty badly when I was walking beans. She wouldn't pay for the doctor. I limped a little because of that."

I worked hard to remain neutral as June talked. . . . "I was the black sheep. Once my stepbrother asked me why I lived with his family." (paras. 17–18)

Flow

One of the most frequently mentioned dimensions of the flow [optimal] experience is that, while it lasts, one is able to forget all the unpleasant aspects of life. . . .

As a young basketball player explains: "The court—that's all that matters. . . . Sometimes out on the court I think of a problem, like fighting with my [girlfriend], and I think that's nothing compared to the game. You can think about a problem all day but as soon as you get in the game, the hell with it!" . . .

A mountaineer expands on the same theme: "When you're [climbing] you're not aware of other problematic life situations. It becomes a world unto its own. . . ."

A similar sensation is reported by a dancer: "I get a feeling that I don't get anywhere else. . . . I have more confidence in myself than any other time. Maybe an effort to forget my problems. Dance is like therapy. If I am troubled about something, I leave it out of the door as I go in [the dance studio]." (paras. 20, 23–25)

Why do you think Pipher quoted June? Why do you think Csikszentmihalyi quoted the people he did? How effective did you find each writer's use of quotation?

Writing: Your Turn

1. Write your own case study of someone who has achieved happiness despite significant obstacles. If you're able to interview that person, you'll have more information and thus more options as a writer. When you write your case study, make a deliberate choice about whether or not to use quotations. Also make a deliberate choice about whether to state your point early or toward the end—or whether to leave it unstated. Share your case study with your classmates to see if it evokes the emotions you want it to evoke. Also ask your classmates if they learned anything from the case study that they might apply to their own lives. Consider their responses to your questions when you revise, along with any other ideas that they shared with you.

2. Write a reflection on "June." How did you feel about June? Did you learn anything from the case study that might affect your own life? Share your reflection with some classmates, and discuss whether or not they had the same response to "June" that you did. Also get their feedback on which passages in your reflection might be worth expanding when you revise. For tips on writing a reflection, see p. 27.

From *Flow: The Psychology of Optimal Experience*

Mihaly Csikszentmihalyi

The classic book *Flow: The Psychology of Optimal Experience* (1990) was written by psychology professor Mihaly Csikszentmihalyi to help people experience "flow," or the enjoyment that arises when people concentrate deeply on a challenging task. In the introduction to *Flow*, Csikszentmihalyi explains that "the best moments in our lives . . . usually occur when a person's body or mind is stretched to its limits in a voluntary effort to accomplish something difficult and worthwhile" (p. 3). Csikszentmihalyi, who has published widely for both academic and general audiences, is a professor at Claremont Graduate University in California.

Focus on Genre　Aimed at a general audience, *Flow* could be described as a summary or an argument; Csikszentmihalyi summarizes his research on flow, and he argues that we can improve our lives by learning from this research.

While you're reading, notice how carefully organized and focused Csikszentmihalyi's writing is. He generally states his points at the beginnings of paragraphs (using topic sentences), and he often closes paragraphs by referring back to his larger point. As you read, think about whether his attention to organization makes it easier for him to persuade you that his research might help you enhance the quality of your life.

Also consider how persuasive you find Csikszentmihalyi's use of evidence, and speculate on what type of research he might have conducted to yield this evidence. Finally, think about whether the deep concentration required for flow might be more difficult to achieve in this era of texting and the Internet than it was in the 1970s and 1980s, when Csikszentmihalyi conducted much of his research.

—◄○►—

THE ELEMENTS OF ENJOYMENT

A Challenging Activity That Requires Skills

In all the activities people in our study reported engaging in, enjoyment comes at a very specific point: whenever the opportunities for action perceived by the individual are equal to his or her capabilities. Playing tennis, for instance, is not enjoyable if the two opponents are mismatched. The less skilled player will feel anxious, and the better player will feel bored. The same is true of every other activity: a piece of music that is too simple relative to one's listening skills will be boring, while music that is too complex will be frustrating. Enjoyment appears at the boundary between boredom and anxiety, when the challenges are just balanced with the person's capacity to act.

The golden ratio between challenges and skills does not only hold true for human activities. Whenever I took our hunting dog, Hussar, for a walk in the open fields he liked to play a very simple game—the prototype of the most culturally widespread game of human children, escape and pursuit. He would run circles around me at top speed, with his tongue hanging out and his eyes warily watching every move I made, daring me to catch him. Occasionally I would take a lunge, and if I was lucky I got to touch him. Now the interesting part is that whenever I was tired, and moved halfheartedly, Hussar would run much tighter circles, making it relatively easy for me to catch him; on the other hand, if I was in good shape and willing to extend myself, he would enlarge the diameter of his circle. In this way, the difficulty of the game was kept constant. With an uncanny sense for the fine balancing of challenges and skills, he would make sure that the game would yield the maximum of enjoyment for us both.

The Merging of Action and Awareness

When all a person's relevant skills are needed to cope with the challenges of a situation, that person's attention is completely absorbed by the activity. There is no excess psychic energy left over to process any information but what the activity offers. All the attention is concentrated on the relevant stimuli.

As a result, one of the most universal and distinctive features of optimal experience takes place: people become so involved in what they are doing that the activity becomes spontaneous, almost automatic; they stop being aware of themselves as separate from the actions they are performing.

A dancer describes how it feels when a performance is going well: "Your 5 concentration is very complete. Your mind isn't wandering, you are not thinking of something else; you are totally involved in what you are doing. . . . Your energy is flowing very smoothly. You feel relaxed, comfortable, and energetic."

A rock climber explains how it feels when he is scaling a mountain: "You are so involved in what you are doing [that] you aren't thinking of yourself as separate from the immediate activity. . . . You don't see yourself as separate from what you are doing."

A mother who enjoys the time spent with her small daughter: "Her reading is the one thing that she's really into, and we read together. She reads to me, and I read to her, and that's a time when I sort of lose touch with the rest of the world, I'm totally absorbed in what I'm doing."

A chess player tells of playing in a tournament: ". . . the concentration is like breathing—you never think of it. The roof could fall in and, if it missed you, you would be unaware of it."

It is for this reason that we called the optimal experience "flow." The short and simple word describes well the sense of seemingly effortless movement. The following words from a poet and rock climber apply to all the thousands of interviews collected by us and by others over the years: "The mystique of rock climbing is climbing; you get to the top of a rock glad it's over but really wish it would go on forever. The justification of climbing is climbing, like the justifica-tion of poetry is writing; you don't conquer anything except things in yourself. . . . The act of writing justifies poetry. Climbing is the same: recognizing that you are a flow. The purpose of the flow is to keep on flowing, not looking for a peak or utopia but staying in the flow. It is not a moving up but a continuous flowing; you move up to keep the flow going. There is no possible reason for climbing except the climbing itself; it is a self-communication."

Although the flow experience appears to be effortless, it is far from being so. It often requires strenuous physical exertion, or highly disciplined mental activity. It does not happen without the application of skilled performance. Any lapse in concentration will erase it. And yet while it lasts consciousness works smoothly, action follows action seamlessly. In normal life, we keep interrupting what we do with doubts and questions. "Why am I doing this? Should I per-haps be doing something else?" Repeatedly we question the necessity of our actions, and evaluate critically the reasons for carrying them out. But in flow there is no need to reflect, because the action carries us forward as if by magic.

10

Clear Goals and Feedback

The reason it is possible to achieve such complete involvement in a flow experience is that goals are usually clear, and feedback immediate. A tennis player always knows what she has to do: return the ball into the opponent's court. And each time she hits the ball she knows whether she has done well or not. The chess player's goals are equally obvious: to mate the opponent's king before his own is mated. With each move, he can calculate whether he has come closer to this objective. The climber inching up a vertical wall of rock has a very simple goal in mind: to complete the climb without falling. Every second, hour after hour, he receives information that he is meeting that basic goal.

Of course, if one chooses a trivial goal, success in it does not provide enjoyment. If I set as my goal to remain alive while sitting on the living-room sofa, I also could spend days knowing that I was achieving it, just as the rock climber does. But this realization would not make me particularly happy, whereas the climber's knowledge brings exhilaration to his dangerous ascent.

Certain activities require a very long time to accomplish, yet the components of goals and feedback are still extremely important to them. One example was given by a sixty-two-year-old woman living in the Italian Alps, who said her most enjoyable experiences were taking care of the cows and tending the orchard: "I find special satisfaction in caring for the plants: I like to see them grow day by day. It is very beautiful." Although it involves a period of patient waiting, seeing the plants one has cared for grow provides a powerful feedback even in the urban apartments of American cities. . . .

The goals of an activity are not always as clear as those of tennis, and the feedback is often more ambiguous than the simple "I am not falling" information processed by the climber. A composer of music, for instance, may know that he wishes to write a song, or a flute concerto, but other than that, his goals are usually quite vague. And how does he know whether the notes he is writing down are "right" or "wrong"? The same situation holds true for the artist painting a picture, and for all activities that are creative or open-ended in nature. But these are all exceptions that prove the rule: unless a person learns to set goals and to recognize and gauge feedback in such activities, she will not enjoy them.

In some creative activities, where goals are not clearly set in advance, a   15
person must develop a strong personal sense of what she intends to do. The artist might not have a visual image of what the finished painting should look like, but when the picture has progressed to a certain point, she should know whether this is what she wanted to achieve or not. And a painter who enjoys painting must have internalized criteria for "good" or "bad" so that after each brush stroke she can say: "Yes, this works; no, this doesn't." Without such internal guidelines, it is impossible to experience flow.

Sometimes the goals and the rules governing an activity are invented, or negotiated on the spot. For example, teenagers enjoy impromptu interactions in which they try to "gross each other out," or tell tall stories, or make fun of their teachers. The goal of such sessions emerges by trial and error, and is rarely made explicit; often it remains below the participants' level of awareness. Yet it is clear that these activities develop their own rules and that those who take part have a clear idea of what constitutes a successful "move," and of who is doing well. In many ways this is the pattern of a good jazz band, or any improvisational group. Scholars or debaters obtain similar satisfaction when the "moves" in their arguments mesh smoothly, and produce the desired result.

What constitutes feedback varies considerably in different activities. Some people are indifferent to things that others cannot get enough of. For instance, surgeons who love doing operations claim that they wouldn't switch to internal medicine even if they were paid ten times as much as they are for doing surgery, because an internist never knows exactly how well he is doing. In an operation, on the other hand, the status of the patient is almost always clear: as long as there is no blood in the incision, for example, a specific procedure has been successful. When the diseased organ is cut out, the surgeon's task is accomplished; after that there is the suture that gives a gratifying sense of closure to the activity. And the surgeon's disdain for psychiatry is even greater than that for internal medicine: to hear surgeons talk, the psychiatrist might spend ten years with a patient without knowing whether the cure is helping him.

Yet the psychiatrist who enjoys his trade is also receiving constant feedback: the way the patient holds himself, the expression on his face, the hesitation in his voice, the content of the material he brings up in the therapeutic hour—all these bits of information are important clues the psychiatrist uses to monitor the progress of the therapy. The difference between a surgeon and a psychiatrist is that the former considers blood and excision the only feedback worth attending to, whereas the latter considers the signals reflecting a patient's state of mind to be significant information. The surgeon judges the psychiatrist to be soft because he is interested in such ephemeral goals; the psychiatrist thinks the surgeon crude for his concentration on mechanics.

The *kind* of feedback we work toward is in and of itself often unimportant: What difference does it make if I hit the tennis ball between the white lines, if I immobilize the enemy king on the chessboard, or if I notice a glimmer of understanding in my patient's eyes at the end of the therapeutic hour? What makes this information valuable is the symbolic message it contains: that I have succeeded in my goal. Such knowledge creates order in consciousness, and strengthens the structure of the self. . . .

Concentration on the Task at Hand

One of the most frequently mentioned dimensions of the flow experience is that, while it lasts, one is able to forget all the unpleasant aspects of life. This feature of flow is an important by-product of the fact that enjoyable activities require a complete focusing of attention on the task at hand—thus leaving no room in the mind for irrelevant information.

20

In normal everyday existence, we are the prey of thoughts and worries intruding unwanted in consciousness. Because most jobs, and home life in general, lack the pressing demands of flow experiences, concentration is rarely so intense that preoccupations and anxieties can be automatically ruled out. Consequently the ordinary state of mind involves unexpected and frequent episodes of entropy interfering with the smooth run of psychic energy. This is one reason why flow improves the quality of experience: the clearly structured demands of the activity impose order, and exclude the interference of disorder in consciousness.

A professor of physics who was an avid rock climber described his state of mind while climbing as follows: "It is as if my memory input has been cut off. All I can remember is the last thirty seconds, and all I can think ahead is the next five minutes." In fact, any activity that requires concentration has a similarly narrow window of time.

But it is not only the temporal focus that counts. What is even more significant is that only a very select range of information can be allowed into awareness. Therefore all the troubling thoughts that ordinarily keep passing through the mind are temporarily kept in abeyance. As a young basketball player explains: "The court—that's all that matters. . . . Sometimes out on the court I think of a problem, like fighting with my [girlfriend], and I think that's nothing compared to the game. You can think about a problem all day but as soon as you get in the game, the hell with it!" And another: "Kids my age, they think a lot . . . but when you are playing basketball, that's all there is on your mind—just basketball. . . . Everything seems to follow right along."

A mountaineer expands on the same theme: "When you're [climbing] you're not aware of other problematic life situations. It becomes a world unto its own, significant only to itself. It's a concentration thing. Once you're into the situation, it's incredibly real, and you're very much in charge of it. It becomes your total world."

A similar sensation is reported by a dancer: "I get a feeling that I don't get anywhere else. . . . I have more confidence in myself than any other time. Maybe an effort to forget my problems. Dance is like therapy. If I am troubled about something, I leave it out of the door as I go in [the dance studio]." 25

On a larger time scale, ocean cruising provides an equivalent merciful oblivion: "But no matter how many little discomforts there may be at sea, one's real cares and worries seem to drop out of sight as the land slips behind the horizon. Once we were at sea there was no point in worrying, there was nothing we could do about our problems till we reached the next port. . . . Life was, for a while, stripped of its artificialities; [other problems] seemed quite unimportant compared with the state of the wind and the sea and the length of the day's run."

Edwin Moses, the great hurdler, has this to say in describing the concentration necessary for a race: "Your mind has to be absolutely clear. The fact that you have to cope with your opponent, jet lag, different foods, sleeping in hotels, and personal problems has to be erased from consciousness—as if they didn't exist."

Although Moses was talking about what it takes to win world-class sports events, he could have been describing the kind of concentration we achieve when we enjoy *any* activity. The concentration of the flow experience—together with clear goals and immediate feedback—provides order to consciousness. . . .

THE CONDITIONS OF FLOW

Flow Activities

. . . In our studies, we found that every flow activity, whether it involved competition, chance, or any other dimension of experience, had this in common: It provided a sense of discovery, a creative feeling of transporting the person into a new reality. It pushed the person to higher levels of performance, and led to previously undreamed-of states of consciousness. In short, it transformed the self by making it more complex. In this growth of the self lies the key to flow activities.

A simple diagram might help explain why this should be the case. Let us   30
assume that the figure below represents a specific activity— for example, the game of tennis. The two theoretically most important dimensions of the experience, challenges and skills, are represented on the two axes of the diagram. The letter A represents Alex, a boy who is learning to play tennis. The diagram shows Alex at four different points in time. When he first starts playing (A_1), Alex has practically no skills, and the only challenge he faces is hitting the ball over the net. This is not a very difficult feat, but Alex is likely to enjoy it because the difficulty is just right for his rudimentary skills. So at this point he will probably be in flow. But he cannot stay there long. After a while, if he keeps practicing, his skills are bound to improve, and then he will grow bored just batting the ball over the net (A_2). Or it might happen that he meets a more practiced opponent, in which case he will realize that there are much harder challenges for him than just lobbing the ball—at that point, he will feel some anxiety (A_3) concerning his poor performance.

Neither boredom nor anxiety are positive experiences, so Alex will be motivated to return to the flow state. How is he to do it? Glancing again at the diagram, we see that if he is bored (A_2) and wishes to be in flow again, Alex has essentially only one choice: to increase the challenges he is facing. (He also has a second choice, which is to give up tennis altogether—in which case A would simply disappear from the diagram.) By setting himself a new and more difficult

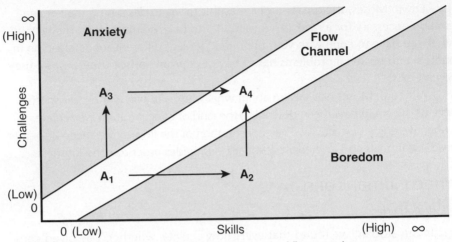

Why the complexity of consciousness increases as a result of flow experiences

goal that matches his skills—for instance, to beat an opponent just a little more advanced than he is—Alex would be back in flow (A_4).

If Alex is anxious (A_3), the way back to flow requires that he increase his skills. Theoretically he could also reduce the challenges he is facing, and thus return to flow where he started (in A_1), but in practice it is difficult to ignore challenges once one is aware that they exist.

The diagram shows that both A_1 and A_4 represent situations in which Alex is in flow. Although both are equally enjoyable, the two states are quite different in that A_4 is a more *complex* experience than A_1. It is more complex because it involves greater challenges and demands greater skills from the player.

But A_4, although complex and enjoyable, does not represent a stable situation, either. As Alex keeps playing, either he will become bored by the stale opportunities he finds at that level, or he will become anxious and frustrated by his relatively low ability. So the motivation to enjoy himself again will push him to get back into the flow channel, but now at a level of complexity even *higher* than A_4.

It is this dynamic feature that explains why flow activities lead to growth and discovery. One cannot enjoy doing the same thing at the same level for long. We grow either bored or frustrated; and then the desire to enjoy ourselves again pushes us to stretch our skills, or to discover new opportunities for using them.

It is important, however, not to fall into the mechanistic fallacy and expect that, just because a person is objectively involved in a flow activity, she will necessarily have the appropriate experience. It is not only the "real" challenges

35

presented by the situation that count, but those that the person is aware of. It is not skills we actually have that determine how we feel, but the ones we think we have. One person may respond to the challenge of a mountain peak but remain indifferent to the opportunity to learn to play a piece of music; the next person may jump at the chance to learn the music and ignore the mountain. How we feel at any given moment of a flow activity is strongly influenced by the objective conditions, but consciousness is still free to follow its own assessment of the case. The rules of games are intended to direct psychic energy in patterns that are enjoyable, but whether they do so or not is ultimately up to us. A professional athlete might be "playing" football without any of the elements of flow being present: he might be bored, self-conscious, concerned about the size of his contract rather than the game. And the opposite is even more likely—that a person will deeply enjoy activities that were intended for other purposes. To many people, activities like working or raising children provide more flow than playing a game or painting a picture, because these individuals have learned to perceive opportunities in such mundane tasks that others do not see.

Notes

p. 320. The balanced **ratio between challenges and skills** was recognized from the very beginning as one of the central conditions of the flow experience (e.g., Csikszentmihalyi 1975, pp. 49–54). The original model assumed that enjoyment would occur along the entire diagonal, that is, when challenges and skills were both very low, as well as when they were both very high. Empirical research findings later led to a modification of the model. People did not enjoy situations in which their skills and the outside challenges were both lower than their accustomed levels. The new model predicts flow only when challenges and skills are relatively in balance, and above the individual's mean level—and this prediction is confirmed by the studies conducted with the Experience Sampling Method (Carli 1986, Csikszentmihalyi & Nakamura 1989, Massimini, Csikszentmihalyi, & Carli 1987). In addition, these studies have shown that the condition of anxiety (high challenge, low skills) is relatively rare in everyday life, and it is experienced as much more negative than the condition of boredom (low challenge, high skills).

p. 320–21. **"Your concentration . . . ,"** **"You are so involved . . . ,"** and **". . . the concentration . . ."** are from Csikszentmihalyi (1975, p. 39). **"Her reading . . ."** is from Allison and Duncan (1988, p. 129). The relationship between focused attention and enjoyment was clearly perceived four centuries ago by Montaigne (1580 [1958], p. 853): "I enjoy . . . [life] twice as much as others, for the measure of enjoyment depends on the greater or lesser attention that we lend it." **"The mystique of rock climbing . . ."** is from Csikszentmihalyi (1975, pp. 47–48).

p. 322. **"I find special satisfaction . . ."** is from Delle Fave & Massimini (1988, p. 197). **Painting.** The distinction between more and less original artists is that the former start painting with a general and often vague idea of what they want to accomplish, while the latter tend to start with a clearly visualized picture in mind. Thus original artists must discover as they go along what it is that they will do, using feedback from the developing work to suggest new approaches. The less original artists end up painting the picture in their heads, which has no chance to grow and develop. But to be successful in his open-ended process of creation, the original artist must have well-internalized criteria for what is good art, so that he can choose or discard the right elements in the developing painting (Getzels & Csikszentmihalyi 1976).

p. 323. **Surgery** as a flow experience is described in Csikszentmihalyi (1975, 1985b).

p. 324. "**It is as if . . .**" is from Csikszentmihalyi (1975, p. 40). "**The court . . .**" and "**Kids my age . . .**" are from Csikszentmihalyi (1975, pp. 40–41); "**When you're [climbing] . . .**" is from ibid., p. 81, and "**I get a feeling . . .**" from ibid., p. 41. "**But no matter how many . . .**" is from Crealock (1951, pp. 99–100), quoted in Macbeth (1988, pp. 221–22). The quotation from Edwin Moses is in Johnson (1988, p. 6).

p. 325–26. **Flow and discovery.** When asked to rank 16 very different activities as being more or less similar to flow, the groups of highly skilled rock climbers, composers of music, chess players, and so on studied by Csikszentmihalyi (1975, p. 29) listed the item "Designing or discovering something new" as being the most similar to their flow activity. **Flow and growth.** The issue of how flow experiences lead to growth of the self are discussed in Deci & Ryan (1985) and Csikszentmihalyi (1982, 1985a). Anne Wells (1988) has shown that women who spend more time in flow have a more positive self-concept.

References

Allison, M. T., & Duncan, M. C. 1998. Women, work, and flow. In M. Csikszentmihalyi & I. S. Csikszentmihalyi, eds., *Optimal experience: Studies of flow in consciousness* (pp. 118–37). New York: Cambridge University Press.

Carli, M. 1986. Selezione psicologica e qualita dell'esperienza. In F. Massimini & P. Inghilleri, eds., *L'esperienza quotidiana* (pp. 285–304). Milan: Franco Angeli.

Crealock, W. I. B. 1951. *Vagabonding under sail.* New York: David McKay.

Croce, B. 1902 (1909). *Aesthetics.* New York: Macmillan.

Csikszentmihalyi, M. 1975. *Beyond boredom and anxiety.* San Francisco: Jossey-Bass.

----. 1982. Learning, flow, and happiness. In R. Gross, ed., *Invitation to life-long learning* (pp. 167–87). New York: Fowlett.

----. 1985a. Emergent motivation and the evolution of the self. In D. Kleiber & M. H. Maehr, eds., *Motivation in adulthood* (pp. 93–113). Greenwich, Conn.: JAI Press.

----. 1985b. Reflections on enjoyment. *Perspectives in Biology and Medicine* 28(4):469–97.

Csikszentmihalyi, M., & Nakamura, J. 1989. The dynamics of intrinsic motivation. In R. Ames & C. Ames, eds., *Handbook of motivation theory and research,* vol. 3 (pp. 45–71). New York: Academic Press.

Deci, E. L., & Ryan, R. M. 1985. *Intrinsic motivation and self-determination in human behavior.* New York: Plenum Press.

Delle Fave, A., & Massimini, F. 1988. Modernization and the changing contexts of flow in work and leisure. In M. Csikszentmihalyi & I. S. Csikszentmihalyi, eds., *Optimal experience: Studies of flow in consciousness* (pp. 193–213). New York: Cambridge University Press.

Getzels, J. W., & Csikszentmihalyi, M. 1976. *The creative vision: A longitudinal study of problem finding in art.* New York: Wiley Interscience.

Johnson, R. 1988. Thinking yourself into a win. *American Visions* 3:6–10.

MacBeth, J. 1988. Ocean cruising. In M. Csikszentmihalyi & I. S. Csikszentmihalyi, eds., *Optimal experience: Psychological studies of flow in consciousness* (pp. 214–31). New York: Cambridge University Press.

Massimini, F., Csikszentmihalyi, M., & Carli, M. 1987. The monitoring of optimal experience: A tool for psychiatric rehabilitation. *Journal of Nervous and Mental Disease* 175(9):545–49.

Montaigne, M. de. 1580 (1958). *The complete essays of Montaigne.* Trans. Donald M. Frame. Stanford: Stanford University Press.

Wells, A. 1988. Self-esteem and optimal experience. In M. Csikszentmihalyi & I. S. Csikszentmihalyi, eds., *Optimal experience: Psychological studies of flow in consciousness* (pp. 327–41). New York: Cambridge University Press.

Questions for Critical Reading

1. Did Csikszentmihalyi's use of evidence persuade you that you can enhance your quality of life by increasing the amount of flow you experience? Do you think he uses enough evidence — and an appropriate type of evidence — to persuade the audience that he's targeting? Why or why not?

2. Csikszentmihalyi tries to persuade readers not only by using evidence but also by establishing his credibility as a researcher. Although he doesn't describe his research methodology in the excerpt included here, he does so in a passage appearing earlier in *Flow.* Take a couple of minutes to consider this passage, assessing how well you think Csikszentmihalyi establishes his credibility as a researcher — and thus how seriously you want to take his claim in the final sentence of the passage:

> [The knowledge of what makes experience enjoyable] is based on long interviews, questionnaires, and other data collected over a dozen years from several thousand respondents. Initially we interviewed only people who spent a great amount of time and effort in activities that were difficult, yet provided no obvious rewards, such as money or prestige: rock climbers, composers of music, chess players, amateur athletes. Our later studies included interviews with ordinary people, leading ordinary existences; we asked them to describe how it felt when their lives were at their fullest, when what they did was most enjoyable. These people included urban Americans—surgeons, professors, clerical and assembly-line workers, young mothers, retired people, and teenagers. They also included respondents from Korea, Japan, Thailand, Australia, various European cultures, and a Navajo reservation. On the basis of these interviews we can now describe what makes an experience enjoyable, and thus provide examples that all of us can use to enhance the quality of life. (p. 4)

Does Csikszentmihalyi's description of his research persuade you to consider his claim that "we can now describe what makes an experience enjoyable, and thus provide examples that all of us can use to enhance the quality of life"? Why or why not?

3. Consider another research method Csikszentmihalyi used to obtain much of his data, the experience sampling method. As he describes this method in the book's introduction, research participants wear a pager for a week and write down how they feel and what they're thinking when the pager activates, approximately eight times a day at random intervals (p. 4). Does knowing about the experience sampling method change how seriously you take Csikszentmihalyi's research? Why or why not?

4. The research Csikszentmihalyi summarizes in *Flow* is widely regarded as seminal; it has significantly influenced — and continues to influence — academics and laypeople across the globe. However, most of this research was conducted in the 1970s and 1980s, well before the advent of texting. Given that deep, sustained concentration is key to flow — and that people's use of modern technology may undermine their ability to concentrate — consider whether flow should be researched again now. What's your hypothesis about whether the interruptions of texting might undermine flow? Take a couple of minutes to sketch out how you would test your hypothesis. What research methodology would you use, and why?

5. Recall that subheadings are used in many genres to emphasize main points and to give readers a big-picture sense of how the writing is organized. Genres that discuss complex ideas sometimes even have multiple levels of subheadings, as does *Flow*. Consider the effect of the following top-level subheading (in capital letters) and the secondary subheadings (italicized):

THE ELEMENTS OF ENJOYMENT

A Challenging Activity That Requires Skills

The Merging of Action and Awareness

Clear Goals and Feedback

Concentration on the Task at Hand

How helpful did you find these subheadings when you were reading Csikszentmihalyi? Would you have preferred the reading without them, or with different subheadings? Why? When in your own writing will you want to use subheadings? (Although subheadings are used more often in some disciplines than others, even professors in disciplines that don't generally use them tend not to object to them; thus, they are a real option, even though many students don't realize it.)

6. Recall that maintaining a sharp focus — both on the paragraph level and on the whole-text level — is important in many genres. Just as Csikszentmihalyi's subheadings help maintain focus on a whole-text level, the opening and closing sentences of his paragraphs help maintain focus on a paragraph level. Compare the following paragraph, from the section "Clear Goals and Feedback," to the altered version; the difference (a concluding sentence at the end of the original phrase) is italicized.

Original Passage	Altered Passage
In some creative activities, where goals are not clearly set in advance, a person must develop a strong personal sense of what she intends to do. The artist might not have a visual image of what the finished painting should look like, but when the picture has progressed to a certain point, she should know whether this is what she wanted to achieve or not. And a painter who enjoys painting must have internalized criteria for "good" or "bad" so that after each brush stroke she can say: "Yes, this works; no, this doesn't." *Without such internal guidelines, it is impossible to experience flow.* (para. 15)	In some creative activities, where goals are not clearly set in advance, a person must develop a strong personal sense of what she intends to do. The artist might not have a visual image of what the finished painting should look like, but when the picture has progressed to a certain point, she should know whether this is what she wanted to achieve or not. And a painter who enjoys painting must have internalized criteria for "good" or "bad" so that after each brush stroke she can say: "Yes, this works; no, this doesn't."

Which paragraph do you think maintains a sharper focus on the larger point? Did the presence or absence of a concluding sentence make a difference to you as a reader? Why or why not?

Still considering the original and altered passages, imagine that Csikszentmihalyi had originally written the passage on the right and then asked himself "So what? Why should readers care about what I just wrote?" Imagine him coming up with several different answers to this question and picking the one that best reinforced his thesis. Find an example of another paragraph where Csikszentmihalyi uses this strategy to take us back to a larger point. Do you think he uses this strategy often enough? Why or why not?

7. Regardless of genre, readers are persuaded not only by words but also by visuals. To what extent do you think the diagram on p. 326 helps Csikszentmihalyi reinforce his point? Why?

Making Connections

8. Recall that whether they're aware of it or not, writers are faced with a choice between depth and breadth — between discussing a small number of things in depth or discussing a larger number of things in less detail. Mary Pipher, author of "June" (p. 311), opted to write *Reviving Ophelia* as a series of case studies so that she could go into depth with each person she discusses. In "June," for instance, she provides enough depth to enable many readers to feel they know June and to understand just how hard June's life was. Readers don't, however, get enough breadth to have a sense of whether or not June's approach to overcoming hardship would work for others.

Writing

In the excerpt from *Flow*, Csikszentmihalyi opts for another approach: he doesn't go into enough depth for readers to feel they know anyone he discusses, but he provides enough breadth to give readers the sense that what he's describing applies to many people, not just one or two. How would you have responded if Csikszentmihalyi had taken the approach used in "June" — if he had focused on describing the flow experiences of one or two people in depth? Do you think you would have preferred this approach? Why or why not?

Writing: Your Turn

1. Write a reflection on how applicable Csikszentmihalyi's ideas are to your own life. Do you experience "flow" in the same conditions that he describes? Is there a way that you could integrate more flow into your life? Share your reflection with some classmates so that they can learn from your insights and give you ideas for revision. For ideas on writing a reflection, see p. 27.

2. Write a critique of the excerpt from *Flow* that's addressed to an audience of classmates. How valid do you find Csikszentmihalyi's argument? To what extent do you think it's possible for all people to do what he's suggesting? In formulating your critique, you might look at Csikszentmihalyi's subheadings; consider, for instance, whether/how everyone would be able to find activities that have "clear goals and feedback" and whether/how everyone (regardless of circumstance) would be able to "concentrate on the task at hand." If you would find it helpful, draw on Maslow (p. 293) or "The Waltz" (p. 298) when writing your critique. After you're done writing, get feedback from some classmates to see how you could make your critique even more persuasive; ask them where you might provide more evidence or anticipate readers' objections. Since a critique is a type of argument, refer to p. 42 for ideas.

Act the Way You Want to Feel
From *The Happiness Project*

Gretchen Rubin

In the words of author Gretchen Rubin, *The Happiness Project* recounts "daily adventures in pursuit of happiness." Rubin used the blog as the basis of a book of the same name, which became so popular that it quickly rose to number one on the *New York Times* bestseller list. She has also written a second book, entitled *Happier at Home*. Before she made writing about happiness her life's work, Rubin was a lawyer.

Focus on Genre Blogs provide a good case study of how technology shapes genre — of how technological advances can allow new genres to emerge and shape what writers in those genres are able to do. The technological advancement of links, for example, enables bloggers to let readers choose for themselves how much additional information they want, thus addressing a key problem writers face: deciding how to meet the needs of a variety of readers, some of whom want additional information and some of whom don't. As you read "Act the Way You Want to Feel," notice which words are linked and which ones aren't.

Another technologically enabled feature of blogs is the comment section, which distinguishes blogs from many older genres that don't generally give readers the chance to encounter multiple viewpoints on an issue. As you read the comments on Rubin's blog, think about which ones you find most persuasive and which ones you find least persuasive, and consider the degree to which the comments give readers a more nuanced sense of how complex Rubin's topic is.

Like other genres, "Act the Way You Want to Feel" is embedded in a web of multiple genres. Not only do Rubin's links point us to different genres — and not only did the blog morph into a book — but Rubin's promotion of her book has been accomplished by turning to other genres and media: Facebook, Twitter, YouTube, a daily e-mail, and a monthly electronic newsletter. If you find yourself interested in what Rubin has to say, you might consider looking at one or more of these other genres and thinking about how her ideas are adapted to work within them.

◄◦►

One of the most surprising, and useful, things I've learned from my happiness project is my <u>Third Commandment</u>:* **Act the way I want to feel.**

Although we presume that we *act* because of the way we *feel*, in fact, we often *feel* because of the way we *act*. More than a century ago, philosopher and psychologist William James described this phenomenon: "Action seems to follow feeling, but really action and feeling go together; and by regulating the action, which is under the more direct control of the will, we can indirectly regulate the feeling, which is not." By acting as if you feel a certain way, you induce that emotion in yourself.

I use this strategy on myself. If I feel shy, I act friendly. If I feel irritated, I act lovingly. This is much harder to do than it sounds, but it's uncannily effective.

Lately, I've been feeling low. I had various justifications for my blue mood, but just last night it occurred to me—maybe it's due to my persistent case of viral conjunctivitis (which has been <u>on my mind</u>† a lot).

As a consequence of the conjunctivitis, my eyes well up constantly, and I   5
wipe tears off my face many times through the day. Maybe *that's* contributing to my feelings of sadness.

It sounds far-fetched—that I feel sad because my eyes are watering as a result of eye inflammation—but I have indeed caught myself wondering, "Why am I feeling so emotional, why am I tearing up?" My mind was searching for an explanation that justified such a tearful response.

Actions, even involuntary actions, influence feelings. Studies show that an artificially induced smile can prompt happier emotions, and an <u>experiment</u>‡ suggests that people who use Botox are less prone to anger, because they can't make angry, frowning faces.

Usually, however, I invoke the act-the-way-I-want-to-feel principle not in the context of involuntary action, like tearful eyes, but in the context of self-regulation. When I'm feeling an unpleasant feeling, I counteract it by behaving the way I *wish* I felt—when I feel like yelling at my children, I make a joke; when I feel annoyed with a sales clerk, I start acting chatty.

It really works. When I can make myself do it.

How about you? Have you ever experienced a situation where a change in   10
your actions has changed your emotions?

---

* This phrase links to a previous post where Rubin discusses another example of this "commandment" in use.

† This link goes to a post where Rubin describes how her conjunctivitis helped her gain another insight into happiness.

‡ flThis link goes to an article in *Discover* magazine that describes the experiment.

COMMENTS

live aloha 1 year ago

There once was a person whom I used to despise for the things she did to my friends and colleagues (claiming credit for work of others, hogging the limelight, making threatening phone calls to those who opposed her, destroying reputations of those she saw as threats).

Because of our work, I ran into her all the time. Although I was never harmed by her directly, I perceived her as a threat because she ran a competing organization and I was never trusting of her actions in network settings. Anything she did, I would interpret only in the most negative light. But at the suggestion of a teacher/mentor, I started meditating and wishing her peace and happiness in her life. It was the exact opposite of what I felt like doing, but I did it.

Amazing results—she starting fading into the background of my mind. After I stopped thinking about her, I had so much more energy to promote our own work and our organization grew and prospered. Her organization has since faded, but the organization I had worked to build is thriving.

positivelypresent 1 year ago

When I first started reading your blog, I learned about the idea of acting the way you want to feel. I started doing it and it really does work!!

Pilar 3 months ago

When I feel sad or when I am dealing with hardships, the best thing that I can do for myself, is to put on my walking shoes and take a long hard walk-run. Walking can do for me what drugs do for other people. As I walk I can sometimes lose myself in the beauty of nature. [It's] hard to feel bad when I look all around and I listen to the outdoors' songs. When I get home, all tired, sweaty and energized, things don't look or feel quite so bad.   15

saranaut 7 months ago

A psychologist once told me that, just as you can "think yourself into" a bad mood (where depressed thoughts eventually present as physical symptoms), the opposite is also true: you can start a good feeling in your body, which can then manifest physically. For example, if you smile even though you feel low, your brain gets signals from the muscles involved in smiling that make it transmit the "feel-good chemicals" that smiling usually elicits. Obviously, that's an extremely simplified description, but it seems a real phenomenon as evidenced by all posts here. :-)

Ed Tseng 11 months ago

Great article . . . I talk about "act how you want to feel and you will feel the way you act" in my book, as well . . . I can't wait to read your new book! Book swap?!?

barcodesnow 11 months ago

This is often true, but not always. It's interesting how much a behavior can influence how you are feeling. Psychologists have done research on this. If you hold a pencil between your teeth while doing something you will enjoy it more than if you did not hold a pencil between your teeth = because holding a pencil between your teeth forces your mouth into a smile, and when you are smiling you subconsciously tend to assume you must be happy. . . .

One problem I have with the assertion that we FEEL because of the way we ACT is that it isn't entirely that simple, and you are in danger of guilt-blaming people for feeling a certain way. Sometimes acting a certain way won't make you feel any different. Getting out of bed in the morning is a good thing to do if you feel depressed, because it might help, but it is certainly not guaranteed to help. The danger is you are telling shy/anxious/distrustful people that it is their fault they feel that way. "If only you did X behavior" you would no longer feel that way. It is telling them their feelings are not really legitimate—or telling them they feel that way because they WANT to feel that way.

> **barcodesnow** 11 months ago in reply to barcodesnow
>
> This is definitely something to think about. I am trying to act differently to   20
> how I feel sometimes, maybe doing that can help me. I know going for a
> run when I feel down helps, but that's because it causes endorphins to be
> released in my body.

halseytailor 1 year ago

I took an acting class to learn how to laugh more spontaneously. And it is true as the cognitive psychologists say, that if you say it or act it, eventually your thinking and actions follow more genuinely. For example, if you give false compliments to your husband every day, "you look so good today," even though you don't originally feel that is true, over time you do come to feel it more genuinely.

> **gretchenrubin** 1 year ago in reply to halseytailor
>
> It never ceases to amaze me how effective this is! You start out fake, but
> then it turns sincere.

rush 1 year ago

I had this very conversation today with a friend of mine, who asked me the question that I would [have] absolutely hate[d] for anyone to ask me maybe about 6 months ago.

She asked me about my self-harming and now, after having stopped for a few months, now it was okay to answer. I smiled, and I answered eloquently—I actually made the person who asked understand instead of jump to accusations—mostly because my response wasn't defensive, and so theirs didn't have to be either.

Out of the conversation, though, I got a whole lot more. Because I opened up   25
so much, the girl who asked felt comfortable in opening up to me as well, and out of the conversation we came up with a point that we both agreed on, as it related to our own personal circumstances: "Your state of mind determines your state of reality."

I decided then that that would be my life's mantra—because it's that type of thinking that has gotten me where I am today; even though I have a good way to go in my pursuit of happiness, with this mantra, I am already halfway there. =]

Your post was inspiring—I could truly, truly relate.

....

Laura G 1 year ago

I wonder if this is one of those things (like positive self-talk) that just isn't compatible with depression? I work in customer service, and behave in a friendly, cheerful manner all day, and when I get home, I certainly don't feel better—most often, I feel grumbly and occasionally like picking a fight. Granted, I typically feel OK *at* work, but then it's like crashing off a sugar high—the pendulum swings back, if you don't mind a mixed metaphor.

....

HappinessNLove 1 year ago

@live aloha, your comment is simply beautiful.......I shall use this to resolve my own issues with people I find difficult to deal with.

That's a great article Gretchen. I too have noticed this happens . . . . . and   30
you know . . . at times when I find it really difficult to "act the way I want to feel" . . . I found that not thinking helps. If I just stop thinking about it, actually it is better if you can just relax and kind of stop thinking about anything at all for a while, I can get to the way I want to feel much faster . . .

....

Leanne 1 year ago

I do think that this works in some things and some cases . . . but I have also seen that acting incongruently with feelings can be very problematic. I once dated someone who had lost their job, but didn't want to tell anyone about it and I wasn't to either. It was excruciating watching this person tell jokes and be the life of the party, and not get any support for what she was going through. She felt alone and isolated but was perceived as fun. Everyone said what a joy she must be to date, but it was horrid . . . it took so much energy to be so fun when she was afraid and tense inside, that when we were alone she was very hard to be around.

Similarly I didn't date someone more than once who seemed sad but I never saw her do anything but smile . . . it was like a mask. I asked why she acted so happy all the time, and she said "one has to." I found out years later she had been going through a particularly rough time. I found the "acting happy" unnerving and impossible to be real around.

And again, after a breakup, I was asked all the time why my ex kept making jokes that turned out to be pointed, or hurtful or just not funny. Again, I think it was an attempt to change feelings by acting differently. But the real anger, sadness and hurt would seep out anyways or be present as an undercurrent.

I do think that it can work for a lot of things like feeling unmotivated, depressed, feeling lonely or unproductive. If one acts motivated, engaged, friendly or productive, in fact one changes one's interface with the world, and the results of these actions can change our feelings, which are then based on very real productivity and engagement in the world. Which reminds me, if I stop slouching right now, I'll probably feel much more alert!

anamen 1 year ago in reply to Leanne

I agree, Leanne.

35

Personally I find the idea of everyone plastering on a big fake smile, in spite of obvious reasons to be sad, a bit chilling. Obviously we can't be happy if we are wallowing in anger, depression, loneliness, or sadness all the time, but that doesn't make these emotions so unacceptable that we must never permit ourselves to feel them. How may I offer comfort to my friends if they are never honest about their feelings of sadness? How will I know what I am doing that drives everyone crazy if no one ever even frowns about it? How will my kids figure out that the consequence of behaving hurtfully is the seemingly obvious fact that people will feel hurt if I am always pretending otherwise?

I think there needs to be a moment when we ask ourselves WHY we are feeling the way we do before we immediately start trying to feel better.

Leanne 1 year ago in reply to anamen

AnaMen,

I think also that we often give an outside "face" to the world, and sometimes when we neglect to, and express what is wrong or what we really feel, that others can reach out. If you show sadness when someone decides not to spend time with you, they might rethink their day, realizing how much they mean to you. If you act happy and fine, because you wish to feel happy and fine, they may just continue to spend their time in front of the nintendo etc., or even think you must not care about them very much at all.

Also, I have gotten great support from unexpected quarters when letting my feelings show instead of smiling and saying things are fine. When I discover that others will offer help, solace etc., then I no longer have to ACT to feel better, I DO feel better, and it is based on actual new ties to people around me, and not just feeling I am no longer alone, but knowing it through the real actions of others.

Conversely, when I have asked others why I am not offered help, I often get the answer: well you seem to do fine by yourself, and not in need of help at all. Even asking for help, in a calm friendly way (vs crying and looking stressed out) can lead to being turned down, as friends and neighbors assess your outward appearance and actions and decide they themselves, or others who DO look more needy, will get their time and a hand. 40

Indeed, I feel I am too emotional, and have been called an open book, but often I have received admiration from unexpected places, when I am praised for just that: being able to be open, vulnerable, real.

But I do not reject this premise entirely. Indeed I am often down, feeling either sad or depressed, and acting differently will indeed make me feel much much better.

Jeffrey Tang 1 year ago in reply to Leanne

I think acting how you want to feel, like many other things, is only good if used judiciously. There are times when it's helpful (such as when you yourself are the biggest obstacle to being happy), and times when it's not so helpful (when you put on a mask to quash your emotions). Knowing the difference isn't always easy though . . .

Questions for Critical Reading

1. Like creative nonfiction, blogs that discuss personal experience are often more successful when writers reflect on their experience in such a way that readers might learn from it. Do you think Rubin succeeded in doing this? Why or why not?

2. One problem blog writers face is deciding which words to link and what to link them to. Rubin's third link, "experiment," goes to an article in *Discover* magazine that describes the experiment she's referring to in more detail. The *Discover* article in turn links to an abstract in *Cerebral Cortex*, the peer-reviewed scholarly journal in which the original research was published. Read the following excerpts from both the *Discover* magazine article and the abstract in the peer-reviewed journal, and consider whether you would have preferred that Rubin link to the *Cerebral Cortex* abstract instead of the *Discover* article.

Discover article ("Why Darwin Would Have Loved Botox")

Recently Bernhard Haslinger at the Technical University of Munich realized that he could test the facial feedback theory in a new way. He could temporarily paralyze facial muscles and then scan people's brains as they tried to make faces. To block facial feedback [in some of the research participants], Haslinger used Dysport, a Botox-like drug. . . . [Participants were asked to make angry faces, and in those whose facial muscles *weren't* paralyzed by Dysport], a region known as the amygdala—a key brain region for processing emotions—became active. In the women with Dysport, who could not use their frown muscles, the amygdala was quieter. Haslinger also found another change, in the connections between the amygdala and the brain stem, where signals can trigger many of the feelings that go along with emotions: Dysport made that connection weaker.

Cerebral Cortex abstract ("The Link between Facial Feedback and Neural Activity within Central Circuitries of Emotion—New Insights from Botulinum Toxin–Induced Denervation of Frown Muscles")

Afferent feedback from muscles and skin has been suggested to influence our emotions during the control of facial expressions. . . . Yet, the physiological interaction between this limbic activation and facial feedback remains unclear. To study . . . facial feedback effects on limbic brain responses during intentional imitation of facial expressions, we applied botulinum toxin (BTX)–induced denervation of frown muscles in combination with functional magnetic resonance imaging. . . . We show that, during imitation of angry facial expressions, reduced feedback due to BTX treatment attenuates activation of the left amygdala. . . . These findings demonstrate that facial feedback modulates neural activity within central circuitries of emotion during intentional imitation of facial expressions. Given that people tend to mimic the emotional expressions of others, this could provide a potential physiological basis for the social transfer of emotion.

Would you have preferred a link to the scholarly abstract in *Cerebral Cortex* instead of the magazine article? Why or why not? Given that some of Rubin's readers probably had one preference while others likely had the opposite preference, what decision would you have made in Rubin's shoes? Why?

3. While Rubin chose to provide a link when she mentioned the Botox experiment, she chose *not* to provide one when she mentioned the studies showing "that an artificially induced smile can prompt happier emotions" (para. 7). If you were Rubin, would you have made the same choice? Why or why not?

4. Some blog readers consider the comment section an important part of the blog experience; it's a forum where other voices can be heard. Find a few comments that you think are effective and a few that you think are less effective. What do the effective ones have in common? What do the less effective ones have in common?

5. The comment section can work like good peer response in a writing class — as a way to get different opinions on an issue so that a more nuanced picture can ultimately emerge. Although some of the comments on Rubin's post merely agree with her idea, others provide caveats, pointing to potential limitations of her idea. How would you summarize a few of these caveats? If you were Rubin and you were writing a book based on this blog, which caveats would you integrate into your book? Why?

Making Connections

6. Regardless of genre, writers are faced with choices at every turn. Before choosing words, and before choosing how to organize those words, writers choose topics. One useful strategy in choosing a topic is to think about something that surprised you — because if it surprised you, it may also surprise your readers, who would probably rather read about something new to them than something they already know. In short, ideas that are unsurprising tend to be boring, while ideas that are surprising tend to be more interesting.

Writers across genres sometimes even use the words "surprise" or "surprising" to pique readers' interest, and others imply the idea of surprise by suggesting that their point is unexpected. To get a sense of whether you would want to do this in your own writing, consider the following two passages, one from Rubin's blog and one from Pipher's "June" (p. 311). Compare the original passages to the altered versions that don't mention or imply surprise:

Original Passage	Altered Passage
One of the most surprising . . . things I've learned from my happiness project is my Third Commandment: **Act the way I want to feel.** (Rubin, para. 1)	One of the things I've learned from my happiness project is my Third Commandment: **Act the way I want to feel.**
Almost all our psychological theories would predict that June would turn out badly. But as happens more frequently than we psychologists generally acknowledge, adversity built her character. (Pipher, para. 31)	Adversity built June's character.

How might you have responded differently if the writers hadn't emphasized that they were telling you something unexpected? Think of something you've written that might have benefited from mentioning or implying the notion of surprise; how could you have conveyed this notion?

7. Recall that punctuation might influence how long readers pause — and thus how much emphasis certain words and ideas receive. For example, both Rubin and Mary Beth Ellis, author of the creative nonfiction essay "The Waltz" (p. 298), sometimes use periods to break what could have been one longer sentence into two shorter ones. The additional period likely prompts some readers to pause longer than they otherwise might have, and thus the emphasis changes. Compare the following two passages from their writing to altered passages that combine sentences, thus eliminating a period; consider whether or not the difference affects you:

Original Passage	Altered Passage
It really works. When I can make myself do it. (Rubin, para. 9)	It really works when I can make myself do it.
The other course of action is to ingest staggering amounts of government-regulated mind-altering substances. I was all for this. (Ellis, para. 37)	The other course of action is to ingest staggering amounts of government-regulated mind-altering substances, and I was all for this.

Like many subtle choices writers make, these differences may affect some readers more than others. Did you respond differently to the original passages compared to the altered passages? If so, how?

(Note that if you want to emulate the strategy used in Rubin's original passage, it helps to be aware of how formal the genre is; in informal genres such as blogs, most readers won't object to sentence fragments such as "When I can make myself do it." In more formal genres, however, some readers may get annoyed by fragments.)

Writing: Your Turn

1. Write a blog post like Rubin's — one in which you discuss a time you were unhappy (or happy) and speculate about the cause(s) of the emotion you felt. Try to reflect on your experience in such a way that others might learn from it. After you write the post, make a list of a few questions to ask some classmates about their response to your post, and consider their feedback when you revise. For ideas on writing a blog post, see p. 90.

2. Go to www.happiness-project.com and browse the archives of Rubin's blog (scroll down the sidebar on the right). Read several of Rubin's posts, and write a rhetorical analysis of the blog. Consider questions such as the following: What do many of the posts have in common, and what might be the purpose underlying these common elements? Who seems to be the target audience, and what leads you to think so? What do you take to be the purpose of the blog? To what extent do you think the blog is fulfilling its purpose for the intended audience? For ideas on writing a rhetorical analysis, see p. 31 — and, based on what you read there, make a list of questions to ask your classmates about your draft. Consider their feedback when you revise.

writing

Depression: Move Your Mood

From *Spark: The Revolutionary New Science of Exercise and the Brain*

John Ratey, MD

The following selection is an excerpt from *Spark: The Revolutionary New Science of Exercise and the Brain* by John Ratey, MD. The chapter excerpted here focuses on the biology of mood—in particular, the biological mechanisms by which exercise can boost people's moods. Ratey is an associate clinical professor of psychiatry at Harvard Medical School who has published over sixty papers in peer-reviewed journals.

Focus on Genre   As a synthesis of medical research for laypeople, "Depression: Move Your Mood" presents us with carefully organized discussions of medical research on the biology of mood. Rather than organizing his writing randomly around a list of research studies ("Here's one study . . . Here's another study . . ."), Ratey organizes it around points ("These studies illustrate this point . . . These other studies illustrate a related point . . ."). As you read, think about how Ratey's organization might help his readers make sense of a complex topic.

Also consider how Ratey interweaves brief case studies with his synthesis of research, ultimately using both to advance an overarching argument. See if you can discern what his argument is, and consider how persuasive you find his evidence to be.

◄O►

B ill didn't know he was missing out. When he turned fifty, he realized he was twenty pounds overweight, and he decided to go on a diet and start running. Before long, he began losing weight, and he noticed some dramatic side effects: he became less critical—of himself and of others—and less of a grouch. His wife and his children picked up on the shift and wanted to spend more time with him, which made him feel good and further improved his attitude. Bill had never had depression, per se, but there was no doubt he felt more passionate about life once he got into an exercise routine. He discovered, entirely by accident, that he could be happier.

Our understanding of depression followed a similar path. Pure serendipity led to our first antidepressants, when in the 1950s it was discovered that an experimental tuberculosis drug made people "inappropriately happy." A few years later, a new antihistamine produced similar mood-elevating effects and spawned a class of drugs called tricyclic antidepressants. Suddenly there were medical treatments that could soothe symptoms of depression. It was the first real hint at the radical notion that there might be a biological explanation for what had been considered an entirely psychological problem. This led to a search for how the brain controls the mind, and the entire landscape of the field changed.

In the fifty years since then, mood disorders have been the focal point of psychiatric research. We still don't know what causes depression, but we've made great strides in describing the brain activity underlying emotions. And the more we've learned about the biology of mood, the more we've come to understand how aerobic exercise alters it. In fact, it's largely through depression research that we know as much as we do about what exercise does for the brain. It counteracts depression at almost every level.

In Britain, doctors now use exercise as a first-line treatment for depression, but it's vastly underutilized in the United States, and that's a shame. According to the World Health Organization, depression is the leading cause of disability in the United States and Canada, ahead of coronary heart disease, any given cancer, and AIDS. About 17 percent of American adults experience depression at some point in their lives, to the tune of $26.1 billion in health care costs each year. It's impossible to know how many people try to commit suicide, but, tragically, in the United States someone succeeds about every seventeen minutes. For this reason, and also because 74 percent of depression patients experience some other disorder—including anxiety, substance abuse, and dementia—it's an urgent problem. Unfortunately, it's not getting any better.

One of the hurdles to conquering depression is that the disorder encom- passes such a broad array of symptoms, most of which all of us experience at some point. Who doesn't feel grouchy, irritable, pessimistic, lethargic, apathetic,

5

self-critical, or melancholy on occasion? Sadness, for instance, is a normal aspect of the human condition—a response to a loss. But being sad isn't the same as being depressed, unless the feeling never goes away or comes along with a certain number of the other symptoms.

And what's the difference between a symptom and a personality trait? My patient Bill had been critical and negative most of his life. He wasn't sick, technically, but he had what I would call a shadow syndrome of depression and was a perfect candidate for a lifestyle change to benefit his Eeyore-like outlook. Prescribing medicine to make people "better than well" is the subject of a long-standing ethical debate, and this is one area where exercise offers a huge advantage over antidepressants. Just because you don't have all the symptoms of depression doesn't mean you can't feel better. Bill's a happier guy because he started running. As I'll explain, the same would probably hold true if he were clinically depressed. Aerobic exercise has a positive impact on the entire range of depressive symptoms, regardless of whether they come individually, in the form of a mild episode, or conspire to form a disorder. Overall, I think of depression as an erosion of connections—in your life as well as between your brain cells. Exercise reestablishes those connections.

Within the spectrum of symptoms, there are distinctly different types of depression. I've had patients who don't eat and can't sleep, and others who eat too much and are so fatigued they feel like they can't get out of bed in the morning. Some can't make even the simplest decision, and they quietly withdraw from the world in a posture of helplessness, while others shout and challenge everything and everyone. Such contradictions make treatment difficult. If you have breast cancer, a biopsy can determine the best treatment. If you have depression, you may take a psychological test, and then it's a matter of trial and error to find a drug that might work; there is no blood test for depression.

Which brings us back to the quest to find a biological culprit. By reverse engineering our original, accidental antidepressants, we discovered that they increase the activity of the so-called monoamine neurotransmitters: norepinephrine, dopamine, and serotonin. When a research psychiatrist at Massachusetts Mental Health Center named Joseph Schildkraut found in 1965 that a breakdown product of norepinephrine, called methoxyhydroxyphenylglycol (MHPG), was reduced in depressed patients, we got excited about the idea that there was something to measure. If we could quantify the imbalance, we should be able to diagnose and attack the disease at the fundamental level of biology. His pioneering work led to the monoamine hypothesis, which holds that depression is caused by a deficit of these three neurotransmitters. Most of our treatments and research since then have been about trying to reverse that deficit.

CONVERGING PATHS

When the blockbuster drug Prozac came along, it was the first antidepressant that corrected the chemical imbalance of just one of the suspect neurotransmitters. Prozac is the mother of a class known as selective serotonin reuptake inhibitors (SSRIs), which prevent serotonin from being recycled at the synapse, leaving more available for use, and theoretically restoring normal transmission in the brain. Prozac was exciting because it worked for a lot of people and it pointed to a single problem that could be fixed. It had a huge impact because it didn't just squelch negativity, it boosted self-esteem which is a different dimension of the disease.

Twenty years later, it's evident that Prozac and its SSRI daughters don't   10
work for everyone, nor do antidepressants that target norepinephrine, dopamine, or any combination of the three. One of the issues is side effects. To take an example, a good portion of my patients on SSRIs develop problems with their sex lives after a few months. Some estimates suggest that more than 50 percent complain of sexual side effects, ranging from lack of interest to lack of functionality. (It says something that SSRIs are often used as a treatment for premature ejaculation and for sexual offenders.) Sexual problems are easy for people to miss or dismiss, especially when they're otherwise feeling good, but they can sneak up on us and lead to other issues. Sexual feelings and passions are primary drivers in all of us, and muzzling them can leave us with a general lack of passion for life or a lack of intimacy or maybe a list of missed opportunities. On balance, the side effects are certainly outweighed by the most serious consequences of depression, but they get in the way for a lot of people. Now SSRIs carry a warning that they may increase the risk of suicidal thoughts and actions in children and adolescents, a finding that is still in question. And stories are coming out about the difficulty of withdrawing from this class of drugs, especially from venlafaxine (Effexor).

Recently, I started treating a successful entrepreneur whose life was a mess. He and his wife were separated because he'd had an affair, and he'd also lost his business. He came to me to find out more about an issue that had cropped up in couple's therapy, where it became clear that he suffered from ADHD.

Dead set against the idea of putting anything "unnatural" into his body, he resisted medication. But he finally agreed to try a stimulant, mostly because his wife was pressuring him, and he felt terribly guilty about cheating. We tried several different drugs, but we quickly stopped all of them. He got headaches, stomachaches, muscle pain.

His attention problems aside, the primary issue, I told him, was that he was depressed. He was inactive, unmotivated, and he felt hopeless. He had done nothing to sort out his work situation, and although it had been months, he denied there was a problem. Then one day, he came in, and I could see his demeanor had deteriorated. Typically very neat, he was unshaven and unkempt and told me he was having a hard time getting out of bed.

I insisted that he try an antidepressant, and I put him on the SSRI escitalopram (Lexapro). He had a severe reaction—he felt nauseated and started throwing up—and said he didn't want to try another.

He'd been physically active in the past, and I told him that he should   15
really be exercising every day. I'd been talking about it all along, but after the Lexapro episode, I explained what an enormous effect exercise has on the brain, and I gave him several relevant studies in an appeal to his professional sensibility.

Two weeks later, he looked like a different man. He was smiling and confident, and he felt good about the fact that he had been running nearly every day. Over the course of the next month, I saw him take up his job search in earnest and make strides in reconciling with his wife. And for the first time, he said he was hopeful that they might get back together. More than anything, he was amazed that he could feel so different and sustain that feeling.

Aside from elevating endorphins, exercise regulates all of the neurotransmitters targeted by antidepressants. For starters, exercise immediately elevates levels of Schildkraut's favorite neurotransmitter, norepinephrine, in certain areas of the brain. It wakes up the brain and gets it going and improves self-esteem, which is one component of depression.

Exercise also boosts dopamine, which improves mood and feelings of wellness and jump-starts the attention system. Dopamine is all about motivation and attention. Studies have shown that chronic exercise increases dopamine storage in the brain and also triggers the production of enzymes that create dopamine receptors in the reward center of the brain, and this provides a feeling of satisfaction when we have accomplished something. If the demand is there, the dopamine genes get activated to produce more, and the overall effect is a more stable regulation of these pathways, which are important to controlling addictions.

Serotonin is equally affected by exercise, and it's important for mood, impulse control, and self-esteem. It also helps stave off stress by counteracting cortisol, and it primes the cellular connections in the cortex and hippocampus that are important for learning.

THE TRUE TEST

We've known for a while that exercise influences the same chemicals as anti-   20
depressants do, but nobody had done a scientifically sound head-to-head

comparison until researchers at Duke University took up the task in 1999. In a landmark study affectionately called SMILE (Standard Medical Intervention and Long-term Exercise), James Blumenthal and his colleagues pitted exercise against the SSRI sertraline (Zoloft) in a sixteen-week trial. They randomly divided 156 patients into three groups: Zoloft, exercise, or a combination of the two. The exercise group was assigned to supervised walking or jogging, at 70 to 85 percent of their aerobic capacity, for thirty minutes (not including a ten-minute warm-up and a five-minute cool-down) three times a week. The results? All three groups showed a significant drop in depression, and about half of each group was completely out of the woods—in remission. Another 13 percent experienced fewer symptoms but didn't fully recover.

Blumenthal concluded that exercise was as effective as medication. This is the study I photocopy for patients who are skeptical of the idea that exercise changes their brain chemistry enough to help their depression, because it puts the issue in terms that are as black-and-white as psychiatry can hope to deliver, at least for now. The results should be taught in medical school and driven home with health insurance companies and posted on the bulletin boards of every nursing home in the country, where nearly a fifth of the residents have depression. If everyone knew that exercise worked as well as Zoloft, I think we could put a real dent in the disease. . . .

THE BEST FIX

When we talk about depression, we don't use the word *cure* because we only have subjective measures for behavior and emotions. About a third of patients with depression achieve full remission of their symptoms with antidepressants. Another third feel much better with medication, but they may continue to have problems with motivation, lethargy, and fatigue. The bad thoughts are gone, but even though they're able to get out of bed, they're still not knocking on the door for a new job or doing what they should be doing. They're feeling less than well, lingering in the shadows of depression. The current *Diagnostic and Statistical Manual of Mental Disorders* lists nine symptoms for depression, and you need to have six to receive a diagnosis of depression. Say you can't concentrate, can't sleep, feel worthless, and aren't interested in anything. That's four. Technically, you aren't depressed. What are you, then? Just miserable? My point is, with any degree of depression, you need to snuff it out completely. And exercise is starting to be taken very seriously in this regard.

Madhukar Trivedi, a clinical psychiatrist who is the director of the Mood Disorders Research Program at the University of Texas Southwestern Medical School, has been researching the effectiveness of using exercise to augment antidepressants. In 2006 he published a pilot study showing that patients who weren't responding to antidepressants lowered their scores on a common depression test by 10.4 points on a 17-point scale—a huge drop—after twelve weeks of exercise. All seventeen patients were deeply depressed and had been taking antidepressants for at least four months. The drugs weren't working, but they stayed on them for the experiment.

Trivedi enlisted the Cooper Institute to set up the exercise protocol. Then they let the patients, who were inactive to begin with, exercise at home, either walking or riding a stationary bike as often and as rigorously as they wanted. The only requirement was that they expend a certain amount of energy each week. Most chose to walk an average of fifty-five minutes three days a week. Nine people dropped out, which isn't unusual, but of the eight who completed the exercise program, five achieved full remission. Even the patients who stuck with the program for only a few weeks showed an improvement in symptoms.

The numbers were small, but Trivedi's results were huge. At least for some people, when drugs don't work, exercise does. It begs the question, why wouldn't you add exercise right from the beginning? Especially if you're play- ing trial and error with a host of other medications? But the allure of the magic pill is powerful, and it takes a long time to overturn attitudes. Just ask T. Byram Karasu, who was in charge of the American Psychiatric Association's work group on major depressive disorders. He pushed to get the APA to formally adopt exercise in its treatment guidelines for depression and suggested that psychia- trists tell every patient to walk three to five miles a day or do some other type of vigorous exercise. The APA balked, presumably because, while most doctors acknowledge the anecdotal evidence that exercise improves mood, they say there isn't enough scientific evidence. In this age of deconstructing the brain and unlocking the secrets of the life and death of cells, it's difficult for psychia- trists to consider such a holistic strategy as exercise a treatment.

Any doctor will tell you that the worst patients are other doctors. Imagine the difficulty, then, in convincing a patient of mine with a medical degree to exercise for her depression. Grace, who has a history of mild bouts of depres- sion, also happens to be a psychiatrist with a sophisticated knowledge of medicine. Even so, we haven't been able to find an antidepressant without side effects. SSRIs seem to work best for her, but she would try one and then stop because they all made her gain weight very quickly. She's brilliant and well aware of the biology of exercise—at least some of it—but she just didn't do it.

Last summer, she injured her back and ended up immobilized in bed for a period. Purely for physical rehabilitation, she started swimming. It was the only thing she could do, and it felt good because the water supported her body and eased her pain. She enjoyed it and began exercising in the pool for three hours a day. Not only did her pain decrease, but she also started seeing some long-lost muscle tone and she felt good about herself.

Then the pool shut down for the winter, her back flared up, and her mood took a dive again. This time she also got angry. Flat on her back with few options for exercise, she started lifting weights—just three-pound dumbbells that she would pump up and down fast enough to get her heart rate up several times a day. Even that minor activity helped, and more important, the experience sparked a shift in her brain and in her mind. I've been seeing Grace for years, but there was something about this situation that put exercise into perspective for her.

She's worked out the kinks in her back and has been very steady with her swimming routine. She says she's able to think and write more creatively, and she feels a newfound sense of vigor that hasn't gone unnoticed by her family and friends. Not that it should have surprised her: She recalled that when she was training every day for the tae kwon do team in college, she did some of her best work. Then as a young doctor in Boston, she got into running marathons. Like many people, it was only after she started a family that she fell out of the habit of exercise. "I just got too busy and forgot the benefits of working out," she says. "Now I feel like I have my brain back."

HOLES IN THE THEORY

It wasn't until we were able to take good pictures of the brain that we really   30
began to understand how various medical treatments and exercise break us out of the bonds of depression. In the early 1990s, using MRI, we noticed bright patches on brain scans of certain depressed patients. The hyperintensities, as they are known, appeared in the white matter, the portion of densely bundled axons that connect neurons in the gray matter of the cortex. Zooming in further, we found differences in the volume of the cortex—the gray matter was physically shrunken. Gray matter is the thin, wrinkly covering of the brain made up of cells that direct all of our complex functions such as attention, emotions, memory, and consciousness. The MRI scans pointed toward a radical notion: that chronic depression may cause structural damage in the thinking brain.

Related research showed that depressed patients also had measurable changes in the amygdala and the hippocampus, crucial players in the stress response. We knew the amygdala was central to our emotional life, but we were just discovering that the memory center was also involved in stress and depression. In 1996 Yvette Sheline of Washington University in St. Louis compared ten patients with depression to ten healthy controls of the same physical stature and educational background, and she found that the hippocampus of depressed patients was up to 15 percent smaller compared to that of the controls. She also found evidence that the degree of shrinkage was directly related to the length of depression, and this was news. It might explain why so many patients with depression complain of learning and memory trouble, and why mood deteriorates in Alzheimer's, the neurodegenerative disease that begins with erosion of the hippocampus.

High levels of the stress hormone cortisol kill neurons in the hippocampus. If you put a neuron in a petri dish and flood it with cortisol, its vital connections to other cells retract. Fewer synapses develop and the dendrites wither. This causes a communication breakdown, which, in the hippocampus of a depressed brain, could partly explain why it gets locked into thinking negative thoughts—it's recycling a negative memory, perhaps because it can't branch out to form alternative connections.

Neuroimaging has cracked open an entirely new view of the biology of depression. The picture was—and still is—crude and fuzzy, but now positron-emission tomography (PET) scans and functional MRI (fMRI) scans allow scientists to go beyond snapshots and see the brain at work. At the same time, we learned that new nerve cells are born every day in the hippocampus and possibly in the prefrontal cortex—two areas shriveled in depression. The new tools and new discoveries led to a reformulation of the neurotransmitter theory.

Our understanding hasn't junked the old theory, just expanded it. Now we see depression as a physical alteration of the brain's emotional circuitry. Norepinephrine, dopamine, and serotonin are essential messengers that ferry information across the synapses, but without enough good connections in place, these neurotransmitters can only do so much. As far as the brain is concerned, its job is to transfer information and constantly rewire itself to help us adapt and survive. In depression, it seems that in certain areas, the brain's ability to adapt grinds to a halt. The shutdown in depression is a shutdown of learning at the cellular level. Not only is the brain locked into a negative loop of self-hate, but it also loses the flexibility to work its way out of the hole.

Redefining depression as a connectivity issue helps explain the wide range of symptoms people experience. It's not just a matter of feeling empty, helpless, and hopeless. It affects learning, attention, energy, and motivation—disparate systems that involve different parts of the thinking brain. Depression also affects the body, shutting down the drive to sleep, eat, have sex, and generally look after ourselves on a primitive level. Psychiatrist Alexander Niculescu sees depression as a survival instinct to conserve resources in an environment void of hope—"to keep still and stay out of harm's way," he wrote in a 2005 article in *Genome Biology*. It's a form of hibernation: When the emotional landscape turns wintry, our neurobiology tells us to stay inside. Except that it can last much longer than a season. It's as if our entire being has said, there's nothing out there for me, so I may as well quit. Thus the atrophy, the halt of neuroplasticity, neurogenesis, and overall lack of connectedness. It's no wonder we haven't been able to define depression as a single problem.

THE UNDERLYING CONNECTION

If depression is primarily a communication breakdown, or a loss of the brain's ability to adapt, it's very good news for the value of exercise. We learned in the early 1990s that brain-derived neurotrophic factor (BDNF) protects neurons against cortisol in areas that control mood, including the hippocampus. It is the fertilizer that encourages neurons to connect to one another and grow, making it vital for neuroplasticity and neurogenesis. While extremely high levels of cortisol can decrease BDNF, antidepressants and especially exercise do just the opposite. BDNF is the rope in a tug of war between chronic stress and adaptability. The Miracle-Gro molecule became the new serotonin, and we began measuring, blocking, increasing, and otherwise tweaking it in every way imaginable, to see how it affected mood in mice and men.

We can't ask a rodent if it's depressed, but we can see how it reacts to inescapable stress. If its feet are shocked, does it attempt to escape or does it freeze? This is the experimental model for learned helplessness, a popular way of describing human depression that implies an inability to cope with adversity and to take the action necessary to survive and flourish. If the lab animal gives up, it's considered to be depressed.

In one such experiment, when BDNF was injected directly into the hippocampi of mice, they were much quicker to try to escape than their nontreated counterparts. The injection seemed to have the same effect as exercise and antidepressants on the animals' behavior. Conversely, scientists have bred mice with genes that produce 50 percent less BDNF and found that they don't respond well to antidepressants, suggesting it's a necessary ingredient for the drugs to work. Such mice were significantly slower to try to escape stress than their peers with normal BDNF function.

In people, scientists are limited to measuring BDNF in the bloodstream, which, at best, offers a rough approximation of levels in the brain. One study of thirty depressed patients showed that every one of them had lower than normal BDNF levels. In another, antidepressants restored depressed patients' BDNF levels to normal, and yet another showed that higher levels correspond to fewer symptoms. In postmortem studies of people with depression who died of suicide, their brains had significantly decreased levels of BDNF. Even in healthy people, low BDNF levels have been correlated with personality traits that make them more vulnerable to depression, such as neuroticism and hostility.

Exercise boosts BDNF at least as much as antidepressants, and sometimes   40 more, in the rat hippocampus. One study showed that combining exercise with antidepressants spiked BDNF by 250 percent. And in humans, we know that exercise raises BDNF, at least in the bloodstream, much like antidepressants do.

As with norepinephrine in the 1960s, BDNF may be the tip of the iceberg. Today, research focuses on BDNF as well as vascular endothelial growth factor (VEGF), fibroblast growth factor (FGF-2), insulin-like growth factor (IGF-1), and all the related chemicals involved in encouraging neuroplasticity and neurogenesis. At the same time, pharmaceutical companies are funding research to mark and measure all these factors, and to map the genes affected by them, so they can figure out how to mimic their actions. BDNF and its neurotrophic brethren are much farther upstream in the neurochemical cascade than serotonin, closer to the source. Ultimately, the genes have to turn on the flow.

The shift from the neurotransmitter hypothesis to the connectivity theory is a move from outside to inside the nerve cell. In addition to working at the synapse, as serotonin does, BDNF turns on genes to produce more neurotransmitters and neurotrophins, puts the brakes on self-destructive cellular activity, releases antioxidants, and provides the proteins used as building material for axons and dendrites. These gene-regulated adaptations of BDNF might go a long way toward explaining the delayed effect of antidepressants.

It can often take three weeks for antidepressants to work. Is it merely a coincidence that the process of neurogenesis—from the time a stem cell is born in the hippocampus until it plugs into the network—takes approximately the same amount of time? Many researchers think not. The latest twist to the connectivity theory is that a shutdown of neurogenesis might be a factor in depression. Some have shown that blocking neurogenesis in rats negates the effect of antidepressants, so it's a possibility. This could provide an even stronger link between exercise and its antidepressant effect, given that exercise clearly elevates BDNF and its sibling growth factors, and that these are essential to the building process of neurogenesis. . . .

OUT OF THE TUNNEL

Science has come a long way since our search for the single culprit began, and the decades' worth of research generated from the monoamine hypothesis has taught us volumes about the biology of emotions. The closer we get to the cause of depression, the more complex it appears. When we began, everyone was fairly certain that the problem was an imbalance of neurotransmitters at the synapses. Now we know for certain that it's not so simple.

Ironically, I think this is precisely why exercise has yet to be embraced as a medical treatment. It doesn't simply raise serotonin or dopamine or norepinephrine. It adjusts all of them, to levels that, we can only presume, have been optimally programmed by evolution. The same goes for exercise's effect on BDNF, IGF-1, VEGF, and FGF-2 which provide the building material and oversight for the construction of new connections and neurons. In short, exercise affects so many variables in the brain that it's nigh impossible to isolate its effect as we'd like—in the name of hard science. But the evidence is there, from the action of microscopic molecules to massive surveys of tens of thousands of people over the years. Yes, exercise is an antidepressant. But it is also much more.

45

Still, it's not surprising that about half the patients in studies on exercise and depression drop out. Perhaps because most of them are inactive to begin with, getting started is that much more challenging. This is critical for doctors to keep in mind when recommending exercise. With people who are already feeling hopeless, it's important to keep expectations reasonable, so as not to reinforce the negative. On the other hand, studies have shown that even people who find the act of exercise inherently unpleasant have a positive mood swing the minute the workout is over. If you know what's on the other side, it's easier to push through the difficulty.

Human beings are social animals, so if you're depressed, it would be ideal to choose a form of exercise that encourages making connections and that can take place outside or in some environment that stimulates the senses. Asking someone to join you in exercise and putting yourself in a new setting will give those newly hatched neurons a powerful reason for being; new connections need to be formed to represent the sensory stimulation. Breaking out of the emptiness that the brain has been locked into provides a sense of purpose and self-worth that evokes a positive future. Once you develop the positive feeling, you need to devote it to something. Then you get the bottom-up motivation and physical boost combined with the top-down reevaluation of yourself. By motivating the body to move, you're encouraging the mind to embrace life.

THE PRESCRIPTION

...In some ways, exercise is even more important for prevention than it is for treatment. One of the first symptoms of depression, even before your mood drops to new lows, is sleep disturbance. Either you can't get up or you can't get to sleep or both. I think of it as sleep inertia—trouble starting or stopping. First you lose your energy, then your interest in things. The key is to get moving immediately. And do not stop. Set up a schedule for a daily walk, run, jog, bike ride, or dance class. If you can't sleep, go for a walk in the dawn light and do it every day. Take the dog out, change your schedule—run from the depression. Burn those 1,400 calories as if your life depended on it, and nip it in the bud.

If you have severe depression, you may feel like you're at the bottom of a pit, in a state of slow death, and that it's almost impossible to make it outside or go to the gym or even think about moving. First, see your doctor about medication and get yourself some omega-3 supplements, which are proven to have antidepressant effects. This will, I hope, loosen up the brain lock enough for you to at least go for a walk. Ask for help. Get a friend or family member to agree to come by every day, at the same time if possible, to escort you outside and around the block. In England and Australia, walking groups for patients with depression have been popular for years, and now they're starting to make their way to the United States, so check the Internet to see if there is one in your area. If that's not an option, and you have the means, set up a regular time with a personal trainer. This might sound crazy, I realize, if you feel like you can't even lift yourself off the couch, but if that's the case, activity is all the more urgent.

Exercise is not an instant cure, but you need to get your brain working again, and if you move your body your brain won't have any choice. It's a process, and the best strategy is to take it one step—and then one stride—at a time. Start slowly and build on it. At its core, depression is defined by an absence of moving toward anything, and exercise is the way to divert those negative signals and trick the brain into coming out of hibernation.

50

Questions for Critical Reading

1. What do you think is Ratey's purpose in synthesizing all this research for us? For you as a reader, did he succeed in achieving his purpose? Why or why not?

2. To appeal to their target audience, many writers across genres think carefully about the age groups of the people they discuss; many believe that the age groups they choose to represent may affect how persuasive their writing is for their target audience. The three patients Ratey discusses all seem to be in about the same age range. Would you have been more persuaded by Ratey's writing if he had discussed people from a variety of age ranges (e.g., a college student, a middle-aged person, and an elderly person), or if he had discussed only people your age? If you were Ratey, what age groups would you have represented? Why?

3. Like many writers seeking to persuade readers, Ratey uses more than one type of evidence in "Depression: Move Your Mood." Imagine for a minute that he had discussed only medical research as evidence. Now imagine that

he had discussed only people who have benefited from exercise. Would you have preferred one of these alternative versions? Why or why not? If you prefer both types of evidence, would you like both types to be equally balanced, or would you prefer more of one type of evidence? Why?

4. Like Ratey, you'll probably be called on to synthesize information from different sources — to take multiple sources and organize them to make points, rather than simply giving readers a random "data dump." In general, your readers will be able to make more sense of your synthesis if you organize it around points — that is, if you select the order of the sources you discuss based on the points you want them to illustrate. Consider how Ratey organizes the following passage. Take a couple of minutes (either by yourself or with some classmates) to make an outline of the points he uses the research to illustrate.

> If depression is primarily a communication breakdown, or a loss of the brain's ability to adapt, it's very good news for the value of exercise. We learned in the early 1990s that brain-derived neurotrophic factor (BDNF) protects neurons against [the stress hormone] cortisol. . . . While extremely high levels of cortisol can decrease BDNF, antidepressants and especially exercise do just the opposite. . . . The Miracle-Gro molecule became the new serotonin, and we began measuring, blocking, increasing, and otherwise tweaking it in every way imaginable, to see how it affected mood in mice and men. (para. 36.)

[Here Ratey provides a paragraph of background information telling us that if a lab animal gives up rather than trying to escape when its feet are shocked, it is considered to be depressed.]

> In one such experiment, when BDNF was injected directly into the hippocampi of mice, they were much quicker to try to escape than their nontreated counterparts. The injection seemed to have the same effect as exercise. . . . Conversely, scientists [in another study] have bred mice with genes that produce 50 percent less BDNF. . . . Such mice were significantly slower to try to escape stress than their peers with normal BDNF function.

> In people, scientists are limited to measuring BDNF in the bloodstream, which, at best, offers a rough approximation of levels in the brain. One study of thirty depressed patients showed that every one of them had lower than normal BDNF levels. In another, antidepressants restored depressed patients' BDNF levels to normal, and yet another showed that higher levels correspond to fewer symptoms. In postmortem studies of people with depression who died of suicide, their brains had significantly decreased levels of BDNF. (paras. 38–39)

Based on your outline, do you think Ratey did a data dump, or do you think he did a good job organizing his sources around points that he wanted to illustrate? Why? Do you think his writing could have been organized even more effectively — and if so, how?

5. Recall that writers across genres need to choose whether to quote people directly or to paraphrase what they wrote. Ratey chooses to quote only one of the patients that he tells us about, Grace. Compare the way he discusses Grace's case to the way he discusses the former entrepreneur's case, focusing on his choice to quote or paraphrase:

> [Grace has] worked out the kinks in her back and has been very steady with her swimming routine. She says she's able to think and write more creatively, and she feels a newfound sense of vigor that hasn't gone unnoticed by her family and friends. Not that it should have surprised her: She recalled that when she was training every day for the tae kwon do team in college, she did some of her best work. . . . Like many people, it was only after she started a family that she fell out of the habit of exercise. "I just got too busy and forgot the benefits of working out," she says. "Now I feel like I have my brain back." (para. 29)

> [After he began exercising,] he looked like a different man. He was smiling and confident, and he felt good about the fact that he had been running nearly every day. Over the course of the next month, I saw him take up his job search in earnest and make strides in reconciling with his wife. And for the first time, he said he was hopeful that they might get back together. More than anything, he was amazed that he could feel so different and sustain that feeling. (para. 16)

Why do you think Ratey might have quoted Grace rather than merely summarizing what she told him? If you were Ratey, would you consider adding a quotation to the paragraph about the man who was looking for a job? Why or why not?

7. Both students and experienced researchers like Ratey often believe that a topic is simpler than it actually turns out to be. Consider the following passage; although Ratey is discussing the biology of emotion, his description could apply to much of the knowledge in almost any field:

> Science has come a long way since our search for the single culprit began, and the decade's worth of research generated from the monoamine hypothesis has taught us volumes about the biology of emotions. *The closer we get to the cause of depression, the more complex it appears.* When we began, everyone was fairly certain that the problem was an imbalance of neurotransmitters at the synapses. *Now we know for certain that it's not so simple.* (para. 44; emphasis added)

Like many writers and researchers across disciplines, Ratey realizes that his field's object of study is more complex than it initially appeared to be.

In the same vein, take a few minutes to list some topics that you've written about, and share your list with a couple of classmates; together, discuss at least one topic from each group member's list, speculating about which topics may have been more complex than you or your classmates initially realized. When you're finished talking with your group, your instructor may ask groups to share an insight or example with the rest of the class.

Making Connections

8. Ratey's realization that "it's not so simple"—that he can't be certain of his field's knowledge—influences which verbs he chooses. (Recall that verbs like "prove" are often avoided in many fields because they imply certainty of knowledge.) Think about the following passages, one from Ratey's "Depression: Move your Mood" and one from Barbara Ehrenreich's critique of positive psychology (p. 374). Consider what assumptions about knowledge are reflected in the choice of verb phrases (italicized):

> **Ratey**
>
> The MRI scans *pointed toward* a radical notion: that chronic depression *may cause* structural damage in the thinking brain. (para. 30)

> **Ehrenreich**
>
> Some of the studies Held has reviewed even conclude that negative traits like pessimism *can be* healthier in the long run than optimism and happiness. . . . [A] longitudinal study of more than a thousand California schoolchildren concluded that optimism *was likely to lead* to an earlier death in middle or old age, possibly because the optimistic people took more risks. (para. 9)

What does each writer seem to assume about the certainty of the knowledge he or she is discussing? How can you tell?

Take a minute to rewrite each passage to reflect the assumption that the writer's knowledge is certain. Share what you wrote with a classmate and discuss when you might want to emulate the original passages and when you might want to emulate your altered versions. Your instructor may ask a few people to share what they wrote with the class, along with their insights on when to emulate the original passages and when to emulate the altered versions.

9. Recall that titles can allow writers both to pique an audience's interest and to establish the focus of their writing. Compare these two titles of books for laypeople, the first of which is the full title of Ratey's book and the second of which is the full title of Barbara Ehrenreich's critique of positive thinking (p. 374):

> *Spark: The Revolutionary New Science of Exercise and the Brain*
>
> *Bright-Sided: How Positive Thinking Is Undermining America*

How would you describe what these titles have in common? How effective do you find each title, and why?

Writing

Writing: Your Turn

1. Drawing on what you see as the most important information from "Depression: Move Your Mood," design and write a brochure to persuade college students that exercise is an important means of maintaining a positive mood. Be sure to cite *Spark* as your source. Test-drive your brochure with some of your classmates to get ideas for revision, and then distribute your revised brochure to at least ten people who aren't in your class. For ideas on designing a brochure, see p. 105.

2. Write a blog post or series of posts on exercise and mood. You might discuss how one or more of the studies referred to in "Depression: Move Your Mood" relates to your life. As part of your discussion, you could link to one of these studies,[1] or you could quote or paraphrase parts of Ratey's summary, making sure to link to *Spark*. Alternatively, you might discuss one of Ratey's case studies of people who have benefited from exercise (again linking to *Spark*), or you might provide your own case study based on an interview of someone you know. Whatever approach you take, be sure to inject your own personal reflection in addition to citing Ratey or others. Before posting, have your classmates read a draft of what you've written and give you feedback for revision. For ideas on writing a blog post, see p. 90.

---

[1] Although Ratey doesn't include a bibliography, he sometimes provides enough information to find a study through a search engine or academic database.

Positive Feeling and Positive Character

From *Authentic Happiness*: *Using the New Positive Psychology to Realize Your Potential for Lasting Fulfillment*

Martin Seligman, PhD

In this excerpt from *Authentic Happiness: Using the New Positive Psychology to Realize Your Potential for Lasting Fulfillment* (2002), Martin Seligman tries to teach us how to become happier by using our "signature strengths." Seligman is a psychology professor at the University of Pennsylvania, where he studies and writes about optimism and motivation. His most recent book is *Flourish: A Visionary New Understanding of Happiness and Well-Being* (2011). He is widely regarded as one of the key figures in positive psychology.

Focus on Genre   A self-help book, *Authentic Happiness* tries to persuade us that we can make ourselves happier by following Seligman's advice, which, he notes, is grounded in research. Seligman makes some moves typical in academic genres but dispenses with others. He doesn't always cite his sources, for example, nor does he recognize complexity as often as he might if he were writing for an academic audience. As you read, consider how Seligman might be simplifying things for a lay audience; for instance, are there any objections you have that he doesn't anticipate or address? Do you think he might be overgeneralizing?

 As always when reading a persuasive genre, consider what the main point is, and try to distinguish the main argument from the subpoints.

◄○►

n 1932, Cecilia O'Payne took her final vows in Milwaukee. As a novice in the School Sisters of Notre Dame, she committed the rest of her life to the teaching of young children. Asked to write a short sketch of her life on this momentous occasion, she wrote:

> God started my life off well by bestowing upon me grace of inestimable value. . . . the past year which I spent as a candidate studying at Notre Dame has been a very happy one. Now I look forward with eager joy to receiving the Holy Habit of Our Lady and to a life of union with Love Divine.

In the same year, in the same city, and taking the same vows, Marguerite Donnelly wrote her autobiographical sketch:

> I was born on September 26, 1909, the eldest of seven children, five girls and two boys. . . . My candidate year was spent in the mother-house, teaching chemistry and second year Latin at Notre Dame Institute. With God's grace, I intend to do my best for our Order, for the spread of religion and for my personal sanctification.

These two nuns, along with 178 of their sisters, thereby became subjects in the most remarkable study of happiness and longevity ever done.

Investigating how long people will live and understanding what conditions shorten and lengthen life is an enormously important but enormously knotty scientific problem. It is well documented, for example, that people from Utah live longer than people from the neighboring state of Nevada. But why? Is it the clean mountain air of Utah as opposed to the exhaust fumes of Las Vegas? Is it the staid Mormon life as opposed to the more frenetic lifestyle of the average Nevadan? Is it the stereotypical diet in Nevada—junk food, late-night snacks, alcohol, coffee, and tobacco—as opposed to wholesome, farm-fresh food, and the scarcity of alcohol, coffee, and tobacco in Utah? Too many insidious (as well as healthful) factors are confounded between Nevada and Utah for scientists to isolate the cause.

Unlike Nevadans or even Utahans, however, nuns lead routine and sheltered lives. They all eat roughly the same bland diet. They don't smoke or drink. They have the same reproductive and marital histories. They don't get sexually transmitted diseases. They are in the same economic and social class, and they have the same access to good medical care. So almost all the usual confounds are eliminated, yet there is still wide variation in how long nuns live and how healthy they are. Cecilia is still alive at age ninety-eight and has never been sick a day in her life. In contrast, Marguerite had a stroke at age fifty-nine and died soon thereafter. We can be sure their lifestyle, diet, and medical care were not the culprits. When the novitiate essays of all 180 nuns were carefully read, however, a very strong and surprising difference emerged. Looking back at what Cecilia and Marguerite wrote, can you spot it?

Sister Cecilia used the words "very happy" and "eager joy," both expressions of effervescent good cheer. Sister Marguerite's autobiography, in contrast, contained not even a whisper of positive emotion. When the amount of positive feeling was quantified by raters who did not know how long the nuns lived, it was discovered that 90 percent of the most cheerful quarter was alive at age eighty-five versus only 34 percent of the least cheerful quarter. Similarly, 54 percent of the most cheerful quarter was alive at age ninety-four, as opposed to 11 percent of the least cheerful quarter.

Was it really the upbeat nature of their sketches that made the difference? 5 Perhaps it was a difference in the degree of unhappiness expressed, or in how much they looked forward to the future, or how devout they were, or how intellectually complex the essays were. But research showed that none of these factors made a difference, only the amount of positive feeling expressed in the sketch. So it seems that a happy nun is a long-lived nun.

College yearbook photos are a gold mine for Positive Psychology researchers. "Look at the birdie and smile," the photographer tells you, and dutifully you put on your best smile. Smiling on demand, it turns out, is easier said than done. Some of us break into a radiant smile of authentic good cheer, while the rest of us pose politely. There are two kinds of smiles. The first, called a Duchenne smile (after its discoverer, Guillaume Duchenne), is genuine. The corners of your mouth turn up and the skin around the corners of your eyes crinkles (like crow's feet). The muscles that do this, the *orbicularis oculi* and the *zygomaticus*, are exceedingly difficult to control voluntarily. The other smile, called the Pan American smile (after the flight attendants in television ads for the now-defunct airline), is inauthentic, with none of the Duchenne features. Indeed, it is probably more related to the rictus that lower primates display when frightened than it is to happiness.

When trained psychologists look through collections of photos, they can at a glance separate out the Duchenne from the non-Duchenne smilers. Dacher Keltner and LeeAnne Harker of the University of California at Berkeley, for example, studied 141 senior-class photos from the 1960 yearbook of Mills College. All but three of the women were smiling, and half of the smilers were Duchenne smilers. All the women were contacted at ages twenty-seven, forty-three, and fifty-two and asked about their marriages and their life satisfaction. When Harker and Keltner inherited the study in the 1990s, they wondered if they could predict from the senior-year smile alone what these women's married lives would turn out to be like. Astonishingly, Duchenne women, on average, were more likely to be married, to stay married, and to experience more personal well-being over the next thirty years. Those indicators of happiness were predicted by a mere crinkling of the eyes.

Questioning their results, Harker and Keltner considered whether the Duchenne women were prettier, and their good looks rather than the genuineness of their smile predicted more life satisfaction. So the investigators went back and rated how pretty each of the women seemed, and they found that looks had nothing to do with good marriages or life satisfaction. A genuinely smiling woman, it turned out, was simply more likely to be well-wed and happy.

These two studies are surprising in their shared conclusion that just one portrait of a momentary positive emotion convincingly predicts longevity and marital satisfaction. The first part of this book is about these momentary positive emotions: joy, flow, glee, pleasure, contentment, serenity, hope, and ecstasy. In particular, I will focus on three questions:

- *Why* has evolution endowed us with positive feeling? What are the functions and consequences of these emotions, beyond making us feel good?
- *Who* has positive emotion in abundance, and who does not? What enables these emotions, and what disables them?
- *How* can you build more and lasting positive emotion into your life?

Everyone wants answers to these questions for their own lives, and it is natural to turn to the field of psychology for answers. So it may come as a surprise to you that psychology has badly neglected the positive side of life. For every one hundred journal articles on sadness, there is just one on happiness. One of my aims is to provide responsible answers, grounded in scientific research, to these three questions. Unfortunately, unlike relieving depression (where research has now provided step-by-step manuals that are reliably documented to work), what we know about building happiness is spotty. On some topics I can present solid facts, but on others, the best I can do is to draw inferences from the latest research and suggest how it can guide your life. In all cases, I will distinguish between what is known and what is my speculation. My most grandiose aim, as you will find out in the next three chapters, is to correct the imbalance by propelling the field of psychology into supplementing its hard-won knowledge about suffering and mental illness with a great deal more knowledge about positive emotion, as well as about personal strengths and virtues.

How do strengths and virtues sneak in? Why is a book about Positive Psychology about anything more than "happiology" or *hedonics*—the science of how we feel from moment to moment? A hedonist wants as many good moments and as few bad moments as possible in his life, and simple hedonic theory says that the quality of his life is just the quantity of good moments minus the quantity of bad moments. This is more than an ivory-tower theory, since many people run their lives based on exactly this goal. But it is a delusion,

10

I believe, because the sum total of our momentary feelings turns out to be a very flawed measure of how good or how bad we judge an episode—a movie, a vacation, a marriage, or an entire life—to be.

Daniel Kahneman, a distinguished professor of psychology at Princeton and the world's leading authority on hedonics, has made a career of demonstrating the many violations of simple hedonic theory. One technique he uses to test hedonic theory is the colonoscopy, in which a scope on a tube is inserted uncomfortably into the rectum and moved up and down the bowels for what seems like an eternity, but is actually only a few minutes. In one of Kahneman's experiments, 682 patients were randomly assigned to either the usual colonoscopy or to a procedure in which one extra minute was added on at the end, but with the colonoscope not moving. A stationary colonoscope provides a less uncomfortable final minute than what went before, but it does add one extra minute of discomfort. The added minute means, of course, that this group gets more total pain than the routine group. Because their experience ends relatively well, however, their memory of the episode is much rosier and, astonishingly, they are more willing to undergo the procedure again than the routine group.

In your own life, you should take particular care with endings, for their color will forever tinge your memory of the entire relationship and your willingness to reenter it. This book will talk about why hedonism fails and what this might mean for you. So Positive Psychology is about the meaning of those happy and unhappy moments, the tapestry they weave, and the strengths and virtues they display that make up the quality of your life. Ludwig Wittgenstein, the great Anglo-Viennese philosopher, was by all accounts miserable. I am a collector of Wittgensteinobilia, but I have never seen a photo of him smiling (Duchenne or otherwise). Wittgenstein was melancholy, irascible, scathingly critical of everyone around him, and even more critical of himself. In a typical seminar held in his cold and barely furnished Cambridge rooms, he would pace the floor, muttering audibly, "Wittgenstein, Wittgenstein, what a terrible teacher you are." Yet his last words give the lie to happiology. Dying alone, he said to his landlady, "Tell them it's been wonderful!"

Suppose you could be hooked up to a hypothetical "experience machine" that, for the rest of your life, would stimulate your brain and give you any positive feelings you desire. Most people to whom I offer this imaginary choice refuse the machine. It is not just positive feelings we want, we want to be *entitled* to our positive feelings. Yet we have invented myriad shortcuts to feeling good; drugs, chocolate, loveless sex, shopping, masturbation, and television are all examples. (I am not, however, going to suggest that you should drop these shortcuts altogether.)

The belief that we can rely on shortcuts to happiness, joy, rapture, comfort, and ecstasy, rather than be entitled to these feelings by the exercise of personal strengths and virtues, leads to legions of people who in the middle of great wealth are starving spiritually. Positive emotion alienated from the exercise of character leads to emptiness, to inauthenticity, to depression, and, as we age, to the gnawing realization that we are fidgeting until we die.

The positive feeling that arises from the exercise of strengths and virtues,   15 rather than from the shortcuts, is authentic. I found out about the value of this authenticity by giving courses in Positive Psychology for the last three years at the University of Pennsylvania. (These have been much more fun than the abnormal psychology courses I taught for the twenty years prior.) I tell my students about Jon Haidt, a gifted young University of Virginia professor who began his career working on disgust, giving people fried grasshoppers to eat. He then turned to moral disgust, observing people's reactions when he asked them to try on a T-shirt allegedly once worn by Adolf Hitler. Worn down by all these negative explorations, he began to look for an emotion that is the opposite of moral disgust, which he calls *elevation*. Haidt collects stories of the emotional reactions to experiencing the better side of humanity, to seeing another person do something extraordinarily positive. An eighteen-year-old freshman at the University of Virginia relates a typical story of elevation:

> We were going home from working at the Salvation Army shelter on a snowy night. We passed an old woman shoveling her driveway. One of the guys asked the driver to let him out. I thought he was just going to take a shortcut home. But when I saw him pick up the shovel, well, I felt a lump in my throat and started to cry. I wanted to tell everyone about it. I felt romantic toward him.

The students in one of my classes wondered if happiness comes from the exercise of kindness more readily than it does from having fun. After a heated dispute, we each undertook an assignment for the next class: to engage in one pleasurable activity and one philanthropic activity, and write about both.

The results were life-changing. The afterglow of the "pleasurable" activity (hanging out with friends, or watching a movie, or eating a hot fudge sundae) paled in comparison with the effects of the kind action. When our philanthropic acts were spontaneous and called upon personal strengths, the whole day went better. One junior told about her nephew phoning for help with his third-grade arithmetic. After an hour of tutoring him, she was astonished to discover that "for the rest of the day, I could listen better, I was mellower, and people liked me much more than usual." The exercise of kindness is a *gratification*, in contrast to a pleasure. As a gratification, it calls on your strengths to rise to an occasion and meet a challenge. Kindness is not accompanied by a separable stream of positive emotion like joy; rather, it consists in total engagement and in the loss of self-consciousness. Time stops. One of the business students volunteered that he had come to the University of Pennsylvania to learn how to make a lot of money in order to be happy, but that he was floored to find that he liked helping other people more than spending his money shopping.

To understand well-being, then, we also need to understand personal strengths and virtues, and this is the topic of the second part of this book. When well-being comes from engaging our strengths and virtues, our lives are imbued with authenticity. Feelings are states, momentary occurrences that need not be recurring features of personality. Traits, in contrast to states, are either negative or positive characteristics that recur across time and different situations, and strengths and virtues are the positive characteristics that bring about good feeling and gratification. Traits are abiding dispositions whose exercise makes momentary feelings more likely. The negative trait of paranoia makes the momentary state of jealousy more likely, just as the positive trait of being humorous makes the state of laughing more likely.

The trait of optimism helps explain how a single snapshot of the momentary happiness of nuns could predict how long they will live. Optimistic people tend to interpret their troubles as transient, controllable, and specific to one situation. Pessimistic people, in contrast, believe that their troubles last forever, undermine everything they do, and are uncontrollable. To see if optimism predicts longevity, scientists at the Mayo Clinic in Rochester, Minnesota, selected 839 consecutive patients who referred themselves for medical care forty years ago. (On admission, Mayo Clinic patients routinely take a battery of psychological as well as physical tests, and one of these is a test of the trait of optimism.) Of these patients, 200 had died by the year 2000, and optimists had 19 percent greater longevity, in terms of their expected life span, compared to that of the pessimists. Living 19 percent longer is again comparable to the longer lives of the happy nuns.

Optimism is only one of two dozen strengths that bring about greater well-being. George Vaillant, a Harvard professor who runs the two most thorough psychological investigations of men across their entire lives, studies strengths he calls "mature defenses." These include altruism, the ability to postpone gratification, future-mindedness, and humor. Some men never grow up and never display these traits, while other men revel in them as they age. Vaillant's two groups are the Harvard classes of 1939 through 1943, and 456 contemporaneous Boston men from the inner city. Both these studies began in the late 1930s, when the participants were in their late teens, and continue to this day, with the men now over eighty. Vaillant has uncovered the best predictors of successful aging, among them income, physical health, and joy in living. The mature defenses are robust harbingers of joy in living, high income, and a vigorous old age in both the largely white and Protestant Harvard group and the much more varied inner-city group. Of the 76 inner-city men who frequently displayed these mature defenses when younger, 95% could still move heavy furniture, chop wood, walk two miles, and climb two flights of stairs without tiring when they were old men. Of the 68 inner-city men who never displayed any of these psychological strengths, only 53% could perform the same tasks. For the Harvard men at age 75, joy in living, marital satisfaction, and the subjective sense of physical health were predicted best by the mature defenses exercised and measured in middle age.

How did Positive Psychology select just twenty-four strengths out of the [20] enormous number of traits to choose from? The last time anyone bothered to count, in 1936, more than eighteen thousand words in English referred to traits. Choosing which traits to investigate is a serious question for a distinguished group of psychologists and psychiatrists who are creating a system that is intended to be the opposite of the *DSM* (the *Diagnostic and Statistical Manual of Mental Disorders* of the American Psychiatric Association, which serves as a classification scheme of mental illness). Valor, kindness, originality? Surely. But what about intelligence, perfect pitch, or punctuality? Three criteria for strengths are as follows:

- They are valued in almost every culture
- They are valued in their own right, not just as a means to other ends
- They are malleable

So intelligence and perfect pitch are out, because they are not very learnable. Punctuality is learnable, but, like perfect pitch, it is generally a means to another end (like efficiency) and is not valued in almost every culture.

While psychology may have neglected virtue, religion and philosophy most assuredly have not, and there is astonishing convergence across the millennia and across cultures about virtue and strength. Confucius, Aristotle, Aquinas, the Bushido samurai code, the *Bhagavad-Gita*, and other venerable traditions disagree on the details, but all of these codes include six core virtues:

- Wisdom and knowledge
- Courage
- Love and humanity
- Justice
- Temperance
- Spirituality and transcendence

Each core virtue can be subdivided for the purpose of classification and measurement. Wisdom, for example, can be broken down into the strengths of curiosity, love of learning, judgment, originality, social intelligence, and perspective. Love includes kindness, generosity, nurturance, and the capacity to *be* loved as well as to love. Convergence across thousands of years and among unrelated philosophical traditions is remarkable, and Positive Psychology takes this cross-cultural agreement as its guide. . . .

When you read about these strengths, you will also find some that are deeply characteristic of you, whereas others are not. I call the former your *signature strengths*, and one of my purposes is to distinguish these from strengths that are less a part of you. I do not believe that you should devote overly much effort to correcting your weaknesses. Rather, I believe that the highest success in living and the deepest emotional satisfaction comes from building and using your signature strengths. For this reason, the second part of this book focuses on how to identify these strengths.

The third part of the book is about no less a question than "What is the good life?" In my view, you can find it by following a startlingly simple path. The "pleasant life" might be had by drinking champagne and driving a Porsche, but not the good life. Rather, the good life is using your signature strengths every day to produce authentic happiness and abundant gratification. This is something you can learn to do in each of the main realms of your life: work, love, and raising children.

One of my signature strengths is the love of learning, and by teaching I have built it into the fabric of my life. I try to do some of it every day. Simplifying a complex concept for my students, or telling my eight-year-old about bidding in bridge, ignites a glow inside me. More than that, when I teach well, it invigorates me, and the well-being it brings is authentic because it comes from what I am best at. In contrast, organizing people is not one of my signature strengths. Brilliant mentors have helped me become more adequate at it, so if I must, I can chair a committee effectively. But when it is over, I feel drained, not invigorated. What satisfaction I derive from it feels less authentic than what I get from teaching, and shepherding a good committee report does not put me in better touch with myself or anything larger.

The well-being that using your signature strengths engenders is anchored in authenticity. But just as well-being needs to be anchored in strengths and virtues, these in turn must be anchored in something larger. Just as the good life is something beyond the pleasant life, the meaningful life is beyond the good life.

What does Positive Psychology tell us about finding purpose in life, about leading a meaningful life beyond the good life? I am not sophomoric enough to put forward a complete theory of meaning, but I do know that it consists in attachment to something larger, and the larger the entity to which you can attach yourself, the more meaning in your life. Many people who want

25

meaning and purpose in their lives have turned to New Age thinking or have returned to organized religions. They hunger for the miraculous, or for divine intervention. A hidden cost of contemporary psychology's obsession with pathology is that it has left these pilgrims high and dry.

Like many of these stranded people, I also hunger for meaning in my life that will transcend the arbitrary purposes I have chosen for myself. Like many scientifically minded Westerners, however, the idea of a transcendent purpose (or, beyond this, of a God who grounds such purpose) has always seemed untenable to me. Positive Psychology points the way toward a secular approach to noble purpose and transcendent meaning — and, even more astonishingly, toward a God who is not supernatural. These hopes are expressed in my final chapter.

Questions for Critical Reading

1. What do you take to be Seligman's main argument, and to what extent do you agree with it? If you were persuaded, what did he do to persuade you? If you weren't persuaded, why weren't you?

2. Writers often transition from sentence to sentence by referring back to the previous sentence. For example, when Seligman tells us in one sentence that George Vaillant studies the "mature defenses," his next sentence reads, "These include altruism, the ability to postpone gratification, future-mindedness, and humor" (para. 19); the word "these" refers back to the mature defenses mentioned in the previous sentence.

Similarly, recall that writers often use the beginning of one paragraph to refer back to the previous paragraph, thus allowing readers to see how the two paragraphs are related. Compare the following two passages, both of which include the end of one paragraph and the beginning of the following paragraph. Consider whether, for you as a reader, one passage shows the relationship between paragraphs more effectively than the other:

> These two nuns, along with 178 of their sisters, thereby became subjects in the most remarkable study of happiness and longevity [length of life] ever done.
> Investigating how long people will live and understanding what conditions shorten and lengthen life is an enormously important but enormously knotty scientific problem. (paras. 1–2)

> For the Harvard men at age 75, joy in living, marital satisfaction, and the subjective sense of physical health were predicted best by the mature defenses exercised and measured in middle age.
> How did Positive Psychology select just twenty-four strengths out of the enormous number of traits to choose from? (paras. 19–20)

Did you find one paragraph-to-paragraph transition easier to navigate than the other one? Why or why not?

3. Regardless of genre, readers are influenced not only by *what* the words are but also by *where* they are—that is, how they fit into the visual design of the page. Bulleted lists, which appear in many genres, are a good example. Compare the following bulleted list from "Positive Feeling and Positive Character" to an altered version that doesn't use bullets. The words are exactly the same; the only difference is the formatting.

Original Passage	Altered Passage
I will focus on three questions: • *Why* has evolution endowed us with positive feeling? What are the functions and consequences of these emotions, beyond making us feel good? • *Who* has positive emotion in abundance, and who does not? What enables these emotions, and what disables them? • *How* can you build more and lasting positive emotion into your life? (para. 9)	I will focus on three questions: *Why* has evolution endowed us with positive feeling? What are the functions and consequences of these emotions, beyond making us feel good? *Who* has positive emotion in abundance, and who does not? What enables these emotions, and what disables them? *How* can you build more and lasting positive emotion into your life?

Did you prefer one version to the other? Why or why not? When in your own writing might you want to use bulleted lists?

Making Connections

4. Consider Seligman's argument—that "the good life is using your signature strengths every day to produce authentic happiness and abundant gratification" (para. 24)—as a way to help Mary Beth Ellis, author of the creative nonfiction piece "The Waltz" (p. 298). Given that Ellis's happiness is undermined by debilitating fear because "insufficient amounts of the neurotransmitter serotonin prevent proper communication between [her] orbital cortex and basal ganglia" (para. 35), to what extent do you think that using her signature strengths daily might help her?

Some of Ellis's readers may not believe that she could become happier by using signature strengths. Do you think that, in light of this potential objection, Seligman would have done well to include a caveat (an admission of the limitations of his argument)? Recall that caveats are often included in academic and persuasive genres to uphold an author's credibility—to show that an author isn't blinded by an ungrounded faith in the infallability of his or her ideas. If you were Seligman and the editor of your book asked you to include a caveat in "Positive Feeling and Positive Character," would you? Why or why not? If you would, where would you add it and how would you phrase it?

5. In genres of academic writing, and in many persuasive genres written for laypeople, writers often use a fair amount of detail when they introduce quotations. Consider the following versions of one of Seligman's introductions to a quotation. In the original passage, he tells us that the quotation will illustrate "a typical story of elevation" (a very positive emotion); in the altered passage, however, we aren't given that information. Consider which introduction to the quotation you prefer. (The difference is italicized.)

Original Passage	Altered Passage
An eighteen-year-old freshman at the University of Virginia *relates a typical story of elevation*:	An eighteen-year-old freshman at the University of Virginia *relates a story*:
We were going home from working at the Salvation Army shelter on a snowy night. We passed an old woman shoveling her driveway. One of the guys asked the driver to let him out. . . . [W]hen I saw him pick up the shovel, well, I felt a lump in my throat and started to cry. (para. 15)	We were going home from working at the Salvation Army shelter on a snowy night. We passed an old woman shoveling her driveway. One of the guys asked the driver to let him out. . . . [W]hen I saw him pick up the shovel, well, I felt a lump in my throat and started to cry.

While some readers of the altered passage may initially wonder why they are reading the quotation, readers of the original passage are more likely to know why they are reading it: to see an example of how a person's virtue can lead to positive emotion. Persuasive genres have points to make, and those points are often reinforced in the introductions to quotations.

In genres that don't make points explicitly, however, quotations are often integrated differently. Sometimes the attribution (the explanation of who said something) comes *after* the quotation, not before it. And recall that in some genres, there may be no attribution at all.

To gain more insight into different ways of integrating quotations, compare another example from Seligman to examples from two other genres, and see if you can explain how the purpose of each might shape how quotations are integrated. Focusing on the italicized words, consider both the amount of detail given and the location of the attribution (before, after, or in the middle of the quotation):

Self-help book ("Positive Feeling and Positive Character")

After an hour of tutoring him, she was astonished to discover that "for the rest of the day, I could listen better, I was mellower, and people liked me much more than usual." (para. 16)

Online news article ("Rating Countries for the Happiness Factor," p. 407)

"The most significant factors [associated with happiness] were health, the level of poverty, and access to basic education," *White says.* (para. 3)

Creative nonfiction ("The Waltz," p. 298)

The therapist closed my file. . . .

[She] was eyeing my hands. "You have dry skin," *she said.*

"I wasn't breast-fed," *I said, nodding.*

"Dry skin on your hands and nowhere else," *she pointed out.* "They're chapped almost raw."

"You know what?" *I said, rising.* "I have a class." (paras. 17–21)

Why might Seligman have chosen to give us a full amount of detail in his introduction to the quotation ("she was astonished to discover that . . ."}? Why might the authors of the news article and the creative nonfiction piece have chosen to write such simple attributions ("White says" and "I said"), and why might they have chosen to put the attributions after the quotations rather than before?

Writing: Your Turn

1. Write a reflection on the extent to which you think Seligman's ideas might be helpful to you or others. Do you think people might really become happier by developing signature strengths and using them more often? Why or why not? Trade reflections with a classmate to learn from each other's ideas and to get ideas for revision. For tips on writing a reflection, see p. 27.

2. Write a brochure informing college students about how they might use Seligman's ideas to become happier. You'll want to discuss what signature strengths are, how they might be identified, and how people might go about using them more often. You'll also want to acknowledge any limitations you see in Seligman's ideas. (If you acknowledge the limitations of his ideas, not only will you have more credibility in the eyes of your readers, but you'll also avoid setting them up with unrealistic expectations.)

Be sure to acknowledge Seligman as the source of your information so that readers will be able to find and read the book for themselves if they want to. Test-drive your brochure with some of your classmates to get ideas for revision, and then distribute the revised brochure to at least ten people who aren't in your class. For ideas on writing and designing a brochure, see p. 105.

Positive Psychology: The Science of Happiness

From *Bright-Sided: How Positive Thinking Is Undermining America*

Barbara Ehrenreich

In this excerpt from her book chapter "Positive Psychology: The Science of Happiness," author Barbara Ehrenreich points to what she sees as the serious limitations of positive psychology, especially as represented by Martin Seligman. "Positive Psychology" originally appeared in Ehrenreich's book *Bright-Sided: How Positive Thinking Is Undermining America* (2009). Ehrenreich has a PhD in cellular immunology from Rockefeller University; however, she is best known as the author of numerous books, including the popular *Nickel and Dimed: On (Not) Getting By in America* (2001) and *Bait and Switch: The (Futile) Pursuit of the American Dream* (2005).

Focus on Genre   As a critique, the following excerpt from *Bright-Sided* seeks to persuade an audience of educated laypeople that the positive psychology movement has serious problems. Critique writers who use this genre generally try to establish their credibility by sounding fair — by recognizing both positive and negative aspects of what they are critiquing. As you read Ehrenreich's critique, consider how fair you think it is. Do you think her characterization of positive psychology — and of Seligman, whom she sees as its most prominent representative — is on target?

   Also consider how persuasive you find Ehrenreich's evidence to be. As do many writers of persuasive genres, Ehrenreich provides multiple types of evidence. Make a mental note of the types of evidence you find most persuasive so that you can use those types when you find yourself in a similar rhetorical situation.

◄O►

HAPPINESS AND HEALTH

The central claim of positive psychology, as of positive thinking generally, is that happiness—or optimism, positive emotions, positive affect, or positive *something*—is not only desirable in and of itself but actually useful, leading to better health and greater success. One book on positive psychology states that "happiness . . . is more than pleasant, it is beneficial," and Seligman begins *Authentic Happiness* by summarizing a few studies showing that happy (or positive) people live longer than unhappy ones.[1] In other words, you should make an effort to be happy, if only because the consequences of unhappiness may include poor health and lower achievement. Would happiness stop being an appealing goal if it turned out to be associated with illness and failure? Isn't it possible to imagine being gloriously contented with a life spent indulging unhealthy habits, like the proverbially happy "pigs in shit"? Nothing underscores the lingering Calvinism of positive psychology more than this need to put happiness to work—as a means to health and achievement, or what the positive thinkers call "success."

Happy, or positive, people—however that is measured—do seem to be more successful at work. They are more likely to get a second interview while job hunting, get positive evaluations from superiors, resist burnout, and advance up the career ladder. But this probably reflects little more than the corporate bias in favor of a positive attitude and against "negative" people. A widely cited review article entitled "The Benefits of Frequent Positive Affect: Does Happiness Lead to Success?" coauthored by Ed Diener, makes no mention of this bias and hence appears to do little more than to confirm it.[2]

When it comes to the proposed health benefits of a positive outlook, the positive psychologists would seem to be on firmer ground. As we have seen, a positive outlook cannot cure cancer, but in the case of more common complaints, we tend to suspect that people who are melancholy, who complain a lot, or who ruminate obsessively about every fleeting symptom may in fact be making themselves sick. Recall the miraculous cures worked on chronic invalids by Phineas Quimby and others in the nineteenth century, simply by encouraging them to get up out of bed and start thinking of themselves as healthy people. We don't have "neurasthenics" today, but there are plenty of ills with a psychosomatic component, some of which may indeed yield to a "mind over matter" approach. When John E. Sarno, a professor of rehabilitation medicine, published a book proposing that lower back pain was caused by repressed anger rather than a physical abnormality and that it was curable by mental exercises, thousands testified that they were helped, including the well-known health guru Andrew Weil.[3]

In contrast to the flimsy research linking attitude to cancer survival, there are scores of studies showing that happy or optimistic people are likely to be healthier than those who are sour-tempered and pessimistic. Most of these studies, however, only establish correlations and tell us nothing about causality: Are people healthy because they're happy or happy because they're healthy? To sort out which comes first, you need longitudinal studies carried out over time. Three such studies are cited frequently by positive psychologists, and none is exactly airtight.

One, the 2001 "nun study," which Seligman calls "the most remarkable study of happiness and longevity ever done," purports to show that happier nuns live longer than less happy ones—into their nineties as opposed to their seventies or eighties.[4] The questionable thing here is the measure of happiness. In the early 1930s, when the nuns were about twenty-two years old, they had written brief sketches of their lives and commitment to the religious life. Some of these sketches contained a high "positive emotional content," as judged by the researchers, with statements such as "I look forward with eager joy to receiving the Holy Habit of Our Lady and to a life of union with Love Divine." As it turned out, the nuns who registered high in positive emotional content outlived the ones who had written such matter-of-fact statements as "with God's grace, I intend to do my best for our Order, for the spread of religion and for my personal sanctification." But since not everyone is capable of expressing their emotions vividly in writing, there's a leap between "positive emotional content" and subjective happiness. One might just as well conclude that the key to longevity lies in good writing, and an earlier study by one of the authors seemed to suggest just that: nuns who, in their youth, wrote complex sentences with high "idea density" turned out to be less likely to succumb to Alzheimer's disease in old age.[5]

A second longitudinal study, also cited by Seligman at the beginning of *Authentic Happiness*, does not even bear directly on the proposition that happiness leads to better health. In this case, happiness was measured by the apparent authenticity of smiles. Poring over the class photos in two mid-twentieth-century yearbooks for Mills College, a private liberal arts school for women, the researchers found that about half the young women smiled "authentically," with eyes crinkled and the corners of their mouths turned up, and that decades later these happy smilers reported being more happily married and generally satisfied with their lives. Whatever the relevance of this finding, it could not be replicated in a similar study of high school yearbook pictures from Wisconsin.[6] For the less elite population in the high school photos, happy smiles did not predict happy lives.

Finally, the positive psychologists like to cite a study of older Mexican Americans—sixty-five and up—that found that people who reported being happy were likely to live longer and experience less frailty than those who did not.[7] In *Authentic Happiness*, Seligman writes that this study, combined with the nun and Mills College studies, creates "an unambiguous picture of happiness as a prolonger of life and improver of health."[8] But even here, a question can be raised. The study controlled for income, education, weight, smoking, and drinking but not for physical activity, which is a known predictor of health and strength in old age. It could be that the happier Mexican Americans were healthier simply because they were more likely to walk, dance, exercise, or engage in physical labor—a possibility that one of the authors of the study tells me they are now looking into.

Adding further ambiguity to the "picture of happiness as a prolonger of life and improver of health" are a number of studies showing that happiness or other positive emotional states may have no effect on one's health. As we saw in chapter 1, an improved mental outlook—generated in support groups or through psychotherapy—does not extend the lives of breast cancer patients, and the same has been found for those suffering from throat and neck cancer. Nor, it turns out, does optimism add to the longevity of lung cancer patients.[9] The evidence that positive emotions can protect against coronary heart disease seems sturdier, although I am not in a position to evaluate it. At least a list of articles on heart disease and emotional states compiled for me by Seligman included a number of studies finding that optimism and other positive states can both protect against heart disease and hasten recovery from it.[10] But others on Seligman's list were more equivocal, and one study cited by Barbara Held found that people high in "trait negative affect" do more complaining about angina but are at no greater risk of pathology than cheerful people.[11]

Some of the studies Held has reviewed even conclude that negative traits like pessimism can be healthier in the long run than optimism and happiness.[12] For example, a 2002 study found that women who are mildly depressed are more likely to live longer than nondepressed or very depressed women. Somewhat alarmingly, a longitudinal study of more than a thousand California schoolchildren concluded that optimism was likely to lead to an earlier death in middle or old age, possibly because the optimistic people took more risks. Another, more recent, study found that preteenagers who were realistic about their standing among their peers were less likely to become depressed than those who held positive illusions about their popularity.[13] But the most surprising case for pessimism comes from a 2001 study coauthored by Seligman himself, finding that, among older people, pessimists were less likely to fall into depression following a negative life event, such as the death of a family member.[14] This study goes unmentioned in *Authentic Happiness*, but at the time it led Seligman to comment to the *New York Times* that "it's important that

optimism not be footless [probably meaning "footloose"] and unwarranted."[15]
So realism has its uses after all.

But the results that go out to the public through the media tend to be   10
spun toward the positive effects of positive emotions on health. Partly, this represents a long-standing media bias away from "null results": a study finding, for
example, that there is no sex difference in the ability to sprint or solve quadratic
equations is likely to be judged less newsworthy than a study reporting that
one sex left the other in the dust. In the case of positive psychology, a 2002
New York Times article cited two studies linking optimism to longevity—and
four studies tracing longevity to such other traits as "conscientiousness," calmness, pessimism, and even cantankerousness. Yet the article was headlined
"Power of Positive Thinking Extends, It Seems, to Aging."[16] Some positive
psychologists acknowledge the pressure to feed the media positive-sounding
results, with the editors of the *Handbook of Positive Psychology* warning that:

> In the excitement that may be associated with this new and invigorating
> approach [positive psychology], it may be tempting to overextrapolate so as
> to convey a sense of the progress that is being made. This can be even more
> possible when a person from the news media is almost putting words in
> our mouths about the supposed discoveries and advances that already have
> occurred.[17]

The positive spin on positive psychology cannot be blamed entirely on
overeager reporters. Consider a 2005 review article entitled "Does Positive
Affect Influence Health?" the summary of which says in its entirety:

> This review highlights consistent patterns in the literature associating posi-
> tive affect (PA) and physical health. However, it also raises serious conceptual
> and methodological reservations. Evidence suggests an association of trait
> PA and lower morbidity and of state and trait PA and decreased symptoms
> and pain. Trait PA is also associated with increased longevity among older
> community-dwelling individuals. The literature on PA and surviving serious
> illness is inconsistent. Experimentally inducing intense bouts of activated state
> PA triggers short-term rises in physiological arousal and associated (potentially
> harmful) effects on immune, cardiovascular, and pulmonary function. However,
> arousing effects of state PA are not generally found in naturalistic ambulatory
> studies in which bouts of PA are typically less intense and often associated with
> health protective responses. A theoretical framework to guide further study is
> proposed.[18]

Yet when asked in an interview to "summarize the significance of your paper
in layman's terms," the authors set aside all their "reservations" and concerns
about "inconsistent" literature and "potentially harmful" effects to respond
cheerily that "the paper provides preliminary evidence that persons who more

often experience positive emotions such as happiness, enthusiasm, and calmness, are less likely to develop a range of diseases, live longer, and experience fewer symptoms and less pain."[19]

Another case of positive self-spinning is provided by Suzanne Segerstrom, a researcher at the University of Kentucky, who won the 2002 Templeton Foundation Award for Positive Psychology for her work on what may be the holy grail of positive psychology—the possible link between positive emotions and the immune system. Although the immune system plays no clear role in cancer, it is definitely important in fighting off colds and other infectious illnesses. Whether there is a link between positive emotions and the immune system is another matter. Martin Seligman asserts such a link, writing that "happy people" have "feistier immune systems than less happy people." In a 1998 paper, Segerstrom reported that optimism was correlated with greater immune competence, as measured by levels of key immune cell types. But in a second study, published three years later, she found that "some contradictory findings have emerged" and that, in some circumstances, more optimistic people "fare worse immunologically" than pessimists.[20]

You would not know, however, that her results were negative or at best "mixed" from reading her newspaper accounts of her work. In a 2002 interview with the *New York Daily News*, she stated that the health benefits of optimism are "significant" and that not only do "optimists almost always have better emotional adjustments," but "most optimists show higher immune responses to illness."[21] When I interviewed Segerstrom by phone in 2007, she insisted that she had been under no pressure from the media, or anyone else, to downplay her negative results. But when I brought up her award a little later on in our talk, she told me, "To get the Templeton award . . . You don't get anything for a null result."

THE TEMPLETON CONNECTION

The Templeton Foundation, which contributed $2.2 million to Seligman's Positive Psychology Center in the first decade of the twenty-first century, as well as about $1.3 million to miscellaneous positive-psychology research projects on such matters as gratitude, humility, and connectedness, is probably best known for its efforts to put religion on an equal intellectual footing with science. Founded by billionaire investor Sir John Templeton in 1972, the foundation gives out an annual Templeton Prize for Progress in Religion, which was designed to fill a gap left by the Nobel prizes and pointedly pays more than they do. (In 2002, perhaps reflecting a certain lack of progress in religion, it was renamed the Templeton Prize for Progress toward Research or Discoveries

about Spiritual Realities.) The foundation's campaign to bring scientific legiti-
macy to religion has led to some dubious ventures, including funding in 1999
for a conference on intelligent design as an alternative to evolution. More cau-
tiously, in recent years, the foundation has backed away from intelligent design
and expressed its "spiritual" orientation through funding for research into the
efficacy of prayer—another null result—as well as various abstract qualities
like "character" and "humility." Until his death in 2008, Sir John Templeton was
fond of bringing scientists and theologians together with the aim of finding
common ground in luxurious tropical resorts.

    Templeton might have been attracted to positive psychology's claim that   15
positive emotions can influence physical health—a "mind over matter" proposition that can be found in just about any form of American spiritualism since
the nineteenth century. But there is another, more intriguing connection. Templeton was an acolyte of Norman Vincent Peale and a minor positive-thinking
guru himself. According to the Templeton Foundation's 2004 "Capabilities
Report," he "credits Norman Vincent Peale's book, *The Power of Positive Thinking*, read 70 years ago, with making him realize that 'what I had become in my
short lifetime was mainly dependent on my mental attitudes—a mental attitude of looking for the good will bring good to you; a mental attitude of giving
love will bring love to you.'"[22] Templeton wrote a number of books in the self-
help genre, some of them conveniently published by his foundation, including
*The Templeton Plan: 21 Steps to Personal Success and Real Happiness, Worldwide
Laws of Life: 200 Eternal Spiritual Principles*, and *Discovering the Laws of Life.* The
last one came with an endorsement from Robert Schuller and an introduction
by Norman Vincent Peale himself, who described Templeton as "the greatest
layman of the Christian church in our time." Surely, the possibility that positive
psychology might eventually provide scientific undergirding for positive thinking was not lost on Templeton.

    But Templeton was not just another positive-thinking businessman. He was
something of a political ideologue, as is, to an even greater degree, his son and,
since 1995, successor at the foundation. John Templeton Jr. is a major Republican donor and activist, having helped fund a group called Let Freedom Ring,
which worked to get out the evangelical vote for George Bush in 2004. In 2007,
he contributed to Freedom's Watch, which paid for television commercials supporting the war in Iraq, often by conflating Iraq with al Qaeda. More recently,
he supported the Romney and then the McCain campaigns for the presidency
and was the second-largest individual donor to the campaign for California's
Proposition 8, banning same-sex marriage.[23]

    The foundation itself is, of course, nonpartisan but is strongly biased in
favor of "free enterprise." Over the years, it has given cash awards to a number

of conservative scholars, including Milton Friedman and Gertrude Himmelfarb, and grants to a long list of conservative organizations, including the Heritage Foundation, the Manhattan Institute, the Jesse Helms Center Foundation, the Federalist Society, and the National Association of Scholars, which is best known for its battle against "political correctness" and academic liberalism.[24] Another recipient, the Association of Private Enterprise Education, states on its Web site that "the danger is very real that demagogues, while reviling 'the rich,' will loot the private wealth that is society's seed corn. The defense against demagogues is understanding and commitment to the principles of private enterprise. These are abstract principles and are not readily obvious." In its 2006 report, we learn that the Templeton Foundation "supports a wide range of programs and research initiatives to study the benefits of competition, specifically how free enterprise and other principles of capitalism can, and do, benefit the poor."[25] The words "and do" suggest a foregone conclusion, although the report goes on to raise the plaintive question *"Why should half the world's population live in circumstances of relative squalor when it has been demonstrated that the principles of the market and free enterprise can lead to sustained economic development?"* (italics in original).

This is not to suggest that positive psychology, or positive anything, is part of a right-wing conspiracy. Pop positive thinking has a mixed political lineage: Norman Vincent Peale was an outspoken conservative, at least until his attacks on a Catholic candidate, John F. Kennedy, resulted in charges of bigotry. On the other hand, perhaps the most famous contemporary promoter of positive thinking is Oprah Winfrey, whom we normally think of as a liberal. As for positive psychology, Seligman himself certainly leans to the right. He is famously impatient with "victims" and "victimology," saying, for example, in a 2000 interview: "In general when things go wrong we now have a culture which supports the belief that this was done to you by some larger force, as opposed to, you brought it on yourself by your character or your decisions."[26] It also turns out that he has spoken about his "learned helplessness" experiments with dogs at one of the military's SERE (Survival, Evasion, Resistance, Escape) schools, which were originally designed to help U.S. troops survive capture but changed their mission, post-9/11, to devising new forms of torture for suspected terrorists.[27] (Seligman denies he was contributing to torture, writing in a 2008 e-mail that "I strongly disapprove of torture and have never and would never provide assistance in its process.") As for rank-and-file positive psychologists, a rising star in the positive psychology firmament, Jonathan Haidt of the University of Virginia, insisted to me that most positive psychologists are probably liberal in their personal outlooks. Certainly many of them see themselves as rebels against a hidebound establishment of psychologists still obsessed with "negative" subjects such as depression, neurosis, and suffering.

But positive psychology seems to have exhausted its rebellious spirit in the battle against "negative psychology" and today offers much to warm the most conservative hearts, including its finding that married and highly religious people—preferably fundamentalists—are happier than other people, as are political conservatives.[28] Happiness, after all, is generally measured as reported satisfaction with one's life—a state of mind perhaps more accessible to those who are affluent, who conform to social norms, who suppress judgment in the service of faith, and who are not overly bothered by societal injustice. Strangely though, the arrival of children—which one would expect to result from fundamentalist marriages—actually decreases the happiness of the parents, and, according to Harvard psychologist Daniel Gilbert, "the only known symptom of 'empty nest syndrome' is increased smiling."[29]

The real conservativism of positive psychology lies in its attachment to the status quo, with all its inequalities and abuses of power. Positive psychologists' tests of happiness and well-being, for example, rest heavily on measures of personal contentment with things as they are. Consider the widely used "Satisfaction with Life Scale" developed by Diener and others, which asks the respondent to agree or disagree with the following propositions:

> In most ways my life is close to my ideal.
> The conditions of my life are excellent.
> I am satisfied with my life.
> So far I have gotten the important things I want in life.
> If I could live my life over, I would change almost nothing.[30]

One could imagine positive psychology, or a more liberal version thereof, spawning a movement to alter social arrangements in the direction of greater happiness—by advocating more democratically organized workplaces, to suggest just one example. Instead, positive psychology seems to have weighed in on the side of the employers, with Seligman collaborator Chris Peterson telling the *Cleveland Plain Dealer* in 2008 that business executives are particularly enthused about the new happiness science: "Hard-headed corporate culture is becoming interested in how to get more work out of fewer workers. They're realizing that if their workers are happy, they will work harder and more productively. So they're leading the charge."[31] As for social action against societal injustice, the American Psychological Association's *Monitor* reported in 1998: "Seligman asserts that . . . those who reproach others and side with the underdog may feel better in the short term, . . . but such good feelings are transient."[32] Why social activism should produce only fleeting good feelings—compared with performing other virtuous deeds, viewing Monets, or reading Richard Russo—is not explained.

Like pop positive thinking, positive psychology attends almost solely to the changes a person can make internally by adjusting his or her own outlook. Seligman himself explicitly rejects social change, writing of the role of "circumstances" in determining human happiness: "The good news about circumstances is that some do change happiness for the better. The bad news is that changing these circumstances is usually impractical and expensive."[33] This argument—"impractical and expensive"—has of course been used against almost every progressive reform from the abolition of slavery to pay equity for women.

Positive psychologists' more important contribution to the defense of the status quo has been to assert or "find" that circumstances play only a minor role in determining a person's happiness. In their misbegotten equation— $H=S+C+V$—"C," for circumstances, is generally judged to make a small contribution to the total, only around 8 to 15 percent.[34] A variety of studies are usually cited in support of the inconsequence of C, finding, for example, that people who lose their jobs or who are rendered paraplegic by severe spinal-cord injuries quickly revert to their original levels of happiness. When I interviewed Seligman, he said that new evidence shows that paraplegics and the unemployed "do not go back to where they were," and he estimated that C could be as high as 25 percent, adding that "there is a lot of controversy over the size of C, since it brings up the question of whether policy matters."

Indeed, if circumstances play only a small role—even 25 percent—in human happiness, then policy is a marginal exercise. Why advocate for better jobs and schools, safer neighborhoods, universal health insurance, or any other liberal desideratum if these measures will do little to make people happy? Social reformers, political activists, and change-oriented elected officials can all take a much-needed rest. And since no one is talking about using gene therapy to raise "S," a person's happiness "set point," that leaves only "V," one's voluntary efforts, to tinker with. In the great centuries-long quest for a better world, the baton has passed to the practitioners of "optimism training," the positive psychologists, and the purveyors of pop positive thinking.

Notes

1. Biswas-Diener and Dean, *Positive Psychology Coaching*, 31.
2. Sonja Lyubomirsky, Laura King, and Ed Diener, "The Benefits of Frequent Positive Affect: Does Happiness Lead to Success?" *Psychological Bulletin* 131 (2005): 803–55.
3. Mike McGrath, "When Back Pain Starts in Your Head: Is Repressed Anger Causing Your Back Pain?" http://www.prevention.com/cda/article/when-back-pain-starts-in-your-head/727b7e643f803110VgnVCM10000013281eac_____/health/conditions.treatments/back.pain.

4. Seligman, *Authentic Happiness*, 3; Deborah D. Danner, David A. Snowdon, and Wallace V. Friesen, "Findings from the Nun Study, University of Kentucky," *Journal of Personality and Social Psychology* 80 (2001): 804–13.

5. Gina Kolata, "Research Links Writing Style to the Risk of Alzheimer's," *New York Times*, Feb. 21, 1996, http://www.nytimes.com/1996/02/21/us /research-links-writing-style-to-the-risk-of-alzheimers.html?sec=health.

6. LeeAnne Harker and Dacher Keltner, "Expressions of Positive Emotion in Women's College Yearbook Pictures and Their Relationship of Personality and Life Outcomes across Adulthood," University of California, Berkeley, http://ist-socrates.berkeley .edu/~keltner/publications/harker.jpsp.2001.pdf; Jeremy Freese, Sheri Meland, and William Irwin, "Expressions of Positive Emotion in Photographs, Personality, and Later-Life Marital and Health Outcomes," *Journal of Research in Personality*, 2006, http://www.jeremyfreese.com/docs/FreeseMelandIrwin%20-%20JRP%20-%20 ExpressionsPositiveEmotionInPhotographs.pdf.

7. Glenn V. Ostir, Kenneth J. Ottenbacher, and Kyriakos S. Markides, "Onset of Frailty in Older Adults and the Protective Role of Positive Affect," *Psychology and Aging* 19 (2004): 402–8.

8. Seligman, *Authentic Happiness*, 40.

9. James Coyne et al., "Emotional Well-Being Does Not Predict Survival in Head and Neck Cancer Patients," *Cancer*, Dec. 1, 2007; Merritt McKinney, "Optimism Doesn't Improve Lung Cancer Survival," *Reuters Health*, Feb. 9, 2004.

10. See, for example, L. B. Kubansky and I. Kawachi, "Going to the Heart of the Matter: Do Negative Emotions Cause Coronary Heart Disease?" *Journal of Psychosomatic Research* 48 (2000): 323–37.

11. Held, "Negative Side of Positive Psychology."

12. Ibid.

13. Melissa Healy, "Truth Is, It's Best If They Know," Oct. 30, 2006, http://www.latimes .com/features/health/la-he-realists30oct30,0,141646.story?coll=la-home-health.

14. Derek M. Isaacowitz, with M. E. P. Seligman, "Is Pessimistic Explanatory Style a Risk Factor for Depressive Mood among Community-Dwelling Older Adults?" *Behaviour Research and Therapy* 39 (2001): 255–72.

15. Mary Duenwald, "Power of Positive Thinking Extends, It Seems, to Aging," *New York Times*, Nov. 19, 2002.

16. Ibid.

17. Quoted in B. Held, "The 'Virtues' of Positive Psychology," *Journal of Theoretical and Philosophical Psychology* 25 (2005): 1–34.

18. Sarah D. Pressman and Sheldon Cohen, "Does Positive Affect Influence Health?" *Psychological Bulletin* 131 (2005): 925–71.

19. http://esi-topics.com/fbp/2007/june07-Pressman_Cohen.html.

20. Seligman, *Authentic Happiness*, 40; Suzanne C. Segerstrom, "Optimism, Goal Conflict, and Stressor-Related Immune Change," *Journal of Behavioral Medicine* 24, no. 5 (2001).

21. Susan Ferraro, "Never a Cloudy Day: The Link between Optimism and Good Health," *New York Daily News*, June 17, 2002.

22. http://www.templeton.org/capabilities_2004/pdf/the_joy_of_giving.pdf.

23. http://latimesblogs.latimes.com/Washington/2008/10/a-big-donor-goe.html.

24. John Templeton Foundation, Form 990, 2005.

25. John Templeton Foundation, Capabilities Report, 2006, 77.

26. Freedman, interview with Martin E. P. Seligman.

27. Jane Mayer, "The Experiment: The Military Trains People to Withstand Interrogation. Are Those Methods Being Misused at Guantánamo?" *New Yorker,* July 11, 2005, 60.

28. David Montgomery, "A Happiness Gap: Doomacrats and Republigrins," *Washington Post,* Oct. 24, 2008.

29. Daniel Gilbert, *Stumbling on Happiness* (New York: Vintage, 2007), 243.

30. Biswas-Diener and Dean, *Positive Psychology Coaching,* 229.

31. Sam Fulwood III, "Poised for Joy: Life Coaches Teach How to Be Happy," *Cleveland Plain Dealer,* Feb. 9, 2008.

32. Sara Martin, "Seligman Laments People's Tendency to Blame Others," *APA Monitor,* Oct. 1998.

33. Seligman, *Authentic Happiness,* 50.

34. Brad Lemley, "Shiny Happy People: Can You Reach Nirvana with the Aid of Science?" *Discover,* Aug. 2006, http://discovermagazine.com/2006/aug/shinyhappy.

Questions for Critical Reading

1. Did Ehrenreich's critique persuade you that there are serious problems with positive psychology? Do you agree with all of her points, some of her points, or none of them? Why?

2. Writers who want to shed light on problems generally aim not just to critique but to critique in a way that readers perceive as fair. (Otherwise, their credibility may be undermined and their critiques dismissed.) To this end, Ehrenreich makes several concessions; she admits that there's some validity to what she's critiquing. What might be interesting to you as a writer is what Ehrenreich does *after* she makes a concession. Consider what the following two passages have in common; the sentences after the concessions are italicized:

> Happy, or positive, people—however that is measured—do seem to be more successful at work. They are more likely to get a second interview while job hunting, get positive evaluations from superiors, resist burnout, and advance up the career ladder. *But this probably reflects little more than the corporate bias in favor of a positive attitude and against "negative" people.* (para. 2)

> The evidence that positive emotions can protect against coronary heart disease seems sturdier. . . . At least a list of articles on heart disease and emotional states compiled for me by Seligman included a number of studies finding that optimism and other positive states can both protect against heart disease and hasten recovery from it. *But others on Seligman's list were more equivocal.* (para. 8)

How would you describe the move that Ehrenreich makes after she concedes a point? When might you as a writer want to make this move?

3. Recall that readers of persuasive genres, including critiques, may be more persuaded when writers use not just one type of evidence but multiple types. Consider the evidence Ehrenreich uses to support her claim that reporters are biased toward reporting the health benefits of positive emotions—that they tend *not* to acknowledge other reasons for good health. To support her claim of media bias, Ehrenreich not only analyzes a newspaper headline in terms of how it fails to reflect the contents of the article but also quotes the editors of the *Handbook of Positive Psychology*. As you read the following passage, consider how persuasive you find each type of evidence:

> In the case of positive psychology, a 2002 *New York Times* article cited two studies linking optimism to longevity—and four studies tracing longevity to such other traits as "conscientiousness," calmness, *pessimism, and even cantankerousness*. Yet the article was headlined "Power of Positive Thinking Extends, It Seems, to Aging." Some positive psychologists acknowledge the pressure to feed the media positive-sounding results, with the editors of the *Handbook of Positive Psychology* warning that:
>
> > In the excitement that may be associated with . . . [positive psychology], it may be tempting to overextrapolate so as to convey a sense of the progress that is being made. This can be even more possible when a person from the news media is almost putting words in our mouths about the supposed discoveries and advances that already have occurred. (para. 10; *emphasis added*)

Would you have found the passage less persuasive if Ehrenreich had provided only the first type of evidence (the example of the headline she sees as misleading)? How much persuasive value do you think the second type of evidence (the block quotation) adds—a little? a lot? Why?

4. Given that readers often evaluate critiques in terms of their fairness, evaluate the fairness of the following passage:

> As for social action against societal injustice, the American Psychological Association's *Monitor* reported in 1998: "Seligman asserts that . . . those who reproach others and side with the underdog may feel better in the short term, . . . but such good feelings are transient." Why social activism should produce only fleeting good feelings—compared with performing other virtuous deeds, viewing Monets, or reading Richard Russo—is not explained. (para. 21)

Ehrenreich includes an endnote that tells us some important information: she's quoting an article entitled "Seligman Laments People's Tendency to Blame Others." If Seligman is indeed referring to "reproach[ing] others" in terms of blaming others, then one might reasonably critique Ehrenreich for implying that "reproach[ing] others and sid[ing] with the underdog" is the same as social activism; in other words, Ehrenreich characterizes Seligman as claiming that *social activism* doesn't produce lasting good feelings, even though he may in fact only be saying that *blaming others* doesn't produce lasting good feelings. Do you think Ehrenreich's implied critique is fair? Why or why not? If you don't have enough information to judge Ehrenreich's fairness, what additional information would you want?

Making Connections

5. One problem Ehrenreich sees with positive psychology is that, in its focus on how people can make themselves happier, it doesn't pay enough attention to the role people's circumstances play in their happiness. Recall that she agrees with Seligman when she quotes him as saying that "there is a lot of controversy over [the extent to which people's circumstances affect their happiness], since it brings up the question of whether policy matters" (quoted in para. 23).

Pretending to believe in positive psychology, Ehrenreich asks — and then answers — a key question about policy:

> Why advocate for better jobs and schools, safer neighborhoods, universal health insurance, or any other liberal desideratum if these measures will do little to make people happy? Social reformers, political activists, and change-oriented elected officials can all take a much-needed rest. (para. 24)

Arthur Brooks's "Inequality and (Un)Happiness in America" (p. 389) confirms what Ehrenreich is suggesting: that assumptions about what makes people happy influence ideas about policy. Discussing happiness and poverty, Brooks argues that "[income] inequality does *not* cause unhappiness" (para. 6; emphasis original). Brooks goes on to suggest that, because poverty doesn't cause unhappiness, we don't need policies that set a minimum wage nor do we need a welfare program. Although you may not want to take a stand on minimum wage or welfare before reading Brooks's argument, what do you believe about the role that circumstances (such as poverty) play in happiness? Do you agree with Brooks's claim that poverty doesn't affect happiness or with Ehrenreich's assumption that it does? (Or do you think there's a valid third position?) Regardless of whether you agree with Brooks or Ehrenreich, do you believe that assumptions about what causes happiness should drive policy?

Writing: Your Turn

1. Write a reflection on the role that you believe circumstances play in your own happiness. Do you think your happiness depends mostly on circumstances? partly on circumstances? partly on your response to circumstances? Do you think you could be happy regardless of circumstances? Share what you wrote with some classmates so that they can point to places where an example or more explanation might benefit readers. Consider their feedback when you revise. For ideas on writing a reflection, see p. 27.

2. Write an argument, addressed to an audience of classmates, that takes a stand on Ehrenreich's critique of Seligman. You might argue that her critique is unfounded, that it is valid, or that some of her points are valid while others are not. You might also extend her critique; that is, you might agree with what she says and take it a step further, perhaps arguing that there are still more problems with Seligman's work. So that your argument can be persuasive, use ample evidence to support your claims. Share what you wrote with some classmates so that they can learn from your ideas and give you feedback; make a list of a few questions you want to ask them and consider their responses when you revise. For ideas on writing an argument, see p. 42.

Inequality and (Un)Happiness in America

From *Gross National Happiness: Why Happiness Matters for America — and How We Can Get More of It*

Arthur Brooks

In the following excerpt from "Inequality and (Un)Happiness in America," Arthur Brooks suggests that public policy should be driven by our knowledge of what causes happiness, and he argues that happiness is affected by beliefs about income mobility (people's ability to move from one economic class to another). "Inequality and (Un)Happiness in America" is from Brooks's book *Gross National Happiness: Why Happiness Matters for America — and How We Can Get More of It* (2008). Brooks is president of the think tank American Enterprise Institute for Public Policy Research.

Focus on Genre   A public policy argument, *Gross National Happiness* relies on statistical evidence to support a double-layered thesis. The first layer of Brooks's thesis makes a causal argument, asserting that one thing causes another. The second layer of his thesis argues that this causality should determine public policy — in this case, policies regarding welfare, taxes for the rich, and the minimum wage.

Although it's important to critically assess the evidence used to support any argument, it's especially important in the case of causal arguments. Arguments about one thing causing another are difficult to support, largely because many things result not just from one cause but rather from a multitude of causes that interact with one another. In fact, many professors from a variety of disciplines tend to avoid the word *cause*, instead suggesting that one thing *contributes* to another, *shapes* it, or *influences* it.

As you read Brooks's argument, carefully assess the evidence he uses to support his claims of causality. Because his claims are often supported by a numbered citation, it's a good idea to refer to the appropriate endnote when you come across a citation. Assess the degree to which each source cited seems to "match" the claim being made, and see if you can generate any rival hypotheses (alternative explanations) that might provide other accounts of what causes what. Finally, assess Brooks's implicit claims about who is responsible for the problems he discusses.

Many intellectuals and scholars have built whole careers around the subject of income inequality. It is practically an academic article of faith that inequality per se is socially destructive and should be avoided wherever and whenever possible. The prevailing view is that the fairest, least envious societies—that is, the *happiest* societies—are the most economically equal ones. And thus, if we want a happier citizenry, we need less economic inequality.

Perhaps they're right—after all, equality appears side by side with happiness in the U.S. Declaration of Independence: "We hold these truths to be self-evident, that all men are created equal, that they are endowed by their Creator with certain unalienable Rights, that among these are Life, Liberty and the pursuit of Happiness." To be sure, most people understand this sentence as referring to political equality, or equality before the law. But a loose interpretation that includes income equality doesn't necessarily make someone a utopian leftist.

But there are good reasons to question the supposed link between inequality and unhappiness. For one thing, the prevailing intellectual view on inequality doesn't seem to match the views expressed by most normal, nonacademic folks. Although some ordinary people of my acquaintance might complain about the enormous compensation of CEOs, I rarely have heard them express any shock or outrage at the great wealth of America's richest people: successful entrepreneurs. On the contrary, they say they hope their *kids* might become the next Bill Gates or Warren Buffett. Most people I know actually admire those successful folks and don't begrudge them their success.

More convincing than my personal experiences are the data showing no link at all between rising inequality and unhappiness. If inequality were so depressing for us, we would expect to see American happiness falling. Yet average happiness has *not* fallen. Remember that, in 1972, 30 percent of the population said they were very happy with their lives. In 1982, 31 percent reported this level of happiness; in 1993, 32 percent; and in 2004, 31 percent. This total lack of significant change in average reported happiness occurred over the same period in which income inequality increased by nearly half. Statistically, income inequality does not explain any of the fluctuations in happiness or unhappiness over the past three decades.[1]

Nor does income inequality explain happiness differences between American communities. Looking at 30,000 households in forty-nine American communities in 2000, we see that the variation between income levels in communities explained nothing about how many people in each stated that they were very happy. Take two very different communities: the Latino community in Cleveland, Ohio, and the city of Boulder, Colorado. Boulder is characterized

5

by far higher income inequality than Cleveland's Hispanic community, yet its citizens are more than twice as likely—45 percent versus 18 percent—to say they are very happy. Income inequality does not lie anywhere behind this happiness gap.[2]

So is this inequality bad for our nation's happiness, or not? Despite all the rhetoric from populist politicians and egalitarian academics, a good hard look at the best available data tells us that, in fact, inequality does *not* cause unhappiness in America. And efforts to diminish economic inequality—without creating economic opportunity—will actually lower America's gross national happiness, not raise it. . . .

About half of all American adults think economic inequality is a major problem, and about half of them do not. Do these two groups differ in some way that might explain the contrasting attitudes? As it turns out, their opinions cannot be explained by income, class, race, or education. Instead, what best predicts an individual's views on income inequality is his or her beliefs about income *mobility*—that is, about whether Americans have opportunities to get ahead economically. And it is these beliefs about mobility, not beliefs about income inequality, that lie directly behind much happiness and unhappiness. Those who believe that they and other Americans can get ahead with hard work and perseverance—that America offers paths to success—are generally happy and unfazed by economic inequality. Those who think that economic mobility in the United States is an illusion are relatively unhappy and tend to complain about income inequality.

In other words, some Americans are unhappy because they don't believe they have opportunities to succeed, but they complain about income inequality, as if this were the root cause of their problem. If our leaders focus on getting rid of income inequality, however, the underlying problem—lack of income mobility—will not improve, nor will happiness. (In fact, it will get worse, because the treatment for inequality exacerbates problems with mobility.) They are mistaking a symptom for a root cause.

People mistake symptoms for root causes all the time. If I am an alcoholic, my relationship with my spouse will probably suffer, and that will make me unhappy. I might complain about the bad relationship, even though my drinking is the real problem. I can work on the relationship all I want, but as long as I keep drinking, things probably won't get better. In fact, the longer I ignore the root cause, the worse it will get and the less likely I am to get back the happiness in my relationship.

And so it goes with inequality, immobility, and happiness. Let's look at the evidence. 10

First, feelings about mobility and inequality go together. Imagine you are asked the following question: "How much upward mobility—children doing better than the family they come from—do you think there is in America: a lot, some, or not much?" If you think there is not much upward mobility in America—you are not a big believer in American opportunity—you will be 46 percent more likely than people who believe there is a lot of mobility to say that income differences in our society are too large. In addition, you will be 63 percent more likely to say that income inequality is a "serious problem," and you will be 71 percent more likely to say that the government should do more to reduce inequality. Perceived immobility is what drives concern about income inequality, pure and simple.[3]

Or take the following statement: "While people may begin with different opportunities, hard work and perseverance can usually overcome those disadvantages." Imagine two people who are identical with respect to income, education, race, sex, religious participation, and family situation. The only difference is that the first person agrees with that statement, while the second disagrees. The optimist about work and perseverance will be 31 percentage points less likely than the pessimist to say inequality in America is too high. He will also be 39 points less likely to say that inequality is a big problem, and 32 points less likely to advocate for more government intervention to lower inequality. Note that this difference is *not* due to the fact that the optimist is more economically successful, better educated, or of a different race than the pessimist—the two are identical in these ways. This is purely a difference in views about opportunity.[4]

This pessimism about opportunity is clearly linked to unhappiness. In 2004, 700 American adults were presented with a statement about opportunity and asked whether they agreed or disagreed. The statement was: "The way things are in America, people like me and my family have a good chance of improving our standard of living." Those who agreed were 44 percent more likely than those who disagreed to say they were very happy in life. The optimists were also 40 percent less likely than the pessimists to say they felt like they were "no good at all" at times, and they were 20 percent less likely to say they felt like a failure.[5]

As we have found again and again, happiness follows earned success (not money) and a sense of control in our lives. Indeed, people who feel they do not have control over their own successes are generally miserable. In 2001, people who said they did not feel responsible for their own successes—whether they enjoyed successes or not, mind you—spent about 25 percent more time feeling sad than those who said they did feel responsible for their own successes.[6]

Pessimism about mobility and worries about income inequality are both associated with unhappiness. But only the former is the *cause* of unhappiness.

15

Imagine two demographically identical people who have the same beliefs about mobility. The inequality they personally experience—the difference between their own incomes and average incomes in their communities—is uncorrelated with their happiness. But what happens when one person believes that his family has a chance of improving its standard of living while the other person does not? The believer in mobility will be 12 percentage points more likely to be very happy than the nonbeliever.[7]

In other words, people who feel economically immobile are generally unhappier than those who feel more mobile. If we ask them about income inequality, they will say they don't like it. But it is not inequality that is driving their unhappiness—it is their perceived immobility. To confuse the two is to commit what economists call the "association-causation fallacy." It is like saying that height leads to intelligence just because, on average, we see that tall kids in developing countries do the best in school. (The real reason is that taller kids, on average, have better nutrition than shorter kids, which leads to both height and intellectual ability.)

It works something like this. Imagine you have a job at a factory, and have no other realistic employment opportunities. Seventy-five percent of the workers, like you, earn a low wage, although enough to get by. The other quarter are no more talented (in your opinion)—nor do they appear to work any harder than you do—yet they earn twice as much as you and live in relative luxury. What would you like? Obviously, the opportunity to make it into the privileged class. But since this is impossible, you instead complain about the unfairness of the difference between your wage and theirs. But if there were a clear path to the upper class and a realistic prospect of making it there if you worked hard enough, you wouldn't complain about inequality. In fact, you might even like inequality, because it would demonstrate what you could attain.

British researchers have found this to be precisely the case: People's happiness rises when the average income increases relative to their own income, if they believe they have opportunities to succeed; they interpret the income average as a measure of their own potential. The fact that Bill Gates is so rich probably raises the happiness of America's optimists, because it demonstrates to them what somebody can do with hard work, good ideas, great luck, and a system that protects free enterprise. Gates is not a duke or a prince; there is no evidence that God especially likes him. He simply had a lot of opportunities and made the most of them.[8]

In contrast, it is depressing to think that no matter how hard you work or how clever you are, you can never get ahead. This is why, when people feel there is a lack of opportunity to advance at their workplace, they often quit their jobs. Indeed, 70 percent of those who say their chances for promotion are good are very satisfied with their jobs, versus just 42 percent who say their chances for promotion are not good. We need clear paths to success, not guarantees of income equality, to be happy. Guarantees of equality actually take us in the wrong direction.[9]

The true relationship between mobility and happiness explains why happiness levels in America have not fallen over time, even though income inequality has risen. Unequal as it is, economically speaking, America is still a happy land of opportunity. 20

Those who are unhappy about income inequality favor public policies that redistribute resources. Seventy percent of people who feel that income inequality is a serious problem say the government should do more than it is doing at present to reduce the income gap. Only 33 percent of those who believe it is less than a serious problem think the government should do more.

There are a number of ways that government can do more to bring about greater equality—by instituting, for example, the kinds of policies advocated by Senator [John] Edwards. Funding welfare programs and other kinds of income support for the poor is one way. Another type of redistributive policy seeks to mandate minimum wages for the poor, placing the burden (policymakers believe) on private companies. And since equality can be achieved not just by giving to the poor, but also by bringing the top down, we can get greater equality by increasing income taxes on the rich, a redistributive policy we will no doubt see after 2008 if a Democratic candidate is elected. Democrats are also generally enthusiastic about increasing the estate tax, which limits the amount of wealth passed on from one generation to the next.

A major problem with all these policies is that they tend to have dramatic unintended consequences that hurt those they are intended to help. Welfare programs have a long history of inducing misery—provoking dependency among beneficiaries, for example, and disengaging money from earned success. Minimum wages create unemployment disproportionately among the least skilled, most at-risk members of the workforce. At the same time, policies that bring the top down change the incentives of the wealthy in ways that hurt the poor as well. Punitive income taxes reduce entrepreneurship, meaning fewer jobs created, less economic growth, less in tax revenues, and less charitable giving—all to the detriment of those left behind.[10]

Ironically, these inequality policies don't even address our main problem, if a happy society is our goal. We know that inequality per se simply does not lie directly behind life satisfaction. In some cases—even among people of modest means—inequality can actually raise happiness by holding out the promise of rewards for future success. Rather, what makes people unhappy, either intrinsically or by way of social strife and ill-health, is immobility. Those left behind in the economy will almost certainly *not* become happier if we simply redistribute more income.

This is why egalitarian policies always hold out the promise of happiness   25
but never deliver on that promise. Every movement to stamp out economic inequality has looked toward, as George Orwell termed it in *1984*, "our new happy life." Yet that happiness is always out in the future, never in the present. Stalin called himself in Soviet propaganda the "Constructor of Happiness" — a moniker that would be comical today were it not for the tens of millions of Soviet citizens who died as a result of the repression that accompanied his pursuit of egalitarian projects such as the push to collectivized farming.[11]

Furthermore, policies to redress income inequality hardly affect *true* inequality at all. Policymakers and economists rarely denounce the scandal of inequality in work effort, creativity, talent, or enthusiasm. We almost never hear about the outrage that is America's inequality in time with friends, love, faith, or fun — even though these are things most of us care about more than we do money. We know that married people, for example, tend to have much happier lives than singles, but no progressive politician I know of is out there declaring war on bachelor life. To believe that we truly redress inequality in our society by moving cash around is to take a materialistic — and totally unrealistic — view of life. To focus on income redistribution is to profess a mechanistic and impoverished understanding of the resources Americans truly value. . . .

It is absolutely true that there is economic inequality in America — in fact, the gap between the richest and poorest members of society is far wider than in many other developed countries. But there is also far more opportunity, which is what is fundamentally important to both our personal happiness and our gross national happiness. Hard work and perseverance *do* hold the key to jumping from one economic class to the next. While it is true we must solve the problems of absolute deprivation, such as hunger and homelessness, we must also recognize that the promise of rewards for hard work render the remaining inequality benign at worst — and a positive stimulant to achievement at best. Redistribution and taxation, beyond that necessary to pay for some key services, can weaken America's willingness and ability to progress.

Knowing this, we should direct our policies not at wiping out economic inequality, but at enhancing economic mobility. This means improving educational opportunities; aggressively addressing cultural impediments to success; enhancing the fluidity of labor markets; encouraging the investor revolution, which reaches further and further down the income-distribution chain every decade; and stimulating the climate of American entrepreneurship.

Many people, particularly on the political left, will call me a Pollyanna for claiming that Americans can really get ahead with hard work and perseverance. They will point out that those who reject the idea of opportunity and mobility might be *unhappy*—but that doesn't necessarily make them *wrong*. They will even point to some oft-cited research to show that not everyone enjoys equal access to the American Dream. For example, one famous study from the early 1970s looked at the economic success of schoolchildren as they grew up and concluded that school quality could not do much to redress inequalities in income. The author of the study asserted that deeper factors—such as discrimination and cultural problems—were largely to blame for ongoing economic gaps. If schools don't bring the bottom up in America, many have thus argued, isn't equal opportunity really just an illusion? And if the disease is incurable, shouldn't we just move right to the symptoms and lower economic inequality?[12]

Subsequent studies have greatly weakened such arguments, however. Whatever the limitations of our education system for improving the lives of the underprivileged, there is in fact an amazing amount of economic mobility in America. Research from the U.S. Census Bureau, the Federal Reserve, and the U.S. Treasury Department have all shown that, as a general rule, about one-fifth of the people in the lowest income quintile will move to a higher quintile within a year, and about half will rise within a decade. To be sure, this tells us that about half will *not* have risen, and the research also says that a significant proportion of people will fall to a lower quintile over the same period (which must be true, mathematically). But all in all, it puts paid to the claim that economic mobility is in any way unusual in America. Millions and millions of poor Americans climb out of the ranks of poverty every year.[13]

While there are a few prominent conservatives who complain about income inequality, it is an issue owned primarily by the political left. Rank-and-file liberals are more than twice as likely as conservatives to say income inequality is a "serious problem." This is not just because of income differences: Seventy-seven percent of liberals with above-average incomes think inequality is a serious problem, but only 40 percent of conservatives with below-average incomes agree with them.[14]

This is not to say that liberals care *only* about inequality and not about opportunity. Liberals do worry about social mobility. But they're far more pessimistic about it: Even liberals who have themselves succeeded are less convinced than conservatives—including poorer conservatives—that economic

30

mobility is actually possible in America. And this difference is one of the biggest reasons American conservatives are happier than American liberals today. Forty-eight percent of lower-income conservatives believe there's a lot of upward income mobility in America, versus 26 percent of upper-income liberals. And 90 percent of the poorer—but optimistic—conservatives said that hard work and perseverance can overcome disadvantage, versus just 65 percent of richer liberals. If a liberal and a conservative are identical in terms of income, education, sex, family situation, and race, the liberal will be 20 percentage points less likely than the conservative to say that hard work leads to success among the disadvantaged.[15]

These attitudes are exhibited every day in egalitarian policies promoted by the Democratic Party, which broadcasts the message that there is little opportunity for certain groups, who must instead fight for redistributive policies. According to the Democratic National Committee, "The federal minimum wage is so disgracefully low that now, during a period of extraordinary prosperity for the nation's corporations and wealthiest families, the average CEO earns as much in just a few hours on the first workday of the year as a full-time minimum wage worker earns the entire year."[16]

Democratic officials no doubt only want to help the poor when they make such statements. But these statements are nonetheless depressing—and not just to me. Research shows that messages have an effect not only on those they reach, but also on those who deliver them. In one provocative study, researchers found that when they asked normal, happy human subjects in an experiment to repeat depressing sentences, the subjects quickly began to show signs of depression. It requires no stretch of the imagination to conclude that an unhappy message about America's lack of opportunity and mobility will make the proponents of this message unhappy.[17]

In contrast, the happy political right in America reinforces its good mood whenever conservatives express faith in the American promise that anyone can get ahead with hard work and perseverance. This view is evidence of a light heart, not a hard one. What our nation must do is work tirelessly to ensure that this promise never becomes hollow.

Notes

1. General Social Surveys (GSS) 1972–2004; *Statistical Abstract of the United States* (various years).
2. *Social Capital Community Benchmark Survey* (SCCBS) [machine-readable data file] (Cambridge, Mass.: Saguaro Seminar at the John F. Kennedy School of Government, Harvard University [producer]; Storrs, Conn.: The Roper Center for Public Opinion Research, University of Connecticut [distributor], 2000). I regressed the percentage saying in each family that they were "very happy" on the income variance in each

community as well as on the mean income level in each community. The coefficient on the variance was insignificant; the mean income level, in contrast, was significant, at the 10 percent level.

3. Campbell Public Affairs Institute, The Maxwell Poll on Civic Engagement and Inequality [dataset] (Syracuse, N.Y.: Maxwell School of Citizenship and Public Affairs, 2005).

4. Ibid. These results are based on probit models in which the beliefs about inequality are regressed on beliefs about the importance of work and perseverance, as well as a vector of the demographics listed. The marginal coefficients are estimated at the mean values of the regressors.

5. 2004 GSS.

6. John Mirowsky and Catherine E. Ross, "Aging, Status, and Sense of Control (ASOC), 1995, 1998, 2001," Computer file ICPSR03334-v2 (Columbus: Ohio State University [producer], 2001; Ann Arbor, Mich.: Inter-University Consortium for Political and Social Research [distributor], 2005-12-15). In this study, people were asked whether they agreed or disagreed with the statement that they were responsible for their own successes. Those who "agreed" or "agreed strongly" said they felt sad, on average, 0.96 days per week. Those who "disagreed" or "disagreed strongly" were sad an average of 1.2 days per week.

7. 2004 GSS. To measure the actual inequality people experience, we compare their income with that of others of their same sex, age, and education level—what economists call their "reference group." This analysis regresses a dummy variable indicating that someone says he or she is "very happy" on household income, the absolute distance of income to the reference income, the amount by which income exceeds (or falls short of) the reference, a dummy for a response that the person agrees that he or she has a good chance of improving living standards, and a vector of demographics. The marginal effects are estimated as the probit coefficients evaluated at the mean values of the regressors. Models in which each income measure is estimated separately (to ensure against collinearity problems in the full model) produce virtually identical results.

8. Andrew E. Clark, "Inequality-Aversion and Income Mobility: A Direct Test," Centre National de la Recherche Scientifique (CNRS) and Department and Laboratory of Applied and Theoretical Economics (DELTA)–Fédération Jourdan Working Paper 2003-11 (2003); Claudia Senik, "What Can We Learn from Subjective Data? The Case of Income and Well-Being," CNRS and DELTA–Fédération Jourdan Working Paper 2003-06 (2003).

9. 2002 GSS.

10. As Irving Kristol put it, "The problem with our current welfare programs is not that they are costly—which they are—but that they have such perverse consequences for people they are supposed to benefit." Irving Kristol, "A Conservative Welfare State," *Wall Street Journal*, June 14, 1993.

11. George Orwell, *1984* (New York: New American Library, 1983), p. 40; Darrin M. McMahon, *Happiness: A History* (New York: Atlantic Monthly Press, 2006), p. 403.

12. Christopher Jencks, *Inequality: A Reassessment of the Effect of Family and Schooling in America* (New York: Basic Books, 1972). Jencks's work grew out of James S. Coleman's 1966 "Coleman Report" ("Equality of Educational Opportunity [Coleman] Study [EEOS]" [Washington, D.C.: U.S. Department of Health, Education, and Welfare, Office of Education/National Center for Education Statistics, 1966].)

13. Bruce Bartlett, "Income Mobility Belies Liberal Myth," National Center for Policy Analysis, August 23, 2000, http://www.ncpa.org/oped/bartlett/aug2300.html; "Movin' On Up" (editorial), *Wall Street Journal*, November 13, 2007, p. A24.
14. 2005 Maxwell Poll.
15. Ibid. These results are based on a probit model in which the beliefs about the importance of hard work are regressed on political views as well as a vector of demographics. The marginal coefficients are estimated at the mean values of the regressors.
16. Democratic National Committee, "Stop the Diversionary Tactics and Raise the Minimum Wage!" 2006, http://www.democrats.org/a/2006/08/stop_the_divers.php.
17. Stefan Klein describes this study in his book *The Science of Happiness: How Our Brains Make Us Happy—and What We Can Do to Get Happier* (New York: Marlowe, 2006), p. 185.

Questions for Critical Reading

1. Were you persuaded by Brooks's arguments that unhappiness is caused not by income *inequality* but by beliefs about income *mobility*—and that policies such as welfare, a mandated minimum wage, and higher taxes for the rich are counterproductive? Why or why not?

2. Public policy arguments such as Brooks's could be organized by first advocating for a policy and then providing reasons and evidence—or, conversely, by first providing reasons and evidence and then advocating for a policy (or policies), as Brooks does. Why do you think Brooks didn't start the chapter by claiming that policies such as welfare, a mandated minimum wage, and higher taxes for the rich are counterproductive? What might he have gained by waiting until later in the chapter to argue that these policies are problematic?

3. Recall that because people's beliefs about causality (what causes what) can influence both public policy and people's behavior, it's important to question claims of causality, whether they are made by Brooks or anyone else.

When Brooks claims that pessimism about income mobility "is the *cause* of unhappiness" (para. 15; emphasis original), he says that we need to avoid commiting the association-causation fallacy (para. 16)—that we shouldn't be fooled into thinking that a third factor, income inequality, causes unhappiness just because income inequality may happen to occur along with unhappiness. Although Brooks considers and argues against this rival hypothesis (alternative explanation), he doesn't consider the following rival hypotheses. As you read this list, consider whether any of these rival hypotheses might be valid:

- Instead of pessimism about income mobility causing unhappiness, as Brooks claims, it could be the reverse—that unhappiness makes people more likely to be pessimistic about income mobility.

- It could be that the causality works in both directions—that there is a vicious cycle in which unhappiness makes people more likely to be pessimistic about income mobility and this pessimism about income mobility makes people even unhappier.
- It could be that pessimism about income mobility merely correlates with unhappiness—that there is no causality involved. There might be another influence that leads to both unhappiness and pessimism about income mobility. (Brooks might be falling into the very association-causation fallacy that he warns us against.)
- It could be that several different influences—not just pessimism about income mobility—work together to contribute to unhappiness.

Do you think any of these rival hypotheses might have some validity? Why or why not? What other rival hypotheses might be added to the list? (Note that generating rival hypotheses is an invaluable strategy; consider doing this whenever you encounter claims of causality.)

4. Readers of many genres tend to expect that arguments will be organized around claims and support—that most or all claims made will be accompanied by supporting evidence. Consider how persuasively Brooks supports his claims in the following paragraph; count the number of claims he makes, and assess whether or not each claim is supported.

> A major problem with all these policies is that they tend to have dramatic unintended consequences that hurt those they are intended to help. Welfare programs have a long history of inducing misery—provoking dependency among beneficiaries, for example, and disengaging money from earned success. Minimum wages create unemployment disproportionately among the least skilled, most at-risk members of the workforce. At the same time, policies that bring the top down change the incentives of the wealthy in ways that hurt the poor as well. Punitive income taxes reduce entrepreneurship, meaning fewer jobs created, less economic growth, less in tax revenues, and less charitable giving—all to the detriment of those left behind.[10] (para. 23)

To assess Brooks's support, consider the endnote that accompanies this paragraph:

10. As Irving Kristol put it, "The problem with our current welfare programs is not that they are costly—which they are—but that they have such perverse consequences for people they are supposed to benefit." Irving Kristol, "A Conservative Welfare State," *Wall Street Journal*, June 14, 1993.

How many claims did you see Brooks making? Which claims do you think he supported? Overall, how persuasive did you find this paragraph to be? Why?

5. Either implicitly or explicitly, policy arguments sometimes assign responsibility for a problem to particular people or behaviors. Some readers might critique Brooks for assigning the responsibility for poverty and unhappiness to the poor themselves. When Brooks tells us, for example, that "[h]ard work and perseverance *do* hold the key to jumping from one economic class to the next" (para. 27), he arguably implies that people who cannot jump to a higher economic class don't work hard or persevere. Some readers might also critique Brooks for blaming the poor in this passage:

> [P]olicies to redress income inequality hardly affect *true* inequality at all. Policymakers and economists rarely denounce the scandal of inequality in work effort, creativity, talent, or enthusiasm. (para. 26)

Do you think it's warranted to critique Brooks for blaming poverty on the poor? Why or why not?

Making Connections

6. Recall that different genres tend to use different types of evidence. Mary Pipher's case study "June" (p. 311), for instance, uses information about June's life as evidence, while Gretchen Rubin's blog post "Act the Way You Want to Feel" (p. 333) uses personal experience, a quotation from an expert, and a citation of research. In contrast, Brooks's policy argument relies primarily on statistical research. If you were to "translate" Brooks's argument into another genre — say, a blog post — would you add any additional type(s) of evidence? Why or why not? If so, what type(s) of evidence would you add?

7. Consider Brooks's claim that income inequality doesn't cause unhappiness in light of Maslow's claim (p. 293) that people aren't able to pursue happiness if basic needs such as food and shelter aren't met. To what extent do you agree with each claim? Why?

Writing: Your Turn

1. Write a summary of "Inequality and (Un)Happiness in America," making sure to distinguish between Brooks's overarching argument and his subpoints. When you finish your summary, give it to some classmates and ask them for feedback on whether it accurately distills Brooks's most important points. Consider your classmates' ideas — along with ideas of your own — when you revise. For strategies to use when writing a summary, see p. 23.

2. Write a critique of this excerpt from *Gross National Happiness.* When you write a critique, you're essentially making an argument about someone else's argument; thus, you should assess the author's points, not summarize them. Before you start writing, it might help to reread the selection, referring to the appropriate endnote whenever you come across a citation used to support a point. As you read, make a list of Brooks's points, noting whether or not you agree with them, and whether you believe they are adequately supported.

After you have a list of Brooks's points and your assessments of them, decide which points are important enough to address in your critique. Consider the order in which you want to address these points, and craft a thesis that provides readers with an overview of your argument.

Before you start writing, you'll also find it helpful to brainstorm ideas for how you might support your argument about Brooks's argument; rather than merely agreeing or disagreeing, you'll want to provide reasons and evidence to support your argument.

After you finish writing and revising, share your critique with some of your classmates to see how successfully you persuaded them, and get their ideas on how you might make your critique even more persuasive. A sample critique (from Barbara Ehrenreich's *Bright-Sided*) can be found on p. 374. Since a critique is a type of argument, you might also refer to p. 42 for ideas.

LINKED
READING
PAGE 407

University of Leicester Produces the First Ever World Map of Happiness

The following two selections discuss research on world happiness conducted by social psychologist Adrian White. The first selection is a 2006 press release from White's employer, the University of Leicester, to promote his work.

Focus on Genre   The following press release discusses the research White did to develop a "happiness map." Press releases promote research, products, events, and the like; organizations send them out to newspapers and online news venues in hopes that the press release will become the basis for a news article, thus giving the organization free publicity. Indeed, a press release is written as if it *were* a news article, and sometimes a paper or news Web site will simply reprint part or all of it as is. Other times, a news writer will take the information in the press release and rework it, sometimes doing more research to add to the article. Often, of course, press releases are simply ignored.

On the surface, press releases seem to have a single purpose: to inform. However, press-release authors also want to persuade papers and news Web sites that what they're writing about is newsworthy. As you read, try to identify strategies the writer uses to make White's research sound newsworthy.

—◄o►—

HAPPINESS IS . . . BEING HEALTHY, WEALTHY AND WISE

A University of Leicester psychologist has produced the first ever "world map of happiness."

Adrian White, an analytic social psychologist at the University's School of Psychology, analysed data published by UNESCO, the CIA, the New Economics Foundation, the WHO, the Veenhoven Database, the Latinbarometer, the Afrobarometer, and the UNHDR, to create a global projection of subjective well-being: the first world map of happiness.

The projection, which is to be published in a Psychtalk in March 2007, will be presented at a conference later in the year. Participants in the various studies were asked questions related to happiness and satisfaction with life. The meta-analysis is based on the findings of over 100 different studies around the world, which questioned 80,000 people worldwide. For this study data has also been analysed in relation to health, wealth and access to education.

Whilst collecting data on subjective well-being is not an exact science, the measures used are very reliable in predicting health and welfare outcomes. It can be argued that whilst these measures are not perfect they are the best we have so far, and these are the measures that politicians are talking of using to measure the relative performance of each country.

The researchers have argued that regular testing as a collaboration between   5
academics in different countries would enable us to track changes in happiness, and what events may cause that. For example what effect would a war, or famine, or national success have on a country's members' happiness.

Adrian White said:

"The concept of happiness, or satisfaction with life, is currently a major area of research in economics and psychology, most closely associated with new developments in positive psychology. It has also become a feature in the current political discourse in the UK.

"There is increasing political interest in using measures of happiness as a national indicator in conjunction with measures of wealth. A recent BBC survey found that 81% of the population think the government should focus on making us happier rather than wealthier.

"It is worth remembering that the UK is doing relatively well in this area, coming 41st out of 178 nations.

"Further analysis showed that a nation's level of happiness was most closely associated with health levels (correlation of .62), followed by wealth (.52), and then provision of education (.51).

"The three predictor variables of health, wealth and education were also very closely associated with each other, illustrating the interdependence of these factors.

"There is a belief that capitalism leads to unhappy people. However, when people are asked if they are happy with their lives, people in countries with good healthcare, a higher GDP per capita, and access to education were much more likely to report being happy.

"We were surprised to see countries in Asia scoring so low, with China 82nd, Japan 90th and India 125th. These are countries that are thought as having a strong sense of collective identity, which other researchers have associated with well-being.

"It is also notable that many of the largest countries in terms of population do quite badly. With China 82nd, India 125th and Russia 167th it is interesting to note that larger populations are not associated with happy countries."

"The frustrations of modern life, and the anxieties of the age, seem to be much less significant compared to the health, financial and educational needs in other parts of the world. The current concern with happiness levels in the UK may well be a case of the 'worried well.'"

"I have used data on happiness published by the New Economics Foundation (Marks, N., Abdallah, S., Simms, A., Thompson, S. [2006]. The Happy Planet Index. London: New Economics Foundation). I have also sourced data from UNESCO on access to schooling, from the WHO on life expectancy, and from the CIA on GDP per capita. I have then performed a new analysis with this data to come to a unique and novel set of results; specifically the extent of correlation between measures of poverty, health and education, and the variable of happiness. I have also presented the data on happiness in the form of a global projection, the 'World Map of Happiness.'"

The twenty happiest nations in the world are:

1. Denmark	8. Bhutan	15. The Netherlands
2. Switzerland	9. Brunei	16. Antigua and
3. Austria	10. Canada	Barbuda
4. Iceland	11. Ireland	17. Malaysia
5. The Bahamas	12. Luxembourg	18. New Zealand
6. Finland	13. Costa Rica	19. Norway
7. Sweden	14. Malta	20. The Seychelles

Other notable results include:

23. USA	62. France	125. India
35. Germany	82. China	167. Russia
41. UK	90. Japan	

The three least happy countries were:

176. Democratic Republic of the Congo
177. Zimbabwe
178. Burundi

Note to Newsdesk:

Adrian White, Analytic Social Psychologist at the University of Leicester, produces first ever global projection of international differences in subjective well-being; the first ever World Map of Happiness.

UK 41st out of 178 countries for happiness.

Happiness is found to be most closely associated with health, followed by wealth and then education.

Online news article

Rating Countries for the Happiness Factor

Marina Kamenev

Like the previous selection, this one discusses the "happiness map" developed by social psychologist Adrian White. It was originally published online at *Bloomberg Businessweek* on October 11, 2006.

Focus on Genre   The preceding press release became the basis of several news articles, including the following selection, "Rating Countries for the Happiness Factor." This news article provides a good example of how press releases can be reworked into news. As you read, pay attention to which aspects of the original press release the writer decided to keep and which aspects she changed. Note the differences in how each piece opens and how each is organized, and think about why the news writer might have made the changes she did.

—◄○►—

A study pulled together from sources and surveys found that good health care and education are as important as wealth to modern happiness

F eeling sad? Researchers at Britain's University of Leicester reckon you might just be in the wrong country. According to Adrian White, an analytic social psychologist at Leicester who developed the first "World Map of Happiness," Denmark is the happiest nation in the world.

White's research used a battery of statistical data, plus the subjective responses of 80,000 people worldwide, to map out well-being across 178 countries. Denmark and four other European countries, including Switzerland, Austria, and Iceland, came out in the top 10, while Zimbabwe and Burundi pulled up the bottom.

Not surprisingly, the countries that are happiest are those that are healthy, wealthy, and wise. "The most significant factors were health, the level of poverty, and access to basic education," White says. Population size also plays a role. Smaller countries with greater social cohesion and a stronger sense of national identity tended to score better, while those with the largest populations fared worse. China came in No. 82, India ranked 125, and Russia was 167. The U.S. came in at 23.

IT'S SUBJECTIVE.

White's study, to be published later this year, was developed in part as a response to the British media's fascination with life satisfaction. A recent BBC survey concluded that 81% of Britain's population would rather the government make them happier than richer.

Despite its often bleak weather, England ranked relatively happy at   5
41. "There is increasing political interest in using measures of happiness as a national indicator along with measures of wealth," White says. "We wanted to illustrate the effects of global poverty on subjective well-being to remind people that if they want to address unhappiness as an issue the need is greatest in other parts of the world."

To produce the "Happy Map," White dug deep. He analyzed data from a variety of sources including UNESCO, the CIA, The New Economics Foundation, and the World Health Organization. He then examined the responses of 80,000 people surveyed worldwide.

MONEY STILL COUNTS.

Good health may be the key to happiness, but money helps open the door. Wealthier countries, such as Switzerland (2) and Luxembourg (12), scored high on the index. Not surprisingly, most African countries, which have little of either, scored poorly. Zimbabwe, which has an AIDS rate of 25%, an average life expectancy of 39, and an 80% poverty rate, ranked near the bottom at 177. Meanwhile, the conflict between the Hutus and Tutsis gave fellow Africans in Burundi, ranked 178, even less to smile about, despite their having a slightly lower poverty rate of 68%.

Capitalism, meanwhile, fared quite well. Free-market systems are sometimes blamed for producing unhappiness due to insecurity and competition, but the U.S. was No. 23 and all the top-ranking European countries are firmly capitalist—albeit of a social-democratic flavor.

White says the only real surprise in his findings was how low many Asian countries scored. China is 82, Japan 90, and India an unhappy 125. "These are countries that are thought as having a strong sense of collective identity, which other researchers have associated with well-being," he says.

ARE WE HAPPY YET?

White admits that happiness is subjective. But he defends his research on the grounds that his study focused on life satisfaction rather than brief emotional states. "The frustrations of modern life, and the anxieties of the age, seem to be much less significant compared to the health, financial, and educational needs in other parts of the world." 10

One of the study's intentions was to see how Britain, given media preoccupation with well-being, fared compared to other parts of the globe. His conclusion: "The current concern with happiness levels in the U.K. may well be a case of the 'worried well.'"

Questions for Critical Reading

1. Just as press releases want to persuade news venues that they're announcing something newsworthy, so too do news venues want to persuade readers that they're reporting on something important. Considering the press release, identify passages where you think the author is trying to persuade news venues that White's research is newsworthy, and then identify passages from the news article where you think the writer is trying to persuade *Businessweek* readers of the same thing. Do you think each writer is successful in establishing newsworthiness? Why or why not?

2. News writers generally try to craft an attention-grabbing lead—an opening that will entice people to continue reading. Compare the lead of the press release to the lead of the news article, and consider why the news writer might have chosen to write her own lead (even though it's considered acceptable for a news article to be a word-for-word reprint of a press release):

> **Press release**
>
> A University of Leicester psychologist has produced the first ever "world map of happiness."

> **News article**
>
> Feeling sad? Researchers at Britain's University of Leicester reckon you might just be in the wrong country.

Which lead do you prefer? Why do you think the news writer chose to craft a different lead?

3. Instead of writing down pieces of information in the same order they were learned, recall that authors across genres often manipulate the order of ideas and information to better achieve their purposes. Note, for example, that although the press release author spreads out the reporting of White's results across several paragraphs (starting in para. 8), the news writer chooses to tell us the most important results right away, in the first two paragraphs:

> [Y]ou might just be in the wrong country. According to Adrian White, an analytic social psychologist at Leicester who developed the first "World Map of Happiness," Denmark is the happiest nation in the world.
>
> White's research used a battery of statistical data, plus the subjective responses of 80,000 people worldwide, to map out well-being across 178 countries. Denmark and four other European countries, including Switzerland, Austria, and Iceland, came out in the top 10, while Zimbabwe and Burundi pulled up the bottom.

Why do you think the news writer might have chosen to tell us White's results sooner than the press release author did? How might your response as a reader have been different had she waited until much later in the article to tell you White's results?

4. Like blogs, online news articles generally offer readers the option of clicking through to related articles, which can provide not only additional information but also different hypotheses and points of view. For instance, "Rating Countries for the Happiness Factor" is prefaced by an editor's note referring readers to another news article reporting on global happiness research, "Survey Says: People Are Happier." This article, written by Matt Mabe, offers a different theory of what makes people happy. Mabe quotes University of Michigan political scientist Ronald Inglehart: "Most of the earlier studies, including my own, were based on economic factors, which are something you can simply pull off a bookshelf and look up. . . . If that's all you look at, then that's all you find" (para. 7). The article continues:

> Social tolerance is [an] important factor in how happy a country rates itself. Over the last quarter-century, growing gender equality and acceptance of minorities and homosexuals has played a major role in those European countries found to be the most content. No. 7–ranked Switzerland, for instance, has elected two women as head of state in the last 10 years, while No. 4–ranked Iceland has recently passed laws guaranteeing virtually all the same rights to gay couples that married couples enjoy. . . . Tolerance simply has a rippling effect that makes people happier. (para. 11)

Although the article seems to base these claims on only the two-question World Values Survey ("How would you rate your happiness?" and "How satisfied are you with your life these days?") — and although it doesn't consider rival hypotheses — it might inspire some readers to think about happiness in a different light. To what extent does reading the claim about social tolerance and happiness affect your interpretation of "Rating Countries for the Happiness Factor" (and the press release it's based on)? Do you agree that there might be more to the story than health care, education, and wealth?

5. A news article sometimes makes a claim of causality even when the research it's summarizing only *speculates* about causality — or even when the original research makes no causal claim at all. Note that, in the extensive quotations of researcher Adrian White in the press release, he's careful to establish that health, wealth, and education are *associated* with happiness, not that they necessarily *cause* happiness. He says, for instance, that "a nation's level of happiness [is] *most closely associated* with health levels (correlation of .62), followed by wealth (.52), and then provision of education (.51)"; he also notes that the "three predictor variables of health, wealth and education [are] also *very closely associated with each other, illustrating the interdependence of these factors*" (paras. 9–10; emphasis added).

    Take a minute to find an example of how the online news article turns White's claim of association into a claim of causality. When you were reading the news article, did you notice this difference? Either then or now, does it bother you? Why or why not?

Making Connections

6. Recall that establishing whether or not a relationship is causal — whether one thing really does cause another — is important because beliefs about causality can drive behavior and policy. If, for example, a government believes that poverty causes unhappiness, it may try harder to reduce poverty. Similarly, if individuals believe that something will cause them to be happy, they're more likely to pursue it — whether it be money, social status, or material goods. Because there are consequences to beliefs about causality, it's important to be aware of how we can go wrong when we make causal claims. In

"Inquality and (Un)Happiness in America" (p. 389), Arthur Brooks provides a useful example of how we can be led astray when we look at causality:

> To confuse [something that is merely associated with something else for its cause] is to commit [a fallacy]. It is like saying that height leads to intelligence just because, on average, we see that tall kids in developing countries do the best in school. (The real reason is that taller kids, on average, have better nutrition than shorter kids, which leads to both height and intellectual ability.) (para. 16)

Recall that when you encounter a causal claim (such as "height leads to intelligence"), it's good to generate a rival hypothesis — to find another way to explain the connection (such as "better nutrition leads to both height and intellectual ability"). While the height example illustrates a rival hypothesis involving a third influence, it's also good to consider rival hypotheses that reverse the direction of causality. For example, consider the causal claims in both "Rating Countries for the Happiness Factor" and the other news article linked to in the editor's note, and then consider each rival hypothesis. See whether you think any of the rival hypotheses might be worth considering.

Original Hypothesis	Rival Hypothesis
Good health may be the key to happiness. (Kamenev, para. 7)	Happiness may contribute to better health.
[M]oney helps open the door [to happiness]. (Kamenev, para. 7)	If one is happy, one is more likely to find a job and work hard at that job.
Tolerance [of women, minorities, and homosexuals] simply has a rippling effect that makes people happier. (Mabe, para. 11)	When people are happier, they are more likely to be tolerant.

Do you believe each original claim, or its rival hypothesis — or do you believe there could be some truth to both? Might there be still other factors to consider (such as nutrition in Brooks's example)?

7. Clichés — worn-out expressions such as "I have butterflies in my stomach" and "my heart is in my throat" — tend to appear more often in some genres than in others. For instance, you might occasionally notice clichés in news articles, but they are generally avoided in creative nonfiction, a genre that prizes originality. In the creative nonfiction essay "The Waltz" (p. 298), Mary Beth Ellis does *not* tell us, "Although I take Luvox and go through life with my heart in my throat, most people don't know that I have OCD until I tell

them." Instead of using this cliché, she tells us that "for all the Luvox and the neurons and the occasional field trips to the fetal position, most people don't know that I have OCD until I tell them" (para. 53).

Unlike Ellis, the writers of the press release and the news article don't mind clichés; the press release tells us in the subtitle that "Happiness Is . . . Being Healthy, Wealthy and Wise," and the news article likewise informs us that "the countries that are happiest are those that are healthy, wealthy, and wise" (para. 3). If you were the author of the press release or the news article, would you revise this cliché, or would you let it go since clichés do sometimes appear in these genres? Why? If you would revise it, what would you say instead?

Writing: Your Turn

1. Just as Kamenev did, turn a press release on happiness into a news article. Visit a press release Web site such as www.eurekalert.org, type "happiness" in the search box, and sort the results by date so that you can easily tell which ones are recent. After you find an interesting press release, consider the following questions:

   - How will you craft an attention-grabbing lead?
   - What information will you keep, and what will you omit?
   - How will you change the order of the information you're keeping?

   After you finish a draft of your news article, show it—along with the original press release—to some of your classmates to get their opinion on how successful you were in crafting an interesting article. Consider their feedback when you revise, and submit the revision to your college newspaper (along with a note about the source of your information).

2. Write an argument on the role that you think health, wealth, and education play in happiness. Do you believe, as the news article suggests, that there is a causal relationship—that health, wealth, and access to education actually *cause* happiness, or do you think there might be a more complex interrelationship? Recall that it can be hard to find evidence of definitive causality; rather than trying to persuade readers that one thing directly causes another (and that there are no other contributing factors), it's often easier to persuade people that two or more phenomena co-occur or that one might contribute to the other. To support your thesis, considering drawing on the press release, any rival hypotheses you might have, any credible sources you find, and/or your personal experience or knowledge of others' experiences. Address your argument to an audience of classmates, and, after you finish writing, get feedback on how you could make your argument even more persuasive when you revise. For ideas on writing an argument, see p. 42.

Visualizing Genre

Greeting Cards

Apple executive Scott Forstall introduces the company's new greeting card app on October 4, 2011. The app enables senders to individualize paper cards by selecting their own pictures and adding their own words.

These American Greetings holiday cards enable a sender to upload up to fifty pictures, producing a slideshow that begins when the receiver opens the card.

To see these greeting cards in color, visit the e-Pages for *Real Questions* at bedfordstmartins.com/realquestions/epages.

Like other card manufacturers, Hallmark produces numerous cards specifically for Valentine's Day.

To save senders the trouble of finding a stamp, Hallmark collaborated with the U.S. Postal Service to produce a line of postage-paid greeting cards.

Congratulations on getting married. Don't let those pesky little divorce statistics ruin your fun.

This card, produced by Sick Chicks Ink, features pink flowers in a photo that is otherwise black and white.

Questions for Critical Reading

1. The genre of greeting cards is very much associated with happiness. One purpose of sending cards is to make people happy — to make them feel connected to the sender and possibly even to make them laugh or smile. In addition to trying to prompt happiness, greeting cards often depict it, featuring images and words that people might associate with happiness. How do you think the cards pictured here depict happiness? Which cards seem to use similar strategies for depicting happiness? What are some of the differences in the way the cards depict happiness?

2. Recall that different genres present different problems and limitations. Greeting cards present a paradoxical problem: they are mass produced, yet their senders generally want to send a personal message. The assumption is that cards that are personalized in some way — whether it be through careful selection or a handwritten note inside — have better odds of accomplishing their purposes.

    The problem of making mass-produced cards seem personal, combined with changes in technology, is prompting greeting card manufacturers to experiment with the genre. Among the pictured cards, for instance, you'll notice not only traditional mass-produced cards but also two alternatives that can be electronically individualized. The digital slide-show holiday cards ("Holiday Happiness" and "Merry Christmas"), for example, allow senders to upload up to fifty of their own pictures. When the receiver opens the card, the slide show begins, along with a soundtrack of upbeat instrumental holiday music. Apple's Cards app also allows senders to individualize a physical card. Using an iPhone or an iPod touch, senders select one of their own photos for the cover of the card and add their own words. Apple then mails the card to the recipient.

    Do you think this experimentation with the genre solves the problem of mass-produced cards not being personal enough? Do you think the additional personalization enabled by technology increases the odds that cards will accomplish their purposes? Why or why not?

3. Since it's not uncommon for genres to evolve and continue evolving, what other potential changes in the greeting-card genre can you envision? Why?

Pulling It All Together

BROCHURE

Drawing on the readings in this chapter, write and design a brochure discussing strategies people might use to become happier. What might people do to change their thoughts? their beliefs? their actions? How might these changes help them become happier? Be sure to include caveats (cautions) so that your readers don't have false expectations. (If people have expectations that aren't fulfilled, they might, in the face of unexpected obstacles, give up on the strategies outlined in the brochure.)

Although not all brochures cite sources, some do. You should too; readers will be more likely to trust the information you provide, and they'll have additional resources that they can consult themselves. You don't necessarily need to use footnotes or endnotes; you could write something to the effect of, "In [title], [author] suggests . . ." and provide a list of works consulted on the back panel.

After you design and write your brochure—and do a round of revision on your own—share it with some of your classmates for ideas on how you might make it even more compelling. After you've revised several times, distribute your brochure to at least ten people who aren't in your class. For ideas on writing a brochure, see p. 105.

ARGUMENT

Drawing on the readings in this chapter and perhaps also on your personal experience or independent research, write an argument about happiness addressed to an audience of your choosing. If you don't already have an argument in mind, you might address one of the following questions to help you formulate a thesis:

- To what extent might it be possible to become happier? In what situations—if any—is it reasonable to expect that people should be able to make themselves happier?

- Should trying to enable people's happiness be a goal of a society? If so, who should be responsible for this goal? To what extent should the responsibility fall on the government? other institutions? people themselves?

After you finish writing and doing an initial round of revision on your own, share your argument with some classmates. Ask them if they learned anything from reading your work or if your writing persuaded them to change their minds about anything. If they found your work persuasive, ask them how it might be more so; if they didn't, ask them what their objections are so that you can address them in your next revision. For strategies to use when writing an argument, see p. 42.

4

When is eating a social issue?

What does food mean to us?
Creative nonfiction, page **429**

What are we doing to be more informed eaters?
Review essay, page **435**   Magazine feature, page **451**

What are the moral implications
of our food choices?
Multi-genre trade book, page **507**   Op-ed, page **545**
Letter to the editor, page **548**

Where does our food come from?
Manifesto, page **460**   Wikipedia article, page **527**

How does the food industry market itself?
Magazine infographic, page **475**   Newsletter interview, page **481**
Researched argument, page **493**

"To eat the typical American diet is to participate in the biggest experiment in human nutrition ever conducted."

—Frances Moore Lappé (1982)

"Today one sits down to breakfast, spreads out a napkin of Irish linen, opens the meal with a banana from Central America, follows with a cereal of Minnesota sweetened with the product of Cuban cane, and ends with a Montana lamb chop and a cup of Brazilian coffee. Our daily life is a trip around the world, yet the wonder of it gives us not a single thrill. We are oblivious."

—Edward East (1924)

"We are paying for the foolishness of yesterday while we shape our own tomorrow. Today's white bread may force a break in the levees and flood New Orleans next spring. This year's wheat from Australia's eroding slopes may flare into a Japanese war three decades hence. . . . We must develop our sense of time and think of the availability of beefsteaks not only for this Saturday but for the Saturdays of our old age, and of our children."

—William Vogt (1948)

"In our every deliberation we must consider the impact of our decisions on the next seven generations."
—The Great Law of the Iroquois Confederacy (18th century)[1]

Some thinkers and cultures have long been aware that we can't take food for granted; indeed, each bite we take has a history, often one involving many laborers, chemicals, and gallons of fuel. More and more, people are coming to realize that eating is about more than just pleasing our taste buds; it's also about politics, ethics, our identity, our culture, and our environment.

The readings in this chapter look at food from several angles. Taken together, they address questions such as the following: How is food intertwined with our family life and our social life? What changes, if any, should be made to the way our food is produced and consumed? Should college campuses change what they serve and how they serve it? Is factory farming an ethical and environmental disaster? Should we eat less meat or abstain from eating it entirely? How do pesticides affect people and the environment? Regardless of whether or not food is organic, how can we trust food labels to accurately represent what's inside? Why have Americans gained so much weight since the 1980s? Should our weight gain and resultant health problems be addressed through changes to public policy, through modification of individuals' behavior, or through other changes?

In addition to reading about these issues in a variety of genres, you'll be hearing an assortment of voices, including a Romanian exchange student; a biologist; a factory farmer; a medical doctor and former FDA commissioner; a professor of psychology, epidemiology, and public health; college students; and well-known food journalists. Regardless of whether or not these voices prompt you to change your mind or your eating habits, reading the selections in this chapter will leave you with a better understanding of how what we eat affects ourselves as well as others.

Case Study: *Food Labeling Chaos*

The 2010 report *Food Labeling Chaos: The Case for Reform* provides a case study in how a genre can change — and how changes to a genre can result in changes in the world. The report was published by an influential nonprofit health advocacy organization, the Center for Science in the Public

---

[1] All quotations are courtesy of Warren Belasco and can be found in *Teaching Food: Agriculture, Food and Society Syllabi and Course Materials Collection*, published by the Association for the Study of Food and Society and the Agriculture, Food and Human Values Society (2003).

Interest (CSPI), and it argues that health claims on food labels need more stringent regulation, that ingredient labels need to be modernized, and that the Nutrition Facts Panel needs to be simplified and improved.

Ultimately, the report calls for the FDA and the USDA to mandate (by law) a change in the genre of food labels, thus illustrating how changes in a genre can result not only from evolving

beliefs and technology but also from changes in the law. Indeed, the genre of the Nutrition Facts Panel exists in the first place because of a law, the 1990 Nutrition Labeling and Education Act (NLEA)

As you'll read in the following excerpt, this law didn't just create any genre — it created a genre that ultimately extended many people's lives. As you'll also read, subsequent changes to the genre saved even more lives. It's no wonder that CSPI is lobbying for still more changes to the genre.

The excerpt from *Food Labeling Chaos* includes a brief literature review (a synthesis of published research) on the impact of past labeling reforms. The literature review is preceded by two annotated examples: one of a current food label and one of a "better" label, which illustrates the revisions that CSPI is lobbying for. You'll notice that these proposed revisions are typical of the changes writers often make when they revise: some information has been omitted, some has been added, and some has been better emphasized.

The proposed revisions encompass two key aspects of the food label: content and design. As you read, think about the possible effects of both the content and design revisions — effects that might range from changes in individuals' purchases to changes in the healthfulness and proportions of ingredients used by the food industry. Bear in mind that, even though much of the same information appears in both the current and revised labels, what gets emphasized is different. Consider whether this difference in emphasis could bring about a change in public health as significant as the one described in the literature review.

To see these food labels in color, visit the e-Pages for *Real Questions* at **bedfordstmartins.com/realquestions/epages.**

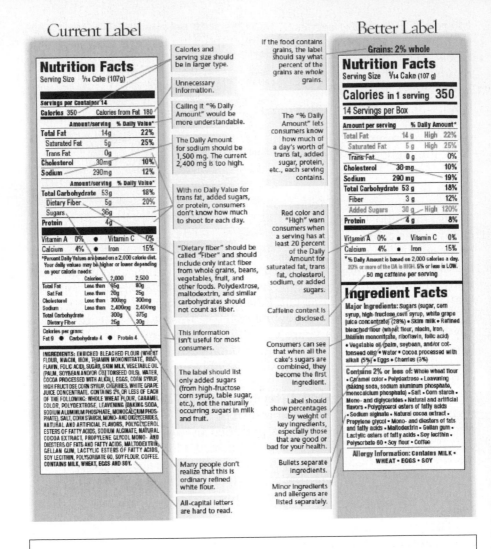

Economic Impact of Past Labeling Reforms

The economic impact of food labeling reforms has been extensively studied. The FDA's major economic impact analysis of its regulations implementing the 1990 NLEA concluded that "[E]stimates of the number of discounted life years gained nationwide for the first 20 years after implementation of the act range from a high of nearly 1.2 million to a low of 40,000." According to this study, the value of life years saved by mandatory nutrition labeling ranged from more than $106 billion to $3.6 billion over the same 20-year period based on 1988 dollars. Thus, the FDA concluded that "[R]elatively small changes in nutrient intakes may generate substantial public health benefits."[1]

A later estimate of a modification to the Nutrition Facts Panel in 2006, which required manufacturers to disclose the number of grams of trans fatty acids per serving, found that in three years, this single change alone would prevent from 600 to 1,200 cases of coronary heart disease and prevent from 240 to 480 deaths annually. It would also result in total benefits ranging from $4.1 billion to $8.3 billion per year.[2] Those were likely gross underestimates, because the FDA assumed that only a small fraction of trans fat would be eliminated; in fact, probably more than half of trans fat has been eliminated.

> "The FDA concluded that '[R]elatively small changes in nutrient intakes may generate substantial public health benefits.'"

Although the protocols for these two economic impact analyses were different, they both concluded that changes that provide consumers with certain better and more easily understood nutrition information on food labels would be cost-beneficial.

Consumer research has shown that many consumers use the Nutrition Facts Panel and that, while cause-and-effect relationships are difficult to establish, the use of nutrition labeling is associated with healthier diets.[3]

Notes

1. Gary A. Zarkin, PhD, et al., *Potential health benefits of nutrition label changes*, 83 Am. J. of Pub. Health 717-724 (May 1993).
2. Food labeling: Trans fatty acids in nutrition labeling, nutrient content claims, and health claims, 68 Fed. Reg. 41434, 41488, 41,467 (July 11, 2003).
3. *See* Sung-Yong Kim et al., *The effect of food label use on nutrient intakes: An endogenous switching regression analysis*, 25 Journal of Agricultural and Resource Economics 215 (July 2000) (finding that nutrition label users consume fewer calories from fat, less cholesterol and sodium, and more fiber, than non-label users); Alan R. Kristal et al., *Predictors of self-initiated healthful dietary change*, 101 J. Am. Diet Assoc. 762-765 (2000) (finding that the use of food labels is strongly associated with fat reduction); Alan D. Mathios, *The impact of mandatory disclosure laws on product choices: An analysis of the salad dressing market*, J. Law & Econ. 651-677 (2000) (finding that the addition of the NFP to food packages reduced the sale of high fat foods); The American Dietetic Association, *Nutrition Trends Survey 1997* (Sept. 1997) (finding that approximately two-thirds of those reading the NFP reported that they stopped or started buying a food product because of something they read on the label, and 56% of consumers said the information on the nutrition label had caused them to switch brands). Some of those studies found associations between reading labels and healthier diets, but could not establish cause and effect.

Questions for Critical Reading

1. Do you think any of the proposed changes to the Nutrition Facts Panel might make a difference in people's eating habits or in the ingredients used by the food industry? Why or why not?

2. Looking at the current label and the "better" label, what do you think are the most significant changes in content? Why?

3. Again considering both labels, what do you think are the most significant changes in design (e.g., font size and use of boldface, bullets, dividing lines, and uppercase vs. lowercase letters)? Why?

4. Take a minute to consider the pull quote (the large-type quotation) in the literature review following the two food labels. Many genres tend to feature pull quotes in order to highlight key information for readers. If you were the author of the report, would you have chosen the same sentence for the pull quote, or would you have chosen another sentence? Why?

5. Literature reviews, such as the one in *Food Labeling Chaos*, are common in industry reports as well as in several academic genres. Such literature reviews often appear in introductions to provide context for what follows; however, the one in *Food Labeling Chaos* appeared on the nineteenth page of the report, after the two food labels. Although it's difficult to assess organization without having the whole report in front of you, would you have rather had some or all of the information from the literature review earlier, before you read the annotated food labels? Why or why not?

As previously mentioned, *Food Labeling Chaos* provides a good illustration of how a change in a genre can effect real change in the world. Especially noteworthy is the literature review's discussion of research on the 2006 revision requiring manufacturers to disclose amounts of trans fat on labels: "this single change alone would prevent from 600 to 1,200 cases of coronary heart disease and prevent from 240 to 480 deaths annually" (para. 2).[2] While most revisions to a genre won't be this profound, the trans fat revision reminds us that, as writers and as consumers, we should never be content with the status quo if we believe that a change in a genre might bring about a change in the world.

About the Readings

While *Food Labeling Chaos* lobbies to change a genre, the bulk of this chapter's readings use particular genres to lobby for change in the food industry. All of the readings explore an aspect of eating that goes beyond the simple act of putting food in our mouths. Flavius Stan's creative nonfiction essay "The Night of Oranges" illustrates how food can be intertwined with family relationships and with systems of government, and it celebrates the power of a simple food, oranges. Michael

---

[2] Despite this revision to the genre, amounts of trans fat less than half a gram can be listed on the Nutrition Facts Panel as zero; thus, the genre doesn't always alert consumers that they are eating trans fat. Trans fat, which appears as a "partially hydrogenated" oil in ingredients lists, is believed by many to contribute to aggression and depression as well as heart disease. Some would argue, then, that the genre needs to be revised yet again.

Pollan's review essay "The Food Movement, Rising" complements Stan's piece by looking at highly processed foods and by examining the high cost of these foods to our health, environment, and culture. As a result of these high costs, says Pollan, we are in the middle of a "food movement" — one that is demanding change in a broad range of food arenas.

One such arena is addressed by Anna Lappé's magazine feature "Cafeteria Consciousness," which discusses how thousands of college students across the nation have mobilized to lobby for food that reflects values of fairness and sustainability. The theme of sustainability is echoed in biologist Sandra Steingraber's genre-bending essay "The Organic Manifesto," which weaves elements of creative nonfiction into a researched argument for organic agriculture. Rebecca Clarren's infographic "Is Your Eco-Label Lying?" looks at organic food labeling alongside other labeling that makes claims of sustainability and fairness, ultimately providing us with a better sense of which labels we can trust.

Processed food and the U.S.'s unprecedented weight gain are addressed by former FDA commissioner David A. Kessler's researched argument from *The End of Overeating*, as well as by Bonnie Liebman's newsletter interview "In Your Face: How the Food Industry Drives Us to Eat." Taken together, these two pieces shed light on why Americans have gained so much weight since the 1980s, and they provide insight into what we might do to address the problem.

Factory farming and the consumption of meat are addressed by the final selections in the chapter. In the excerpt from Jonathan Safran Foer's "Hiding/Seeking," you'll encounter factory farming through a mix of genres: a creative nonfiction adventure, a business letter, and oral histories — including one from an animal rights activist, another from a factory farmer, and still another from one of the few remaining traditional poultry farmers.

A more straightforward approach to the topic of industrial meat production is provided by the Wikipedia article "Factory Farming," which sheds light not only on factory farming but also on the ways that collaborative authorship might influence genre. Finally, Michael Fitzpatrick and Claire Miller debate the virtues of vegetarianism. Fitzpatrick's *Brown Daily Herald* op-ed piece, "The Vegetarian Delusion," argues that "moral vegetarianism" is "a failure as a form of activism," and Miller responds in a letter to the editor, arguing that "any individual vegetarian is still making a difference in the lives of animals and the health of our environment."

All these genres and voices confirm that food is far more than just a substance that fends off hunger. Alice P. Julier, president of the

Association for the Study of Food and Society, sums up the role of food in our lives:

> We are linked by what is on our plates and by how we think about who made it, where it came from, how it was grown and transported and transformed, served, and, indeed, eaten. Awareness of that process makes us . . . better eaters, better citizens, and ultimately, better people.[3]

There is no better way to achieve this awareness than by reading and writing about the many ways that food influences our lives—and the many ways that you, in turn, can influence how your food gets grown, produced, and consumed.

🇪 For additional readings in online and multimedia genres related to the chapter theme, see the e-Pages online at **bedfordstmartins.com /realquestions/epages.**

---

[3] From *Teaching Food: Agriculture, Food and Society Syllabi and Course Materials Collection,* published by the Association for the Study of Food and Society and the Agriculture, Food and Human Values Society (2003).

The Night of Oranges

Flavius Stan

When he wrote "The Night of Oranges," Flavius Stan was a 17-year-old exchange student who had just moved to New York City from his home country of Romania. In the essay, Stan recounts the story of giving his little brother oranges for Christmas when "the ice [was] still dirty from the boots of the Romanian revolution." Originally written as the first part of a two-part college application essay, "The Night of Oranges" was published in the *New York Times* in 1995. Many people have made a tradition of reading the essay aloud every year during the holiday season.

After attending college and graduate school in the U.S., Stan advised and directed businesses and non-profits in the U.S., Africa, and Europe. Currently living in Spain and working for the European Union institutions, Stan is committed to making a difference for less fortunate children in Romania and elsewhere.

Focus on Genre   "The Night of Oranges" seems to be a simple recounting of a personal experience — yet Stan's writing is highly crafted. Indeed, he notes that the essay went through "a serious process of thinking and re-thinking, writing and re-writing, of every paragraph, every sentence and literally every word."[4] His painstaking revision enabled him to add evocative details, cut words and sentences that didn't pull their weight, and draw out important moments.

As you read, pay special attention to Stan's pacing — to the way he devotes more space to describing certain moments than he does to others. One moment might be described in a sentence, while another might take a paragraph. Together, these moments make up a scene, the basic building block of creative nonfiction. Like most good scenes, the scene Stan describes happens at a very specific place and time; he skillfully gives us details that help us feel as if we are there with him at this place and time. As you read, consider what his purpose may have been in giving us these details — and in telling us his story in the first place.

◄O►

---

[4] From an e-mail to Kathryn Evans dated August 20, 2012.

It is Christmas Eve in 1989 in Timisoara and the ice is still dirty from the boots of the Romanian revolution. The dictator Nicolae Ceausescu had been deposed a few days before, and on Christmas Day he would be executed by firing squad. I am in the center of the city with my friends, empty now of the crowds that prayed outside the cathedral during the worst of the fighting. My friends and I still hear shots here and there. Our cold hands are gray like the sky above us, and we want to see a movie.

There is a rumor that there will be oranges for sale tonight. Hundreds of people are already waiting in line. We were used to such lines under the former Communist Government—lines for bread, lines for meat, lines for everything. Families would wait much of the day for rationed items. As children, we would take turns for an hour or more, holding our family's place in line.

But this line is different. There are children in Romania who don't know what an orange looks like. It is a special treat. Having the chance to eat a single orange will keep a child happy for a week. It will also make him a hero in the eyes of his friends. For the first time, someone is selling oranges by the kilo.

Suddenly I want to do something important: I want to give my brother a big surprise. He is only eight years old, and I want him to celebrate Christmas with lots of oranges at the table. I also want my parents to be proud of me.

So I call home and tell my parents that I'm going to be late. I forget about going to the movie, leave my friends and join the line.

People aren't silent, upset, frustrated, as they were before the revolution; they are talking to one another about life, politics and the new situation in the country.

The oranges are sold out of the back doorway of a food shop. The clerk has gone from anonymity to unexpected importance. As he handles the oranges, he acts like a movie star in front of his fans.

He moves his arms in an exaggerated manner as he tells the other workers where to go and what to do. All I can do is stare at the stack of cardboard boxes, piled higher than me. I have never seen so many oranges in my life.

Finally, it is my turn. It is 8 o'clock, and I have been waiting for six hours. It doesn't seem like a long time because my mind has been flying from the oranges in front of me to my brother and then back to the oranges. I hand over the money I was going to spend on the movie and watch each orange being thrown into my bag. I try to count them, but I lose their number.

I am drunk with the idea of oranges. I put the bag inside my coat as if I want to absorb their warmth. They aren't heavy at all, and I feel that this is going to be the best Christmas of my life. I begin thinking of how I am going to present my gift.

I get home and my father opens the door. He is amazed when he sees the oranges, and we decide to hide them until dinner. At dessert that night, I give my brother the present. Everyone is silent. They can't believe it.

My brother doesn't touch them. He is afraid even to look at them. Maybe they aren't real. Maybe they are an illusion, like everything else these days. We have to tell him he can eat them before he has the courage to touch one of the oranges.

I stare at my brother eating the oranges. They are my oranges. My parents are proud of me.

Questions for Critical Reading

1. Creative nonfiction writers generally want their stories to have a larger significance; they want to affect readers in some way. Consider why some of Stan's readers have made it a tradition to read "The Night of Oranges" aloud to friends and family during the holiday season. What might prompt them to do so? How did Stan's story affect you as a reader, and why?

2. Recall that many subgenres of creative nonfiction make points implicitly rather than stating them directly. Stan takes this approach as well. Consider, for instance, his final paragraph: "I stare at my brother eating the oranges. They are my oranges. My parents are proud of me." Think about how you would have responded to a more direct approach, something to the effect of "This experience shows that a special food can be a way to let your family know how important they are, and that we shouldn't take food for granted." Would you have preferred a more direct approach such as this? Why or why not?

3. Recall that the basic building block of creative nonfiction is the scene: a detailed recounting, sometimes including dialogue, of things that happened in a single time and place. In addition to scenes, sometimes you'll also find brief summaries or reflections in this genre—passages in which writers describe general conditions, beliefs, or actions that have been repeated. Unlike scenes, summaries do *not* take place in a particular time and place. Because creative nonfiction tends to be more powerful if there is more scene than summary, it's helpful to be able to distinguish between the two. Consider the following two paragraphs from Stan's essay and identify which sentences are *scene* and which ones are *summary*:

> There is a rumor that there will be oranges for sale tonight. Hundreds of people are already waiting in line. We were used to such lines under the former Communist Government—lines for bread, lines for meat, lines for everything. Families would wait much of the day for rationed items. As

children, we would take turns for an hour or more, holding our family's place in line.

But this line is different. There are children in Romania who don't know what an orange looks like. It is a special treat. Having the chance to eat a single orange will keep a child happy for a week. It will also make him a hero in the eyes of his friends. For the first time, someone is selling oranges by the kilo. (paras. 2–3)

You may have noticed that the last three sentences of the top paragraph, and all but the first and last sentences of the bottom paragraph, are summary. However, this is the only summary in the entire essay; the other eleven paragraphs depict only scene — only things that are happening at a single time and place.

Now imagine that the reverse were true — that there were fewer than two paragraphs depicting a scene and that the rest of the essay consisted of summary. In this scenario, the author might have made more generalizations about living under communism, such as "Life was grueling before the revolution; people tended to be depressed and discouraged all the time." (Note that, as a generalization, this sentence does not take place at a specific time and place.) The author might also have made more generalizations about oranges — "I have heard that oranges are sweet and juicy" — and about his family: "My parents like it when I do things for my brother, and he appreciates it too." How might you have responded differently if the majority of the essay had been summary such as this? Why?

4. After creative nonfiction writers reduce the amount of summary and focus on crafting scenes, they need to adjust the pacing of those scenes — that is, they need to decide whether to condense each scene, leave it as is, or draw it out. (In general, less important moments are condensed, and more important ones are expanded.) Assess Stan's pacing by comparing his original essay to the following condensed essay; this is an example of how the entire story could have been told with more compressed pacing:

It is Christmas Eve in 1989 in Timisoara and the ice is still dirty from the boots of the Romanian revolution. I am in the center of the city with my friends, and we want to see a movie.

There is a rumor that there will be oranges for sale tonight. Suddenly I want to do something important: I want to give my brother a big surprise. So I call home and tell my parents that I'm going to be late. I forget about going to the movie, leave my friends, and join the line for oranges. Finally, it is my turn. I hand over the money I was going to spend on the movie and watch each orange being thrown into my bag.

I put the bag inside my coat, and I begin thinking of how I am going to present my gift. I get home and my father opens the door. He is amazed when he sees the oranges, and we decide to hide them until dinner. At dessert that night, I give my brother the present. My parents are proud of me.

Which essay do you prefer? What's the effect of this more compressed pacing? What's the effect of the more drawn-out pacing of the original?

5. Similes (comparisons using the words *like* or *as*) are common in creative non-fiction. Unfortunately, similes can be a breeding ground for clichés; consider "sweet as candy," "clear as day," and "cuts like a knife." To gain insight into when a simile might sound clichéd, compare the following original and altered similes (italicized) from Stan's essay:

Original Passage	Altered Passage
Our cold hands are *gray like the sky above us* . . . (para. 1)	Our gray hands are *as cold as ice.*

Which simile do you prefer? Why? If you had to explain to someone how to revise away a cliché, what would you say?

Making Connections

6. Recall that you'll sometimes see a move typical of one genre being made in another genre. Consider the following two creative nonfiction opening sentences — one from Stan's "Night of Oranges" and one from Jonathan Safran Foer's "Hiding/Seeking" (p. 507) — and compare them to the opening sentence of Anna Lappé's magazine feature "Cafeteria Consciousness" (p. 451):

"The Night of Oranges"

It is Christmas Eve in 1989 in Timisoara and the ice is still dirty from the boots of the Romanian revolution.

"Hiding/Seeking"

I'm wearing black in the middle of the night in the middle of nowhere.

"Cafeteria Consciousness"

It was a little after midnight, long after the official conference had ended and the 500-plus attendees of the 2007 Food and Society annual get-together had turned in for the night.

Why might all three authors have decided to open their pieces in this way? When might you as a writer want to open a piece by establishing a setting (a time and place)?

7. Think about "The Night of Oranges" in light of the next reading selection, Michael Pollan's review essay "The Food Movement, Rising" (p. 435). In this essay, Pollan describes the experience many people in the United States have with food:

The supermarkets brim with produce summoned from every corner of the globe, a steady stream of novel food products (17,000 new ones each year) crowds the middle aisles, and in the freezer case you can find "home meal

Writing

replacements" in every conceivable ethnic stripe, demanding nothing more of the eater than opening the package and waiting for the microwave to chirp. Considered in the long sweep of human history, in which getting food dominated not just daily life but economic and political life as well, having to worry about food as little as we do, or did, seems almost a kind of dream. (para. 2)

Just as this passage encapsulates the experience of many people in a country, so too do some of the passages in Stan's essay. Take a minute to find a passage in "The Night of Oranges" that you think might encapsulate how many Romanians experienced food. Juxtaposing the passage you find in Stan's essay with the one from Pollan's essay, how would you describe the difference between the two? What does the juxtaposition of the two passages prompt you to think about your own experience with food?

Writing: Your Turn

1. Write a reflection on how Stan's experience with food is similar to or different from your own. Have you ever had to put as much time and energy into procuring food as Stan did? Has food ever played an important role in your family life? Is food something you tend to take for granted? Trade reflections with some classmates so that you can learn from each other's ideas and discuss revision strategies. For ideas on writing a reflection, see p. 27.

2. Write your own creative nonfiction piece about a memorable encounter (or series of related encounters) that you've had with food. Try to select an encounter that might teach readers something or help them see that not everyone has the same relationship to food that they do. Share your essay with some classmates so that they can give you feedback on whether they grew in some small way from reading your essay. For ideas on writing creative nonfiction, see p. 77.

The Food Movement, Rising

Michael Pollan

The following selection appeared in 2010 in the *New York Review of Books*. In it, award-winning food journalist Michael Pollan gives an overview of the food movement, ultimately suggesting that food plays a larger role in our lives than we may have realized and that, conversely, we as eaters and consumers can ultimately play a role in the way that food production affects our communities and our planet.

Focus on Genre   "The Food Movement, Rising" is a review essay — an essay that discusses several books. Unlike a typical book review, which discusses one book with the aim of giving readers enough information to decide whether or not to read it, review essays sometimes focus less on reviewing and more on using books to support an argument the author wants to make. That is Pollan's approach in this essay.

Unlike many other genres, and even unlike some other review essays, "The Food Movement, Rising" favors breadth over depth; rather than focusing deeply on a narrow topic — say, organic food or factory farming — Pollan covers a lot of territory, arguing that all the topics he discusses fall under the rubric of "the food movement" — a movement that will, he hopes, ultimately succeed in addressing the array of serious problems surrounding the food we eat. If Pollan's essay discusses a topic that doesn't interest you, stick with it; rest assured that his discussion of that topic will be brief and that it will serve a larger purpose. Pollan's brief discussion of the political history of food starting with President Nixon, for instance, sheds light on how our "food problem" came about — and to address a problem, as he hopes we will, it's important to understand how the problem arose.

As you read, notice the strategies Pollan uses to keep a sharp focus. Try to locate his thesis — the place where he gives an overview of his argument. Readers of academic genres are used to finding the thesis at the end of the introduction, but that isn't where Pollan put it. See if you can locate the thesis, and if you can, try to articulate how you know that it is indeed the thesis. Then consider the strategies Pollan uses throughout the rest of the essay to maintain the focus established by the thesis.

◄O►

1. FOOD MADE VISIBLE

It might sound odd to say this about something people deal with at least three times a day, but food in America has been more or less invisible, politically speaking, until very recently. At least until the early 1970s, when a bout of food price inflation and the appearance of books critical of industrial agriculture (by Wendell Berry, Francis Moore Lappé, and Barry Commoner, among others) threatened to propel the subject to the top of the national agenda, Americans have not had to think very hard about where their food comes from, or what it is doing to the planet, their bodies, and their society.

Most people count this a blessing. Americans spend a smaller percentage of their income on food than any people in history—slightly less than 10 percent—and a smaller amount of their time preparing it: a mere thirty-one minutes a day on average, including clean-up. The supermarkets brim with produce summoned from every corner of the globe, a steady stream of novel food products (17,000 new ones each year) crowds the middle aisles, and in the freezer case you can find "home meal replacements" in every conceivable ethnic stripe, demanding nothing more of the eater than opening the package and waiting for the microwave to chirp. Considered in the long sweep of human history, in which getting food dominated not just daily life but economic and political life as well, having to worry about food as little as we do, or did, seems almost a kind of dream.

The dream that the age-old "food problem" had been largely solved for most Americans was sustained by the tremendous postwar increases in the productivity of American farmers, made possible by cheap fossil fuel (the key ingredient in both chemical fertilizers and pesticides) and changes in agricultural policies. Asked by President Nixon to try to drive down the cost of food after it had spiked in the early 1970s, Agriculture Secretary Earl Butz shifted the historical focus of federal farm policy from supporting prices for farmers to boosting yields of a small handful of commodity crops (corn and soy especially) at any cost.

The administration's cheap food policy worked almost too well: crop prices fell, forcing farmers to produce still more simply to break even. This led to a deep depression in the farm belt in the 1980s followed by a brutal wave of consolidation. Most importantly, the price of food came down, or at least the price of the kinds of foods that could be made from corn and soy: processed foods and sweetened beverages and feedlot meat. (Prices for fresh produce have increased since the 1980s.) Washington had succeeded in eliminating food as a political issue—an objective dear to most governments at least since the time of the French Revolution.

* * *

But although cheap food is good politics, it turns out there are significant 5
costs—to the environment, to public health, to the public purse, even to the
culture—and as these became impossible to ignore in recent years, food has
come back into view. Beginning in the late 1980s, a series of food safety scandals opened people's eyes to the way their food was being produced, each one
drawing the curtain back a little further on a food system that had changed
beyond recognition. When BSE, or mad cow disease, surfaced in England in
1986, Americans learned that cattle, which are herbivores, were routinely being
fed the flesh of other cattle; the practice helped keep meat cheap but at the
risk of a hideous brain-wasting disease.

The 1993 deaths of four children in Washington State who had eaten
hamburgers from Jack in the Box were traced to meat contaminated with
E. coli 0157:H7, a mutant strain of the common intestinal bacteria first identified in feedlot cattle in 1982. Since then, repeated outbreaks of food-borne
illness linked to new antibiotic-resistant strains of bacteria (campylobacter,
salmonella, MRSA) have turned a bright light on the shortsighted practice of
routinely administering antibiotics to food animals, not to treat disease but simply to speed their growth and allow them to withstand the filthy and stressful
conditions in which they live.

In the wake of these food safety scandals, the conversation about food
politics that briefly flourished in the 1970s was picked up again in a series of
books, articles, and movies about the consequences of industrial food production. Beginning in 2001 with the publication of Eric Schlosser's *Fast Food Nation*,
a surprise best-seller and, the following year, Marion Nestle's *Food Politics*, the
food journalism of the last decade has succeeded in making clear and telling
connections between the methods of industrial food production, agricultural
policy, food-borne illness, childhood obesity, the decline of the family meal
as an institution, and, notably, the decline of family income beginning in the
1970s.

Besides drawing women into the work force, falling wages made fast food
both cheap to produce and a welcome, if not indispensible, option for pinched
and harried families. The picture of the food economy Schlosser painted
resembles an upside-down version of the social compact sometimes referred
to as "Fordism": instead of paying workers well enough to allow them to buy
things like cars, as Henry Ford proposed to do, companies like Wal-Mart and
McDonald's pay their workers so poorly that they can afford *only* the cheap,
low-quality food these companies sell, creating a kind of nonvirtuous circle
driving down both wages and the quality of food. The advent of fast food (and
cheap food in general) has, in effect, subsidized the decline of family incomes
in America.

2. FOOD POLITICS

Cheap food has become an indispensable pillar of the modern economy. But it is no longer an invisible or uncontested one. One of the most interesting social movements to emerge in the last few years is the "food movement," or perhaps I should say "movements," since it is unified as yet by little more than the recognition that industrial food production is in need of reform because its social/environmental/public health/animal welfare/gastronomic costs are too high.

As that list suggests, the critics are coming at the issue from a great many   10
different directions. Where many social movements tend to splinter as time goes on, breaking into various factions representing divergent concerns or tactics, the food movement starts out splintered. Among the many threads of advocacy that can be lumped together under that rubric we can include school lunch reform; the campaign for animal rights and welfare; the campaign against genetically modified crops; the rise of organic and locally produced food; efforts to combat obesity and type 2 diabetes; "food sovereignty" (the principle that nations should be allowed to decide their agricultural policies rather than submit to free trade regimes); farm bill reform; food safety regula-tion; farmland preservation; student organizing around food issues on campus; efforts to promote urban agriculture and ensure that communities have access to healthy food; initiatives to create gardens and cooking classes in schools; farm worker rights; nutrition labeling; feedlot pollution; and the various efforts to regulate food ingredients and marketing, especially to kids.

It's a big, lumpy tent, and sometimes the various factions beneath it work at cross-purposes. For example, activists working to strengthen federal food safety regulations have recently run afoul of local food advocates, who fear that the burden of new regulation will cripple the current revival of small-farm agriculture. Joel Salatin, the Virginia meat producer and writer who has become a hero to the food movement, fulminates against food safety regulation on libertarian grounds in his *Everything I Want to Do Is Illegal: War Stories from the Local Food Front*. Hunger activists like Joel Berg, in *All You Can Eat: How Hungry Is America?*, criticize supporters of "sustainable" agriculture—i.e., producing food in ways that do not harm the environment—for advocating reforms that threaten to raise the cost of food to the poor. Animal rights advocates occa-sionally pick fights with sustainable meat producers (such as Joel Salatin), as Jonathan Safran Foer does in his recent vegetarian polemic, *Eating Animals*.

But there are indications that these various voices may be coming together in something that looks more and more like a coherent movement. Many in the animal welfare movement, from PETA to Peter Singer, have come to see that a smaller-scale, more humane animal agriculture is a goal worth fighting for, and surely more attainable than the abolition of meat eating. Stung by charges of elitism, activists for sustainable farming are starting to take seriously the problem of hunger and poverty. They're promoting schemes and policies to make fresh local food more accessible to the poor, through programs that give vouchers redeemable at farmers' markets to participants in the Special Supplemental Nutrition Program for Women, Infants, and Children (WIC) and food stamp recipients. Yet a few underlying tensions remain: the "hunger lobby" has traditionally supported farm subsidies in exchange for the farm lobby's support of nutrition programs, a marriage of convenience dating to the 1960s that vastly complicates reform of the farm bill—a top priority for the food movement.

The sociologist Troy Duster reminds us of an all-important axiom about social movements: "No movement is as coherent and integrated as it seems from afar," he says, "and no movement is as incoherent and fractured as it seems from up close." Viewed from a middle distance, then, the food movement coalesces around the recognition that today's food and farming economy is "unsustainable"—that it can't go on in its current form much longer without courting a breakdown of some kind, whether environmental, economic, or both.

For some in the movement, the more urgent problem is environmental: the food system consumes more fossil fuel energy than we can count on in the future (about a fifth of the total American use of such energy) and emits more greenhouse gas than we can afford to emit, particularly since agriculture is the one human system that *should* be able to substantially rely on photosynthesis: solar energy. It will be difficult if not impossible to address the issue of climate change without reforming the food system. This is a conclusion that has only recently been embraced by the environmental movement, which historically has disdained all agriculture as a lapse from wilderness and a source of pollution.[1] But in the last few years, several of the major environmental groups have come to appreciate that a diversified, sustainable agriculture—which can sequester large amounts of carbon in the soil—holds the potential not just to mitigate but actually to help solve environmental problems, including climate change. Today, environmental organizations like the Natural Resources Defense Council and the Environmental Working Group are taking up the cause of food system reform, lending their expertise and clout to the movement.

* * *

But perhaps the food movement's strongest claim on public attention today is   15
the fact that the American diet of highly processed food laced with added fats and sugars is responsible for the epidemic of chronic diseases that threatens to bankrupt the health care system. The Centers for Disease Control estimates that

fully three quarters of US health care spending goes to treat chronic diseases, most of which are preventable and linked to diet: heart disease, stroke, type 2 diabetes, and at least a third of all cancers. The health care crisis probably cannot be addressed without addressing the catastrophe of the American diet, and that diet is the direct (even if unintended) result of the way that our agriculture and food industries have been organized. . . .

The political ground is shifting, and the passage of health care reform may accelerate that movement. The bill itself contains a few provisions long promoted by the food movement (like calorie labeling on fast food menus), but more important could be the new political tendencies it sets in motion. If health insurers can no longer keep people with chronic diseases out of their patient pools, it stands to reason that the companies will develop a keener interest in preventing those diseases. They will then discover that they have a large stake in things like soda taxes and in precisely which kinds of calories the farm bill is subsidizing. As the insurance industry and the government take on more responsibility for the cost of treating expensive and largely preventable problems like obesity and type 2 diabetes, pressure for reform of the food system, and the American diet, can be expected to increase.

3. BEYOND THE BARCODE

It would be a mistake to conclude that the food movement's agenda can be reduced to a set of laws, policies, and regulations, important as these may be. What is attracting so many people to the movement today (and young people in particular) is a much less conventional kind of politics, one that is about something more than food. The food movement is also about community, identity, pleasure, and, most notably, about carving out a new social and economic space removed from the influence of big corporations on the one side and government on the other. As the Diggers used to say during their San Francisco be-ins during the 1960s, food can serve as "an edible dynamic"—a means to a political end that is only nominally about food itself.

One can get a taste of this social space simply by hanging around a farmers' market, an activity that a great many people enjoy today regardless of whether they're in the market for a bunch of carrots or a head of lettuce. Farmers' markets are thriving, more than five thousand strong, and there is a lot more going on in them than the exchange of money for food. Someone is collecting signatures on a petition. Someone else is playing music. Children are everywhere, sampling fresh produce, talking to farmers. Friends and acquaintances stop to chat. One sociologist calculated that people have ten times as many conversations at the farmers' market than they do in the supermarket.

Socially as well as sensually, the farmers' market offers a remarkably rich and appealing environment. Someone buying food here may be acting not just as a consumer but also as a neighbor, a citizen, a parent, a cook. In many cities and towns, farmers' markets have taken on (and not for the first time) the function of a lively new public square.

Though seldom articulated as such, the attempt to redefine, or escape, the traditional role of consumer has become an important aspiration of the food movement. In various ways it seeks to put the relationship between consumers and producers on a new, more neighborly footing, enriching the kinds of information exchanged in the transaction, and encouraging us to regard our food dollars as "votes" for a different kind of agriculture and, by implication, economy. The modern marketplace would have us decide what to buy strictly on the basis of price and self-interest; the food movement implicitly proposes that we enlarge our understanding of both those terms, suggesting that not just "good value" but ethical and political values should inform our buying decisions, and that we'll get more satisfaction from our eating when they do.

That satisfaction helps to explain why many in the movement don't greet   20
the spectacle of large corporations adopting its goals, as some of them have begun to do, with unalloyed enthusiasm. Already Wal-Mart sells organic and local food, but this doesn't greatly warm the hearts of food movement activists. One important impetus for the movement, or at least its locavore wing—those who are committed to eating as much locally produced food as possible—is the desire to get "beyond the barcode"—to create new economic and social structures outside of the mainstream consumer economy. Though not always articulated in these terms, the local food movement wants to decentralize the global economy, if not secede from it altogether, which is why in some communities, such as Great Barrington, Massachusetts, local currencies (the "BerkShare") have popped up.

In fact it's hard to say which comes first: the desire to promote local agriculture or the desire to promote local economies more generally by cutting ties, to whatever degree possible, to the national economic grid.[2] This is at bottom a communitarian impulse, and it is one that is drawing support from the right as well as the left. Though the food movement has deep roots in the counterculture of the 1960s, its critique of corporate food and federal farm subsidies, as well as its emphasis on building community around food, has won it friends on the right. In his 2006 book *Crunchy Cons*, Rod Dreher identifies a strain of libertarian conservatism, often evangelical, that regards fast food as anathema to family values, and has seized on local food as a kind of culinary counterpart to home schooling.

* * *

It makes sense that food and farming should become a locus of attention for Americans disenchanted with consumer capitalism. Food is the place in daily life where corporatization can be most vividly felt: think about the homogenization of taste and experience represented by fast food. By the same token, food offers us one of the shortest, most appealing paths out of the corporate labyrinth, and into the sheer diversity of local flavors, varieties, and characters on offer at the farmers' market.

Put another way, the food movement has set out to foster new forms of civil society. But instead of proposing that space as a counterweight to an overbearing state, as is usually the case, the food movement poses it against the dominance of corporations and their tendency to insinuate themselves into any aspect of our lives from which they can profit. As Wendell Berry writes, the corporations

> will grow, deliver, and cook your food for you and (just like your mother) beg you to eat it. That they do not yet offer to insert it, prechewed, into your mouth is only because they have found no profitable way to do so.

The corporatization of something as basic and intimate as eating is, for many of us today, a good place to draw the line.

The Italian-born organization Slow Food, founded in 1986 as a protest against the arrival of McDonald's in Rome, represents perhaps the purest expression of these politics. The organization, which now has 100,000 members in 132 countries, began by dedicating itself to "a firm defense of quiet material pleasure" but has lately waded into deeper political and economic waters. Slow Food's founder and president, Carlo Petrini, a former leftist journalist, has much to say about how people's daily food choices can rehabilitate the act of consumption, making it something more creative and progressive. In his new book *Terra Madre: Forging a New Global Network of Sustainable Food Communities*, Petrini urges eaters and food producers to join together in "food communities" outside of the usual distribution channels, which typically communicate little information beyond price and often exploit food producers. A farmers' market is one manifestation of such a community, but Petrini is no mere locavore. Rather, he would have us practice on a global scale something like "local" economics, with its stress on neighborliness, as when, to cite one of his examples, eaters in the affluent West support nomad fisher folk in Mauritania by creating a market for their bottarga, or dried mullet roe. In helping to keep alive such a food tradition and way of life, the eater becomes something more than a consumer; she becomes what Petrini likes to call a "coproducer."

Ever the Italian, Petrini puts pleasure at the center of his politics, which 25 might explain why Slow Food is not always taken as seriously as it deserves to be. For why *shouldn't* pleasure figure in the politics of the food movement?

Good food is potentially one of the most democratic pleasures a society can offer, and is one of those subjects, like sports, that people can talk about across lines of class, ethnicity, and race.

The fact that the most humane and most environmentally sustainable choices frequently turn out to be the most delicious choices (as chefs such as Alice Waters and Dan Barber have pointed out) is fortuitous to say the least; it is also a welcome challenge to the more dismal choices typically posed by environmentalism, which most of the time is asking us to give up things we like. As Alice Waters has often said, it was not politics or ecology that brought her to organic agriculture, but rather the desire to recover a certain taste—one she had experienced as an exchange student in France. Of course democratizing such tastes, which under current policies tend to be more expensive, is the hard part, and must eventually lead the movement back to more conventional politics lest it be tagged as elitist.

But the movement's interest in such seemingly mundane matters as taste and the other textures of everyday life is also one of its great strengths. Part of the movement's critique of industrial food is that, with the rise of fast food and the collapse of everyday cooking, it has damaged family life and community by undermining the institution of the shared meal. Sad as it may be to bowl alone, eating alone can be sadder still, not least because it is eroding the civility on which our political culture depends.

*   *   *

That is the argument made by Janet Flammang, a political scientist, in a provocative new book called *The Taste for Civilization: Food, Politics, and Civil Society.* "Significant social and political costs have resulted from fast food and convenience foods," she writes, "grazing and snacking instead of sitting down for leisurely meals, watching television during mealtimes instead of conversing"— 40 percent of Americans watch television during meals—"viewing food as fuel rather than sustenance, discarding family recipes and foodways, and denying that eating has social and political dimensions." The cultural contradictions of capitalism—its tendency to undermine the stabilizing social forms it depends on—are on vivid display at the modern American dinner table.

In a challenge to second-wave feminists who urged women to get out of the kitchen, Flammang suggests that by denigrating "foodwork"—everything involved in putting meals on the family table—we have unthinkingly wrecked one of the nurseries of democracy: the family meal. It is at "the temporary democracy of the table" that children learn the art of conversation and acquire the habits of civility—sharing, listening, taking turns, navigating differences, arguing without offending—and it is these habits that are lost when we eat alone and on the run. "Civility is not needed when one is by oneself."[3]

These arguments resonated during the Senate debate over health care   30
reform, when *The New York Times* reported that the private Senate dining room,
where senators of both parties used to break bread together, stood empty.
Flammang attributes some of the loss of civility in Washington to the aftermath
of the 1994 Republican Revolution, when Newt Gingrich, the new Speaker of
the House, urged his freshman legislators *not* to move their families to Washington. Members now returned to their districts every weekend, sacrificing opportunities for socializing across party lines and, in the process, the "reservoirs of
good will replenished at dinner parties." It is much harder to vilify someone
with whom you have shared a meal.

Flammang makes a convincing case for the centrality of food work and
shared meals, much along the lines laid down by Carlo Petrini and Alice Waters,
but with more historical perspective and theoretical rigor. A scholar of the
women's movement, she suggests that "American women are having second thoughts" about having left the kitchen.[4] However, the answer is not for
them simply to return to it, at least not alone, but rather "for everyone—men,
women, and children—to go back to the kitchen, as in preindustrial days, and
for the workplace to lessen its time demands on people." Flammang points out
that the historical priority of the American labor movement has been to fight
for money, while the European labor movement has fought for time, which she
suggests may have been the wiser choice.

At the very least this is a debate worth having, and it begins by taking food
issues much more seriously than we have taken them. Flammang suggests that
the invisibility of these issues until recently owes to the identification of food
work with women and the (related) fact that eating, by its very nature, falls on
the wrong side of the mind-body dualism. "Food is apprehended through the
senses of touch, smell and taste," she points out,

> which rank lower on the hierarchy of senses than sight and hearing, which are
> typically thought to give rise to knowledge. In most of philosophy, religion, and
> literature, food is associated with body, animal, female, and appetite—things
> civilized men have sought to overcome with reason and knowledge.

Much to our loss. But food is invisible no longer and, in light of the mount-
ing costs we've incurred by ignoring it, it is likely to demand much more of
our attention in the future, as eaters, parents, and citizens. It is only a matter
of time before politicians seize on the power of the food issue, which besides
being increasingly urgent is also almost primal, indeed is in some deep sense
proto-political. For where do all politics begin if not in the high chair?—at that
fateful moment when mother, or father, raises a spoonful of food to the lips of
the baby who clamps shut her mouth, shakes her head no, and for the very first
time in life awakens to and asserts her sovereign power.

Notes

1. Al Gore's *An Inconvenient Truth* made scant mention of food or agriculture, but in his recent follow-up book, *Our Choice: A Plan to Solve the Climate Crisis* (2009), he devotes a long chapter to the subject of our food choices and their bearing on climate.

2. For an interesting case study about a depressed Vermont mining town that turned to local food and agriculture to revitalize itself, see Ben Hewitt, *The Town That Food Saved: How One Community Found Vitality in Local Food* (Rodale, 2009).

3. See David M. Herszenhorn, "In Senate Health Care Vote, New Partisan Vitriol," *New York Times*, December 23, 2009: "Senator Max Baucus, Democrat of Montana and chairman of the Finance Committee, said the political—and often personal—divisions that now characterize the Senate were epitomized by the empty tables in the senators' private dining room, a place where members of both parties used to break bread. 'Nobody goes there anymore,' Mr. Baucus said. 'When I was here 10, 15, 30 years ago, that was the place you would go to talk to senators, let your hair down, just kind of compare notes, no spouses allowed, no staff, nobody. It is now empty.'"

4. The stirrings of a new "radical homemakers" movement lends some support to the assertion. See Shannon Hayes's *Radical Homemakers: Reclaiming Domesticity from a Consumer Culture* (Left to Write Press, 2010).

Questions for Critical Reading

1. What did you take to be Pollan's thesis, and why? Were you persuaded that his thesis had some validity? Why or why not?

2. Not all review essays cover as much ground as Pollan's; some focus more narrowly on a single issue. Consider Pollan's choice in opting for breadth over depth—in covering a lot of ground instead of picking one narrow topic and delving deeply into it. For you as a reader, did Pollan's breadth-over-depth approach work? Why or why not?

3. One reason some readers may be less persuaded by the breadth-over-depth approach is that the sheer number of topics covered means there's less room for evidence to support claims. The amount of evidence a reader needs depends on many things, including the credibility of the writer and what the reader has previously read. Recall that Pollan's essay appeared in the *New York Review of Books*, a publication with an audience of avid readers—many of whom would have read Pollan's previous work since he's published numerous articles and books on food. Given their familiarity with Pollan's work, these readers might not have needed support for every claim.

Because, unlike Pollan, you probably haven't been widely published (at least not yet!), an instructor might tell you that opting for breadth over depth is too risky for a student to attempt; in other words: don't try this at home. At this point in your career, would you heed that advice, or can you imagine a scenario in which you might want to risk a project as broad as Pollan's? Why or why not?

4. One of the greatest challenges of working in most genres is to keep a sharp focus—to show readers that there's an overarching purpose tying all your paragraphs together. This is a challenge because, as a writer, you need to walk a fine line: you don't want to repeat entire sentences, but you *do* want to refer back to previous points often enough for readers to see how everything is connected. Some students find it especially tricky to refer back to their thesis at the end of an essay without repeating it word for word. Assess whether or not Pollan does this successfully when you look at a version of his thesis followed by a sentence from the beginning of his conclusion. Recall this version of his thesis:

> [A]lthough cheap food is good politics, it turns out there are significant costs—to the environment, to public health, to the public purse, even to the culture—and as these became impossible to ignore in recent years, food has come back into view. (para. 5)[5]

Consider whether this sentence from the beginning of Pollan's conclusion works well to keep the focus established by the thesis, or whether it's too repetitious for your taste:

> [F]ood is invisible no longer and, in light of the mounting costs we've incurred by ignoring it, it is likely to demand much more of our attention in the future, as eaters, parents, and citizens. (para. 33)

Do think Pollan succeeds in referring back to his thesis without sounding too repetitious? Why or why not?

5. While Pollan refers back to his thesis at the beginning of his conclusion, he uses the *end* of the conclusion to reinforce a specific subargument that he thinks is important. Here, he is more subtle in referring back to a previous point; compare his original statement of the subargument, made in the middle of his essay, to the way he reinforces it with a symbolic image in the final sentences of the essay. See if the connection between the two passages is too subtle for you or if it works:

Original statement of the subargument

> [The food movement encourages] us to regard our food dollars as "votes" for a different kind of agriculture. . . . The modern marketplace would have us decide what to buy strictly on the basis of price and self-interest; the food movement implicitly proposes that we enlarge our understanding of both those terms, suggesting that not just "good value" but ethical and political values should inform our buying decisions. (para. 19)

---

[5] Note that another version of Pollan's thesis appears in paragraph 9.

Connections

Reference back to the subargument (final sentences of the essay)

It is only a matter of time before politicians seize on the power of the food issue, which besides being increasingly urgent is also almost primal, indeed is in some deep sense proto-political. For where do all politics begin if not in the high chair?—at that fateful moment when mother, or father, raises a spoonful of food to the lips of the baby who clamps shut her mouth, shakes her head no, and for the very first time in life awakens to and asserts her sovereign power. (para. 33)

For you as a reader, did the symbolic image of the baby shaking her head no succeed in reinforcing Pollan's point that we should vote with our food dollars—that we should sometimes say no to food?[6] Why or why not?

Making Connections

6. Regardless of genre, readers tend to have an easier experience if they can quickly figure out who said the words in each quotation. To this end, recall that when you're writing academic genres, you'll generally want to avoid floating quotations, or quotations that take up a whole sentence, unanchored by any of your own words. When you're writing creative nonfiction, however, you'll probably *want* to use some floating quotations, and sometimes you may also want to use them in journalistic genres.

To help you gain more insight into both when you'd want to use floating quotations and when you'd want to avoid them, consider the following three passages—one from Pollan's essay, one from Anna Lappé's magazine feature "Cafeteria Consciousness" (p. 451), and one from the creative nonfiction section of Jonathan Safran Foer's "Hiding/Seeking" (p. 507). Each passage contains both regular quotations and floating quotations (italicized). Consider whether some of the floating quotations work better than others, or if they all work for you:

Pollan's review essay (para. 29)

Flammang suggests that by denigrating "foodwork"—everything involved in putting meals on the family table—we have unthinkingly wrecked one of the nurseries of democracy: the family meal. It is at "the temporary democracy of the table" that children learn the art of conversation and acquire the habits of civility—sharing, listening, taking turns, navigating differences, arguing without offending—and it is these habits that are lost when we eat alone and on the run. *"Civility is not needed when one is by oneself."*[3]

[Note that endnote 3 begins "See David M. Herszenhorn, 'In Senate Health Care Vote, New Partisan Vitriol,' *New York Times* . . ." and goes on to quote a passage from Herszenhorn's article. The actual quotation about civility is from Flammang.]

---

[6] For another example of ending an essay with a symbolic image, see "Black Men and Public Space" (p. 223).

Lappé's magazine feature (para. 6)

The Campus Climate Challenge served as inspiration for the Real Food Challenge founders, who were interested in channeling student excitement in a new direction. "There was a lot of momentum around climate change on campuses. Al Gore had swept onto the scene," said Galarneau. *"But the activism lacked a connection with the food system."*

Foer's creative nonfiction (paras. 6–9, 11–12)

"Bull," I half-echoed, half-asked, with no obvious linguistic intent.

"Male cow," she said brusquely, as she sorted through a bag of what appeared to be dental equipment.

"And if you and I should, tonight, encounter a bull?"

"We won't." . . .

"Hypothetically."

"Stand very still," C advised. *"I don't think they see stationary objects."*

Do Foer's floating quotations work for you? Does Lappé's? Pollan's? In your own writing, how will you decide when to let a quotation float alone as its own sentence and when to anchor it by adding some of your own words to the sentence? (Just remember to be cautious about using floating quotations in academic genres unless you check with your professor first; many professors frown on them.)

7. With any genre, it's useful to look at punctuation when you revise. In addition to affecting your credibility as a writer, recall that punctuation helps writers control emphasis and can help readers make connections more quickly. In the three passages that follow—one from "The Food Movement, Rising," one from Flavius Stan's creative nonfiction essay "The Night of Oranges" (p. 429), and one from Anna Lappé's magazine feature "Cafeteria Consciousness" (p. 451)—the authors chose to use semicolons (;) rather than periods. (When semicolons are used correctly, as they are in these examples, they can be replaced by periods; this is a useful test to do with your own writing if you use semicolons.) See whether you prefer the original passages or the altered passages, which replace the semicolons with periods.

Original Passage	Altered Passage
In helping to keep alive such a food tradition and way of life, the eater becomes something more than a consumer; she becomes what Petrini likes to call a "coproducer." (Pollan, para. 24)	In helping to keep alive such a food tradition and way of life, the eater becomes something more than a consumer. She becomes what Petrini likes to call a "coproducer."

Original Passage	Altered Passage
People aren't silent, upset, frustrated, as they were before the revolution; they are talking to one another about life, politics, and the new situation in the country. (Stan, para. 6)	People aren't silent, upset, frustrated, as they were before the revolution. They are talking to one another about life, politics, and the new situation in the country.
[Schwartz and Steel] sensed that students were hankering to speak up more loudly for sustainable food; they just needed an effective way to do so. (Lappé, para. 2)	[Schwartz and Steel] sensed that students were hankering to speak up more loudly for sustainable food. They just needed an effective way to do so.

Given the choice between a semicolon and a period, would you have made the same decision that each author did? Why or why not?

Writing: Your Turn

1. Take a stance on one of Pollan's points by agreeing, disagreeing, or arguing that there is only limited truth to the point. Choose any of the following points:

   - "[N]ot just 'good value' but ethical and political values should inform our buying decisions." (para. 19)
   - "Food is the place in daily life where corporatization can be most vividly felt: think about the homogenization of taste and experience represented by fast food." (para. 22)
   - "[W]ith the rise of fast food and the collapse of everyday cooking, [food that is produced by companies rather than people] has damaged family life and community by undermining the institution of the shared meal." (para. 27)

   As evidence to support your argument, use (as your instructor directs) your personal experience or that of people you know and/or evidence that you find through your own research. Share your work with your classmates to see if you've used enough evidence to persuade them and to get other ideas for revision. For tips on making an argument, see p. 42.

2. Since Pollan opted for breadth over depth, resulting in several passages that aren't fully developed, select a passage he wrote and elaborate on it, filling in (after having spent a bit of time on the web or in the library) some of the details that he's missing. You may pick any passage in his essay, but if you want a list to choose from, consider one of the following (and note that the

questions posed after each passage provide only one way to elaborate; you may find other ways):

- "Americans spend a smaller percentage of their income on food than any people in history — slightly less than 10 percent — and a smaller amount of their time preparing it: a mere thirty-one minutes a day on average, including clean-up" (para. 2). What percentage of income do/did other peoples spend on food? How much time do/did other peoples spend on food preparation and clean-up? Was there a time when Americans spent more time and money on food than they do now?

- "[T]he food system . . . emits more greenhouse gas than we can afford to emit" (para. 14). How much greenhouse gas does the food system emit? What parts of the food system emit gas? What evidence is there that these food-system emissions are indeed harmful?

- "[S]everal of the major environmental groups have come to appreciate that a diversified, sustainable agriculture — which can sequester large amounts of carbon in the soil — holds the potential . . . to help solve environmental problems, including climate change" (para. 14). How can large amounts of carbon be sequestered in the soil? What environmental groups are advocating this? Is there any evidence that this could really work?

- "[T]he American diet of highly processed food laced with added fats and sugars is responsible for the epidemic of chronic diseases" (para. 15). What evidence is there to support this claim? Couldn't other things be contributing to the epidemic of chronic diseases?

After you've written several paragraphs elaborating on one of Pollan's sentences, share your work with some of your classmates so that they can both learn from what you wrote and tell you if there's any more information that readers might appreciate. Also ask them to give you feedback on clarity and organization.

Cafeteria Consciousness

Anna Lappé

In "Cafeteria Consciousness," Anna Lappé discusses the Real Food Challenge, a student-run initiative whose mission is to bring fairly and sustainably produced food to college campuses. Originally published in the *Nation*, "Cafeteria Consciousness" is adapted from Lappé's book *Diet for a Hot Planet: The Climate Crisis at the End of Your Fork and What You Can Do about It* (2010).

Lappé, a highly regarded food journalist, has written numerous articles and is also coauthor of the books *Hope's Edge: The Next Diet for a Small Planet* (2002) and *Grub: Ideas for an Urban Organic Kitchen* (2006). She is on the advisory council for the Real Food Challenge.

Focus on Genre   Journalistic genres are typically written to inform readers; many pieces of journalism, however, have other purposes as well. This is often true of feature articles like "Cafeteria Consciousness," which, rather than focusing on breaking news, discuss people, organizations, or movements — things that are interesting whether someone reads about them today, next week, or next month. While on the surface, feature articles seek to inform readers, an implicit purpose of this genre is often to persuade readers to feel a certain way about the writer's topic. As you read "Cafeteria Consciousness," see if you can discern how Lappé wants you to feel about the Real Food Challenge. Also notice how Lappé handles paragraphs — whether they are focused and, if they are, what strategies she uses to make them so.

◄○►

*Concerned about global warming, students are
pushing for change — in their dining halls.*

I t was a little after midnight, long after the official conference had ended and
the 500-plus attendees of the 2007 Food and Society annual get-together
had turned in for the night. Tim Galarneau of the California Student Sustainability Coalition; Anim Steel from the Food Project, a Boston-based food and
farming nonprofit; David Schwartz from Brown University; and a few other
young people were still talking. Hunched over a table in an empty meeting
room at the Grand Traverse Resort in Traverse City, Michigan, the group had
already been together for hours, continuing a conversation that had been
going on for more than a year.

What was keeping them up so late? They were comparing notes. Each was
witnessing a burgeoning student movement on college campuses to bring
sustainably and fairly raised food into dining halls. From coast to coast, a similar
energy and enthusiasm seemed to be bubbling up. Galarneau was seeing it
in the massive effort to transform university food across California's esteemed
public university system. Schwartz was seeing it back in Providence at Brown,
where students were getting increasingly vocal about finding sustainable food.
And Steel, a leader in the food-justice movement, had a frontline view from the
Food Project's youth-run farm in Boston. From their unique perspectives, both
sensed that students were hankering to speak up more loudly for sustainable
food; they just needed an effective way to do so. Out of this ongoing conversation, the group would launch the Real Food Challenge.

The concept is simple, really. Students, some who pay as much as
$100,000, or more, for four years at a private college, should have a say in
what grub their schools serve — and that food should reflect shared values of
fairness and sustainability. The Real Food Challenge provides an organizing tool
to empower students to persuade their schools to make a move. Schools that
join the challenge pledge to shift at least 20 percent of school food to "real
food" — sustainably raised, grown with fairness, and from local and regional
farms — by 2020.

In addition to this concrete goal, the Challenge also offers schools and
student organizers a support network, resources for finding sources of real
food, organizer training and a "real food calculator." The calculator provides
campuses with a mechanism for quantifying real food, for determining the
percentage of real food they currently serve and assessing improvement
over time.

The excitement about the Real Food Challenge, Galarneau said, is partly   5
that it taps into students' energy to address the global warming impact of their
campuses. One strategy of student environmental activists has been to focus

on persuading their schools to reduce their global warming impact through rethinking institutional energy use and turning to renewable-energy sources. One of the most successful campus-based efforts to date is the Campus Climate Challenge. The initiative has helped young people in colleges and high schools across the United States and Canada organize to campaign for—and win—100 percent clean-energy policies at their schools.

The Campus Climate Challenge served as inspiration for the Real Food Challenge founders, who were interested in channeling student excitement in a new direction. "There was a lot of momentum around climate change on campuses. Al Gore had swept onto the scene," said Galarneau. "But the activism lacked a connection with the food system." And yet the global food system, from seed to plate to landfill, is responsible for as much as one-third of all greenhouse-gas emissions, largely because it is the single greatest force behind deforestation and soil degradation, both of which release carbon dioxide into the atmosphere. Indeed, livestock production alone is responsible for 18 percent of the world's emissions, more than those produced by all transportation—every SUV, steamer ship and jet plane combined.

"Many young people are realizing that the food system is a key contributor to global warming. They know that we've got to talk about food if we're going to advance a broader sustainability agenda," Galarneau noted.

It would take another year and a half of conversations like the one back in that stuffy meeting room before the Real Food Challenge was officially launched in September 2008. But within a month, the original crew had hard proof that their hunch had been right.

The Challenge launched with eleven pilot schools. Organizers hoped several hundred more would soon join. "During one of our conference calls that first month, we checked to see how many campuses had come on board. We had hoped for maybe 200," said Galarneau. "We already had 230. That's when we knew we'd hit a nerve. People were biting."

By the end of that first year, 329 campuses had joined the network, from   10
Brown University to City College of New York to DeAnza Community College in San Mateo, California. The determined young people who lead the Challenge expect that in another year that number could grow to 1,000, about a quarter of all the two- and four-year colleges and universities in the country. To put the potential impact in context, US colleges and universities currently spend more than $4 billion annually on school food. (Roughly half of school food is contracted out to food-service companies; the rest is managed by the schools themselves.) If it's successful, and the participating schools shift 20 percent of their purchases, the Real Food Challenge will have helped to move nearly $1 billion of food purchases toward sustainability by 2020.

"We're talking about shaking up the system," said Galarneau, "and young people like that."

Connecting the overarching mission of the Real Food Challenge—increasing the amount of fairly and sustainably raised local foods on campuses—to the effort to combat climate change is a complex challenge. First and foremost, there's the problem of quantifying the impact. Unlike getting data on campus energy use—emissions are relatively easy to measure and are usually the direct result of action (or inaction)—getting data on food is difficult. Campuses rarely know the full life story of the food they purchase. In part that's because food-related emissions mostly occur during production, processing and distribution—long before the food shows up in the cafeteria. Plus, even for the "direct" emissions—energy used in dining halls, food waste ending up in landfills—schools often don't have systems in place yet for accurate measurement.

But a data gap doesn't have to mean an action gap. The Real Food Challenge stresses that there are guiding principles for planet-friendly choices schools can make, including cutting back on meat and dairy, reducing waste and packaging, and choosing more sustainably raised and local foods, for instance.

*   *   *

It was not long before the Real Food Challenge piqued the interest of food-service companies. In that initial launch month, said Galarneau, they were contacted by Aramark, Sodexo, and Bon Appétit—some of the biggest players in college food service. "They were calling to say they wanted to partner with the Challenge," he said. But Galarneau and the other organizers were wary of official corporate partnerships, concerned that companies would just be latching on to the initiative without actually changing their practices. They'd already seen food-service companies pay lip service to sustainability in their contracts without embracing broad change in the dining halls. As we talked, Galarneau described a 135-page food-service contract he was reviewing, hunting for language that would provide the company loopholes to skirt sustainability. "The devil is in the details," he said.

(On its own, Bon Appétit, which serves 80 million meals a year at campus and corporate facilities, has launched a low-carbon diet initiative, reducing food waste, promoting composting, educating guests about their food choices and cutting back on beef purchases by 33 percent systemwide between 2007 and 2009.)

Organizers of the Real Food Challenge say their primary focus is on building student engagement. Because food-service directors typically don't have time to make the needed changes, schools need students to help make it happen. Plus, as Steel says, "no matter how committed many of these companies say they are, they can only go as far as students push them."

* * *

The Challenge, while popular among students on participating campuses, still faces many hurdles, including getting the ear of administrators facing one of the worst economic downturns in generations. But as the organizers like to point out, many of the climate-friendly principles actually help schools save money. Students at Stanford, for example, borrowed the Love Food, Hate Waste campaign from the United Kingdom to develop a way for people on campus to compost their waste easily. Erin Gaines, former sustainable-foods coordinator at Stanford Dining and Hospitality, and an active member of the Real Food Challenge, told me about their success. In 2007, thanks to the campaign, the school composted 1.2 million pounds of food from campus dining halls and cafes. That's 1.2 million pounds that would have gone into a landfill. Instead, the scraps were taken to a local composting facility, and half of the compost was returned to the school to be used on its gardens and grounds.

Galarneau offered an example from the University of California system. In response to student campaigning, the Santa Cruz campus decided to go "trayless" to address the pile-on phenomenon: students grabbing more food than their stomachs can hold. No trays means less washing. The school has already calculated a savings of more than 1 million gallons of water a year. And no trays means less food waste. Since the policy was introduced, the campus has seen food waste decline by one-third, and it is committed to diverting the remaining waste to compost. "The mantra is 'upcycling,'" said Galarneau, "reducing waste before it becomes waste and then reintegrating waste, through composting, so that it never becomes waste." This one step has helped reduce energy consumption (less dishwater to heat), saving the school money, which in turn leaves more resources to invest in sustainable food choices.

Galarneau cited an observation economists have made: that once a consumer trend reaches 20 percent of a market, it can become an unstoppable force. What the young people in the Challenge are doing, says Galarneau, is "testing that theory with a push towards purchases that value justice and sustainability." When I talked with Katrina Norbom, a Real Food Challenge member at the University of North Florida, she said "No matter what, it comes down to the students. If we can create enough support, we can make it happen."

This determination is making an impact well beyond the campus. Alumni   20
of the Real Food Challenge are heading into communities where they're using their passion and organizing skills to expand the market for real food across the country. When I asked Galarneau and Steel for examples, they

rattled off a bunch: Sue DeBlieck from Iowa State University is running a farm-to-school project in Maine; Sam Lipschultz, a 2009 Sarah Lawrence graduate, is starting a youth-run farmers' market in one of Brooklyn's poorest neighborhoods; and UC Irvine's Hai Vo, who had been consulting with other youth-empowerment projects after college, just sent in his applications for programs in farm apprenticeship.

The organizers know that shifting 20 percent of school food to "real food" by 2020 is ambitious; but their vision is even bolder—and broader—than that. Currently less than 2 percent of food on most campuses is "real." Nationwide, the figure isn't much different. As Steel said, "If we can't make the shift happen on a campus, how can we expect it to happen elsewhere? And if we *can* do it on campuses, then we can start asking, "Why can't we do that everywhere?""

Questions for Critical Reading

1. What's your opinion of the Real Food Challenge? What did Lappé do to help shape your opinion?

2. Some of the academic genres you use probably call on you to organize your paragraphs around points (often stated in topic sentences at the beginnings of paragraphs). However, not all genres use topic sentences in every paragraph. Journalistic genres, including magazine features such as "Cafeteria Consciousness," use topic sentences only sometimes.

Since an important purpose of a topic sentence is to establish the focus of a paragraph, the challenge when *not* using one is to nonetheless write a paragraph that's focused—that doesn't confuse readers by shifting from one topic to another. Consider the following three paragraphs from "Cafeteria Consciousness"; take note of whether each paragraph opening (italicized) is a topic sentence summarizing the point of the paragraph. If the italicized sentence *doesn't* summarize the point of the paragraph, assess whether the paragraph is focused despite the lack of a topic sentence.

> *The Challenge launched with eleven pilot schools.* Organizers hoped several hundred more would soon join. "During one of our conference calls that first month, we checked to see how many campuses had come on board. We had hoped for maybe 200," said Galarneau. "We already had 230. That's when we knew we'd hit a nerve. People were biting." (para. 9)

> *Connecting the overarching mission of the Real Food Challenge—increasing the amount of fairly and sustainably raised local foods on campuses—to the effort to combat climate change is a complex challenge.* First and foremost, there's the problem of quantifying the impact. Unlike getting data on campus energy use . . . getting data on food is difficult. Campuses rarely know the full life story of the food they purchase. In part that's because food-related emissions mostly occur during production, processing and

distribution—long before the food shows up in the cafeteria. Plus, even for the "direct" emissions—energy used in dining halls, food waste ending up in landfills—schools often don't have systems in place yet for accurate measurement. (para. 12)

But a data gap doesn't have to mean an action gap. The Real Food Challenge stresses that there are guiding principles for planet-friendly choices schools can make, including cutting back on meat and dairy, reducing waste and packaging, and choosing more sustainably raised and local foods, for instance. (para. 13)

Do you think the paragraph that didn't open with a topic sentence still managed to maintain its focus? If so, how did Lappé pull it off? When might you want to use topic sentences in your own writing, and when might you want to use other strategies to maintain paragraph focus?

3. To write successfully using any genre, it's helpful to be aware of the level of detail you're providing. Many writers, regardless of genre, notice while revising that it would be good to add even more detail. One of the most detailed passages in Lappé's article is the one in which she describes how UC Santa Cruz went trayless; compare two versions of that passage—one with less detail (which might resemble a first draft) and one with more detail (the one that was good enough to publish).

Imagined first draft

In response to student campaigning, the Santa Cruz campus decided to go "trayless" to address the pile-on phenomenon: students grabbing more food than their stomachs can hold. No trays means less washing. And no trays means less food waste. Since the policy was introduced, the campus has seen food waste decline, and it is committed to diverting the remaining waste to compost.

Published paragraph

In response to student campaigning, the Santa Cruz campus decided to go "trayless" to address the pile-on phenomenon: students grabbing more food than their stomachs can hold. No trays means less washing. The school has already calculated a savings of more than 1 million gallons of water a year. And no trays means less food waste. Since the policy was introduced, the campus has seen food waste decline by one-third and it is committed to diverting the remaining waste to compost. "The mantra is 'upcycling,'" said Galarneau, "reducing waste before it becomes waste and then reintegrating waste, through composting, so that it never becomes waste." This one step has helped reduce energy consumption (less dishwater to heat), saving the school money, which in turn leaves more resources to invest in sustainable food choices. (para. 18)

Which version do you prefer—or would you prefer a "middle" version? Why?

4. Many writers find that deciding how to end a piece, regardless of genre, can be tricky. One strategy used across genres is to end with a call to action—a suggestion that readers *do* something. Another strategy, also commonly used across genres, is to end with an important quotation. In "Cafeteria Consciousness," Lappé combines these strategies, providing us with a quotation that might inspire some readers to take action:

> As Steel said, "If we can't make this shift happen on a campus, how can we expect it to happen elsewhere? And if we *can* do it on campuses, then we can start asking, 'Why can't we do it everywhere?'" (para. 21)

Do you think this ending is effective in helping Lappé achieve her purpose? Why or why not? In what situations might you plan to end with a quotation or a call to action (or a quotation that works like a call to action)?

Making Connections

5. Subtitles are common in journalistic genres. Consider the subtitles (underneath the headlines) of two magazine pieces, "Cafeteria Consciousness" and Rebecca Clarren's "Is Your Eco-Label Lying?" (p. 475); think about why they might have been added:

CAFETERIA CONSCIOUSNESS

Concerned about global warming, students are pushing for change—in their dining halls.

IS YOUR ECO-LABEL LYING?

Sure, it says it's green. But what's that really mean?

What do you take to be the purpose of these subtitles? Did you find them effective? Why or why not?

6. Writers across genres sometimes list multiple examples in the same sentence. When you do this, you'll want to choose the relationship between those examples carefully. Sometimes it may suit your purposes to have the examples in a list be similar; other times it may be better to choose examples based on their diversity. Consider the following two passages, one from "Cafeteria Consciousness" and the other from Sandra Steingraber's essay "The Organic Manifesto" (p. 460). The original passages list diverse examples, while the altered versions list similar examples.

Original Passage	Altered Passage
By the end of that first year, 329 campuses had joined the network, from Brown University to City College of New York to DeAnza Community College in San Mateo, California. (Lappé, para. 10)	By the end of that first year, 329 campuses had joined the network, from the University of Florida to the University of Georgia to Valdosta State University in Valdosta, Georgia.
For nearly two decades, I lived the life of a gypsy biologist—investigating the interactions between organisms and the environments they inhabit in places as varied as Costa Rican rainforests, Sudanese deserts, Mexican tidal pools, and Minnesota pine forests. (Steingraber, para. 1)	For nearly two decades, I lived the life of a gypsy biologist—investigating the interactions between organisms and the environments they inhabit in places ranging from the Sahara to Death Valley to the Mohave.

Do you think the types of examples each writer chose helped her better achieve her purpose? Why or why not?

Writing: Your Turn

1. Go to the Real Food Challenge Web site at http://realfoodchallenge.org and browse, looking for any information that you think might have been good for Lappé to include in her article. Write a reflection on what you learned from the site; if there's information you think would have been good for Lappé to include, explain why. Share your reflection with some classmates so that they can learn from it and give you feedback for revision. For ideas on writing a reflection, see p. 27.

2. Write a rhetorical analysis of "Cafeteria Consciousness," discussing how well you think it achieves its purpose. You might address questions such as the following: Does Lappé provide enough evidence to support her claims? Are there any additional details or explanations she could have provided? How effective do you think her use of numbers is (see paragraphs 6, 9, 10, 17, 18, and 21)?

Before you revise, ask some classmates for feedback on whether you provide enough quotations to support your claims and whether your analysis of those quotations illustrates *how* the quotations support your claims. (For example, you might claim that Lappé uses numbers effectively and quote passages in which she uses numbers, but you'll be more likely to persuade readers if you also explain *why* you find the numbers in those passages to be effective.) For ideas on writing a rhetorical analysis, see p. 31.

The Organic Manifesto

Sandra Steingraber, PhD

Written by biologist and author Sandra Steingraber, "The Organic Manifesto" appears on the Organic Valley Web site and was republished in *In Good Tilth*. *In Good Tilth* is the magazine of Oregon Tilth, a nonprofit organization whose mission is "to educate gardeners, farmers, legislators, and the general public about the need to develop and use sustainable growing practices." Steingraber has taught at Cornell University and Ithaca College and is the author of six books, most recently *Raising Elijah: Protecting Our Children in an Age of Environmental Crisis* (2011).

Focus on Genre Manifestos are public declarations of motive, policy, intention, or belief. They are often calls to action or arguments for change. Steingraber's manifesto is innovative in that it uses elements of creative nonfiction to ultimately make a researched argument. Many manifestos don't cite research, as Steingraber does, nor do many of them use creative nonfiction strategies. Steingraber's essay, then, provides a good example of how genre is flexible — of how a writer can bend a genre and make it incorporate elements of other genres. As you read, look for elements of creative nonfiction, such as evocative detail, setting, and characterization (of Steingraber and her children). Also look for elements of a researched argument; notice especially the way Steingraber explicitly states her thesis, cites sources, and establishes her credibility as a scientist.

◄O►

For nearly two decades, I lived the life of a gypsy biologist—investigating the interactions between organisms and the environments they inhabit in places as varied as Costa Rican rainforests, Sudanese deserts, Mexican tidal pools, and Minnesota pine forests. I slept in tents, dormitories, farm houses, huts with grass roofs, and at least one military bunker. I left for airports at 4 AM. I never balanced my checkbook.

And then I eloped with a sculptor and got pregnant. Now, well into my forties, I am wife to a man with a lot of power tools and mother to a four-year-old daughter and a one-year-old son. Now, I live in a log cabin in rural upstate New York and have seen the same basswood trees bloom four times. Now, I make my living as an environmental writer, analyzing the data of other scientists rather than generating my own. These days, my field research extends about as far as the backyard birdfeeder, which services migrating songbirds heading north to Canadian pine forests or south to Latin American rainforests.

"I'm no longer one of you," I laugh while watching them refuel for their journeys. I teach their calls to my daughter Faith, to whom I have bequeathed my grubby ornithology guide. I whisper their names to my son Elijah, as I nurse him in the old rocking chair that is stationed near the picture window. And when we all sleep upstairs in the big bed together—one child holding on to my hair, the other flung across my chest, I know that I never lived more symbiotically. A source of food, a place of comfort, mattress for napping, I myself am now a habitat.

And I balance my checkbook.

Having children after twenty years of a childless adult life has brought with it at least two revelations. One is an acute awareness of the brevity of infancy. You only get a four-month-old for a month. And even at 4 AM when baby-ness seems eternal, it still passes more quickly than you can believe. So Jeff and I compete to be the primary parent. We don't want to miss anything. 5

The second is the realization that young children—in spite of all kinds of advertising to the contrary—require few possessions. What they do need, in seemingly unquenchable quantities, is the loving attention of their parents. Which brings me to the checkbook. In our household, with its two self-employed adults, money is a means to buy time with Faith and Elijah. The farther I can stretch a dollar, the more hours I have for berry-picking, story-reading, and line dances around the kitchen table.

To this end, Jeff and I recently sought out the advice of a financial counselor. We thought a third pair of eyes looking over our household budget might identify places where we could take up even more slack. And Becky Bilderback—who runs a bed and breakfast, cans her own garden produce, and sews her own curtains—seemed to possess the ideal eyes for the job.

Becky wasted no time scanning down the list of our monthly expenses. But, to both our relief and disappointment, she couldn't find much room for improvement. We own one car, buy clothes at consignment shops, pay off our credit card in full each month. And there wasn't much that could be done about those health insurance premiums. Finally, she tapped her finger on one of our line items. "Here," said Becky. "Right here. This seems high to me." We leaned over the table. It was our groceries: $140 per week for food for a family of four. "And another thing," she said. "I don't see a line item for charitable giving." Was this, she wondered, an expense that we had perhaps overlooked?

I took a deep breath. It wasn't. Indeed, the absence of charitable donations and our generous food budget were directly related to each other. Virtually all the groceries Jeff and I buy for our family are organically grown. As well as an investment in a healthy environment for my children, directing my food dollars toward organic farmers is part of my spiritual practice. Simply put, we choose to support an agricultural system that does not rely on toxic chemicals to produce the food we eat. In attempting to articulate the depth of my commitment toward organic food, I realized it was time to write my organic manifesto, complete with all the reasons why I believe the decision to buy organic is rational, ethical, and in the long run, cost effective. And here it is.

1. ORGANIC FOOD CONTAINS FEWER PESTICIDE RESIDUES THAN CONVENTIONAL FOOD.

This might seem a self-evident truth. After all, organic farming prohibits the use of synthetic pesticides and intends to offer crops virtually free of residues. And yet the evidence to support this claim has only been available since spring 2002, when a peer-reviewed scientific journal published the first systematic comparison of pesticide residues in organic and non-organic foods.[1] Examining the data from more than 90,000 samples of produce, the authors of this study found that nearly three-quarters of conventionally grown foods had detectable pesticide residues. Three-quarters of organic crops had none. And among the one-quarter of organic samples that did test positive, levels of pesticide contamination were far lower. Conventionally grown foods were also more likely to test positive for multiple pesticides than were their organic counterparts.

2. CHILDREN FED ORGANIC FOOD HAVE LOWER RESIDUES OF CERTAIN PESTICIDES IN THEIR BODIES THAN CHILDREN FED CONVENTIONALLY GROWN FOOD.

Organophosphate insecticides kill by attacking the nervous systems of insect pests. They are frequently used in fruit and vegetable farming. A 2003 study measured levels of these chemicals in the urine of pre-school children living in Seattle. Children with conventional diets had, on average, nine times more organophosphate insecticides in their urine than children fed organic produce.[2] So, are organic foods healthier for our kids? Here is where science yields to mother wisdom. We in the scientific community do not yet know what levels of pesticide exposure are sufficient to endanger the health of human adults, and we know even less about their effects on children. Thus, the wide gray area called "uncertain risk."

The reasons for our ignorance are many. When researching my book, *Living Downstream*, I discovered that many pesticides on the market have never been adequately screened for their ability to cause cancer. Even less thoroughly have we tested their ability to affect fetal brain growth, contribute to miscarriages, disrupt hormonal signaling, alter the onset of puberty, or undermine fertility. Evidence from animal studies suggests we have reason to be concerned about these possibilities and investigate them further.

I also learned that most human dietary studies of pesticide exposure presume adult eating habits. And yet, as any mother will testify, children dine on fewer foods in proportionally higher quantities than their parents do. (I do not routinely consume two bananas and two avocados a day. My 27-pound son does.) Finally, consider that children lack many of the biological defenses that protect adults against the toxic effects of pesticides. All of us grown-ups, for example, possess a blood-brain barrier. It works quite well to keep neurological poisons from entering the gray matter of our brains. However, we did not acquire this cerebral suit of armor until we reached the age of six months. Infants are thus far more susceptible to the brain-addling potential of insecticides and at much lower doses.

Pesticides, by design, are poisons. The science shows us that most organic produce is free from pesticide residues and most conventionally grown produce is not. The science shows that children fed organic produce have significantly lower pesticide residues in their bodies than children fed conventional produce. Whatever we do or don't know about threshold levels for harm, my intuition tells me that food with no poison is better for my children's developing minds and bodies than food with some.

3. ORGANIC AGRICULTURE IS PART OF GOOD PRENATAL CARE.

Women's bodies are the first environment. So says native American midwife, Katsi Cook. This simple truth became the starting point of my book *Having Faith*, which explores the intimate ecology of pregnancy. It was a project that I began during the first month of my pregnancy with the real-life Faith and finally finished a week before I gave birth to her younger brother. Those four

15

years of research and writing can really be summed up in two simple sentences: If the world's environment is contaminated, so too is the ecosystem of a mother's body. If a mother's body is contaminated, so too is the child who inhabits it.

The placenta, which does such an admirable job at keeping bacteria and viruses out of the womb's watery habitat, is ill-equipped to serve as a barrier to toxic chemicals. Pesticides that are made up of smaller molecules are afforded free passage. They slip easily from the mother's bloodstream into the blood of the baby's umbilical cord. Pesticides made of bigger, heavier molecules are partly broken down by the placenta's enzymes before they pass through. But, ironically, this transformation sometimes renders them even *more* toxic.[3]

We have much to learn about the reproductive effects of pesticides in use today. In the meantime, organic farming—like sobriety, seatbelts, and not smoking—makes good prenatal sense.

4. ORGANIC AGRICULTURE PROTECTS AIR AND WATER.

Last year, I received a phone call from a reporter at my hometown newspaper. He asked me to comment on the news that herbicide drift had now made it all but impossible to grow grapes commercially in central Illinois.[4] In other words, in the place where I grew up, the wind itself now contains so much weed killer (2,4-D) that grape leaves curl up and die. Illinois's cherry trees are perishing for the same reason. Looking out at my son stacking blocks on our back deck, a spring breeze ruffling the blond feathers of his hair, I wondered what effect this pesticide-laden air was having on the children who were breathing it.

After I hung up, I thought about my pregnancy with my daughter Faith, the first five months of which were spent in downstate Illinois. While researching the drinking water data for the town in which I was living, I discovered that two herbicides—alachlor and atrazine—were routinely found in the tap water there. Neither had ever exceeded its legal maximum contaminant level. However, I was not entirely reassured. These limits were never set with human embryos and fetuses in mind.

Pesticides do not adhere to the fields in which they are sprayed. They   20
evaporate and rise into the jetstream. They drift for miles in the wind. They fall in the rain. They are detectable in fog. They insinuate themselves into the crystalline structures of snowflakes. They follow storm run-off into gullies and streambeds. They descend through soil into groundwater.

Organic agriculture does not poison wells and reservoirs. It does not bring ruin to vineyards and orchards. It is respectful of snow, fog, wind, and rain—our life support system.

5. ORGANIC AGRICULTURE PROTECTS WILDLIFE.

My most beloved landscape, the Illinois River valley near Peoria, is an ecologically diminished place. Poisoned by insecticide run-off, the river's fingernail
clams disappeared in 1955. The diving ducks that depended on the clams for
their food source soon followed. Ring-necks. Canvasbacks. Scaups. They are
all gone now. Then, poisoned by herbicide run-off, the river's lush vegetation
vanished from the shallows. Wild celery. Coontail. Sago. The seeds of these
aquatic plants fed the river's dabbling ducks. And so they vanished too—the
wigeons and the gadwells. By the time I was born in 1959, the riverbank near
my home had become an eerily silent place. I learned to identify native Illinois
ducks not by direct observation but by studying stuffed specimens in ornithology labs. I learned their calls by listening to instructional tapes. I felt myself a
natural historian of ghosts.

New studies identify pesticides as a leading suspect in the ongoing decline
of North America's frog populations. For example, trace exposures to certain
common weed killers emasculate male tadpoles. They do so by stimulating an
enzyme that converts male hormone into female hormone. Thus altered, male
tadpoles metamorphose into hermaphroditic adults.[5] Similarly, nitrates from
synthetic fertilizers can trigger deformities in developing tadpoles or kill them
outright—at levels well below their legal limits in drinking water.[6]

Faith and I are sometimes kept awake April nights by the shrill EEP! EEP! of
the spring peepers who inhabit the wetlands out behind our cabin. Peepers are
a cricket-sized species of tree frog with a piercingly loud method of finding suitable mates. The peepers' cries, which signal the advent of spring more reliably
than any bird song, are soon joined by the quieter ZZZIPPP . . . ZZZIPPP of the
chorus frog, whose call most closely resembles a finger drawn over the tines of
a comb. Later in the season comes the loudspeaker JUG-O-RUM of the bullfrog,
whose booming pronouncements make Elijah jump and laugh out loud. I want
the songs of frogs to remain as familiar to my children as the lullabies we sing
together. I want my grocery-buying habits to help sustain the annual spring
amphibian festival in our backyard. Let frogs keep us up all night. No more
animal ghosts.

6. ORGANIC AGRICULTURE PROMOTES PUBLIC HEALTH.

Farmers have higher rates of certain cancers than the general population. So   25
do farmers' children.[7] An emerging body of evidence suggests that exposure to
pesticides on farms may be part of the reason.

Other studies have revealed possible links between agricultural use of
pesticides and birth defects. For example, according to a recent California study,

living near agricultural fields where pesticides are sprayed raises the risk of stillbirths due to birth defects. Researchers found the largest risk among babies whose mothers lived within one mile of such areas during their first trimester of pregnancy. Similarly, a Minnesota study found that the children of farmers, as well as those born to families living in agricultural areas, have elevated rates of birth defects. Similar findings come from Iowa.[8]

All dread, grief, and human suffering aside, cancer and birth defects are expensive. And here lies the economic sense of organic agriculture.

Food that is grown organically often does cost more than conventionally grown foods. There are at least three reasons for this higher price tag. Organic foods are more strictly regulated. Organic farming practices require more labor. And organic farms tend to be smaller. However, conventionally grown foods carry with them many indirect costs. The price of cleaning up contaminated water, the loss of wildlife, and the increased health care needs of farm families are just a few. These costs may not be incorporated in the price we pay in the grocery store, but they are reflected in our tax bills and insurance premiums.

As the demand for organic food rises, prices at the cash register will fall. In the meantime, here is how I make organic food more affordable for my family: instead of donating to the American Cancer Society or the March of Dimes, I fold my charitable giving into my grocery bill. By buying organic, I feed my own family and, at the same time, work towards the prevention of cancer and birth defects in rural America.

7. ORGANIC FARMS PROMOTE COMMUNITY.

Rising just west of our cabin is Snyder Hill, a long, steep rocky ridge that blocks the afternoon sun far sooner than I'd like during the too-short days of the too-long winters here. On top of that hill is a flat, wide expanse of good drainage and good views that is also the location of an organic vegetable farm. We are grateful to this farm, as the snow and rain that falls on its fields eventually descend the slopes of Snyder Hill and seep into the hollow where we live, recharging our drinking water well and filling up our froggy swamp. Our home shares a watershed with this agricultural operation.   30

In addition to this ecological link, we are also joined economically. Organized on the principle of community supported agriculture (CSA), the farm atop our hill sells its produce directly to consumer-members who purchase a share of the season's harvest in early spring. As shareholders, Jeff and I help pay for seeds, machinery, and labor, thereby guaranteeing the farmers' production expenses. This investment is returned throughout the months that follow, in the form of a parade of fresh produce. Our farm, as Faith calls it, also provides us flowers, berries, honey, herbs, and eggs.

Once a week we gather in the barn to collect our share. Some of the crops are picked and packed for us. Some lie out in the fields for us to harvest ourselves.

Along with the food has come other intangible benefits. My four-year-old knows how to pick green beans. She knows about how many potatoes make a pound. My one-year-old can recognize a tomato vine at twenty paces. They both know the joy of fresh raw sugar peas. And I see them coming to understand the relationship between those who eat the food and those who grow it, between the dinner on the table and the land from which the dinner comes. When a summer cloudburst cut short a family expedition last July, my daughter said cheerily, "Our carrots are drinking now."

And our farm provides us a sense of community. Among its hundred or so members, recipes are exchanged along with child care. Last summer, some fathers got together and constructed a children's play area out by the bean fields. Monthly potluck dinners are organized, with offerings so dependably delicious that I insisted on attending one of them when Elijah was only three days old. A year later, at another late-summer farm feast, I found myself dancing with my sweetheart while a bluegrass band played in the barnyard and a yellow moon rose over the fields. Around us, a stream of sticky-mouthed children, including two of our own, ran and scattered in the tall grass.

I thought back to that household budget of ours. "And another thing," I 35 imagined telling our financial advisor, "organic agriculture saves us a bundle on entertainment."

Sources

1. B.P. Baker et al., "Pesticide Residues in Conventional, Integrated Pest Management (IPM)-grown and Organic Foods: Insights from Three US Data Sets," *Food Additives and Contaminants* 19 (2002): 427-46.
2. C.L. Curt et al., "Organophosphorus Pesticide Exposures of Urban and Suburban Pre-school Children with Organic and Conventional Diets," *Environmental Health Perspectives* 111 (2003): 377-82.
3. R.G. Gupta, "Environmental Agents and Placental Toxicity: Anticholinesterases and Other Insecticides," in B.V. Rama Sastry, ed., *Placental Toxicology* (Boca Raton: CRC Press, 1995), pp. 257-78.
4. S. Tarter, "Grapes Struggle in Illinois Due to Chemical Drift, Overspray," *Peoria Journal Star*, April 30, 2002.
5. T. Hayes et al., "Herbicides: Feminization of Male Frogs in the Wild," *Nature* 419 (2002): 895-96.
6. A. Marco et al., "Sensitivity to Nitrate and Nitrite in Pond-Breeding Amphibians from the Pacific Northwest, USA," *Environmental Toxicology and Chemistry* 18 (1999): 2836-39.
7. Cancers found in excess among U.S. farmers include blood and nervous system cancers. Cancers found in excess among their children include brain cancers, leukemias,

Wilms' tumor, Ewing's sarcoma, and germ cell tumors. L.E. Fleming et al., "National Health Interview Survey Mortality Among US Farmers and Pesticide Applicators," *American Journal of Industrial Medicine* 43 (2003): 227-33; L.M. O'Leary et al., "Parental Occupational Exposures and Risk of Childhood Cancer: A Review," *American Journal of Industrial Medicine* 20 (1991): 17-35; J.L. Daniels et al., "Pesticides and Childhood Cancers," *Environmental Health Perspectives* 105 (1997): 1068-77.

8. E.M. Bell et al., "A Case-Control Study of Pesticides and Fetal Death Due to Congenital Anomalies," *Epidemiology* 12 (2001): 148-56; V.F. Garry et al., "Pesticide Appliers, Biocides, and Birth Defects in Rural Minnesota," *Environmental Health Perspectives* 104 (1996): 394-99; R. Munger et al., "Birth Defects and Pesticide-Contaminated Water Supplies in Iowa," *American Journal of Epidemiology* 136 (1992): 959. Birth defects associated with pesticide exposure include cleft lip and palate, limb defects, heart malformations, spina bifida, hydrocephaly, undescended testicles, and hypospadias. See also G. Solomon et al., *Pesticides and Human Health: A Resource for Health Care Professionals* (San Francisco: Physicians for Social Responsibility, 2000), pp. 40-42.

Online Resources

Birth Defect Research for Children, Inc.
Learn more about the National Birth Defects Registry, a research program that studies associations between birth defects and environmental contaminants.
www.birthdefects.org

Beyond Pesticides
Learn more about alternatives to pesticides in homes, gardens, and schools.
www.beyondpesticides.org

Northwest Coalition for Alternatives to Pesticides
Learn more about the hazards of pesticides and their alternatives.
www.pesticide.org

Organic Trade Association
Learn more about the economics of organic and conventional agriculture.
www.ota.com

Organic Valley Web site
Learn more about the farmers and organic products of the Organic Valley cooperative.
www.organicvalley.com

Pesticide Action Network
Learn more about worldwide efforts to advance alternatives to pesticides.
www.panna.org

Robin Van En Center for CSA Resources
Learn more about community-supported agriculture and locate a CSA in
your area.
www.csacenter.org

Questions for Critical Reading

1. What did you take to be Steingraber's thesis? Did her strategy of interweaving elements of both creative nonfiction and a researched argument
ultimately persuade you that her thesis had at least some validity? Why or
why not?

2. Unlike many manifestos, "The Organic Manifesto" has a preface; Steingraber
uses the first nine paragraphs to give us background information on herself
and what led her to write the manifesto. She tells us, for instance, how her
life changed:

> And then I eloped with a sculptor and got pregnant. Now, well into my
> forties, I am wife to a man with a lot of power tools and mother to a four-
> year-old daughter and a one-year-old son. . . . Now, I make my living as
> an environmental writer, analyzing the data of other scientists rather than
> generating my own. These days, my field research extends about as far as
> the backyard birdfeeder, which services migrating songbirds heading north
> to Canadian pine forests or south to Latin American rainforests.
>
> "I'm no longer one of you," I laugh while watching them refuel for their jour-
> neys. I teach their calls to my daughter Faith, to whom I have bequeathed
> my grubby ornithology guide. I whisper their names to my son Elijah, as I
> nurse him in the old rocking chair that is stationed near the picture window.
> (paras. 2–3)

Consider how the manifesto would have worked if Steingraber had dispensed
with this personal information — and the rest of the personal information in
the preface — and instead opened with the point stated at the end of the preface: "I realized it was time to write my organic manifesto, complete with all
the reasons why I believe the decision to buy organic is rational, ethical, and
in the long run, cost-effective. And here it is" (para. 9). Would you have preferred that Steingraber cut to the chase, omitting the personal information?
Why or why not? What purpose do you think the personal information
serves?

3. Recall that writers across genres often acknowledge uncertainty. To gain
insight into when you might want to do this yourself, compare the following
two passages. In the original version, Steingraber acknowledges uncertainty
in the italicized sentences; in the altered version, uncertainty isn't
acknowledged.

Original Passage	Altered Passage
So, are organic foods healthier for our kids? Here is where science yields to mother wisdom. *We in the scientific community do not yet know what levels of pesticide exposure are sufficient to endanger the health of human adults, and we know even less about their effects on children. Thus, the wide gray area called "uncertain risk."* *The reasons for our ignorance are many. When researching my book,* Living Downstream, *I discovered that many pesticides on the market have never been adequately screened for their ability to cause cancer. Even less thoroughly have we tested their ability to affect fetal brain growth, contribute to miscarriages, disrupt hormonal signaling, alter the onset of puberty, or undermine fertility.* Evidence from animal studies suggests we have reason to be concerned about these possibilities and investigate them further. (paras. 11–12)	So, are organic foods healthier for our kids? Evidence from animal studies suggests we have reason to be concerned about pesticides causing cancer, affecting fetal brain growth, contributing to miscarriages, disrupting hormonal signaling, altering the onset of puberty, and undermining fertility.

Which passage do you prefer, and why? In what situations might you as a writer want to acknowledge uncertainty?

4. Some readers might lose trust in Steingraber when they realize there are some objections she doesn't acknowledge. For example, she doesn't acknowledge the research suggesting that nonorganic food is no more harmful to our bodies than is organic food; she could have mentioned this research and then explained why she doesn't find it to be valid. Moreover, she doesn't acknowledge that many small farms practicing community-supported agriculture (CSA) aren't officially organic and yet don't use synthetic pesticides, herbicides, or fungicides. (Recognition as an organic farm requires an expensive certification process that many small farms can't afford. Thus, even though these farms aren't organic, they offer the same benefits of the organic CSA that Steingraber describes in paragraphs 30–35.)

If you were Steingraber, would you acknowledge these potential objections? Why or why not? Do you think the original venue of publication (the Web site of an organic food company) may have influenced her choice not to acknowledge these objections? Why or why not?

5. Use of specific detail serves different purposes in different genres. In researched arguments, specific detail generally supports claims, and Steingraber uses it in this capacity; in creative nonfiction, it often draws readers in, allowing their senses and thus their minds to become more engaged — and Steingraber uses it in this capacity as well. Inexperienced writers sometimes think of detail in black-and-white terms — either you have it or you don't — but in reality, detail lies on a continuum, a ladder with many rungs.

Compare the continuum of detail for the passages that follow; the passages on the left have the most detail, the middle passages have less, and the passages on the right have still less. Consider which version of each passage you prefer:

Original Passage	Less Detailed Passage	Least Detailed Passage
Now, I live in a log cabin in rural upstate New York and have seen the same basswood trees bloom four times. (para. 2)	Now, I live in a cabin in upstate New York and have seen the same trees bloom four times.	Now, I live in upstate New York and have lived there for four years.
The farther I can stretch a dollar, the more hours I have for berry-picking, story-reading, and line dances around the kitchen table. (para. 6)	The farther I can stretch a dollar, the more hours I have for fruit-picking, reading, and dancing.	The farther I can stretch a dollar, the more time I have to spend as I please.

Which version of each passage did you prefer? Why? In your own writing, how will you decide when to use the level of detail that Steingraber does, when to use a little less, and when to use very little?

6. The version of Steingraber's essay reproduced here is the one that was published by Organic Valley; the version published in the magazine *In Good Tilth* doesn't cite any sources. Take a minute to look the essay over again, noting a few of the places where Steingraber cites sources (paras. 10, 11, 16, 18, 23, 25, and 26) and imagining how the essay might affect you differently if the notes were removed. Why do you think the magazine removed them? Which version would you prefer? Why?

Making Connections

7. Recall that creative nonfiction differs from other nonfiction genres in that it uses literary techniques also used in fiction — techniques such as establishing a setting, which is often evoked not only in the opening sentences but also throughout a piece. Consider the following creative nonfiction passages from

"The Organic Manifesto," Flavius Stan's "The Night of Oranges" (p. 429), and Jonathan Safran Foer's piece "Hiding/Seeking" (p. 507). Articulate a theory about why all three authors intersperse details about setting (italicized) throughout their writing:

"The Organic Manifesto"

Looking out at my son stacking blocks *on our back deck, a spring breeze* ruffling the blond feathers of his hair, I wondered what effect this pesticide-laden air was having on the children who were breathing it. (para. 18)

"The Night of Oranges"

The oranges are sold out of the back doorway of a food shop. The clerk has gone from anonymity to unexpected importance. As he handles the oranges, he acts like a movie star in front of his fans.

He moves his arms in an exaggerated manner as he tells the other workers where to go and what to do. *All I can do is stare at the stack of cardboard boxes, piled higher than me.* I have never seen so many oranges in my life.

Finally, it is my turn. *It is 8 o'clock,* and I have been waiting for six hours. (paras. 7–9)

"Hiding/Seeking"

The farm is set up in a series of seven sheds, each about 50 feet wide by 500 feet long, each holding in the neighborhood of 25,000 birds—although I don't yet know these facts.

Adjacent to the sheds is a massive granary, which looks more like something out of Blade Runner *than* Little House on the Prairie. *Metal pipes spiderweb the outsides of the buildings, massive fans protrude and clang, and floodlights plow weirdly discrete pockets of day.* . . . [B]efore me is the kind of farm that produces roughly 99 percent of the animals consumed in America. . . .

The surface is lunarlike. With each step, my feet sink into a compost of animal waste, dirt, and I-don't-yet-know-what-else that has been poured around the sheds. I have to curl my toes to keep my shoes from being left behind in the glutinous muck. (paras. 30–31, 33)

Why do you think each author provided these details about when and where things happen? Considering what you take to be each writer's purpose, do you think each passage effectively integrates details about setting? Why or why not?

8. Like setting, characterization is important in creative nonfiction. Characterization is the means by which writers give readers insight into who characters are as people, including what they value. In first-person pieces such as "The Organic Manifesto," the speaking "I" is generally a central character, and often there are other important characters as well. Characterization can be accomplished in a number of ways, including dialogue and description of a character's thoughts or actions. Consider the effect of

writing

the characterization in the following passages, one from "The Organic Manifesto" and one from Stan's creative nonfiction essay "The Night of Oranges" (p. 429).

"The Organic Manifesto"

[W]hen we all sleep upstairs in the big bed together—one child holding on to my hair, the other flung across my chest, I know that I have never lived more symbiotically. A source of food, a place of comfort, a mattress for napping, I myself am now a habitat. (para. 3)

"The Night of Oranges"

Suddenly I want to do something important: I want to give my brother a big surprise. He is only eight years old, and I want him to celebrate Christmas with lots of oranges at the table. I also want my parents to be proud of me.

So I call home and tell my parents that I'm going to be late. I forget about going to the movie, leave my friends, and join the line. (paras. 4–5)

What do you think these passages reveal about the characters? What do you think is the effect of the way that each writer characterizes himself or herself?

Writing: Your Turn

1. Write a rhetorical analysis of "The Organic Manifesto," discussing how well you think it achieves its purpose for its intended audience. You might discuss a subset of the following (along with anything else you notice): evidence, the credibility of the author, setting, characterization, the interweaving of strategies from multiple genres, use of sensory detail, use of repetition, and use of short sentences interspersed among longer ones. Share what you wrote with your classmates so that they can both learn from it and give you feedback on which parts of your analysis could be more fully developed. For tips on writing a rhetorical analysis, see p. 31.

2. Write a blog post about "The Organic Manifesto." If you have your own blog, think about posting what you write there, or pick a blog that accepts posts from multiple authors, making sure to target what you write to that blog. One possibility is *Organic on the Green* (http://organiconthegreen.wordpress .com), which is often looking for contributions. To learn more about contributing to this blog, go to the "About" tab on the main page and make use of the contact information provided for potential contributors. In your post, you might do any of the following:

- Summarize "The Organic Manifesto"
- Read one of the sources it cites and summarize that source
- Critique "The Organic Manifesto"

Writing

- Discuss what you liked about "The Organic Manifesto"
- Quote a specific passage and discuss that passage
- Discuss another aspect of the organic movement or another advantage of organic food (e.g., taste, nutrition) that Steingraber doesn't mention

After you write your post, share it with your classmates so that they can give you ideas for revision before you go public. For ideas on writing a blog post, see p. 90.

Is Your Eco-Label Lying?

Rebecca Clarren

Published in the magazine *Mother Jones*, "Is Your Eco-Label Lying?"[7] aims to provide readers with enough information about "eco-labels" (such as "natural" and "made with organic ingredients") so that we have a better sense of which labels we can trust. *Mother Jones* is a national newsmagazine that covers politics, culture, and the environment.

Focus on Genre   The following excerpt from the magazine infographic "Is Your Eco-Label Lying?" illustrates not only conventions that are common in magazine writing but also conventions typical of food labels, including the use of small circular or oval-shaped seals. Indeed, seals on food labels might be considered a genre unto themselves; as you read, look for what they have in common and think about the purpose(s) that might be served by these common elements.

Also think about the strategies that Clarren uses for emphasis, including the manipulation of word order and the use of italics. Finally, consider why Clarren (or the magazine editors) may have decided to use an infographic instead of conveying information in paragraph form.

◄○►

---

[7] Note that this article was originally printed in color, with the labels toward the top of each arrow in green ("Biodynamic," "100% Organic," "Certified Organic," "Certified Humane Raised & Handled," "Leaping Bunny," "Certified Biodegradable," "Compostable," and "Marine Stewardship Council"), some labels below them in yellow ("Food Alliance," "Made with organic ingredients," and "Dolphin Safe Tuna"), and the rest of the labels in red ("Natural," "No additives," "Hormone free," "Cruelty free," "Free range," and "Biodegradable"). To see this magazine infographic in color, visit the e-Pages for *Real Questions* at **bedfordstmartins.com /realquestions/epages**.

Is Your Eco-Label Lying?

Sure, it *says* it's green. But what's that really mean?

YOUR SHAMPOO BOTTLE is covered with labels proclaiming that its contents are all natural, cruelty free, and biodegradable, but is that actually true? There are more than 300 eco-labels out there, and not all are created equal. Official-looking seals created by industry groups can be misleading. Reassuring claims may be based solely on the manufacturer's word. And some feel-good terms are so broad as to be meaningless. Below, we peel back some common eco-labels and rate them: Green means clean, yellow is okay, and red means buyer beware.

FOOD/ORGANICS

Biodynamic Demeter's standard for "beyond organic" biodynamic food and wine requires biodiversity and zero pesticides on farms.

100% Organic The real deal for produce and packaged food.

Certified Organic Confusingly uses the same logo as 100% Organic and applies only to packaged foods and wine. Contents can be no more than 5% nonorganic.

Food Alliance Requires farms to avoid GMO veggies or livestock, but they can still use pesticides.

"Made with organic ingredients" The label that gave us (thank God) organic Oreos. USDA requires products' total contents to be at least 70% organic.

"Natural" USDA-approved "natural" meat doesn't contain artificial flavoring, preservatives, or synthetic ingredients. But "natural" steak can still have antibiotics and hormones.

"No additives" Implies a product doesn't have ingredients like Red No. 40 or MSG. Or not—the maker decides what it means.

"Hormone free" Bull. Producers can call beef "hormone free" even if it contains hormones such as testosterone. By law, pork and poultry must be hormone free anyway.

> **GREEN:** Best of the bunch
> **YELLOW:** Better than nothing
> **RED:** Virtually meaningless

ANIMAL CRUELTY

Certified Humane Raised & Handled Meat came from an animal that lived a happy (as far as we know) life with space to move around.

Leaping Bunny Cocreated by the Humane Society, this label is for cosmetics and cleaners without ingredients tested on animals.

"Cruelty free" No set standards.

"Free range" No set standards for beef, pork, or eggs. The USDA lets poultry producers make this claim if chickens have "access" to the outdoors for 51% of their lives, not if they actually go out.

BIODEGRADABILITY

Certified Biodegradable Soaps and cleaners with this third-party-certified label won't hurt fish and will break down quickly.

Compostable This label for eco-plastics adheres to stringent scientific guidelines.

"Biodegradable" Under FTC rules, biodegradable products must "return to nature" when left to the elements. No one enforces this overly broad standard.

FISH/SEAFOOD

Marine Stewardship Council For seafood that isn't endangered or overfished. The only real eco-label for fish.

Dolphin Safe Tuna Means dolphins aren't dying in tuna nets. But sea turtles, sharks, and other endangered species might be.

Questions for Critical Reading

1. What do you take to be the purpose of "Is Your Eco-Label Lying?" For you as a reader, did it accomplish this purpose? Why or why not?

2. In magazine and newspaper genres, infographics are relatively common. Why do you think this is the case? How might you have responded differently to "Is Your Eco-Label Lying?" if, instead of using the infographic, Clarren had conveyed the information in paragraph form?

3. It has been said that "[w]ords carry with them the places they have been"[8]—and we might say the same about shapes and images. Consider the shape of the small circle or oval as it appears in many of the eco-labels. Why do you think this shape—as opposed to, say, a triangle—appears on so many of the eco-labels? What do you take to be the purpose of the words or graphics inside the circles and ovals?

4. Although many genres tend to avoid the second person ("you," "your," "yours"), it's often used in several genres. Compare the original lead (opening) of "Is Your Eco-Label Lying?" to an altered version that doesn't use the second person, and consider why Clarren might have chosen to use the second person (italicized).

Original Passage	Altered Passage
Your shampoo bottle is covered with labels proclaiming that its contents are all natural, cruelty free, and biodegradable, but is that actually true? (para. 1)	Shampoo bottles are covered with labels proclaiming that their contents are all natural, cruelty free, and biodegradable, but is that actually true?

Why do you think Clarren chose to use the second person? Did you have a preference for one version over the other? Why or why not? (Note: if you are considering using the second person in an academic genre, check with your professor first; the second person tends to be avoided in many academic genres.)

---

[8] This is Adam Zachary Newton's paraphrase of Roland Barthes (on p. 171 of *The Elsewhere*, 2005). Newton notes that Barthes bears comparison to Mikhail Bakhtin. A similar paraphrase of Bakhtin appears on p. 535 of Lester Faigley's classic article "Competing Theories of Process: A Critique and a Proposal" (*College English*, 1986).

Making Connections

5. In many genres, writers often use numbers to quantify how common or widespread something is. Consider, for example, the statistics used in the following passages, which are from the introductions of "Is Your Eco-Label Lying?" and Bonnie Liebman's newsletter interview "In Your Face: How the Food Industry Drives Us to Eat" (p. 481). To help you assess when to use numbers in your own writing, compare the original passages with the altered versions that don't use numbers.

Original Passage	Altered Passage
There are more than 300 eco-labels out there, and not all are created equal. (Clarren)	There are numerous eco-labels out there, and not all are created equal.
Two out of three American adults—and one out of three children—are overweight or obese. Why? (Liebman, para. 1)	Most American adults—and many children—are overweight or obese. Why?

How did the statistics in each original passage affect you as a reader? When might you want to use statistics in your own introductions? (Note that in academic genres, readers generally expect writers to disclose the sources of any statistics they cite, and they expect those sources to be credible.)

6. Recall that regardless of genre, how much emphasis a word or phrase gets depends on where in the sentence or paragraph it appears. Consider the following original and altered passages from "Is Your Eco-Label Lying?" and the Wikipedia article "Factory Farming" (p. 527). See if the original passages affect you differently than the altered passages do. Each original and altered passage pair has the same words—just in different places.

Original Passage	Altered Passage
USDA-approved "natural" meat doesn't contain artificial flavoring, preservatives, or synthetic ingredients. But "natural" steak can still have antibiotics and hormones. (Clarren, para. 7)	USDA-approved "natural" steak can still have antibiotics and hormones. But "natural" meat doesn't contain artificial flavoring, preservatives, or synthetic ingredients.
Although being dangerous to humans, CC398 [a bacterium] is often asymptomatic in food-producing animals. (Wikipedia, para. 16)	Although often asymptomatic in food-producing animals, CC398 is dangerous to humans.

Did the difference in word order affect your response to each passage? If so, how?

Now take a minute to find a couple of other passages in "Is Your Eco-Label Lying?" and "flip" them. Do you think that, given her purpose, Clarren's choice of word order was generally effective? Why or why not?

7. Like word order, italics is a tool for emphasis used by writers across genres. Consider the specific purposes of the italics in the following sentences from "Is Your Eco-Label Lying" and Jonathan Safran Foer's multi-genre book chapter "Hiding/Seeking" (p. 507):

"Is Your Eco-Label Lying?"

Sure, it *says* it's green. But what's that really mean? (subtitle)

"Hiding/Seeking"

Now, you said you don't *think* bulls see stationary objects. Wouldn't this qualify, though, as one of those things that you absolutely need to *know*? (para. 17)

What do you take to be the purpose of the italics in these sentences? Would you have responded differently to either passage if italics hadn't been used? Why or why not?

Writing: Your Turn

1. Because "Is Your Eco-Label Lying?" is a one-page article, Clarren didn't have much space to provide a full explanation of each eco-label. Pick two of the labels and do some additional research on them, using what you learn to expand Clarren's explanation.

As with any research, it will help to have specific questions in mind that you want to answer. If you're researching "biodynamic," for example, your research might be guided by the question: what exactly is biodiversity, and why is it important? If you're researching the "Food Alliance" label, you might be guided by the question: what exactly does GMO refer to, and does avoiding GMO vegetables and livestock really make a difference?

After you use your research to write fuller explanations of two eco-labels, share what you wrote with some classmates so that they can both learn from your work and give you feedback for revision (especially feedback on which passages could benefit from even more elaboration).

2. Write a reflection speculating on the meaning of some other claims appearing on food labels (claims that Clarren *doesn't* discuss). If you have access to a kitchen or grocery store, see how many other claims you can find. If not, you might consider some of these claims: "heart healthy," "fresh," "preservative free," "no artificial ingredients," "all natural," "premium," "light," "reduced fat," "restaurant quality," "farm style," "traditionally brewed," "no fillers," "tested quality," "produced under the highest standards of food safety," "made with whole wheat," and "made with real fruit/cheese/meat."

In your reflection, list at least five claims, and speculate on possible loopholes or areas for wiggle room that may exist when manufacturers make these claims. Although you'll just be speculating, this activity will allow you to exercise your critical-thinking skills.

Share what you write with some classmates; see if they have any ideas on possible loopholes that you might have missed, and have fun comparing notes on who is the most cynical. For ideas on writing a reflection, see p. 27.

In Your Face: How the Food Industry Drives Us to Eat

Bonnie Liebman

In Q & A interview format, "In Your Face: How the Food Industry Drives Us to Eat" discusses public policy changes that would address our "toxic food environment." "In Your Face" was published in the health newsletter *Nutrition Action,* a publication of the consumer advocacy group Center for Science in the Public Interest (CSPI). Based in Washington, D.C., CSPI focuses on the issues of nutrition and health, food safety, and alcohol consumption.

Focus on Genre   Although the bulk of this newsletter article is an interview, its purpose is less to inform than to persuade; there's even an overview of its argument at the end of the introduction, just as there is in many academic genres. As you read, bear in mind that readers are persuaded not by content in a vacuum but by how much emphasis that content gets. Recall that journalistic genres often use graphic elements to emphasize content; in this case, consider the effect of the text box surrounding the brief biography of the interviewee. Also consider the two levels of headings. Notice that the interview questions are in boldface, in effect allowing them to work as subheadings, and that on top of these subheadings is still another layer of headings in all caps. As you read, think about how these headings and subheadings draw more attention to the content and, in so doing, potentially increase its persuasive power. Finally, consider the amount of evidence provided to support claims, and notice whether you find yourself being persuaded by these claims.

◄○►

Kelly Brownell is a professor in the department of psychology at Yale University. He is also a professor of epidemiology and public health. Brownell co-founded and directs Yale's Rudd Center for Food Policy and Obesity, which works to improve the world's diet, prevent obesity, and reduce weight stigma. Brownell, who is a member of *Nutrition Action*'s scientific advisory board, has published more than 300 scientific articles and chapters and 14 books, including *Food Fight: The Inside Story of the Food Industry, America's Obesity Crisis, and What We Can Do About It* (McGraw-Hill). He spoke to *Nutrition Action*'s Bonnie Liebman from New Haven.

Two out of three American adults—and one out of three children—are overweight or obese. Why?

The answers are everywhere: In the Starbucks Zucchini Walnut Muffin (490 calories), the Turkey Artichoke Panini at Panera (750 calories), the Wild Mushroom and Grilled Chicken Pizza at California Pizza Kitchen (1,300 calories), and the small unbuttered popcorn at Regal Theatres (670 calories).

Yet many people (not to mention the food industry) blame the overweight for eating too much and exercising too little.

"It's difficult to avoid obesity in a toxic food environment," says Yale University psychologist Kelly Brownell. "There's tremendous pressure on people to overeat."

Excess pounds raise the risk of diabetes, heart disease, stroke, cancer (of the breast, colon, esophagus, kidney, and uterus), gallbladder disease, arthritis, and more. And once people gain weight, the odds of losing it and keeping it off are slim.

"Estimates are that this generation of children may be the first to live fewer years than their parents," says Kelly Brownell. "Health care costs for obesity are now $147 billion annually."

What are we doing about it? Not enough.

"The conditions that are driving the obesity epidemic need to change," says Brownell. Here's why and how.

Q: Why do you call our food environment toxic?

A: Because people who are exposed to it get sick. They develop chronic diseases like diabetes and obesity in record numbers.

Q: How does the environment influence what we eat?

A: When I was a boy, there weren't aisles of food in the drugstore, and gas stations weren't places where you could eat lunch. Vending machines in workplaces were few and far between, and schools didn't have junk food. Fast food restaurants didn't serve breakfast or stay open 24 hours. Today, access to unhealthy choices is nearly ubiquitous.

Burgers, fries, pizza, soda, candy, and chips are everywhere. Apples and bananas aren't. And we have large portion sizes—bigger bagels, burgers, steaks, muffins, cookies, popcorn, and sodas. We have the relentless marketing of unhealthy food, and too little access to healthy foods.

Q: Does the price structure of food push us to buy more?

A: Yes. People buy a Value Meal partly because that large burger, fries, and soft   15
drink cost less than a salad and bottle of water. A large popcorn doesn't cost much more than a small. A Cinnabon doesn't cost much more than a Minibon.

Q: And most stores are pushing junk food, not fresh fruit?

A: Yes. There's a Dunkin' Donuts at our Stop 'n Shop supermarket and at the Wal-Mart near us. And if you look at retail stores, they're set up in ways that maximize the likelihood of impulse purchases.

For example, the candy is on display at the checkout line at the supermarket. And when you go to a modern drugstore, the things you usually go to a drugstore to buy—like bandages, cough medicine, pain reliever, your prescriptions—are all at the back. People typically have to walk by the soda, chips, and other junk food to navigate their way there and back.

OLD GENES, NEW WORLD

Q: You've said that our biology is mismatched with the modern world. How?

A: Thousands of years ago, our ancestors faced unpredictable food supplies and   20
looming starvation. Those who adapted ate voraciously when food was available and stored body fat so they could survive times of scarcity.

Our bodies were programmed to seek calorie-dense foods. They were exquisitely efficient calorie-conservation machines, which matched nicely with a scarce food supply.

But now we have an abundance. And there's no need for the extreme physical exertion that our ancestors needed to hunt and gather food. It's a mismatch.

Q: How do ads encourage overeating?

A: Overeating is written into the language that companies use—names like Big Gulp, Super Gulp, Extreme Gulp. At one point, Frito-Lay sold dollar bags of snack foods called the Big Grab. The burger companies describe their biggest burgers with words like the Monster Burger, the Whopper, the Big Mac. The industry capitalizes on our belief that bigger is better and promotes large amounts of their least healthy foods.

Q: Why do we want a good deal on a bad food?   25

A: Everybody likes value. Getting more of something for your money isn't a bad idea. You like to do that when you buy an automobile or clothing or laundry detergent or anything.

But when the incentives are set up in a way that offers value for unhealthy food, it's a problem. If you buy the big bag of Cheetos, you get a better deal than if you buy the little bag. A big Coke is a better deal than a little Coke. But if you buy six apples, you don't always get a better deal than if you buy three.

Q: Is indulgence a code word for overeating?

A: Right. You deserve a reward and we're here to offer it to you. And ads describe food as sinful. Or we make light of eating too much, like the ad that said "I can't believe I ate the whole thing."

ARE WE IRRESPONSIBLE?

Q: How does the food industry blame people for the obesity epidemic?   30

A: The two words it uses most frequently are personal responsibility. It plays well in America because of this idea that people should take charge of their own lives and because some people have the biological fortune to be able to resist our risky environment.

But it also serves to shift blame from the industry and government to the individuals with a weight problem. It's right out of the tobacco-industry playbook.

Q: What else is in the food industry's playbook?

A: Industry spokespeople raise fears that government action usurps personal freedom. Or they vilify critics with totalitarian language, characterizing them as the food police, leaders of a nanny state, and even food fascists, and accuse them of trying to strip people of their civil liberties.

They also criticize studies that hurt the food industry as "junk science." And   35 they argue that there are no good or bad foods—only good or bad diets. That way, soft drinks, fast foods, and other foods can't be targeted for change.

Q: So people think it's their fault?

A: Many people who struggle with weight problems believe it's their own fault anyway. So exacerbating that is not helpful. But removing the mandate for business and government to take action has been very harmful.

For example, if you look at funding to reduce obesity, it has lagged far behind the extent of the problem. It's because of this idea that people are responsible for the way they are, so why should government do anything about it?

Q: Are people irresponsible?

A: There's been increasing obesity for years in the United States. It's hard to believe that people in 2010 are less responsible than they were 10 or 20 years ago. You have increasing obesity in literally every country in the world. Are people in every country becoming less responsible?

We looked into the literature to find data on other health behaviors like mammograms, seat belt use, heavy drinking, and smoking. All those other behaviors have remained constant or have improved in the U.S. population.

If irresponsibility is the cause of obesity, one might expect evidence that people are becoming less responsible overall. But studies suggest the opposite.

So if people are having trouble acting responsibly in the food arena, the question is why? There must be enormous pressure bearing down on them to override their otherwise responsible behavior.

Q: It's not as though society rewards obesity.

A: No. Obesity is stigmatized. Overweight people, especially children, are teased and victimized by discrimination. Obese children have lower self-esteem and a higher risk of depression. They're less likely to be admitted to college. And obese adults are less likely to be hired, have lower salaries, and are often viewed as lazy and less competent. So the pressure to overeat must be overwhelming.

Q: Are the pressures worse for children?

A: Yes. Kids don't have the natural cognitive defenses against marketing. And they're developing brand loyalty and food preferences that can last a lifetime.

To allow the food industry to have free range with our children has come at a tremendous cost. A third of kids are now overweight or obese. And when you project ahead to the adult diseases that will cause, it's incredible. Someday, our children may wonder why we didn't protect them from the food companies.

Q: Do we do anything to protect kids?

A: We do some nutrition education in schools, but it's a drop against the tidal wave of what the food industry is doing to educate our children.

The Robert Wood Johnson Foundation is by far the biggest funder of work on childhood obesity, and it's now spending $100 million a year on the problem. The food industry spends that much every year by January 4th to market unhealthy food to children. There's no way the government can compete with that just through education.

If parents ate every meal with their children, that would amount to 1,000 teaching opportunities per year. Yet the average child sees 10,000 food ads each year. And parents don't have Beyoncé, LeBron, and Kobe on their side.

Q: So if irresponsibility isn't to blame, what is?

A: When you give lab animals access to the diets that are marketed so aggressively in the United States, they become obese. We have abundant science that the environment is the causative agent here. So the environment needs to be changed.

That's what public policy is all about. We require that children get vaccinated and ride in child safety seats. We have high taxes on cigarettes. Your car has an air bag. The government could educate us to be safe drivers and hope for the best. Or it could just put an air bag in every car. Those are examples of government taking action to create better defaults.   55

KEEPING IT OFF

Q: Why is it so important to prevent obesity?

A: Because it's so difficult to fix. The results of studies on treating obesity are very discouraging, especially if one looks at long term results. The exception is surgery, but that's expensive and can't be used on a broad scale. So this is a problem that screams out to be prevented.

Q: Why is it so hard to keep weight off?

A: There's good research, much of it done by Rudolph Leibel and colleagues at Columbia University, that shows that when people are overweight and lose weight, their biology changes in a way that makes it hard to keep the weight off.

Take two women who weigh 150 pounds. One has always weighed 150 and the other was 170 and reduced down to 150. Metabolically, they look very different. To maintain her 150-pound weight, the woman who has dropped from 170 is going to have to exist on about 15 percent fewer calories than the woman who was always at 150.   60

Q: Why?

A: It's as if the body senses that it's in starvation mode so it becomes more metabolically efficient. People who have lost weight burn fewer calories than those who haven't, so they have to keep taking in fewer calories to keep the weight off. That's tough to do day after day, especially when the environment is pushing us to eat more, not less.

And Leibel and others have shown that there are changes in hormones, including leptin, that explain why people who lose weight are hungry much of the time.

Q: Are you saying that our bodies think we're starving when we lose just ten percent of our body weight?

A: Right. It's not hopeless, but the data can be discouraging. The results of weight-loss studies are clear. Not many people lose a significant amount of   6 weight and keep it off. All these environmental cues force people to eat, and then this biology makes it hard to lose weight and keep it off.

Q: Does genetics play a role in obesity?

A: Yes. Genetics can help explain why some people are prone to gain weight and some are not. But genetics can't explain why there are so many overweight people. The reason we have more obesity than Somalia, let's say, is not because we're genetically different. The fact that so many people are overweight is all environment.

ADDICTIVE FOODS

Q: Are some foods addictive?

A: My prediction is that the issue of food and addiction will explode onto the scene relatively soon, because the science is building almost by the day and it's very compelling. I think it's important to put the focus on the food, rather than the person. There are people who consider themselves food addicts, and they might be, but the more important question is whether there's enough addictive properties in some foods to keep people coming back for more and more. That's where the public health problem resides.

Q: What are those properties?

70

A: What's been studied most so far is sugar. There are brain-imaging studies in humans and a variety of animal studies showing that sugar acts on the brain very much like morphine, alcohol, and nicotine. It doesn't have as strong an effect, but it has a similar effect on reward pathways in the brain. So when kids get out of school and they feel like having a sugared beverage, how much of that is their brain calling out for this addictive substance? Are we consuming so many foods of poor nutrient quality partly because of the addictive properties of the food itself?

Q: What do you mean by reward pathways?

A: There are pathways in the brain that get activated when we experience pleasure, and drugs of abuse like heroin hijack that system. The drugs take over the system to make those substances extremely reinforcing and to make us want those things when we don't have them.

The drugs do that by setting up withdrawal symptoms when we don't have them. The drugs set up the addiction by creating tolerance, so you need more over time to produce the same effect. The drugs set us up to have cravings. The same reward system is activated by foods, especially foods high in sugar.

Q: Do we need more research in people?   75

A: Yes, but we already have animal and human studies, some done by highly distinguished researchers. I think this is a top priority because if we get to the point where we say that food can be addictive, the whole landscape can change.

Think of the morality or legality of marketing these foods to children. Could the industry ever be held accountable for the intentional manipulation of ingredients that activate the brain in that way? The stakes are very high.

Q: How much does exercise matter to losing weight?

A: Exercise has so many health benefits that it's hard to count them. It lowers the risk for cancer, heart disease, and cognitive impairment as people age. There's a very long list of reasons to be physically active, but weight control may not be one of them. Recent studies have suggested that the food part of the equation is much more important than the activity part.

Q: Because you can undo an hour of exercise with one muffin?   80

A: Yes. The food industry has been front and center in promoting exercise as the way to address the nation's obesity problem. The industry talks about the importance of physical activity continuously, and they've been quite involved in funding programs that emphasize physical activity. The skeptics claim that that's the way to divert attention away from food.

ANSWERS

Q: So what's the answer to the obesity epidemic?

A: The broad answer is to change the environmental conditions that are driving obesity. Some of the most powerful drivers are food marketing and the economics of food, so I would start there. I don't think we have much chance of succeeding with the obesity problem unless the marketing of unhealthy foods is curtailed.

Q: Not just to kids?

A: No, but children would be a great place to start. Second would be to   85
change the economics so that healthy food costs less and unhealthy food costs more. So a small tax on sugar-sweetened beverages—say, one penny per ounce—would be part of that effort.

Ideally, the tax revenues would be used to subsidize the cost of fruit and vegetables. That creates a better set of economic defaults. Now, especially if you're poor, all the incentives are pushing you toward unhealthy foods.

Q: Like zip codes where there are no grocery stores?

A: That's a great example of a bad default. Another, which applies not just to the poor, would be what children have available in schools. You can sell a lot of junk in schools and then try to educate your way out of it. Or you can just get rid of the junk food and kids will have healthier defaults. They'll eat healthier food if that's what's available. You can inspire that just by changing the default.

Imagine the optimal environment to combat obesity. We would have affordable and healthful food, especially fresh fruits and vegetables, easily accessible to people in low-income neighborhoods. TV commercials for children would encourage them to eat fresh fruits and vegetables rather than pushing processed snacks that are associated with TV and movie characters. And every community would have safe sidewalks and walking trails to encourage physical activity.

Q: So people wouldn't have to struggle to avoid eating junk?

90

A: Right. We have a terrible set of defaults with food: big portions, bad marketing, bad food in schools. These conditions produce incentives for the wrong behaviors. So the question is: can we create an environment that supports healthy eating, rather than undermines it?

If you count the number of places where you can buy sugared beverages and salty snack foods and candy, it's enormous. If you count the number of places where you can buy baby carrots and oranges, it's a fraction of that.

So if you were creating an environment from scratch, you would do the opposite of what we have. The population deserves a better set of defaults.

Questions for Critical Reading

1. In many genres, the credibility of a source is typically established by a phrase (e.g., "Kelly Brownell, professor of psychology, epidemiology, and public health at Yale Universiy"); however, "In Your Face" provides both the graphic element of the text box and an entire paragraph about Brownell's credentials (p. 482). How much do you think the text box and the bio inside it increase the odds that readers will be persuaded by the rest of the article? Why?

How much of the persuasive effect do you think can be traced to the words? How much do you think can be traced to the box calling attention to the words?

2. The boxed bio establishing Brownell's expertise might be seen as a way to counterbalance the lack of support for some of his claims; recall that unlike many academic genres, journalistic genres often make unsupported claims.

Consider the following claims that Brownell makes, and recall whether you found them persuasive despite the lack of support:

> Kids don't have the natural cognitive defenses against marketing. And they're developing brand loyalty and food preferences that can last a lifetime. (para. 47)

Although you'd be expected to explain how you know this if you were writing in most academic genres, many readers of this newsletter probably *didn't* expect Brownell to explain how he knows this. Similarly, many readers probably didn't expect him to provide supporting examples. Did you find Brownell's claims to be persuasive even though he doesn't explain where his knowledge comes from or provide examples? Why or why not?

3. Consider how Brownell's claims about marketing and brand loyalty fit into the broader argument made in "In Your Face." How would you summarize this argument, and how persuasive did you find it? Why?

4. Recall that journalistic genres often use not just one but multiple visual strategies for emphasizing content. In effect, the boldface interview questions act as subheadings to the superordinate all-cap headings ("OLD GENES, NEW WORLD," "ARE WE IRRESPONSIBLE?" "KEEPING IT OFF," "ADDICTIVE FOODS," and "ANSWERS"). Do you think this extra layer of headings is an effective tool for emphasis? Why or why not? Which of the headings work best for you as a reader, and why?

5. If you look at the article again, you'll notice that some of the sections shift focus toward the end, straying from the topic specified in the all-caps heading. Take a few minutes to find one or two sections that shift focus. If you were an editor at *Nutrition Action*, would you add any additional all-caps headings to address this shift in focus and to emphasize more points? Why or why not? If you would add headings, what would they be and where would you put them?

Making Connections

6. In many journalistic and academic genres, writers try to make their arguments seem motivated by adding tension—by making it clear that there are conflicting views on an issue. When readers know that people disagree on an issue, the writer's argument seems more motivated; in other words, readers see that there's a *reason* the writer is making this argument at this time. Consider the following original and altered versions of the openings of "In Your Face" and Michael Pollan's review essay "The Food Movement, Rising" (p. 435). Compare the original passages (with the tension italicized) to the altered passages, which don't have tension. See if the tension makes a difference in your experience as a reader.

Original Passage	Altered Passage
The [reasons for obesity] are everywhere: in the Starbucks Zucchini Walnut Muffin (490 calories), the Turkey Artichoke Panini at Panera (750 calories), the Wild Mushroom and Grilled Chicken Pizza at California Pizza Kitchen (1,300 calories), and the small unbuttered popcorn at Regal Theatres (670 calories).	The [reasons for obesity] are everywhere: in the Starbucks Zucchini Walnut Muffin (490 calories), the Turkey Artichoke Panini at Panera (750 calories), the Wild Mushroom and Grilled Chicken Pizza at California Pizza Kitchen (1,300 calories), and the small unbuttered popcorn at Regal Theatres (670 calories).
Yet many people (not to mention the food industry) blame the overweight for eating too much and exercising too little. "It's difficult to avoid obesity in a toxic food environment," says Yale University psychologist Kelly Brownell. "There's tremendous pressure on people to overeat." (Liebman, paras. 2–4)	"It's difficult to avoid obesity in a toxic food environment," says Yale University psychologist Kelly Brownell. "There's tremendous pressure on people to overeat."
Washington [DC] had succeeded in eliminating food as a political issue — an objective dear to most governments at least since the time of the French Revolution. *But although cheap food is good politics,* it turns out there are significant costs — to the environment, to public health, to the public purse, even to the culture. (Pollan, para. 4–5)	It turns out that cheap food has significant costs — to the environment, to public health, to the public purse, even to the culture.

Do you prefer the versions with or without tension? Why? When in your own writing might you want to establish tension? (Note that using words such as *yet* and *although*, as in the original passages, will help you establish tension.)

7. Recall that in many journalistic and academic genres, writers often tell readers about the consequences, or costs, of a problem they are discussing. Read the following excerpts from "In Your Face" and from Sandra Steingraber's "The Organic Manifesto" (p. 460); think about *why* both writers might have chosen to enumerate the costs of the problems they were discussing and whether their writing would have affected you differently if they hadn't discussed these costs:

"In Your Face"

Excess pounds raise the risk of diabetes, heart disease, stroke, cancer (of the breast, colon, esophagus, kidney, and uterus), gallbladder disease, arthritis, and more. . . .

"Estimates are that this generation of children may be the first to live fewer years than their parents," says Kelly Brownell. "Health care costs for obesity are now $147 billion annually." (paras. 5–6)

"The Organic Manifesto"

My most beloved landscape, the Illinois River valley near Peoria, is an ecologically diminished place. Poisoned by insecticide run-off, the river's fingernail clams disappeared in 1955. The diving ducks that depended on the clams for their food source soon followed. Ring-necks. Canvasbacks. Scaups. They are all gone now. Then, poisoned by herbicide run-off, the river's lush vegetation vanished from the shallows. Wild celery. Coontail. Sago. The seeds of these aquatic plants fed the river's dabbling ducks. And so they vanished too—the wigeons and the gadwells. By the time I was born in 1959, the riverbank near my home had become an eerily silent place. (para. 22)

"In Your Face" could have simply established the prevalence of obesity, analyzed the cause of the problem, and proposed solutions—all without mentioning what obesity costs in terms of both health problems and actual dollars. Similarly, "The Organic Manifesto" could have simply stated that organic agriculture is better for the environment without mentioning what insecticides and herbicides cost in terms of dead wildlife. Why do you think the authors of both pieces chose to emphasize the costs of the problems under discussion? When in your own writing might you want to emphasize the cost of a problem?

Writing: Your Turn

1. In paragraphs 24 and 29, Brownell does a brief rhetorical analysis of a few product names (Big Gulp, Big Mac) and advertisements for food ("I can't believe I ate the whole thing"). Do a more in-depth rhetorical analysis, listing more ads or product names and describing their common elements. In your analysis, address the following questions (or any others you think are relevant): What assumptions are made about eating large quantities? How does the language make light of eating too much, validate eating too much, or validate eating unhealthy food? Share your draft with your classmates to see what additional insights they can offer. For instance, they might come up with more examples or push you to develop an insight in greater depth. For ideas on writing a rhetorical analysis, see p. 31.

2. Write an argument, addressed to an audience of classmates, that takes a stance on one of the issues raised in "In Your Face." You might address one or two of the following questions: To what extent do we really live in a "toxic food environment"? What do you think is the most important action (or set of actions) we can take to make our food environment less toxic? To what extent is the epidemic of obesity the responsibility of the food industry? As evidence to support your claims, draw on what Brownell says in the interview, other readings in this chapter, personal experience, and/or your own research. Share your argument with some classmates, and ask them how you might make it even more persuasive. For ideas on writing an argument, see p. 42.

From *The End of Overeating: Taking Control of the Insatiable American Appetite*

David A. Kessler, MD

In this excerpt from *The End of Overeating: Taking Control of the Insatiable American Appetite,* former FDA comissioner David Kessler accounts for why North Americans have gained so much weight since the 1980s; he asks, "What . . . happened in such a short time to add so many millions of pounds to so many millions of people?" and he responds by telling us that there's "an unexpected answer."

Focus on Genre   *The End of Overeating* is a trade (general audience) book that synthesizes both primary and secondary research to make an argument about the cause of North America's weight gain. In making his argument, Kessler draws on others' previously published work (secondary research), and he also discusses what he learned from interviewing people himself (primary research). As you read, think about whether you find his primary research or his secondary research to be more persuasive, or whether you think they both contribute equally to his persuasive power.

Since Kessler is making a causal argument, be sure to consider rival hypotheses or other explanations for the weight gain that he doesn't consider. Recall that whenever you encounter a causal argument, it's useful to play devil's advocate and think about other explanations; there are often several causes of a phenomenon, which may or may not be interrelated.

Also notice that, as the author of a book rather than a short journalistic piece, Kessler is able to favor depth over breadth. Although he sometimes makes a new point when he starts a new paragraph, he often takes several paragraphs to develop a single point in depth. As you read, consider what you think of this approach; given your needs as a reader, does he get it right? Does he have a sense of when you as a reader appreciate multiple paragraphs of support and when one paragraph does the trick for you?

Finally, notice how Kessler uses numbers, which often play a crucial role in arguments. Consider how persuasive you find Kessler's use of numbers and whether you would have wanted him to use a table or graph to better emphasize any of these numbers.

◄○►

SOMETHING CHANGED . . . NORTH AMERICA GAINED WEIGHT

For thousands of years human body weight stayed remarkably stable. Throughout adulthood we basically consumed no more than the food we needed to burn. People who were overweight stood apart from the general population. Millions of calories passed through our bodies, yet with the rare exceptions our weight neither rose nor fell by any significant amount. A perfect biological system seemed to be at work

Then, in the 1980s, something changed.

Katherine Flegal was one of the first to recognize the trend, but like many good researchers faced with an unexpected finding, she thought her numbers must be wrong. A senior research scientist at the U.S. Centers for Disease Control and Prevention, Flegal had been studying data from an enormous federal government survey of the health and nutritional status of American households. Her figures indicated that the number of people who were overweight had spiked dramatically.

Researchers had never seen such extreme numbers. In earlier decades, American adults typically gained a couple of pounds between the ages of twenty and forty and then lost a couple of pounds in their sixties and seventies.

The shift that riveted Katherine Flegal's attention came from government survey data collected from 1988 to 1991, which revealed that fully one-third of the population aged twenty to seventy-four weighed too much. In fewer than a dozen years, 8 percent more Americans—about 20 million people, roughly the population of New York State—had joined the ranks of the overweight.   5

Her training and professional experience had taught Flegal to be cautious. In a complex and ambitious survey, errors can creep in at many points, and data often show anomalies that disappear with further scrutiny. She knew her information had to be accurate before she sounded an alarm.

"We checked it to a fare-thee-well," she said, describing her research team's review of regional analyses, time trends, and quality-control techniques. Nothing seemed out of place. The evidence of an abrupt increase in the number of overweight Americans appeared to be valid.

Still, she was nervous, especially since no one else seemed particularly aware that Americans as a group were becoming heavier. Hoping to find studies confirming these provocative data, her team scoured the published literature, but few journal articles were relevant. At professional meetings Flegal casually asked other researchers what they thought was happening with weight in America. Most thought it was the same as it had always been.

Americans were gaining millions of extra pounds, yet at first these pounds remained invisible. The medical community, the scientific community, and the federal government were not quick to notice the trend.

And so Flegal's team wrote up its data and went to press. The study,   10
published in the July 1994 issue of the *Journal of the American Medical Association*, reported that a comparison of current and earlier data on the weight of Americans had revealed "dramatic increases in all race/sex groups." When a respected academic journal calls something dramatic, it's the equivalent of a red alert. The results were consistent virtually across the board—among men and women, young and old, black and white. The rate of obesity in America had evidently exploded.

I asked Katherine Flegal to tell me how average weight had changed over time. Her graphs showed that the population had gotten bigger over the decades. In 1960, when weight was still relatively stable in America, women ages twenty to twenty-nine averaged about 128 pounds; by 2000, the average weight of women in that age group had reached 157.

A similar trend was apparent in the forty-to-forty-nine-year-old group, where the average weight had jumped from 142 pounds in 1960 to 169 in 2000.

Also striking was the evidence that we were entering into our adult years at a significantly higher weight, reflecting the gains that had taken place during childhood and adolescence. And from age twenty to age forty, many of us kept gaining. Rather than a few pounds, the average adult man was gaining more than a dozen pounds in those years.

Flegal observed something else. While on average everyone was getting heavier, the heaviest people in the population were gaining disproportionately more weight than others. The spread between those at the upper end of the weight curve and those at the lower end was widening. Weight gain was primarily about overweight people becoming more overweight.

A shift in Canada, while not quite as dramatic, is equally apparent. Three   15
decades ago, one in ten Canadians was obese. One in four is obese today. And the number of obese and overweight children has jumped 300% between 1981 and 2001.

What had happened in such a short time to add so many millions of pounds to so many millions of people? Many years of research led me to an unexpected answer.

Certainly food had become more readily available in the 1970s and 1980s: We have larger portion sizes, more chain restaurants, more neighborhood food outlets, and a culture that promotes more out-of-home eating. But having food available doesn't mean we have to eat it. What's been driving us to overeat?

It is not a want born out of fear that food shortages lie ahead. Once this had been so. In the Bible, seven years of plenty were inevitably followed by seven years of famine, so we needed to build storehouses of fat in preparation. But in North America, where even northern supermarkets are filled with summer fruits much of the year, that logic doesn't apply.

Nor is it a want rooted in hunger or the love of exceptional food. That kind of logic is not what's driving the out-of-control eating we see.

We know, too, that overeating is not the sole province of those who are overweight. Even people who remain lean feel embattled by their drive for food. For them, it takes the most determined restraint to resist what feels like an almost overpowering push to eat.

Little help has been available. Family members, friends, and colleagues have not had the knowledge to offer support. Many, including doctors and health care professionals, still think that weight gainers merely lack willpower, or perhaps self-esteem. Few medical personnel or nutritionists, few psychological experts or public health advocates, have recognized the distinctive pattern of overeating that has become widespread in the population. No one has seen loss of control as its most defining characteristic.

Those who have succumbed to the pull of food are spending billions of dollars in search of a cure, determined to rid their bodies of the burden of weight. But they are squandering most of their money, finding only short-term weight loss and a vain hope that it will last.

That is because we have not understood why eating certain foods only makes us want to eat more of them. No one has recognized what's really happening. Let me try to explain.

SUGAR, FAT, AND SALT MAKE US EAT MORE SUGAR, FAT, AND SALT

To understand how eating promotes more eating—and why homeostasis is under sustained assault—we must first understand the concept of "palatability" as the term is used scientifically. In everyday language, we call food palatable if it has an agreeable taste. But when scientists say a food is palatable, they are referring primarily to its capacity to stimulate the appetite and prompt us to eat more. Palatability does involve taste, of course, but crucially, it also involves the motivation to *pursue* that taste. It is the reason we want more.

Palatability is largely based on how food engages the full range of our senses. Usually, the most palatable foods contain some combination of sugar, fat, and salt. The sensory properties of palatable foods—the cold, creamy pleasure of a milkshake, the aroma of chocolate cake, the texture of crispy chicken wings sweetened with honey-mustard dipping sauce—all stimulate the appetite. And it's that stimulation, or the anticipation of that stimulation, rather than genuine hunger, that makes us put food in our mouths long after our caloric needs are satisfied. . . .

The combination of sugar and fat is what people prefer, and it's what they'll eat most. The art of pleasing the palate is in large part a matter of combining them in optimal amounts. That can do more than make food palatable. It can make food "hyperpalatable." . . .

* * *

Eating foods high in sugar, fat, and salt makes us eat *more* foods high in sugar, fat, and salt. We see this clearly in both animal and human research.

Barry Levin, a physician and professor at the New Jersey Medical School, demonstrated this principle with rats. He bred one strain to overfeed when a high-calorie diet was available, producing an obesity-prone rat. The other strain did not ordinarily overfeed—an obesity-resistant rat. After a period of eating extra calories, the obesity-resistant rats typically cut back their food consumption much faster than obesity-prone rats.

But when both groups of rats were offered a rich, creamy liquid high in sugar and fat, those patterns changed. All the animals ate without restraint. Levin said that when they were given such a palatable combination, "they will just gorge themselves." Increasing only the fat content of a resistant rat's diet won't make the animal overeat or become obese. But feed it a high-fat high-sugar diet, and it will grow just as fat as an obesity-prone rat on a high-calorie diet.

Variety and ready availability further amplify overeating. Anthony Sclafani   30 was a graduate student at the University of Chicago in the late 1960s when he started trying to understand what promoted excess consumption. When he fed animals high-fat foods, they gained more weight than those fed chow pellets (the bland food that's typically given to laboratory rats), but his results weren't particularly dramatic.

Then, by chance, he put a rat on a lab bench near some fallen Froot Loops, the high-calorie, high-sugar cereal. He was struck by how fast the animal picked up the cereal and started to eat it.

Sclafani turned that casual observation into a more formal experiment. After familiarizing test animals with the taste of Froot Loops, he let them loose in an open field. Rats prefer to stay in corners and won't readily venture across a field to eat chow pellets, but when Froot Loops were available, they scurried over to them.

Next, Sclafani studied the effect of a "supermarket diet." The mix of foods he fed animals could be purchased at any grocery store: sweetened condensed milk, chocolate-chip cookies, salami, cheese, bananas, marshmallows, milk chocolate, and peanut butter. After ten days, animals that were fed the supermarket diet weighed significantly more than rats that were fed bland chow. And the rats on the supermarket diet continued to gain weight, eventually becoming twice as heavy as their control counterparts. Sclafani concluded that feeding adult rats "a variety of highly palatable supermarket foods was a particularly effective way of producing dietary obesity."

Why did they keep on eating? What happened to the homeostatic ability to balance energy consumption and expenditure? Why did rats fail to defend themselves from weight gain?

Sclafani answered those questions in a single sentence: "In the normal rat, free access to palatable foods is a sufficient condition to promote excessive weight."   35

Coupled with evidence collected by other scientists, Sclafani's results support the idea that the biological system that's designed to maintain energy balance can go awry when animals have easy access to a variety of foods that are high in sugar and fat.

Experiments with humans show much the same thing, especially when they're offered foods they prefer. In one study, participants were asked to keep track of the foods they ate for seven days and to rate their preference for each meal on a scale of 1 to 7. Most people gave higher ratings to foods with higher levels of fat and sugar. Unsurprisingly, they also ate more of them, consuming almost 44 percent more food at meals they rated a 7 than at those rated a 3 or below.

In another study, researchers at the U.S. National Institutes of Health confined male subjects to a ward in which their food intake could be monitored. For the first few days the men were fed a diet designed to keep them at their current body weight; since many of them were significantly overweight, that meant an average of just under 3,000 calories a day. (Approximately 50 percent of those calories came from carbohydrates, 30 percent from fat, and 20 percent from protein.)

The participants were then allowed to eat whatever they wished from two free vending machines that contained a variety of entrées and snacks. This gave them twenty-four-hour-a-day access to meats, cheese, and bread; tortillas and pinto beans; cereal, pastry, and desserts; french fries, popcorn, and chips; fruits, vegetables, nuts, and beverages. The men were asked to follow their typical eating patterns as closely as possible.

You've probably guessed the result. Given the opportunity to eat without restriction, participants consumed an average of 4,500 calories daily— 150 percent of what they actually needed to maintain a stable weight. One person consumed almost 7,000 calories, the equivalent of about seventeen quarter-pound hamburgers. In general, the study subjects also ate substantially more fat and less protein during the period of unrestrained eating; the typical diet contained 48 percent carbohydrates, 40 percent fat, and 12 percent protein.   40

All of this demonstrates scientifically what most of us know from experience: When offered a varied selection and large portions of high-sugar, high-fat, high-salt foods, many of us will eat them in excessive amounts.

THE BUSINESS OF FOOD: CREATING HIGHLY REWARDING STIMULI

"Higher sugar, fat, and salt make you want to eat more," a high-level food industry executive told me. I had already read this in the scientific literature and heard it in conversations with neuroscientists and psychologists. Now an insider was saying the same thing.

My source was a leading food consultant, a Henry Ford of mass-produced food who had agreed to part the curtain for me, at least a bit, to reveal how his industry operates. To protect his business, he did not want to be identified.

But he was remarkably candid, explaining that the food industry creates dishes to hit what he called the "three points of the compass." Sugar, fat, and salt make a food compelling, said the consultant. They make it indulgent. They make it high in hedonic value, which gives us pleasure.

"Do you design food specifically to be highly hedonic?" I asked.   45

"Oh, absolutely," he replied without a moment's hesitation. "We try to bring as much of that into the equation as possible."

* * *

During the past two decades there has been an explosion in our ability to access and afford highly palatable foods. Restaurants—where Americans spend 50 percent of today's food dollar—sit at the epicenter of this explosion.

Countless new foods have been introduced in restaurants, and most of them hit the three points of the compass. Sugar, fat, and salt are either loaded onto a core ingredient (such as meat, vegetable, potato, or bread), layered on top of it, or both. Deep-fried tortilla chips are an example of loading—the fat is contained in the chip itself. When a potato is smothered in cheese, sour cream, and sauce, that's layering.

I asked the food consultant to describe the ingredients in some foods commonly found in popular restaurants today.

Potato skins, for example: Typically the potato is hollowed out and the skin   50 is fried, which provides a substantial surface area for what he calls "fat pickup." Then some combination of bacon bits, sour cream, and cheese is added. The result is fat on fat on fat on fat, much of it loaded with salt.

Cheese fries "take a high-fat food and put more fat on top of it," he said. The potato base is simple carbohydrate, which quickly breaks down to sugar in the body. Once it's fried and layered with cheese, we're eating salt on fat on fat on sugar.

Buffalo wings start with the fatty parts of a chicken, which get deep-fried. Then they're served with creamy or sweet dipping sauce that's heavily salted. Usually they're par-fried at a production plant, then fried again at the restaurant, which essentially doubles the fat. That gives us sugar on salt on fat on fat on fat.

"Spinach dip" is a misnomer. The spinach provides little more than color and a bit of appeal; a high-fat, high-salt dairy product is the main ingredient. It's a tasty dish of salt on fat.

Chicken tenders are so loaded with batter and fat that my source jokes that they're a UFO—an unidentified fried object. Salt and sugar are loaded into the fat.

The White Chocolate Mocha Frappuccino served at Starbucks is coffee diluted with a mix of sugar, fat, and salt. The whipped cream is optional.

Bloomin' Onions—the trademark Outback Steakhouse dish—are very popular, and they too provide plenty of surface area to absorb fat. Fried in batter and topped with sauce, their flavor comes from salt on sugar on fat.

Salads contain vegetables, of course, but in today's restaurants they're more likely to be smothered in a cream-based ranch dressing and flavored with cheese chunks, bacon bits, and oily croutons. The food consultant calls this "fat with a little lettuce," although there's salt in the salad as well. Even lettuce has become a vehicle for fat.

I began reading the Cheesecake Factory menu to my industry source. He called the chain, known for its vast spaces and equally vast portions, "an icon of indulgence."

We started with the appetizers.

"Tex Mex Eggrolls: Spicy chicken, corn, black beans, peppers, onions and melted cheese. Served with avocado cream and salsa," I read. The food consultant said that the avocado alone is about 15 to 20 percent fat, and that's before any mayonnaise or heavy cream is loaded in. A fried outer layer wraps fat and salt around more fat.

"Roadside Sliders: Bite-sized burgers on mini-buns served with grilled onions, pickles, and ketchup." The words suggest a cute, little hamburger, but he said there's salt and fat in the meat, and sugar and salt in the caramelized onions and the ketchup. In reality, this dish is fat surrounded by layers of sugar on salt on sugar on salt, making it another grand slam.

"Chicken Pot Stickers: Oriental dumplings pan-fried in the classic tradition. Served with our soy dipping sauce." Frying the pot stickers replaces the water in the wrapper with fat. The layer of meat inside is loaded with salt, while the outside layer of sauce is rich with sugar and salt. "That's hitting all the points," my source said, sounding almost rueful.

"Buffalo Blasts: Chicken breast, cheese, and our spicy buffalo sauce, all stuffed in a spiced wrapper and fried until crisp. Served with celery sticks and blue cheese dressing."

For a moment the food consultant just laughed. "What can I say? That's fat, sugar, and salt." Chicken breast allows us to suspend our guilt because it suggests a low-fat dish, and the celery sticks also hint at something healthy. But the cheese layer is at least 50 percent fat and carries a load of salt, and the buffalo sauce adds a layer of sugar on salt. The dough wrapper—a simple carbohydrate—is fried and so absorbent that he calls it "a fat bomb."

Just as chicken becomes the carrier for fat in the Buffalo Blasts, pizza crust can be a carrier for sugar and fat. Caesar salads are built as an excuse to carry fat and salt. We double-fry french fries, first at the manufacturing plant and then in the restaurant. Our hamburgers are layered with bacon and cheese. We add cheese to spinach, batter our fish before frying it, and slather our Mexican food with cheese. As we do, each one of these foods "become more compelling, more hedonic," said the consultant. 65

As our conversation wound down, he walked me to the door of his office and paused, as if choosing his words carefully. Then, with the certainty of an insider, he observed that the food industry is "the manipulator of the consumers' minds and desires."

WE ARE WIRED TO FOCUS ATTENTION ON THE MOST SALIENT STIMULI

Animals, humans included, seem to have a built-in preference for features larger than those that occur naturally. Ethologists, scientists who study animal behavior, have tried to understand the attraction of "supernormal stimuli."

Consider the oystercatcher, a shorebird with black-and-white plumage, a red bill, and brightly colored legs. Back in the 1950s, Dutch ethologist Nikolaas Tinbergen conducted now-classic studies of the bird's incubation behavior and discovered something astonishing: When presented with a choice between brooding its own small egg and the giant egg of a much larger bird, the oystercatcher invariably chose to sit on the giant one.

Research with the herring gull and the greylag goose uncovered much the same thing. Both of these birds prefer an egg that is biologically impossible for them to have laid.

We also see this with butterflies. When a male is courting, he'll be drawn to 70
the female by the rate at which she flickers her wings. But when a butterfly is

presented with some kind of artificial stimuli that flickers even faster, that's what he'll prefer.

Most of the relevant research about supernormal stimuli was conducted decades ago, although some contemporary writers and scientists have taken on the topic as it relates to food in recent years as well. I wanted to talk to one of the original researchers in the field. John Staddon, now a professor of biology and neurobiology at Duke University in North Carolina, seemed startled to be tracked down as an expert on the subject. "I wrote some stuff on this years and years ago," he told me, surprised that I had uncovered his work.

His early findings seemed to deserve new scrutiny as I considered the possible analogies to food.

Staddon and I talked about the concepts of "asymmetrical selection pressure." From the standpoint of evolution, a bird's preference for a larger egg over a smaller one makes sense. Smaller eggs are more likely to be nonviable, so birds that consistently choose them would not have been likely to survive as a species. Their preference for a giant egg is a logical extension of a preference for the egg that seems most likely to be viable.

I asked Staddon about the kind of food we eat today. "Now I'm eating very energy-dense sugar and fat," I said. "And I've artificially created it. It didn't exist in the wild. Is it a supernormal stimulus?"

It would be, said Staddon. "It is not only exaggerated, it has also never been seen in nature." Those features define the term.   75

"Why do I prefer an exaggerated stimulus?" I asked.

"Your ancestors were punished for preferring a smaller-than-normal stimulus but not punished for preferring a larger-than-normal stimulus," explained Staddon, harkening back to asymmetrical selection pressure. He talked about the "gradient of preference" established by evolution—whether it's a gigantic egg or a hyperpalatable food, a lot seems to be more desirable than a little. An entertainment spectacle, such as Disneyland or Las Vegas, attracts us in much the same way.

Today's choices only push us farther along the gradient. "In the selection pressures acting on the species, more sugar was always better than less," said Staddon. The amount of sugar in food today goes beyond the level we could have experienced naturally—and that just means we desire it all the more.

Questions for Critical Reading

1. Recall that when people argue that there's a single cause for something, there are often actually multiple causes (if indeed there is true causality rather than just correlation). Did Kessler succeed in persuading you that the only cause of our weight gain is the unnatural amount of sugar, fat, and salt in processed foods, or do you think there might be some additional contributing factors? Why?

2. Like many general audience books, *The End of Overeating* supports its claims by referring to published research (secondary research), but Kessler also did his own original (primary) research: he interviewed the authors of published studies as well as a high-level food industry executive. How persuasive did you find this combination of both primary and secondary research? Do you think you might have been *less* persuaded if Kessler had used only secondary research — or if he had only used primary research? Why or why not?

3. Recall that in many genres, including books such as Kessler's as well as a number of journalistic and academic genres, writers establish that there is a gap in our knowledge — something we don't know — and then tell us that their work will address this gap. Consider the end of Kessler's first section to see how well this strategy works for you as a reader:

> Little help [for those who want to lose weight] has been available. Family members, friends, and colleagues have not had the knowledge to offer support. Many, including doctors and health care professionals, still think that weight gainers merely lack willpower, or perhaps self-esteem. Few medical personnel or nutritionists, few psychological experts or public health advocates, have recognized the distinctive pattern of overeating that has become widespread. . . .
>
> That is because we have not understood why eating certain foods only makes us want to eat more of them. No one has recognized what's really happening. Let me try to explain. (paras. 21–23)

How might you have responded differently if, instead of establishing a gap in our knowledge, Kessler had simply started by announcing his topic: "Let me try to explain why so many people have gained weight"? When might you want to make a similar move in your own writing?

4. Although writers across genres emphasize points through visuals such as tables and graphs, Kessler sticks with words. Consider this passage and think about whether, if you'd written it, you would have added a table or graph to complement the words:

> In 1960, when weight was still relatively stable in America, women ages twenty to twenty-nine averaged about 128 pounds; by 2000, the average weight of women in that age group had reached 157.
>
> A similar trend was apparent in the forty-to-forty-nine-year-old group, where the average weight had jumped from 142 pounds in 1960 to 169 in 2000. (paras. 11–12)

Make a guess about the numbers for the thirty to thirty-nine age group, and take a minute to sketch a table or graph that would illustrate the data for all three age groups. If you have time in class, trade visual aids with a classmate for comparison. Would you have included your (or your classmate's) visual aid along with the passage if you were Kesslor, or would you have decided to convey the data through a visual aid alone or words alone? Why?

Making Connections

5. Recall that in some genres — including some journalistic genres as well as the five-paragraph essays you probably wrote in high school — it's not uncommon to see a point discussed in one paragraph and then dropped. In other genres, however, points are more likely to be developed over the course of several paragraphs. Compare the following paragraph from the newsletter interview "In Your Face" (p. 481) to a much longer passage from Kessler's book. Despite the difference in length, each passage makes only one point — the same point, in fact. First, consider the paragraph from the newsletter interview:

> When you give lab animals access to the diets that are marketed so aggressively in the United States, they become obese. *We have abundant science that the environment is the causative agent here.* So the environment needs to be changed. (para. 54)

Now consider paragraphs 27–41 (pp. 497–99) from Kessler's book, and take a few minutes to jot down what you see as the advantages and disadvantages of both the one-paragraph approach and the multiparagraph approach.

When might you as a writer want to use the one-point-per-paragraph approach taken in the newsletter interview? When, on the other hand, might you want to develop a point over the course of several paragraphs?[9]

6. One pattern you'll occasionally see across genres is this: a writer will ask a question and, before answering it, will proceed to tell us what the answer is *not*. In the following passages, you'll see this move being made by Kessler in *The End of Overeating* and by Jonathan Safran Foer in the multi-genre book chapter "Hiding/Seeking" (p. 507). Consider why each writer might have made this move:

The End of Overeating

What's been driving us to overeat?

It is not a want born of fear that food shortages lie ahead. Once this had been so. In the Bible, seven years of plenty were inevitably followed by seven years of famine, so we needed to build storehouses of fat in preparation. But

---

[9] Bear in mind that although the point-per-paragraph approach is common in some genres and the opposite approach is common in other genres, many genres are flexible enough to accommodate a combination approach; Kessler, for example, sometimes takes the one-point-per-paragraph approach, and the newsletter interview occasionally develops one point over multiple paragraphs.

Writing

in North America, where even northern supermarkets are filled with summer fruits much of the year, that logic doesn't apply.

Nor is it a want rooted in hunger or the love of exceptional food. That kind of logic is not what's driving the out-of-control eating we see. (paras. 17–19)

"Hiding/Seeking"

Why would a farmer lock the doors of his turkey farm?

It can't be because he's afraid someone will steal his equipment or animals. There's no equipment to steal in the sheds, and the animals aren't worth the herculean effort it would take to illicitly transport a significant number. A farmer doesn't lock his doors because he's afraid his animals will escape. (Turkeys can't turn doorknobs.) And despite the signage, it isn't because of biosecurity, either. (Barbed wire is enough to keep out the merely curious.) So why? (paras. 37–38)

How did this move — a question followed by what the answer is *not* — affect you as a reader? Why do you think each writer might have chosen to make this move?

7. Even an offhand mention of something (not a main point) can have an effect on a reader. In the following passages, both Kessler and Jonathan Safran Foer happen to mention the length of time they spent working on their books:

The End of Overeating

What had happened in such a short time to add so many millions of pounds to so many millions of people? Many years of research led me to an unexpected answer. (para. 16)

"Hiding/Seeking"

In the three years I will spend immersed in animal agriculture, nothing will unsettle me more than the locked doors. (para. 39)

How did the references to "many years of research" and "three years" affect you as a reader? Why do you think each writer might have included this information?

Writing: Your Turn

1. Write a brochure that summarizes what you see as the most useful information in the excerpt from *The End of Overeating*. Target the brochure to an audience of college students, and be sure to refer to Kessler's book so that readers know where to turn if they want more information. Share what you wrote with some classmates to get ideas on where you might add information, where you might cut or condense information, and where you might refine the design. After you've revised your brochure, distribute it to at least ten *writing*

other people (*not* classmates, who already know the information conveyed in the brochure). For tips on writing and designing a brochure, see p. 105.

2. Write a reflection on the excerpt from *The End of Overeating*. Does any of it resonate with your own experience? If you were persuaded by Kessler's argument about the cause of North America's weight gain, what might a solution (or at least a partial solution) look like? (Note that Kessler does propose solutions at the end of his book; you might decide to read it if you get the chance.) Share your reflection with some classmates to get feedback on which passages you might clarify or develop in greater depth. For ideas on writing a reflection, see p. 27.

Hiding/Seeking

From *Eating Animals*

Jonathan Safran Foer

In this excerpt from "Hiding/Seeking," Jonathan Safran Foer examines factory farming, or the practice of mass-producing animals — raising large numbers of them, often in confined areas, with the ultimate goal of optimizing the production of meat, milk, and eggs. "Hiding/Seeking" is from Foer's first nonfiction book, *Eating Animals* (2009). Foer is also the author of the highly regarded novels *Everything Is Illuminated* (2002) and *Extremely Loud and Incredibly Close* (2005).

Focus on Genre   "Hiding/Seeking" is from a trade book aimed at a fairly broad audience of laypeople. Despite this, Foer takes an experimental approach; he uses a variety of genres and voices. In this excerpt, you'll encounter a visual argument consisting of a rectangle and its caption, a creative nonfiction adventure, a business letter, and oral histories (the italicized first-person narratives that Foer transcribed from his interviews of several people). As you read, consider Foer's purpose in writing "Hiding/Seeking" and whether drawing on this wide variety of genres and voices helps him achieve it.

In addition to using a variety of genres and voices, Foer uses humor. As you read, consider why he might have tried to make us laugh even though he is addressing a serious topic. (Note: to fully appreciate Foer's humor, you'll need to know that Cujo, a dog in a Stephen King horror novel, had rabies and inflicted a reign of terror on an entire town.)

◄○►

Hiding/
Seeking

In the typical cage for egg-laying
hens, each bird has 67 square inches
of space—the size of the rectangle
above. Nearly all cage-free birds have
approximately the same amount of
space.

1. I'M NOT THE KIND OF PERSON WHO FINDS HIMSELF ON A STRANGER'S FARM IN THE MIDDLE OF THE NIGHT

I'm wearing black in the middle of the night in the middle of nowhere. There are surgical booties around my disposable shoes and latex gloves on my shaking hands. I pat myself down, quintuple-checking that I have everything: red-filtered flashlight, picture ID, $40 cash, video camera, copy of California penal code 597e, bottle of water (not for me), silenced cell phone, blow horn. We kill the engine and roll the final thirty yards to the spot we scouted out earlier in the day on one of our half-dozen drive-bys. This isn't the scary part yet.

I am accompanied tonight by an animal activist, "C." It wasn't until I picked her up that I realized I'd been picturing someone who inspired confidence. C is short and wispy. She wears aviator glasses, flip-flops and a retainer.

"You have a lot of cars," I observed, as we pulled away from her house.

"I live with my parents for now."

As we drove down the highway known to locals as Blood Run because of   5
both the frequency of accidents and the number of trucks that use the road to transport animals to slaughter, C explained that sometimes "entry" is as simple as walking through an open gate, although this has become increasingly rare, given concerns about biosecurity and "troublemakers." More often, these days, fences have to be hiked. Occasionally lights go on and alarms go off. Every now and then there are dogs, every now and then unleashed. She once encountered a bull that was left to roam among the sheds, waiting to impale snooping vegetarians.

"Bull," I half-echoed, half-asked, with no obvious linguistic intent.

"Male cow," she said brusquely, as she sorted through a bag of what appeared to be dental equipment.

"And if you and I should, tonight, encounter a bull?"

"We won't."

A tailgater forced me behind a truck packed tight and piled high with   10
chickens on their way to slaughter.

"Hypothetically."

"Stand very still," C advised. "I don't think they see stationary objects."

If the question is, *Have things ever gone seriously wrong on one of C's night visits?* the answer is yes. There was the time she fell into a manure pit, a dying rabbit under each arm, and found herself up to her neck (literally) in (literally) deep shit. And the night she was forced to spend in construction-paper blackness with twenty thousand miserable animals and their fumes, having accidentally locked herself in the shed. And the near-fatal case of campylobacter one of her cohorts picked up from picking up a chicken.

Feathers were collecting on the windshield. I turned on the wipers and asked, "What's all that stuff in your bag?"

"In case we need to make a rescue." 15

I had no idea what she was referring to, and I didn't like it.

"Now, you said you don't *think* bulls see stationary objects. Wouldn't this qualify, though, as one of those things that you absolutely need to *know?* I don't mean to belabor the point, but—"

—*but what the hell have I gotten myself into?* I am not a journalist, activist, veterinarian, lawyer, or philosopher—as, to my knowledge, have been the others who have made such a trip. I am not up for anything. And I am not someone who can stand very still in front of a guard bull.

We come to a gravelly stop at the planned-upon spot and wait for our synchronized watches to click over to 3:00 A.M., the planned-upon time. The dog we'd seen earlier in the day can't be heard, although that's hardly a comfort. I take the scrap of paper from my pocket and read it one last time—

> In case any domestic animal is at any time . . . impounded and continues to be without necessary food and water for more than twelve consecutive hours, it is lawful for any person, from time to time, as may be deemed necessary, to enter into and upon any pound in which the animal is confined, and supply it with necessary food and water so long as it remains so confined. Such person is not liable for the entry . . .

—which, despite being state law, is about as reassuring as Cujo's silence. I'm imagining some roused-from-REM-sleep-and-well-armed farmer coming upon I-know-the-difference-between-arugula-and-rugelach me scrutinizing the living conditions of his turkeys. He cocks his double-barrel, my sphincter relaxes, and then what? I whip out California penal code 597e? Is that going to make his trigger finger more or less itchy?

It's time. 20

We use a series of dramatic hand signals to communicate what a simple whisper would have done just as well. But we've taken vows of silence: not a word until we're safely on the way home. The twirl of a latexed index finger means *Let's roll.*

"You first," I blurt.

And now for the scary part.

Your Continued Consideration

To Whom It May Concern at Tyson Foods:

I am following up on my previous letters of January 10, February 27, March 25 15, April 20, May 15, and June 7. To reiterate, I am a new father, eager to learn as much as I can about the meat industry, in an effort to make informed decisions about what to feed my son. Given that Tyson Foods is the world's largest processor and marketer of chicken, beef, and pork, your company is an obvious place to start. I would like to visit some of your farms and speak with company representatives about everything from the nuts and bolts of how your farms operate, to animal welfare and environmental issues. If possible, I would also like to speak with some of your farmers. I can make myself available at just about any time, and on relatively short notice, and am happy to travel as is needed.

Given your "family-centered philosophy" and recent "It's What Your Family Deserves" advertising campaign, I assume you'll appreciate my desire to see for myself where my son's food comes from.

Thanks so much for your continued consideration.

Best,

Jonathan Safran Foer

The Whole Sad Business

The farm is set up in a series of seven sheds, each about 50 feet wide by   30
500 feet long, each holding in the neighborhood of 25,000 birds — although I don't yet know these facts.

Adjacent to the sheds is a massive granary, which looks more like something out of *Blade Runner* than *Little House on the Prairie*. Metal pipes spiderweb the outsides of the buildings, massive fans protrude and clang, and floodlights plow weirdly discrete pockets of day. Everyone has a mental image of a farm, and to most it probably includes fields, barns, tractors, and animals, or at least one of the above. I doubt there's anyone on earth not involved in farming whose mind would conjure what I'm now looking at. And yet before me is the kind of farm that produces roughly 99 percent of the animals consumed in America.

With her astronaut's gloves, C spreads the harp of barbed wire far enough apart for me to squeeze through. My pants snag and rip, but they are disposable, purchased for this occasion. She passes the gloves through to me, and I hold open the wires for her.

The surface is lunarlike. With each step, my feet sink into a compost of animal waste, dirt, and I-don't-yet-know-what-else that has been poured around the sheds. I have to curl my toes to keep my shoes from being left behind in the glutinous muck. I'm squatting, to make myself as small as possible, and holding my hands against my pockets to keep their contents from jingling. We shuffle quickly and quietly past the clearing and into the rows of sheds, whose cover allows us to move about more freely. Huge fan units — maybe ten fans, each about four feet in diameter — come on and shut off intermittently.

We approach the first shed. Light spills from under its door. This is both good and bad news: good because we won't have to use our flashlights, which, C told me, scare the animals, and in a worse case could get the entire flock squawking and agitated; bad because should someone open the door to check on things, it will be impossible for us to hide. I wonder: Why would a shed full of animals be brightly lit in the middle of the night?

I can hear movement from inside: the hum of machines blends with what   35
sounds a bit like a whispering audience or a chandelier shop in a mild earthquake. C wrestles with the door and then signals that we should move to the next shed.

We spend several minutes like this, looking for an unlocked door.

Another why: Why would a farmer lock the doors of his turkey farm?

It can't be because he's afraid someone will steal his equipment or animals. There's no equipment to steal in the sheds, and the animals aren't worth the herculean effort it would take to illicitly transport a significant number. A farmer doesn't lock his doors because he's afraid his animals will escape. (Turkeys can't turn doorknobs.) And despite the signage, it isn't because of biosecurity, either. (Barbed wire is enough to keep out the merely curious.) So why?

In the three years I will spend immersed in animal agriculture, nothing will unsettle me more than the locked doors. Nothing will better capture the whole sad business of factory farming. And nothing will more strongly convince me to write this book.

As it turns out, locked doors are the least of it. I never heard back from   40
Tyson or any of the companies I wrote to. (It sends one kind of message to say no. It sends another not to say anything at all.) Even research organizations with paid staffs find themselves consistently thwarted by industry secrecy. When the prestigious and well-heeled Pew Commission decided to fund a two-year study to evaluate the impact of factory farming, they reported that

> there have been some serious obstacles to the Commission completing its review and approving consensus recommendations. . . . In fact, while some industrial agriculture representatives were recommending potential authors for the technical reports to Commission staff, other industrial agriculture representatives were discouraging those same authors from assisting us by threatening to withhold research funding for their college or university. We found significant influence by the industry at every turn: in academic research, agriculture policy development, government regulation, and enforcement.

The power brokers of factory farming know that their business model depends on consumers not being able to see (or hear about) what they do.

The Rescue

Men's voices drift over from the granary. Why are they working at 3:30 in the morning? Machines engage. What kinds of machines? It's the middle of the night and things are happening. What is happening?

"Found one," C whispers. She slides open the heavy wooden door, releasing a parallelogram of light, and enters. I follow, sliding the door shut behind me. The first thing that catches my attention is the row of gas masks on the near wall. Why would there be gas masks in a farm shed?

We creep in. There are tens of thousands of turkey chicks. Fist-sized with feathers the color of sawdust, they're nearly invisible on the sawdust floor. The chicks are huddled in groups, asleep beneath the heat lamps installed to replace the warmth their broody mothers would have provided. Where are the mothers?

There is a mathematical orchestration to the density. I pull my eyes from the birds for a moment and take in the building itself: lights, feeders, fans, and heat lamps evenly spaced in a perfectly calibrated artificial day. Besides the animals themselves, there is no hint of anything you might call "natural"—not a patch of earth or a window to let in moonlight. I'm surprised by how easy it is to forget the anonymous life all around and simply admire the technological symphony that so precisely regulates this little world-unto-itself, to see the efficiency and mastery of the machine, and then to understand the birds as extensions of, or cogs in, that machine—not beings, but parts. To see it any other way requires effort.

I look at a particular chick, how it is struggling to get from the outside of   45
the pile around the heat lamp to its center. And then at another one, immediately under the lamp, seemingly content as a dog in a patch of sunlight. Then another, which isn't moving at all, not even with the undulations of breath.

At first the situation doesn't look too bad. It's crowded, but they seem happy enough. (And human babies are kept in crowded indoor nurseries, right?) And they're cute. The exhilaration of seeing what I came to see, and confronting all of these baby animals, has me feeling pretty good.

C is off giving water to some dreary-looking birds in another part of the shed, so I tiptoe around and explore, leaving vague bootie prints in the sawdust. I'm starting to feel more comfortable with the turkeys, willing to get closer to them, if not to handle them. (C's first commandment was never to touch them.) The closer I look, the more I see. The ends of the beaks of the chicks are blackened, as are the ends of their toes. Some have red spots on the tops of their heads.

Because there are so many animals, it takes me several minutes before I take in just how many dead ones there are. Some are blood matted; some are covered in sores. Some seem to have been pecked at; others are as desiccated and loosely gathered as small piles of dead leaves. Some are deformed. The dead are the exceptions, but there are few places to look without seeing at least one.

I walk over to C—it's been the full ten minutes, and I'm not eager to push our luck. She is kneeling over something. I approach and kneel beside her. A chick is trembling on its side, legs splayed, eyes crusted over. Scabs protrude from bald patches. Its beak is slightly open, and its head is shaking back and forth. How old is it? A week? Two? Has it been like this for all of its life, or did something happen to it? What could have happened to it?

C will know what to do, I think. And she does. She opens her bag and   50
removes a knife. Holding one hand over the chick's head—is she keeping it still or covering its eyes?—she slices its neck, rescuing it.

2. I AM THE KIND OF PERSON WHO FINDS HERSELF ON A STRANGER'S FARM IN THE MIDDLE OF THE NIGHT

That turkey chick I euthanized on our rescue, that was hard. . . .

I'm not a radical. In almost every way, I'm a middle-of-the-road person. I don't have any piercings. No weird haircut. I don't do drugs. Politically, I'm liberal on some issues and conservative on others. But see, factory farming is a middle-of-the-road issue—something most reasonable people would agree on if they had access to the truth.

I grew up in Wisconsin and Texas. My family was typical: My dad was (and is) into hunting; all of my uncles trapped and fished. My mom cooked roasts every Monday night, chicken every Tuesday, and so on. My brother was All-State in two sports.

The first time I was exposed to farming issues was when a friend showed me some films of cows being slaughtered. We were teenagers, and it was just gross-out shit, like those "Faces of Death" videos. He wasn't a vegetarian—no one was vegetarian—and he wasn't trying to make me one. It was for a laugh. . . .

I wanted to know if that video was exceptional. I suppose I wanted a way out   55
of having to change my life. So I wrote letters to all of the big farm corporations, asking for tours. Honestly, it never crossed my mind that they would say no or not respond. When that didn't work, I started driving around and asking any farmers I saw if I could look in their sheds. They all had reasons for saying no. Given what they're doing, I don't blame them for not wanting anyone to see. But given their secrecy about something so important, who could blame me for feeling that I needed to do things my own way?

The first farm I entered at night was an egg facility, maybe a million hens. They were packed into cages that were stacked several rows high. My eyes and lungs burned for days after. It was less violent and gory than what I'd seen in the video, but it affected me even more strongly. That really changed me, when I realized that an excruciating life is worse than an excruciating death.

The farm was so bad that I assumed it, too, had to be exceptional. I guess I couldn't believe that people would let that kind of thing happen on so large a scale. So I got myself into another farm, a turkey farm. By chance I'd come just a few days before slaughter, so the turkeys were full grown and jammed body to body. You couldn't see the floor through them. They were totally crazy: flapping, squawking, going after each other. There were dead birds everywhere, and half-dead birds. It was sad. I didn't put them there, but I felt ashamed just to be a person. I told myself it had to be exceptional. So I entered another farm. And another. And another.

Maybe on some deep level, I kept doing this because I didn't want to believe that the things I'd seen were representative. But everyone who cares to know about this stuff knows that factory farms are nearly all there is. Most people aren't able to see these farms with their own eyes, but they can see them through mine. I've videotaped conditions at chicken and egg factories, turkey factories, a couple of hog farms (those are basically impossible to get into now), rabbit farms, drylot dairies and feedlots, livestock auctions, and in transport trucks. I've worked in a few slaughterhouses. Occasionally the footage will make its way onto the evening news or into the newspaper. A few times it's been used in animal cruelty court cases.

That's why I agreed to help you. I don't know you. I don't know what kind of book you're going to write. But if any part of it is bringing what happens inside those farms to the outside world, that can only be a good thing. The truth is so powerful in this case it doesn't even matter what your angle is.

Anyway, I wanted to be sure that when you write your book you don't make it 60 *seem like I kill animals all the time. I've done it four times, only when it couldn't be avoided. Usually I take the sickest animals to a vet. But that chick was too sick to be moved. And it was suffering too much to leave be. Look, I'm pro-life. I believe in God, and I believe in heaven and hell. But I don't have any reverence for suffering. These factory farmers calculate how close to death they can keep the animals without killing them. That's the business model. How quickly can they be made to grow, how tightly can they be packed, how much or little can they eat, how sick can they get without dying. . . .*

3. I AM A FACTORY FARMER

When people ask me what I do, I tell them I'm a retired farmer. I started milking cows when I was six. We lived in Wisconsin. My daddy had a small herd—fifty, give or take—which back then was pretty typical. I worked every day until I left home, worked hard. I thought I'd had enough of it at that point, thought there must be a better way.

After high school, I got a degree in animal science and went to work for a poultry company. I helped service, manage, and design turkey breeder farms. Bounced around some integrated companies after that. I managed large farms, a million birds. Did disease management, flock management. Problem solving, you could say. Farming is a lot of problem solving. Now I specialize in chicken nutrition and health. I'm in agribusiness. Factory farming, some people might say, but I don't care for the term.

It's a different world from the one I grew up in. The price of food hasn't increased in the past thirty years. In relation to all other expenses, the price of protein stayed put. In order to survive—I don't mean get rich; I mean put food on your table, send your kids to school, get a new car as needed—the farmer had to produce more and more. Simple math. Like I said, my daddy had fifty cows. The model now for a viable dairy is twelve hundred cows. That's the smallest that can stay in business. Well, a family can't milk twelve hundred cows, so you gotta get four or five employees, and each of them will have a specialized job: milking, managing illness, tending the crops. It's efficient, yeah, and you can squeeze out a living, but a lot of people became farmers because of the diversity of farm life. And that's been lost.

Another part of what's happened in response to the economic squeeze is that you gotta make an animal that produces more of the product at a lower cost. So you breed for faster growth and improved feed conversion. As long as food continues to get cheaper and cheaper relative to everything else, the farmer has no choice but to produce food at a lower production cost, and genetically he's going to move toward an animal that accomplishes that task, which can be counterproductive to its welfare. The loss is built into the system. It's assumed that if you have fifty thousand broilers in a shed, thousands are going to die in the first weeks. My daddy couldn't afford to lose an animal. Now you begin by assuming you'll lose 4 percent right off the bat.

I've told you the drawbacks because I'm trying to be up-front with you. But in fact, we've got a tremendous system. Is it perfect? No. No system is perfect. And if you find someone who tells you he has a perfect way to feed billions and billions of people, well, you should take a careful look. You hear about free-range eggs and grass-fed cattle, and all of that's good. I think it's a good direction. But it ain't gonna feed the world. Never. You simply can't feed billions of people free-range eggs. And when you hear people talking about small farming as a model, I call that the Marie Antoinette syndrome: if they can't afford bread, let them eat cake. High-yield farming has allowed everyone to eat. Think about that. If we go away from it, it may improve the welfare of the animal, it may even be better for the environment, but I don't want to go back to China in 1918. I'm talking about starving people. . . .

People have no idea where food comes from anymore. It's not synthetic, it's not created in a lab, it actually has to be grown. What I hate is when consumers act as if farmers want these things, when it's consumers who tell farmers what to grow.

65

They've wanted cheap food. We've grown it. If they want cage-free eggs, they have to pay a lot more money for them. Period. It's cheaper to produce an egg in a massive laying barn with caged hens. It's more efficient and that means it's more sustainable. Yes, I'm saying that factory farming can be more sustainable, though I know that word is often used against the industry. From China to India to Brazil, the demand for animal products is growing—and fast. Do you think family farms are going to sustain a world of ten billion?

A friend of mine had an experience a few years ago where two young guys came and asked if they could take some footage for a documentary about farm life. Seemed like nice guys, so he said sure. But then they edited it to make it look like the birds were being abused. They said the turkeys were being raped. I know that farm. I've visited it many times, and I can tell you those turkeys were being cared for as well as they needed to survive and be productive. Things can be taken out of context. And novices don't always know what they're looking at. This business isn't always pretty, but it's a bad mistake to confuse something unpleasant with something wrong. Every kid with a video camera thinks he's a veterinary scientist, thinks he was born knowing what takes years and years to learn. I know there's a necessity to sensationalize stuff in order to motivate people, but I prefer the truth.

In the eighties, the industry tried to communicate with animal groups, and we got burned real bad. So the turkey community decided there would be no more of it. We put up a wall, and that was the end. We don't talk, don't let people onto the farms. Standard operating procedure. PETA doesn't want to talk about farming. They want to end farming. They have absolutely no idea how the world actually works. For all I know, I'm talking to the enemy right now.

But I believe in what I'm telling you. And it's an important story to tell, a story that's getting drowned out by the hollering of the extremists. I asked you not to use my name, but I have nothing to be ashamed of. Nothing. You just have to understand that there's a bigger picture here. And I've got bosses. I gotta put food on the table, too.

Can I make a suggestion to you? Before you rush off trying to see everything you can, educate yourself. Don't trust your eyes. Trust your head. Learn about animals, learn about farming and the economics of food, learn the history. Start at the beginning.

* * *

5. I AM THE LAST POULTRY FARMER

My name is Frank Reese and I'm a poultry farmer. It's what I've given my whole life to. I don't know where that comes from. I went to a little one-room country school. Mother said one of the first things I wrote was a story titled "Me and My Turkeys."

I just always loved the beauty of them, the majesticness. I like how they strut. I don't know. I don't know how to explain it. I just love their feather patterns. I've always loved the personality of them. They're so curious, so playful, so friendly and full of life. . . .

A lot of people slow down when they pass my farm. Get a lot of schools and churches and 4-H kids. I get kids asking me how a turkey got in my trees or on my roof. I tell 'em, "He flew there!" And they don't believe me! Turkeys used to be raised out on fields like this by the millions in America. This kind of turkey is what everybody had on their farms for hundreds of years, and what everybody ate. And now mine are the only ones left, and I'm the only one doing it this way.

Not a single turkey you can buy in a supermarket could walk normally, much less jump or fly. Did you know that? They can't even have sex. Not the antibiotic-free or organic, or free-range or anything. They all have the same foolish genetics, and their bodies won't allow for it anymore. Every turkey sold in every store and served in every restaurant was the product of artificial insemination. If it were only for efficiency, that would be one thing, but these animals literally can't reproduce naturally. Tell me what could be sustainable about that?

These guys here, cold weather, snow, ice—doesn't hurt 'em. With the modern industrial turkey it would be a mess. They couldn't survive. My guys could maneuver through a foot of snow without any trouble. And my turkeys all have their toenails; they all have their wings and beaks—nothing's been cut off; nothing's been destroyed. We don't vaccinate, don't feed antibiotics. No need to. Our birds exercise all day. And because their genes haven't been messed with, they have naturally strong immune systems. We never lose birds. If you can find a healthier flock, anywhere in the world, you take me to it and then I'll believe you. What the industry figured out—and this was the real revolution—is that you don't need healthy animals to make a profit. Sick animals are more profitable. The animals have paid the price for our desire to have everything available at all times for very little money.

We never needed biosecurity before. Look at my farm. Anyone who wants to can visit, and I wouldn't have a second thought about taking my animals to shows and fairs. I always tell people to visit an industrial turkey farm. You may not even have to go into the building. You'll smell it before you get there. But people don't want to hear those things. They don't want to hear that these big turkey factories have incinerators to burn all the turkeys that die every day. They don't care to hear that when the industry sends turkeys off to be processed, it knows and accepts that it's gonna lose 10 to 15 percent of them in transport—the DOAs at the plant. You know my DOA rate this Thanksgiving? Zero. But these are just numbers, not anything anyone gets excited about. It's all about nickels and dimes. So 15 percent of the turkeys suffocate. Throw them in the incinerator.

75

Why are entire flocks of industrial birds dying at once? And what about the people eating those birds? Just the other day, one of the local pediatricians was telling me he's seeing all kinds of illnesses that he never used to see. Not only juvenile diabetes, but inflammatory and autoimmune diseases that a lot of the docs don't even know what to call. And girls are going through puberty much earlier, and kids are allergic to just about everything, and asthma is out of control. Everyone knows it's our food. We're messing with the genes of these animals and then feeding them growth hormones and all kinds of drugs that we really don't know enough about. And then we're eating them. Kids today are the first generation to grow up on this stuff, and we're making a science experiment out of them. Isn't it strange how upset people get about a few dozen baseball players taking growth hormones, when we're doing what we're doing to our food animals and feeding them to our children? . . .

People care about these things. And I don't mean rich city people. Most of the folks who buy my turkeys are not rich by any means; they're struggling on fixed incomes. But they're willing to pay more for the sake of what they believe in. They're willing to pay the real price. And to those who say it's just too much to pay for a turkey, I always say to them, "Don't eat turkey." It's possible you can't afford to care, but it's certain you can't afford not to care.

Everyone's saying buy fresh, buy local. It's a sham. It's all the same kind of bird, and the suffering is in their genes. When the mass-produced turkey of today was designed, they killed thousands of turkeys in their experiments. Should it be shorter legs or shorter keel bone? Should it be like this or like this? In nature, sometimes human babies are born with deformities. But you don't aim to reproduce that generation after generation. But that's what they did with turkeys.

Michael Pollan wrote about Polyface Farm in The Omnivore's Dilemma like it   80
was something great, but that farm is horrible. It's a joke. Joel Salatin is doing industrial birds. Call him up and ask him. So he puts them on pasture. It makes no difference. It's like putting a broken-down Honda on the Autobahn and saying it's a Porsche. KFC chickens are almost always killed in thirty-nine days. They're babies. That's how rapidly they're grown. Salatin's organic free-range chicken is killed in forty-two days. 'Cause it's still the same chicken. It can't be allowed to live any longer because its genetics are so screwed up. Stop and think about that: a bird that you simply can't let live out of its adolescence. So maybe he'll just say he's doing as much right as he can, but it's too expensive to raise healthy birds. Well, I'm sorry if I can't pat him on the back and tell him what a good guy he is. These aren't things, they're animals, so we shouldn't be talking about good enough. Either do it right or don't do it.

I do it right from beginning to end. Most important, I use the old genetics, the birds that were raised a hundred years ago. Do they grow slower? Yes. Do I have to feed them more? Yes. But you look at them and tell me if they're healthy.

I don't allow baby turkeys to be shipped through the mail. Lots of people don't care that half their turkeys are going to die under the stress of going through the *mail, or that those that do live are going to be five pounds lighter in the end than those that you give food and water to immediately. But I care. All my animals get as much pasture as they want, and I never mutilate or drug them. I don't manipulate lighting or starve them to cycle unnaturally. I don't allow my turkeys to be moved if it's too cold or too hot. And I have them transported in the night, so they'll be calmer. I only allow so many turkeys on a truck, even though I could pack many, many more in. My turkeys are always carried upright, never hung by their feet, even if that means it takes much longer. At our processing plant they have to slow everything down. I pay them twice as much to do it half as fast. They have to get the turkeys off the trailers safely. No broken bones and no unnecessary stress. Everything is done by hand and carefully. It's done right every time. The turkeys are stunned before they're shackled. Normally they're hung live and dragged through an electrical bath, but we don't do that. We do one at a time. It's a person doing it, handheld. When they do it one by one, they do it well. My big fear is having live animals put in the boiling water. My sister worked at a large poultry plant. She needed the money. Two weeks, and that was all she could take. This was years and years ago, and she's still talking about the horrors she saw there.*

People care about animals. I believe that. They just don't want to know or to pay. A fourth of all chickens have stress fractures. It's wrong. They're packed body to body, and can't escape their waste, and never see the sun. Their nails grow around the bars of their cages. It's wrong. They feel their slaughters. It's wrong, and people know it's wrong. They don't have to be convinced. They just have to act differently. I'm not better than anyone, and I'm not trying to convince people to live by my standards of what's right. I'm trying to convince them to live by their own.

Endnotes

The identifying characteristics of a character, and the timing and location of and participants in some of the events, in this chapter have been changed.

509. **sixty-seven square inches** . . . The United Egg Producers recommends that hens be given at least 67 square inches per hen. HSUS reports that this minimum is what is typically used. "United Egg Producers Animal Husbandry Guidelines for U.S. Egg Laying Flocks," United Egg Producers Certified (Alpharetta, GA: United Egg Producers, 2008), http://www.uepcertified.com/program/guidelines/ (accessed June 24, 2009); "Cage-Free Egg Production vs. Battery-Cage Egg Production," Humane Society of the United States, 2009, http://www.hsus.org/farm/camp/nbe/compare.html (accessed June 23, 2009).

512. **seven sheds, each about 50 feet wide** . . . These numbers are representative of a typical turkey factory farm in California (or most anywhere). John C. Voris, "Poultry Fact Sheet No. 16c: California Turkey Production," Cooperative Extension, University of California, September 1997, http://animalscience.ucdavis.edu/Avian/pfsl6C.htm (accessed August 16, 2009).

516. *I AM A FACTORY FARMER* . . . This monologue is derived from the statements of more than one factory farmer interviewed for this book.

517. ***4 percent right off the bat*** . . . Mortality rates in chicken production are typically around 1 percent a week, which would yield a 5 percent mortality rate over the life of most broiler chickens. This is seven times the mortality rate seen in laying hens of the same age, and this large number of deaths is attributed largely to their rapid rate of growth. "The Welfare of Broiler Chickens in the EU," Compassion in World Farming Trust, 2005, http://www.ciwf.org.uk/includes/documents/cm_docs/2008/w/welfare_of_broilers_in_the_eu_2005.pdf (accessed August 16, 2009).

Questions for Critical Reading

1. After reading "Hiding/Seeking," what's your stance on factory farming? Are you more inclined to see the issue from the animal activist C's perspective, from the perspective of the factory farmer, or from a middle ground? What did Foer do to influence your belief?

2. Consider the effect of the rectangle on pp. 508–9, along with its caption:

> In the typical cage for egg-laying hens, each bird has 67 square inches of space—the size of the rectangle above. Nearly all cage-free birds have approximately the same amount of space.

Did the rectangle, working in conjunction with the caption, affect you more than words alone would have? Why or why not?

3. Consider why Foer drew on so many genres and why he might have used the following order:

- Diagram of the rectangle with a caption
- Creative nonfiction: "I'm Not the Kind of Person Who Finds Himself on a Stranger's Farm in the Middle of the Night"
- Business letter: "Your Continued Consideration"
- Creative nonfiction: "The Whole Sad Business" and "The Rescue"
- Oral history: "I Am the Kind of Person Who Finds Herself on a Stranger's Farm in the Middle of the Night"
- Oral history: "I Am a Factory Farmer"[10]
- Oral history: "I Am the Last Poultry Farmer"

---

[10] Foer notes that the factory farmer's monologue is a composite derived from interviews with more than one factory farmer.

Given all these genres and voices (an animal activist, a factory farmer, and a traditional poultry farmer), do you think Foer's purpose is to inform us — to help us understand the complexity of factory farming and to help us see the issue from multiple angles? Do you think he's ultimately making an argument about factory farming, and if so, what is he arguing? Why do you think what you do?

4. Recall that humor is used as a tool in many genres. Take a minute to find a couple of passages that amused you, and compare notes with a classmate. How did these passages affect each of you? Why do you think Foer chose to use humor?

Making Connections

5. Many writers who use creative nonfiction strategies write in the present tense rather than the past tense, although both tenses are common. Read the different versions of the following passages, one from "Hiding/Seeking" and one from Flavius Stan's "The Night of Oranges" (p. 429). The original versions are in the present tense, and the altered versions are in the past tense. Consider whether this difference in tense affects your experience as a reader:

Original Passage	Altered Passage
With her astronaut's gloves, C spreads the harp of barbed wire far enough apart for me to squeeze through. My pants snag and rip, but they are disposable, purchased for this occasion. She passes the gloves through to me, and I hold open the wires for her. (Foer, para. 32)	With her astronaut's gloves, C spread the harp of barbed wire far enough apart for me to squeeze through. My pants snagged and ripped, but they were disposable, purchased for this occasion. She passed the gloves through to me, and I held open the wires for her.
I am drunk with the idea of oranges. I put the bag inside my coat as if I want to absorb their warmth. They aren't heavy at all, and I feel that this is going to be the best Christmas of my life. I begin thinking of how I am going to present my gift. (Stan, para. 10)	I was drunk with the idea of oranges. I put the bag inside my coat as if I wanted to absorb their warmth. They weren't heavy at all, and I felt that this was going to be the best Christmas of my life. I began thinking of how I was going to present my gift.

Did the change in tense make a difference in your experience as a reader? Why or why not? If you write creative nonfiction, how will you decide which tense to use?

6. Regardless of genre, your writing will have a more pronounced effect on readers if you're able to integrate both long and short quotations.[11] When working with long quotations, you'll want to use the block quotation format, in which quotations are indented so that readers don't get distracted by wondering whether they or the writer missed the closing quotation mark. Read the following original and altered passages from "Hiding/Seeking" and from the Wikipedia article "Factory Farming" (p. 527). Note that the words leading up to the quotations are the same in both the original and altered passages; it's only the length of the quotations (italicized) that's different. Consider why the authors might have chosen to use long block quotations rather than selecting shorter excerpts to quote:

Original Passage	Altered Passage
We come to a gravelly stop at the planned-upon spot and wait for our synchronized watches to click over to 3:00 A.M., the planned-upon time. The dog we'd seen earlier in the day can't be heard, although that's hardly a comfort. I take the scrap of paper from my pocket and read it one last time— *In case any domestic animal is at any time . . . impounded and continues to be without necessary food and water for more than twelve consecutive hours, it is lawful for any person, from time to time, as may be deemed necessary, to enter into and upon any pound in which the animal is confined, and supply it with necessary food and water so long as it remains so confined. Such person is not liable for the entry . . .* —which, despite being state law, is about as reassuring as Cujo's silence. (Foer, para. 19)	We come to a gravelly stop at the planned-upon spot and wait for our synchronized watches to click over to 3:00 A.M., the planned-upon time. The dog we'd seen earlier in the day can't be heard, although that's hardly a comfort. I take the scrap of paper from my pocket and read it one last time— *"In case any domestic animal is . . . impounded and continues to be without necessary food and water for more than twelve consecutive hours, it is lawful for any person . . . to enter . . . any pound"* —which, despite being state law, is about as reassuring as Cujo's silence.

---

[11] What counts as "long" depends on the citation style you're using; MLA, for instance, considers "long" to be over four lines, while the cut-off for APA is over forty words. To indent a long (block) quotation, simply go to a new line, type the quotation, select it, and then use the ruler at the top of your screen to drag it an inch for MLA and a half inch for APA. Note that regardless of the citation style you're using, if you're writing an academic genre, it's important to provide page numbers after all quotations. If you're not using a block quotation and the quotation comes at the end of your sentence, put the period *after* the page number in parentheses; if you're using a block quotation, however, put the period *before* the page number in parentheses. Also note that regardless of what citation style you're using, you don't need quotation marks with block quotations; the indentation is what marks it as a quotation.

Original Passage	Altered Passage
At one farm (Farm 2105) run by Carrolls Foods of North Carolina, the second-largest pig producer in the U.S., twenty pigs are kept per pen and each confinement building or "hog parlor" holds 25 pens. The company's chief executive officer, F.J. "Sonny" Faison, . . . states: *They're in state-of-the-art confinement facilities. The conditions that we keep these animals in are much more humane than when they were out in the field. Today they're in housing that is environmentally controlled in many respects. And the feed is right there for them all the time, and water, fresh water. They're looked after in some of the best conditions, because the healthier and [more] content that animal, the better it grows. So we're very interested in their well-being—up to an extent.* (Wikipedia, para. 4)	At one farm (Farm 2105) run by Carrolls Foods of North Carolina, the second-largest pig producer in the U.S., twenty pigs are kept per pen and each confinement building or "hog parlor" holds 25 pens. The company's chief executive officer, F.J. "Sonny" Faison, . . . states: *"They're in state-of-the-art confinement facilities. The conditions that we keep these animals in are much more humane than when they were out in the field."*

Why do you think each author chose to quote the long passage rather than selecting a shorter excerpt? How will you as a writer decide when to use a long quotation and when to use a shorter excerpt?

Writing: Your Turn

1. Drawing on Foer—including the oral histories that he provides—make an argument addressed to an audience of classmates that takes a stance on factory farming. As with any argument, you don't necessarily need to take a position on one pole or another ("Factory farming is wrong" or "Factory farming is necessary"); instead, feel free to make a more nuanced argument that recognizes complexity and acknowledges objections. Share what you wrote with your classmates to get ideas on how you might add even more evidence and address any objections that you may not have originally anticipated. For ideas on writing an argument, see p. 42.

2. Write a rhetorical analysis of "Hiding/Seeking." Taking into consideration Foer's purpose and audience, analyze how effectively he uses language. In your analysis, you might consider any combination of the following (as well as anything else you notice): paragraph length; use of multiple genres and points of view; and use of dialogue, suspense, characterization, humor, verbs, detail, and punctuation (including dashes and colons).

Share your rhetorical analysis with some classmates so that they can both learn from it and give you feedback on places where you might need to provide more evidence (in the form of quotations) or places where you might need to more thoroughly analyze your evidence (explain how you arrived at your interpretation of the quotations). For ideas on writing a rhetorical analysis, see p. 31.

Factory Farming

Wikipedia

This excerpted Wikipedia article discusses several aspects of factory farming, including the ethical issues involved, the exemption of farmed animals from animal cruelty laws, and the impact of factory farming on both the environment and human and animal health. Launched in 2001, Wikipedia is one of the most popular sites on the web, receiving about 2.7 billion page views per month in the United States alone.[12]

Focus on Genre   As a Wikipedia article, "Factory Farming" is available on the web to be read—or revised—by anyone at any time. Wikipedia provides a good example of how changes in technology can lead to changes in genres; because technology allows anyone to add to a Wikipedia article at any time, these articles are sometimes substantially longer than other online encyclopedia articles. (However, sometimes Wikipedia articles are short since the amount—and quality—of the information provided depends on who has the time and interest to contribute to any given article.)

Consider additional ways that the technological advances necessary to allow open, multiple authorship might influence what you read on Wikipedia. Note whether there is any repetition in "Factory Farming," and notice whether paragraphs and sections maintain a sharp focus or shift focus. Do you think that having open, multiple authorship might affect an article's organization and focus?

Just as anyone can add words to Wikipedia, so too can anyone add photographs. Photographs are an important aspect of Wikipedia since they, along with other visual elements, have the potential to shape a reader's opinion. As you read, take note of how the three photos shape your experience as a reader. Finally, consider the paradox of Wikipedia: because everyone in the world with web access can contribute, there's a lot of expertise and knowledge—but because everyone in the world with web access can contribute, readers don't always know how much they should trust the information provided. How will this paradox affect your reading?

◄○►

---

[12] From Hunter Walk's *TechCrunch* article "Please Read: A Personal Appeal to Wikipedia Founder Jimmy Wales" (available at http://techcrunch.com/2011/02/05/wikipedia-affiliate-links; published on February 5, 2011, and accessed on August 20, 2012).

Factory farming is a term referring to the process of raising
livestock in confinement at high
stocking density, where a farm
operates as a factory — a practice
typical in industrial farming by
agribusinesses.[1,2,3,4,5] The main
product of this industry is meat,
milk and eggs for human consumption.[6] However, there have
been issues regarding whether
factory farming is sustainable and
ethical.[7]

A commercial chicken house raising broiler pullets
for meat.

Confinement at high stocking
density is one part of a systematic
effort to produce the highest output at the lowest cost by relying
on economies of scale, modern
machinery, biotechnology, and
global trade. Confinement at high
stocking density requires antibiotics and pesticides to mitigate the
spread of disease and pestilence

Factory farming near Hemelte, Germany

exacerbated by these crowded living conditions.[8] In addition, antibiotics are
used to stimulate livestock growth by killing intestinal bacteria.[9] There are differences in the way factory farming techniques are practiced around the world.
There is a continuing debate over the benefits and risks of factory farming. The
issues include the efficiency of food production; animal welfare; whether it is
essential for feeding the growing global human population; the environmental
impact and the health risks.

Distinctive Characteristics

Factory farms hold large numbers of animals, typically cows, pigs, turkeys, or
chickens, often indoors, typically at high densities. The aim of the operation
is to produce as much meat, eggs, or milk at the lowest possible cost. Food
is supplied in place, and a wide variety of artificial methods are employed to
maintain animal health and improve production, such as the use of antimicrobial agents, vitamin supplements, and growth hormones. Physical restraints
are used to control movement or actions regarded as undesirable. Breeding
programs are used to produce animals more suited to the confined conditions
and able to provide a consistent food product. *citation needed*

The distinctive characteristic of factory farms is the intense concentration of livestock. At one farm (Farm 2105) run by Carrolls Foods of North Carolina, the second-largest pig producer in the U.S., twenty pigs are kept per pen and each confinement building or "hog parlor" holds 25 pens.[10] The company's chief executive officer, F.J. "Sonny" Faison, has said, "It's all a supply-and-demand price question . . .

Cows in a factory farm in the U.S.

The meat business in this country is just about perfect, uncontrolled supply-and-demand free enterprise. And it continues to get more and more sophisticated, based on science. Only the least-cost producer survives in agriculture."[11] Faison states:

> They're in state-of-the-art confinement facilities. The conditions that we keep these animals in are much more humane than when they are out in the field. Today they're in housing that is environmentally controlled in many respects. And the feed is right there for them all the time, and water, fresh water. They're looked after in some of the best conditions, because the healthier and [more] content that animal, the better it grows. So we're very interested in their well-being—up to an extent.[12]

KEY ISSUES

Ethics

The large concentration of animals, animal waste, and the potential for dead animals in a small space poses ethical issues. It is recognized that some techniques used to sustain intensive agriculture can be cruel to animals.[13] As awareness of the problems of intensive techniques has grown, there have been some efforts by governments and industry to remove inappropriate techniques.

Farm Sanctuary defines factory farming as "an attitude that regards animals and the natural world merely as commodities to be exploited for profit." The group contends "this attitude has led to institutionalized animal cruelty, massive environmental destruction and resource depletion, and animal and human health risks.[14]

In the UK, the Farm Animal Welfare Council was set up by the government to act as an independent advisor on animal welfare in 1979[15] and expresses

5

its policy as five freedoms: from hunger and thirst; from discomfort; from pain, injury, or disease; to express normal behavior; from fear and distress.

There are differences around the world as to which practices are accepted and there continue to be changes in regulations with animal welfare being a strong driver for increased regulation. For example, the EU is bringing in further regulation to set maximum stocking densities for meat chickens by 2010, where the UK Animal Welfare Minister commented, "The welfare of meat chickens is a major concern to people throughout the European Union. This agreement sends a strong message to the rest of the world that we care about animal welfare."[16]

However, given the assumption that intensive farming techniques are a necessity, it is recognized that some apparently cruel techniques are better than the alternative. For example, in the UK, debeaking of chickens is deprecated, but it is recognized that it is a method of last resort, seen as better than allowing vicious fighting and ultimately cannibalism.[13] Between 60 and 70 percent[17] of six million breeding sows in the U.S. are confined during pregnancy, and for most of their adult lives, in 2 ft (0.61 m) by 7 ft (2.1 m) gestation crates.[3,18] According to pork producers and many veterinarians, sows will fight if housed in pens. The largest pork producer in the U.S. said in January 2007 that it will phase out gestation crates by 2017.[3] They are being phased out in the European Union, with a ban effective in 2013 after the fourth week of pregnancy.[19] With the evolution of factory farming, there has been a growing awareness of the issues amongst the wider public, not least due to the efforts of animal rights and welfare campaigners.[20] As a result gestation crates, one of the more contentious practices, are the subject of laws in the U.S.,[21] Europe[22] and around the world to phase out their use as a result of pressure to adopt less confined practices.

Human Health Impact

According to the U.S. Centers for Disease Control and Prevention (CDC),   10
farms on which animals are intensively reared can cause adverse health reactions in farm workers. Workers may develop acute and chronic lung disease, musculoskeletal injuries, and may catch infections that transmit from animals to humans (such as tuberculosis).[23]

Pesticides are used to control organisms which are considered harmful[24] and they save farmers money by preventing product losses to pests.[25] In the US, about a quarter of pesticides used are used in houses, yards, parks, golf courses, and swimming pools[26] and about 70% are used in agriculture.[25] However, pesticides can make their way into consumers' bodies which can cause health problems. One source of this is bioaccumulation in animals raised on factory farms.[27,28]

The CDC writes that chemical, bacterial, and viral compounds from animal waste may travel in the soil and water. Residents near such farms report problems such as unpleasant smell, flies and adverse health effects.[29]

The CDC has identified a number of pollutants associated with the discharge of animal waste into rivers and lakes, and into the air. The use of antibiotics may create antibiotic-resistant pathogens; parasites, bacteria, and viruses may be spread; ammonia, nitrogen, and phosphorus can reduce oxygen in surface waters and contaminate drinking water; pesticides and hormones may cause hormone-related changes in fish; animal feed and feathers may stunt the growth of desirable plants in surface waters and provide nutrients to disease-causing micro-organisms; trace elements such as arsenic and copper, which are harmful to human health, may contaminate surface waters.[29]

In the European Union, growth hormones are banned on the basis that there is no way of determining a safe level. The UK has stated that in the event of the EU raising the ban at some future date, to comply with a precautionary approach, it would only consider the introduction of specific hormones, proven on a case by case basis.[30] In 1998, the European Union banned feeding animals antibiotics that were found to be valuable for human health. Furthermore, in 2006 the European Union banned all drugs for livestock that were used for growth promotion purposes. As a result of these bans, the levels of antibiotic resistance in animal products and within the human population showed a decrease.[31,32]

The various techniques of factory farming have been associated with a number of European incidents where public health has been threatened or large numbers of animals have had to be slaughtered to deal with disease. Where disease breaks out, it may spread more quickly, not only due to the concentrations of animals, but because modern approaches tend to distribute animals more widely.[33, citation needed] The international trade in animal products increases the risk of global transmission of virulent diseases such as swine fever,[34] BSE, foot and mouth and bird flu.

Methicillin-resistant Staphylococcus aureus (MRSA) has been identified in pigs and humans raising concerns about the role of pigs as reservoirs of MRSA for human infection. One study found that 20% of pig farmers in the United States and Canada in 2007 harbored MRSA.[35] A second study revealed that 81% of Dutch pig farms had pigs with MRSA and 39% of animals at slaughter carried the bug where all of the infections were resistant to tetracycline and many were resistant to other antimicrobials.[36] A more recent study found that MRSA ST398 isolates were less susceptible to tiamulin, an antimicrobial used in agriculture, than other MRSA or Methicillin susceptible S. aureus.[37] Cases of MRSA have increased in livestock animals. CC398 is a new clone of MRSA that has emerged in animals and is found in intensively reared production animals (primarily pigs, but also cattle and poultry), where it can be transmitted to humans. Although being dangerous to humans, CC398 is often asymptomatic in food-producing animals.[38]

A 2011 study reported that according to a nationwide study nearly half of the meat and poultry sold in U.S. grocery stores—47 percent—was contaminated with S. aureus, and more than half of those bacteria—52 percent—were resistant to at least three classes of antibiotics. Although Staph should be killed with proper cooking, it may still pose a risk to consumers through improper food handling and cross-contamination in the kitchen. The senior author of the study said, "The fact that drug-resistant S. aureus was so prevalent, and likely came from the food animals themselves, is troubling, and demands attention to how antibiotics are used in food-animal production today."[39]

In April 2009, lawmakers in the Mexican state of Veracruz accused large-scale hog and poultry operations of being breeding grounds of a pandemic swine flu, although they did not present scientific evidence to support their claim. A swine flu which quickly killed more than 100 infected persons in that area, appears to have begun in the vicinity of a Smithfield subsidiary pig CAFO (concentrated animal feeding operation).[40]

Animal Health Impact

Confinement and overcrowding of animals results in a lack of exercise and natural locomotory behavior, which weakens their bones and muscles. An intensive poultry farm provides the optimum conditions for viral mutation and transmission—thousands of birds crowded together in a closed, warm, and dusty environment is highly conducive to the transmission of a contagious disease. Selecting generations of birds for their faster growth rates and higher meat yields has left birds' immune systems less able to cope with infections and there is a high degree of genetic uniformity in the population, making the spread of disease more likely. Further intensification of the industry has been suggested by some as the solution to avian flu, on the rationale that keeping birds indoors will prevent contamination. However, this relies on perfect fail-safe biosecurity—and such measures are near impossible to implement. Movement between farms by people, materials, and vehicles poses a threat and breaches in biosecurity are possible. Intensive farming may be creating highly virulent avian flu strains. With the frequent flow of goods within and between countries, the potential for disease spread is high.[41] Confinement and overcrowding of animals' environment presents the risk of contamination of the meat from viruses and bacteria. Feedlot animals reside in crowded conditions and often spend their time standing in their own waste.[42] A dairy farm with 2,500 cows may produce as much waste as a city of 411,000 people, and unlike a city in which human waste ends up at a sewage treatment plant, livestock waste is not treated. As a result, feedlot animals have the potential of exposure to various viruses and bacteria via the manure and urine in their environment. Furthermore, the animals often have residual manure on their bodies when they go to slaughter.[43]

Confinement at high stocking density requires antibiotics and pesticides to mitigate the spread of disease and pestilence exacerbated by these crowded living conditions.[8] In addition, antibiotics are used to stimulate livestock growth by killing intestinal bacteria.[9] According to a February 2011 FDA report, nearly 29 million pounds of antimicrobials were sold in 2009 for both therapeutic and non-therapeutic use for all farm animal species.[44] The Union of Concerned Scientists estimates that 70% of that amount is for non-therapeutic use.[45]

Environmental Impact

Concentrating large numbers of animals in factory farms is a major contribution to global environmental degradation, through the need to grow feed (often by intensive methods using excessive fertiliser and pesticides), pollution of water, soil and air by agrochemicals and manure waste, and use of limited resources (water, energy).[46]

Livestock production is also particularly water-intensive in indoor, intensive systems. Eight percent of global human water use goes towards animal production, including water used to irrigate feed crops.[46]

Industrial production of pigs and poultry is an important source of GHG [green house gas] emissions and is predicted to become more so. On intensive pig farms, the animals are generally kept on concrete with slats or grates for the manure to drain through. The manure is usually stored in slurry form (slurry is a liquid mixture of urine and faeces). During storage on farm, slurry emits methane and when manure is spread on fields it emits nitrous oxide and causes nitrogen pollution of land and water. Poultry manure from factory farms emits high levels of nitrous oxide and ammonia.[46]

Organic pig meat production has a lower global warming potential per kg than does intensive pig meat production. The energy input for free-range poultry meat and eggs is higher than for factory-farmed poultry meat and eggs, but GHG emissions are lower.[46]

Environmental impacts of factory farming can include:

- Deforestation for animal feed production
- Unsustainable pressure on land for production of high-protein/high-energy animal feed

- Pesticide, herbicide and fertilizer manufacture and use for feed production
- Unsustainable use of water for feed-crops, including groundwater extraction
- Pollution of soil, water and air by nitrogen and phosphorus from fertiliser used for feed-crops and from manure
- Land degradation (reduced fertility, soil compaction, increased salinity, desertification)
- Loss of biodiversity due to eutrophication, acidification, pesticides and herbicides
- Worldwide reduction of genetic diversity of livestock and loss of traditional breeds
- Species extinctions due to livestock-related habitat destruction (especially feed-cropping)[46]

Animal Welfare Impact

Animal welfare impacts of factory farming can include:

- Close confinement systems (cages, crates) or lifetime confinement in indoor sheds
- Discomfort and injuries caused by inappropriate flooring and housing
- Restriction or prevention of normal exercise and most of natural foraging or exploratory behaviour
- Restriction or prevention of natural maternal nesting behaviour
- Lack of daylight or fresh air and poor air quality in animal sheds
- Social stress and injuries caused by overcrowding
- Health problems caused by extreme selective breeding and management for fast growth and high productivity
- Reduced lifetime (longevity) of breeding animals (dairy cows, breeding cows)
- Fast-spreading infections encouraged by crowding and stress in intensive conditions[46]
- Debeaking (beak trimming or shortening) in the poultry and egg industry to avoid pecking in overcrowded quarters[47]
- Sexual and physical abuse at the hands of workers[48]
- Forced and over feeding (by inserting tubes into the throats of ducks) in the production of foie gras[49]

Labor

Small farmers are often absorbed into factory farm operations, acting as contract growers for the industrial facilities. In the case of poultry contract growers, farmers are required to make costly investments in construction of sheds to house the birds, buy required feed and drugs—often settling for slim profit margins, or even losses. Factory farm workers also cite the repetitive actions and high line speeds that are features of the large-scale slaughtering and processing facilities that characterize the factory farming poultry sectors, as causing injuries and illness to workers.[50] Forced labor is another problem encountered in factory farming system. Greenpeace's report Eating Up the Amazon described a set of poor labor conditions at Roncador Farm in Mato Grosso, where workers are responsible for maintaining more than 100,000 cattle and 4,000 ha (9,000 ac) of soybeans: "Working 16 hours a day, seven days a week, the laborers were forced to live in plastic shanties with no beds or sanitary provision. Water for washing, cooking and drinking came from a cattle watering hole and was stored in barrels previously used for diesel oil and lubricants. There was no opportunity to leave the farm. Goods had to be bought from the farm shop at extortionate prices, putting laborers into ever-increasing debt, which they would never be able to pay off—a form of slavery known as debt bondage."[51]

FARMED ANIMALS AND THE LAW

Main Article: Animal Law

In the United States, farmed animals are excluded by half of all state animal cruelty laws including the federal Animal Welfare Act. The 28 hour law, enacted in 1873 and amended in 1994 states that when animals are being transported for slaughter, the vehicle must stop every 28 hours and the animals must be let out for exercise, food, and water. The United States Department of Agriculture claims that the law does not apply to birds. The Humane Methods of Livestock Slaughter Act is similarly limited. Originally passed in 1958, the Act requires that livestock be stunned into unconsciousness prior to slaughter. This Act also excludes birds, who make up more than 90 percent of the animals slaughtered for food, as well as rabbits and fish. Individual states all have their own animal cruelty statutes; however many states have a provision to exempt standard agricultural practices.[52]

Notes

1. Sources discussing "intensive farming," "intensive agriculture," or "factory farming":
   - Fraser, David. *Animal welfare and the intensification of animal production: An alternative interpretation*, Food and Agriculture Organization of the United Nations, 2005.
   - Turner, Jacky. "History of factory farming," United Nations: "Fifty years ago in Europe, intensification of animal production was seen as the road to national food security and a better diet . . . The **intensive systems**—called '**factory farms**'—were characterised by confinement of the animals at high stocking density, often in barren and unnatural conditions."

- Simpson, John. "Why the organic revolution had to happen," *The Observer*, April 21, 2001: "Nor is a return to 'primitive' farming practices the only alternative to **factory farming** and highly **intensive agriculture.**"
- Baker, Stanley. "Factory farms — the only answer to our growing appetite?," *The Guardian*, December 29, 1964: "**Factory farming**, whether we like it or not, has come to stay . . . In a year which has been as uneventful on the husbandry side as it has been significant in economic and political developments touching the future of food procurement, the more far-seeing would name the growth of **intensive farming** as the major development." (Note: Stanley Baker was the Guardian's agriculture correspondent.)
- "Head to head: Intensive farming", BBC News, March 6, 2001: "Here, Green MEP Caroline Lucas takes issue with the **intensive farming** methods of recent decades . . . In the wake of the spread of BSE from the UK to the continent of Europe, the German Government has appointed an Agriculture Minister from the Green Party. She intends to end **factory farming** in her country. This must be the way forward and we should end **industrial agriculture** in this country as well."

2. Sources discussing "industrial farming," "industrial agriculture" and "factory farming":
   - "Annex 2. Permitted substances for the production of organic foods", Food and Agriculture Organization of the United Nations: "'**Factory' farming** refers to **industrial management systems** that are heavily reliant on veterinary and feed inputs not permitted in organic agriculture.
   - "Head to head: Intensive farming", BBC News, March 6, 2001: "Here, Green MEP Caroline Lucas takes issue with the **intensive farming** methods of recent decades . . . In the wake of the spread of BSE from the UK to the continent of Europe, the German Government has appointed an Agriculture Minister from the Green Party. She intends to end **factory farming** in her country. This must be the way forward and we should end **industrial agriculture** in this country as well."

3. [abc] Kaufmann, Mark. "Largest Pork Processor to Phase Out Crates", *The Washington Post*, January 26, 2007.
4. "EU tackles BSE crisis", *BBC News*, November 29, 2000.
5. "Is factory farming really cheaper?" in *New Scientist*, Institution of Electrical Engineers, New Science Publications, University of Michigan, 1971, p. 12.
6. Danielle Nierenberg (2005) *Happier Meals: Rethinking the Global Meat Industry.* Worldwatch Paper 121: 5
7. Duram, Leslie A. (2010). *Encyclopedia of Organic, Sustainable, and Local Food.* ABC-CLIO. p. 139. ISBN 0313359636.
8. [ab] "Factory farming," *Encyclopædia Britannica*, 2007.
9. [ab] [1] Doug Gurian-Sherman. April 2008. CAFOs Uncovered: The Untold Costs of Confined Animal Feeding Operations, Union of Concerned Scientists, Cambridge, MA.
10. Scully, Matthew. *Dominion*, St. Martin's Griffin, pp. 259.
11. Scully, Matthew. *Dominion*, St. Martin's Griffin, 2002, pp. 255–256.
12. Scully, Matthew. *Dominion*, St. Martin's Griffin, 2002, p. 258.
13. [ab] http://www.kt.iger.bbsrc.ac.uk/FACT%20sheet%20PDF%20files/kt32.pdf UK DEFRA comment on de-beaking recognizing it as cruel
14. Farm Sanctuary FactoryFarming.com

15. Farm Animal Welfare Council
16. DEFRA press release
17. Barnett JL, Hemsworth PH, Cronin GM, Jongman EC, and Hutson GD. 2001. "A review of the welfare issues for sows and piglets in relation to housing," *Australian Journal of Agricultural Research 52:1–28.* Cited in: Pajor EA. 2002. "Group housing of sows in small pens: advantages, disadvantages and recent research," In: Reynells R (ed.), *Proceedings: Symposium on Swine Housing and Well-being* (Des Moines, Iowa: U.S. Department of Agriculture Agricultural Research Service, June 5, pp. 37–44). In: An HSUS Report: Welfare Issues with Gestation Crates for Pregnant Sows, Humane Society of the United States.
18. *a* The Welfare of Sows in Gestation Crates: A Summary of the Scientific Evidence., Farm Sanctuary.
19. "An HSUS Report: Welfare Issues with Gestation Crates for Pregnant Sows," The Humane Society of the United States, January 6, 2006.
20. Hickman, Martin (January 4, 2008). "The true cost of cheap chicken". *The Independent* (London). http://news.independent.co.uk/uk/this_britain/article3307570.ece. Retrieved May 2, 2010.
21. Animal rights concerns grow in California
22. Washington Post: Largest Pork Processor to Phase Out Crates
23. "Factory Farming: The Impact of Animal Feeding Operations on the Environment and Health of Local Communities." http://www.cdc.gov/nceh/conference/2006_conference/abstracts/session_D1.html. Retrieved 2009-12-13.
24. The benefits of pesticides: A story worth telling. Purdue.edu. Retrieved on September 15, 2007.
25. *ab* Kellogg RL, Nehring R, Grube A, Goss DW, and Plotkin S (February 2000), Environmental indicators of pesticide leaching and run-off from farm fields. United States Department of Agriculture Natural Resources Conservation Service. Retrieved on 3 October 2007.
26. *ab* Miller GT (2004), *Sustaining the Earth,* 6th edition. Thompson Learning, Inc. Pacific Grove, California. Chapter 9, Pages 211–216.
27. Sustainable Table article *Pesticides*
28. Pesticides In the Environment. Pesticide fact sheets and tutorial, module 6. cornell .edu. Retrieved on September 19, 2007.
29. *ab* "Concentrated animal feeding operations", Centers for Disease Control and Prevention, United States Department of Health and Human Services.
30. Food Standards Agency – VPC report on growth hormones in meat
31. Schneider K, Garrett L (June 19, 2009). "Non-therapeutic Use of Antibiotics in Animal Agriculture, Corresponding Resistance Rates, and What Can be Done About It". http://www.cgdev.org/content/article/detail/1422307/.
32. "Denmark's Case for Antibiotic-Free Animals". *CBS News.* February 10, 2010. http://www.cbsnews.com/stories/2010/02/10/eveningnews/main6195054.shtml.
33. The Hidden Link Between Factory Farms, Toxic Chemicals and Human Illness
34. EU–AGRINET article *Fighting swine fever in Europe* (Project Coordinator: Dr Trevor Drew at Veterinary Laboratories Agency)
35. T. Khannaa, R. Friendshipa, C. Deweya and J.S. Weeseb (PDF). *Methicillin resistant Staphylococcus aureus colonization in pigs and pig farmers.* http://www.mrsa-net .nl/de/files/file-bron-ant-10055-0-Khanna.pdf. Retrieved 2010-11-14.

36. de Neeling AJ, van den Broek MJ, Spalburg EC, van Santen-Verheuvel MG, Dam-Deisz WD, Boshuizen HC, van de Giessen AW, van Duijkeren E, Huijsdens XW. (PDF). *High prevalance methicillin resistant Staphylococcus aureus in pigs.* https://mrsa.rivm.nl/flash/Publicatie%20over%20MRSA%20bij%20varkens%20in%20slachthuizen.pdf. Retrieved 2010-11-14.

37. Rubin, JE; Ball KR, Chirino-Trejo M (In Press). "Decreased susceptibility of MRSA ST398 to tiamulin". *Veterinary Microbiology.* doi:10.1016/j.vetmic.2011.03.030.

38. "Joint scientific report of ECDC, EFSA and EMEA on methicillin resistant Staphylococcus aureus (MRSA) in livestock, companion animals and food". 2009-06-16. http://www.efsa.europa.eu/EFSA/Report/biohaz_report_301_joint_mrsa_en,0.pdf. Retrieved 2009-09-19.

39. http://www.sciencedaily.com/releases/2011/04/110415083153.htm

40. David Kirby (2009-04-28). "Mexican Lawmaker: Factory Farms Are "Breeding Grounds" of Swine Flu Pandemic". *The Huffington Post.* http://www.huffingtonpost.com/david-kirby/mexican-lawmaker-factory_b_191579.html. Retrieved 2009-04-28.

41. Compassion in World Farming—Animal health and disease

42. http://science.nationalgeographic.com/science/health-and-human-body/human-body/food-safety.html#page=1

43. "Food Safety Consequences of Factory Farms". Food & Water Watch. March, 2007. http://www.foodandwaterwatch.org:8080/Plone/food/factoryfarms/FoodSafetyFactoryFarms.pdf.

44. http://www.fda.gov/downloads/ForIndustry/UserFees/AnimalDrugUserFeeActADUFA/UCM231851.pdf

45. http://www.ucsusa.org/news/press_release/new-fda-data-confirm-what-ucs-0481.html

46. abcdef Compassion in World Farming—Environment & sustainability

47. http://www.mercyforanimals.org/4outrage04.html

48. http://www.peta.org/tv/videos/graphic/822806665001.aspx

49. http://www.humanesociety.org/issues/force_fed_animals/

50. Contract Farming in the World's Poultry Industry. Grain, Seedling, January 2008

51. Greenpeace (2006) Eating up the Amazon, 32.

52. [2] ALDF Farmed Animals and the Law

Questions for Critical Reading

1. As reflected in "Factory Farming," what do you see as the advantages and disadvantages of a public encyclopedia that anyone can write and edit?

2. Although anyone can contribute to any Wikipedia article, Wikipedia does have core principles that contributors should observe, one of which is "neutral point of view." Consider whether "Factory Farming" succeeds in having a neutral point of view, at least as explained by Wikipedia: "Articles mustn't *take* sides, but should *explain* the sides, fairly and without bias."[13]

---

[13] From http://en.wikipedia.org/wiki/Wikipedia:Neutral_point_of_view, accessed August 15, 2011.

Wikipedia goes on to note that being careful about "due and undue weight" is an important means of achieving a neutral point of view: "Neutrality requires that each article . . . fairly represents all significant viewpoints that have been published by reliable sources, in proportion to the prominence of each viewpoint."[14] Do you think "Factory Farming" succeeds in achieving a neutral point of view? Why or why not?

3. Because contributors don't always observe Wikipedia's policies—especially the policy that articles should be based on reliable, published sources—many professors discourage their students from using Wikipedia as a source in their writing. If you find a Wikipedia article helpful, however, you might read some of the sources cited in the article (if you think they're credible) and then cite those sources. Take a look at some of the sources for "Factory Farming"; if you were writing about this topic, which sources do you think might be credible enough to cite? Why?

4. Readers of many genres may often look to the opening sentence of a paragraph to tell them how the paragraph is connected to the larger topic. Consider the opening sentences of the first few paragraphs in the section entitled "Human Health Impact"; assess how well each paragraph opening maintains the focus on human health:

Human Health Impact

According to the U.S. Centers for Disease Control and Prevention (CDC), farms on which animals are intensively reared can cause adverse health reactions in farm workers. (para. 10)

Pesticides are used to control organisms which are considered harmful and they save farmers money by preventing product losses to pests. (para. 11)

The CDC writes that chemical, bacterial, and viral compounds from animal waste may travel in the soil and water. (para. 12)

Which paragraph openings did you feel clearly established a connection to the subheading "Human Health Impact"? Were there any that left you feeling a bit unsure of the connection?

Often, when writers think a reader might be confused about a connection, they either cut the information or rework it so that the connection becomes clearer. If you were to revise this section of "Factory Farming," what changes would you make, and why?

5. Recall that just as writers across genres typically want readers to see how each paragraph connects to the larger topic, they also want readers to see how sentences within a paragraph connect to the topic of that paragraph. Compare the following two paragraphs to see if, for you as a reader, one does

---

[14] From http://en.wikipedia.org/wiki/Wikipedia:Neutral_point_of_view#Undue_weight, accessed August 15, 2011.

a better job of sticking to the topic announced in the opening sentence (italicized):

> *There are differences around the world as to which practices are accepted and there continue to be changes in regulations with animal welfare being a strong driver for increased regulation.* For example, the EU is bringing in further regulation to set maximum stocking densities for meat chickens . . . where the UK Animal Welfare Minister commented, "The welfare of meat chickens is a major concern to people throughout the European Union. This agreement sends a strong message to the rest of the world that we care about animal welfare." (para. 8)

> *However, given the assumption that intensive farming techniques are a necessity, it is recognized that some apparently cruel techniques are better than the alternative.* For example, in the UK, de-beaking of chickens is deprecated, but it is recognized that it is a method of last resort, seen as better than allowing vicious fighting and ultimately cannibalism. Between 60 and 70 percent of six million breeding sows in the U.S. are confined during pregnancy, and for most of their adult lives, in 2 ft (0.61 m) by 7 ft (2.1 m) gestation crates. According to pork producers and many veterinarians, sows will fight if housed in pens. The largest pork producer in the U.S. said in January 2007 that it will phase out gestation crates by 2017. They are being phased out in the European Union, with a ban effective in 2013 after the fourth week of pregnancy. With the evolution of factory farming, there has been a growing awareness of the issues amongst the wider public, not least due to the efforts of animal rights and welfare campaigners. As a result gestation crates, one of the more contentious practices, are the subject of laws in the U.S., Europe and around the world to phase out their use as a result of pressure to adopt less confined practices. (para 9)

Which paragraph do you think better maintains the focus established in the opening sentence? Why? How would you revise the less focused paragraph to give it a sharper focus? If you have time in class, revise the less focused paragraph and trade revisions with a classmate to see if you had similar or different approaches to addressing the problem. If you or one of your classmates produces an especially focused revision, consider sharing it with the rest of the class.

6. Pictures can be useful across genres, in part because readers tend to notice them before they read the words on a page. What effect did the photos in "Factory Farming" have on you? Do you think they worked well with the content of the encyclopedia entry, or do you see them as a missed (or partially missed) opportunity? Why?

7. Just as experienced writers cut out words and phrases that don't advance their purposes, so too do experienced photographers crop out parts of photos that don't advance their purposes. Taking away part of a picture (or a piece of writing) can put greater emphasis on what remains. Consider how the

photos in "Factory Farming" might have been cropped differently; imagine a cropping of the chicken house photo that would cut out the empty space in front of and behind the chickens, leaving just the birds. Now imagine that the photo of the factory farm in Germany had been cropped to cut out the big tree, the field, and most of the sky. Would the different cropping of the pictures affect your experience as a reader? Why or why not?

Making Connections

8. Writers across genres use lists, which can be invaluable tools for providing an overview of an argument or for fitting a fair amount of information into a sentence smoothly. One key to writing effective lists is to use parallel structure — to write, for instance, "I like texting, reading, and watching movies" rather than "I like texting, to read, and watching movies."[15] Look at the following four lists — from Flavius Stan's creative nonfiction piece "The Night of Oranges" (p. 429), Michael Pollan's review essay "The Food Movement, Rising" (p. 435), Michael Fitzpatrick's op-ed "The Vegetarian Delusion" (p. 545), and Claire Miller's letter to the editor "Eating Vegetarian and Making a Difference" (p. 548) — and compare them to the list reprinted from "Factory Farming." See if you can apply the conventions of parallelism used in the first four examples to help you revise the list from "Factory Farming."

"The Night of Oranges"

We were used to such lines under the former Communist Government — lines for bread, lines for meat, lines for everything. (para. 2)

"The Food Movement, Rising"

But although cheap food is good politics, it turns out there are significant costs — to the environment, to public health, to the public purse, even to the culture — and as these became impossible to ignore in recent years, food has come back into view. (para. 5)

"The Vegetarian Delusion"

Animals eat other animals — lions eat antelope, eagles eat rabbits, dolphins eat fish. (para. 8)

---

[15] Note that different punctuation marks may be used before and within lists. If a list is introduced by an independent clause — that is, a clause that could stand as a sentence by itself — then writers generally use a colon (:) to introduce the list (e.g., "There are lots of things on my bucket list: seeing the Eiffel Tower, climbing Mount Everest . . ."). If a list *isn't* preceded by a clause that could be a sentence by itself (e.g., "I want to see the Eiffel Tower, climb Mount Everest . . ."), then *no* punctuation is needed before the list. To separate items within a list, writers usually use commas (sometimes skipping the comma before the last item in the list). However, if some items in the list have internal commas, then writers typically use semicolons to separate items in the list (e.g., "I introduced that evening's speakers: Ms. Huang, a nutritionist; Dr. Weiskopf, a pediatrician; and Dr. Nagpaul, an oncologist").

Connections

"Eating Vegetarian and Making a Difference"

If [living compassionately] means eating vegetarian a couple times a week, checking for the "not tested on animals" label or choosing pleather . . . over dead skin, it's making a difference. (para. 6)

"Factory Farming"

In the UK, the Farm Animal Welfare Council was set up by the government to act as an independent advisor on animal welfare in 1979 and expresses its policy as five freedoms: from hunger & thirst; from discomfort; from pain, injury or disease; to express normal behavior; from fear and distress. (para. 7)

Take a few minutes to revise the list from "Factory Farming." Compare notes with a few classmates and decide if you like the revisions better than the original. Which do you prefer? Why?

9. Regardless of genre, comma usage can affect a writer's credibility and can also affect the smoothness of a reader's experience. Unfortunately, many online genres don't have professional editors to help smooth out comma glitches. Consider the pattern of comma usage in three different sentences from a published book (Kessler's *End of Overeating*, p. 493), and see if you can use your knowledge of that pattern to supply a missing comma from "Factory Farming":

The End of Overeating

He bred one strain [of rats] to overfeed when a high-calorie diet was available, producing an obesity-prone rat. (para. 28)

[T]hey also ate more of them, consuming almost 44 percent more food at meals. (para. 37)

[T]his dish is fat surrounded by layers of sugar on salt on sugar on salt, making it another grand slam. (para. 61)

"Factory Farming"

[MRSA] has been identified in pigs and humans raising concerns about the role of pigs as reservoirs of MRSA for human infection. (para. 16)

Where in the "Factory Farming" excerpt would you put a comma? When you first read the "Factory Farming" sentence, did the missing comma affect your reading experience? Why or why not?

10. Now try your hand at revising another commonly seen comma glitch. This time, consider the pattern of commas in Sandra Steingraber's "The Organic Manifesto" (p. 460), and, based on what you notice, try adding commas to the sentences from "Factory Farming":

"The Organic Manifesto"

Children with conventional diets had, on average, nine times more organophosphate insecticides in their urine than children fed organic produce. (para. 11)

Pesticides, by design, are poisons. (para. 14)

The placenta, which does such an admirable job at keeping bacteria and viruses out of the womb's watery habitat, is ill-equipped to serve as a barrier to toxic chemicals. (para. 16)

The peepers' cries, which signal the advent of spring more reliably than any bird song, are soon joined by the quieter ZZZIPPP . . . ZZZIPPP of the chorus frog. (para. 24)

"Factory Farming"

A swine flu which quickly killed more than 100 infected persons in that area, appears to have begun in the vicinity of a Smithfield subsidiary pig CAFO. (para. 18)

The 28 hour law, enacted in 1873 and amended in 1994 states that when animals are being transported for slaughter, the vehicle must stop every 28 hours and the animals must be let out for exercise, food, and water. (para. 28)

Where in the "Factory Farming" sentences would you put commas? When you first read these sentences, did the missing commas affect your reading experience? Why or why not?

Writing: Your Turn

1. Since anyone can revise "Factory Farming" at any time, the version that's online now is probably different from the one printed here. Go to http://en.wikipedia.org/wiki/Factory_farming to see how it's been changed, and write a reflection on the changes. Is there any new information that you think is important or that you think shouldn't be there? Why do you appreciate (or not appreciate) this new information? Has anything been taken away, and if so, how do you feel about the omission? Share your reflection with your classmates so that they can hear your opinions and tell you whether or not they agree with you. For ideas on writing a reflection, see p. 27.

2. Write a rhetorical analysis of "Factory Farming" (either the version that appears here or the version that's now online, as your instructor directs). Consider how well the article accomplishes the purpose of informing readers about factory farming. You might address any subset of the following questions: Does the article succeed in achieving a neutral point of view? Is citation used appropriately? What about quotation? Is the article focused, both on the whole-text level and on the paragraph level? Is it well organized, without too much repetition? Is coherence achieved through smooth paragraph-to-paragraph and sentence-to-sentence transitions? Share your rhetorical analysis with some classmates so that they can give you feedback on where you might need to add more evidence to support your claims. For ideas on writing a rhetorical analysis, see p. 31.

3. To address any problems you see, revise a section of "Factory Farming" (either the version printed here or the current online version), and then write a preface to your revision discussing what changes you made to the section and why you made them. Share your preface and revision with some classmates to see if they prefer your revision to the original and to see if they have any ideas about further revision.

If you revised the current online version of "Factory Farming" and your classmates like your revision better than the original, consider going to Wikipedia and typing in some or all of your revisions. Before you do, however, it would be good to review Wikipedia's policies at http://en.wikipedia.org /wiki/Wikipedia:List_of_policies. Observing these policies will increase the likelihood that your revisions will "stick" rather than being removed.

To type in your revisions, simply click the "edit" link beside each subheading. To access the entire article at once, click the "Edit" tab at the top of the page. If you're making substantive changes to the content, it's advisable to discuss these changes with other contributors before making them. To access the discussion forum, simply click the "Talk" tab at the top of the page.

Making changes to Wikipedia articles is relatively simple, but if there's anything you don't know how to do, go to http://en.wikipedia.org/wiki /Wikipedia:FAQ/Editing for tips.

The Vegetarian Delusion

Michael Fitzpatrick

Michael Fitzpatrick's op-ed "The Vegetarian Delusion" appeared in 2009 in the *Brown Daily Herald,* Brown University's student newspaper. In it, Fitzpatrick tells us that moral vegetarianism "is not only a failure as a form of activism; it's a failure as a lifestyle choice." Following the op-ed is a letter to the editor that takes issue with it, written by Claire Miller and published in the same newspaper.

Focus on Genre Op-eds (sometimes simply labeled "opinion") allow members of a newspaper staff to make a timely argument and support it with evidence. Many newspapers also accept op-eds from outside contributors; indeed, you might find yourself writing one if you ever want to persuade people to consider an issue that's important to you. Because newspapers typically post much of their content online, op-eds often have a wide readership.

Op-eds tend to adapt to local circumstances; in some newspapers, for instance, they may have a harsher tone than in others. See what you think of Fitzpatrick's tone (e.g., his attitude toward others as implied by his word choice). Also consider what Fitzpatrick's main point is and why he states it where he does. (Op-eds often state the main point in the first paragraph, but that's not where Fitzpatrick puts it.) Finally, consider whether or not you agree with Fitzpatrick's argument, and why.

◄O►

Anyone who wandered through the Main Green this past week was granted a rare opportunity to see some profoundly horrifying images: a seal being brutally clubbed to death for its fur; an innocent piglet being castrated; a poor cat being pinned down on a dissecting table.

In a stunning juxtaposition of moral outrage and disgust-inducing tastelessness, the Brown Animal Rights Club, in conjunction with People for the Ethical Treatment of Animals, brought to our campus an exhibition of the Animal Liberation Project. In a nutshell, the ALP seeks to inform the public—in particular, the youth—about the injustices that human beings inflict upon animals.

Armed with an arsenal of hyper-sentimental quotes from human rights leaders such as Gandhi and Martin Luther King Jr., the group has launched a campaign against societal tolerance of speciesism—the belief that other species are inferior to our own. The campaign fashions itself as a revival of older liberation fronts, from abolition to feminism. But instead of boycotts, protest marches and petitions, the Animal Liberation Project proposes a decidedly unorthodox protest method: vegetarianism.

Vegetarianism? Are they trying to waste our time?

To clarify, I have nothing wrong with dietary vegetarianism. Nutritionally   5
speaking, vegetables are far more valuable than animal flesh as sources of fiber, vitamins and minerals. Moral vegetarianism, on the other hand, is not only a failure as a form of activism; it's a failure as a lifestyle choice.

Let's focus on vegetarian activism for a moment. Vegetarian activism operates on the same principle as a boycott: activists refuse to purchase a product or use a service and urge others to do the same. To convince others to make that sacrifice, activists need to make a statement about their cause. Unfortunately, swearing off meat isn't a particularly powerful statement when other people do it for selfish reasons, like improving their diet or fulfilling their religious obligations.

Compare this with Mahatma Gandhi, a vegetarian who went on several hunger strikes to promote peaceful resistance to British rule in India. Vegetarianism was his lifestyle, but self-starvation was his protest method. It brought the attention he wanted. After all, apart from the occasional anorexic teenager, people generally don't starve themselves unless they want to make a point.

Furthermore, vegetarianism constricts the focus of the animal-welfare cause. If you refuse to eat meat, any reasonable person would assume that you protest the killing of animals for their flesh, or the harvesting of animal byproducts (e.g., eggs, milk and honey) for food. But in terms of cruelty, eating animals is relatively mild compared to other inhumane activities. Animals eat other animals—lions eat antelope, eagles eat rabbits, dolphins eat fish. Eating is a natural process.

Humans, on the other hand, are exclusively guilty of killing animals for reasons other than eating. Remember that seal clubber? He's going to leave the skinned seal carcass on the ice pack for some polar bear to eat. Eating meat has nothing to do with the fur industry, vivisection or animal abuse, because in those cases the animals do not end up on your plate.

To be an effective vegetarian activist, you need to loudly proclaim to every-   10
one within earshot that (a) you refuse to eat meat because it's cruel, and (b) you also strongly disapprove of fur coats, experimentation and animal abuse. But would you believe me if I told you that you also had to grow your own food?

That's right: millions of rabbits, mice and other rodents die each year when wheat combines and other farm equipment harvest the crops. The problem is that machines do not pause to allow the vermin to escape. Only handpicked food is truly safe for animals, and that means finding a way to hire millions of farm workers to gather, process and package your dinner without forcing the farmers into bankruptcy.

But you could grow your own food, right? Subsistence gardening is extremely eco-friendly and you can harvest on your own terms. You'll never have to kill another rabbit again, unless you find the little backstabbers munching on your vegetables. For those that remember Beatrix Potter's "The Tales of Peter Rabbit" . . . Well, you'll suddenly feel a strong sympathetic connection with nasty old Mr. McGregor as you chase the vermin away with a rake.

In terms of animal welfare, moral vegetarianism is an insufficient response to animal cruelty. It exists as a cheap alternative for people who are too apathetic to participate in a real protest against a real problem. Do something productive with your time: protest the seal clubbing, the experimentation and the abuse . . . and please pass me a steak knife.

LINKED
READING
PAGE 545

| Letter to the editor |

Eating Vegetarian and Making a Difference

Claire Miller

Written in response to Fitzpatrick's op-ed "The Vegetarian Delusion," Claire Miller's letter to the editor appeared in the *Brown Daily Herald*, two days after the op-ed. Miller takes issue with Fitzpatrick's position, arguing that "any individual vegetarian is still making a difference in the lives of animals and the health of our environment."

Focus on Genre   Letters to the editor tend to be shorter than op-eds, although they often share the purpose of trying to persuade readers. Letters are often written in response to an op-ed or something else that's been published; they might disagree with an argument, thank the paper for publishing a piece and state why the piece was important, or point out additional information that the writer thinks is relevant.

Like op-eds, letters tend to adapt to local circumstances; for example, they tend to be shorter in some papers and longer in others—a variation that affects the amount of evidence writers can use. Consider the evidence Miller uses to support her claims—whether you find it persuasive and whether you think there's enough of it. Finally, think about Miller's tone. A writer's tone might be dismissive of others, respectful of others, or somewhere in between; consider how you'd describe Miller's tone and whether or not it affects your openness to being persuaded by her.

◄○►

To the Editor:

Animals do have the ability to suffer and feel pain just as we do, so why do we continue to exploit them?

There are many great reasons to be vegetarian, including health, religion, the environment and — of course — the moral aspect. Although some of these may not be in an effort to better the world, any individual vegetarian is still making a difference in the lives of animals and the health of our environment. Michael Fitzpatrick ("The vegetarian delusion," Oct. 6) states in his column that "eating is a natural process" and compares our consumption of flesh to a lion eating an antelope. This is a gross assumption. There is nothing natural about the way meat, dairy and eggs get to our plates today.

The general public is completely disconnected from food production and takes no responsibility for the harm caused in the process. Ethical vegetarianism could simply be about not killing any being in order to please our taste buds, but there's a much larger problem at hand: the horrifying, filthy conditions that animals in factory farms are forced to endure. What we're consuming supports cruelty to animals.

In his column, Fitzpatrick suggests that vegetarians grow their own food 5 because of the millions of rodents killed each year from harvesting grains. This criticism is rather backwards: 80 percent of the farmed land in the U.S. is used to support the animal by-product industries. Sixteen pounds of grain goes into producing only one pound of meat. By not eating meat, I'm not only boycotting the slaughter of 27 billion animals each year for food, but I'm also massively cutting back on the animals that get run over by tractors in the fields.

We all can live as compassionately as possible, within our own capabilities. If that means eating vegetarian a couple times a week, checking for the "not tested on animals" label or choosing pleather (which is often cheaper) over dead skin, it's making a difference.

I commend Fitzpatrick for reminding us that ethical vegetarianism is not an end all to the abuses of animals. We have never implied that vegetarianism is a panacea, and our audience understands that abstaining from meat doesn't stop seal-clubbing.

Animal abuse is pervasive, but each step towards a more compassionate lifestyle is worthwhile. While I choose to be vegan in all aspects of my life, I know not everyone will. All I hope is that people will take time to consider the suffering of animals and live as kindly as possible.

Claire Miller '11
President, Brown Animal Rights Club
Oct. 6

Questions for Critical Reading

1. Do you agree with Fitzpatrick or with Miller, or do you think there's an alternative position? If you were persuaded by one or both of them, what did they do to persuade you? If you weren't persuaded by either of them, what could they have done to persuade you?

2. Unlike some op-ed authors, Fitzpatrick waits several paragraphs to state his main argument. What did you take to be his argument, and why do you think he waited to tell us? If you were Fitzpatrick, would you have stated your main argument earlier? Why or why not?

3. The organization of Miller's letter to the editor also differs from that of some other letters. While not all letters to the editor are written in response to an op-ed or an article, those that are tend to name the piece they're responding to in the first sentence. Compare the following original and altered openings of Miller's letter, and see if you have a preference for one over the other.

Original Passage	Altered Passage
Animals do have the ability to suffer and feel pain just as we do, so why do we continue to exploit them? There are many great reasons to be vegetarian, including health, religion, the environment and—of course—the moral aspect. Although some of these may not be in an effort to better the world, any individual vegetarian is still making a difference in the lives of animals and the health of our environment. Michael Fitzpatrick ("The vegetarian delusion," Oct. 6) states in his column that "eating is a natural process" and compares our consumption of flesh to a lion eating an antelope. This is a gross assumption. There is nothing natural about the way meat, dairy and eggs get to our plates today. (paras. 1–2)	Michael Fitzpatrick ("The vegetarian delusion," Oct. 6) states in his column that "eating is a natural process" and compares our consumption of flesh to a lion eating an antelope. This is a gross assumption. There is nothing natural about the way meat, dairy and eggs get to our plates today.

If you were Miller, how would you have opened your letter? Why?

4. If you read a lot of letters to the editor, you'll notice that claims are sometimes supported with evidence and sometimes not. Miller provides support for some of her claims, but others go unsupported. Consider the following two paragraphs from her letter; see if you think one offers better support for its claims:

> The general public is completely disconnected from food production and takes no responsibility for the harm caused in the process. Ethical vegetarianism could simply be about not killing any being in order to please our taste buds, but there's a much larger problem at hand: the horrifying, filthy conditions that animals in factory farms are forced to endure. What we're consuming supports cruelty to animals. (para. 4)

> In his column, Fitzpatrick suggests that vegetarians grow their own food because of the millions of rodents killed each year from harvesting grains. This criticism is rather backwards: 80 percent of the farmed land in the U.S. is used to support the animal by-product industries. Sixteen pounds of grain goes into producing only one pound of meat. By not eating meat, I'm not only boycotting the slaughter of 27 billion animals each year for food, but I'm also massively cutting back on the animals that get run over by tractors in the fields. (para. 5)

Which paragraph do you think offers more support for its claims? If you were Miller, would you add more support to either paragraph? Why or why not? If you would add more support, what would you say, and where would you say it?

Making Connections

5. Regardless of genre, a writer's tone can convey an attitude toward readers (and toward others more generally). How respectful or dismissive a writer's tone is can influence readers to be more — or less — receptive to a writer's points. Think about the different attitudes implied in the original and altered versions of the following passages from Fitzpatrick's op-ed, Miller's letter to the editor, and Jonathan Safran Foer's business letter to Tyson Foods (included in "Hiding/Seeking," p. 507). Compare the different tones of the original and altered passages, and consider whether or not the changes in tone affect your response.

Original Passage	Altered Passage
[M]oral vegetarianism is an insufficient response to animal cruelty. It exists as a cheap alternative for people who are too apathetic to participate in a real protest against a real problem. Do something more productive with your time: protest the seal clubbing, the experimentation and the abuse. (Fitzpatrick, para. 13)	[M]oral vegetarianism is an insufficient response to animal cruelty. People who are concerned enough about animal suffering to be moral vegetarians should also consider protesting the seal clubbing, the experimentation and the abuse.

Original Passage	Altered Passage
I commend Fitzpatrick for reminding us that ethical vegetarianism is not an end all to the abuses of animals. We have never implied that vegetarianism is a panacea, and our audience understands that abstaining from meat doesn't stop seal-clubbing. (Miller, para. 7)	Fitzpatrick clearly misunderstands our position. We have never implied that vegetarianism is a panacea, and our audience understands that abstaining from meat doesn't stop seal-clubbing.
I am following up on my previous letters of January 10, February 27, March 15, April 20, May 15, and June 7. . . . Given your "family-centered philosophy" and recent "It's What Your Family Deserves" advertising campaign, I assume you'll appreciate my desire to see for myself where my son's food comes from. Thanks so much for your continued consideration. (Foer, paras. 25–27)	You failed to respond to my previous letters of January 10, February 27, March 15, April 20, May 15, and June 7. . . . If your "family-centered philosophy" and recent "It's What Your Family Deserves" advertising campaign weren't ploys to make more money, then you would understand my desire to see for myself where my son's food comes from.

Note that the implied attitudes toward others in the original passages may not represent how the writers actually felt; writers often "erase" their negative feelings and craft a respectful tone for rhetorical purposes — to project a more likable persona that they believe will help them better persuade readers. Would you have responded differently to Miller's and Foer's writing if they had used a disrespectful tone? Conversely, would you have responded differently to Fitzpatrick's op-ed if he had been more respectful of moral vegetarians? Why or why not?

Find another passage in Fitzpatrick's op-ed that might be considered disrespectful, and revise it so that it has a more respectful tone. Trade revisions with a classmate to see if you both prefer the revisions to the original.

6. Writers across genres use a hyphen (-) to combine two words that work together to describe a noun.[16] Although many of these hyphenated adjectives are found in everyday phrases (e.g., "high-paying job," "twenty-year-old woman"), writers also have the option of combining words to make their own original adjectives; this is one of many ways writers can have fun being creative. Consider the following passages from Fitzpatrick's op-ed "The Vegetarian Delusion"

---

[16] Compound adjectives are generally hyphenated only when they come before nouns, not when they come after them. There are also some cases in which two words preceding a noun aren't hyphenated (such as when one of the words is an adverb ending in *-ly*).

(p. 545), Michael Pollan's review essay "The Food Movement, Rising" (p. 435), Sandra Steingraber's essay "The Organic Manifesto" (p. 460), and Jonathan Safran Foer's multi-genre book chapter "Hiding/Seeking" (p. 507). Some of the hyphenated adjectives in these passages seek to inform us, others to persuade us, and still others to entertain us or enable us to appreciate an evocative image. (Of course, multiple purposes are often at work too.) Pick one or two hyphenated adjectives that you especially like:

"The Vegetarian Delusion"

In a stunning juxtaposition of moral outrage and disgust-inducing tastelessness, the Brown Animal Rights Club . . . brought to our campus an exhibition of the Animal Liberation Project. (para. 2)

"The Food Movement, Rising"

Americans learned that cattle, which are herbivores, were routinely being fed the flesh of other cattle; the practice helped keep meat cheap but at the risk of a hideous brain-wasting disease. (para. 5)

Since [1982], repeated outbreaks of food-borne illness linked to new antibiotic-resistant strains of bacteria . . . have turned a bright light on the shortsighted practice of routinely administering antibiotics to food animals. (para. 6)

"The Organic Manifesto"

Rising just west of our cabin is Snyder Hill, a long, steep rocky ridge that blocks the afternoon sun far sooner than I'd like during the too-short days of the too-long winters here. (para. 30)

"Hiding/Seeking"

There was . . . the night she was forced to spend in construction-paper blackness with twenty thousand miserable animals. (para. 13)

I'm imagining some roused-from-REM-sleep-and-well-armed farmer coming upon I-know-the-difference-between-arugula-and-rugelach me scrutinizing the living conditions of his turkeys. (para. 19)

There were dead birds everywhere, and half-dead birds. (para. 57)

In almost every way, I'm a middle-of-the-road person. I don't have any piercings. No weird haircut. I don't do drugs. . . . [s]ee, factory farming is a middle-of-the-road issue—something most reasonable people would agree on if they had access to the truth. (para. 52)

To get a sense of the value of hyphenated adjectives, take your favorite adjective from one of the passages and rewrite the sentence that it's in *without* the hyphenated adjective; for example, "half-dead birds" could be rewritten as "birds that were half dead." Consider your rewritten version alongside a few classmates' rewritten versions, and compare these versions to the original passages. What does your comparison tell you about the potential value (or potential limitations) of hyphenated adjectives?

Writing: Your Turn

1. Write a letter to the editor in response to Fitzpatrick's op-ed. Although it wouldn't make sense to actually submit it to the *Brown Daily Herald* since Fitzpatrick's op-ed wasn't published this week, writing the letter will allow you to stretch your writing muscles — and Miller's letter by no means exhausts everything there is to say in response to Fitzpatrick's argument. Share your letter with some classmates to get ideas on how you might strengthen it, and then revise it. For tips on writing a letter to the editor, see p. 62.

2. Look through your campus newspaper or your local town/city paper to find an article about food (including restaurant reviews), and write a letter to the editor in response to it. You might take issue with something the author wrote, point out something else that's relevant to the topic, or thank the paper for publishing the article and explain why you think the article is important. If you can't find an article to respond to, write a letter making a timely argument about food that will be relevant to many of the paper's readers. Share your letter with some classmates to get ideas on how you might strengthen it, and then revise it and submit it to the newspaper. (Note that most papers accept letters electronically.) For tips on writing a letter to the editor, see p. 62.

Visualizing Genre

Food Packaging

:e: To see these food packages in color, visit the e-Pages for *Real Questions* at **bedfordstmartins.com /realquestions/epages.**

Questions for Critical Reading

1. What kind of consumers seem to be targeted by the packaging of each food pictured here? How can you tell?

2. The genre of food boxes has a predictable purpose: to persuade people to buy the product. Because nutrition is something many consumers care about, much food packaging seeks to persuade us that the food being sold is nutritious. On the surface, this would seem to be a difficult task, since most food in a package or box is processed, unlike the whole foods that many consider to be more nutritious.[17]

   Many of the food boxes pictured here try to persuade us that the food inside is nutritious by featuring a picture of a whole food on the package. For instance, strawberries are pictured on the packaging for Pop Tarts, Cheerios, Special K bars, and Special K cereal. Similarly, onions and tomatoes are pictured on the Pringles BBQ package, and representations of a whole grain (imagine a field of wheat) are pictured on the Kashi cracker box, the Cheerios box, and the Annie's macaroni and cheese box. Do you think this strategy of picturing whole foods on the packaging of processed foods might subtly work to attract some consumers? Why or why not?

3. Besides the images of whole foods on the processed-food packaging, what other strategies do you see the food manufacturers using to attract their target audiences?

---

[17] If you're not sure how to tell the difference between processed foods and whole foods, think of the number of ingredients: processed foods generally have numerous ingredients, while whole foods — say, strawberries, or raw almonds — generally have one ingredient.

Pulling It All Together

ARGUMENT

Drawing on more than one of the readings in this chapter, and perhaps also on your personal experience or independent research, write an argument addressed to an audience of college students about an aspect of food that you find interesting. If you don't already have an argument in mind, you might address these questions to help you formulate a thesis: What is an especially significant problem regarding food? What are the consequences of this problem, and how might it be addressed?

After you finish writing and doing a round of revision on your own, share your argument with some classmates; ask them if they learned anything from reading it and if it persuaded them to change their minds about anything. If they found your work persuasive, ask them how it might be more so; if they didn't, ask what their objections are so that you can address them in your revision. For ideas on writing an argument, see p. 42.

OP-ED AND LETTER TO THE EDITOR

In pairs, write your own op-ed and letter to the editor. First, write an op-ed about a food issue that affects your campus or your city/town, and then swap op-eds with a partner and write a letter to the editor in response to your partner's op-ed.

Before you write your op-ed, target it to a specific newspaper, and make sure you find out what the paper's op-ed guidelines are. When you write the op-ed, have a specific purpose in mind (for example, making readers aware of an issue or persuading them to take a particular action).

Be sure to begin your op-ed with a timely "hook" — that is, open by referring to something that just happened. For instance, if you want to argue that your cafeteria should serve fresher food, you might describe that day's salad bar, or if you want to argue that restaurant patrons should ask restaurants to offer at least one organic menu item, you might refer to a recent study on the benefits of organic food. (If you look, you can find recent news on virtually any topic.[18]) After you've crafted a timely hook, transition into your argument and support it with evidence. When you're done writing, give your op-ed to your partner so that she or he can write a letter to the editor in response to it, and then write your own letter in response to your partner's op-ed.

After your partner finishes his or her letter, use it to give you ideas on how to revise your op-ed. For example, if your partner disagrees with one of your points, you might decide to rebut his or her objection or add more evidence. For ideas on writing an op-ed and a letter to the editor, see p. 62.

---

[18] To find a timely angle for your op-ed hook, try http://www.google.com/alerts; type "food," or a more specific term, into the top box ("Preview results"). You might also look at recent press releases on http://www.eurekalert.org/; click on "Agriculture" and then "Food/Food Science." Another resource for press releases is http://www.sciencedaily.com/; click on "Health and Medicine" and then on "Nutrition" or "Obesity," or click on "Plants and Animals" and then on "Agriculture and Food."

5

How is social media
affecting our relationship
with the world around us?

How does spending so much time
online affect our brains?

Are screen-based technologies stressing us out?

How does technology both connect and isolate us?

Is there such a thing as Facebook Depression?

What does it mean to be "addicted" to texting and social media?

"You're never where you are. But you're not anywhere else either. You're nowhere," said one professor in a conversation about the pull of texting and the Internet. Indeed, some professors have noticed a significant change since texting and other cell phone–enabled technologies have come on the scene. In the pre–cell phone era, these professors claim, students were more likely to talk with one another before class, whereas now many of them are hunched over cell phones before class starts, silently touching screens or pushing buttons. Some professors have also noticed that what happens after class tends to be different as well: students are now more likely, they say, to leave the room single file — again silently touching screens and pushing buttons — rather than leaving the room chatting in pairs or small groups.

The changes that characterize the time spent in class are equally noticeable, many say. Some professors who used to be able to facilitate lively class discussions now say that engaging students in an interesting discussion can be difficult. Perhaps this is partly because students' attention is captured by surreptitious texting and partly because even when students aren't texting, they're less able to pay attention for sustained periods of time.

Indeed, one of the reading selections in this chapter, a study conducted at the University of Maryland entitled "A Day without Media," quotes numerous students who say that when they attempted to go twenty-four hours without their cell phones, computers, and other media, they were almost unbearably bored—both in and outside of class. One of the students quoted contrasts her life with cell phones, television, and the Internet to her parents' lives: "My parents grew up without any of these things and said that as teenagers, they never felt bored" (para. 60). There is arguably a vicious cycle: people's attention spans may have become shorter because they are used to being interrupted by texts and zooming from one Web site to another, and this shorter attention span may then compel them to spend even more time texting and seeking out online destinations.

The compulsion to text and access the Internet isn't limited to students, as MIT professor Sherry Turkle notes in one of the reading selections in this chapter, an excerpt from her general audience book *Alone Together: Why We Expect More from Technology and Less from Each Other.* Turkle describes how the advent of technology has also influenced many older adults, including several she saw at a memorial service who used their programs to hide their cell phones as they texted during the service. Although the texting was especially upsetting to Turkle because the service was for one of her closest friends, she writes that "compassion is due to those of us—and there are many of us—who are so dependent on our devices that we cannot sit still for a funeral service or a lecture or a play. We now know that our brains are rewired every time we use a phone to search or surf or multitask. As we try to reclaim our concentration, we are literally at war with ourselves" (para. 65). Turkle concludes: "We deserve better. When we remind ourselves that it is we who decide how to keep technology busy, we shall have better" (para. 66).

Turkle makes an important point when she notes that we are the ones who decide how to use technology, not the other way around. As you read the selections in this chapter, remember that it's too simple to blame or credit technology alone for any changes that people believe to be affecting our world. Keep this in mind as you consider the following questions raised by the readings: How does our use of technology shape our relationships with others? How does it shape our sense of self? Why do some people believe that recent technology has benefited them while others believe that it has hurt them? What might we learn about the role of technology in our lives by temporarily unplugging? What might we do to more actively shape the influence of technology in our lives?

Case Study: Twitter

Besides influencing our lives in the ways already discussed, our use of technology has given rise to new genres that we encounter with great frequency. The immediacy of the Internet and smaller devices for reading on the go require writers to carefully consider how to reach an audience used to being bombarded with streams of texts, e-mails, status updates, and spam.

Consider the popular microblogging site Twitter, which requires posts to be limited to 140 characters. Within that character limit, writers can make a number of moves: they can address specific audiences, keyword their tweets for searchability, incorporate sources, and respond in real time.

Take a look at some sample tweets from the *Chronicle of Higher Education,* an online and print news source for issues related to higher education. Annotations have been added to illustrate different aspects of the *Chronicle's* tweets.

To read and answer questions about these tweets online, visit the e-Pages for *Real Questions* at **bedfordstmartins.com/realquestions/epages.**

Chronicle @chronicle
'Me.edu': the coming personalization of #highered.
http://chroni.cl/Jdg9H9

Each tweet on the *Chronicle's* feed shows the writer's username and @reply handle to allow users to reply to their tweets.

This tweet uses a hashtag [#] so that users who follow "highered" as a topic will see it in their feed.

Chronicle @chronicle
Thanks @UofT_Teaching @DPUTC @mary_carmichael @iampatrickw and @SooOh! We love the new Tumblr too: http://bit.ly/Jbp5j3

Users can reference other Twitter accounts in their feed (with links to those accounts) by including "@" and the account name in their tweets.

Chronicle @chronicle
2 former Kaplan employees settle lawsuit and withdraw whistle-blower case: http://chroni.cl/HyBvTo #4profit

Many tweets include shortened URLs to alert followers to news stories of interest. Why would Twitter be a popular tool for news agencies themselves?

Brad Wolverton @bradwolverton
4 of top 10 wealthiest NCAA programs, plus other biggies, opposed multiyear scholarships: http://chroni.cl/xZR37x
Retweeted by Chronicle

This tweet by Brad Wolverton shows up in the *Chronicle's* feed because Twitter allows users to retweet posts from other users. In addition, many users head retweeted posts "RT" to note that the post has been retweeted.

Questions for Critical Reading

1. Think about the purpose(s) of these four tweets from the *Chronicle's* feed: the first and last ones link to *Chronicle* blog posts, the second one thanks the Twitter accounts that have linked to the *Chronicle's* Tumblr feed, and the

third one links to a *Chronicle* news article. What do you take to be the purpose(s) of each tweet, and why?

2. Compare the purposes of the four *Chronicle* tweets to what you take to be the purposes of some other tweets. If Web sites can be projected onto a screen in your classroom, sample tweets can be shown to everyone by accessing https://twitter.com/search-home and clicking on one of the trends listed under the search box. Take a minute to read a few of the tweets and consider what might have prompted the authors to post. Do you think any of their reasons for posting might differ from the *Chronicle*'s? Why or why not?

3. In what ways is the format of Twitter limiting? What do you think are the effects of Twitter's constraints?

4. What might be some of the advantages of having to write within a 140-character limit? Why?

About the Readings

The reading selections in this chapter discuss several facets of our technology use. In his op-ed "How to Survive the Age of Distraction," Johann Hari draws on several thinkers to argue that it's becoming harder to read books — that the space they used to occupy is "being eroded by the thousand Weapons of Mass Distraction that surround us all" (para. 3). Hari suggests a digital diet, telling us that "most humans have a desire to engage in deep thought and deep concentration." Nicholas Carr makes a similar argument in his magazine feature "Is Google Making Us Stupid?" but the longer length enabled by the genre allows him to draw on more research and spend more time discussing personal experience; seeing two similar arguments in different genres will shed light on some of the ways that genre shapes what writers are able to accomplish.

Carr's article is critiqued in Trent Batson's "Response to Nicholas Carr's 'Is Google Making Us Stupid?'" Batson, writing for the Web site *Campus Technology*, claims that rather than being worried about "how we 'skim' and 'bounce' around in our reading" (para. 10), we should celebrate how Google and the Internet help us "re-claim our human legacy of learning through a rapid exchange of ideas in a social setting" (para. 11).

The excerpt from Sherry Turkle's *Alone Together* examines not only how technology can affect our attention span but also how it can affect our stress levels and our relationships. Turkle draws on both primary and secondary research to argue that some people's use of technology can profoundly affect their lives.

Also drawing on primary and secondary research, former Microsoft and Apple executive Linda Stone focuses on the stress that, she claims, can affect those who are inundated with e-mail or who multitask (e.g., texting while carrying on a conversation). In both of her blog posts, "Beyond Simple Multi-Tasking: Continuous Partial Attention" and "Diagnosis: Email

Apnea," Stone focuses on the biology of the stress response, and she emphasizes her points by coining two new terms: "continuous partial attention"
and "email apnea." These terms have made their way into many people's
vocabulary and have been widely cited in both online and print publications, including the *New York Times*. The widespread use of these terms is
largely due to Stone's choice of genre; because blog posts are easy to link
to, they have the potential to be highly influential.

A broader discussion of the effects of technology use — both positive
and negative — is provided by the peer-reviewed journal *Pediatrics* in a
literature review entitled "Clinical Report: The Impact of Social Media on
Children, Adolescents, and Families," by Gwenn Schurgin O'Keeffe,
Kathleen Clarke-Pearson, and the Council on Communications and Media.
Unlike most peer-reviewed journal articles, which generally cite original
research reports, the *Pediatrics* report also cites media coverage of research
reports. In citing these secondhand sources, the report breaks from the
conventions of the genre and, according to John Grohol's blogged critique "*Pediatrics* Gets It Wrong about 'Facebook Depression,'" forfeits any
credibility it might have otherwise had. Because Grohol chose to present
his critique in a blog format that allowed for comments, it was easy for
lead author Gwenn O'Keeffe to reply — and for Grohol, along with
researcher Joanne Davila, to reply back to her. These multiple exchanges
will make it easier for you to critically assess the validity of the original
article as well as Grohol's critique of it.

The final cluster of readings centers around "A Day without Media,"
the web-published research report on the University of Maryland study
that asked students to go a day without cell phones, computers, and other
media. You'll be able to compare this original research report to a blogged
column that covers it, Jenna Johnson's "Fighting a Social Media Addiction." Media coverage such as Johnson's is critiqued by media psychologist Pamela Brown Rutledge, who notes in her blog that the original study
did *not* demonstrate that college students are addicted to social media.
Rutledge argues that people are too cavalier about using the word "addiction," which she notes "is a serious psychological diagnosis based on specific and seriously life-impairing criteria" (para. 3).

As you're reading these selections, recall that, contrary to what some
of the authors may imply, recent technology by itself can't be credited or
blamed for the ways our world has changed since it came on the scene.
Rather, it's *how we interact with technology* that shapes our world. The
voices and genres in this chapter may or may not inspire you to use technology differently, but they will at least shed light on the many ways that
you and others are affected by the roles it plays in our lives.

For additional readings in online and multimedia genres related to
the chapter theme, see the e-Pages online at **bedfordstmartins.com
/realquestions/epages.**

How to Survive the Age of Distraction

Johann Hari

Johann Hari's op-ed "How to Survive the Age of Distraction" appeared in 2011 in the British newspaper the *Independent*. Hari, who was on the *Independent's* staff when he wrote the op-ed, argues that in the "age of the internet, physical paper books are a technology we need more, not less." Hari has also written for the *Huffington Post* and a variety of other publications.

Focus on Genre   Like most op-ed authors, Hari cites a recent event that prompts him to give his opinion — in this case, an opinion on the effects that recent technology is having on our ability to read books. As you read Hari's op-ed, notice his organization: while some op-eds refer to the prompting event right away (in the first paragraph), Hari waits until the second paragraph to refer to it. Consider why he might have done this and whether you would have made the same decision if you'd been in his shoes.

Also consider how Hari draws on a larger organizational pattern common to many genres: the problem/solution organization. See if you agree with Hari's articulation of the problem — as well as his suggested solution. Finally, think about why Hari waits until the very end of the piece to propose a solution, rather than offering one earlier.

◄o►

In the 20th century, all the nightmare-novels of the future imagined that books would be burnt. In the 21st century, our dystopias imagine a world where books are forgotten. To pluck just one, Gary Shteyngart's novel *Super Sad True Love Story* describes a world where everybody is obsessed with their electronic Apparat—an even more omnivorous iPhone with a flickering stream of shopping and reality shows and porn—and have somehow come to believe that the few remaining unread paper books let off a rank smell. The book on the book, it suggests, is closing.

I have been thinking about this because I recently moved flat, which for me meant boxing and heaving several Everests of books, accumulated obsessively since I was a kid. Ask me to throw away a book, and I begin shaking like Meryl Streep in *Sophie's Choice* and insist that I just couldn't bear to part company with it, no matter how unlikely it is I will ever read (say) a 1,000-page biography of little-known Portuguese dictator Antonio Salazar. As I stacked my books high, and watched my friends get buried in landslides of novels or avalanches of polemics, it struck me that this scene might be incomprehensible a generation from now. Yes, a few specialists still haul their vinyl collections from house to house, but the rest of us have migrated happily to MP3s, and regard such people as slightly odd. Does it matter? What was really lost?

The book—the physical paper book—is being circled by a shoal of sharks, with sales down 9 per cent this year alone. It's being chewed by the e-book. It's being gored by the death of the bookshop and the library. And most importantly, the mental space it occupied is being eroded by the thousand Weapons of Mass Distraction that surround us all. It's hard to admit, but we all sense it: it is becoming almost physically harder to read books.

In his gorgeous little book *The Lost Art of Reading—Why Books Matter in a Distracted Time,* the critic David Ulin admits to a strange feeling. All his life, he had taken reading as for granted as eating—but then, a few years ago, he "became aware, in an apartment full of books, that I could no longer find within myself the quiet necessary to read." He would sit down to do it at night, as he always had, and read a few paragraphs, then find his mind was wandering, imploring him to check his email, or Twitter, or Facebook. "What I'm struggling with," he writes, "is the encroachment of the buzz, the sense that there's something out there that merits my attention."

I think most of us have this sense today, if we are honest. If you read a book with your laptop thrumming on the other side of the room, it can be like trying to read in the middle of a party, where everyone is shouting to each other. To read, you need to slow down. You need mental silence except for the words. That's getting harder to find.

5

No, don't misunderstand me. I adore the web, and they will have to wrench my Twitter feed from my cold dead hands. This isn't going to turn into an antediluvian rant against the glories of our wired world. But there's a reason why that word—"wired"—means both "connected to the internet" and "high, frantic, unable to concentrate."

In the age of the internet, physical paper books are a technology we need more, not less. In the 1950s, the novelist Herman Hesse wrote: "The more the need for entertainment and mainstream education can be met by new inventions, the more the book will recover its dignity and authority. We have not yet quite reached the point where young competitors, such as radio, cinema, etc., have taken over the functions from the book it can't afford to lose."

We have now reached that point. And here's the function that the book—the paper book that doesn't beep or flash or link or let you watch a thousand videos all at once—does for you that nothing else will. It gives you the capacity for deep, linear concentration. As Ulin puts it: "Reading is an act of resistance in a landscape of distraction. . . . It requires us to pace ourselves. It returns us to a reckoning with time. In the midst of a book, we have no choice but to be patient, to take each thing in its moment, to let the narrative prevail. We regain the world by withdrawing from it just a little, by stepping back from the noise."

A book has a different relationship to time than a TV show or a Facebook update. It says that something was worth taking from the endless torrent of data and laying down on an object that will still look the same a hundred years from now. The French writer Jean-Philippe De Tonnac says "the true function of books is to safeguard the things that forgetfulness constantly threatens to destroy." It's precisely because it is not immediate—because it doesn't know what happened five minutes ago in Kazakhstan, or in Charlie Sheen's apartment—that the book matters.

That's why we need books, and why I believe they will survive. Because most humans have a desire to engage in deep thought and deep concentration. Those muscles are necessary for deep feeling and deep engagement. Most humans don't just want mental snacks forever; they also want meals.

I'm not against e-books in principle—I'm tempted by the Kindle—but the more they become interactive and linked, the more they multitask and offer a hundred different functions, the less they will be able to preserve the aspects of the book that we actually need. An e-book reader that does a lot will not, in the end, be a book. The object needs to remain dull so the words—offering you the most electric sensation of all: insight into another person's internal life—can sing.

10

So how do we preserve the mental space for the book? We are the first generation to ever use the internet, and when I look at how we are reacting to it, I keep thinking of the Inuit communities I met in the Arctic, who were given alcohol and sugar for the first time a generation ago, and guzzled them so rapidly they were now sunk in obesity and alcoholism. Sugar, alcohol and the web are all amazing pleasures and joys—but we need to know how to handle them without letting them addle us.

The idea of keeping yourself on a digital diet will, I suspect, become mainstream soon. Just as I've learned not to stock my fridge with tempting carbs, I've learned to limit my exposure to the web—and to love it in the limited window I allow myself. I have installed the programme "Freedom" on my laptop: it will disconnect you from the web for however long you tell it to. It's the Ritalin I need for my web-induced ADHD. I make sure I activate it so I can dive into the more permanent world of the printed page for at least two hours a day, or I find myself with a sense of endless online connection that leaves you oddly disconnected from yourself.

T. S. Eliot called books "the still point of the turning world." He was right. It turns out, in the age of super-speed broadband, we need dead trees to have fully living minds.

Questions for Critical Reading

1. Do you agree with Hari's assessment of the problem we face in this digital age? Why or why not?

2. Like works in many genres, Hari's op-ed has a problem/solution organization. While some problem/solution pieces devote several paragraphs or pages to the solution, Hari discusses his solution in one paragraph toward the end:

> The idea of keeping yourself on a digital diet will, I suspect, become mainstream soon. Just as I've learned not to stock my fridge with tempting carbs, I've learned to limit my exposure to the web—and to love it in the limited window I allow myself. I have installed the programme "Freedom" on my laptop: it will disconnect you from the web for however long you tell it to. It's the Ritalin I need for my web-induced ADHD. I make sure I activate it so I can dive into the more permanent world of the printed page for at least two hours a day, or I find myself with a sense of endless online connection that leaves you oddly disconnected from yourself. (para. 13)

Why do you think Hari waited until the very end to propose the solution of the digital diet when he could have proposed it much earlier? Did he succeed in persuading you that the digital diet is a good solution? Why or why not?

3. As an example of the flexibility of genre, it's interesting to note that while some op-eds refer to a recent event that motivates the writer's argument in the first paragraph, Hari doesn't do so until the second paragraph. Consider the first paragraph and the beginning of the second, and see if you can come up with a theory about why Hari waited until the second paragraph to discuss the event that prompted him to write:

> In the 20th century, all the nightmare-novels of the future imagined that books would be burnt. In the 21st century, our dystopias imagine a world where books are forgotten. To pluck just one, Gary Shteyngart's novel *Super Sad True Love Story* describes a world where everybody is obsessed with their electronic Apparat—an even more omnivorous i-Phone with a flickering stream of shopping and reality shows and porn—and have somehow come to believe that the few remaining unread paper books let off a rank smell. The book on the book, it suggests, is closing.
>
> I have been thinking about this because I recently moved flat, which for me meant boxing and heaving several Everests of books, accumulated obsessively since I was a kid. (paras. 1–2)

Why do you think Hari waits to discuss the event that prompted him to write? Would you have preferred that he refer to that event at the very beginning (with an opening sentence such as "I have been thinking about the decline of the book because I recently moved flat, which for me meant boxing and heaving several Everests of books, accumulated obsessively since I was a kid")? Why or why not?

4. In journalistic genres—especially newspaper writing—it's not uncommon to encounter short sentences (although short sentences can pack a punch in any genre). Consider which version of Hari's last paragraph you prefer—the original, with one medium-length sentence and two short ones, or the altered version, which conveys the same information in one longer sentence:

Original Passage	Altered Passage
T. S. Eliot called books "the still point of the turning world." He was right. It turns out, in the age of super-speed broadband, we need dead trees to have fully living minds. (para. 14)	T. S. Eliot was right to call books "the still point of the turning world," and it turns out, in the age of super-speed broadband, we need dead trees to have fully living minds.

Did you have a preference, and if so, which version did you prefer? Why? What might you as a writer have to gain by occasionally using short sentences? Take a minute to find another example of a short sentence. Did it work for you as a reader? Why or why not?

Making Connections

5. Examine the three types of evidence used in each of the following three genres: Hari's op-ed, John Grohol's blogged critique "*Pediatrics* Gets It Wrong about 'Facebook Depression'" (p. 644), and Nicholas Carr's magazine feature "Is Google Making Us Stupid?" (p. 574):

Hari's op-ed, "How to Survive the Age of Distraction"

A book has a different relationship to time than a TV show or a Facebook update. It says that something was worth taking from the endless torrent of data and laying down on an object that will still look the same a hundred years from now. The French writer Jean-Philippe De Tonnac says "the true function of books is to safeguard the things that forgetfulness constantly threatens to destroy." (para. 9)

Grohol's blogged critique, "*Pediatrics* Gets It Wrong about 'Facebook Depression'"

There are a multitude of studies that disagree with [the authors'] point of view...One longitudinal study (Kraut et al., 1998) found that, over a period of 0–12 months, both loneliness and depression increased with time spent online among adolescent and adult first-time Internet users. In a one-year follow-up study (Kraut et al., 2002), however, the observed negative effects of Internet use had disappeared. (para. 10)

Carr's magazine feature, "Is Google Making Us Stupid?"

[A] recently published study of online research habits, conducted by scholars from University College London, suggests that we may well be in the midst of a sea change in the way we read and think. As part of the five-year research program, the scholars examined computer logs documenting the behavior of visitors to two popular research sites, one operated by the British Library and one by a U.K. educational consortium, that provide access to journal articles, e-books and other sources of written information. They found that people using the sites exhibited "a form of skimming activity," hopping from one source to another and rarely returning to any source they'd already visited. They typically read no more than one or two pages of an article or book before they would "bounce" out to another site. Sometimes they'd save a long article, but there's no evidence that they ever went back and actually read it. The authors of the study report:

> It is clear that users are not reading online in the traditional sense; indeed there are signs that new forms of "reading" are emerging as users "power browse" horizontally through titles, contents pages and abstracts going for quick wins. It almost seems that they go online to avoid reading in the traditional sense. (para. 7)

How would you describe each author's use of evidence, and why do you think each author chose the type of evidence he did? How effective did you find each author's use of evidence, and why?

6. Making analogies (comparisons) is a strategy that writers across genres use for a variety of purposes. The following analogies come from four different genres: Hari's op-ed; Nicholas Carr's magazine feature "Is Google Making Us Stupid?" (p. 574); Jenna Johnson's blogged column "Fighting a Social Media Addiction" (p. 659); and Pamela Brown Rutledge's blogged critique of news coverage like Johnson's, "Social Media Addiction: Engage Brain before Believing" (p. 662). As you read the analogies (italicized), consider why writers across such a wide variety of genres might make comparisons, and see if you like some of the analogies better than others:

> **"How to Survive the Age of Distraction"**
>
> *Ask me to throw away a book, and I begin shaking like Meryl Streep in* Sophie's Choice. (para. 2)
>
> [M]ost humans have a desire to engage in deep thought and deep concentration. Those muscles are necessary for deep feeling and deep engagement. *Most humans don't just want mental snacks forever; they also want meals.* (para. 10)
>
> [The program "Freedom" is] *the Ritalin I need for my web-induced ADHD.* (para. 13)
>
> **"Is Google Making Us Stupid?"**
>
> *Once I was a scuba diver in the sea of words. Now I zip along the surface like a guy on a Jet Ski.* (para. 4)
>
> **"Fighting a Social Media Addiction"**
>
> But just read the blogs these students wrote after the traumatic experience [of unplugging]—*it's very easy to confuse these students with crack addicts who went cold-turkey, smokers not given the comfort of a patch while quitting, alcoholics forced to dry up.* (para. 3)
>
> **"Social Media Addiction: Engage Brain before Believing"**
>
> There is no way to . . . have someone else vet all the material you read. You have to do it yourself. *Think of it like defensive driving.* (para. 12)

Why do you think these writers, representing such a wide variety of genres, all decided to use analogies? Did you find all the analogies equally effective, or did some work better than others for you? Why?

Writing: Your Turn

1. Write a letter to the editor responding to Hari's op-ed. Although the *Independent* probably wouldn't publish it since Hari's article was written a couple of years ago, it's useful to have experience writing this important genre. In your letter, state your response to Hari's op-ed, and provide evidence (ideally evidence not used by Hari) to support your point. Note that you might respond to the overarching argument Hari makes or to a specific sentence, paragraph, or point he makes. After you write your letter, trade with some classmates to get feedback on how to make your letter even more persuasive. For ideas on writing a letter to the editor, see p. 62.

2. Using Hari's op-ed as a model, write your own op-ed on the issue he discusses (or a similar issue). Before you start writing, target a specific newspaper or other venue, and be sure to find out about its op-ed guidelines — for example, does it accept op-eds from nonstaffers and does it have a length limit? For a list of U.S. newspapers by state, see www.newslink.org/statnews .html, but also bear in mind your campus paper as well as online venues.

When you write your op-ed, have a specific purpose in mind (e.g., making readers aware of an issue or persuading them to take a particular action), but begin your piece with a timely hook; you might, for instance, tell a story about a recent event that illustrates how a certain technology affects you or others, or you might refer to some recent news (e.g., "Facebook/Twitter, etc., now has _____ users"). Alternatively, you could find a recent study that's relevant to the technology you're interested in.[1] After you've crafted a timely hook, lead into your argument and support it with evidence.

When you're done writing the op-ed, give it to some classmates so they can give you feedback on how to make it even more persuasive. After revising, submit your op-ed to the publication you've targeted. For more ideas on writing an op-ed, see p. 62.

---

[1] To find a timely angle for your op-ed hook, go to www.google.com/alerts and type the name of the topic you want to write about into the top box. You might also look at recent press releases on www.eurekalert.org by clicking on "Technology & Engineering." Another resource for press releases is www.sciencedaily.com; scroll all the way down to the bottom of the page to find a search box.

Magazine feature

Is Google Making Us Stupid?

Nicholas Carr

In his well-known article "Is Google Making Us Stupid?" Nicholas Carr argues that our brains are being rewired by our use of the Internet. Published in the *Atlantic* in 2008, the article was a seed that later became a book titled *The Shallows: What the Internet Is Doing to Our Brains,* a finalist for the 2011 Pulitzer Prize for General Nonfiction. Carr is also the author of the blog *Rough Type* (www.roughtype.com) and several other books, including *The Big Switch: Rewiring the World, from Edison to Google* (2008).

Following "Is Google Making Us Stupid?" you'll find a critique of it written by Trent Batson.

Focus on Genre   As a feature in a magazine like the *Atlantic*, "Is Google Making Us Stupid?" has the luxury of being able to be longer than pieces in many other genres and venues, including many other magazines. (Magazines are aimed at very specific audiences and thus tend to vary in article length, among other things. The *Atlantic* is a highly respected magazine aimed at an educated readership.)

The additional length afforded by the *Atlantic* allows Carr to accomplish much that he couldn't in other genres, including situating his argument within a brief history of technology, recognizing more complexity, and drawing on both his personal experience and previously published research to support his claims. The longer length also allows Carr to devote more than one paragraph to developing a point, thus potentially enabling him to better persuade readers. As you read, think about how Carr's individual paragraphs fit into his overarching argument and whether you find his article more persuasive than you might if it were compressed to, say, a five-paragraph essay.

Your initial insight into Carr's argument can be gleaned from the title, "Is Google Making Us Stupid?" When you consider what Carr's argument is, bear in mind that his title refers to a specific example, Google, as a way of representing a much broader category, the Internet (and, some would say, texting).

◄○►

"Dave, stop. Stop, will you? Stop, Dave. Will you stop, Dave?" So the super-computer HAL pleads with the implacable astronaut Dave Bowman in a famous and weirdly poignant scene toward the end of Stanley Kubrick's *2001: A Space Odyssey*. Bowman, having nearly been sent to a deep-space death by the malfunctioning machine, is calmly, coldly disconnecting the memory circuits that control its artificial brain. "Dave, my mind is going," HAL says, for-lornly. "I can feel it. I can feel it."

I can feel it, too. Over the past few years I've had an uncomfortable sense that someone, or something, has been tinkering with my brain, remapping the neural circuitry, reprogramming the memory. My mind isn't going—so far as I can tell—but it's changing. I'm not thinking the way I used to think. I can feel it most strongly when I'm reading. Immersing myself in a book or a lengthy article used to be easy. My mind would get caught up in the narrative or the turns of the argument, and I'd spend hours strolling through long stretches of prose. That's rarely the case anymore. Now my concentration often starts to drift after two or three pages. I get fidgety, lose the thread, begin looking for something else to do. I feel as if I'm always dragging my wayward brain back to the text. The deep reading that used to come naturally has become a struggle.

I think I know what's going on. For more than a decade now, I've been spending a lot of time online, searching and surfing and sometimes adding to the great databases of the Internet. The Web has been a godsend to me as a writer. Research that once required days in the stacks or periodical rooms of libraries can now be done in minutes. A few Google searches, some quick clicks on hyperlinks, and I've got the telltale fact or pithy quote I was after. Even when I'm not working, I'm as likely as not to be foraging in the Web's info-thickets—reading and writing e-mails, scanning headlines and blog posts, watching videos and listening to podcasts, or just tripping from link to link to link. (Unlike footnotes, to which they're sometimes likened, hyperlinks don't merely point to related works; they propel you toward them.)

For me, as for others, the Net is becoming a universal medium, the conduit for most of the information that flows through my eyes and ears and into my mind. The advantages of having immediate access to such an incredibly rich store of information are many, and they've been widely described and duly applauded. "The perfect recall of silicon memory," *Wired*'s Clive Thompson has written, "can be an enormous boon to thinking." But that boon comes at a price. As the media theorist Marshall McLuhan pointed out in the 1960s, media are not just passive channels of information. They supply the stuff of thought, but they also shape the process of thought. And what the Net seems to be doing is chipping away my capacity for concentration and contemplation. My mind now expects to take in information the way the Net distributes it: in a swiftly moving stream of particles. Once I was a scuba diver in the sea of words. Now I zip along the surface like a guy on a Jet Ski.

I'm not the only one. When I mention my troubles with reading to friends   5 and acquaintances—literary types, most of them—many say they're having similar experiences. The more they use the Web, the more they have to fight to stay focused on long pieces of writing. Some of the bloggers I follow have also begun mentioning the phenomenon. Scott Karp, who writes a blog about online media, recently confessed that he has stopped reading books altogether. "I was a lit major in college, and used to be [a] voracious book reader," he wrote. "What happened?" He speculates on the answer: "What if I do all my reading on the web not so much because the way I read has changed, i.e. I'm just seeking convenience, but because the way I THINK has changed?"

Bruce Friedman, who blogs regularly about the use of computers in medicine, also has described how the Internet has altered his mental habits. "I now have almost totally lost the ability to read and absorb a longish article on the web or in print," he wrote earlier this year. A pathologist who has long been on the faculty of the University of Michigan Medical School, Friedman elaborated on his comment in a telephone conversation with me. His thinking, he said, has taken on a "staccato" quality, reflecting the way he quickly scans short passages of text from many sources online. "I can't read *War and Peace* anymore," he admitted. "I've lost the ability to do that. Even a blog post of more than three or four paragraphs is too much to absorb. I skim it."

Anecdotes alone don't prove much. And we still await the long-term neurological and psychological experiments that will provide a definitive picture of how Internet use affects cognition. But a recently published study of online research habits, conducted by scholars from University College London, suggests that we may well be in the midst of a sea change in the way we read and think. As part of the five-year research program, the scholars examined computer logs documenting the behavior of visitors to two popular research sites, one operated by the British Library and one by a U.K. educational consortium, that provide access to journal articles, e-books and other sources of written information. They found that people using the sites exhibited "a form of skimming activity," hopping from one source to another and rarely returning to any source they'd already visited. They typically read no more than one or two pages of an article or book before they would "bounce" out to another site. Sometimes they'd save a long article, but there's no evidence that they ever went back and actually read it. The authors of the study report:

> It is clear that users are not reading online in the traditional sense; indeed there are signs that new forms of "reading" are emerging as users "power browse" horizontally through titles, contents pages and abstracts going for quick wins. It almost seems that they go online to avoid reading in the traditional sense.

Thanks to the ubiquity of text on the Internet, not to mention the popularity of text-messaging on cell phones, we may well be reading more today than we did in the 1970s or 1980s, when television was our medium of choice. But it's a different kind of reading, and behind it lies a different kind of thinking—perhaps even a new sense of the self. "We are not only *what* we read," says Maryanne Wolf, a developmental psychologist at Tufts University and the author of *Proust and the Squid: The Story and Science of the Reading Brain.* "We are *how* we read." Wolf worries that the style of reading promoted by the Net, a style that puts "efficiency" and "immediacy" above all else, may be weakening our capacity for the kind of deep reading that emerged when an earlier technology, the printing press, made long and complex works of prose commonplace. When we read online, she says, we tend to become "mere decoders of information." Our ability to interpret text, to make the rich mental connections that form when we read deeply and without distraction, remains largely disengaged.

Reading, explains Wolf, is not an instinctive skill for human beings. It's not etched into our genes the way speech is. We have to teach our minds how to translate the symbolic characters we see into the language we understand. And the media or other technologies we use in learning and practicing the craft of reading play an important part in shaping the neural circuits inside our brains. Experiments demonstrate that readers of ideograms, such as the Chinese, develop a mental circuitry for reading that is very different from the circuitry found in those of us whose written language employs an alphabet. The variations extend across many regions of the brain, including those that govern such essential cognitive functions as memory and the interpretation of visual and auditory stimuli. We can expect as well that the circuits woven by our use of the Net will be different from those woven by our reading of books and other printed works.

*   *   *

Sometime in 1882, Friedrich Nietzsche bought a typewriter—a Malling-Hansen 10 Writing Ball, to be precise. His vision was failing, and keeping his eyes focused on a page had become exhausting and painful, often bringing on crushing headaches. He had been forced to curtail his writing, and he feared that he would soon have to give it up. The typewriter rescued him, at least for a time. Once he had mastered touch-typing he was able to write with his eyes closed, using only the tips of his fingers. Words could once again flow from his mind to the page.

But the machine had a subtler effect on his work. One of Nietzsche's friends, a composer, noticed a change in the style of his writing. His already terse prose had become even tighter, more telegraphic. "Perhaps you will through this instrument even take to a new idiom," the friend wrote in a letter, noting that, in his own work, his "'thoughts' in music and language often depend on the quality of pen and paper."

"You are right," Nietzsche replied, "our writing equipment takes part in the forming of our thoughts." Under the sway of the machine, writes the German media scholar Friedrich A. Kittler, Nietzsche's prose "changed from arguments to aphorisms, from thoughts to puns, from rhetoric to telegram style."

The human brain is almost infinitely malleable. People used to think that our mental meshwork, the dense connections formed among the 100 billion or so neurons inside our skulls, was largely fixed by the time we reached adulthood. But brain researchers have discovered that that's not the case. James Olds, a professor of neuroscience who directs the Krasnow Institute for Advanced Study at George Mason University, says that even the adult mind "is very plastic." Nerve cells routinely break old connections and form new ones. "The brain," according to Olds, "has the ability to reprogram itself on the fly, altering the way it functions."

As we use what the sociologist Daniel Bell has called our "intellectual technologies"—the tools that extend our mental rather than our physical capacities—we inevitably begin to take on the qualities of those technologies. The mechanical clock, which came into common use in the 14th century, provides a compelling example. In *Technics and Civilization*, the historian and cultural critic Lewis Mumford described how the clock "disassociated time from human events and helped create the belief in an independent world of mathematically measurable sequences." The "abstract framework of divided time" became "the point of reference for both action and thought."

The clock's methodical ticking helped bring into being the scientific mind and the scientific man. But it also took something away. As the late MIT computer scientist Joseph Weizenbaum observed in his 1976 book, *Computer Power and Human Reason: From Judgment to Calculation*, the conception of the world that emerged from the widespread use of timekeeping instruments "remains an impoverished version of the older one, for it rests on a rejection of those direct experiences that formed the basis for, and indeed constituted, the old reality." In deciding when to eat, to work, to sleep, to rise, we stopped listening to our senses and started obeying the clock.

The process of adapting to new intellectual technologies is reflected in the changing metaphors we use to explain ourselves to ourselves. When the mechanical clock arrived, people began thinking of their brains as operating "like clockwork." Today, in the age of software, we have come to think of them as operating "like computers." But the changes, neuroscience tells us, go much deeper than metaphor. Thanks to our brain's plasticity, the adaptation occurs also at a biological level.

The Internet promises to have particularly far-reaching effects on cognition. In a paper published in 1936, the British mathematician Alan Turing proved that a digital computer, which at the time existed only as a theoretical machine, could be programmed to perform the function of any other information-processing device. And that's what we're seeing today. The Internet, an immeasurably powerful computing system, is subsuming most of our other intellectual technologies. It's becoming our map and our clock, our printing press and our typewriter, our calculator and our telephone, and our radio and TV.

When the Net absorbs a medium, that medium is re-created in the Net's image. It injects the medium's content with hyperlinks, blinking ads, and other digital gewgaws, and it surrounds the content with the content of all the other media it has absorbed. A new e-mail message, for instance, may announce its arrival as we're glancing over the latest headlines at a newspaper's site. The result is to scatter our attention and diffuse our concentration.

The Net's influence doesn't end at the edges of a computer screen, either. As people's minds become attuned to the crazy quilt of Internet media, traditional media have to adapt to the audience's new expectations. Television programs add text crawls and pop-up ads, and magazines and newspapers shorten their articles, introduce capsule summaries, and crowd their pages with easy-to-browse info-snippets. When, in March of this year, the *New York Times* decided to devote the second and third pages of every edition to article abstracts, its design director, Tom Bodkin, explained that the "shortcuts" would give harried readers a quick "taste" of the day's news, sparing them the "less efficient" method of actually turning the pages and reading the articles. Old media have little choice but to play by the new-media rules.

Never has a communications system played so many roles in our lives—or   20
exerted such broad influence over our thoughts—as the Internet does today. Yet, for all that's been written about the Net, there's been little consideration of how, exactly, it's reprogramming us. The Net's intellectual ethic remains obscure.

*   *   *

About the same time that Nietzsche started using his typewriter, an earnest young man named Frederick Winslow Taylor carried a stopwatch into the Midvale Steel plant in Philadelphia and began a historic series of experiments aimed at improving the efficiency of the plant's machinists. With the approval of Midvale's owners, he recruited a group of factory hands, set them to work on various metalworking machines, and recorded and timed their every movement as well as the operations of the machines. By breaking down every job into a sequence of small, discrete steps and then testing different ways of performing each one, Taylor created a set of precise instructions—an "algorithm," we might say today—for how each worker should work. Midvale's employees grumbled about the strict new regime, claiming that it turned them into little more than automatons, but the factory's productivity soared.

More than a hundred years after the invention of the steam engine, the Industrial Revolution had at last found its philosophy and its philosopher. Taylor's tight industrial choreography—his "system," as he liked to call it—was embraced by manufacturers throughout the country and, in time, around the world. Seeking maximum speed, maximum efficiency, and maximum output, factory owners used time-and-motion studies to organize their work and configure the jobs of their workers. The goal, as Taylor defined it in his celebrated 1911 treatise, *The Principles of Scientific Management*, was to identify and adopt, for every job, the "one best method" of work and thereby to effect "the gradual substitution of science for rule of thumb throughout the mechanic arts." Once his system was applied to all acts of manual labor, Taylor assured his followers, it would bring about a restructuring not only of industry but of society, creating a utopia of perfect efficiency. "In the past the man has been first," he declared; "in the future the system must be first."

Taylor's system is still very much with us; it remains the ethic of industrial manufacturing. And now, thanks to the growing power that computer engineers and software coders wield over our intellectual lives, Taylor's ethic is beginning to govern the realm of the mind as well. The Internet is a machine designed for the efficient and automated collection, transmission, and manipulation of information, and its legions of programmers are intent on finding the "one best method"—the perfect algorithm—to carry out every mental movement of what we've come to describe as "knowledge work."

*   *   *

Google's headquarters, in Mountain View, California—the Googleplex—is the Internet's high church, and the religion practiced inside its walls is Taylorism. Google, says its chief executive, Eric Schmidt, is "a company that's founded around the science of measurement," and it is striving to "systematize everything" it does. Drawing on the terabytes of behavioral data it collects through its search engine and other sites, it carries out thousands of experiments a day, according to the *Harvard Business Review*, and it uses the results to refine the algorithms that increasingly control how people find information and extract meaning from it. What Taylor did for the work of the hand, Google is doing for the work of the mind.

The company has declared that its mission is "to organize the world's information and make it universally accessible and useful." It seeks to develop "the perfect search engine," which it defines as something that "understands exactly what you mean and gives you back exactly what you want." In Google's view, information is a kind of commodity, a utilitarian resource that can be mined and processed with industrial efficiency. The more pieces of information we can "access" and the faster we can extract their gist, the more productive we become as thinkers.

Where does it end? Sergey Brin and Larry Page, the gifted young men who founded Google while pursuing doctoral degrees in computer science at Stanford, speak frequently of their desire to turn their search engine into an artificial intelligence, a HAL-like machine that might be connected directly to our brains. "The ultimate search engine is something as smart as people—or smarter," Page said in a speech a few years back. "For us, working on search is a way to work on artificial intelligence." In a 2004 interview with *Newsweek*, Brin said, "Certainly if you had all the world's information directly attached to your brain, or an artificial brain that was smarter than your brain, you'd be better off." Last year, Page told a convention of scientists that Google is "really trying to build artificial intelligence and to do it on a large scale."

Such an ambition is a natural one, even an admirable one, for a pair of math whizzes with vast quantities of cash at their disposal and a small army of computer scientists in their employ. A fundamentally scientific enterprise, Google is motivated by a desire to use technology, in Eric Schmidt's words, "to solve problems that have never been solved before," and artificial intelligence is the hardest problem out there. Why wouldn't Brin and Page want to be the ones to crack it?

Still, their easy assumption that we'd all "be better off" if our brains were supplemented, or even replaced, by an artificial intelligence is unsettling. It suggests a belief that intelligence is the output of a mechanical process, a series of discrete steps that can be isolated, measured, and optimized. In Google's world, the world we enter when we go online, there's little place for the fuzziness of contemplation. Ambiguity is not an opening for insight but a bug to be fixed. The human brain is just an outdated computer that needs a faster processor and a bigger hard drive.

The idea that our minds should operate as high-speed data-processing machines is not only built into the workings of the Internet, it is the network's reigning business model as well. The faster we surf across the Web—the more links we click and pages we view—the more opportunities Google and other companies gain to collect information about us and to feed us advertisements. Most of the proprietors of the commercial Internet have a financial stake in collecting the crumbs of data we leave behind as we flit from link to link—the more crumbs, the better. The last thing these companies want is to encourage leisurely reading or slow, concentrated thought. It's in their economic interest to drive us to distraction.

* * *

Maybe I'm just a worrywart. Just as there's a tendency to glorify technological   30
progress, there's a countertendency to expect the worst of every new tool or
machine. In Plato's *Phaedrus*, Socrates bemoaned the development of writing. He feared that, as people came to rely on the written word as a substitute
for the knowledge they used to carry inside their heads, they would, in the
words of one of the dialogue's characters, "cease to exercise their memory
and become forgetful." And because they would be able to "receive a quantity of information without proper instruction," they would "be thought very
knowledgeable when they are for the most part quite ignorant." They would
be "filled with the conceit of wisdom instead of real wisdom." Socrates wasn't
wrong—the new technology did often have the effects he feared—but he
was shortsighted. He couldn't foresee the many ways that writing and reading
would serve to spread information, spur fresh ideas, and expand human knowledge (if not wisdom).

The arrival of Gutenberg's printing press, in the 15th century, set off
another round of teeth gnashing. The Italian humanist Hieronimo Squarciafico
worried that the easy availability of books would lead to intellectual laziness,
making men "less studious" and weakening their minds. Others argued that
cheaply printed books and broadsheets would undermine religious authority,
demean the work of scholars and scribes, and spread sedition and debauchery.
As New York University professor Clay Shirky notes, "Most of the arguments
made against the printing press were correct, even prescient." But, again, the
doomsayers were unable to imagine the myriad blessings that the printed word
would deliver.

So, yes, you should be skeptical of my skepticism. Perhaps those who dismiss critics of the Internet as Luddites or nostalgists will be proved correct, and
from our hyperactive, data-stoked minds will spring a golden age of intellectual
discovery and universal wisdom. Then again, the Net isn't the alphabet, and
although it may replace the printing press, it produces something altogether
different. The kind of deep reading that a sequence of printed pages promotes
is valuable not just for the knowledge we acquire from the author's words but
for the intellectual vibrations those words set off within our own minds. In the
quiet spaces opened up by the sustained, undistracted reading of a book, or by
any other act of contemplation, for that matter, we make our own associations,
draw our own inferences and analogies, foster our own ideas. Deep reading, as
Maryanne Wolf argues, is indistinguishable from deep thinking.

If we lose those quiet spaces, or fill them up with "content," we will sacrifice something important not only in our selves but in our culture. In a recent
essay, the playwright Richard Foreman eloquently described what's at stake:

I come from a tradition of Western culture, in which the ideal (my ideal) was the complex, dense and "cathedral-like" structure of the highly educated and articulate personality—a man or woman who carried inside themselves a personally constructed and unique version of the entire heritage of the West. [But now] I see within us all (myself included) the replacement of complex inner density with a new kind of self—evolving under the pressure of information overload and the technology of the "instantly available."

As we are drained of our "inner repertory of dense cultural inheritance," Foreman concluded, we risk turning into "'pancake people'—spread wide and thin as we connect with that vast network of information accessed by the mere touch of a button."

I'm haunted by that scene in *2001*. What makes it so poignant, and so weird, is the computer's emotional response to the disassembly of its mind: its despair as one circuit after another goes dark, its childlike pleading with the astronaut—"I can feel it. I can feel it. I'm afraid"—and its final reversion to what can only be called a state of innocence. HAL's outpouring of feeling contrasts with the emotionlessness that characterizes the human figures in the film, who go about their business with an almost robotic efficiency. Their thoughts and actions feel scripted, as if they're following the steps of an algorithm. In the world of *2001*, people have become so machinelike that the most human character turns out to be a machine. That's the essence of Kubrick's dark prophecy: as we come to rely on computers to mediate our understanding of the world, it is our own intelligence that flattens into artificial intelligence.

LINKED
READING
PAGE 574

Critique

Response to Nicholas Carr's "Is Google Making Us Stupid?"

Trent Batson

Trent Batson's "Response to Nicholas Carr's 'Is Google Making Us Stupid?'" appeared in the Viewpoints section of *Campus Technology*, the companion Web site for the magazine of the same name. Batson is a former English professor who is now the executive director for the Association for Authentic, Experiential and Evidence-Based Learning (AAEEBL), a nonprofit educational organization that works with educators to promote the use of e-portfolios.

Focus on Genre   As you read Batson's critique of Carr, see whether you agree with Batson or Carr — or whether you think both authors make some valid points. Are Batson's points and Carr's points mutually exclusive?

Also consider how Batson's piece works as a critique. Note that before Batson critiques Carr, he's careful both to establish that Carr's views are commonly held and to find several positive things to say about Carr. Why might he make these moves?

Finally, consider how and why Batson summarizes Carr's argument before critiquing it. When Batson discusses Carr's ideas at length, can you tell that he's still talking about Carr's ideas and not his own ideas? Why do you think he bothers to summarize Carr in so much detail?

◄O►

Criticism of the Web most often questions whether we are becoming more superficial and scattered in our thinking. In the July–August 2008 *Atlantic* magazine, Nicholas Carr published "Is Google Making Us Stupid?" (http://www .theatlantic.com/doc/200807/google). Like other critics, he sees change as loss and not as gain. But, his own criticism is superficial and misses the humanizing impact of Web 2.0.

Nicholas Carr is an important voice today in pointing to the nervousness that many people have about technology. He recently published *The Big Switch: Rewiring the World, from Edison to Google*, which is in its seventh printing. His blog is well worth reading regularly: http://www.roughtype.com/. His views are carefully constructed and researched. He is a skilled writer and is widely read.

And, academics often express the same concerns Carr does in his *Atlantic* article. Our concerns are about the qualitative differences in how net-gen students think and write and learn. Nicholas Carr is giving voice to these concerns. This article is about one skill that he believes is being eroded, that of reading:

> I'm not thinking the way I used to think. I can feel it most strongly when I'm reading. Immersing myself in a book or a lengthy article used to be easy. My mind would get caught up in the narrative or the turns of the argument, and I'd spend hours strolling through long stretches of prose. That's rarely the case anymore. Now my concentration often starts to drift after two or three pages. I get fidgety, lose the thread, begin looking for something else to do. I feel as if I'm always dragging my wayward brain back to the text. The deep reading that used to come naturally has become a struggle.

He says this change is because of all the time he spends online. As a writer, he finds the Web a valuable tool, but he thinks it's having a bad effect on his concentration. He says "Once I was a scuba diver in the sea of words. Now I zip along the surface like a guy on a Jet Ski." He refers to a 5-year study in the UK, which found that people visiting their sites "exhibited 'a form of skimming activity,' hopping from one source to another and rarely returning to any source they'd already visited."

Carr admits that we, as a culture, read a lot more because of the Web, but 5 laments that "our ability to interpret text, to make the rich mental connections that form when we read deeply and without distraction, remains largely disengaged." And he highlights a quote from an essay by the playwright Richard Foreman:

> I come from a tradition of Western culture, in which the ideal (my ideal) was the complex, dense and 'cathedral-like' structure of the highly educated and articulate personality—a man or woman who carried inside themselves a personally constructed and unique version of the entire heritage of the West.

> [But now] I see within us all (myself included) the replacement of complex
> inner density with a new kind of self—evolving under the pressure of infor-
> mation overload and the technology of the 'instantly available.'

As an advocate for technology in higher education over the past 20 years,
I've heard similar warnings for years. Indeed, some people reading this article
may believe that Carr has hit the nail on the head. There is no question that
our habits are changing: The Web has captured our attention and is now
the default starting point for almost all work. The Web is different in almost
all aspects from a book. Printed books have contained the essential truths of
humanity for half a millennium. The Web is where we look for knowledge that
usually exists not in final, authoritative, single-author text blocks but in the
aggregate of wisdom from many sites.

Carr sees only one side of the change we are going through, the loss of
book habits. But, for us over our thousands of years of learning, the book is the
anomaly, not the Web. The book led us to think that one person could write a
permanent compilation of truth. Books lived on over the years, separated from
their authors, a single voice, implying that knowledge is a thing or a commodity, creating the legal fiction that one person "owned" the ideas in a book as
though the author had grown up in isolation from all other humans and all the
ideas had sprung, fully-formed, from his or her brain.

Books are heavy and expensive and take a long time to produce. Knowledge based in books, therefore, is slow to develop, hard to respond to, and is
scarce. People responded to books with reviews, with articles, and with new
books. Human gregariousness was therefore slowed to a snail's pace as conversation around a book was carried out in the lengthy print process. Books built
our culture, don't get me wrong, and have provided wonderful wealth, but ultimately they also undervalued and ignored the natural ways that humans learn:
through oral interaction and in a group.

It is easy to criticize a new technology; it is much harder to understand
how the new technology can help create new abilities in humans. And even
much harder to understand how technology can actually recapture and
re-enable human abilities.

What Carr describes and is most worried about, how we "skim" and
"bounce" around in our reading, is actually a kind of new orality: We are
reading as we speak when we are in a group. We "listen" to one statement,
then another and another in quick succession: Our reading on the Web is like
listening to a bunch of people talking. It's hybrid orality. We find ourselves
once again the naturally gregarious humans we always were. We find ourselves
creating knowledge continually and rapidly as our social contacts on the Web
expand. We have re-discovered new ways to enjoy learning in a social setting.

No, Google is not making us stupid. What Google and the Web are doing is helping us re-claim our human legacy of learning through a rapid exchange of ideas in a social setting. Google is, indeed, making us smarter as we re-discover new ways to learn.

Questions for Critical Reading

1. How would you summarize Carr's and Batson's arguments? Did you agree with one writer more than the other, or do you think both writers make some valid (or invalid) points? Why?

2. Like authors of other critiques, Batson is careful to situate Carr's argument; that is, he establishes how Carr's argument is related to what other people believe. Look at the following examples from Batson's critique and consider why he does this; note that the relevant phrases are italicized:

> *Like other critics,* [Carr] sees change as loss and not as gain. (para. 1)
>
> *Academics often express the same concerns* Carr does. (para. 3)
>
> *I've heard similar warnings* [to Carr's] for years. (para. 6)

Why do you think Batson so carefully establishes that Carr's concerns are common? When in your own writing might you want to establish that the beliefs of someone you're critiquing are commonly held?

3. Like other authors of researched arguments, Carr doesn't just cite a barrage of sources to support his claims; he also discusses his own personal experience:

> Over the past few years I've had an uncomfortable sense that someone, or something, has been tinkering with my brain, remapping the neural circuitry, reprogramming the memory. My mind isn't going—so far as I can tell—but it's changing. I'm not thinking the way I used to think. I can feel it most strongly when I'm reading. Immersing myself in a book or a lengthy article used to be easy. My mind would get caught up in the narrative or the turns of the argument, and I'd spend hours strolling through long stretches of prose. That's rarely the case anymore. . . .
>
> I think I know what's going on. For more than a decade now, I've been spending a lot of time online, searching and surfing and sometimes adding to the great databases of the Internet. . . .
>
> . . . And what the Net seems to be doing is chipping away my capacity for concentration and contemplation. (paras. 2–4)

Why do you think Carr discusses his personal experience before he discusses the research he's found? Would you have found his article more persuasive if he hadn't told us about his personal experience or if he had told us about it *after* discussing the research on the topic? Why or why not?

Questions

4. Like many other genres of researched argument, "Is Google Making Us Stupid?" might be considered an "anti-five-paragraph essay," for it lets its argument unfold and breathe, unconstrained by being limited to just an introductory paragraph, three body paragraphs, and a concluding paragraph. (Note that many professors rejoice when students can get beyond a five-paragraph essay and make a more in-depth argument.)

To get a sense of what is lost and perhaps gained by the genre of the five-paragraph essay, translate the following outline of the crux of Carr's argument into an outline for a five-paragraph essay:

para. 1	"Dave, stop" (quotes the movie *2001: A Space Odyssey*).
paras. 2–3	Discusses how it's become harder for him to read books since he's been spending a lot of time online.
para. 4	Speculates, drawing on media theorist Marshall McLuhan, that media not only "supply the stuff of thought, but they also shape the process of thought."
paras. 5–6	Notes that he's "not the only one"—that his friends and acquaintances, as well as bloggers Scott Karp and Bruce Friedman, have also started to have trouble staying focused on long pieces of writing since they've been spending time online.
para. 7	Notes that "anecdotes alone don't prove much" and cites research conducted by scholars from University College London suggesting that, as a result of the time we spend online, "we may well be in the midst of a sea change in the way we read and think."
para. 8	Notes that reading text on the Internet and text messages on cell phones is a different type of reading, and draws on developmental psychologist Maryanne Wolf to suggest that "the style of reading promoted by the Net" diminishes our "ability to interpret text, to make the rich mental connections that form when we read deeply and without distraction."
para. 9	Continues to draw on Wolf to note that reading isn't instinctive—that "we have to teach our minds how to translate the symbolic characters we see" and that "media or other technologies we use in . . . reading play an important part in shaping the neural circuits inside our brains." Discusses experiments demonstrating that readers of ideograms develop a different mental circuitry for reading, and argues that "we can expect as well that the circuits woven by our use of the Net will be different from those woven by our reading of books and other printed works."

| paras. 10–12 | Discusses Nietzsche: when Nietzsche used a different technology to write, the quality of the thoughts expressed in his writing changed. |
| para. 13 | Draws on neuroscience professor James Olds to suggest that the neural networks in our brain can change—that, in the words of Olds, "the brain has the ability to reprogram itself on the fly, altering the way it functions." |

Compare your outline for a five-paragraph essay to some of your classmates' outlines. Are there any five-paragraph versions of Carr's article that you would prefer to his original article? Why or why not? When might you as a writer choose to make an argument in five-paragraph form, and when might you choose to write a longer, more in-depth argument?

5. In most genres that draw on sources—whether those sources are interviews or published research—writers who draw on the same source over the course of a paragraph or more will generally use attribution tags (e.g., "Smith writes" or "Smith believes") *repeatedly* throughout a passage, not just once. Compare the original versions of the following passages—one from Carr and one from Batson—to altered versions that use only one attribution tag, and see if you can develop a theory about why these authors might have used so many attribution tags (italicized):

Original Passage	Altered Passage
"We are not only what we read," *says Maryanne Wolf,* a developmental psychologist at Tufts University. . . . "We are how we read." *Wolf worries* that the style of reading promoted by the Net, a style that puts "efficiency" and "immediacy" above all else, may be weakening our capacity for the kind of deep reading that emerged when an earlier technology, the printing press, made long and complex works of prose commonplace. When we read online, *she says,* we tend to become "mere decoders of information." (Carr, para. 8; emphasis altered)	"We are not only what we read," *says Maryanne Wolf,* a developmental psychologist at Tufts University. . . . "We are how we read." The style of reading promoted by the Net, a style that puts "efficiency" and "immediacy" above all else, may be weakening our capacity for the kind of deep reading that emerged when an earlier technology, the printing press, made long and complex works of prose commonplace. When we read online, we tend to become "mere decoders of information."

Connections

Original Passage	Altered Passage
[Carr] says this change is because of all the time he spends online. *As a writer, he finds* the Web a valuable tool, but *he thinks* it's having a bad effect on his concentration. *He says* "Once I was a scuba diver in the sea of words. Now I zip along the surface like a guy on a Jet Ski." *He refers* to a 5-year study in the UK, which found that people visiting their sites "exhibited 'a form of skimming activity,' hopping from one source to another and rarely returning to any source they'd already visited."	*[Carr] says* this change is because of all the time he spends online. The Web is a valuable tool, but it's having a bad effect on his concentration. "Once I was a scuba diver in the sea of words. Now I zip along the surface like a guy on a Jet Ski." A 5-year study in the UK found that people visiting their sites "exhibited 'a form of skimming activity,' hopping from one source to another and rarely returning to any source they'd already visited."
Carr admits that we, as a culture, read a lot more because of the Web, but *laments* that "our ability to interpret text, to make the rich mental connections that form when we read deeply and without distraction, remains largely disengaged." (Batson, paras. 4–5)	As a culture, we read a lot more because of the Web, but "our ability to interpret text, to make the rich mental connections that form when we read deeply and without distraction, remains largely disengaged."

Why do you think both authors used so many attribution tags? How did your experience reading the original passages differ from your experience reading the altered passages? When might you as a writer want to use multiple attribution tags as Carr and Batson do?

Making Connections

6. Recall that writers in many genres try to avoid making simple black-and-white arguments ("X is great" or "X is terrible"); instead, they try to recognize complexity and nuance, acknowledging that even when something is problematic, it can have benefits — or, conversely, that even when something is beneficial, it can have disadvantages. Consider why Carr, Batson, and Johann Hari, author of the op-ed "How to Survive the Age of Distraction" (p. 566), all make this move:

    ### Carr

    The advantages of having immediate access to such an incredibly rich store of information are many, and they've been widely described and duly applauded. . . . But that boon comes at a price. (para. 4)

Batson

Books built our culture, don't get me wrong, and have provided wonderful wealth, but ultimately they also undervalued and ignored the natural ways that humans learn: through oral interaction and in a group. (para. 8)

Hari

I adore the web, and they will have to wrench my Twitter feed from my cold dead hands. This isn't going to turn into an antediluvian rant against the glories of our wired world. But there's a reason why that word — "wired" — means both "connected to the internet" and "high, frantic, unable to concentrate." (para. 6)

How might you have responded differently had each author not acknowledged the flip side of his argument? When might you as a writer want to recognize the positive aspects of something you're arguing against or the negative aspects of something you're arguing for?

7. Recall that writers across genres often provide some basic identifying information about the people they refer to, quote, or paraphrase. Consider the following three passages — one from "Is Google Making Us Stupid?," one from Johann Hari's op-ed "How to Survive the Age of Distraction" (p. 566), and one from Pamela Brown Rutledge's blogged critique "Social Media Addiction: Engage Brain before Believing" (p. 662) — and notice how the identifying information (italicized) about the people being quoted or referred to affects your reading of the passages:

Carr

[T]he historian and cultural critic Lewis Mumford described how the clock "disassociated time from human events and helped create the belief in an independent world of mathematically measurable sequences." (para. 14)

Hari

In the 1950s, *the novelist* Herman Hesse wrote: "The more the need for entertainment and mainstream education can be met by new inventions, the more the book will recover its dignity and authority. We have not yet quite reached the point where young competitors, such as radio, cinema, etc., have taken over the functions from the book it can't afford to lose." (para. 7)

Rutledge

The web-published results were a thoughtful qualitative analysis by a team headed by *University of Maryland professor* Dr. Susan Moeller. (para. 5)

Why do you think all three authors chose to tell us some identifying information about the people they referred to or quoted? When might you as a writer want to provide identifying information about a source?

Writing

Writing: Your Turn

1. Referring to Carr, write a reflection on whether you think your attention span is affected by the Internet. When you're done writing, trade reflections with some classmates so that you can all get a sense of whether or not your experience is typical, and so that you can give one another feedback to use in revision. Before you give your draft to your classmates, make a list of a few specific points or passages that you'd like feedback on. For strategies to use when writing a reflection, see p. 27.

2. Make an argument, addressed to an audience of classmates, that takes a stance on the Carr-Batson debate. You might agree with Carr or with Batson, or you might argue that the two writers' positions aren't mutually exclusive—that both make valid (or invalid) points. Be sure to support your claims with evidence. After you're done writing, trade with some classmates to get feedback on how clear your argument is and how well you support it with evidence. For ideas on writing an argument, see p. 42.

3. As a way of gaining insight into the genre Carr is using and the genre of the five-paragraph essay, translate Carr's article into a five-paragraph essay, and then write a paragraph reflecting on what was lost or gained in translation. You might find it helpful to refer to question 4 to guide your translation. After you're done writing and doing a round of revision on your own, get feedback from your classmates on how your essay might be even stronger, and see if they have any additional insight into what was lost or gained in translation. Since five-paragraph essays generally make an argument, see p. 42 for strategies you can use in your essay.

From *Alone Together: Why We Expect More from Technology and Less from Each Other*

Sherry Turkle

MIT professor Sherry Turkle, who has a joint doctorate in sociology and personality psychology, published the book *Alone Together: Why We Expect More from Technology and Less from Each Other* (2011) to share her research with a general audience. Although Turkle doesn't provide a full discussion of how she conducted her research, she does say in an author's note (not included in the following excerpt) that she spent fifteen years doing the research and that over 450 people participated in her study, which involved both field research and detailed interviews. Turkle also states in a footnote that she studied teenagers from a wide range of economic, social, and ethnic backgrounds.

Focus on Genre   As you read this excerpt from *Alone Together,* consider how the book-length genre Turkle is using helps her advance an argument that a broad audience might find persuasive. Think about what her main point (thesis) is, and assess her use of evidence. Notice that she uses two types of evidence to support her points; how would you describe these two types of evidence, and how persuasive do you think each type is for her intended audience? Also notice the weighting of the two types of evidence, and consider why Turkle might have chosen to rely more heavily on one type than the other.

Finally, think about the solution Turkle proposes toward the end of the selection. Do you believe it would successfully address the problem she identifies in her thesis? Why or why not?

◄◦►

ALWAYS ON

The New State of the Self: Multitasking and the Alchemy of Time

In the 1980s, the children I interviewed about their lives with technology often did their homework with television and music in the background and a handheld video game for distraction. Algebra and Super Mario were part of the same package. Today, such recollections sound almost pastoral. A child doing homework is usually—among other things—attending to Facebook, shopping, music, online games, texting, videos, calls, and instant messages. Absent only is e-mail, considered by most people under twenty-five a technology of the past, or perhaps required to apply to college or to submit a job application.

Subtly, over time, multitasking, once seen as something of a blight, was recast as a virtue. And over time, the conversation about its virtues became extravagant, with young people close to lionized for their ability to do many things at once. Experts went so far as to declare multitasking not just a skill but *the* crucial skill for successful work and learning in digital culture. There was even concern that old-fashioned teachers who could only do one thing at a time would hamper student learning.[1] Now we must wonder at how easily we were smitten. When psychologists study multitasking, they do not find a story of new efficiencies. Rather, multitaskers don't perform as well on any of the tasks they are attempting.[2] But multitasking feels good because the body rewards it with neurochemicals that induce a multitasking "high." The high deceives multitaskers into thinking they are being especially productive. In search of the high, they want to do even more. In the years ahead, there will be a lot to sort out. We fell in love with what technology made easy. Our bodies colluded. . . .

Our networked devices encourage a new notion of time because they promise that one can layer more activities onto it. Because you can text while doing something else, texting does not seem to take time but to give you time. This is more than welcome; it is magical. We have managed to squeeze in that extra little bit, but the fastest living among us encourage us to read books with titles such as *In Praise of Slowness*.[3] And we have found ways of spending more time with friends and family in which we hardly give them any attention at all.

We are overwhelmed across the generations. Teenagers complain that parents don't look up from their phones at dinner and that they bring their phones to school sporting events. Hannah, sixteen, is a solemn, quiet high school junior. She tells me that for years she has tried to get her mother's attention when her mother comes to fetch her after school or after dance lessons. Hannah says, "The car will start; she'll be driving still looking down, looking at her messages, but still no hello." We will hear others tell similar stories.

Parents say they are ashamed of such behavior but quickly get around to   5
explaining, if not justifying, it. They say they are more stressed than ever as
they try to keep up with e-mail and messages. They always feel behind. They
cannot take a vacation without bringing the office with them; their office is
on their cell phone.[4] They complain that their employers require them to be
continually online but then admit that their devotion to their communications
devices exceeds all professional expectations. . . .

In a tethered world, too much is possible, yet few can resist measuring success against a metric of what they could accomplish if they were always available. Diane, thirty-six, a curator at a large Midwestern museum, cannot keep
up with the pace set by her technology.

> I suppose I do my job better, but my job is my whole life. Or my whole life
> is my job. When I move from calendar, to address book, to e-mail, to text
> messages, I feel like a master of the universe; everything is so efficient. I am a
> maximizing machine. I am on my BlackBerry until two in the morning. I don't
> sleep well, but I still can't keep up with what is sent to me.
>
> Now for work, I'm expected to have a Twitter feed and a Facebook presence
> about the museum. And do a blog on museum happenings. That means me in
> all these places. I have a voice condition. I keep losing my voice. It's not from
> talking too much. All I do I type, but it has hit me at my voice. The doctor says
> it's a nervous thing.

Diane, in the company of programs, feels herself "a master of the universe."
Yet, she is only powerful enough to see herself as a "maximizing machine"
that responds to what the network throws at her. She and her husband have
decided they should take a vacation. She plans to tell her colleagues that
she is going to be "off the grid" for two weeks, but Diane keeps putting off
her announcement. She doesn't know how it will be taken. The norm in the
museum is that it is fine to take time off for vacations but not to go offline during them. So, a vacation usually means working from someplace picturesque.
Indeed, advertisements for wireless networks routinely feature a handsome man
or beautiful woman sitting on a beach. Tethered, we are not to deny the body
and its pleasures but to put our bodies somewhere beautiful while we work.
Once, mobile devices needed to be shown in such advertisements. Now, they
are often implied. We know that the successful are always connected. On vacation, one vacates a place, not a set of responsibilities. In a world of constant
communication, Diane's symptom seems fitting: she has become a machine for
communicating, but she has no voice left for herself.

As Diane plans her "offline vacation," she admits that she really wants to
go to Paris, "but I would have no excuse not to be online in Paris. Helping to
build houses in the Amazon, well, who would know if they have Wi-Fi? My

new nonnegotiable for a vacation: I have to be able to at least pretend that there is no reason to bring my computer." But after her vacation to remote Brazil finally takes place, she tells me, "Everybody had their BlackBerries with them. Sitting there in the tent. It was as though there was some giant satellite parked in the sky."

Diane says she receives about five hundred e-mails, several hundred texts, and around forty calls a day. She notes that many business messages come in multiples. People send her a text and an e-mail, then place a call and leave a message on her voicemail. "Client anxiety," she explains. "They feel better if they communicate." In her world, Diane is accustomed to receiving a hasty message to which she is expected to give a rapid response. She worries that she does not have the time to take her time on the things that matter. And it is hard to maintain a sense of what matters in the din of constant communication.

The self shaped in the world of rapid response measures success by calls   10
made, e-mails answered, texts replied to, contacts reached. This self is cali-brated on the basis of what technology proposes, by what it makes easy. But in the technology-induced pressure for volume and velocity, we confront a paradox. We insist that our world is increasingly complex, yet we have created a communications culture that has decreased the time available for us to sit and think uninterrupted. As we communicate in ways that ask for almost instan-taneous responses, we don't allow sufficient space to consider complicated problems.

Trey, a forty-six-year-old lawyer with a large Boston firm, raises this issue explicitly. On e-mail, he says, "I answer questions I can answer right away. And people want me to answer them right away. But it's not only the speed. . . . The questions have changed to ones that I *can* answer right away." Trey describes legal matters that call for time and nuance and says that "people don't have patience for these now. They send an e-mail and they expect something back fast. They are willing to forgo the nuance; really, the client wants to hear some-thing now, and so I give the answers that can be sent back by return e-mail . . . or maybe answers that will take me a day, max. . . . I feel pressured to think in terms of bright lines." He corrects himself. "It's not the technology that does this, of course, but the technology sets expectations about speed." We are back to a conversation about affordances and vulnerabilities. The technology primes us for speed, and overwhelmed, we are happy to have it help us speed up. Trey reminds me that "we speak in terms of 'shooting off' an e-mail. Nobody 'shoots something off' because they want things to proceed apace."

Trey, like Diane, points out that clients frequently send him a text, an e-mail, and a voicemail. "They are saying, 'Feed me.' They feel they have the right." He sums up his experience of the past decade. Electronic communication has been liberating, but in the end, "it has put me on a speed-up, on a treadmill, but that isn't the same as being productive."

I talk with a group of lawyers who all insist that their work would be impossible without their "cells"—that nearly universal shorthand for the smartphones of today that have pretty much the functionality of desktop computers and more. The lawyers insist that they are more productive and their mobile devices "liberate" them to work from home and to travel with their families. The women, in particular, stress that the networked life makes it possible for them to keep their jobs and spend time with their children. Yet, they also say that their mobile devices eat away at their time to think. One says, "I don't have enough time alone with my mind." Others say, "I have to struggle to make time to think." "I artificially make time to think." "I block out time to think." These formulations all depend on an "I" imagined as separate from the technology, a self that is able to put the technology aside so that it can function independently of its demands. This formulation contrasts with a growing reality of lives lived in the continuous presence of screens. This reality has us, like the MIT cyborgs, learning to see ourselves as one with our devices. To make more time to think would mean turning off our phones. But this is not a simple proposition since our devices are ever more closely coupled to our sense of our bodies and minds.[5] They provide a social and psychological GPS, a navigation system for tethered selves. . . .

Fearful Symmetries

When I speak of a new state of the self, itself, I use the word "itself" with purpose. It captures, although with some hyperbole, my concern that the connected life encourages us to treat those we meet online in something of the same way we treat objects—with dispatch. It happens naturally: when you are besieged by thousands of e-mails, texts, and messages—more than you can respond to—demands become depersonalized. Similarly, when we Tweet or write to hundreds or thousands of Facebook friends as a group, we treat individuals as a unit. Friends become fans. A college junior contemplating the multitudes he can contact on the Net says, "I feel that I am part of a larger thing, the Net, the Web. The world. It becomes a thing to me, a thing I am part of. And the people, too, I stop seeing them as individuals, really. They are part of this larger thing."

With sociable robots, we imagine objects as people. Online, we invent   15
ways of being with people that turn them into something close to objects. The self that treats a person as a thing is vulnerable to seeing itself as one. It is important to remember that when we see robots as "alive enough" for us, we give them a promotion. If when on the Net, people feel just "alive enough" to

be "maximizing machines" for e-mails and messages, they have been demoted. These are fearful symmetries. . . .

I interview Sanjay, sixteen. We will talk for an hour between two of his class periods. At the beginning of our conversation, he takes his mobile phone out of his pocket and turns it off.[6] At the end of our conversation, he turns the phone back on. He looks at me ruefully, almost embarrassed. He has received over a hundred text messages as we were speaking. Some are from his girlfriend who, he says, "is having a meltdown." Some are from a group of close friends trying to organize a small concert. He feels a lot of pressure to reply and begins to pick up his books and laptop so he can find a quiet place to set himself to the task. As he says goodbye, he adds, not speaking particularly to me but more to himself as an afterthought to the conversation we have just had, "I can't imagine doing this when I get older." And then, more quietly, "How long do I have to continue doing this?"

GROWING UP TETHERED

Presentation Anxiety

. . . Early in my study, a college senior warned me not to be fooled by "anyone you interview who tells you that his Facebook page is 'the real me.' It's like being in a play. You make a character." Eric, a college-bound senior at Hadley, a boys' preparatory school in rural New Jersey, describes himself as savvy about how you can "mold a Facebook page." Yet, even he is shocked when he finds evidence of girls using "shrinking" software to appear thinner on their profile photographs. "You can't see that they do it when you look at the little version of the picture, but when you look at the big picture, you can see how the background is distorted." By eighteen, he has become an identity detective. The Facebook profile is a particular source of stress because it is important to high school social life. Some students feel so in its thrall that they drop out of Facebook, if only for a while, to collect themselves.

Brad, eighteen, a senior at Hadley, is about to take a gap year to do community service before attending a small liberal arts college in the Midwest. His parents are architects; his passion is biology and swimming. Brad wants to be part of the social scene at Hadley, but he doesn't like texting or instant messaging. He is careful to make sure I know he is "no Luddite." He has plenty of good things to say about the Net. He is sure that it makes it easier for insecure people to function. Sometimes the ability to compose his thoughts online "can be reassuring," he says, because there is a chance to "think through, calculate, edit, and make sure you're as clear and concise as possible." But as our conversation continues, Brad switches gears. Even as some are able to better function because they feel in control, online communication also offers an opportunity to ignore other people's feelings. You can avoid eye contact. You can elect not to hear how "hurt or angry they sound in their voice." He says, "Online, people miss your body language, tone of voice. You are not really you." And worst of all, online life has led him to mistrust his friends. He has had his instant messages "recorded" without his knowledge and forwarded on "in a cut-and-paste world."

In fact, when I meet Brad in the spring of his senior year, he tells me he has "dropped out" of online life. "I'm off the Net," he says, "at least for the summer, maybe for my year off until I go to college." He explains that it is hard to drop out because all his friends are on Facebook. A few weeks before our conversation, he had made a step toward rejoining but immediately he felt that he was not doing enough to satisfy its demands. He says that within a day he felt "rude" and couldn't keep up. He felt guilty because he didn't have the time to answer all the people who wrote to him. He says that he couldn't find a way to be "a little bit" on Facebook—it does not easily tolerate a partial buy-in. Just doing the minimum was "pure exhaustion."

In the world of Facebook, Brad says, "your minute movie preferences mat-   20
ter. And what groups you join. Are they the right ones?" Everything is a token, a marker for who you are:

> When you have to represent yourself on Facebook to convey to anyone who doesn't know you what and who you are, it leads to a kind of obsession about minute details about yourself. Like, "Oh, if I like the band State Radio and the band Spoon, what does it mean if I put State Radio first or Spoon first on my list of favorite musical artists? What will people think about me?" I know for girls, trying to figure out, "Oh, is this picture too revealing to put? Is it prudish if I don't put it?" You have to think carefully for good reason, given how much people will look at your profile and obsess over it. You have to know that everything you put up will be perused very carefully. And that makes it necessary for you to obsess over what you do put up and how you portray yourself . . . . And when you have to think that much about what you come across as, that's just another way that. . . . you're thinking of yourself in a bad way.

For Brad, "thinking of yourself in a bad way" means thinking of yourself in reduced terms, in "short smoke signals" that are easy to read. To me, the smoke signals suggest a kind of reduction and betrayal. Social media ask us to represent ourselves in simplified ways. And then, faced with an audience, we feel pressure to conform to these simplifications. On Facebook, Brad represents himself as cool and in the know—both qualities are certainly part of who he is.

But he hesitates to show people online other parts of himself (like how much he likes Harry Potter). He spends more and more time perfecting his online Mr. Cool. And he feels pressure to perform him all the time because that is who he is on Facebook.

At first Brad thought that both his Facebook profile and his college essays had gotten him into this "bad way" of thinking, in which he reduces himself to fit a stereotype. Writing his Facebook profile felt to him like assembling cultural references to shape how others would see him. The college essay demanded a victory narrative and seemed equally unhelpful: he had to brag, and he wasn't happy. But Brad had a change of heart about the value of writing his college essays. "In the end I learned a lot about how I write and think—what I know how to think about and some things, you know, I really can't think about them well at all." I ask him if Facebook might offer these kinds of opportunities. He is adamant that it does not: "You get reduced to a list of favorite things. 'List your favorite music'—that gives you no liberty at all about how to say it." Brad says that "in a conversation, it might be interesting that on a trip to Europe with my parents, I got interested in the political mural art in Belfast. But on a Facebook page, this is too much information. It would be the kiss of death. Too much, too soon, too weird. And yet . . . it is part of who I am, isn't it? . . . You are asked to make a lot of lists. You have to worry that you put down the 'right' band or that you *don't* put down some Polish novel that nobody's read." And in the end, for Brad, it is too easy to lose track of what is important:

> What does it matter to anyone that I prefer the band Spoon over State Radio? Or State Radio over Cake? But things like Facebook . . . make you think that it really does matter. . . . I look at someone's profile and I say, "Oh, they like these bands." I'm like, "Oh, they're a poser," or "they're really deep, and they're into good music." We all do that, I think. And then I think it doesn't matter, but . . . the thing is, in the world of Facebook it *does* matter. Those minute details *do* matter.

Brad, like many of his peers, worries that if he is modest and doesn't put down all of his interests and accomplishments, he will be passed over. But he also fears that to talk about his strengths will be unseemly. None of these conflicts about self presentation are new to adolescence or to Facebook. What is new is living them out in public, sharing every mistake and false step. Brad, attractive and accomplished, sums it up with the same word Nancy uses: "Stress. That's what it comes down to for me. It's just worry and stressing out about it." Now Brad only wants to see his friends in person or talk to them on the telephone. "I can just act how I want to act, and it's a much freer way." But who will answer the phone?

NO NEED TO CALL

"So many people hate the telephone," says Elaine, seventeen. Among her friends at Roosevelt High School, "it's all texting and messaging." She herself writes each of her six closest friends roughly twenty texts a day. In addition, she says, "there are about forty instant messages out, forty in, when I'm at home on the computer." Elaine has strong ideas about how electronic media "levels the playing field" between people like her—outgoing, on the soccer team, and in drama club—and the shy: "It's only on the screen that shy people open up." She explains why: "When you can think about what you're going to say, you can talk to someone you'd have trouble talking to. And it doesn't seem weird that you pause for two minutes to think about what you're going to say before you say it, like it would be if you were actually talking to someone."

Elaine gets specific about the technical designs that help shy people   25 express themselves in electronic messaging. The person to whom you are writing shouldn't be able to see your process of revision or how long you have been working on the message. "That could be humiliating." The best communication programs shield the writer from the view of the reader. The advantage of screen communication is that it is a place to reflect, retype, and edit. "It is a place to hide," says Elaine.

The notion that hiding makes it easier to open up is not new. In the psychoanalytic tradition, it inspired technique. Classical analysis shielded the patient from the analyst's gaze in order to facilitate free association, the golden rule of saying whatever comes to mind. Likewise, at a screen, you feel protected and less burdened by expectations. And, although you are alone, the potential for almost instantaneous contact gives an encouraging feeling of already being together. In this curious relational space, even sophisticated users who know that electronic communications can be saved, shared, and show up in court, succumb to its illusion of privacy. Alone with your thoughts, yet in contact with an almost tangible fantasy of the other, you feel free to play. At the screen, you have a chance to write yourself into the person you want to be and to imagine others as you wish them to be, constructing them for your purposes.[1] It is a seductive but dangerous habit of mind. When you cultivate this sensibility, a telephone call can seem fearsome because it reveals too much.

Elaine is right in her analysis: teenagers flee the telephone. Perhaps more surprisingly, so do adults. They claim exhaustion and lack of time; always on call, with their time highly leveraged through multitasking, they avoid voice communication outside of a small circle because it demands their full attention when they don't want to give it.

Technologies live in complex ecologies. The meaning of any one depends on what others are available. The telephone was once a way to touch base or ask a simple question. But once you have access to e-mail, instant messaging, and texting, things change. Although we still use the phone to keep up with those closest to us, we use it less outside this circle.[2] Not only do people say that a phone call asks too much, they worry it will be received as demanding too much. Randolph, a forty-six-year-old architect with two jobs, two young children, and a twelve-year-old son from a former marriage, makes both points. He avoids the telephone because he feels "tapped out. . . . It promises more than I'm willing to deliver." If he keeps his communications to text and e-mail, he believes he can "keep it together." He explains, "Now that there is e-mail, people expect that a call will be more complicated. Not about facts. A fuller thing. People expect it to take time—or else you wouldn't have called." . . .

Overwhelmed across the Generations

. . . Dan, a law professor in his mid-fifties, explains that he never "interrupts" his colleagues at work. He does not call; he does not ask to see them. He says, "They might be working, doing something. It might be a bad time." I ask him if this behavior is new. He says, "Oh, yes, we used to hang out. It was nice." He reconciles his view that once collegial behavior now constitutes interruption by saying, "People are busier now." But then he pauses and corrects himself. "I'm not being completely honest here: it's also that *I* don't want to talk to people now. *I* don't want to be interrupted. I think I should want to, it would be nice, but it is easier to deal with people on my Blackberry."[3]

This widespread attitude makes things hard for Hugh, twenty-five, who   30
says that he "needs more than e-mails and Facebook can provide." If his friends don't have time to see him, he wants them to talk to him on the phone so that he can have "the full attention of the whole person." But when he texts his friends to arrange a call, Hugh says that he makes his intentions clear: he wants "private cell time." He explains, "This is time when the person you are calling makes a commitment that they will not take calls from other people. They are not doing anything else." He says he feels most rejected when, while speaking on the phone with a friend, he becomes aware that his friend is also texting or on Facebook, something that happens frequently. "I don't even want them to be walking. I can't have a serious conversation with someone while they are on their way from one sales meeting to another. Private cell time is the hardest thing to get. People don't want to make the commitment."

Some young people—aficionados of the text message and the call to "touch base"—echo Hugh's sentiments about the difficulty of getting "full attention." One sixteen-year-old boy says, "I say to people, talk to *me*. Now is my time." Another tries to get his friends to call him from landlines because it means they are in one place as they speak to him, and the reception will be clear. He says, "The best is when you can get someone to call you back on a landline. . . . That is the best." Talking on a landline with no interruptions used to be an everyday thing. Now it is exotic, the jewel in the crown. . . .

The barrier to making a call is so high that even when people have something important to share, they hold back. Tara, the lawyer who admits to "processing" her friends by dealing with them on e-mail, tells me a story about a friendship undermined. About four times a year, Tara has dinner with Alice, a classmate from law school. Recently, the two women exchanged multiple e-mails trying to set a date. Finally, after many false starts, they settled on a time and a restaurant. Alice did not come to the dinner with good news. Her sister had died. Though they lived thousands of miles apart, the sisters had spoken once a day. Without her sister, without these calls, Alice feels ungrounded.

At dinner, when Alice told Tara about her sister's death, Tara became upset, close to distraught. She and Alice had been e-mailing for months. Why hadn't Alice told her about this? Alice explained that she had been taken up with her family, with arrangements. And she said, simply, "I didn't think it was something to discuss over e-mail." Herself in need of support, Alice ended up comforting Tara.

As Tara tells me this story, she says that she was ashamed of her reaction. Her focus should have been—and should now be—on Alice's loss, not on her own ranking as a confidant. But she feels defensive as well. She had, after all, "been in touch." She'd e-mailed; she'd made sure that their dinner got arranged. Tara keeps coming back to the thought that if she and Alice had spoken on the telephone to set up their dinner date, she would have learned about her friend's loss. She says, "I would have heard something in her voice. I would have suspected. I could have drawn her out." But for Tara, as for so many, the telephone call is for family. For friends, even dear friends, it is close to being off the menu. . . .

THE NOSTALGIA OF THE YOUNG

Cliff, a Silver Academy sophomore, talks about whether it will ever be possible to get back to what came "before texting." Cliff says that he gets so caught up in the back-and-forth of texting that he ends up wasting time in what he thinks are superficial communications "just to get back." I ask him about when, in his view, there might be less pressure for an immediate response. Cliff thinks of two: "Your class has a test. Or you lost your signal." Conspicuously absent—you are doing something else, thinking something else, with someone else.

We have seen young people walk the halls of their schools composing messages to online acquaintances they will never meet. We have seen them feeling more alive when connected, then disoriented and alone when they leave their screens. Some live more than half their waking hours in virtual places. But they also talk wistfully about letters, face-to-face meetings, and the privacy of pay phones. Tethered selves, they try to conjure a future different from the one they see coming by building on a past they never knew. In it, they have time alone, with nature, with each other, and with their families.

Texting is too seductive. It makes a promise that generates its own demand.[1] The promise: the person you text will receive the message within seconds, and whether or not he or she is "free," the recipient will be able to see your text. The demand: when you receive a text, you will attend to it (during class, this might mean a glance down at a silenced phone) and respond as soon as possible. Cliff says that in his circle of friends, that means, "ten minutes, maximum."

> I will tell you how it is at this school. If something comes in on our phone and it's a text, you feel you have to respond. They obviously know you got it. With IM, you can claim you weren't at the computer or you lost your Internet connection and all that. But if it's a text, there's no way you didn't get it. Few people look down at their phone and then walk away from it. Few people do that. It really doesn't happen. . . . Texting is pressure. I don't always feel like communicating. Who says that we always have to be ready to communicate?

Indeed, who says? Listening to what young people miss may teach us what they need.

Spontaneity

In a discussion of online life among seniors at the Fillmore School, Brendan says he is lonely. He attempts humor, describing a typical day as "lost in translation": "My life is about 'I'll send you a quick message, you send me another one in fifteen minutes, an hour, whatever. And then I'll get back to you when I can." His humor fades. Texting depresses him. It doesn't make him "feel close," but he is certain that it takes him away from things that might. Brendan wants to see friends in person or have phone conversations in which they are not all rushing off to do something else. Here again, nostalgia circles around attention, commitment, and the aesthetic of doing one thing at a time. Truman, one of Brendan's classmates, thinks his friend is asking too much. Truman says, "Brendan . . . calls me up sometimes, and it's really fun, and I really enjoy it, but it's something I can't really imagine myself doing. . . . Well, it seems like an awkward situation to me, to call someone up just to talk." Truman wants to indulge his friend, but he jokes that Brendan shouldn't "bet on long telephone conversations anytime soon." Truman's remarks require some unpacking. He says he likes the telephone, but he doesn't really. He says conversation is fun, but it's mostly stressful. For Truman, anything other than "a set-up call, a call to make a plan, or tell a location" presumes you are calling someone who has time for you. He is never sure this is the case. So, he worries that this kind of call intrudes. It puts you on the line. You can get hurt.

When young people are insecure, they find ways to manufacture love   40
tests—personal metrics to reassure themselves. These days I hear teenagers measuring degrees of caring by type of communication. An instant message puts you in one window among many. An extended telephone call or a letter—these rare and difficult things—demonstrates full attention. Brad, the Hadley senior taking a break from Facebook, says, "Getting a letter is so special because it is meant only for you. . . . It feels so complimentary, especially nowadays, with people multitasking more and more, for someone to actually go out of their way and give their full attention to something for your sake for five or ten minutes. What is flattering is that they take that amount of time . . . that they're actually giving up that time."

Herb, part of the senior group at Fillmore, feels similarly; he and his girlfriend have decided to correspond with letters: "The letter, like, she wrote it, she took her time writing it, and you know it came from her. The e-mail, it's impersonal. Same with a text message, it's impersonal. Anyone, by some chance, someone got her e-mail address, they could've sent it. The fact that you can touch it is really important. . . . E-mails get deleted, but letters get stored in a drawer. It's real; it's tangible. Online, you can't touch the computer screen, but you can touch the letter." His classmate Luis agrees: "There is something about sending a letter. You can use your handwriting. You can decorate a letter. Your handwriting can show where you are." It comes out he has never received a personal letter. He says, "*I miss those days even though I wasn't alive.*" He goes on, a bit defensively because he fears his fondness of handwriting might make him seem odd: "Before, you could just feel that way, it was part of the culture. Now, you have to feel like a throwback to something you really didn't grow up with."

Brad says that digital life cheats people out of learning how to read a person's face and "their nuances of feeling." And it cheats people out of what he calls "passively being yourself." It is a curious locution. I come to understand that he means it as shorthand for authenticity. It refers to who you are when you are not "trying," not performing. It refers to who you are in a simple conversation, unplanned. His classmate Miguel likes texting as a "place to hide," but to feel close to someone, you need a more spontaneous medium:

> A phone conversation is so personal because you don't have time to sit there and think about what you're going to say. What you have to say is just going to come out the way it's meant to. If someone sends you a text message, you

have a couple minutes to think about what you're going to say, whereas if you're in a conversation, it'd be a little awkward if you didn't say anything for two minutes, and then came up with your answer. . . . That's why I like calls. I'd rather have someone be honest with you. . . . If you call, you're putting yourself out there, but it is also better.

At Fillmore, Grant says of when he used to text, "I end[ed] up feeling too lonely, just typing all day." He has given it up, except texting his girlfriend. He returns her long text messages with a "k," short for "okay," and then holds off on further communication until he can talk to her on the phone or see her in person. He says, "When someone sends you a text or IM, you don't know *how* they're saying something. They could say something to you, and they could be joking, but they could be serious and you're not really sure."

These young men are asking for time and touch, attention and immediacy. They imagine living with less conscious performance. They are curious about a world where people dealt in the tangible and did one thing at a time. This is ironic. For they belong to a generation that is known, and has been celebrated, for never doing one thing at a time.

Erik Erikson writes that in their search for identity, adolescents need a place   45
of stillness, a place to gather themselves.[2] Psychiatrist Anthony Storr writes of solitude in much the same way. Storr says that in accounts of the creative process, "by far the greater number of new ideas occur during a state of reverie, intermediate between waking and sleeping. . . . It is a state of mind in which ideas and images are allowed to appear and take their course spontaneously . . . the creator need[s] to be able to be passive, to let things happen within the mind."[3] In the digital life, stillness and solitude are hard to come by. . . .

The Perils of Performance

Brad says, only half jokingly, that he worries about getting "confused" between what he "composes" for his online life and who he "really" is. Not yet con-firmed in his identity, it makes him anxious to post things about himself that he doesn't really know are true. It burdens him that the things he says online affect how people treat him in the real. People already relate to him based on things he has said on Facebook. Brad struggles to be more "himself" there, but this is hard. He says that even when he tries to be "honest" on Facebook, he cannot resist the temptation to use the site "to make the right impression." On Face-book, he says, "I write for effect. I sit down and ask, 'If I say this, will it make me sound like I'm too uptight? But if I say this, will it make me sound like I don't care about anything?'" He makes an effort to be "more spontaneous on Face-book . . . to actively say, 'This is who I am, this is what I like, this is what I don't like,'" but he feels that Facebook "perverts" his efforts because self-revelation should be to "another person who cares." For Brad, it loses meaning when it is broadcast as a profile.

The Internet can play a part in constructive identity, although, as we have seen, it is not so easy to experiment when all rehearsals are archived. But Brad admits that on Facebook he only knows how to play to the crowd. We've seen that he anguishes about the cool bands and the bands that are not so cool. He thinks about the movies he should list as favorites and the ones that will pin him as boring or sexist. There is a chance that admitting he likes the Harry Potter series will read positively—he'll be seen as someone in touch with the whimsy of his childhood. But more likely, it will make him seem less sexy. Brad points out that in real life, people can see you are cool even if you like some uncool things. In a profile, there is no room for error. You are reduced to a series of right and wrong choices. "Online life," he says, "is about premeditation." Brad sums up his discontents with an old-fashioned word: online life inhibits "authenticity." He wants to experience people directly. When he reads what someone says about themselves on Facebook, he feels that he is an audience to their performance of cool.

Brad has more than a little of Henry David Thoreau in him. In *Walden*, published in 1854, Thoreau remarks that we are too much in contact with others and in ways that are random. We cannot respect each other if we "stumble over one another."[4] He says, we live "thick," unable to acquire value for each other because there is not enough space between our times together. "Society," writes Thoreau, "is commonly too cheap."[5] It would be better, he says, to learn or experience something before we join in fellowship with others. We know what Thoreau did about his opinions. He took his distance. He found communion with nature and simple objects. He saw old friends and made new ones. All of these sustained him, but he did not live "thick." In the end, Brad decides to leave his digital life for his own private Walden. When he wants to see a friend, he calls, makes a plan, and goes over to visit. He says that life is beginning to feel more natural. "Humans learn to talk and make eye contact before they learn to touch-type, so I think it's a more basic, fundamental form of communication," he says. Abandoning digital connection, he says, he is "sacrificing three hollow conversations" in favor of "one really nice social interaction with one person." He acknowledges that "not doing IM reduces the amount of social interacting you can do in one day," but doesn't mourn the loss: "Would you rather have thirty kind-of somewhat-good friends or five really close friends?"

I meet other teenagers, like Brad, who go on self-imposed media "fasts." Some give up texting, some IM. Because of its centrality to social life, the most decisive step they can think of is to leave Facebook.[6] Some, like Brad, are exhausted by its pressure for performance. Some say they find themselves being "cruel"—online life suppresses healthy inhibitions. Others say they lose touch with their "real" friends as they spend hours keeping up contacts with the "friended." Some, not yet many, rebel against the reality that Facebook owns (in the most concrete terms) the story of their lives. Some believe that the site encourages them to judge themselves and others in superficial ways. They agonize over what photographs to post. They digitally alter their Facebook photographs to look more appealing. But even after so much time, writing profiles and editing photos, the fiction of a Facebook page is that it is put up with a kind of aristocratic nonchalance. Luis says, "It's like a girl wearing too much makeup, trying too hard. It's supposed to look like you didn't care. But no one believes this myth of 'Oh, I just threw some stuff up on my page. . . . I'm very cool. I have so much else to do.' You see that they are on their Facebook page all day. Who are they kidding?" His tone turns wistful: "It must have been nice when you could just discover a person by talking to them." For all of these reasons, dropping out comes as something of a relief.

The terms of these refusals—to find oneself and others more directly and   50
to live a less-mediated life, to move away from performances and toward something that feels more real—suggest the refusals that brought Henry David Thoreau to Walden Pond nearly two centuries before.

Walden 2.0

In his essay about his two years of retreat, Thoreau writes, "I went to the woods because I wished to live deliberately, to front only the essential facts of life, and see if I could not learn what it had to teach, and not, when I came to die, discover that I had not lived. I did not wish to live what is not life, living is so dear; nor did I wish to practise resignation, unless it was quite necessary."[7] Thoreau's quest inspires us to ask of our life with technology: Do we live deliberately? Do we turn away from life that is not life? Do we refuse resignation?

Some believe that the new connectivity culture provides a digital Walden. A fifteen-year-old girl describes her phone as her refuge. "My cell phone," she says, "is my only individual zone, just for me." Technology writer Kevin Kelly, the first editor of *Wired*, says that he finds refreshment on the Web. He is replenished in its cool shade: "At times I've entered the web just to get lost. In that lovely surrender, the web swallows my certitude and delivers the unknown. Despite the purposeful design of its human creators, the web is a wilderness. Its boundaries are unknown, unknowable, its mysteries uncountable. The bramble of intertwined ideas, links, documents, and images create an otherness as thick as a jungle. The web smells like life."[8]

But not everyone is as refreshed as Kelly. Brad talks about the "throwaway friendships" of online life. Hannah wonders what she really has to show for the time she has spent hanging out with a small, sarcastic in-crowd and with a best friend who she fears will simply not show up again. It is hard to accept that online friends are not part of your life; yet, they can make themselves disappear just as you can make them vanish. Anxiety about Internet friendships makes people cherish the other kind. The possibility of constant connection makes people value a bit of space. Pattie, fourteen, no longer carries her cell phone. "It feels good," she says, "to have people *not* reach you."

That bit of space could leave room for a child to be a child a bit longer. One of the privileges of childhood is that some of the world is mediated by adults. Hillary, sixteen, is taking a long break from her cell phone. She doesn't want to be on call, and so she leaves it at home. "I don't like the feeling of being reachable all the time . . . of knowing about everything in real time." For a child—and for this purpose, adolescents are still children—one cost of constant connectivity is that adults lose the ability to act as a buffer against the world. Only a few months before, Hillary was at a party to celebrate the release of a new volume in the Harry Potter series when her father suffered a seizure. She didn't learn about it until she was at home and with family. She was glad for this. Without a cell phone, the bad news waited until there was an adult there to support her, to put it in context. She didn't want to hear it alone, holding a phone.

Hillary is fond of movies but drawn towards "an Amish life minus certain   55 exceptions [these would be the movies] . . . but I wouldn't mind if the Internet went away." She asks, "What could people be doing if they weren't on the Internet?" She answers her own question: "There's piano; there's drawing; there's all these things people could be creating." Hillary talks about how hard it is to keep up "all the different sites you have to keep up," and above all, how time-consuming it is to feed Facebook. These tiring performances leave little space for creativity and reflection: "It really is distracting." There is not much room for what Thoreau meant by a life lived deliberately.

There is nothing more deliberate than the painstaking work of constructing a profile or having a conversation on instant messenger in which one composes and recomposes one's thoughts. And yet, most of the time on the Net, one floats and experiments, follows links, and sends out random feelers. One flips through the photo albums of friends—and then the albums of their friends. One comments on the postings of people one hardly knows. Thoreau complained that people are too quick to share an opinion. Online, social networks instruct us to share whenever there's "something on our mind," no matter how ignorant or ill considered, and then help us broadcast it to the widest possible audience. Every day each of us is bombarded by other people's random thoughts. We start to see such effusions as natural. So, although identity construction on the Net begins in a considered way, with the construction of a profile or an avatar, people can end up feeling that the only deliberate act is the decision to hand oneself over to the Net. After that, one is swept along. . . .

When Thoreau considered "where I live and what I live for," he tied together location and values. Where we live doesn't just change how we live; it informs who we become. Most recently, technology promises us lives on the screen. What values, Thoreau would ask, follow from this new location? Immersed in simulation, where do we live, and what do we live for?

CONCLUSION: NECESSARY CONVERSATIONS

Forbidden Experiments

. . . Some would say that we have already completed a forbidden experiment, using ourselves as subjects with no controls, and the unhappy findings are in: we are connected as we've never been connected before, and we seem to have damaged ourselves in the process. A 2010 analysis of data from over fourteen thousand college students over the past thirty years shows that since the year 2000, young people have reported a dramatic decline in interest in other people. Today's college students are, for example, far less likely to say that it is valuable to try to put oneself in the place of others or to try to understand their feelings.[1] The authors of this study associate students' lack of empathy with the availability of online games and social networking. An online connection can be deeply felt, but you only need to deal with the part of the person you see in your game world or social network. Young people don't seem to feel they need to deal with more, and over time they lose the inclination. One might say that absorbed in those they have "friended," children lose interest in friendship.

These findings confirm the impressions of the psychotherapists — psychiatrists, psychologists, and social workers — who talk to me about the increasing numbers of patients who present in the consulting room as detached from their bodies and seem close to unaware of the most basic courtesies. Purpose-driven, plugged into their media, these patients pay little attention to those around them. In others, they seek what is of use, an echo of that primitive world of "parts." Their detachment is not aggressive. It is as though they just don't see the point.[2]

Early Days

It is, of course, tempting to talk about all of this in terms of addiction. Adam, who started out playing computer games with people and ends up feeling compelled by a world of bots, certainly uses this language. The addiction metaphor fits a common experience: the more time spent online, the more one wants to spend time online. But however apt the metaphor, we can ill afford the luxury of using it. Talking about addiction subverts our best thinking because it suggests that if there are problems, there is only one solution. To combat addiction, you have to discard the addicting substance. But we are not going to "get rid" of the Internet. We will not go "cold turkey" or forbid cell phones to our children. We are not going to stop the music or go back to television as the family hearth.

I believe we will find new paths towards each other, but considering ourselves victims of a bad substance is not a good first step. The idea of addiction, with its one solution that we know we won't take, makes us feel hopeless. We have to find a way to live with seductive technology and make it work to our purposes. This is hard and will take work. Simple love of technology is not going to help. Nor is Luddite impulse.

What I call *realtechnik* suggests that we step back and reassess when we hear triumphalist or apocalyptic narratives about how to live with technology. *Realtechnik* is skeptical about linear progress. It encourages humility, a state of mind in which we are most open to facing problems and reconsidering decisions. It helps us acknowledge costs and recognize the things we hold inviolate. . . .

The networked culture is very young. Attendants at its birth, we threw ourselves into its adventure. This is human. But these days, our problems with the Net are becoming too distracting to ignore. At the extreme, we are so enmeshed in our connections that we neglect each other. We don't need to reject or disparage technology. We need to put it in its place. . . .

When we are at our best, thinking about technology brings us back to questions about what really matters. When I recently travelled to a memorial service for a close friend, the program, on heavy cream-colored card stock, listed the afternoon's speakers, told who would play what music, and displayed photographs of my friend as a young woman and in her prime. Several around me used the program's stiff, protective wings to hide their cell phones as they sent text messages during the service. One of the texting mourners, a woman in her late sixties, came over to chat with me after the service. Matter-of-factly, she offered, "I couldn't stand to sit that long without getting my phone." The point of the service was to take a moment. This woman had been schooled by a technology she'd had for less than a decade to find this close to impossible.[3] Later, I discussed the texting with some close friends. Several shrugged. One said, "What are you going to do?"

A shrug is appropriate for a stalemate. That's not where we are. It is too early to have reached such an impasse. Rather, I believe we have reached a point of inflection, where we can see the costs and start to take action. We will begin with very simple things. Some will seem like just reclaiming good

65

manners. Talk to colleagues down the hall, no cell phones at dinner, on the playground, in the car, or in company. There will be more complicated things: to name only one, nascent efforts to reclaim privacy would be supported across the generations. And compassion is due to those of us—and there are many of us—who are so dependent on our devices that we cannot sit still for a funeral service or a lecture or a play. We now know that our brains are rewired every time we use a phone to search or surf or multitask.[4] As we try to reclaim our concentration, we are literally at war with ourselves. Yet, no matter how difficult, it is time to look again toward the virtues of solitude, deliberateness, and living fully in the moment. We have agreed to an experiment in which we are the human subjects. Actually, we have agreed to a series of experiments: robots for children and the elderly, technologies that denigrate and deny privacy, seductive simulations that propose themselves as places to live.[5]

We deserve better. When we remind ourselves that it is we who decide how to keep technology busy, we shall have better.

NOTES

Always On

1. Media theorist Henry Jenkins is an eloquent spokesperson for the significance of multitasking. See "The Skill of the Future: In a Word 'Multitasking,'" PBS.org, www .pbs.org/wgbh/pages/frontline/digitalnation/living-faster/split-focus/the-skill -of-the-future.html? (accessed November 16, 2009). His other online interviews on the Digital Nation website beautifully capture a vision of schools bending to new media sensibilities. See "The Tech Fix," PBS.org, www.pbs.org/wgbh/pages /frontline/digitalnation/learning/schools/the-tech-fix.html?play (accessed November 14, 2009), and "Defenders of the Book," PBS.org, www.pbs.org/wgbh/pages /frontline/digitalnation/learning/literacy/defenders-of-the-book.html?play (accessed November 14, 2009).

2. The literature on the downside of multitasking is growing. An influential and much-reported study is Eyal Ophir, Clifford Nass, and Anthony Wagner, "Cognitive Control in Media Multitaskers," *Proceedings of the National Academy of Sciences* 106 (2009): 15583–15587, www.pnas.org/content/106/37/15583 (accessed August 10, 2010). This study found that when people multitask, everything they do is degraded in quality. An excellent work on the general topic is Maggie Jackson, *Distracted: The Erosion of Attention and the Coming Dark Age* (New York: Prometheus, 2008). On the practical downside of thinking that we can do more than one thing at once, see, for example, the nine-part series on the *New York Times* website titled "Driven to Distraction," covering such topics as doing office work while driving 60 mph, drivers and legislators dismissing cell phone risks, and New York taxi drivers ignoring the ban on cell phone use while driving. "Driven to Distraction," *New York Times*, http:// topics.nytimes.com/topics/news/technology/series/driven_to_distraction /index.html (accessed November 14, 2009).

    Teenagers routinely drive and text; we know this because their automobile accidents are traced back to texting and cell phone use. A 2009 study on twenty-one teenagers showed them changing speed and weaving in and out of lanes while texting. Eastern Virginia Medical School, "Texting While Driving Can Be Deadly, Study Shows," *ScienceDaily*, May 5, 2009, www.sciencedaily.com/releases/2009 /05/090504094434.htm (accessed January 4, 2010). A larger study of nine hundred teenagers in 2007 showed 50 percent of them texted while driving despite the fact that 36 percent of them thought this was dangerous. See Steve Vogel, "Teen Driver Menace: Text-Messaging," Suite101, October 2, 2007, http://parentingteens.suite101.com/article.cfm/teen_driver_menace_textmessaging (accessed January 4, 2009).

Adults also text while driving. Trains collide while conductors text. A plane flies past its destination airport because its pilots are absorbed in a new computer program. In October 2009, pilots attending to their laptop computers—behavior in defiance of safety regulations—were the cause of an aircraft overshooting its Minneapolis destination by 150 miles. "The pilots told the National Transportation Safety Board that they missed their destination because they had taken out their personal laptops in the cockpit, a violation of airline policy, so the first officer, Richard I. Cole, could tutor the captain, Timothy B. Cheney, in a new scheduling system put in place by Delta Air Lines, which acquired Northwest last fall." See Micheline Maynard and Matthew L. Wald, "Off-Course Pilots Cite Computer Distraction," *New York Times*, October 26, 2009, www.nytimes.com/2009/10/27/us/27plane.html?_r=1 (accessed November 16, 2009).

3. The first book club selection by Arianna Huffington for the *Huffington Post*'s book club was Carl Honoré's *In Praise of Slowness: How a Worldwide Movement Is Challenging the Cult of Speed* (New York: HarperCollins, 2004).

4. Diana B. Gant and Sara Kiesler, "Blurring the Boundaries: Cell Phones, Mobility and the Line Between Work and Personal Life," in *Wireless World: Social and Interactional Aspects of the Mobile Age*, ed. N. G. R. H. Brown (New York: Springer, 2001).

5. Donna Haraway, "A Cyborg Manifesto," in *Simians, Cyborgs, and Women: The Reinvention of Nature* (New York, Routledge, 1991), 149–181.

6. I studied teenagers from a wide range of economic, social, and ethnic backgrounds. They attended seven different schools: two private boys' preparatory schools, one in an urban center (Fillmore) and one in a rural setting (Hadley), one urban private girls school (Richelieu), an urban Catholic coeducational high school (Silver Academy), a private urban coeducational high school (Cranston), and two public high schools, one suburban (Roosevelt) and one urban (Branscomb). All students, from wealthy to disadvantaged, had cell phones with texting capability. Class distinctions showed themselves not in whether students possessed a phone but in what kind of contract they had with their providers. Teenagers with fewer resources, such as Julia in the following chapter, tended to have plans that constrained who they could text for free. Free texts are most usually for people on the same network. Ever resourceful, students with restricted plans try to get their friends to sign up with their cell providers. We shall see that teenagers don't care much about who they can call. I often hear, "I never use my calling minutes." On teenagers and digital culture, see Mizuko Ito et al., *Hanging Out, Messing Around, and Geeking Out: Kids Learning and Living with New Media* (Cambridge, MA: MIT Press, 2010) and Danah Boyd, "Why Youth (Heart) Social Network Sites: The Role of Networked Publics in Teenage Social Life," MacArthur Foundation Series on Digital Learning—Youth, Identity, and Digital Media, ed. David Buckingham (Cambridge, MA: MIT Press 2007), 119–142.

No Need to Call

1. In the object relations tradition of psychoanalysis, an object is that which one relates to. Usually, objects are people, especially a significant person who is the object or target of another's feelings or intentions. A whole object is a person in his or her entirety. It is common in development for people to internalize part objects, representations of others that are not the whole person. Online life provides an environment that makes it easier for people to relate to part objects. This puts relationships at risk. On object relations theory, see, for example, Stephen A. Mitchell and Margaret J. Black, *Freud and Beyond: A History of Modern Psychoanalytic Thought* (New York: Basic Books, 1995).

2. See Stefana Broadbent, "How the Internet Enables Intimacy," Ted.com, www.ted.com/talks/stefana_broadbent_how_the_internet_enables_intimacy.html (accessed August 8, 2010). According to Broadbent, 80 percent of calls on cell phones are made to four people, 80 percent of Skype calls are made to two people, and most Facebook exchanges are with four to six people.

3. Dan is aware of his withdrawal, but a new generation takes machine-mediated communication simply as the nature of things. Two young girls, ten and twelve, trapped inside a storm drain turned to Facebook for help instead of calling the police. They used their mobile phones to update their Facebook statuses. Even with their lives at risk, these girls saw Facebook as their portal to the world. Firefighters eventually rescued the pair after being contacted by one of their male school friends, who had been online and saw they were trapped. The news report read as follows:

   "The drama happened near Adelaide, Australia. Firefighter Glen Benham, who took part in the rescue, said 'These girls were able to access Facebook on their mobile phones so they could have called emergency services. It seems absolutely crazy but they updated their status rather than call us directly. We could have come to their rescue much faster than relying on someone else being online, then replying to them, then calling us. It is a worrying development. Young people should realize it's better to contact us directly. Luckily they are safe and well. It's awful to think what could have happened because of the delay.'"

   See "Girls Trapped in Storm Drain Use Facebook to Call for Help," *Daily Mail*, September 8, 2009, www.dailymail.co.uk/news/worldnews/article-1211909.Girls-trapped-storm-drain-use-Facebook-help-instead-phoning-emergency-services.html#ixzzoT9iWpeNR (accessed October 6, 2009).

The Nostalgia of the Young

1. This recalls how French psychoanalyst Jacques Lacan talks about the analytic encounter. The offer to listen creates a demand to be heard. "In short, I have succeeded in doing what in the field of ordinary commerce people would dearly like to be able to do with such ease: with supply, I have created demand." See Jacques Lacan, "The Direction of the Treatment and the Principles of Its Power," *Ecrits: A Selection*, trans. Alan Sheridan (New York: W.W. Norton, 1977), 254. For a discussion of Lacan and the "intransitive demand," see Sherry Turkle, *Psychoanalytic Politic: Jacques Lacan and Freud's French Revolution* (1978; New York: Guilford Press, 1992), 85.

2. David Andersen, "Erik H. Erikson's Challenge to Modernity" (PhD diss., Bowling Green State University, 1993). After writing this chapter and the next, I found Alan Lightman's elegant essay, "Prisoner of the Wired World," which evokes many of the

themes I treat here. In *A Sense of the Mysterious: Science and the Human Spirit* (New York: Pantheon, 2005), 183–208.

3. Anthony Storr, *Solitude: A Return to the Self* (New York, Random House, 1988), 198.

4. Henry David Thoreau, "Where I Lived and What I Lived For," in *Walden* (1854; New York: American Renaissance Books, 2009), 47. I thank Erikson biographer Lawrence J. Friedman for his insights on Erikson and "stillness."

5. Thoreau, "Where I Lived," 47.

6. Katy Hafner, "To Deal with Obsession, Some Defriend Facebook," *New York Times*, December 20, 2009, www.nytimes.com/2009/12/21/technology/internet /21facebook.html?_r=1 (accessed January 6, 2009).

7. Thoreau, "Where I Lived," 47.

8. Kevin Kelly, "Technophilia," The Technium, June 8, 2009, www.kk.org/thetechnium /archives/2009/06/technophilia.php (accessed December 9, 2009).

Conclusion: Necessary Conversations

1. A University of Michigan study found that today's college students have less empathy than those of the 1980s or 1990s. Today's generation scored about 40 percent lower in empathy than their counterparts did twenty or thirty years ago. Sarah Konrath, a researcher at the University of Michigan's Institute for Social Research, conducted, with University of Michigan graduate student Edward O'Brien and undergraduate student Courtney Hsing, a meta-analysis that looked at data on empathy, combining the results of seventy-two different studies of American college students conducted between 1979 and 2009. Compared to college students of the late 1970s, the study found, college students today are less likely to agree with statements such as "I sometimes try to understand my friends better by imagining how things look from their perspective" and "I often have tender, concerned feelings for people less fortunate than me." See "Empathy: College Students Don't Have As Much As They Used To," EurekAlert!, May 28, 2010, www.eurekalert .org/ pub_releases / 2010-05 / uom-ecso52610.php (accessed June 4, 2010).

2. I thank my psychotherapist colleagues for ongoing conversations on these matters. In particular I acknowledge the adolescent psychiatrist John Hamilton and the panels on "Adolescence in Cyberspace" on which we have collaborated at the Annual Meetings of the American Academy of Child and Adolescent Psychiatry in October 2004 and October 2008; the participants in the MIT working group, "Whither Psychoanalysis in Digital Culture" Initiative on Technology and Self, 2003–2004; and participants at the Washington Institute for Psychoanalysis's "New Directions" Conference, April 30, 2010.

3. Matt Richtel, "Hooked on Gadgets and Paying a Mental Price," *New York Times*, July 7, 2010, http://community.nytimes.com/comments/www.nytimes .com/2010/06/07/technology/07brain.html?sort=oldest&offset=2 (accessed July 7, 2010).

4. Nicholas Carr, *The Shallows: What the Internet Is Doing to Our Brains* (New York: W. W. Norton and Company, 2010). Here, the argument is that online activities— surfing, searching, jumping from e-mail to text—actually change the nature of the brain. The more time we spend online, the more we are incapable of quiet reverie, not because of habits of mind but because of a rewiring of our circuitry. This area of research is, happily, getting more and more public attention. See Matt Richtel,

"Your Brain on Computers: Outdoor and Out of Reach, Studying the Brain," *New York Times*, August 16, 2010, www.nytimes.com/2010/08/16/technology/16brain .html (accessed August 16, 2010).

5. Of course, one of my concerns is that the moment to summon ourselves to action might pass. We are at a point at which, when robots are proposed as companions for the elderly or as babysitters, we can still have a conversation that challenges these ideas. We still remember why they are problematic. I am concerned that in twenty years, one may simply boast, "I'm leaving my kid with the nanny bot." After the cost of purchase, it will be free and reliable. It will contact you if there is any deviation from the plan you have left for your child—be these deviations in your child's temperature or in a range of acceptable behaviors. I vividly remember leading an MIT seminar in 2001, one that was part of a celebration at the release of Steven Spielberg's *A.I.: Artificial Intelligence*, when for the first time, I was the only person in a room of thirty who did not see any issue at all with the prospect of a computer psychotherapist. Moments when big steps with technology seem problematic have a way of passing.

Questions for Critical Reading

1. Remember that when you encounter the common problem/solution organization used by Turkle and other writers across genres, it's good to consider both how persuasive you find the analysis of the problem *and* how well the writer's proposed solution would address the problem. How would you describe Turkle's analysis of the problem? How would you describe her proposed solution? Were you persuaded that what she sees as a problem really *is* a problem and that her proposed solution would address it? Why or why not?

2. Like writers in other genres, Turkle doesn't rely on just one type of evidence to support her claims; rather, she gives us quotations and rich details about the people who participated in her study, *and* she provides footnotes referring us to a wide variety of sources. Consider how effectively these two types of evidence are used in the following passage, in which Turkle provides us with both a quotation from one of her research participants and a citation of an academic source:

> We are overwhelmed across the generations. Teenagers complain that parents don't look up from their phones at dinner and that they bring their phones to school sporting events. Hannah, sixteen, is a solemn, quiet high school junior. She tells me that for years she has tried to get her mother's attention when her mother comes to fetch her after school or after dance lessons. Hannah says, "The car will start; she'll be driving still looking down, looking at her messages, but still no hello." We will hear others tell similar stories.

Parents say they are ashamed of such behavior but quickly get around to explaining, if not justifying, it. . . . They cannot take a vacation without bringing the office with them; their office is on their cell phone.[4] (paras 4–5)

---

[4] Diana B. Gant and Sara Kiesler, "Blurring the Boundaries: Cell Phones, Mobility and the Line Between Work and Personal Life," in *Wireless World: Social and Interactional Aspects of the Mobile Age*, ed. N. G. R. H. Brown (New York: Springer, 2001).

How persuasive did you find Turkle's use of evidence, and why? Why do you think she used both types of evidence? Find another passage that uses multiple types of evidence, and evaluate how effectively Turkle uses those types of evidence in that passage.

3. Writers who use multiple types of evidence sometimes deliberately give more weight to one type of evidence — that is, they use one type more than others. How would you describe the type of evidence that Turkle favors? Would you have been more persuaded by her writing if she had given more weight to another kind of evidence, or did you prefer the weighting she chose? Why? When might you as a writer decide to use one type of evidence more than another kind?

4. Since an idea can be expressed through different genres, writing involves not only the careful crafting of words appropriate for the genre but also — before that — the careful selection of the genre itself. Consider whether you, like the people Turkle quotes in the following passage, might respond differently to a letter than you would to an electronic genre:

> These days I hear teenagers measuring degrees of caring by type of communication. An instant message puts you in one window among many. An extended telephone call or a letter—these rare and difficult things—demonstrates full attention. Brad, the Hadley senior taking a break from Facebook, says, "Getting a letter is so special because it is meant only for you. . . . It feels so complimentary, especially nowadays, with people multitasking more and more, for someone to actually go out of their way and give their full attention to something for your sake. . . ."
>
> Herb . . . feels similarly; he and his girlfriend have decided to correspond with letters: "The letter . . . she took her time writing it, and you know it came from her. The e-mail, it's impersonal. Same with a text message, it's impersonal. . . . The fact that you can touch it is really important. . . . E-mails get deleted, but letters get stored in a drawer. It's real; it's tangible." (paras. 40–41)

Do you agree with Brad and Herb that genre (shaped by medium of communication) matters — that you can measure "degrees of caring by type of communication"? Why or why not?

5. Turkle isn't the only one who has argued that our relationships are shaped by the genres we use; in fact, this argument has been made in multiple genres, including postcards. Take a moment to envision a postcard with the message

"The Internet often disconnects us . . . a postcard reconnects us!" accompanied by the visual pun of a cat glaring, claws extended, at a computer mouse.

What do you think the cat-and-mouse postcard might enable the writer and designer to accomplish that Turkle couldn't? Conversely, what do you think Turkle was able to accomplish by writing her book that couldn't have been accomplished with a postcard?

Making Connections

6.   Given the importance of looking for connections among the different things you read, you may have noticed a recurrent claim in several of the genres in this chapter — the claim that technology shapes our sense of self. Consider the following passages, one from Nicholas Carr's magazine feature "Is Google Making Us Stupid?" (p. 574) and several from *Alone Together*; note that the claims about technology and selfhood are italicized. In a small group with some of your classmates, make a list of the different ways that — according to the authors and the people they quote — technology is giving rise to a new sense of self.

"Is Google Making Us Stupid?"

The kind of deep reading that a sequence of printed pages promotes [and that the Internet makes difficult] is valuable not just for the knowledge we acquire from the author's words but for the intellectual vibrations those words set off within our own minds. In the quiet spaces opened up by the sustained, undistracted reading of a book, or by any other act of contemplation, . . . we make our own associations, draw our own inferences and analogies, foster our own ideas. . . .

If we lose those quiet spaces, or fill them up with "content," we will sacrifice something important not only in our selves but in our culture. In a recent essay, the playwright Richard Foreman eloquently described what's at stake:

> I come from a tradition of Western culture, in which the ideal (my ideal) was the complex, dense and "cathedral-like" structure of the highly educated and articulate personality—a man or woman who carried inside themselves a personally constructed and unique version of the entire heritage of the West. [But now] *I see within us all (myself included) the replacement of complex inner density with a new kind of self—evolving under the pressure of information overload and the technology of the "instantly available."*

As we are drained of our "inner repertory of dense cultural inheritance," Foreman concluded, *we risk turning into "'pancake people'—spread wide and thin* as we connect with that vast network of information accessed by the mere touch of a button." (paras. 32–33)

Alone Together

The self shaped in a world of rapid response measures success by calls made, e-mails answered, texts replied to, contacts reached. The self is calibrated on the basis of what technology proposes, by what it makes easy. But in the technology-induced pressure for volume and velocity, we confront a paradox. We insist that our world is increasingly complex, yet we have created a communications culture that has decreased the time available for us to sit and think uninterrupted. As we communicate in ways that ask for almost instantaneous responses, we don't allow sufficient space to consider complicated problems. (para. 10)

. . .

When I speak of a new state of the self, itself, I use the word "itself" with purpose. It captures . . . my concern that the connected life encourages us to treat those we meet online in something of the same way we treat objects—with dispatch. It happens naturally: when you are besieged by thousands of e-mails, texts, and messages—more than you can respond to—demands become depersonalized. Similarly, when we Tweet or write to hundreds or thousands of Facebook friends as a group, we treat individuals as a unit. . . .

. . . Online, we invent ways of being with people that turn them into something close to objects. The self that treats a person as a thing is vulnerable to seeing itself as one. (paras. 14–15)

. . .

[Brad] says, "Online, people miss your body language, tone of voice. *You are not really you.*" (para. 18)

. . .

For Brad, "thinking of yourself in a bad way" means thinking of yourself in reduced terms, in "short smoke signals" that are easy to read. To me, the smoke signals suggest a kind of reduction and betrayal. *Social media ask us to represent ourselves in simplified ways. . . .*

. . . Brad says that "in a conversation, it might be interesting that on a trip to Europe with my parents, I got interested in the political mural art in Belfast. But on a Facebook page, this is too much information. It would be the kiss of death. Too much, too soon, too weird. *And yet . . . it is part of who I am, isn't it?*" (paras. 21–22)

After your group makes a list of the different claims about how technology affects selfhood, compare notes with the other groups in your class, perhaps pooling your lists of claims into one master list. Do you agree with any of the claims on this master list? Why or why not?

Writing: Your Turn

1. In light of Turkle's claim that the genre one chooses can affect a reader's response (see question 4), write a letter and translate it into an electronic genre, such as an e-mail, a series of texts, or one of the genres commonly used in social media. Alternatively, you could write the message using an electronic genre and then translate it into a letter. After you write the same

Writing

message using two different genres, write a reflection on how the genre used might shape the reader's (or readers') responses to what you wrote.

Share everything you wrote with some classmates to see if they have similar or different theories about how the choice of genre might affect readers' responses. For ideas on writing a reflection, see p. 27.

2. To deepen your understanding of Turkle's argument about how technology affects us, as well as her argument about what we can do to address the problem she perceives, write a summary of the excerpt from her book, making sure to distinguish between her main point and her secondary points. At the end of your summary, write a brief statement discussing your response to Turkle. Share what you wrote with some classmates to see if there are any nuances of Turkle's argument that you missed and to hear any other revision ideas they might have. For tips on writing a summary, see p. 23.

Beyond Simple Multi-Tasking: Continuous Partial Attention *and* Diagnosis: Email Apnea

Linda Stone

In the two blog posts that follow, former Microsoft and Apple executive Linda Stone argues that our interaction with screen-based technologies can trigger our fight or flight response, largely because we have so many competing demands on our attention. Both posts, dated November 30, 2009, appear on Stone's blog *The Attention Project*. Stone explains her reason for focusing on attention:

> Attention is the most powerful tool of the human spirit. We can enhance or augment our attention with practices like meditation and exercise, diffuse it with technologies like email and Blackberries, or alter it with pharmaceuticals. In the end, though, we are fully responsible for how we choose to use this extraordinary tool.[2]

In addition to appearing on *The Attention Project*, "Diagnosis: Email Apnea" was republished in the *Huffington Post* and *O'Reilly Radar* (where the version reprinted here was obtained).

Focus on Genre   Like many blog posts, Stone's two posts are sharply focused; that is, rather than letting paragraphs shift to somewhat unrelated topics, Stone makes the paragraphs in each post work together to advance the larger purpose of the post. To this end, she coins new terms that have since become part of many people's vocabulary: "continuous partial attention" and "email apnea." As you read, think about why Stone coined each of these terms and how each one helps her fulfill her purpose. Also consider whether the term "email apnea" (holding one's breath or breathing shallowly while doing e-mail) might apply not just to e-mail but also to other screen-based activities, such as texting.

◄○►

---

[2] From www.lindastone.net; accessed May 8, 2012.

BEYOND SIMPLE MULTI-TASKING: CONTINUOUS PARTIAL ATTENTION

What I call continuous partial attention is referred to as complex multi-tasking in cognitive science. Most of us don't walk around distinguishing between simple and complex multi-tasking when we talk about our day: "I multi-tasked all afternoon and I'm exhausted." "Yes, I multi-task when I drive." "A good chef has to multi-task."

Were those examples of simple or complex multi-tasking? There's no way to know. The differences between simple and complex multi-tasking are profound. So, when I noticed that complex multi-tasking was increasingly pervasive in our culture, I took the liberty of giving it a new name: continuous partial attention. <u>WordSpy,</u> a fun site that tracks new words and phrases, recognizes cpa, and so does <u>Wikipedia.</u>

Continuous partial attention and multi-tasking are two different attention strategies, motivated by different impulses. When we multi-task we are motivated by a desire to be more productive and more efficient. Each activity has the same priority—we eat lunch AND file papers. We stir the soup AND talk on the phone. With simple multi-tasking, one or more activities is somewhat automatic or routine, like eating lunch or stirring soup. That activity is then paired with another activity that is automatic, or with an activity that requires cognition, like writing an email or talking on the phone. At the core of simple multi-tasking is a desire to be more productive. We multi-task to CREATE more opportunity for ourselves—time to DO more and time to RELAX more.

An image that comes to mind for me here is the contrast between *the organization man* (Whyte, 1956): a dutiful employee who ate lunch in a cafeteria or restaurant and certainly not at his desk; and the entrepreneur of the late 1960's, early 1970's, who ate lunch at his/her desk or while filing papers, in order to get more done in a day.

Simple multi-tasking made it possible to cram more into our workday, and often, helped create a little more free time for drinks with friends, or time with family, or a favorite television show.

In the case of continuous partial attention, we're motivated by a desire not to miss anything. We're engaged in two activities that *both* demand cognition. We're talking on the phone and driving. We're writing an email and participating in a conference call. We're carrying on a conversation at dinner and texting under the table on the Blackberry or iPhone.

Continuous partial attention also describes a state in which attention is on a priority or primary task, while, at the same time, scanning for other people, activities, or opportunities, and replacing the primary task with something that seems, in this next moment, more important. When we do this, we may have the feeling that our brains process multiple activities in parallel. Researchers say that while we can rapidly shift between activities, our brains process serially.

Continuous partial attention involves a kind of vigilance that is not characteristic of multi-tasking. With cpa, we feel most alive when we're connected, plugged in, and in the know. We constantly SCAN for opportunities—activities or people—in any given moment. With every opportunity we ask, "What can I gain here?"

Why care about the difference between multi-tasking and cpa?

Continuous partial attention is an always on, anywhere, anytime, any place   10
behavior that creates an artificial sense of crisis. We are always in high alert. We are demanding multiple cognitively complex actions from ourselves. We are reaching to keep a top priority in focus, while, at the same time, scanning the periphery to see if we are missing other opportunities. If we are, our very fickle attention shifts focus. What's ringing? Who is it? How many emails? What's on my list? What time is it in Bangalore?

In this state of always-on crisis, our adrenalized "fight or flight" mechanism kicks in. This is great when we're being chased by tigers. How many of those 500 emails a day is a TIGER? How many are flies? Is everything an emergency? Our way of using the current set of technologies would have us believe it is.

Over the last twenty years, we have become expert at continuous partial attention and we have pushed ourselves to an extreme that I call continuous continuous partial attention. There are times when cpa is the best attention strategy for what we're doing; and, in small doses, continuous partial attention serves us well. There are times when cpa and ccpa compromise us.

The "shadow side" of cpa is over-stimulation and lack of fulfillment. The latest, greatest powerful technologies are now contributing to our feeling increasingly powerless. Researchers are beginning to tell us that we may actually be doing tasks more slowly and poorly.

And that's not all. We have more attention-related and stress-related diseases than ever before. Continuous continuous partial attention and the fight or flight response associated with it can set off a cascade of stress hormones, starting with norepinephrine and its companion, cortisol. As a hormone, cortisol is a universal donor. It can attach to any receptor site. As a result, dopamine and serotonin—the hormones that help us feel calm and happy—have nowhere to go because cortisol has taken up the available spaces. The abundance of cortisol in our systems has contributed to our turning to pharmaceuticals to calm us down and help us sleep. Read about email apnea to understand how our relationship with screen-based activities plays a role in this fight or flight response.

DIAGNOSIS: EMAIL APNEA

I've just opened my email and there's nothing out of the ordinary there. It's the usual daily flood of schedule, project, travel, information, and junk mail. Then I notice. I'm holding my breath.

As the email spills onto my screen, as my mind races with thoughts of what I'll answer first, what can wait, who I should call, what should have been done two days ago, I've stopped the steady breathing I was doing only moments earlier in a morning meditation and now, I'm holding my breath.

And here's the deal: You're probably holding your breath, too.

I wanted to know—how widespread is *email apnea*?* I observed others on computers and BlackBerries: in their offices, their homes, at cafes. The vast majority of people held their breath, or breathed very shallowly, especially when responding to email. I watched people on cell phones, talking and walking, and noticed that most were mouth-breathing and hyperventilating. Consider also, that for many, posture while seated at a computer can contribute to restricted breathing.

Does it matter? How was holding my breath affecting me?   5

I called Dr. Margaret Chesney, at the National Institutes of Health (NIH). Research conducted by Dr. Margaret Chesney and NIH research scientist Dr. David Anderson demonstrated that breath-holding contributes significantly to stress-related diseases. The body becomes acidic, the kidneys begin to re-absorb sodium, and as the oxygen (O_2), carbon dioxide (CO_2), and nitric oxide (NO) balance is undermined, our biochemistry is thrown off.

Breath-holding and hyperventilating disturb our body's balance of oxygen, CO_2, and NO. Nitric oxide, not to be confused with the nitrous oxide used in dental offices, plays an important role in our health. From a briefing document prepared for the Royal Society and Association of British Science Writers, Pearce Wright explains, "The immune system uses nitric oxide in fighting viral, bacterial and parasitic infections, and tumors. Nitric oxide transmits messages between nerve cells and is associated with the processes of learning, memory, sleeping, feeling pain, and, probably, depression. It is a mediator in inflammation and rheumatism."

As I researched the literature, and spoke with physicians and researchers about breath-holding, a relationship to the vagus nerve emerged. The vagus nerve is one of the major cranial nerves, and wanders from the head, to the neck, chest and abdomen. Its primary job is to mediate the autonomic nervous system, which includes the sympathetic ("fight or flight") and parasympathetic ("rest and digest") nervous systems.

---

*Email apnea—a temporary absence or suspension of breathing, or shallow breathing, while doing email (Linda Stone, February 2008).

The parasympathetic nervous system governs our sense of hunger and satiety, flow of saliva and digestive enzymes, the relaxation response, and many aspects of healthy organ function. Focusing on diaphragmatic breathing enables us to down-regulate the sympathetic nervous system, which then causes the parasympathetic nervous system to become dominant. Shallow breathing, breath-holding and hyperventilating trigger the sympathetic nervous system, in a "fight or flight" response.

The activated sympathetic nervous system causes the liver to dump glucose and cholesterol into our blood, our heart rate to increase, our sense of satiety to be compromised, and our bodies to anticipate and resource for the physical activity that, historically, accompanied a physical fight or flight response. Meanwhile, when the only physical activity is sitting and responding to email, we're sort of "all dressed up with nowhere to go."

Some breathing patterns favor our body's move toward parasympathetic functions, and other breathing patterns favor a sympathetic nervous system response. Diaphragmatic breathing, Buteyko breathing (developed by a Russian M.D., http://en.wikipedia.org/wiki/Buteyko_method), some of Andy Weil's breathing exercises, and certain martial arts and yoga breathing techniques all have the potential to soothe us, and to help our bodies differentiate when fight or flight is really necessary and when we can rest and digest.

Now I want to know: Is it only the Big Mac that makes us fat? Or, are we more obese and diabetic because of a combination of holding our breath off and on all day and then failing to move when our bodies have prepared us to do so? Can 15 minutes of diaphragmatic breathing before a meal tune us in to when we're full? If, when we're doing sedentary work, and O_2, CO_2, and NO are optimally balanced, through healthy breathing, will we escape the ravages of an always-on sympathetic nervous system? Can daily breathing exercises contribute to helping reduce asthma, ADD, depression, obesity, and a host of other stress-related conditions?

I predict, within the next five-to-seven years, breathing exercises will be a significant part of every fitness regime. In the meantime, why not breathe while doing email? Awareness is the first step toward wiping out email apnea!

COMMENTS

Deva Hazarika

Linda, you should do some reading on Pranayama, a yoga breath control technique.

http://en.wikipedia.org/wiki/Pranayama

There have been a wide range of claims made in India about the benefits of these techniques, ranging from some that have been well documented and researched to others that are somewhat outlandish.

http://www.yogapranayama.com is one prominent yogi focusing on these techniques.

Linda

Thanks, Deva. One of my fact-checkers for the piece is an Indian physician. We absolutely reviewed both scientific research on various Pranayama practices as well as popular literature. Some of these techniques HAVE been researched and some have not. The way we breathe—or do not—fundamentally impacts our health and resilience. That we unintentionally compromise this when we engage with technology is a good thing to know—it means that we can INTENTIONALLY shift toward what would serve us better.

Jo

I lived in New Zealand for a while and the physiotherapists there have built up an understanding of the phenomenon you describe.

Patients present to them with painful chest and back muscles brought about by prolonged mild hyperventilation. The worst of it all is that you don't notice when you are hyperventilating. You are coping after all. It is the syndrome of a frog in water brought slowly to boiling point. Your partner won't notice either because it happens so slowly. It takes a stranger who is looking out for it because they have seen it so often. . .

20

aakriti

Hey Linda,

What you've mentioned is something we all experience but are not cognizant of the side effects it may lead to.

Do try Pranayama, twenty mins a day is effective enough to show you results.

Thanks for the good post!

Steve de Brun

If our devices and applications (computers, cell phones, PDAs, etc.) potentially contribute to shallow breathing and an activated sympathetic nervous system, I have to wonder if we will come up with ways that our devices will counteract these responses. I think of an iPhone app that has some kind of biofeedback mechanism, or cell phone that helps me calm down. If we must use these devices so much, then we must harness their potential power to calm us down.

25

Jen, writer MembershipMillionaire.com

I have also noticed the same thing a few months ago. However, I wasn't checking my mail when I discovered it. I realized I hold my breath while exercising, watching a certain program on television. Sometimes, I hold my breath while putting on makeup. And the strangest thing of all is that I never really noticed it before. Even when I finally did, I would still catch myself holding my breath. I used to wonder why and now I have a better understanding of it. Thanks for sharing!

Linda

Jen, an inhale and short breath hold is not uncommon when we are in a state of anticipation. Following it with an exhale keeps us in "balance." Inhales without much exhaling, constant shallow breathing, and constant (and frequent, long duration) breath holding appears to stress our bodies. The great thing about this is that, with intention, we can shift the behavior—we can learn a breathing technique, we can catch ourselves and do more diaphragmatic breathing, we can exercise, then enjoy the parasympathetic response that follows that, we can get an adjustable desk and stand some (standing posture better supports healthy breathing patterns) and sit some when we work . . .

Elf M. Sternberg

I don't think it's just email. My wife has long commented on my tendency to breathe oddly when I write, even long-form essays or fiction. I breathe in cadence with my thought processes, with the speed and demands of the piece, and have these odd little pauses and gasps all throughout.

Targeting email is cheap and easy, but it's not the whole of the story. There's something about the act of typing thoughtfully that makes one forget to do less important things, like breathing.

Dave W.

ADD (and ADHD) are not stress-related disorders. They are neurological disorders.

30

Sacha D.

From your description (and my ten minutes of experimentation) I think a more accurate term would be "poor breathing control while processing information," but e-mail apnea sounds so much more lyrical (and medical-sounding)!

http://blog.renewlab.com/2008/02/email-apnea-poor-breath-control-while.html

Linda

Elf—correct. Not just email. I chose to focus on email because so many of us do it and once alerted, would be likely to notice whether or not we breathe optimally, and if not, improve our posture, improve our breathing or do some follow-on activity that supports healthy breathing. A bonus if we notice, in some other aspect of our life, we might also apply this information.

Sacha—I used dictionary.com to help me come up with a more memorable and less awkward phrase than "breath holding while doing email," which is where I started.

Dave—I'm not an expert on ADD. I do believe, after doing months of research   35
on this, that "healthy" breathing can probably contribute in a positive way to just about anyone in any condition.

Stephen Lark

The following link is in a collection of articles published by Reader's Digest in 1951 called *Keys To Happiness*.

Tension's Little Trigger Men—One of the secrets of good health is to escape the tyranny of telephone, clock and calendar [https://slark.jottit.com/tension's_little_trigger_men]

Les Posen

Hi Linda,

I have watched and listened to your presentations since "discovering" you on IT Conversations some years back.

I'm a psychologist who specialises in anxiety, especially fear of flying (flightwise   40
.com.au). But I also teach psychologists about trends in technology and how they may affect their practices and so of course have included info on Continuous Partial Attention and reference to your talks.

But I read your recent article on email apnea and have used the printout to give to my patients when it comes time to introduce them to the concept of Heart Rate Variability (HRV), and how raising it through Diaphragmatic Breathing exercises, using biofeedback, can help moderate anxiety and depression, and numerous psychosomatic complaints.

Your article was a most cogent distillation of how the ANS, SNS and PNS work in sync. I talk about Formula 1 racing car drivers (the Australian Grand Prix is held a mile or two from my practice) using a deft combination of brake and accelerator to eke maximum speeds around corners, compared to suburban drivers who just shift their right foot from brake to accelerator.

The putative link between breathing and obesity is a curious one. There is some discussion in the literature also of oxygen stress and more talk about neurocardiology, the link between the heart and brain mediated by the vagus nerve. No surprise, I also give workshops to psychologists here in Melbourne, on HRV and the technologies to measure it, and use Apple's Keynote to make the workshops engaging and interactive.

BTW, the HRV equipment I use comes from the US, from heartmath.org and I get a very good response from IT pros who come to me as patients and see the data displayed on my wall via a data projector. Very effective tool for those less aware of the power of the affective system to influence health and behaviour.

Many thanks again for your article,

Best wishes

Les Posen
Fellow, Australian Psychological Society
President, Internet Macintosh User Group, Melbourne

Questions for Critical Reading

1. Did Stone succeed in persuading you to consider the role of continuous partial attention (CPA) in your life? Did she succeed in persuading you to consider whether you have e-mail apnea? Why or why not?

2. Making a move that isn't uncommon to see across genres, Stone coins new terms, "continuous partial attention" and "email apnea." Consider the term "continuous partial attention" as a case study in coining terms. Like other writers who coin terms, Stone has an underlying purpose for coining this particular term; there's a reason she thinks it should replace the cognitive science term "complex multi-tasking." What do you think her reason is? Do you think coining this term was a good move on her part? Why or why not?

3. Now consider the other term Stone coined, "email apnea." When she mentions e-mail apnea in the last sentence of her CPA post, she suggests that the term encompasses more than just e-mail by referring more broadly to "screen-based activities" (para. 14). Moreover, she responds to a reader's comment that "Targeting e-mail is cheap and easy, but it's not the whole story" (para. 21) by acknowledging the point: "correct. Not just email" (para. 24). Stone goes on to defend her choice of the term "email apnea":

> I chose to focus on email because so many of us do it and, once alerted, would be likely to notice whether or not we breathe optimally, and if not, improve our posture, improve our breathing or do some follow-on activity that supports healthy breathing. A bonus if we notice, in some other aspect of our life, [where] we might also apply this information. (para. 33)

Did you find Stone's defense of her choice persuasive? Why or why not? Can you think of a term you like better than "email apnea"? If so, what would it be?

4. Recall that while scholarly research reports tend to include descriptions of how the research was conducted, many nonacademic genres don't. Indeed, in the version of the email apnea post appearing in *O'Reilly Radar,* Stone devotes only one sentence to her methodology: "I observed others on computers and BlackBerries: in their offices, their homes, at cafes" (para. 4).

However, Stone does provide a bit more detail about her methodology in a post with the same title on her individual blog, *The Attention Project.* Read how she describes her methodology in this post and consider whether you would have wanted her to include this description in her *O'Reilly Radar* post:

> I spent the next 6–7 months observing and interviewing over 200 people. I watched and spoke with people in their offices, in cafes, in their homes, and roughly 80% of this sample appeared to have what I called **email apnea**.

Would you have found the *O'Reilly Radar* post more persuasive if Stone had included this information? Why or why not? Is there anything else you would have wanted to know about how Stone conducted her research and, if so, what?

5. Recall that letting readers know why they should care about your topic is an important move made in many genres — and indeed, Stone explicitly makes this move in both blog posts. In her CPA post, she asks, "Why care about the difference between multi-tasking and CPA?" (para. 9), and she then proceeds to answer the question.

Similarly, in her e-mail apnea post, she tells us that she's observed people holding their breath or breathing shallowly while using technology, and then she asks — and answers — the question "Does it matter?" (para. 5).

Why do you think Stone makes this move in both posts? When in your own writing might you want to make such a move? (Note that this move can also be made without actually asking the question explicitly; many writers simply skip the question and proceed directly to providing the answer.)

6. When Stone answers the questions "Why care?" in her CPA post and "Does it matter?" in her e-mail apnea post, she does so at different points in each piece: in the email apnea post she answers the question toward the beginning, while in the CPA post she answers it toward the end. Indeed, it's not until we're more than halfway through the CPA post that Stone tells us why we should care about the difference between simple multitasking and continuous partial attention: "Continuous partial attention is an always on, anywhere, anytime, any place behavior that creates an artificial sense of crisis" (para. 10). Would you have preferred to get this information earlier in the post? Why or why not?

If you liked this information where it was, did Stone say something near the beginning of the post to inspire you to trust that the term "continuous partial attention" would be important in some way (to tide you over until she fully explained its importance)? If so, where and how did she inspire your trust that this would be an important term?

7. Recall that comments on a blog post sometimes help readers see that the post doesn't fully recognize complexity — that there are nuances the author doesn't address. Which comment(s) on "Diagnosis: Email Apnea" do you think recognized important nuances that were missing from the original piece of writing? If you were Stone and you decided to revise "Diagnosis: Email Apnea," would you recognize any of the nuances pointed out in the comments? Why or why not?

Making Connections

8. Like writers across genres who discuss their personal experience, Stone claims that her experience is typical. Nicholas Carr, author of the magazine feature "Is Google Making Us Stupid?" (p. 574), also tells us that his personal experience is representative. Consider why both authors might have made this move:

   ### "Diagnosis: Email Apnea"

   As the email spills onto my screen, as my mind races with thoughts of what I'll answer first, what can wait, who I should call, what should have been done two days ago, I've stopped the steady breathing I was doing only moments earlier in a morning meditation and now, I'm holding my breath.

   And here's the deal: You're probably holding your breath, too. (paras. 2–3)

   ### "Is Google Making Us Stupid?"

   I'm not the only one. When I mention my troubles with reading to friends and acquaintances — literary types, most of them — many say they're having similar experiences. . . . Some of the bloggers I follow have also begun mentioning the phenomenon. (para. 5)

   Why do you think both writers tell us that their experiences are typical? When you discuss your personal experience in your own writing, in what situations might you want to note that it's typical? In what situations might you want to note that it's *not* typical?

9. Recall that in some genres (especially blogs and news genres), you're likely to encounter unsupported claims such as "researchers found" and "scientists say"; in other genres, however, writers are more likely to elaborate on such claims, supporting them by providing details from an actual study or a named expert. However, as with most aspects of writing, there can be variation within a genre; for instance, Stone provides supporting details about a source in one of her posts but not in the other.

   To get a sense of how stark the difference between these two approaches is, compare the following three passages, one from Stone's CPA post, one from her e-mail apnea post, and one from Carr's magazine feature "Is Google

writing

Making Us Stupid?" (p. 574). Note that each passage includes the ending of the paragraph and that the sentences referring to research or to expert knowledge are italicized.

"Beyond Simple Multi-Tasking: Continuous Partial Attention" (blog post)

The latest, greatest powerful technologies are now contributing to our feeling increasingly powerless. *Researchers are beginning to tell us that we may actually be doing tasks more slowly and poorly.* (para. 13)

"Diagnosis: Email Apnea" (blog post)

Breath-holding and hyperventilating disturb our body's balance of oxygen, CO_2, and NO. Nitric oxide . . . plays an important role in our health. *From a briefing document prepared for the Royal Society and Association of British Science Writers, Pearce Wright explains, "The immune system uses nitric oxide in fighting viral, bacterial and parasitic infections, and tumors. Nitric oxide transmits messages between nerve cells and is associated with the processes of learning, memory, sleeping, feeling pain, and, probably, depression. It is a mediator in inflammation and rheumatism."* (para. 7)

"Is Google Making Us Stupid?" (magazine feature)

People used to think that our [brain's neural connections were] largely fixed by the time we reached adulthood. *But brain researchers have discovered that that's not the case. James Olds, a professor of neuroscience who directs the Krasnow Institute for Advanced Study at George Mason University, says that even the adult mind "is very plastic." Nerve cells routinely break old connections and form new ones. "The brain," according to Olds, "has the ability to reprogram itself on the fly, altering the way it functions."* (para. 13)

Did the unsourced claim in the first example affect you differently than the claims followed by information about the source? Why or why not? How will you as a writer decide when to support claims by referring to an actual study or expert?

Writing: Your Turn

1. Using as models the comments on "Diagnosis: Email Apnea" that you find to be especially detailed, write your own responses to both of Stone's blog posts. In your responses, you might take issue with one or more of Stone's claims; extend one of her points (suggesting, for instance, that it applies even more broadly); point out that a phenomenon is more complex than she claims; discuss how her ideas apply to you personally (or to people you know); or respond in yet another way that is thoughtfully considered. Share your responses with your classmates to get feedback on how you could make them even stronger.

2. Using Stone's blog posts as models, write your own blog post coining a term that describes how some people interact with technology. Share your post with some classmates to see if you persuaded them that you're accurately describing a common phenomenon—and to see if they understand the purpose underlying your coining of the term. (Stone, for instance, coined the term "continuous partial attention" to draw our attention to a way in which we're creating "an artificial sense of crisis" (para. 10); she didn't make up the term just for the sake of making up a term.) For ideas on writing a blog post, see p. 90.

LINKED
READING
PAGE 644

Literature review

Clinical Report: The Impact of Social Media on Children, Adolescents, and Families

Gwenn Schurgin O'Keeffe, MD; Kathleen Clarke-Pearson, MD; and Council on Communications and Media

Published in the peer-reviewed[3] journal *Pediatrics*, "Clinical Report: The Impact of Social Media on Children, Adolescents, and Families" provides an overview of the effects of social media aimed at an audience of pediatricians—and indeed, the lead author, Dr. Gwenn O'Keeffe, is a pediatrician herself. After you read "Clinical Report: The Impact of Social Media," you'll find a blogged critique of it written by John Grohol.

Focus on Genre   "The Impact of Social Media" attempts to advance the field of pediatrics by providing pediatricians with a literature review of research on how social media affects children, teenagers, and their families. Literature reviews don't present new research; rather, their value lies in the authors' ability to insightfully discuss and synthesize previously published research. Literature reviews can be useful to readers who are familiar with the previously published research but who haven't looked at it in the same light as the authors have. They can also be useful for readers who haven't read all the research but who are interested in learning about it. Although literature reviews can be difficult for readers who aren't part of the intended audience, reading a well-done literature review can be a helpful way to understand, at a glance, the current state of knowledge in a particular area. When you read literature reviews, it's important to think about how thoroughly the authors have looked for sources, how they have chosen which sources to discuss and which ones to omit, and how carefully they represent the sources they do discuss.

◄○►

---

[3] Recall that "peer-reviewed" refers to the method by which journal editors evaluate work to determine whether it's suitable for publication; experts in a given field are asked to consider whether submitted articles convey new knowledge or synthesize previously published knowledge in a new and useful way.

ABSTRACT

Using social media Web sites is among the most common activity of today's children and adolescents. Any Web site that allows social interaction is considered a social media site, including social networking sites such as Facebook, MySpace, and Twitter; gaming sites and virtual worlds such as Club Penguin, Second Life, and the Sims; video sites such as YouTube; and blogs. Such sites offer today's youth a portal for entertainment and communication and have grown exponentially in recent years. For this reason, it is important that parents become aware of the nature of social media sites, given that not all of them are healthy environments for children and adolescents. Pediatricians are in a unique position to help families understand these sites and to encourage healthy use and urge parents to monitor for potential problems with cyberbullying, "Facebook Depression," sexting, and exposure to inappropriate content. Pediatrics *2011; 127:800–804*

SOCIAL MEDIA USE BY TWEENS AND TEENS

Engaging in various forms of social media is a routine activity that research has shown to benefit children and adolescents by enhancing communication, social connection, and even technical skills.[1] Social media sites such as Facebook and MySpace offer multiple daily opportunities for connecting with friends, classmates, and people with shared interests. During the last 5 years, the number of preadolescents and adolescents using such sites has increased dramatically. According to a recent poll, 22% of teenagers log on to their favorite social media site more than 10 times a day, and more than half of adolescents log on to a social media site more than once a day.[2] Seventy-five percent of teenagers now own cell phones, and 25% use them for social media, 54% use them for texting, and 24% use them for instant messaging.[3] Thus, a large part of this generation's social and emotional development is occurring while on the Internet and on cell phones.

Because of their limited capacity for self-regulation and susceptibility to peer pressure, children and adolescents are at some risk as they navigate and experiment with social media. Recent research indicates that there are frequent online expressions of offline behaviors, such as bullying, clique-forming and sexual experimentation,[4] that have introduced problems such as cyberbullying,[5] privacy issues, and "sexting."[6] Other problems that merit awareness include Internet addiction and concurrent sleep deprivation.[7]

Many parents today use technology incredibly well and feel comfortable and capable with the programs and online venues that their children and adolescents are using. Nevertheless, some parents may find it difficult to relate to their digitally savvy youngsters online for several reasons. Such parents may lack a basic understanding of these new forms of socialization, which are integral to their children's lives.[8] They frequently do not have the technical abilities or time needed to keep pace with their children in the ever-changing Internet landscape.[8] In addition, these parents often lack a basic understanding that kids' online lives are an extension of their offline lives. The end result is often a knowledge and technical skill gap between parents and youth, which creates a disconnect in how these parents and youth participate in the online world together.[9]

BENEFITS OF CHILDREN AND ADOLESCENTS USING SOCIAL MEDIA

Socialization and Communication

Social media sites allow teens to accomplish online many of the tasks that are important to them offline: staying connected with friends and family, making new friends, sharing pictures, and exchanging ideas. Social media participation also can offer adolescents deeper benefits that extend into their view of self, community, and the world, including:[1,10]

1. opportunities for community engagement through raising money for charity and volunteering for local events, including political and philanthropic events;
2. enhancement of individual and collective creativity through development and sharing of artistic and musical endeavors;
3. growth of ideas from the creation of blogs, podcasts, videos, and gaming sites;
4. expansion of one's online connections through shared interests to include others from more diverse backgrounds (such communication is an important step for all adolescents and affords the opportunity for respect, tolerance, and increased discourse about personal and global issues); and
5. fostering of one's individual identity and unique social skills.[11]

Enhanced Learning Opportunities

Middle and high school students are using social media to connect with one another on homework and group projects.[11] For example, Facebook and similar social media programs allow students to gather outside of class to collaborate and exchange ideas about assignments. Some schools successfully use blogs as teaching tools,[12] which has the benefit of reinforcing skills in English, written expression, and creativity.

Accessing Health Information

Adolescents are finding that they can access online information about their health concerns easily and anonymously. Excellent health resources are increasingly available to youth on a variety of topics of interest to this population, such as sexually transmitted infections, stress reduction, and signs of depression. Adolescents with chronic illnesses can access Web sites through which they can develop supportive networks of people with similar conditions.[13] The mobile technologies that teens use daily, namely cell phones, instant messaging, and text messaging, have already produced multiple improvements in their health care, such as increased medication adherence, better disease understanding, and fewer missed appointments.[14] Given that the new social media venues all have mobile applications, teenagers will have enhanced opportunities to learn about their health issues and communicate with their doctors. However, because of their young age, adolescents can encounter inaccuracies during these searches and require parental involvement to be sure they are using reliable online resources, interpreting the information correctly, and not becoming overwhelmed by the information they are reading. Encouraging parents to ask about their children's and adolescents' online searches can help facilitate not only discovery of this information but discussion on these topics.

RISKS OF YOUTH USING SOCIAL MEDIA

Using social media becomes a risk to adolescents more often than most adults realize. Most risks fall into the following categories: peer-to-peer; inappropriate content; lack of understanding of online privacy issues; and outside influences of third-party advertising groups.

Cyberbullying and Online Harassment

Cyberbullying is deliberately using digital media to communicate false, embarrassing, or hostile information about another person. It is the most common online risk for all teens and is a peer-to-peer risk.

Although "online harassment" is often used interchangeably with the term "cyberbullying," it is actually a different entity. Current data suggest that online harassment is not as common as offline harassment,[15] and participation in social networking sites does not put most children at risk of online harassment.[16] On the other hand, cyberbullying is quite common, can occur to any young person online, and can cause profound psychosocial outcomes including depression, anxiety, severe isolation, and, tragically, suicide.[17]

10

Sexting

Sexting can be defined as "sending, receiving, or forwarding sexually explicit messages, photographs, or images via cell phone, computer, or other digital devices."[18] Many of these images become distributed rapidly via cell phones or the Internet. This phenomenon does occur among the teen population; a recent survey revealed that 20% of teens have sent or posted nude or semi-nude photographs or videos of themselves.[19] Some teens who have engaged in sexting have been threatened or charged with felony child pornography charges, although some states have started characterizing such behaviors as juvenile-law misdemeanors.[20,21] Additional consequences include school suspension for perpetrators and emotional distress with accompanying mental health conditions for victims. In many circumstances, however, the sexting incident is not shared beyond a small peer group or a couple and is not found to be distressing at all.[4]

Facebook Depression

Researchers have proposed a new phenomenon called "Facebook depression," defined as depression that develops when preteens and teens spend a great deal of time on social media sites, such as Facebook, and then begin to exhibit classic symptoms of depression.[22–27] Acceptance by and contact with peers is an important element of adolescent life. The intensity of the online world is thought to be a factor that may trigger depression in some adolescents. As with offline depression, preadolescents and adolescents who suffer from Facebook depression are at risk for social isolation and sometimes turn to risky Internet sites and blogs for "help" that may promote substance abuse, unsafe sexual practices, or aggressive or self-destructive behaviors.

PRIVACY CONCERNS AND THE DIGITAL FOOTPRINT

The main risk to preadolescents and adolescents online today are risks from each other, risks of improper use of technology, lack of privacy, sharing too much information, or posting false information about themselves or others.[28] These types of behavior put their privacy at risk.

When Internet users visit various Web sites, they can leave behind evidence of which sites they have visited. This collective, ongoing record of one's Web activity is called the "digital footprint." One of the biggest threats to young people on social media sites is to their digital footprint and future reputations. Preadolescents and adolescents who lack an awareness of privacy issues often post inappropriate messages, pictures, and videos without understanding that "what goes online stays online."[8] As a result, future jobs and college acceptance may be put into jeopardy by inexperienced and rash clicks of the mouse. Indiscriminate Internet activity also can make children and teenagers easier for marketers and fraudsters to target.

INFLUENCE OF ADVERTISEMENTS ON BUYING

Many social media sites display multiple advertisements such as banner ads,   15
behavior ads (ads that target people on the basis of their Web-browsing behavior), and demographic-based ads (ads that target people on the basis of a specific factor such as age, gender, education, marital status, etc.) that influence not only the buying tendencies of preadolescents and adolescents but also their views of what is normal. It is particularly important for parents to be aware of the behavioral ads, because they are common on social media sites and operate by gathering information on the person using a site and then targeting that person's profile to influence purchasing decisions. Such powerful influences start as soon as children begin to go online and post.[29] Many online venues are now prohibiting ads on sites where children and adolescents are participating. It is important to educate parents, children, and adolescents about this practice so that children can develop into media-literate consumers and understand how advertisements can easily manipulate them.

ON TOO YOUNG: MIXED MESSAGES FROM PARENTS AND THE LAW

Many parents are aware that 13 years is the minimum age for most social media sites but do not understand why. There are 2 major reasons. First, 13 years is the age set by Congress in the Children's Online Privacy Protection Act (COPPA), which prohibits Web sites from collecting information on children younger than 13 years without parental permission. Second, the official terms of service for many popular sites now mirror the COPPA regulations and state that 13 years is the minimum age to sign up and have a profile. This is the minimum age to sign on to sites such as Facebook and MySpace. There are many sites for preadolescents and younger children that do not have such an age restriction, such as Disney sites, Club Penguin, and others.

It is important that parents evaluate the sites on which their child wishes to participate to be sure that the site is appropriate for that child's age. For sites without age stipulations, however, there is room for negotiation, and parents should evaluate the situation via active conversation with their preadolescents and adolescents.

In general, if a Web site specifies a minimum age for use in its terms of service, the American Academy of Pediatrics (AAP) encourages that age to be respected. Falsifying age has become common practice by some preadolescents and some parents. Parents must be thoughtful about this practice to be sure that they are not sending mixed messages about lying and that online safety is always the main message being emphasized.

THE ROLE OF PEDIATRICIANS

Pediatricians are in a unique position to educate families about both the complexities of the digital world and the challenging social and health issues that online youth experience by encouraging families to face the core issues of bullying, popularity and status, depression and social anxiety, risk-taking and sexual development. Pediatricians can help parents understand that what is happening online is an extension of these underlying issues and that parents can be most helpful if they understand the core issues and have strategies for dealing with them whether they take place online, offline, or, increasingly, both. Some specific ways in which pediatricians can assist parents include:

1. Advise parents to talk to their children and adolescents about their online use and the specific issues that today's online kids face.
2. Advise parents to work on their own participation gap in their homes by becoming better educated about the many technologies their youngsters are using.
3. Discuss with families the need for a family online-use plan that involves regular family meetings to discuss online topics and checks of privacy settings and online profiles for inappropriate posts. The emphasis should be on citizenship and healthy behavior and not punitive action, unless truly warranted.
4. Discuss with parents the importance of supervising online activities via active participation and communication, as opposed to remote monitoring with a "net-nanny" program (software used to monitor the Internet in the absence of parents).

In addition, the AAP encourages all pediatricians to increase their knowledge of digital technology so that they can have a more educated frame of reference for the tools their patients and families are using, which will aid in providing timely anticipatory media guidance as well as diagnosing media-related issues should they arise.

To assist families in discussing the more challenging issues that kids face online, pediatricians can provide families with reputable online resources, including "Social Media and Sexting Tips" from the AAP (www.aap.org /advocacy/releases/june09socialmedia.htm),[30] the AAP Internet safety site (http://safetynet.aap.org),[31] and the AAP public education site, Healthy Children.org (www.healthychildren.org/english/search/pages/results.aspx?Type_Keyword&Keyword_Internet_safety),[32] and encourage parents to discuss these resources with their children. Pediatricians with Web sites or blogs may wish to create a section with resources for parents and children about these issues and may suggest a list of or links to social media sites that are appropriate for the different age groups. In this way, pediatricians can support the efforts of parents to engage and educate youth to be responsible, sensible, and respectful digital citizens.

References

1. Ito M, Horst H, Bittani M. *Living and Learning with New Media: Summary of Findings from the Digital Youth Project.* Chicago, IL: John D. and Catherine T. MacArthur Foundation Reports on Digital Media and Learning; 2008. Available at: http://digitalyouth.ischool.berkeley.edu/files/report/digitalyouth-TwoPageSummary.pdf. Accessed July 16, 2010

2. Common Sense Media. *Is Technology Networking Changing Childhood? A National Poll.* San Francisco, CA: Common Sense Media; 2009. Available at: www.commonsensemedia.org/sites/default/files/CSM_teen_social_media_080609_FINAL.pdf. Accessed July 16, 2010

3. Hinduja S, Patchin J. Offline consequences of online victimization: school violence and delinquency. *J Sch Violence.* 2007; 6(3):89–112

4. Lenhart A. *Teens and Sexting.* Washington, DC: Pew Research Center; 2009. Available at: http://pewinternet.org/Reports/2009/Teens-and-Sexting.aspx. Accessed August 4, 2010

5. Patchin JW, Hinduja S. Bullies move beyond the schoolyard: a preliminary look at cyberbullying. *Youth Violence Juv Justice.* 2006; 4(2):148–169

6. A thin line: 2009 AP-TVT digital abuse study. Available at: www.athinline.org/MTV-AP_Digital_Abuse_Study_Executive_Summary.pdf. Accessed July 16, 2010

7. Christakis DA, Moreno MA. Trapped in the net: will internet addiction become a 21st-century epidemic? *Arch Pediatr Adolesc Med.* 2009; 163(10):959–960

8. Palfrey J, Gasser U, Boyd D. *Response to FCC Notice of Inquiry 09-94: "Empowering Parents and Protecting Children in an Evolving Media Landscape."* Cambridge, MA: Berkman Center for Internet and Society at Harvard University; 2010. Available at: http://cyber.law.harvard.edu/sites/cyber.law.harvard.edu/files/Palfrey_Gasser_boyd_response_to_FCC_NOI_09-94_Feb2010.pdf. Accessed July 16, 2010

9. Jenkins H, Clinton K, Purushotma R, Robinson AJ, Weigel M. *Confronting the Challenges of Participatory Culture: Media Education for the 21st Century.* Chicago, IL: John D. and Catherine T. MacArthur Foundation Reports on Digital Media and Learning; 2006. Available at: http://digitallearning.macfound.org/atf/cf/{7E45C7E0-A3E0-4B89-AC9C-E807E1B0AE4E}/JENKINS_WHITE_PAPER.PDF. Accessed July 16, 2010

10. Boyd D. Why youth (heart) social network sites: the role of networked publics in teenage social life. In: Buckingham D, ed. *MacArthur Foundation Series on Digital Learning: Youth, Identity, and Digital Media Volume.* Cambridge, MA: MIT Press; 2007. Available at: www.danah.org/papers/WhyYouthHeart.pdf. Accessed July 16, 2010

11. Boyd D. *Taken Out of Context: American Teen Sociality in Networked Publics.* Berkeley, CA: University of California; 2008. Available at: www.danah.org/papers /TakenOutOfContext.pdf. Accessed July 16, 2010

12. Borja RR. "Blogs" catching on as tool for instruction: teachers use interactive Web pages to hone writing skills. *Educ Week.* December 14, 2005. Available at: www .iapsych.com/edblogs.pdf. Accessed July 16, 2010

13. Lenhart A, Purcell K, Smith A, Zickur K. *Social Media and Young Adults.* Washington, DC: Pew Research Center; 2010. Available at: http://pewinternet.org/Reports/2010/ Social-Media-and-Young-Adults.aspx. Accessed July 16, 2010

14. Krishna S, Boren SA, Balas EA. Healthcare via cell phones: a systematic review. *Telemed E Health.* 2009; 15(3):231–240

15. Lenhart A. *Cyberbullying.* Washington, DC: Pew Research Center; 2007. Available at: www.pewinternet.org/Reports/2007/Cyberbullying.aspx. Accessed July 16, 2010

16. Ybarra ML, Mitchell KJ. How risky are social networking sites? A comparison of places online where youth sexual solicitation and harassment occurs. *Pediatrics.* 2008; 121(2). Available at: www.pediatrics.org/cgi/content/full/121/2/e350

17. Hinduja S, Patchin JW. Bullying, cyberbullying, and suicide. *Arch Suicide Res.* 2010; 14(3):206–221

18. Berkshire District Attorney. *Sexting.* Pittsfield, MA: Commonwealth of Massachusetts; 2010. Available at: www.mass.gov/?pageID_berterminal&L_3&L0_Home&L1 _Crime_Awareness_%26_Prevention&L2_Parents_%26_Youth&sid_Dber&b_ terminalcontent&f_parents_youth_sexting&csid_Dber. Accessed September 7, 2010

19. National Campaign to Prevent Teen and Unplanned Pregnancy. *Sex and Tech: Results of a Survey of Teens and Young Adults.* Washington, DC: National Campaign to Prevent Teen and Unplanned Pregnancy; 2008. Available at: www .thenationalcampaign.org/SEXTECH/PDF/SexTech_Summary.pdf. Accessed July 16, 2010

20. Gifford NV. *Sexting in the USA.* Washington, DC: Family Online Safety Institute Report; 2009. Available at: www.fosi.org/cms/downloads/resources/Sexting.pdf. Accessed July 16, 2010

21. Walker J. Child's play or child pornography: the need for better laws regarding sexting. *ACJS Today.* 2010; 35(1):3–9. Available at: www.acjs .org/pubs/uploads/ACJSToday_February_2010.pdf. Accessed July 16, 2010

22. Davila J, Stroud CB, Starr LR, et al. Romantic and sexual activities, parent-adolescent stress, and depressive symptoms among early adolescent girls. *J Adolesc.* 2009; 32(4):909–924

23. Selfhout MHW, Branje SJT, Delsing M, ter Bogt TFM, Meeus WHJ. Different types of Internet use, depression, and social anxiety: the role of perceived friendship quality. *J Adolesc.* 2009; 32(4):819–833

24. Melville K. Facebook use associated with depression. *Science A Go Go.* February 3, 2010. Available at: www.scienceagogo.com/news/20100102231001data_trunc _sys.shtml. Accessed September 7, 2010

25. Irvine C. Excessive chatting on Facebook can lead to depression in teenage girls. *Daily Telegraph.* January 31, 2010. Available at: www.telegraph.co.uk/technology /facebook/4405741/Excessive-chatting-on-Facebook-can-lead-to-depression-in -teenage-girls.html. Accessed September 7, 2010

26. Herr J. Internet entangles college students in a web of loneliness and depression. *Truman State University Index.* February 27, 2007. Available at: www.trumanindex .com/2.10111/internet-entangles-college-students-in-a-web-of-loneliness-and -depression-1.1462681. Accessed September 7, 2010

27. Sturm S. Social networking psych studies: research shows teen Facebook users prone to depression. *TrendHunter.* Available at: www.trendhunter.com/trends /depression-from-facebook. Accessed September 7, 2010

28. Barnes S. A privacy paradox: social networking in the United States. *First Monday.* 2006; 11(9). Available at: http://firstmonday.org/htbin/cgiwrap/bin/ojs/index .php/fm/article/view/1394/1312. Accessed July 16, 2010

29. Kunkel D, Wilcox BL, Cantor J, Palmer E, Linn S, Dowrick P. Report of the APA Task Force on Advertising and Children. Section: psychological aspects of commercialization of childhood. February 2004. Available at: www.chawisconsin.org/Obesity /O2ChildAds.pdf. Accessed July 16, 2010

30. American Academy of Pediatrics. Talking to kids and teens about social media and sexting. Available at: www.aap.org/advocacy/releases/june09socialmedia.htm. Accessed September 7, 2010

31. American Academy of Pediatrics. Safety net. Available at: http://safetynet.aap.org. Accessed September 7, 2010

32. American Academy of Pediatrics. Internet safety. Available at: www.healthychildren .org/english/search/pages/results.aspx?Type_Keyword&Keyword_internet_safety. Accessed September 7, 2010

Blogged critique

Pediatrics Gets It Wrong about "Facebook Depression"

John Grohol, PsyD

The *Pediatrics* report you just read is critiqued in John Grohol's blog post "*Pediatrics* Gets It Wrong about 'Facebook Depression.'" Grohol's blog appears on *Psych Central*, a Web site he founded to offer resources on a variety of topics in the field of psychology. Grohol also conducts his own research and sits on the editorial board of *Cyberpsychology, Behavior, and Social Networking*.

Focus on Genre   It is largely for evidence inappropriate to the genre that Grohol critiques the *Pediatrics* report: indeed, part of succeeding in the use of any genre is being aware of readers' expectations, especially their expectations about evidence. If readers don't get what they expect, they are more likely to find fault, as Grohol does with the *Pediatrics* report.

Interestingly enough, Grohol marshals fairly extensive evidence in his blogged critique — even though, as he himself notes, readers don't always expect extensive evidence in blogs. The lesson we might learn is this: although you're open to critique when you provide *less* evidence than readers expect from a genre, you might sometimes be well served by providing *more* evidence than they expect. As you read, consider whether Grohol was indeed well served by providing more evidence than readers might expect from a blog. Also consider whether you agree with Grohol that the evidence in the *Pediatrics* report is problematic.

Finally, bear in mind an important advantage of technologically enabled genres such as blogs: the opportunity for multiple readers to respond to one another — to have a conversation. For instance, the lead author of the *Pediatrics* report, Gwenn O'Keeffe, posted a response to Grohol's critique, and Grohol responded to her response, as did Joanne Davila, one of the researchers cited in the *Pediatrics* report. As you read, assess the evidence used in these responses to Grohl's critique. Which responses did you find persuasive, and why?

—◄O►—

Y ou know it's not good when one of the most prestigious pediatric journals, *Pediatrics*, can't differentiate between correlation and causation.

And yet this is exactly what the authors of a "clinical report" did in reporting on the impact of social media on children and teens. Especially in their discussion of "Facebook depression," a term that the authors simply *made up* to describe the phenomenon observed when depressed people use social media.

Shoddy research? You bet. That's why *Pediatrics* calls it a "clinical report"—because it's at the level of a bad blog post written by people with a clear agenda. In this case, the report was written by Gwenn Schurgin O'Keeffe, Kathleen Clarke-Pearson and the American Academy of Pediatrics Council on Communications and Media (2011).

What makes this a bad report? Let's just look at the issue of "Facebook depression," their made-up term for a phenomenon that doesn't exist.

The authors of the *Pediatrics* report use six citations to support their claim   5
that social media sites like Facebook actually *cause* depression in children and teens. Four of the six citations are third-party news reports on research in this area. In other words, *the authors couldn't even bother with reading the actual research to see if the research actually said what the news outlet reported it said.*

I expect to see this sort of lack of quality and laziness on blogs. Hey, a lot of time we're busy and we just want to make a point—that I can understand.

When you go to the trouble not only of writing a report but also publishing it in a peer-reviewed journal, you'd think you'd go to the trouble of reading the research—not other people's reporting on research.

Here's what the researchers in *Pediatrics* had to say about "Facebook depression":

> Researchers have proposed a new phenomenon called "Facebook depression," defined as depression that develops when preteens and teens spend a great deal of time on social media sites, such as Facebook, and then begin to exhibit classic symptoms of depression.
>
> Acceptance by and contact with peers is an important element of adolescent life. The intensity of the online world is thought to be a factor that may trigger depression in some adolescents. As with offline depression, preadolescents and adolescents who suffer from Facebook depression are at risk for social isolation and sometimes turn to risky Internet sites and blogs for "help" that may promote substance abuse, unsafe sexual practices, or aggressive or self-destructive behaviors.

Time and time again researchers are finding much more nuanced relationships between social networking sites and depression. In the Selfhout et al. (2009) study they cite, for instance, the researchers only found the correlation between the two factors in people with *low quality* friendships. Teens with what the researchers characterized as high quality friendships showed no increase in depression with increased social networking time.

The *Pediatrics* authors also do what a lot of researchers do when promoting a specific bias or point of view—they simply ignore research that disagrees with their bias. Worse, they cite the supposed depression-social networking link as though it were a foregone conclusion—that researchers are all in agreement that this actually exists, and exists in a causative manner.

There are a multitude of studies that disagree with their point of view, however. One longitudinal study (Kraut et al., 1998) found that, over a period of 8–12 months, both loneliness and depression increased with time spent online among adolescent and adult first-time Internet users. In a one-year follow-up study (Kraut et al., 2002), however, the observed negative effects of Internet use had disappeared. In other words, this may not be a robust relationship (if it even exists) and may simply be something related to greater familiarity with the Internet.   10

Other research has shown that college students'—who are often older teens—Internet use was directly and indirectly related to **less depression** (Morgan & Cotten, 2003; LaRose, Eastin, & Gregg, 2001).

Furthermore, studies have revealed that Internet use can lead to online relationship formation, and thereby to more social support ([Nie and Erbring, 2000], [Wellman et al., 2001] and [Wolak et al., 2003])—which may subsequently lead to less internalizing problems.

In another study cited by the *Pediatrics* authors, simply reading the news report should've raised a red flag for them. Because the news report on the study quoted the study's author who specifically noted her study could not determine causation:

> According to Morrison, pornography, online gaming and social networking site users had a higher incidence of moderate to severe depression than other users. "Our research indicates that excessive Internet use is associated with depression, but what we don't know is which comes first—are depressed people drawn to the Internet or does the Internet cause depression? What is clear is that for a small subset of people, excessive use of the Internet could be a warning signal for depressive tendencies," she added.

The other citations in the *Pediatrics* report are equally problematic (and one citation has nothing to do with social networking and depression [Davila, 2009]). None mention the phrase "Facebook depression" (as far as I could determine), and none could demonstrate a **causative relationship between use of Facebook making a teenager or child feel more depressed.** Zero.

I'm certain depressed people use Facebook, Twitter and other social networking websites. I'm certain people who are already feeling down or depressed might go online to talk to their friends, and try and be cheered up. This in no way suggests that by using more and more of Facebook, a person is going to get more depressed. That's just a silly conclusion to draw from the data to date, and we've previously discussed how use of the Internet has not been shown to cause depression, only that there's an association between the two.

If this is the level of "research" done to come to these conclusions about   15 "Facebook depression," the entire report is suspect and should be questioned. This is not an objective clinical report; this is a piece of propaganda spouting a particular agenda and bias.

The problem now is that news outlets everywhere are picking up on "Facebook depression" and suggesting not only that it exists, but that researchers have found the online world somehow "triggers" depression in teens. *Pediatrics* and the American Academy of Pediatrics should be ashamed of this shoddy clinical report, and retract the entire section about "Facebook depression."

References

Davila, J., Stroud, C. B., Starr, L. R., Miller, M. R., Yoneda, A., Hershenberg, R. (2009). Romantic and sexual activities, parent–adolescent stress, and depressive symptoms among early adolescent girls. *Journal of Adolescence, 32(4), 909–924.*

Kraut, R., Kiesler, S., Boneva, B., Cummings, J.N., Helgeson, V., & Crawford, A.M. (2002). Internet paradox revisited. *Journal of Social Issues, 58, 49–74.*

Kraut, R., Patterson, M., Lundmark, V., Kiesler, S., Mukophadhyay, T., & Scherlis, W. (1998). Internet paradox: a social technology that reduces social involvement and psychological well-being? *American Psychologist, 53, 1017–1031.*

LaRose, R., Eastin, M.S., & Gregg, J. (2001). Reformulating the Internet paradox: social cognitive explanations of Internet use and depression. *Journal of Online Behavior, 1, 1–19.*

Morgan, C., & Cotten, S. R. (2003). The relationship between Internet activities and depressive symptoms in a sample of college freshmen. *CyberPsychology and Behavior, 6, 133–142.*

Nie, N. H. & Erbring, L. (2000). Internet and society: A preliminary report, Stanford Inst. of Quant. Study Soc., Stanford, CA.

O'Keeffe et al. (2011). Clinical Report: The Impact of Social Media on Children, Adolescents, and Families (PDF). *Pediatrics. DOI: 10.1542/peds.2011-0054.*

Selfhout, M. H. W., Branje, S. J. T., Delsing, M., ter Bogt, T. F. M., & Meeus, W. H. J. (2009). Different types of Internet use, depression, and social anxiety: The role of perceived friendship quality. *Journal of Adolescence, 32(4), 819–833.*

Wellman, B., Quan-Haase A., Witte, J., & Hampton, K. (2001). Does the Internet increase, decrease, or supplement social capital? Social networks, participation, and community commitment. *American Behavioral Scientist, 45, 436–455.*

Wolak, J., Mitchell, K. J., & Finkelhor, D. (2003). Escaping or connecting? Characteristics of youth who form close online relationships. *Journal of Adolescence, 26, 105–119.*

COMMENTS IN RESPONSE TO "*PEDIATRICS* GETS IT WRONG ABOUT 'FACEBOOK DEPRESSION'"

Joanne Davila, PhD

I am the lead author on the citation that John accurately points out "has nothing to do with social networking and depression [Davila, 2009]." I invite readers to visit my webpage:

http://www.psychology.sunysb.edu/jdavila-/webpage/

where I have posted some information and links to interviews and podcasts on the matter. Thank you.

John M. Grohol, PsyD

CNET is *reporting* that O'Keeffe will at some point issue a response to this editorial.   20

We can't wait to read the justifications and rationalizations for: (1) using third-party media reports about research as references, rather than the actual research itself; (2) using citations that don't support the statements made in the report itself (thanks for the link, Joanne!); (3) ignoring or purposely confusing the difference between data that show a causal relationship (which we take from their use of the word "trigger") and a correlational relationship; (4) and making up a new term ("Facebook depression") to describe what they found by perusing mainstream media reports and a study or two.

Dr. Gwenn O'Keeffe

Dr. Grohol:

I have to take issue with your post about our clinical report. All you have done is add to the media frenzy about this issue.

A Clinical Report is a summary of a clinical situation that augments the clinical practice of pediatrics. It is not a study nor is it intended to be interpreted as such. The only agenda we had in proposing and then writing this report was to assist our colleagues practicing pediatrics to understand the entire landscape of social media today, the positives and the negatives.

As with all AAP reports, for the report to be published, it was subjected to a rigorous review process that included internal and external review groups. These groups were not only top pediatric and psychiatric groups in the country but top social media groups and legal groups. We took great care to be sure our facts were accurate and everyone was on board with the information we were presenting for our colleagues on all sections of the report, including the Facebook Depression section.

The Social Media Clinical Report was carefully and thoughtfully organized in   25
the following way after the introduction and abstract:

Benefits
Risks
Privacy Concerns and the Digital Footprint
Influences of Advertisements on Buying
On Too Young: mixed messages and the law
The Role of the Pediatrician
References

If you took the time to read the full report, you'd notice [that,] of the 5 page report, Facebook Depression is one small paragraph of the Risks section that takes up all 1/6 of a page. So, the clinical report is by no means about Facebook Depression nor do we make that claim ever.

Let me go further and clarify a few of your concerns.

I was most certainly not the first to use the term "Facebook Depression" and I won't be the last. I first noticed the term in widespread use in the mainstream press around 2009 after Dr. Davila's Stonybrook study came out, which you cite below. She not only gave compelling interviews about this topic when her study came out but has done so as recently as two weeks ago. You can review her interviews yourself on the following links:

http://www.telegraph.co.uk/technology/facebook/4405741/Excessive-chatting -on-Facebook-can-lead-to-depression-in-teenage-girls.html [an article quoting Davila in the British newspaper *The Telegraph*] and http://miami.cbslocal.com /2011/03/07/study-social-networking-may-leave-teens-depressed/ [a CBS-Miami newscast featuring brief soundbites from Davila].

Interestingly, one speculation that has been growing is that excessive internet   30
use may be a set up for this phenomenon of "Facebook Depression." Since we submitted our CR [Clinical Report] for approval, more research is coming out supporting that hypothesis. For example, researchers at the University of Leeds have noticed this by following hyper internet users (http://content.karger .com/ProdukteDB/produkte.asp?Aktion=ShowAbstract&ArtikelNr=277001& Ausgabe=253793&ProduktNr=22426) [an abstract of "The Relationship between Excessive Internet Use and Depression," an article published in the peer-reviewed journal *Psychopathology* reporting that "Correlational analyses [found] a close relationship between IA [internet addiction] tendencies and depression, such that IA respondents were more depressed."]

A nice summary of this study is on *Psychiatry Today* by Dr. Jared DeFife (http://www.psychologytoday.com/blog/the-shrink-tank/201002 /depression-in-the-digital-world).

Finally, you will be interested to read AAP Psychiatrist Mike Brody's comments posted yesterday about "Facebook Depression": http://www .myhealthnewsdaily.com/facebook-depression-rare-but-serious-side-effect -of-social-networking—1318/ [a *Health News Daily* article entitled "'Facebook

Depression': Rare but Serious Side Effect of Social Networking," which quotes Brody as saying that Facebook "sets up a competitive thing where kids might feel less than they are because their friends seem to be having a better time than they are."]

Do we know about causality yet? No. But we didn't claim to. All we claimed to note was the existence of a risk that pediatricians needed to note to keep kids healthy—one risk among many others.

In the end, this is not a clinical report for pediatricians about Facebook Depression, Depression or even psychological issues in kids and teens. This is a clinical report about "The Impact of Social Media" on our kids today. For us to do justice to that topic we have a responsibility to be thorough and review the entire landscape, the pluses and minuses. That's the only way for our colleagues to help parents keep their kids healthy and for our colleagues to help parents be the best parents in this evolving digital world.

Why engage in pack journalism when you could actually do a thoughtful analysis and report?   35

For this work in question, I'm proud of the work we've created and stand by it, frenzy and all.

Gwenn O'Keeffe, MD
Lead Author
AAP Clinical Report: The Impact of Social Media on Children, Adolescents, and Families

. . . .

John M. Grohol, PsyD

Dr. O'Keeffe, thank you for your detailed and thoughtful response.

Just so everyone here is clear, Dr. O'Keeffe says:

> As with all AAP reports, for the report to be published, it was subjected to a **rigorous review process** that included internal and external review groups.

Please correct me if I'm reading this wrong, but it appears this means that using random mainstream reports of research is a part of this "rigorous review." I don't understand how so many prestigious individuals can attach their names to a report that reports—second-hand—on actual medical and psychological research. Even when I write a simple blog entry here, I regularly go to the primary research to verify the conclusions stated in a mainstream media news story. How could my standards be higher than the AAP's?

I indeed did read the entire report, but focused on the area I'm most familiar with, your so-called "Facebook depression"—a term you and your co-authors invented specifically for this report.

Any professional who buys into media reports of over-generalization, and confusing causation with correlation and then uses that as a defense for simply "reporting" on trends is sort of missing the point. How are you helping to educate other professionals when you are simply presenting the same mis-representations appearing in the mainstream media to begin with?

I did ask where in the research the term "Facebook depression" was ever used, since, according to the report you co-authored you specifically stated:

> **Researchers** have proposed a new phenomenon called "Facebook depression," defined as depression that develops when preteens and teens spend a great deal of time on social media sites, such as Facebook, and then begin to exhibit classic symptoms of depression.

You didn't say the "mainstream media"—you said researchers. I asked where in the research researchers actually said this? We still have no answer to this question, which supports my claim that you and your co-authors simply invented the term to help better market the AAP report.

Dr. Davila has responded here and elsewhere, noting that her research you originally cited wasn't specifically about Facebook or any social networking website. In actually reading her research (which I assume you've also done), you'll see that to be true (notwithstanding how the media chooses what bits of an interview to publish in an article to support their own particular bias or slant).

Pulling in the controversial "Internet addiction" disorder (your Morrison & Gore citation above) to help prove your point really does just the opposite, since the research in this area is also just sloppy and methodologically poor. And resorting to anecdotal evidence from another AAP professional who was directly involved in creating this report? Sorry, I look to scientific research for evidence—not other AAP professionals who have a vested interest and inherent bias to support the work that has their name on it.

Finally, you state, "Do we know about causality yet? No. But we didn't claim to."

Actually, you did. In context of the "Facebook depression" section, you and your co-authors stated—as a foregone conclusion:

> "The intensity of the online world is thought to be a factor that may trigger depression in some adolescents."

Trigger, as you know, is to cause to function or act. Words should mean something consistent, don't you agree? If you didn't mean Facebook may trigger—or cause to happen—depression, why (a) state it and (b) call the section "Facebook depression"?

I can't say whether the rest of the report is as sloppy as this one small section. But if this section is any indication of what passes for "rigorous review" in the AAP, then I suspect the entire clinical report is of questionable value and should be taken with a healthy grain of salt.

Joanne Davila, PhD

Dr. O'Keeffe continues to cite my "compelling interviews" on facebook depression. Once again, I invite readers to view my website, which I continue to update to further clarify how the media has misinterpreted my research and the importance of focusing on science rather than media reports when disseminating information to the public. Thank you. – Joanne Davila

http://psychology.sunysb.edu/jdavila-/webpage/facebook%20depression%20controversy.htm   50

[The following passage is excerpted from this website]:

Please note that I have not published any data on "Facebook Depression." . . . Regarding the AAP Clinical Report (O'Keeffe et al., 2011, *Pediatrics*), Dr. Gwenn O'Keeffe maintains the following (quoted from her blog post on PsychCentral, March 30, 2011) . . .

> I first noticed the term in widespread use in the mainstream press around 2009 after Dr. Davila's Stonybrook study came out. . . . She not only gave compelling interviews about this topic when her study came out but has done so as recently as two weeks ago. You can review her interviews yourself on the following links:
>
> http://www.telegraph.co.uk/technology/facebook/4405741/Excessive-chatting-on-Facebook-can-lead-to-depression-in-teenage-girls.html
>
> http://miami.cbslocal.com/2011/03/07/study-social-networking-may-leave-teens-depressed/

I invite you to review these interviews. Let me make clear a few things.

First, regarding all of the reports that came out in 2009 — they all said the same exact thing. Why? Because one internet news report picked up on one inaccurately quoted speculation that my colleague Lisa Starr and I made in response to an interviewer's question. Following this, many other media outlets republished the misquotation and the inaccurate conclusion made by the reporter.

A bit of history . . . here is the link to the original article that started this all. If   55
you read it you will see that it says NOTHING about social networking and depression:

http://www.nytimes.com/2008/09/11/fashion/11talk.html [Links to a *New York Times* article entitled "Girl Talk Has Its Limits," which discusses talking rather than social networking]

Following the publication of that article, we were contacted for the *Telegraph* interview (that Dr. O'Keeffe refers to). Here is an excerpt from the article that includes the inaccurately quoted speculation (in italics) that was made in response to the interviewer's direct question about how our findings might apply to social networking:

Psychology professor Dr Joanne Davila and her colleague Lisa Starr, at Stony Brook University in New York, interviewed 83 girls aged around 13—the age when risk of depression starts to increase. They were contacted again a year later to follow them up. On both occasions they were tested for depressive symptoms and asked about romantic experiences considered normal for early teens, such as being asked out on a date and having been kissed. According to the report published in *The Journal of Adolescence*, it found higher levels of discussing problems with friends "significantly" linked with higher levels of depression while more romantic experience was linked both to excessive talking and more depressive symptoms.

Dr Davila said: *"Texting, instant messaging and social networking make it very easy for adolescents to become even more anxious, which can lead to depression."* She added: "Lots of talking can help if those involved have strong problem-solving skills because it helps them reach a solution and it builds friendships." She said many teenagers have not yet developed effective ways of dealing constructively with their troubles, remarking that parents may need to be aware when they are obsessing about a setback.

In the *Telegraph* article, what I was quoted (inaccurately) as saying above got translated into the following by the reporter:

Frequently discussing the same problem can intensify into an unhealthy activity for those who use Facebook and other electronic means to obsess about it, according to the researchers.

Clearly, it was a mistake to speculate. We were not reporting on actual findings. We were SPECULATING and we clearly articulated that to the reporter. However, the media adopted that inaccurate quote and republished it over and over. I DID NOT continue to provide misinformation to the media. The media report took on a life of its own because of inaccurate, irresponsible reporting. Moreover, Lisa Starr and I emailed as many of the writers and news agencies as possible to correct this mistake, to no avail. We also emailed our colleagues in the field, in line with ethical guidelines, to make sure that our scientific findings were not misreported or misunderstood.

That Dr. O'Keeffe and her co-authors trusted media reports rather than the actual scientific data is concerning. It is common knowledge among scientists that the media often misquotes, or at best selectively reports, things that they find potentially newsworthy. I hope that pediatricians and the public will treat the AAP *Pediatrics* report, particularly the part on "facebook depression" and others like it with caution.   60

Regarding my interview with CBS news last month, again that piece included only those parts of a much longer interview that the news editing team found "newsworthy." Unfortunately, the media is not in the habit of having interviewees review and edit the material that will eventually appear in print, online, or on TV. As such, although I agreed to do that interview in order to clarify what my research has and has not demonstrated, yet again, statements that I made as speculations in response to questions by the interviewer were taken out of context.

Questions

... [D]issemination of inaccurate information is dangerous and perhaps worse than no dissemination at all.

And when people who are trusted to provide accurate, guiding information to physicians and the public, information that has the potential to shape how the public views key aspects of behavior—when those people rely on media rather than on the science in their reports, then dissemination is clearly more dangerous than it is worth.

The media should not be creating science. The media should be accurately reporting science.

And scholarly journals should be reporting information based on science, not on media reports.   65

Questions for Critical Reading

1. Did your view of the *Pediatrics* report change after you read Grohol's critique of it? Why or why not? If you were persuaded by Grohol's critique, what evidence did you find most compelling? Why?

2. Did the evidence that O'Keeffe used in her rebuttal of Grohol's critique (p. 648) succeed in persuading you that Grohol's critique was unfounded, or at least partially unfounded? Which parts of O'Keeffe's rebuttal did you find especially persuasive or unpersuasive? Why?

3. How persuasive did you find the evidence (reprinted on pp. 652–53) that Davila linked to in her last response to Grohol's critique? Why?

4. Just as many expert readers do when they read a work that contains a list of references, assess the credibility of the references in the *Pediatrics* report. Which sources seem especially credible? Which ones seem less credible? How can you tell?

5. Since genres are read by particular audiences, the more audience-aware writers are, the more effectively they can communicate with their readers. Think about how writing for an audience of pediatricians rather than an audience of parents might have shaped some of the choices made by the authors of the *Pediatrics* report; consider the following two passages and see if you think there's a difference between how the authors discuss parents' knowledge and how they discuss pediatricians' knowledge:

> Parents often lack a basic understanding that kids' online lives are an extension of their offline lives. (para. 4)

> AAP [American Academy of Pediatrics] encourages all pediatricians to increase their knowledge of digital technology. (para. 19)

What differences did you notice? If you had written the *Pediatrics* report and were going to revise it for an audience of parents, would you revise the first passage? Why or why not? If you would revise it, how would you do so?

6. Recall that in any genre, the order in which writers present ideas can shape readers' responses. Consider the following original passage from the *Pediatrics* report and compare it to the altered version; note that the same information is presented in both versions, just in a different order. The sentence that has been moved is italicized; see how the different order affects your response:

Original Passage	Altered Passage
Some teens who have engaged in sexting have been threatened or charged with felony child pornography charges, although some states have started characterizing such behaviors as juvenile-law misdemeanors. Additional consequences include school suspension for perpetrators and emotional distress with accompanying mental health conditions for victims. *In many circumstances, however, the sexting incident is not shared beyond a small peer group or a couple and is not found to be distressing at all.* (para. 11)	*In many circumstances, the sexting incident is not shared beyond a small peer group or a couple and is not found to be distressing at all.* [In other circumstances], some teens who have engaged in sexting have been threatened or charged with felony child pornography charges, although some states have started characterizing such behaviors as juvenile-law misdemeanors. Additional consequences include school suspension for perpetrators and emotional distress with accompanying mental health conditions for victims.

How did the order of information affect your response to each passage? If you had written this report, would you have opted for the original version or the altered version? Why?

Making Connections

7. Because blogs are a more informal genre, Grohol can — arguably — get away with word choices that might be considered unprofessional in other venues. In more formal venues, and even in some blogs, writers tend to avoid judgmental words such as "bad" and "silly." Consider, for instance, Trent Batson's tone in "Response to Nicholas Carr's 'Is Google Making Us Stupid?'" (p. 584) and Pamela Brown Rutledge's tone in her blogged critique "Social Media Addiction: Engage Brain before Believing" (p. 662):

Batson

Carr sees only one side of the change we are going through. (para. 7)

Rutledge

The headlines in several news articles reporting on the study focused entirely on social media addiction, extrapolated from student comments, not the analysis, and [they] did not mention the profound . . . shifts in behavior and expectations. (para. 8)

If you were Grohol and you were going to adjust the tone of your critique, how would you revise each of the following passages? (Keep in mind that revision means not only changing but also adding or deleting.)

Shoddy research? You bet. That's why *Pediatrics* calls it a "clinical report"—because it's at the level of a bad blog post written by people with a clear agenda. (para. 3)

What makes this a bad report? (para. 4)

I expect to see this sort of lack of quality and laziness on blogs. (para. 6)

That's just a silly conclusion to draw. (para. 14)

Compare revisions with a few classmates. Which ones do you think have an especially professional tone? Why? Do you think that Grohol's original tone was appropriate for a blogged critique, or would you have preferred a more professional tone even in a blog? Why?

8. Note that although there are no sentence fragments (incomplete sentences) in the *Pediatrics* report, there are some in Grohol's blogged critique; as a blog post rather than a document published in a peer-reviewed journal, the critique probably wasn't edited as thoroughly—or it could simply be that Grohol wanted to take advantage of the more informal writing style that characterizes many online genres. Indeed, you'll also notice fragments in Rutledge's blogged critique "Social Media Addiction" (p. 662) and in the web-published research report "A Day without Media" (p. 666). Locate the fragments[4] in each of the following passages and then revise each one to read as you'd want it to appear in a more formal print genre.

"*Pediatrics* Gets It Wrong"

[Not differentiating between correlation and causation] is exactly what the authors of a "clinical report" did in reporting on the impact of social media on children and teens. Especially in their discussion of "Facebook depression," a term that the authors simply *made up* to describe the phenomenon observed when depressed people use social media. (para. 2)

In [a] study cited by the *Pediatrics* authors, simply reading the news report should've raised a red flag for them. Because the news report on the study

---

[4] Recall that you can identify a fragment by tacking "It is true that" onto the beginning of a sentence. If the original phrase makes sense with this temporary addition, it is really a sentence; if it doesn't make sense, it is actually a fragment.

quoted the study's author who specifically noted her study could not determine causation:

> ... "What we don't know is which comes first—are depressed people drawn to the Internet or does the Internet cause depression?" (para. 13)

"Social Media Addiction"

The conclusion had nothing to do with addiction, but made important points about the way social media technologies have been integrated into students' lives, their expectations about frequency of contact, and how that impacts how they relate to the world. From the site:

> The major conclusion of this study is that the portability of all that media stuff has changed students' relationship not just to news and information, but to family and friends—it has, in other words, caused them to make different and distinctive social, and arguably moral, decisions. (ICMPA, 2010, para. 3) (para. 7)

"A Day without Media"

What do the lengthy responses mean? That the students had a lot to say—even though most failed to make it through an entire 24-hour span without succumbing to the lure of media. (para. 65; boldface removed)

Compare your revisions with those of a few classmates so that you can get a sense of the many possibilities available to writers. Which revisions would you select if you were adapting these online passages for a print genre? Why? Are there any revisions that you'd select even for the original online venue? If so, which ones, and why?

Writing: Your Turn

1. Just as O'Keeffe and Davila did, write a comment on Grohol's blog post. Your comment might agree with Grohol's critique, take issue with it, or do some of both, acknowledging what you see as valid while also pointing to any problems you see.

When you write your comment, be sure to support your claims with evidence. Many comments to blog posts use personal experience as evidence, and you should feel free to draw on this resource too. However, you don't want to oversell your personal experience by claiming that it proves anything definitively; it's better for your credibility if you instead claim that your experience suggests a possibility. When you finish writing your comment, give it to a few classmates, along with a list of some of the things you want feedback on.

2. Find one of the references listed at the end of the *Pediatrics* report, read it, and then write about it, being sure to do the following tasks:

- Give a brief summary of the source
- Discuss how credible you think the source is
- Discuss whether you think the *Pediatrics* report represents the source accurately

When you're done, trade with several classmates to get their feedback and to get a sense of how accurately the *Pediatrics* report represents other sources. Ask your classmates for feedback on how clear your summary is and whether they agree with your assessment of both your source's credibility and the accuracy with which it was represented in the *Pediatrics* report. For ideas on writing a summary, see p. 23.

Blogged column

Fighting a Social Media Addiction

Jenna Johnson

In "Fighting a Social Media Addiction" (2010), Jenna Johnson describes a class assignment that asked University of Maryland students to go a day without media, including cell phones and the Internet. The experience, Johnson tells us, was "traumatic" for the students, one of whom reported, "I clearly am addicted and the dependency is sickening (para. 4)." Johnson's account of the students' experiences appeared in her blogged column *Campus Overload*, which appears on the *Washington Post's* Web site. Johnson is an education reporter for the *Post*.

After "Fighting a Social Media Addiction," you'll find Pamela Brown Rutledge's critique of media coverage like Johnson's, and following the critique you'll find "A Day without Media," the web-published research report referred to by both Johnson and Rutledge.

Focus on Genre   Consider "Fighting a Social Media Addiction" as a case study in how journalistic genres represent research reports. Because journalistic genres are typically much shorter than research reports, journalists must decide what information to include and exclude when they report on research. As you read, focus on the information that Johnson presents, which you'll later compare to the information presented in the research report that she's covering.

In addition, try to discern Johnson's attitude toward students and their "media addiction." Finally, note how persuasive you find Johnson's claim that Maryland students — and "American college students" more generally — are indeed addicted to media.

◄○►

Here was the challenge given to 200 University of Maryland students from a variety of majors: Abstain from social media for 24 hours.

That meant no iPhone or text messaging. No laptops or netbooks. No Gchatting or Twittering. No e-mail and absolutely no Facebook. Ah, a return to simplicity.

But just read the blogs these students wrote after the traumatic experience—it's very easy to confuse these students with crack addicts who went cold-turkey, smokers not given the comfort of a patch while quitting, alcoholics forced to dry up. The university's news release on the study last week reported that some descriptions popped up over and over: "In withdrawal. Frantically craving. Very anxious. Extremely antsy. Miserable. Jittery. Crazy."

"I clearly am addicted and the dependency is sickening," one student said. Another student had to fight the urge to check e-mail: "I noticed physically, that I began to fidget, as if I was addicted to my iPod and other media devices, and maybe I am."

The study—["A Day without Media"]—was conducted by the university's   5
International Center for Media & the Public Agenda in late February and early March. Researchers found that American college students struggle to function without their media connection to the world.

"We were surprised by how many students admitted that they were 'incredibly addicted' to media," Susan D. Moeller, a journalism professor and director of the center, said in the university's news report on the study.

Students found themselves surrounded by new technology and blaring TVs, even when they were trying to avoid them. And it was boring to walk around without a soundtrack being piped into their ears from an MP3 player.

"It was really hard for me to go without listening to my iPod during the day because it's kind of my way to zone out of everything and everyone when I walk to class," a student wrote. "It gets my mind right. Listening to music before I go to class or take an exam is my way of getting amped up like a football player before a game. It sounds weird but music really helps to set my mood or fix my mood and without it I had to rely on other people to keep me in a good mood."

But it's not just the entertainment value. When cut off from social media, many students felt cut off from other humans and lived in isolation. The study found that the friendships and relationships these 18- to 21-year-olds had were dependent on technology.

"Going without media meant, in their world, going without their friends   1
and family," Moeller said.

One student wrote that texting and instant messaging friends gives a feeling of comfort: "When I did not have those two luxuries, I felt quite alone and secluded from my life. Although I go to a school with thousands of students, the fact that I was not able to communicate with anyone via technology was almost unbearable."

Being cut off from the wired world also meant being cut off from news and information—not that any of them were regularly watching the news on TV, picking up a newspaper, listening to the news on the radio or visiting a news Web site.

One student who failed the assignment and cracked open a laptop during the 24-hour ban learned about the violent earthquake in Chile from "an informal blog post on Tumblr." Another student suddenly had less information than everyone else about a range of subjects, including sports and news and cultural references.

While students had an insatiable appetite for news, they relied on a broad range of sources, showing little loyalty to any, the university's news report said.

"They care about what is going on among their friends and families and even in the world at large," said researcher Raymond McCaffrey, a Ph.D. student who used to work at the *Washington Post*. "But most of all they care about being cut off from that instantaneous flow of information that comes from all sides and does not seem tied to any single device or application or news outlet."

15

Blogged critique

Social Media Addiction: Engage Brain before Believing

Pamela Brown Rutledge, PhD, MBA

News coverage such as Jenna Johnson's "Fighting a Social Media Addiction" (p. 659) is critiqued by Pamela Brown Rutledge in "Social Media Addiction: Engage Brain before Believing." Rutledge's critique was published on *Positively Media*, a blog appearing on the Web site of popular psychology magazine *Psychology Today*. In addition to blogging, Rutledge teaches in several psychology programs and is the editor of *Media Psychology Review*, an online journal devoted to examining issues related to psychology, technology, and media.

After Rutledge's critique, you will find "A Day without Media," the research report that Rutledge claims is being misrepresented by the media.

Focus on Genre In her critique, Rutledge tells us that people writing the news "don't always read the actual studies before they write" (para. 1), and she calls out specific groups of news consumers:

> Psychologists, parents, educators and politicians frequently talk about how important it is to teach kids media literacy so they can critically use, produce and evaluate media. Evidence suggests that this is not a skill that should be reserved for the young. (para. 2)

In addition to arguing that we need to "engage brain before believing" how the media represent studies such as "A Day without Media," Rutledge performs a rhetorical analysis of popular news genres, analyzing specific words and passages from these genres to demonstrate how news venues think about their audience and purpose in tailoring their messages. As you read Rutledge's critique, note how carefully she analyzes reporting in order to make recommendations about how people should consume news.

◄○►

When you see headlines about social media addiction, take a deep breath. Exhale. I know this sounds radical, but don't go by the news articles. Find the actual study and read it. Don't just read the results; see how the researchers define what they are measuring. This is important because (1) sometimes studies just don't make sense, (2) sometimes things that are only correlated get reported as being a "cause," and (3) the people writing the articles don't always read the actual studies before they write—even when they are real journalists.

Psychologists, parents, educators and politicians frequently talk about how important it is to teach kids media literacy so they can critically use, produce and evaluate media. Evidence suggests that this is not a skill that should be reserved for the young.

There has been a little flurry of news articles and blogs recently about social media addiction. First of all, it concerns me that, as a society, we are very cavalier tossing around the concept of "addiction." Addiction is a serious psychological diagnosis based on specific and seriously life-impairing criteria. (PT Blogger Allen Frances has a good discussion of behavioral addictions as compulsively driven behavior with negative consequences and the problems of getting too loose with clinical diagnoses.) Identifying an addiction of any kind is important. To my knowledge, however, a college student saying "I'm addicted to Facebook" is not adequate diagnostic criteria for addiction any more than someone saying they are addicted to chocolate or *American Idol*.

Of course, as a writer, if you can get the word "addiction" in a headline it will draw eyeballs to your copy because it targets people's fears. (Did it get you to read this?) Since we are all biologically wired to notice danger, especially where kids are concerned, this is a sure-fire way to get someone to read your stuff. I know journalists are all freaking out about the competition from new media. I get the conflict. But this isn't the time to compromise journalistic standards, it's the time to shore them up to prove your point about training and objectivity.

One of the recent studies discussed in the reports about social media addiction was an interesting outgrowth of a class assignment in a journalism course, not an empirically designed research project. The web-published results were a thoughtful qualitative analysis by a team headed by University of Maryland professor Dr. Susan Moeller. The homework assignment was to go without media for 24 hours and then write about it. 5

The results of the analysis of student submissions (along with some notes on methodology) were published online. They included quotes from students that were illustrative of their experience. That is how qualitative studies are done. A quote is not meant to be a common denominator and it is not accompanied by a frequency distribution; it is local color. The report on the website describes how students experienced a new appreciation for how they used media. Some students even used the word "addiction" in their submissions. However, most comments, judging from the data published on the report's site, were reflective of different types of new media use, the shift in the students' reliance on new media relative to traditional forms, and the students' desire to stay connected to friends, family and world events.

The conclusion had nothing to do with addiction, but made important points about the way social media technologies have been integrated into students' lives, their expectations about frequency of contact, and how that impacts how they relate to the world. From the site:

> The major conclusion of this study is that the portability of all that media stuff has changed students' relationship not just to news and information, but to family and friends—it has, in other words, caused them to make different and distinctive social, and arguably moral, decisions. (ICMPA, 2010, para. 3)

The headlines in several news articles reporting on the study focused entirely on social media addiction, extrapolated from student comments, not the analysis, and did not mention the profound, albeit conceptual, shifts in behavior and expectations. Thus when various reporters/writers polled experts for their articles, they asked about social media addiction, not the other implications of the study. One article had a particularly good quote from fellow PT blogger and media psychologist Stuart Fischoff, who reasonably and articulately pointed out that,

> "All these technologies have potential for terrific use and for terrific abuse. . . . Everyone is a potential addict—they're just waiting for their drug of choice to come along, whether heroin, running, junk food or social media. All those substances can be streetcars of desire. . ."

His remarks, evoking some cool imagery and media references, basically said there is potential for addiction with many behaviors. Exactly.

Fischoff's great quote got picked up by WiredPRNews.com when they decided to cover the story about the Maryland study, only now the headline said "Study shows social media withdrawal can occur" and starts out, *"A recent study suggests individuals may go through withdrawal symptoms from abstaining from social media for long periods."* The writer then cites the Maryland study as the source for Fischoff's quote. (At least he still got credit for saying it, even if he hadn't been in the study.) Does this remind anyone of the old "telephone" or "whisper" game?

Another recently quoted report was published online by Retrevo Gadgetology, entitled "Is Social Media a New Addiction?" This is a marketing report by a consumer electronics marketplace. As an academic piece, it has some serious methodological issues and none of the criteria for diagnosing addiction were included in the survey.

That wasn't Retrevo's intention and, to their credit, if you read the actual report you see they responsibly qualify their remarks, are speculative about their conclusion, and do not declare outright an epidemic of social media addiction as the headline might imply:

> We're not qualified to declare a societal, social media crisis but when almost half of social media users say they check Facebook or Twitter sometime during the night or when they first wake up, you have to wonder if these people aren't suffering from some sort of addiction to social media. (Retrevo, 2010, para. 7)

By the time the study got reported by Media Post, however, it was labeled "Social Addiction" and said that the Retrevo study concluded that social media can be habit forming.

We live in a world where information is no longer the purview of the privileged few, but neither is having an opinion. This is a tremendous freedom and opportunity. With it comes responsibility. There is no way to maintain freedom and have someone else vet all the material you read. You have to do it yourself. Think of it like defensive driving. This is a big onus, but in my mind, a price well worth paying.

However, we can't be lazy or blinded by our beliefs instead of engaging our gray matter. If we blithely forward "facts" based on our innate biases and "it seems right to me" conclusions, pull the most sensational quotes to use as headlines, and, as consumers, believe what we see rather than thinking critically and reading original sources, then we will not be able to identify the real issues we need to tackle nor will we be able to see our way to the positive potential these tools can bring.

As Fischoff said in his quote, there is no shortage of things to be addicted to. Social media is just one of many. But just because something is new and having a profound impact on how people behave doesn't by definition mean that it is bad or harmful. Believe it or not, there are actually research studies that report a positive side to social media, too, but they don't make very good headlines.

ICMPA (2010). A Day without Media. Research Project, University of Maryland, Phillip Merrill College of Journalism. Retrieved May 20, 2010 http://withoutmedia .wordpress.com/

Retrevo (2010). Is Social Media a New Addiction? Retrevo Studies. Retrieved May 20, 2010 http://www.retrevo.com/content/blog/2010/03/ social-media-new-addiction%3F

Web-published research report

A Day without Media

International Center for Media and the Public Agenda

"A Day without Media" is the web-published research report discussed by Jenna Johnson and Pamela Brown Rutledge. It was conducted in 2010 by the International Center for Media and the Public Agenda (ICMPA) and students at the Philip Merrill College of Journalism at the University of Maryland, College Park. The study's director, Dr. Susan Moeller, is a professor of media and international affairs.

In the methodology section of the research report (most of which isn't reprinted here), Moeller and six PhD candidates who coauthored the report tell us that a two hundred–student core course was given the assignment to try to go without media for twenty-four hours and then to blog about the experience. The students' blogged reports of their experiences were coded and underwent a qualitative content analysis conducted by the study's authors. The authors tell us that all quotations in the report are from students in the class and that they put some parts of the quotations in bold "to highlight key themes in the students' comments" (para. 12).

Focus on Genre   As a research report, the excerpt that follows is somewhat unconventional. In some ways it resembles the kind of research report you might find in a scholarly journal, but it also takes advantage of web conventions (including tabs on its homepage, links, and clickable images that open larger versions of charts and word clouds). In its original web-published format, the report is able to present summarized information while also giving readers the option of clicking to read further. You can see it in its original format at http://withoutmedia.wordpress.com/.

As you read the research report, focus on assessing how accurately it was represented in Jenna Johnson's "Fighting a Social Media Addiction." Compare the information covered in Johnson's column to that presented in the research report itself; notice what information appears in both pieces and what doesn't. Think about how you would represent the research if you were writing about it. What information would you include, and what would you omit?

◄○►

24 HOURS: UNPLUGGED

What is it like to go without media? What if you had to give up your cell phone, iPod, television, car radio, magazines, newspapers and computer (i.e., no texting, no Facebook or IM-ing)?

Could you do it? Is it even possible?

Well, not really, if you are an American college student today.

According to a new ICMPA study, most college students are not just unwilling, but functionally unable to be without their media links to the world.

"I clearly am addicted and the dependency is sickening," said one student   5
in the study. "I feel like most people these days are in a similar situation, for between having a Blackberry, a laptop, a television, and an iPod, people have become unable to shed their media skin."

This is a "Wordle" data visualization of the over 100,000 words the students in the study wrote about their experiences of going 24 hours without media. This Wordle cloud makes larger those words that appeared most frequently in the students' comments.

This new study conducted by the International Center for Media & the Public Agenda (ICMPA) asked 200 students at the University of Maryland, College Park, to abstain from using all media for 24 hours. After their 24 hours of abstinence, the students were then asked to blog on private class websites about their experiences: to report their successes and admit to any failures. The 200 students wrote over 110,000 words: in aggregate, about the same number of words as a 400-page novel.

What Were the Study's Top 5 Highlights?

1. **Students use literal terms of addiction to characterize their dependence on media.**

   "Although I started the day feeling good, I noticed my mood started to change around noon. I started to feel isolated and lonely. I received several phone calls that I could not answer," wrote one student. "By 2:00 pm. I began to feel the urgent need to check my email, and even thought of a million ideas of why I had to. I felt like a person on a deserted island. . . . I noticed physically, that I began to fidget, as if I was addicted to my iPod and other media devices, and maybe I am."

2. **Students hate going without media. In their world, going without media, means going without their friends and family.**
   "Texting and IM-ing my friends gives me a constant feeling of comfort,"   10
   wrote one student. "When I did not have those two luxuries, I felt quite alone and secluded from my life. Although I go to a school with thousands of students, the fact that I was not able to communicate with anyone via technology was almost unbearable."

3. **Students have only a casual relationship to the originators of news, and in fact don't make fine distinctions between news and more personal information. They get news in a disaggregated way, often via friends. Students show no significant loyalty to a news program, news personality or even news platform.**
   "Although I will admit I do not actively keep up with breaking news every day, I do get a lot of information on a daily basis through social networking, text messaging, and websites such as Gmail, where it does have headlines on the homepage. It is very important to me to have some sense of what is going on in the world on a daily basis."

4. **18–21 year old college students are constantly texting and on Facebook—with calling and email distant seconds as ways of staying in touch, especially with friends.**
   Said one student, "Texting and Facebook allow me to make plans to meet up and act socially, whereas without these two devices I had no easy way of making plans unless I happened to run into the person I wanted to do something with."

5. **Students could live without their TVs and the newspaper, but they can't survive without their iPods.**
   "It was really hard for me to go without listening to my iPod during the day   1
   because it's kind of my way to zone out of everything and everyone when I walk to class. It gets my mind right. Listening to music before I go to class or take an exam is my way of getting amped up like a football player before a game. It sounds weird but music really helps to set my mood or

fix my mood and without it I had to rely on other people to keep me in a good mood," said one student.

STUDY: CONCLUSIONS

"Most schools and colleges spend too much time preparing students for careers and not enough preparing them to make social decisions. . . . In short, modern societies have developed vast institutions [that] have an affinity for material concerns and a primordial fear of moral and social ones."

—*New York Times* columnist David Brooks

The way students CONSUME media is related to "material concerns"—the stuff they have: the iPhones, Droids, iPods, TVs, cars with their radios, etc.

But the impact of what they DO with that stuff has profound "moral and social" implications.

The major conclusion of this study is that the portability of all that   20
media stuff has changed students' relationship not just to news and information, but to family and friends—it has, in other words, caused them to make different and distinctive social, and arguably moral, decisions.

The absence of information—the feeling of not being connected to the world—was among the things that caused the most anxiety in students as they sought to learn about the role of media in their lives—ironically by completing an assignment that asked them to spend a day without using media.

What did they learn by forgoing media for 24 hours?

That they cared about what was going on among their friends and families; they cared about what was going on in their community; they even cared about what was going on in the world at large. But most of all they cared about being cut off from that instantaneous flow of information that comes from all sides and does not seem tied to any single device or application or news outlet.

- "When I officially started the 24 hour period, I walked down the hallway of my dorm, and noticed that the rooms that I passed had TV's blaring, music playing, computers being used for Facebook purposes, and at the end of the hallway someone was talking on the phone. This was in one fifteen second span."

Technology Is about Media

In April 2010, the Pew Research Center's Internet & American Life Project reported that "text messaging has become the primary way that teens reach their friends, surpassing face-to-face contact, email, instant messaging and voice calling as the go-to daily communication tool for this age group," and noting that "half of teens send 50 or more text messages a day, or 1,500 texts a month, and one in three send more than 100 texts a day, or more than 3,000 texts a month."

The ICMPA study noted a similar phenomenon—although the college students, close to 20 years old on average, were even greater senders of text messages, with a number of participants in the almost 200-person study reporting that they sent over 5,000 text messages a month, and one woman reporting that she sends over 9,000 a month.

Both the Pew report and the ICMPA study document that teens and young adults today place an unprecedented priority on cultivating an almost minute-to-minute connection with friends and family. And the ICMPA study shows that much of that energy is going towards cultivating a digital relationship with people who could be met face-to-face—but oftentimes the digital relationship is the preferred form of contact: it's fast and it's controllable.

Two years ago, in 2008, Pew reported that the Internet had overtaken newspapers as the primary source of campaign news in the United States, and that, for the first time, younger Americans sought national and international news as much from online sources as they did from television news outlets. Today, University of Maryland undergraduates not only rarely mention television and newspapers when discussing their news consumption during Media Literacy classes . . .

According to this study, students get their news and information in a disaggregated way, often through friends texting via cell phone, or Facebooking, emailing and IM-ing via their laptops. Students are aware of different media platforms, but students have only a casual relationship to actual news outlets. In fact students rarely make fine distinctions between information that is "news" and information that is "personal."

Media Is about Information

Students reported in this study that while they missed their music and their movies and their TV programs, they found that going media-free resulted in a greater, all-encompassing loss: "**I believe that those who are not tied to this system are missing something**," one student wrote. "**They are missing information.**" And information, they discovered, was a precious commodity--one that they used to define themselves in comparison to their peers. One student said he

25

realized that he suddenly had "less information" than "everyone else," regardless of whether that information involved "news, class information, scores, or what happened on *Family Guy*."

Students also expressed their awareness that information connected them to a larger world, beyond their circle of friends. One student wrote of finally logging on to the computer after going media-free and learning about the earthquake in Chile. A social network site directed her to news sites that gave her more information about the disaster. "Those who aren't connected through media probably have no idea about certain things going on in the world," she wrote.

Information Is about Connection

Again and again, students wrote about the role of media in establishing and cementing social connections--how they used their laptops and phones and myriad devices to communicate with friends, families, and others in their lives. "This technology craze has become so deeply ingrained in each of us we know no other way of living our lives, but to rely on our cell phones, laptops, televisions, and iPods to keep us occupied and connected with the world around us. **I find it [difficult] to fathom someone not being connected through media, because I know no other way**," one student wrote. "It's funny," wrote another, "but I realized we are a social species, and the use of media today helps us to establish a connection with one another."   30

Students also made it clear that socializing and the flow of information were inextricably intertwined. When the earthquake in Chile struck, most students didn't learn about it from newspapers or the evening news. They found out about it first through contacts on social network sites, and that information propelled them to visit mainstream news sites. "People who do not use media as frequently as our society does are probably missing out on important news and social interaction," the student wrote.

Connection Is about Instant Access

Students may differ in their dependency on different devices and their appetite for different media, but an undeniable common denominator that came through in their comments was their demand for and dependency on instant access to information—information so omnipresent that it has become the essential background to their lives. **"The ability to constantly receive information is a privilege that I recognize is a crutch at times but I relish its advantages**," one student wrote.

Information that is not delivered quickly is deemed as obsolete as the delivery method. **"Why would someone take the time to go out and get a** newspaper, when he / she can roll over and open a laptop?" another student asked.

And yet, there were flickers of knowledge that the ease of technology can hide its costs: "**Everything is so accessible and so instantaneous,**" one student wrote, "**that we lose sight of what is behind these snippets of information.**"

This study began as a homework assignment for 200 students. It has not ended, for them, or for the rest of us. A closer look at reactions of these students offers profound insights for universities, developers of media technology and journalists.   35

Lessons Here for Us All

- For **UNIVERSITIES, the takeaway is that students cannot be taught about the role of media in their lives**—how to distinguish between fact and fiction, credible and non-credible sources, important and unimportant information—**if those who teach them do not have a basic comprehension of how students find, share and experience media.**

- For **DEVELOPERS OF MEDIA TECHNOLOGIES, the takeaway is that their grand inventions find a fickle audience, at least among young people.** The students may feel tethered to their favorite devices, like the iPod, or delight in hot new applications, like Droid, or flock to essential Web destinations, like Facebook, but the most important thing of all to them is whatever latest technology can connect them the quickest to the people they most value.

- For **JOURNALISTS, the takeaway is that the readers and viewers of the future see them at once as irrelevant—and indispensable.** Specifically, students don't care about newspapers or TV news broadcasts or even blogs, but covet the information that comes to them through a diverse and circuitous pathway of devices, platforms, applications and sites. A truer mapping of those pathways could provide direction to journalists in their search for relevance in the century ahead.

References

Pew Research Center for the People and the Press. 2008. *Internet Now Major Source of Campaign News.* 31 October.

Pew Research Center for the People and the Press, 2008. *Internet Overtakes Newspapers As News Outlet.* 23 December.

1. USING MEDIA

I want to be connected (to people, to music, to entertainment, to news) NOW
Digital media provide "instant gratification" for students. **But of all the media technologies, most students felt most bereft without their cell phones.** [They] use cell phones not only to call friends and family, but to text others at nearly any time of day. They use their phones to text and tweet and Facebook during lectures, while walking around campus, and whenever they need to coordinate with friends.

- "Basic things like text messages usually plan out my days but **without a phone, the only people I really saw were the people who live in my building or people I accidentally ran into.**"
- "Not having a cell phone created a logistical problem. It was manageable for one day, but I cannot see how life would be possible without one. . . . **the most important aspect of a cell phone seems to be being able to meet up with people. . . . it is problematic having to make up specific times and places to meet up with people: most of us are very accustomed to our flexible by-the-whim lives.**"
- "To me, media is a way to connect to people in ways I never do on a day to day basis. With classes, location, and other commitments it's hard to meet with friends and have a conversation. **Instant messaging, SMS, and Facebook are all ways to make those connections with convenience, and even a heightened sense of openness.** I believe that people are more honest about how they really feel through these media sources because they are not subject to nonverbal signals like in face to face communication."

Tuned in 24/7: I can't live without my iPod
Today's students have a soundtrack to their lives; they are always plugged in; they listen to music all day. **Not having music when they walked to class, when they exercised, or when they studied dramatically disconcerted many students.** There was an upside, however, several students noted: their lack of music actually forced them to have conversations with people they did not know.

40

- "**The hardest part of the 24 hours was not listening to music.**"
- "Walking to and from class was not as relaxing as it usually is for me because I love just walking, thinking about things, and listening to my music."

- "I like listening to music while I study because I like the background noise. If it's too quiet, sometimes it's hard for me to focus."
- "I do believe that the iPod touch is the greatest thing ever invented, having thousands of applications which allow me to check my email, check the weather, play games, and listen to my 16 gigabytes of music, half of which have probably never been played. It is genius, it fits in my pocket, and if there was one thing other than not playing guitar that was going to make this assignment impossible, it was not having my iPod on me."
- "My attempt at the gym without the ear pieces in my iPhone wasn't the same; doing cardio listening to yourself breathe really drains your stamina."

Cellphones: This generation's Swiss army knife
Students' primary multipurpose media tool is the cellphone: especially for calling and texting, but also for email and playing games. Without it, students repeatedly pointed out, they not only couldn't communicate, they literally couldn't operate in the world as they had become accustomed.

- "I really wanted to call home to speak to my mother."
- "Facebook I might be able to do without, but my cell phone is important to me. It creates a link to constant communication and safety. What happens when I need immediate contact with someone, if there is an emergency?"
- "I just got a Droid last month and am very attached to it as I am constantly sending and receiving emails, checking Facebook and playing different games or using applications. Our cell phones have become such a large part of our lives, it is the one thing I always have with me at all times."
- "I literally had to have my friend hide my phone so I wouldn't check it by accident."
- "It becomes a normal task to look at my phone every few minutes, yes minutes."
- "I am constantly on my phone. On average I probably send a text message every minute or so. I am ashamed that I couldn't go without my phone for 24 hours, but communicating with people is one of the most prominent things in my life."

If I'm online, I'm on Facebook (or some other networking site)
Students noted how much they use Facebook to alleviate boredom. While students did mention that they used the Internet for completing class assignments, many said that what they missed about not accessing the Internet was keeping track of their social networking.

- "It is almost second nature to check my Facebook or email; it was very hard for my mind to tell my body not to go on the Internet."

- "I knew that the hardest aspect of ridding myself of media, though, would be not checking Facebook or my emails, so I went ahead and deactivated my Facebook account in advance. **It's pathetic to think that I knew I had to delete my Facebook in order to prevent myself from checking it for one day.**"
- "I began to compare my amount of media usage to that of my friends. I realized that I don't usually check or update Facebook or Twitter like a lot of my friends that have Blackberrys or iPhones. I did however realize that as soon as I get home from class it has become a natural instinct to grab my computer (not to do school work which is the sole reason my parents got me my computer!) but to check my email, Gmail, umd account mail, Facebook account, Twitter account, Skype, AIM, and ELMS: that's six websites and four social networking sites. This in itself is a wake-up call! I was so surprised to think that **I probably spend at least 1–2 hours on these sites alone BEFORE I even make it to attempting my homework and then continue checking these websites while doing my school work.**"

OK, if I had to, I could give up my television set
Students had an **easier time disconnecting from television**. While students did say they watch television, many missed their computers and the Internet more, which they used not only to surf the Web and send e-mails but because they used their computers essentially as a TV: to watch various videos.

- "Not watching TV was probably the easiest media source to not use. The computer was not as easy but not the most difficult. Giving up my cell phone was the most difficult."

Hey, do you have the time? (I don't have my cell phone.)
What came as a surprise to many students was how the assignment played havoc with their sense of time. First, without a cell phone, students who had no watch were late for meetings and classes. And second, without the distraction of media, time seemed to crawl for many.

- "I had to set my alarm clock for the first time this year because I usually use my phone."
- "Interestingly, **not having a way to tell time became one of the biggest stresses of this experiment.** I tried to rely on clocks in campus buildings . . . and it became apparent that many buildings are not made for people without watches/phones. Consequently, I got to my first class 20 minutes early, ate lunch very quickly so I wouldn't get to my next class late (again I was early), and was 15 minutes late meeting up with my boyfriend later in the day. Lesson: I really need a watch in case my cell dies."
- "**The absence of media made life feel a little slower.**"

- "**The day seemed so much longer** and it felt like we were trying to fill it up with things to do as opposed to running out of time to do all of the things we wanted to do."

Writing by hand is so last-century (and so slow)

Some other students also mentioned just the plain inconvenience of going without laptops and cell phones.   45

- "I had to take notes by hand which was difficult for the particular speed in which my professor lectures."
- "I found it harder to keep up with the teacher because I am so used to typing my notes very quickly on my computer, and now I had to handwrite the notes for the lecture."
- "**The convenience of these tools is incomparable. I can make plans for Friday, Saturday, and Sunday within ten minutes worth of phone calls or texts.** Without my phone, I'd have to be making plans months in advance through letters."

2. FEELINGS ABOUT MEDIA

Addicted to media. REALLY. Addicted.

Many students described their reactions to going without media for 24 hours in literally the same terms associated with drug and alcohol addictions: *In withdrawal, Frantically craving, Very anxious, Extremely antsy, Miserable, Jittery, Crazy.*

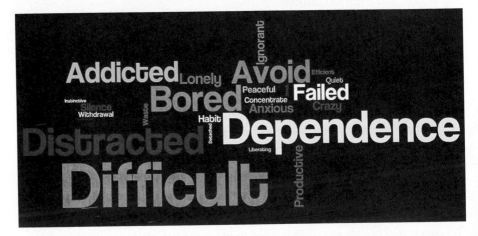

Some said they **hated the media-free period, hated the assignment and hated being away from their cell phones.** Others said they were *lonely* or *sad,* more *irritable* than usual, or *anxious.* Still others noted feeling *isolated, upset, moody, absent, frustrated, flustered* and *annoyed.*

- "Texting and IMing my friends gives me a constant feeling of comfort. When I did not have those two luxuries, I felt quite alone and secluded from my life. Although I go to a school with thousands of students, **the fact that I was not able to communicate with anyone via technology was almost unbearable."**

- **"Honestly, this experience was probably the single worst experience I have ever had."**

- "I got back from class around 5, frantically craving some technology and to look through my phone so I cheated a little bit and checked my phone. From my phone, I accessed text messages, close to a dozen missed calls, glanced at some emails, and acknowledged many twitter @replies from followers wondering where I was and if I was OK. At that moment, **I couldn't take it anymore being in my room . . . alone . . . with nothing to occupy my mind** so I gave up shortly after 5 pm. *I* **think I had a good run for about 19 hours and even that was torture."**

- "My short attention span prevented me from accomplishing much, so I stared at the wall for a little bit. After doing some push-ups, **I just decided to take a few Dramamine and go to sleep to put me out of my misery."**

Students said **they felt** *disconnected,* *anxious* **or** *worried* **they were missing out on something,** *out of the loop,* or *lost.* Taking away their technological means of being in touch clearly put students out of sorts—many used words such as *weird, odd* or *strange* to describe how they felt.

- **"When I don't have [my cell phone] on my person, sometimes it can feel like I am missing a limb** because I feel so disconnected from all the people who I think are calling me, but really they aren't half the time."

And did I mention that I was BORED to distraction?!

Without a digital connection to others, students felt bereft of company as well as cut off from the chief way they amuse themselves. Students noted that especially when they are alone they rely on cell phones and the Internet to fill the hours between classes, entertain them while working out or commuting—even if that commuting just means walking around campus. Without media, they were simply, stunningly, crashingly bored.

- "I then became more bored than I believe I have ever been in my life."

- "On a psychological note, my brain periodically went crazy because I found **at times that I was so bored I didn't know what to do with myself."**

- "Thankfully, the combination of studying and randomly shooting paper clips into my garbage across the room took me all the way until dinner."
- **"After a few hours in class I decided mentally I couldn't last any longer because texting in class keeps me occupied when I am bored** and I was extremely bored in class that day so the effects of no technology took its toll."
- "When I was walking to class I always text and listen to my iPod so **the walk to class felt extremely long and boring** unlike all the other times."
- "On Friday, I had to walk to class and stare at everyone as I passed because I had nothing else to do."
- "I took the longest shower of my life and went to bed early on Sunday night."

3. MEDIA DEPENDENCY

First off, using media is a habit.

Students are swimming in an ocean of media, but are often oblivious to their   50
use of the technology all around them so they take it for granted. It's not only that they are used to listening to music, going online, watching TV, texting and calling friends, it's that the act of doing those things has become invisible—it has come to be an extension of their selves.

- "While I was driving to my friend's house, **I accidentally turned on the radio.**"
- "After dinner **I kind of instinctively opened Safari and started browsing the web.**"
- "A few hours later, I brushed my teeth, came back to my room, opened my laptop, and got on Facebook. **I was on the computer for a good ten minutes before I realized what I was doing.**"
- "Once I got back from the gym I turned on the T.V. and laid down to watch. It didn't even dawn on me that I was breaking the rules until I turned it off to sleep and then realized what I did while I was in bed. **It is just natural for me to turn on the T.V.** I have been doing it since I was about 5."
- "I wish I didn't cheat with the assignment by checking my email and phone, but the anxiety was insane. **I had no clue how connected I was with my friends and the world at all times. I never realized how much I text messaged my friends or checked Perez Hilton until I couldn't.**"

This Wordle gives a snapshot of some of the top terms that the students used to describe how it felt going "Cold Turkey" with media:

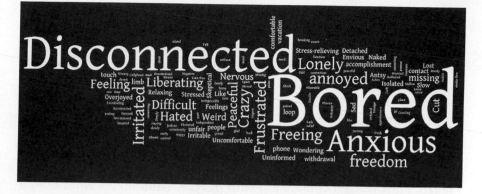

Then there was this weird "Phantom Ringing" phenomenon.

Many students observed that their phones "feel like a part of me"—which for a surprising number resulted in hallucinations that their cells were in their pockets or were turned on, even when they weren't. The disturbing "ringxiety" alerted students that they were "so dependent on these inanimate objects."

- "I thought I would feel my jacket vibrate (usually where I put my phone) and twice I would look for my phone and realize I left it at my apartment."
- "When sitting in the library reading my textbook, **I actually did hear some vibrations in my head and would think my phone was vibrating next to me.**"
- "**I felt phantom vibrations all throughout the day,** especially in my very boring Monday lectures."
- "With full knowledge that my phone was off and tucked away, **I reached into my pocket at least 30 times to pull out a vibrating phone that wasn't there.**"
- "**I definitely felt some psychological effects, such as hearing my cell phone ring even though it was off or typing on a pretend keyboard without realizing it.**"
- "I could swear I heard my phone's sound for when I had a message (which was impossible because the phone itself was turned off). **The experience of 'phantom ringing' was a little disturbing**—it really enforced my dependence on my phone. I still had four hours to go."

It's true. I failed. But I needed to talk to my mom . . .

Baby boomers went to college and entire semesters could slip away without a phone call or a letter exchanged between parent and child. Not so today. Both men and women reported that one of the key functions of their cell phones was to call home. On occasion the phone call home was to report in after a trip away, but for many students, calling or texting a parent (especially a mother) multiple times a day is not just routine, but valued.

- "I slipped up and called my mother."
- "Near the end of my 24 hours I did have to call my mom and let her know that I got back to school safely because **she tends to worry.**"
- "The only exceptions I made were to use my laptop to take notes in class (never connected to the UMD wifi) and to pick up calls only from my mother or father."
- "If I hadn't told my parents I was conducting this experiment, I am sure they would have tried calling me 1,000 times and they probably would have filed a missing persons report."

I failed. I just missed connecting with people. (Hmmm . . . what does it mean that my connections happen over cell and text?)
Over and over again students commented that they absolutely needed the phone to have on-demand 24/7 contact with family and friends. The "inability" for the students to get in touch—and the inability of the students' friends and family to get in touch back—greatly distressed them all. Some cited the need for that connection in case of an emergency, some mentioned a need to be a caretaker, others simply needed the technological and psychological tether.

- "I have grown up in a community where I was constantly surrounded by a need to stay connected. Whether that is through television, cell phones or whatever. The reliance is kind of disturbing, but in the modern American environment **it is a necessity to have constant connection in order to survive.**"
- "My roommate woke up feeling too sick to go to her classes and my phone was her only link to me throughout the day if she needed something."
- "I finally convinced myself to call my sister in case something terrible had happened. Everything was fine, and I realized after the phone call, that **I just simply needed a form of contact with another human being.**"

I failed. I just couldn't stand it.
Quite a few students justified their failure by referencing what they came to see was a kind of addiction.

- "My reasons for giving in was that **I am a sport junkie**, so I have to be up to date with sports."
- "I broke my streak by checking into ESPN.com. **I couldn't stand going an entire day without getting my sports fix.**"
- "I felt like a complete addict on withdrawal mode, once I gave in, I **went all out and felt connected to the world again.**"
- "In retrospect I lasted a solid 12 hours but once sleep was taken out of the equation of counting towards the 24 hours **I only lasted 4 hours.**"

OK, so I'm reliant on media . . . and why is that a bad thing?
Students acknowledged that their inability to go without media was eye-opening. But many said that they didn't mind being so dependent—on balance they enjoyed their reliance on cell phones, the Internet, iPods and other technologies.

- **"While I was upset that I wasn't able to go these twenty-four hours, this truly made me realize how reliant not only society is on media/ technology, but how reliant I am.** I do not even think about it; it has become so natural to me. I am constantly checking my computer, my phone, the TV, etc., all day, and at this point it doesn't even occur to me."
- **"So yes I'm a failure, I love my phone and I don't want to live in a world without technology.** Our society is so technology dependent that I wouldn't want to ask anyone to live without it for 24 hours."
- "I feel that **my life is way happier when I have access to media.**"
- "I took out an old project that I have been working on since before this past winter break—I finished knitting a scarf I planned on giving my mother a few months earlier. I'm glad I am able to knit, or else I would have had literally nothing to do. By the time the clock read 11:55 pm, I was getting so antsy; all I could do was stare at it until it hit 12. You better believe that once it hit 12, I was in my office reconnecting myself to the internet. After that I flung my desk drawer open and grabbed my beloved phone. I missed 20 emails and 3 text messages (from coworkers who wanted me to pick up a shift). . . . **Before I finally fell asleep around 1:00 am, I felt a sense of relief that I was finally back in the loop.**"

4. ADVANTAGES OF UNPLUGGING

Technology's not the problem. It's that I waste my time . . .
Effectively all those who succeeded in the homework challenge said that without the distraction of Facebook, text messages and videos, they **spent more time on course work.**

- "My morning routine was completely different; I couldn't check my phone, email, weather, or watch Sportscenter. My morning was not rushed; it was quiet and seemed slow. It was actually somewhat peaceful. Walking to class all day was different since I couldn't listen to my iPod. This caused me to look around more at other people and actually pay attention to what was going on around me. **Classes went better since I couldn't text or get on the Internet, I took better notes and was more focused. I** ate lunch alone because I couldn't text anyone to meet up. Not only did I eat alone, but I of course couldn't use my phone, iPod, or laptop, so I just sat there until I decided to look through some notes—which was actually productive."

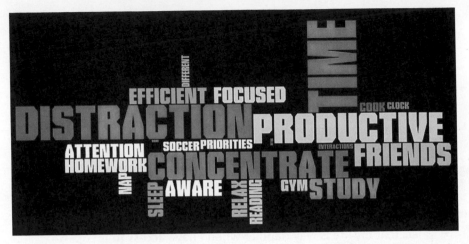

While most didn't enjoy the day off, they reported that they had prepared for exams, settled down to routine homework and read novels. Quite a few students noted their surprise at how productive they actually could be.

- "Studying was a million times more productive without the media distracting me with texts, calls, Facebook, email, games and other random internet sites."
- "Over my 24 hours without media, I finished an entire novel, and started a second one."
- "I was very productive in my schoolwork and I was able to get ahead this week with all my midterms coming up."
- "I spend way too much time on my computer doing basically nothing, and it was actually a relief to step away from that and spend time doing other things."

Surprise! Staying focused in class helps me learn more

Students who use laptops in class aren't only taking notes. While keeping one ear tuned to the professor, they are simultaneously checking emails, updating Facebook, and chatting with friends via instant messages. As the assignment made both laptops and cell phones off limits in other classes, students said that **without the temptation of their computers and cell phones they learned more.**

- "I also found that I paid more attention during lecture without the temptation of Facebook."
- "I found that I was able to pay more attention in class on Monday, instead of checking my Blackberry constantly to see if I got any messages or emails. . . . [and] not having my computer in class was less distracting since I was not tempted to check my Facebook every second."

- "Before I began the 24-hour period with no media, I would have never started to study for a test 3 days before the test. **With more time to study, though, I ended up easily getting an A on my test, something that I have rarely done since getting to college.** *I* actually went into the test feeling prepared and confident."
- "**From this experience I have learned that concentrating fully on the task at hand and not a media distraction [leads] to a more positive result.**"

Who knew that "quality time" meant "media-free" time?

Quite a few observed that they **unexpectedly became aware of aspects of their life which they had been rather oblivious to.** Some students reflected on their media-free experience by saying that they caught up with their priorities and **spent more quality time with their loved ones.** Instead of their normal internet "news" checkup in the morning, they made themselves a "much more balanced" breakfast. Some reported that they had more time and desire to cook a nice dinner for themselves and their families. During their media-free day, student went to the gym and, in general, reported **more face-to-face interactions** with friends.

60

- "It's the easy access, fast connection, and genuine boredom of our society that has caused a day without media to be so difficult. I think about those who aren't connected to media outputs the way Americans, in particular, are, and I find it both a combination of upsetting and lucky. Those people are unable to be as interconnected on a global scale, but probably have **better people-skills because they have their conversations the old-fashioned way, not through texting.**"
- "I definitely picked up on more details and things about the people I live around that I had never noticed before."
- "I usually see a lot of my friends or people I know on my way to class and **not having my iPod on with my earbuds in my ear gave me the excuse to actually have a conversation on my way to class.**"
- "Life is not as boring as it would seem to be without cell phones, television, and the internet. My parents grew up without any of these things and said that as teenagers, they never felt bored. I had a taste of their experiences and **thoroughly enjoyed the alone time I had with my boyfriend.**"
- "I felt like walking to class would be tough without my iPod, which I normally listen to on all my walks. I was wrong though. **It was actually really nice not having my ear buds in. I looked around, saw things I never really looked at before,** and even had a good, silent lunch."
- "I decided to go outside and shoot some baskets like I used to do back when I was in high school."

- "I found a book I had lying around that I had not yet finished, and read for two solid hours. This turned out to be the most enjoyable part of my Sunday. I had completely forgotten how much I enjoyed reading a real book."
- **"I also realized how much media causes me to miss out on physical fitness and healthy eating habits.** I felt so much better about myself after working out and actually eating 3 hearty meals in one day for the first time that I can remember."

On balance, perhaps I learned something . . .

Although the assignment of being media-free for 24 hours stunned most students, at the end most students found a kind of equanimity with the outcome of the media-free day.

There were those students who expressed feeling *relaxed, care-free, peaceful* and *serene*, saying they felt *mellow*, like they were *on vacation*.

- "This assignment allowed me to take a step back and reflect. **I probably had more 'thinking time' that day than any day spent at college.**"
- "After 24 hours of giving up Facebook, I thought I would challenge myself further to do a week. So far I've done it and it actually feels great! I believe that I've been much more productive since giving up Facebook, having more time on my hands to do various chores such as cleaning different parts of my house."
- "I must say a good thing that came out of this assignment was I was able to be more aware and [knowledgeable about] my surroundings while I walked to and from class. **By not being able to listen to my iPod, I could hear natural sounds like birds chirping** or . . . people calling my name."

Others said they didn't enjoy the experience, but they felt proud of themselves for making it through a whole day without using their cell phone or Internet. The best news? Everyone was thrilled when it was over.

- "Overall, it was a good experience to wait 24 hours to use technology, but it is something that I never want to do again!"

111,109 WORDS*

It took 200 students 111,109 words to explain what it was like to go without media for a day.
That's about 550 words per student—250 more words than the assignment asked for. It's unusual for students to spend MORE time on an assignment than they need to.

---

* This section is excerpted from the methodology section of the research report, which follows the conclusion.

What do the lengthy responses mean? That the students had a lot to   65
say—even though **most failed to make it through an entire 24-hour span
without succumbing to the lure of media.**

- Some failed because they just didn't know what to do with themselves
  without the stimulation of media.

- Some failed because they needed to communicate to friends, family or
  professors and couldn't find another way to do so other than by phone or
  text or email. (Students had been told, however, that they could use their
  computers to complete school work and that they could commandeer a
  friend to make a phone call for them, if need be.)

- Some failed because they found that there was no place they could go on-
  or off-campus where they wouldn't be swimming in media: TVs blaring
  in the gym exercise rooms, video games being played by their suitemates,
  music piped into elevators heading up to their doctors' offices.

Many students had been appalled when the assignment was announced.
They were *skeptical* about the purpose and even *fearful* about going without
media for such a "long" period of time. Many students admitted that they
had had *doubts* from the beginning about their ability to complete the assignment—and those students who didn't manage to go the entire 24 hours noted
that they **weren't surprised by their failure** to do so.

**Most students had never known a time when they hadn't had
access to the convenience and on-demand power of media.** And most
admitted that **they hadn't been entirely aware how distracted they were
by all the technology** in their pockets and backpacks. Somewhat abashedly
they wrote about getting more out of their classes because they weren't
texting or Facebooking through lectures. They wrote about getting their
homework done faster without online distractions or the temptations of TV
and video games. A few even noted that they believed that they would be
getting a better grade on an assignment they completed during the 24-hour
period as a result.

At the end of the assignment, many expressed both positive and negative emotions—simultaneously saying they felt *freer* and a *little happy* but also
more disconnected and therefore *more discontented*. A few found the experience
stress-relieving while others said they felt more stressed.

- "Overall, a day without media ends up making you feel very uninformed
  and lost. . . . Not being able to use media also makes you realize how
  much you are missing and how much time you are wasting. **Media
  has a trade-off between its usefulness and its ability to waste your
  time.**"

Questions for Critical Reading

1. Consider the Maryland report alongside Johnson's "Fighting a Social Media Addiction" — especially in light of Rutledge's claim that the report's conclusion "had nothing to do with addiction" (para. 7). To what extent do you think that "Fighting a Social Media Addiction" accurately represents the Maryland study? Why?

2. If you were a journalist reporting on the Maryland study, what information from the study would you include and what information would you exclude? Why? What would your headline be, and why?

3. Regardless of genre, it's useful to assess whether the topics you read about are represented in a positive or negative (or mixed) light. Based on your reading of the Maryland study, would you say that the authors represent students and their technology use as being more positive than negative, or more negative than positive — or would you say that they give approximately equal weight to both the positive and the negative? Why? Take a minute to find some specific passages that support your interpretation, and explain.

    Now consider the same questions for Johnson's "Fighting a Social Media Addiction." How does it compare to "A Day without Media" in this regard?

4. Word clouds are commonly found in a number of online and print genres. In groups, take a few minutes to compare the different word clouds used in "A Day without Media," and consider how well each one conveys the point made in the section in which it appears. Are there any word clouds that you think illustrate the points of sections especially well? If so, summarize the points, and explain why you think they are well illustrated by the word clouds.

    Are there any word clouds that you think are less effective in conveying points? If so, summarize the points that the word clouds are supposed to illustrate, and explain why you think these points aren't well conveyed.

Making Connections

5. Like many media accounts of research, Johnson's "Fighting a Social Media Addiction" is based largely on a press release.[5] Note how one of the quotations of Moeller appears both in Johnson's account and in the press release on which it was based:

    ### "Fighting a Social Media Addiction"

    "We were surprised by how many students admitted that they were 'incredibly addicted' to media," Susan D. Moeller, a journalism professor and director of the center, said in the university's news report on the study. (para. 6)

---

[5] Recall that press releases promote research, products, events, and the like; organizations send them out in hopes that they'll become the basis for media reports, thus giving the organization free publicity. Indeed, press releases are written to read like news articles, and it's common practice for part or all of a press release to be reprinted as is.

Connections

Press release from the University of Maryland[6]

"We were surprised by how many students admitted that they were 'incredibly addicted' to media," noted the project director Susan D. Moeller, a journalism professor at the University of Maryland and the director of the International Center for Media and the Public Agenda which conducted the study. "But we noticed that what they wrote at length about was how they hated losing their personal connections. Going without media meant, in their world, going without their friends and family." (para. 4)

Like Johnson, many journalists reprinted only the first sentence of the Moeller quotation. For you as a reader, what was the effect of the shorter quotation compared to the effect of the longer one?

6. Think about media reporting of the Maryland study in light of what psychology professor Joanne Davila says on the Web site she links to in her blog comment (p. 652):

> It is common knowledge among scientists that the media often misquotes, or at best selectively reports, things that they find potentially newsworthy (para. 60).

Considering "Fighting a Social Media Addiction" alongside the Maryland study — and alongside your experience with other media accounts of research — do you think it's possible for journalistic genres to do justice to research reports, or do you think these genres (at least as they exist currently) shouldn't cover research reports? Alternatively, do you think that journalistic genres can productively cover research *if* readers bear in mind Rutledge's advice to "engage brain before believing" (and if you hold this opinion, how could readers — realistically — be taught to engage their brains)? Why do you hold the opinion you do?

7. Both "A Day without Media" and the selection from Sherry Turkle's *Alone Together* (p. 593) suggest that one important reason people use technology is to maintain relationships — to stay connected to others. Turkle, however, suggests that the time and energy we spend maintaining our many online connections may ultimately weaken our in-person connections:

> A 2010 analysis of data from over fourteen thousand college students over the past thirty years shows that since the year 2000, young people have reported a dramatic decline in interest in other people. Today's college students are, for example, far less likely to say that it is valuable to try to put oneself in the place of others or to try to understand their feelings. The authors of this study associate students' lack of empathy with the availability of online games and social networking. An online connection can be deeply felt, but you only need to deal with the part of the person you see in your game world or social network. Young people don't seem to feel they need to deal with more, and over time they lose the inclination. (para. 58)

---

[6] From "Students Addicted to Social Media—New UM Study," released by the University of Maryland's newsdesk on April 21, 2010; retrieved from http://www.newsdesk.umd.edu /sociss/release.cfm?ArticleID=2144 on August 26, 2012.

Turkle uses Brad, whom she interviewed extensively, to provide detail about what she sees as the sometimes-superficial world of online connection:

> Abandoning digital connection, [Brad says he] is "sacrificing three hollow conversations" in favor of "one really nice social interaction with one person." He acknowledges that "not doing IM reduces the amount of social interacting you can do in one day," but doesn't mourn the loss: "Would you rather have thirty kind-of somewhat-good friends or five really close friends?" (para. 48)

Turkle, then, lays claim to a nuance that the Maryland study does not discuss. While both studies quote people who believe technology can enable personal connections, only Turkle distinguishes between *types* of personal connections: the sometimes-superficial ones enabled by digital interaction and the often more in-depth ones that, she claims, are fostered by phone calls and in-person interaction.

Consider whether the differences between Turkle's findings and the Maryland study's findings might be partially explained by the different research methodologies used — by the fact that the Maryland study looked at two hundred students who blogged about their experience trying to go media-free for one day, while Turkle observed and interviewed more than 450 people over the course of fifteen years. Do you think that the different methodologies used in each study might partially explain the different results? Why or why not?

Finally, consider one last question: do you find the results of one study more compelling than the results of the other study, or do you find both sets of results equally compelling? Why?

Writing: Your Turn

1. Some "digital immigrants" (people who didn't grow up with cell phones and social media) might differ from some "digital natives" (people who did grow up with these technologies). Recall, for instance, a quotation from one of the students in the Maryland study: "My parents grew up without [cell phones, television, and the Internet] and said that as teenagers, they never felt bored" (para. 60).

    If you are a digital native, interview a digital immigrant to see if he or she experienced boredom less (or more) often than you do. Be sure to write down several interview questions before you conduct your interview so that you will go into the interview feeling prepared. When you're done with the interview, write a summary of what you learned. Trade summaries with some classmates to get feedback on what you wrote and to see if there are any commonalities among the digital immigrants who were interviewed. For ideas on writing a summary, see p. 23.

2. After carefully reading "A Day without Media," write a news article—including a headline—that you think is a fair and accurate representation of the study's conclusions. In your article, include some carefully selected quotations from the authors of the study and/or the students they quote. When you're done, write a brief reflection on the process of writing the article: was it hard or easy (or somewhere in between) to represent the study's conclusions fairly and accurately? When you're done with both the article and the reflection, trade documents with some classmates to give them feedback on their work and to see how similar or different your news article is compared to theirs.

Alternatively, you might get in groups of two or three before writing anything and assign each person one of the following versions of a news article:

- One version that focuses on the *negative* side of students' feelings about their media use (which might, for instance, include a quotation such as "I clearly am addicted and the dependency is sickening" from para. 5)

- One version that focuses on the *positive* ways that students in the study use media (which might include a quotation such as "the portability of [media] has changed students' relationship not just to news and information, but to family and friends—it has, in other words, caused them to make different and distinctive social, and arguably moral, decisions" from para. 14)

- One version (if there's a third person in the group) that tries to represent the *complexity* of students' media use and their feelings about media (which might include a quotation such as "media has a trade-off between its usefulness and its ability to waste your time" from para. 59; boldface removed)

After each person in the group writes a different news article, read what everyone has written and provide feedback to each writer so that he or she can revise. Then write a brief reflection on your group's experience. In your reflection, discuss whether or not someone who read only the positive or negative article—and who *hasn't* read the research report—might suspect that the article shows only one side of the story. For ideas on writing a reflection, see p. 27.

JSTOR (jstor.org) offers students and professors from participating institutions access to scholarly journals, books, and primary sources.

To see these Web pages in color, visit the e-Pages for *Real Questions* at **bedfordstmartins .com/realquestions/epages.**

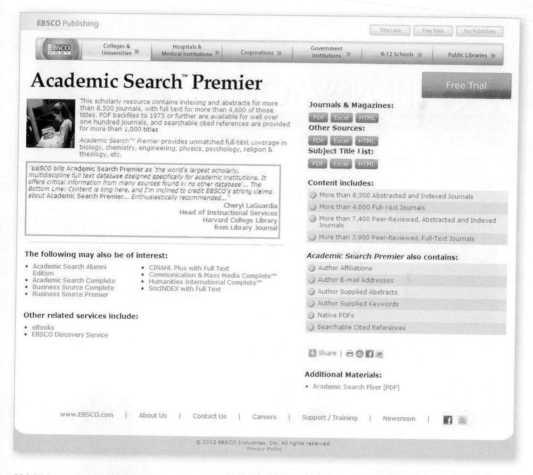

EBSCO's Academic Search Premier (http://www.ebscohost.com/academic/academic-search
-premier) is a subscription site that many colleges and universities use to allow students and
faculty to access scholarly journals.

The *New Yorker* (newyorker.com) is a weekly magazine that features reporting and commentary on a broad range of topics, along with cartoons, fiction, and poetry.

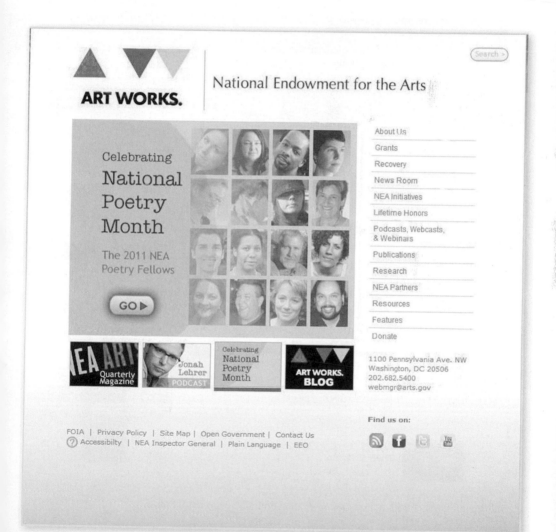

The National Endowment for the Arts (nea.gov) is a government agency that runs grant programs and promotes the arts in the United States.

Mashable (mashable.com) provides news and commentary on social media.

Questions for Critical Reading

1. What do you take to be the purpose of each Web page in this portfolio, and who do you see as the target audience of each page? Why?

2. Think about these and other Web sites you visit regularly. To what extent is each of these sites designed to be shared and with whom? How do these Web sites promote sharing of their content? How are you most likely to share information you find on these Web sites, and why?

3. An especially important aspect of visual design is alignment (how visual elements line up on the page). In the National Endowment for the Arts (NEA) Web page (p. 693), for example, you could draw a straight line down the page connecting the left point of the triangle with several other visual elements: the box that contains the photographs, the smaller box that reads "NEA Quarterly Magazine," and the left margin of the small print at the bottom of the page. Several visual elements on the other side of the page are aligned as well. Compare the number of invisible lines you could draw down this page to the number you could draw down the Mashable Web page (p. 694). Which page has more lines, and how does the number of alignments on each page affect you? How do you think it might affect others? Why?

4. Pick one of the sites from this portfolio and take a few minutes to consider alignment alongside other aspects of the layout. How is the site designed to help users find what they need quickly (search boxes, tool bars, headings, photos, etc.)? Now compare the design of the page you picked to that of the others. If you were redesigning any of these Web sites, would you change any aspects of the design in order to make finding content easier? Why or why not?

Pulling It All Together

BLOG POST

Drawing on the strategies you found to be persuasive in this chapter's blogged critiques (Grohol and Rutledge), write a blog post critiquing one or two of the other reading selections, possibly including one of the Web pages in the visual portfolio. If you decide to critique two selections, select two that are related.

Organize your critique carefully, and provide evidence to support your claims. You should also feel free to add a visual element to your blog post if you can find one that's appropriate. After you draft your post, trade with some classmates to see if they find your critique persuasive and to hear their thoughts on how you could make it even more so. For ideas on writing a blog post, see p. 90.

ARGUMENT

Drawing on two or more of the readings in this chapter, and perhaps also on your personal experience and/or independent research, write an argument about an aspect of screen-based technology that you find interesting. Tailor your argument to an audience of your choosing. If you don't already have ideas about what to write, you might address one of the questions in the chapter introduction (p. 561) to help you formulate a thesis.

In your thesis, try to avoid blanket statements that assume all people interact with screen-based technology in the same way (e.g., "Technology helps us have better relationships" or "Technology hurts relationships"). Instead, try making an argument that is

- specific (for example, what type of screen-based technology are you talking about?), and
- nuanced (for example, in what situations might people's use of this technology enrich their relationships, and in what situations might it hurt their relationships? Does your argument apply to all people or just some people?).

After you revise your argument, share it with a few classmates, and ask them if reading your work prompted them to see anything in a new light. If they found your work to be persuasive, ask them how it might be more so; if they didn't, ask them what their objections are so that you can address them in your revision. For ideas on writing an argument, see p. 42.

Appendix:
Publishing Your Writing

The following is a brief list of some publications that accept student writing. Like most lists, this is just a starting point, but it should provide you with ideas for sharing your work with wider audiences. In many cases, asking a professor or searching your school's Web site will help you find publications affiliated with your school (for example, newspapers, blogs, or literary magazines) to which you can submit your work. Or you may consult the list below for more ideas for places to publish your writing.

For each publication below that you consider, make sure you visit its site and read the submission requirements before you submit your work. Some publications have strict guidelines they will want you to follow in order to be considered for publication. It is also a good idea to read some of the work that appears in a publication so that you can determine whether your writing would be a good fit.

Academic Journals

There are many academic journals — both discipline-specific and general-research journals — that publish undergraduate writing. It is important when submitting your work to an academic journal that you read the guidelines carefully and prepare your work accordingly. Use the citation style preferred by the journal. Many academic journals have a policy against simultaneous submissions; in general, do not submit the same piece of writing to more than one journal at a time unless you have gotten permission to do so. Here is a sampling of academic journals that publish undergraduate research:

American Journal of Undergraduate Research
http://www.ajur.uni.edu/

Journal of Research and Creative Studies
http://www.bw.edu/resources/dean/fscs/jrcs/

Journal of Undergraduate Research
http://www.mnsu.edu/urc/journal/

Journal of Undergraduate Research and Scholarly Excellence
http://jur.colostate.edu/index.cfm

Journal of Undergraduate Sciences
http://www.hcs.harvard.edu/~jus/home.html

Queen City Writers: A Journal of Undergraduate Writing and Composing
http://qc-writers.com/about/

Pittsburgh Undergraduate Review
http://www.pur.honorscollege.pitt.edu/

Undergraduate Journal of Service Learning and Community-Based Research
http://www.bk.psu.edu/Academics/33679.htm

Valley Humanities Review
http://www.lvc.edu/vhr/

Young Scholars in Writing: Undergraduate Research in Writing and Rhetoric
http://cas.umkc.edu/english/publications/youngscholarsinwriting/default.asp

You can find more discipline-specific journals at the Council on Undergraduate Research site, including journals in mathematics, neuroscience, politics, and business: http://www.cur.org/resources/students/undergraduate_journals/.

General Essays and Creative Nonfiction

Most literary journals publish creative nonfiction, particularly memoir. While a few are listed here, you might want to try a site like Duotrope (http://duotrope.com) for finding additional nonfiction publications.

Creative Nonfiction
http://www.creativenonfiction.org/

North Central Review
http://northcentralcollege.edu/academics/distinctive-opportunities/student-publications/north-central-review

River Teeth: A Journal of Nonfiction Narrative
http://www.riverteethjournal.com/

Sphere: International Journal of Student Writing
http://www.spherefdu.org/

Blogs

Many schools maintain group blogs where undergraduates can write about campus issues. You might also try a Google search for a group blog on a topic that interests you. Here are a couple of group blogs that accept submissions:

Feministing
http://community.feministing.com/

Huffington Post College
http://www.huffingtonpost.com/college/

Of course, many bloggers choose to go it alone and run blogs by themselves. There are several free blog services, and most of them are highly customizable, allowing you to tinker with the design and test your technical proficiency.

Conventional Blog Sites

Blogger
http://blogger.com

LiveJournal
http://livejournal.com

WordPress
http://wordpress.com

Microblogging Sites

Jux
http://jux.com

Tumblr
http://tumblr.com

Twitter
http://twitter.com

Op-Eds and Letters to the Editor

Many colleges and universities publish newspapers that cover campus and local events. If you have written about issues on your campus, try contacting your campus newspaper or visiting its Web page to see if it publishes op-eds or other pieces by students.

Most college newspapers also publish a Letters to the Editor section that includes student responses to stories published in the paper as well as brief opinions related to the paper's coverage in general. These pages will contain information about how to submit letters.

Acknowledgments

Text

Amel S. Abdullah. From "Assuming the Best of Others." Reprinted by permission of the author.

Sarah Adams. "Be Cool to the Pizza Dude." By Sarah Adams from the book *This I Believe*, edited by Jay Allison and Dan Gediman. Copyright © 2005 by Sarah Adams, copyright © 2006 by This I Believe, Inc. Reprinted by permission of Henry Holt and Company, LLC.

Tom Bartlett. From "Is Psychology about to Come Undone?" From *The Chronicle of Higher Education*, April 17, 2012. Copyright © 2012 by The Chronicle of Higher Education. Reprinted with permission of the publisher.

Trent Batson. "Response to Nicholas Carr's 'Is Google Making Us Stupid?'" From *Campus Technology*, March 18, 2009, copyright © 2009 by 1105 Media, Inc. All rights reserved. Used by permission and protected by the Copyright Laws of the United States. The printing, copying, redistribution, or retransmission of this Content without express written permission is prohibited.

Arthur C. Brooks. From *Gross National Happiness*. Copyright © 1963 by Arthur C. Brooks. Reprinted by permission of Basic Books, a member of the Perseus Books Group.

Nicholas Carr. "Is Google Making Us Stupid?" First published in the *Atlantic Monthly*, July/August 2008 issue. Copyright © 2008 by The Atlantic Media Co. Distributed by Tribune Media Services.

Rebecca Clarren. "Is Your Eco-Label Lying?" From MotherJones.com, Nov./Dec. 2009. Reprinted courtesy of Mother Jones.

Mihaly Csikszentmihalyi. Excerpts from *Flow: The Psychology of Optimal Experience*. Copyright © 1990 by Mihaly Csikszentmihalyi. Reprinted with permission of HarperCollins Publishers. Electronic rights licensed by Brockman, Inc. on behalf of the author.

Deborah Dean. From *Genre Theory: Teaching, Writing, and Being*. Copyright © 2008 by the National Council of Teachers of English. Reprinted with permission.

Gavin de Becker. From *The Gift of Fear*. Copyright © 1997 by Gavin de Becker. Reprinted by permission of Little, Brown and Company. Electronic rights licensed by the author. All rights reserved.

Raam Dev. "Say Less." Posted Dec. 8, 2011, http://raamdev.com/2011/say-less. Reprinted by permission of the author.

Natasha Diamond. From "Letter to the Editor" of the *Daily Atheneum*, Oct. 8, 2011. Reprinted by permission of the author.

Barbara Ehrenreich. From "Positive Psychology: The Science of Happiness" from the book *Bright-sided: How Positive Thinking Is Undermining America*. Copyright © 2009 by Barbara Ehrenreich. Reprinted by permission of Henry Holt and Company, LLC.

Mary Beth Ellis. "The Waltz." Copyright © 2006 by Mary Beth Ellis. From *20 Something Essays by 20 Something Writers*, edited by Matt Kellogg & Jillian Quint. Used by permission of Random House Trade Paperbacks, a division of Random House, Inc.

Michael Fitzpatrick. "The Vegetarian Delusion." From the *Brown Daily Herald*, Oct. 5, 2009. Reprinted by permission of the publisher.

Cathy Fleischer and Sarah Andrew-Vaughan. From *Writing Outside Your Comfort Zone*. Copyright © 2009 by Cathy Fleischer and Sarah Andrew-Vaughan. Published by Heinemann, Portsmouth, NH. All rights reserved.

Jonathan Safran Foer. From *Eating Animals*. Copyright © 2009 by Jonathan Safran Foer. Reprinted by permission of Little, Brown and Company. All rights reserved.

Malcolm Gladwell. From *Blink*. Copyright © 2005 by Malcolm Gladwell. Reprinted by permission of Little, Brown and Company. All rights reserved.

Gretchen Rubin. "Act the Way You Want to Feel." From *The Happiness Project*, a blog by Gretchen Rubin, with reader comments. Reprinted by permission of Gretchen Rubin.

Pamela Rutledge. "Social Media Addiction: Engage Brain Before Believing." From *Psychology Today*, May 22, 2010. Reprinted by permission of the author, Dr. Pamela Rutledge, Director, Media Psychology Research Center.

Zach Schonfeld. "*New York Times* on Drunk Fruit Flies, Wooly Bear Caterpillars, and Prof. Michael Singer." Originally published on *Wesleying*, a blog about student life at Wesleyan University. Reprinted with permission of Zach Schonfeld.

Martin E. P. Seligman. From *Authentic Happiness: Using the New Positive Psychology to Realize Your Potential for Lasting Fulfillment*. Reprinted and edited with the permission of Free Press, a Division of Simon & Schuster, Inc. Copyright © 2002 by Martin E. P. Seligman. All rights reserved.

Todd K. Shackelford et al. From "When We Hurt the Ones We Love: Predicting Violence against Women from Men's Mate Retention." From *Personal Relationships*, 12 (2005) 447–463. Copyright © 2005 by John Wiley and Sons. Reprinted by permission of the publisher.

Bruce Silverglade. From "Economic Impact of Past Labeling Reforms." Reprinted from "Food Labeling Chaos" by permission of the Center for Science in the Public Interest.

Flavius Stan. "Night of Oranges." First published in the *New York Times*, Dec. 24, 1995. Reprinted by permission of the author.

Brent Staples. "Black Men and Public Space." Reprinted by permission of the author.

Sandra Steingraber. "The Organic Manifesto." Copyright © by Sandra Steingraber. Used with permission. All rights reserved.

Linda Stone. "Beyond Simple Multi-Tasking: Continuous Partial Attention" and "Diagnosis: Email Apnea." Reprinted by permission of Linda Stone. http://LindaStone.net

David Straker. "Attribution Theory." From ChangingMinds.org. Reprinted by permission of the author.

Amy Sutherland. "Modern Love: What Shamu Taught Me about a Happy Marriage." From the *New York Times*, June 25, 2006. Reprinted by permission of the author.

Deborah Tannen. From *You're Wearing That? Understanding Mothers and Daughters in Conversation*. Copyright © 2006 by Deborah Tannen. Used by permission of Ballantine Books, a division of Random House, Inc.

Katherine Taylor. "Meeting Great Expectations." From the *Daily Texan*, Oct. 12, 2011. Reprinted by permission of the publisher.

Studs Terkel. "C. P. Ellis." From *American Dreams: Lost and Found*. Copyright © 1980 by Studs Terkel. Reprinted by permission of Donadio & Olson, Inc.

Maurice Thomas. Letter to the editor of the *Badger Herald*, Oct. 3, 2011. Reprinted by permission of Maurice Thomas.

Sherry Turkle. From *Alone Together*. Copyright © 2011 by Sherry Turkle. Reprinted by permission of Basic Books, a member of the Perseus Books Group.

University of Leicester. Press release, "University of Leicester Produces the First Ever World Map of Happiness." A global projection by Adrian White, Analytic Social Psychologist, University of Leicester, 2006. Press release reprinted by permission of the University of Leicester.

Doug Walp. Excerpt from "Justice for Dead Miners Trumped by Corporate Influence." From the *Daily Athenaeum*, Jan. 9, 2012, and from "Let's Cut the Fat on Obesity Commentary in the U.S." from the *Daily Athenaeum*, Jan. 24, 2012. Reprinted by permission of the publisher.

Kristen Wolfe. "Dear Customer Who Stuck Up for His Little Brother." Originally posted on www.sweetupndown.tumblr.com. Reprinted by permission of the author.

Leslie A. Zebrowitz and Joann M. Montepare. "Social Psychological Face Perception: Why Appearance Matters." From *Social and Personality Psychology Compass*, April 17, 2008. Copyright © 2008 by Leslie A. Zebrowitz and Joann M. Montepare and by Blackwell Publishing Ltd. Reprinted by permission of the publisher.

Art

p. 122: © Tom Cheney/New Yorker Collection/www.cartoonbank.com; **p.124:** By permission of Lab 42, LLC; **pp. 175–179:** © ETR Associates. All rights reserved. Reprinted with permission from ETR Associates, Scotts Valley, California; **p. 193:** Grant Jeffries/MCT via Getty Images; **p. 194:** Lana Sundman/Alamy; **p. 195:** Images-USA/Alamy; **p. 196:** Bob Falcetti/Getty Images; **p. 197:** Justin Sullivan/Getty Images; **p. 200:** Mark Ralston/Getty Images; **p. 285:** Courtesy of the Ad Council and Gay, Lesbian and Straight Education Network "Think Before You Speak" campaign; **p. 286:** Richard Levine /Alamy; **p. 287:** The Ad Council on behalf of United Way; **p. 288:** John Tlumacki/Getty Images; **p. 291:** from *Time Magazine*, 1/17/2005 issue. © 2005 Time Inc. Used under license. **p. 414:** (top) Tim Cook/Getty Images; (bottom) PR Newsphoto/American Greetings Corporation/AP Photo; **p. 415:** Orlin Wagner/AP Photo; **p. 416:** PR Newsphoto Hallmark Cards/AP Photo; **p. 417:** Sick Chick Ink/AP Photo; **p. 420:** AFP Images/Getty Images; **pp. 423–424:** Center for Science in the Public Interest; **p. 555:** (top) Justin Sullivan/Getty Images; (bottom) JB Reed/Bloomberg/Getty Images; **p. 556:** (top) Daniel Acker/Bloomberg/Getty Images; (bottom) Chris Walker/Chicago Tribune/MCT via Getty Images; **p. 557:** Joe Raedle/Getty Images; **p. 560:** iStock photo; **p. 690:** Reprinted courtesy of JSTOR. JSTOR © 2012; **p. 691:** EBSCO HOST; **p. 692:** New Yorker Collection /www.cartoonbank.com; **p. 693:** National Endowment for the Arts Web site homepage; **p. 694:** From Mashable.com, May 3rd, 2012. Mashable, Inc. All rights reserved. Used by permission and protected by the copyright laws of the United States. The printing, copying, redistribution, and retransmission of this Content without express written permission is prohibited.

e-Pages

The Happy Planet Index. Courtesy of wellbeing@neweconomics.org.
Philip Wollen. Courtesy of Phil Wollen/info@kindnesstrust.org.
Sheri White. "Seeing beyond Our Differences." Copyright © 2009 by Sheri White/Audio recording copyright © 2009 by This I Believe, Inc. Part of the This I Believe Essay Collection found at www.thisibelieve.org. Copyright © 2005–2012, This I Believe, Inc. Used with permission.

Index